D1264130

Prose and Poetry for Enjoyment

St. Thomas More Series

PROSE AND POETRY FOR ENJOYMENT

SECOND EDITION

Julian L. Maline, Ph.D.

PROFESSOR OF EDUCATION, WEST BADEN COLLEGE OF LOYOLA UNIVERSITY

Joseph F. Downey, A.M.

FORMERLY INSTRUCTOR IN ENGLISH, ST. XAVIER HIGH SCHOOL, CINCINNATI, OHIO

J. FRANK DEVINE, A.M.

NORMAN W. MOELLER, LITT.B.

THOMAS E. TRESE, A.M.

SYRACUSE, NEW YORK

The L. W. Singer Company, Inc.

THE COVER DESIGN:

"Cardinal Albrecht of Brandenburg as Saint Jerome." This very important panel, showing Saint Jerome in his study, is noted especially for the careful delineation of inanimate objects, the painter's naïve delight in his subject matter, and the charm of the composition. The painting is dated 1526, and signed with a flying dragon. It was painted by Lucas Cranach the Elder, a German painter of the sixteenth century. It is reproduced by permission of The John and Mable Ringling Museum of Art, Sarasota, Florida.

THE FRONTISPIECE:

This is a glazed terracotta Madonna, probably from the workshop of the Florentine sculptor Michelozzo. The period is that of the fifteenth century, which produced many beautiful sculptures, a number of them done in this technique which is an imitation of polished marble. This work of art is in the National Gallery of Art in Washington, D. C.

IMPRIMATUR:

✠ *Paul C. Schulte, Archbishop of Indianapolis*

THE DESIGN:

Stefan Salter

61193

PREFACE

To develop a habit of reading *from the sheer joy of reading* is the purpose of this volume. Although most of the selections are on a fairly mature level, and although some may stretch the minds of ninth-grade readers, all of them were chosen primarily because of their entertainment value for the freshman reader. A wide variety of classical literary types is offered, but literary types as such have not been emphasized. Such emphasis at this early stage of literary development, it is feared, would place another obstacle across the already difficult path to the reading habit. The relatively simple vocabulary of most of the selections, their interesting content, and the variety of setting, character, and action throughout the book will, it is hoped, so attract the students to reading that they will *want* to read similar material even when no longer under classroom compulsion.

The present book endeavors to take the freshman boy or girl as he is; that is, to meet him on his own level of interest and understanding. The constant purpose, therefore, is *teaching to enjoy*. This consideration has determined the organization, the editing, and the material employed throughout this volume.

The organization around centers of interest has considerable merit. It extends the interests of the pupils and at the same time eliminates the danger of stifling reading pleasure by the analysis of types—an activity for which the average freshman is unprepared. Leaving the treatment of literary types for study in the second, third, and fourth years, PROSE AND POETRY FOR ENJOYMENT aims primarily at awakening response to wholesome literature. This awakening is sought through the choice of selections which are truly apt for enjoyment, and through an editing consciously centered on suggesting, testing, and enriching enjoyment.

The editorial matter accompanying each selection is simple and practical. Introductions, footnotes, study questions, book lists, and other aids are directed to the student rather than to the teacher. In place of mystifying academic terms, the editors have tried to use words which are simple, clear, and—where possible—picturesque. The carefully graded program toward building student vocabulary is a feature that the teacher will appreciate, meeting as it does the critical need for developing power over words. The glossary, an added feature of this new edition, will be a ready aid to the pupil in clarifying pronunciations and meanings of words unfamiliar to him.

Like the other three volumes of the ST. THOMAS MORE SERIES, this book is edited from the Catholic point of view, for Catholic students. Every selection—from nonsense verses to Negro spirituals—is integrated with the Catholic philosophy of life. Such integration is possible because wholesome literature, as a comment on life, is essentially in accord with the Christian, and therefore the Catholic, outlook. As Faith does not deny but builds on nature, so necessarily literature of both natural and supernatural inspiration is taken into account in the making of this book. Catholic and non-Catholic authors will be found side by side, but in every instance their comments on life find interpretation in the light of the Catholic Faith and Catholic ideals.

How this integration is achieved will be clear from the table of contents. Selections are related to nine centers of interest in nine successive sections. In order, these centers of interest are Adventure, Humor, Achievement, the Beauty of the World, the Mystery of Pain, the Life of Grace, Family Life, Patriotism, Social Responsibility. These are categories that include basic principles by which Catholic life develops and grows to perfection. Further, special introductions establish the theme of the several sections and direct the student toward a sane and Catholic enjoyment of the different areas of experience.

The inclusion in this edition of a modern novel will add to the appeal and usefulness of the book. Conrad Richter's *The Light in the Forest* is suited in style and story content to ninth-grade readers. To be sure, this is not exactly a Catholic novel. It even smacks of Rousseau's glorification of the man of pure nature. Yet this fact may be all for the best, since challenging comments and questions in the study material will help even the ninth-grade pupil to see that he must learn early to ponder and evaluate everything he reads, in the light of his Catholic philosophy of life.

In every way PROSE AND POETRY FOR ENJOYMENT is suited to be a bridge between the less formal extensive reading program of the junior high-school period and the more traditional approach of the senior high-school years.

CONTENTS

CONTENTS

SWORD OF SORROW

FIRE FROM HEAVEN

UNDER ONE ROOF

CONTENTS BY TYPES

NONFICTION

CONTENTS BY TYPES

PAGE

LYRIC POETRY

THE NOVEL

THE ROYAL ROAD TO ADVENTURE

From the vastness of the sky to the depths of the ocean, adventure lies in wait. Most of us like excitement—real or imaginary. In the poems and stories that follow, you will share many thrilling experiences: with Captain Tremblay you will take over the controls of an airliner in trouble; with Admiral Byrd you will be the first to fly over the South Pole; you'll help a famous detective solve a baffling mystery; you'll click the camera in a lion's face; you'll go a-pirating with Long John Silver.

The red-blooded adventurers you will meet are as tireless and full of life as you are. They have your own unrestrained spirit, your supple muscles, and fresh-air personality. Like yourselves they are a generation born to danger, lusty fellows who know nothing of fear.

The air becomes purer, the sun brighter, and the future more full of promise through the reading of these stories. You become rich with many more daring experiences than you could otherwise have known. Like magic, reading opens a brand-new world before you.

Do not be surprised if this first section fans into flame that vital spark, smouldering in all human beings, which makes life one vast desire for migration and adventure—ending only in Paradise.

H. ARMSTRONG ROBERTS

As heroes of the air Captain Patrick Tremblay and Father Timothy Mulvey had one thing in common: neither had ever piloted an airplane before the events related here. In fact Father Mulvey dislikes flying even as a passenger. In his book, THESE ARE YOUR SONS, *from which this selection was taken, he says: "The mere thought of stepping into a plane leaves me with visions of all the headlines ever printed about air disasters." Nevertheless, he did fly many times while he was in Korea gathering material for his book. It was there that he heard about Captain Tremblay's remarkable adventure.*

DOING A TREMBLAY

TIMOTHY J. MULVEY

The Twenty-fifth Canadian Infantry Brigade was having some difficulty in securing the proper air-to-ground support from the Fifth United States Air Force. The brigade had been in Korea two months and the liaison organization [1] between Division Corps and Army was still spotty.

Captain Patrick Tremblay, a ruddy French Canadian, approached his senior officer and requested an opportunity to go to Fifth Army Headquarters. "I want to study the organization of American air support, sir," Tremblay informed Brigadier Rockingham.

"It's all right, Pat. Take all the time you need," was the answer.

That was the prelude to a flight which the members of three Canadian regiments and the residents of Saguenay County [2] will tell their grandchildren about long after the pips and stars [3] are tarnished.

When Captain Pat arrived at headquarters in Seoul,[4] the Air Force major was sympathetic. "You say you are the Senior Liaison Officer?"

"That's right, sir, but the setup is still rough. I'd like to get an over-all picture of operations."

"If you really want to learn, we'll give you lectures and briefings. We'll let you ride our air spotters and observers. If you wish we'll also give you a hurry-up course on maps and terrains," the major said.

After five or six days of study, Pat felt he was reasonably ready to return to his

[1] LIAISON (lē′ā·zŏn′) ORGANIZATION—An organization that maintains intercommunication between two closely associated units.

[2] SAGUENAY (săg′ĕ·nā′) COUNTY—A county in the province of Quebec, Canada.

[3] PIPS AND STARS—Officers' brass decorations.

[4] SEOUL (sōl)—Capital of South Korea.

Brigade. Some of the information he had already known. He was aware of the fact, for example, that the perfect controller on the ground to direct air support is always a pilot; and conversely, the best pilots for calling in barrages are ex-artillerymen trained for the task.

"So that you'll have a complete picture of operations, Captain, you may want to ride as a passenger in one of our light observation planes," the wing commander at Pyongtak[5] suggested. "I'll be looking for a detailed report on your observations when you return."

The idea sounded like a good one, and Pat attended the briefing. A tall, fair Texan, Captain Wittom, was to be pilot. Fifteen minutes after the briefing, Tremblay and Wittom walked to the plane. It was a T-6 Harvard, about the size of an average fighter. Before they boarded the plane, Wittom spread a map on the wing and ran his finger over the marked areas indicating ack-ack activity.

"When you get up around here, Tremblay, that's when you start to watch and pray," the pilot grinned.

Tremblay climbed into the rear seat, adjusted his earphones, and placed the map across his knee. "I see you have dual mechanism on this ship," Tremblay noted.

"That's right. Sometimes we leave the rear control stick in. Sometimes we remove it to give the observer more room. Is it in your way?"

"It's all right, Captain."

They were airborne quickly. The first thing Tremblay did was to line up his map with the terrain below. He had no difficulty locating Suwon and the MSR.[6] The ground training and the Airborne School at Manitoba[7] were paying dividends now. Pat was actually elated.

Three-quarters of an hour later they were over the front lines. "Know where you are?" Wittom asked.

"Yes. That looks like the first R.O.K.[8] line, Imjin River."

"That's right. We'll fly around Kaesong[9] for a while."

The propeller of the T-6, whirling with its peculiar buzz-saw resonance, sliced off slivers of sound as it beat northward. Tremblay again congratulated himself as he identified landmarks on his map. At Kaesong they circled for a time at a thousand feet. The town, shortly before the peace talks, was comparatively quiet.

"Okay, Tremblay. We're going deeper up the line. You'd better keep your eyes open from now on," Wittom warned.

Tremblay bent forward in his seat searching the land that lay ahead. As the hills rolled under them, the enemy infantry positions began to appear. There was no activity evident, but the slit and crawl trenches were visible scars in the earth.

"Remember," Wittom called over the phone, "we want to establish the position of their guns."

Tremblay scanned the terrain with his binoculars. As yet all the heavy mission guns were well concealed.

[5] PYONGTAK—Pronounced pyûng·tăk′. Probably a Canadian air field.

[6] SUWON AND THE MSR—Suwon is a town in western Korea just south of Seoul. MSR is a military abbreviation for main supply route.

[7] MANITOBA (măn′ĭ·tō′bȧ)—A province in central Canada.

[8] R.O.K.—Republic of Korea.

[9] KAESONG (kă′ĭ·sông′)—A city just north of Seoul.

"Find anything yet, Pat?"

"Not a thing."

"All right. See that hill to the left? Watch it closely."

Pat saw that the hill was heavily wooded, and he noticed also that Wittom was dropping slightly to get a better view. Just as they cleared the crest, a quick shattering burst broke below them. The air was thick with .50-caliber and 20-mm ack-ack. The first blast was the one that did the damage. It pierced the plane between the pilot's and observer's compartments. The glass in the panel dials was shattered.

"Wow, that one was too close for comfort," Pat yelled into the phone.

There was no answer from the pilot's seat.

Pat watched Wittom closely. The pilot's head and part of his shoulders were barely visible above the seat. On the floor, a large red trickle of blood was running into Pat's compartment. Tremblay pushed the button again. The plane was wobbling in a slow half-turn to the left.

"Witt, are you hurt?" Tremblay knew he was hurt.

A faint sound came into the earphones. Wittom was trying to talk. "Wait . . ." the voice said. Then Wittom continued: "mayday . . . mayday."[10] His voice became unintelligible after that.

"Are you hurt, Witt?" Pat yelled again. "Are we going to jump?"

Wittom's head was now hanging limp over the edge of the cockpit. His hand, flung out over the side, had a deathly white pallor. Pat Tremblay, who, in all his life, had never touched the controls of a plane, was riding with a pilot who was either dead or unconscious.

The T-6 with its engine still roaring began to bounce and jiggle. Pat looked in dismay at the switches and dials on the panel. There had been moments in past life when he had imagined being in just this sort of predicament. Pat looked over the side of the plane and noticed with fright that the ground was coming up fast. He reached forward for the stick. There were only two details that Tremblay knew out of the vast science of aeronautics: push the stick forward and the plane goes down; pull it back and the plane rises. The tug he put on the stick zoomed the ship upward like a rocket. "Easy . . . easy . . ." Pat reminded himself in a cold sweat. Steady as she goes. This was trial and error. The last thing he could afford to do was throw the plane into a power stall. Slowly the T-6 moved over, and he was going down again. For the next several minutes, anyone observing the antics of the plane would have been led to believe that the pilot was an old-time roller coaster operator. The Thunderbolt at Palisades Park had dips and twists that were mild compared to Tremblay's charge through these Korean skies.

After Pat brought the plane under some semblance of control by jiggling the foot pedals, his mind shot back to the situation on hand. Wittom was still sagging over the cockpit. He decided that he had the alternative either of jockeying the plane back over friendly territory and ditching it, or, if Wittom were still alive, to take a chance of bringing the ship down. But how was he to

[10] MAYDAY—The distress signal word for radiotelephony.

know if Wittom were still alive, and how would he slow up the plane sufficiently to land it? To pull or push any of these confusing instruments might send the plane into a half dozen different gyrations. Pat did not know the starter from the stopper. Tremblay had problems.

Approaching Kaesong, Pat recognized the terrain. This alone was enough to give him a lift. As the plane drew nearer to friendly lines, Pat measured the bail-out procedure of a free drop as against the attempt to land the plane. What was he going to do?

A few minutes later, Pat knew definitely what he was going to do. Wittom's hand opened slowly. It was a slight movement, but Pat noticed immediately. "Witt, can you hear me? Can you make me out?" Pat called.

No response came back. Tremblay tried several more times but it was of no use.

The sun was bright in his eyes and he had difficulty holding to a level course. If he could only keep the plane flying around until Wittom regained consciousness, there would be a chance for both of them to come out of it safely. While he was thinking of this, Wittom lifted his hand slowly. With apparent effort he twisted himself around and looked at Tremblay. His face was quizzical and pain-racked. He turned his head away from Pat, took one look over the side of the ship, and then flung his hand in a weak gesture toward the left.

"You want me to turn to the left?" Pat shouted.

The hand was raised again. Yes, it was directing Pat to the left.

Tremblay eased down on the foot

pedals. He was not sure whether it was the slant of the stick or the foot pedals that did the trick, but after a few minor jounces and corrections the nose of the ship was pointing east. That's when Pat saw the strips of Kimpo.[11] Tremblay then asked himself what kind of approach he should make. Somewhere down there, there were wind pennants indicating the direction of approach. From where Pat sat, however, Kimpo was a vast blur. The only clear details were the landing strips.

While Pat was still holding on to the stick he was startled by the change of the engine. Somehow through the haze of semiconsciousness, Wittom, who was partially paralyzed with ack-ack fragments in his spinal column, reached out and pushed the button for the landing gear flaps. He knew that Tremblay could not touch choke-off speed. The plane pointed her nose over. Tremblay was working the pedals like mad when he saw they were coming in on the down wind. A Navy fighter plane was heading toward them on a take-off. They were coming in on the strip in what was practically a dive angle. A hard pull on the stick leveled them off but not enough. The plane hit the hard concrete, bounced into the air, and in that fleeting, perilous instant as they were suspended in the air, the fighter plane zoomed under them. The T-6, out of control now, went sprawling into a field, weaving from left to right. It crashed through a four-inch raid-wall that some Koreans were building. Dust and flying debris were thick in the air when it came to a shuddering stop. Flames were licking around the engine when Pat unhooked his harness. Jumping out on the wing, he lifted Wittom from the cockpit. The six-foot-two Texan, whose face was completely smeared with blood, looked more dead than alive. Emergency crash crews rushed to the scene and a few minutes later Wittom was carried away in an ambulance.

"Where are you going, Captain?" a startled fireman asked Tremblay when he saw the Canadian jump up on the wing of the smoking plane.

"I forgot my reports and maps," Tremblay said.

An hour later, Pat Tremblay was flown to Pyongtak where he made his first official report as an observer. He pointed out the co-ordinates on the map to the wing commander, and in a voice flavored slightly with the French Canadian of Chicoutimi,[12] he affirmed, "On this hill, truly, there are gun positions."

The wing commander ran his fingers through his hair. "You say you never flew a plane before?"

"Today was the first time I ever put my hand on a stick."

"How long did you pilot it?"

"About forty-five minutes, sir."

A major who had listened to Pat's story suggested that he be booked for the Distinguished Flying Cross.

"What would I do with a D.F.C.?" Pat asked.

"Oh, I don't know, but for the rest of your life you'd have one whale of a time trying to explain it."

[11] KIMPO (kĭm·pō)—Air field behind the United Nations' lines.

[12] CHICOUTIMI (shĭ·kōō′tĭ·mĭ)—A river port on the Saguenay River.

At this juncture somebody produced a bottle of spirits. "Canadian, of course," Pat explained to me. "You see, in our outfit if anyone goes through a hardship, we figure he needs a shot."

"And what about Wittom?"

"The last I heard, he was doing all right after they took those fragments out of his spine."

This is the kind of story I particularly enjoy. Should it ever have happened to me, and I have flown behind the dual control system of the T-6, the chances are there would have been twin obituaries. But this has never prevented me from dreaming and redreaming my favorite aeronautical emergency. It's an episode where I take over the controls of an airliner.

The ship was a huge DC-6, the Advance Mercury, whizzing westward over Texas. More than fifty passengers were resting comfortably, blissfully unaware of the tragedy that was about to stalk them for the next seven hours. The light over the cabin door flashed red. NO SMOKING, FASTEN YOUR SEAT BELTS—the glass panel warned. The ship began to labor through rough air currents. A cold front had suddenly developed. Conditions behind were as bad as those ahead, so there was nothing to do but proceed. Murky gray clouds surrounded the plane, and lightning began to flash at frequencies of twenty seconds. The blaze of lightning was so brilliant, it blinded the eyes. Ninety-nine times out of a hundred a DC-6 could rise above these disturbances. That night was the one time it could not. Tremendous air pockets developed and the ship dropped and shuddered frightfully on the impacts. The huge tail section began to sway in the grip of high-velocity winds.

Nervous, as usual, I looked about me at the other passengers. The aged couple in front of me were approaching hysteria. The old gentleman would groan audibly every time the ship plunged in a down draft. He kept calling out to the pilot to bring the plane down. The stewardess went forward at a signal from one of the passengers, but halfway down the ship, she was tossed off her feet. Coats, hats, brief cases, blankets, and pillows were strewn all over the plane.

Then the door of the pilot's cabin opened. The second stewardess stood framed in it, pale and shaken. She managed to crawl down the aisle on her hands and knees, and when she reached her companion I overheard the frightful story she told.

"All of them," she cried, "the pilot, co-pilot, and engineer, they're all dead. Electrocuted or asphyxiated or something. What are we going to do, Marjane?"

Immediate panic began to spread among the passengers. I will confess I was shaken myself.

"Wait a minute, everybody," I shouted, standing up and clutching the seat in front of me. "This is an emergency and it's not going to do any of us any good if we start losing our heads. If you'll all be quiet, I'm sure I'll be able to handle this thing."

This, needless to say, was nothing but the rankest lie. As I staggered up the aisle, I felt their strained, terror-bright eyes watching me. "Probably an old pilot from World War II," their eyes were saying. "Probably an ex-Wing Commander of the Berlin airlift." I patted a shaking, white-haired executive on the shoulder as I went by.

I remember it now—those first few moments alone in the pilot's cabin. I placed the bodies of the crew in the engineer's compartment so that I should have room to move around. The door opened behind me. It was the second stewardess. She wanted to know if there was anything she could do.

"Yes," I said. "Which gadget is the radio?"

A fleeting look of suspicion passed over her face. I suspected she knew that I was unacquainted with the technical details of aircraft. After she had indicated the earphones and the microphone, I advised her to go back and offer any assistance necessary to the passengers.

Surprisingly enough we had broken through the cold front and were sailing along in level flight. A few seconds later I sat in the pilot's seat and in a voice that quivered slightly I kept repeating, "SOS—mayday . . . SOS, mayday. This is Advance Mercury."

"Advance Mercury . . . this is Dallas Control."

"Dallas Control . . . this is Advance Mercury reporting pilot, co-pilot, and engineer dead. Advise you clear all air channels. Alert civilian traffic control, and dispatch aircraft to escort ship for directional bearings. Am not acquainted with instrument panel or let-down procedure. Require detailed radio broadcast describing same."

Little did I know then that within a half hour, practically a whole nation would be standing by for the outcome of this hair-raising flight. N.B.C., C.B.S., and M.B.C.[13] had thrown open their networks to record my air-to-tower broadcasts.

"Roger.[14] This is Advance Mercury. Repeat. Which dial is what?"

The voice said: "The dial three inches above your left knee is the fuel indicator. Over."

"Roger. Fuel indicator. What about it? Over."

"How does fuel indicator read?"

I gave a fairly good description of the needle angle and proceeded to request more detailed instructions for let-down procedure. "Roger. This is Advance Mercury. Three Constellations and a C-54 are coming in now at one o'clock[15] . . . they are circling over me. Now they are taking a veering to right. Instruct escort ships to lead me to Mojave Desert.[16] Am just a bit confused about regular airstrip landing you describe. Over."

"Mojave Desert! Why the Mojave Desert? Over."

"Contemplate negotiating belly landing. Will take ship in on the long oblique."[17]

This startling decision I had made evidently caused some confusion back at air

[13] N.B.C., C.B.S., AND M.B.C.—National Broadcasting Company, Columbia Broadcasting System, and Mutual Broadcasting Company.

[14] ROGER—In radio, Roger means *all right, I understand.*

[15] AT ONE O'CLOCK—The planes sent out from Dallas were approaching the nose of the "pilotless" plane at an angle slightly to the right, as the number one on a clock is just to the right of twelve.

[16] MOJAVE (mô·hä'vê) DESERT—An arid region in southern California.

[17] LONG OBLIQUE—A landing pattern in which a pilot makes a long approach to the field and glides in for a landing.

control, but finally the voice came through. "Roger, wilco." [18]

The rest of the story, of course, is what everybody read about in *Life* and *Newsweek.*

> "Like a huge bird that had labored through a storm, it settled slowly . . . slowly while a nation prayed. Below, the sands of the Mojave stretched endlessly. One man alone behind the throttles knew the real agony of this descent. Never in the history of world aviation had there been such a daring gamble with human life. Fifty-three passengers, numbed with suspense, peered from the windows. They also prayed. Constellation pilot, chunky, puckish, William Varian relayed the ACA.[19] 'You are ten feet above sand . . . five feet . . . three feet . . . easy . . . hold it . . .' A slight ripple, then a feathering, swirling spray leaps up where the belly of the ship creases the sand. The Mojave was sweet touchdown to a 'pilotless' airliner. Three minutes later, fifty-three hysterically weeping, laughing passengers surrounded Mulvey. With characteristic shyness he tried to pass it off. His request: 'A glass of water.' Said air-wise stewardess, Marjane: 'I'll fly with him any day.' Repeated Varian: 'The nicest belly landing I've ever seen.' "

This particular story is absolutely true up to a point. I have flown in a DC-6 when it was the one out of the hundredth time that it could not rise above the storm conditions of a cold front. I still have the American Airlines passenger log to prove it. The fact that the pilot, co-pilot, and engineer did not happen to die on this trip was a circumstance beyond my control. A Mitty complex,[20] of which I have more than a modicum, provides me with enough cadavers to render the *Queen Mary* crewless and if *that* isn't a job, trying to bring the big lady through the Narrows [21] all by yourself, then you just don't have any idea of navigation.

[18] WILCO—Will do; will co-operate.

[19] ACA—Air Controlled Approach.

[20] MITTY COMPLEX—In "The Secret Life of Walter Mitty" by James Thurber, Mr. Mitty has frequent daydreams in which he plays a heroic part.

[21] THE NARROWS—A strait connecting Upper New York Bay with Lower New York Bay.

FOR DISCUSSION

1. Why did Captain Tremblay visit the Fifth United States Air Force Headquarters in Seoul? Explain how he happened to be a passenger in a dual-controlled observation plane.

2. Why did Wittom fly low directly over the enemy lines? Describe the situation of the two men after the plane was hit. What were some of the problems that confronted Tremblay?

3. What characteristics of a hero did Captain Tremblay show during the emergency? How might a less courageous or less stable person have behaved under the same circumstances? Do you think he should have been awarded the Distinguished Flying Cross? Give reasons for your opinion.

4. If you know enough about aircraft and flying, evaluate this selection on the basis of possibility or probability. Point out anything in the circumstances or happenings which seemed to you pure luck or unexplained coincidence.

ARMCHAIR HEROICS

Notice that when he introduces the tale of his own exploits, the author speaks of "dreaming and redreaming." What he tells us is not a dream in the usual sense, but a *daydream.* You have probably had similar daydreams in which you imagine yourself the calm resourceful person who takes over in time of emergency.

1. Compare Captain Tremblay's adventure with Father Mulvey's daydream. In

what ways are they similar? How are they different? Tell why you enjoyed one more than the other.

2. In order really to appreciate the last sentence in the selection you should know James Thurber's story, "The Secret Life of Walter Mitty." You might look for the story in the library to read for your own enjoyment or to use as a special report to the rest of the class.

AIR-AGE WORDS

Each discovery or invention brings new words into the language or gives additional meanings to old words. If you are interested in the field of aviation you will do well to develop an air-age vocabulary.

1. If the following italicized words are not already familiar to you, you can probably guess their meanings from their use in the sentences below:

a. "There were only two details that Tremblay knew out of the vast science of *aeronautics*." The prefix *aero* or *aëro*, as it is sometimes written, means *air*. Use the dictionary to make a list of additional air-age words besides *aeronautics* that begin with that prefix.

b. "It is an episode where I take over the controls of an *airliner*." Sometimes the English word *air* itself is used instead of the older prefix. Look under *air* in the dictionary to add to your list of aviation terms.

2. The word *aviation* comes from the Latin word *avis*, which means *bird*. See if you can name two additional words which begin with *avi*.

◇◇◇◇◇

Here is a first-hand account of a life-and-death experience at sea. With great skill, the author has drawn word-pictures which will make this experience as keenly exciting for you as it was for him.

THE BATTLE OF THE GREAT WHITE SHARK

S. ROBERT RUSSELL

Forty miles off shore, in the Gulf of Mexico, our commercial fishing boat, *Celsa*, wallowed soddenly, her dirty canvas hanging limp in the dead calm, her ancient Diesel dead. The four-man crew labored over the stubborn engine and cursed their luck. I could offer only half-hearted sympathy, for as a paying passenger making the trip to study marine life, I felt sure this interlude in calm waters would prove exciting. From my vantage point on top of the cabin, I surveyed the sea.

The blazing August sun made the water transparent for one hundred feet straight down before it fogged into smoky translucence.

Deep down in the haze I spotted a cigar-shaped shadow. It was so small it hardly caught my eye. But as it rose toward the surface a terrifying change took place. That which had seemed only inches long grew to feet, then yards and finally, when the sail-like dorsal[1] broke water, it had become a blood-chilling monster as long as our boat, a full thirty feet from snout to wide-forked tail. It was a great white shark, Carcharodon carcharias.[2]

Gray-white, horrible, he was a direct descendant of gigantic ancestors. Deadly, broad, serrated daggers gleamed ivory-white in the sardonic-grinning, half-opened mouth, as symmetrical as the teeth on a cross-cut saw. Along one side an even row of small round scars, like healed machine gun bullet wounds, gave testimony that a giant sawfish had once driven home a telling blow.

He circled the boat. Down on the deck the men jumped up with a yell when the high, pointed fin passed by, cruising around us.

For a time he swam aimlessly, then, swerving, he streaked toward the large patch of seaweed.

Lying half-awash, comfortably bedded atop the seaweed, was one of nature's weirdest freaks, Mola mola, the oceanic sunfish.

She looked, from small, pouting mouth to high dorsal, much like any full-bodied fish. But from the dorsal where her body should have tapered off into a tail was—nothing. She was almost exactly half a fish, a tailless head and body, something nature had absentmindedly left incomplete. She was small, as such freaks go, measuring only three feet up and down.

Carcharodon skirted the seaweed, scented the thing sheltered on it, reversed in a whirlpool of foam, and struck.

In an instant the seaweed patch erupted into a boiling, foaming maelstrom. Brown clumps flew spinning into the air. Carcharodon's terrifying jaws opened and clamped shut, lightning fast. His battery of jagged-edged knives sheared into Mola mola's leathery skin and locked. Another great swirl and Mola mola disappeared as completely as though she had never existed.

Carcharodon plowed out of the seaweed. Streamers trailed from tight clenched jaws, beardlike.

It was soon after that the engine gave its first thump. As the explosions shattered the quiet and vibrated through the depths the towering dorsal fin sank slowly beneath the surface.

Our cargo was beginning to smell. There was no use taking it in. For a time I helped the fishermen shovel the fish overboard. The exhaust skipped, quit, started and skipped, and the *Celsa* crept toward harbor as I searched the water for another glimpse of the tremendous white shark.

He did not surface again nor could I locate him below us but I visualized him matching our poor speed effortlessly, slashing and gorging on our catch with ravenous gluttony.

Unloading tons of big fish by hand is slow work. The engine constantly balked and stopped. As a result it was late afternoon when the last fish was jettisoned

[1] DORSAL—Dorsal or back fin.

[2] CARCHARODON CARCHARIAS—Pronounced kär·kăr′ō·dŏn kär·kā′rĭ·ăs.

and the Galveston north jetty lay close in, dead ahead. There the engine died finally. The captain sent a man forward to throw the kedge[3] over. We then could signal for a tow in.

I mounted to the deckhouse roof, convinced that the huge shark had followed our trail of fish, and wishing to have a last glimpse of his spine-chilling bulk.

Inshore on the flats lay an old wreck. To seaward of it a school of porpoises surfaced, blew, and fed around a slow moving shrimp trawler. Not far from us a mother porpoise and her pup swam close together.

It was feeding time for the pup. He nudged and butted his mother insistently. Finally yielding, she stopped and rolled over slightly until her starboard flipper came out of the water.

I watched, delighted at the luck my trip had brought, for few men have seen a porpoise pup being nursed.

Then, a commotion twenty yards away attracted my attention. A bull porpoise surfaced noisily with a large flounder held loosely between his jaws. Throwing back his head quickly he sent the fish spinning into the air. He retrieved it almost as it struck the water and repeated the performance again and again. Finally abandoning the shredded fish, he dived and almost instantly zoomed into the air in the series of spectacular leaps that is the main act in a male porpoise's courtship.

Suddenly a tremendous, shadowy form materialized in the depths nearby. It was the great white shark. Possibly the abandoned flounder had settled close enough to be detected by his marvelously acute combination senses of taste and smell.

In any event he swam directly toward the mother porpoise and her nursing pup. He seemed in no hurry and completely unaware of their presence.

But the porpoise, her every nerve alert while nursing, sensed his approach. She whirled, panic-stricken, to an even keel. As she did, her flipper smacked the pup smartly across the head. Frightened, bewildered by the undeserved chastisement, he darted away from her protecting side —straight toward the shark!

Carcharodon saw the tiny porpoise, swerved, and surged ahead to meet it. Death was quick and merciful for the little pup.

The frantic mother, tearing after him, twisted and dived instinctively. That lightning reflex saved her. Her conical teeth were grinders, useless to tear and slash, quite incapable of ripping through the shark's tough, denticle-armored[4] hide. But nature had given her another weapon. The aeons since her forebears had first left land for a marine existence had fused her neck vertebrae into almost solid bone. Her hog-like snout made a perfect battering ram.

She smashed into the shark with the force of three-hundred pounds moving at almost forty miles an hour. His great bulk quivered under the impact. He whirled, jaws clashing. She twisted away from his boiling rush with far superior speed and agility.

As she dodged, the bull porpoise charged to her aid. Nearly twice the weight and infinitely more powerful than the female, he blasted into the shark well

[3] KEDGE—A light anchor.

[4] DENTICLE-ARMORED—Covered with tooth-like scales.

aft, almost at the anal fins. The smash was so terrific that the huge tail was lifted a full yard out of the water.

Then the mother drove in again from the opposite side. She hit the shark above center, slid up the smooth side, shot ten feet into the air, and struck the water on her back. For a split second she floundered, confused. In that brief interval the shark spun, jaws snapping. Knife-edged teeth slashed multiple grooves along her side and chopped the end of her port side flipper.

Around them the water boiled and swirled. Foam spread in a widening circle. Mud from the bottom, only fifteen feet below, slowly changed the clear water to a dirty yellow.

A half mile north the other porpoises had abandoned their feeding and were playing, blowing, and diving around the shrimp boat. Abruptly, as if in response to an inaudible signal, they surfaced and charged in echelon,[5] straight for the boiling, foam-flecked whirlpool.

So great was the urge for speed that they swam almost on the surface, submerging only slightly in long undulating dives. Two flashed cleanly into the air in shallow, speed-accelerating leaps.

Out-weighed and out-weaponed, the female porpoise and her new-found champion fought on desperately. The tide of battle was slowly turning against them. Six inches had been sheared from the great bull's starboard tail-fluke and a row of jagged furrows, from dorsal fin aft, ran red.

He charged in fury, struck high, ricocheted in turn from the plunging, rounded back, and burst into the air in a long shallow flight. His landing split the surface fifty feet distant. The shark plunged toward the weakening female.

He might have caught her but before the chase had run twenty yards, the charging school of porpoises struck with the impact of galloping Cossacks.[6] The

[5] IN ECHELON—In wedge-like formation.

[6] COSSACKS—Members of a Russian people noted for horsemanship and daring.

sound of sodden, smashing blows was like a boxer's dripping gloves smacking against flesh but amplified to thousands of pounds.

For ten explosive, water-churning minutes the porpoises tore in, struck and retreated like a pack of dogs holding a bear at bay. Like a bear the shark would make short slashing stands; then, as his adversaries drew back, attempt to run for safety. And each time the school, circling to seaward, drove him toward the beach.

A blindly charging young bull failed to elude the champing jaws. That was the beginning of the end. As the shark slowed to crush his victim the mother porpoise charged for the monster's most vulnerable spot—his gill slits. She was squarely on target.

At forty miles an hour her hard snout drove through the leather-tough protecting strips on his starboard side as though they were paper. Her head bored in eyes-deep. Her powerful jaws clamped. Thrashing free she brought with her a whole mouthful of crimson gill-tissue, as all important to the shark as lungs to a man.

Blood pumping from the gaping opening dyed the water.

As if on signal the entire school concentrated its attack on both gills. One tough snout after another drove in, lightning fast. Teeth clamped, ripped, and withdrew. Within a minute the port gill was also gushing red.

There was a cataclysmic upheaval. Chunks of mud slung spinning into the air. Silt-yellowed water darkened to reddish brown. A ghastly, sneering head climbed straight out of the water until the huge flippers came into view. It hung there for three long seconds, ruptured gills spouting redly. Frightful jaws gaped wide, then crashed shut with the report of two planks being slapped together. A convulsive shudder shook the crumpling hulk. It toppled backward, quivering weakly, and settled toward the bottom.

One by one the porpoises withdrew, all but the still raging female and the big bull. Time after time she surfaced, then dived, and by the water's turmoil I could visualize her slamming into the flaccid bulk on the bottom. The male, as if in patient understanding, made no effort to dissuade her but circled slowly as if waiting until her fury was spent.

Finally she turned from her vengeance and swam to him. For a long minute they lay quietly. Then swimming side by side they followed the others.

The sun had set, and the quiet bay was purple with the reflection of fading twilight, when a power boat whose skipper had caught our signals finally towed us into port.

"Didja get a good catch?" he asked the member of our crew who tossed him the tow rope. Our man replied in disgust that the trip had been a complete bust. I had the sense to keep quiet, realizing my commercial-minded boat-mates could hardly share my joy in the most rewarding day I had ever spent on the Gulf.

FOR DISCUSSION

1. How good an artist is your imagination? Can you present yourself with pictures of the shark and his first victim? Describe Mola mola.

2. What is the chief weapon of the shark? What, of the porpoises? Which struck first, the shark or the porpoise?

3. Describe the strategy used by the porpoises in defeating Carcharodon.

4. How did the white shark try to escape?

5. Name some reasons why Mr. Russell counts this day as "the most rewarding day" he ever spent on the Gulf.

WHAT DID YOU SEE?

1. How many *picture words* can you find in the paragraph describing the death of the shark? List at least ten.

2. In a sentence or two explain in your own words what each of the following phrases means. Your explanation should prove that you understand the meanings of the words in italics.

a. "I visualized him *gorging* on our catch with ravenous *gluttony*."

b. "She *floundered*, confused."

c. "The young bull failed to *elude* the *champing* jaws."

d. "There was a *cataclysmic* upheaval."

FOR UNDERSTANDING

In an encyclopedia or other reference book, look up the characteristics and activities of the sunfish. Then tell why Mola mola was such an easy prey for Carcharodon.

RELATED READING

In "The Triumph of Scar-Face" by Kenneth Gilbert, you will find another tense story of sea life. Look for it in *American Boy Stories*.

◇◇◇◇◇

Old John Silver, the picturesque pirate of TREASURE ISLAND *fame, represents the bold, baneful, yet cheerful crew that sailed the seas and flourished during the sixteenth century. Read this ballad in the same boasting tone which John Silver would use if he were actually here telling the tale.*

A Ballad of John Silver

JOHN MASEFIELD

We were schooner-rigged and rakish, with a long and lissome hull,
And we flew the pretty colors of the crossbones and the skull;
We'd a big black Jolly Roger flapping grimly at the fore,
And we sailed the Spanish Water in the happy days of yore.

1. SCHOONER-RIGGED AND RAKISH—With masts rigged out in schooner style, and at an angle which suggests speed and illegal trade.
1. LISSOME (lĭs′ŭm)—Trim, graceful.
3. JOLLY ROGER—Name of pirate flag.
4. SPANISH WATER—The Caribbean Sea.

"A Ballad of John Silver" from *Collected Poems* by John Masefield. Reprinted by permission of The Macmillan Company.

We'd a long brass gun amidships, like a well-conducted ship; 5
We had each a brace of pistols and a cutlass at the hip;
It's a point which tells against us, and a fact to be deplored,
But we chased the goodly merchantmen and laid their ships aboard.

Then the dead men fouled the scuppers and the wounded filled the chains,
And the paint work all was spatter-dashed with other people's brains; 10
She was boarded, she was looted, she was scuttled till she sank,
And the pale survivors left us by the medium of the plank.

O! then it was (while standing by the taffrail on the poop)
We could hear the drowning folk lament the absent chicken coop;
Then, having washed the blood away, we'd little else to do 15
Than to dance a quiet hornpipe as the old salts taught us to.

O! the fiddle on the fo'c's'le, and the slapping naked soles,
And the genial "Down the middle, Jake, and curtsy when she rolls!"
With the silver sea around us and the pale moon overhead,
And the lookout not a-looking and his pipe bowl glowing red. 20

Ah! the pig-tailed, quidding pirates and the pretty pranks we played,
All have since been put a stop to by the naughty Board of Trade;
The schooners and the merry crews are laid away to rest,
A little south the sunset in the Islands of the Blest.

9. SCUPPERS—Holes in the side of the ship, at deck level, which drain water and refuse off the deck.
9. CHAINS—Flat ledge on side of ship, to receive strain of the shrouds.
13. TAFFRAIL ON THE POOP—Rail around the rear of the ship.
16. HORNPIPE—Lively dance.
17. FO'C'S'LE—Forecastle, part of the upper deck.
21. QUIDDING—Tobacco-spitting.

FOR DISCUSSION

1. Let us use some modern terms as we discuss Silver's ancient schooner. To what "navy" did the ship belong? What was its "theater of operations"? What was its "objective"? Describe the thoroughness with which it completed its "mission."

2. What is the Board of Trade? Do you agree with Silver that the Board of Trade is "naughty"? Why or why not?

3. Find lines which tell the various ways in which the pirates had fun.

4. The "Spanish Water" seems to be a famous rendezvous for adventurers. If you were to visit these waters today, what would you expect to find or see there? Answer in some detail.

5. Is this ballad meant to be taken seriously? What feeling did it leave with you —amusement, delight, horror, pity? Take a poll of the class to find the reaction of each of your classmates.

IN PICTURES

In order to emphasize the humor in a

situation or to put special emphasis on particular characteristics of an individual he is picturing, the cartoonist uses exaggeration in the details of his drawing. Draw a cartoon of old John himself, or of the battle with the merchantmen, or of any other incident.

RELATED READING

For some gay lines about another famous pirate see "Captain Kidd" in *A Book of Americans* by Rosemary and Stephen Vincent Benét.

◇◇◇◇◇

Adventure is synonymous with the name, Rear Admiral Richard E. Byrd. Here is an excerpt from Byrd's personal account of one of his experiences in the South Polar regions. As you read this account, remember that this hazardous flight was accomplished in 1929. What contrast is there between the planes used then and those that would be used today for such a flight?

FLIGHT TO THE SOUTH POLE

RICHARD E. BYRD

Thanksgiving Day, November 25, [1929] brought what we wanted. At noon the Geological Party[1] radioed a final weather report: "Unchanged. Perfect visibility. No clouds anywhere." Harrison[2] finished with his balloon runs, Haines[3] with his weather charts. The sky was still somewhat overcast, and the surface wind from the east southeast. Haines came into the library, his face grave. Together we went out for a walk and a last look at the weather. What he said exactly I have forgotten, but it was in effect: "If you don't go now, you may never have another chance as good as this." And that was that.

The mechanics, Bubier, Roth, and Demas, went over the plane for the last time, testing everything with scrupulous care. A line of men passed five-gallon cans of gasoline to several men standing on the wing, who poured them into the wing tanks. Another line fed the stream of gear which flowed into the plane. Black weighed each thing before passing it on to McKinley and June, who were stowing the stuff in the cabin. Hanson

[1] GEOLOGICAL PARTY—A section of Byrd's expedition assigned to the study of the earth's structure and surface in the antarctic.

[2] HARRISON—A weather conditions expert assigned to the expedition by the U. S. Weather Bureau.

[3] HAINES—Another Weather Bureau expert.

went over the radio equipment. With De Ganahl [4] I made a careful check of the sextant and the watches and chronometers, which were among the last things put aboard. For days De Ganahl and I had nursed the chronometers, checking them against the time-tick broadcast every night from the United States. We knew their exact loss or gain.

The total weight was approximately 15,000 pounds.

Haines came up with a final report on the weather: "A twenty-mile wind from the south at 2000 feet." I went into my office and picked up a flag weighted with a stone from Floyd Bennett's [5] grave. It seemed fitting that something connected with the spirit of this noble friend, who stood with me over the North Pole, on May 9, 1926, should rest as long as stone endures at the bottom of the world.

There were handshakes all around, and at 3:29 o'clock we were off. The skis were in the air after a run of thirty seconds—an excellent take-off. A calm expectation took hold of my mind.

Had you been there to glance over the cabin of this modern machine which has so revolutionized polar travel, I think you would have been impressed most of all—perhaps first of all—with the profusion of gear in the cabin. There was a small sledge, rolled masses of sleeping bags, bulky food sacks, two pressure gasoline stoves, rows of cans of gasoline packed about the main tank forward, funnels for draining gasoline and oil from the engines, bundles of clothing, tents, and so on *ad infinitum.* There was scarcely room in which to move.

June had his radio in the after bulkhead on the port [6] side. From time to time he flashed reports on our progress to the base. From the ear phones strapped to his helmet ran long cords, so that he might move freely about the cabin without being obliged to take them off. His duties were varied and important. He had to attend to the motion-picture camera, the radio, and the complicated valves of the six gasoline tanks. Every now and then he relieved Balchen [7] at the wheel or helped him to follow the elusive trail.

McKinley had his mapping camera ready for action either on port or starboard side. It was for him and the camera he so sedulously served that the flight was made. The mapping of the corridor between Little America and the South Pole was one of the major objectives of the expedition.

Balchen was forward, bulking large in the narrow compartment, his massive hands on the wheel, now appraising the engines with a critical eye, now the dozen flickering fingers on the dials on the instrument board. Balchen was in his element. His calm fine face bespoke his confidence and sureness. He was anticipating the struggle at the "Hump" [8] almost with eagerness.

It was quite warm forward, behind the engines. But a cold wind swept through the cabin, making one thankful for heavy

[4] DE GANAHL—The navigator.

[5] FLOYD BENNETT—Sole companion of Byrd in his flight over the North Pole in 1926.

[6] PORT—Left side.

[7] BALCHEN—Bernt Balchen, head pilot. He had piloted Amundsen and Ellsworth on their arctic expeditions and Byrd on his transatlantic flight to France.

[8] THE "HUMP"—The sharp rise leading up to the two-mile-high plateau.

clothes. When the skies cleared, a golden light poured into the cabin. The sound of the engines and propellers filled it. One had to shout to make oneself heard. From the navigation table aft, where my charts were spread out, a trolley ran to the control cabin. Over it I shot to Balchen the necessary messages and courses; he would turn and smile his understanding.

That, briefly, is the picture, and a startling one it makes in contrast with that of Amundsen's party,[9] which had pressed along this same course eighteen years before. A wing, pistons, and flashing propellers had taken the place of runner,[10] dogs, and legs. Amundsen was delighted to make twenty-five miles per day. We had to average ninety miles per hour to accomplish our mission. We had the advantages of swiftness and comfort, but we had as well an enlarged fallibility. A flaw in a piece of steel, a bit of dirt in the fuel lines or carburetor jets, a few hours of strong head winds, fog, or storm—these things, remotely beyond our control, could destroy our carefully laid plans and nullify our most determined efforts.

Still, it was not these things that entered our minds. Rather it was the thought of the "Hump," and how we should fare with it.

Soon after passing the crevasses we picked up again the vast escarpment [11] to the right. More clearly than before we saw the white-blue streams of many glaciers discharging into the Barrier,[12] and several of the higher snow-clad peaks glistened so brightly in the sun as to seem like volcanoes in eruption.

Now the Queen Maud Range loomed ahead. I searched again for the "appearance of land" to the east. Still the rolling Barrier—nothing else.

At 8:15 o'clock we had the Geological Party in sight—a cluster of beetles about two dark-topped tents. Balchen dropped overboard the photographs of the Queen Maud Range and the other things we had promised to bring. The parachute canopy to which they were attached fluttered open and fell in gentle oscillations, and we saw two or three figures rush out to catch it. We waved to them, and then prepared for a settlement of the issue at the "Hump."

Up to this time the engines had operated continuously at cruising revolutions. Now Balchen opened them full throttle, and the Ford girded its loins for the long, fighting pull over the "Hump." We rose steadily. We were then about sixty miles north of the western portal of Axel Heiberg,[13] and holding our course steadily on meridian 163° 45′ W. with the sun compass.

I watched the altimeters, of which there were two in the navigation department. The fingers marched with little jumps across the face of the dial—3000 feet, 3500, 4000, 4500. The Ford had her toes in, and was climbing with a vast effort.

Drawing nearer, we had edged 30° to the west of south, to bring not only Axel Heiberg but also Liv Glacier into view. This was a critical period. I was by no means certain which glacier I should

[9] AMUNDSEN'S PARTY—Amundsen traveled the same route to the South Pole by dog sled. He was the first to reach it, December 14, 1911.

[10] RUNNER—That is, of the sleds.

[11] ESCARPMENT—Steep mountain slope.

[12] THE BARRIER—The huge ice sheet stretching beyond the land out into the sea.

[13] AXEL HEIBERG—A large glacier.

choose for the ascent. I went forward and took a position behind the pilots.

The schemes and hopes of the next few minutes were beset by many uncertainties. Which would it be—Axel Heiberg or Liv Glacier?

There was this significant difference between flying and sledging: we could not pause long for decision or investigation. Minutes stood for gasoline, and gasoline was precious. The waste of so little as half an hour of fuel in the fruitless experiment might well overturn the mathematical balance on which the success of the flight depended. The execution of the plan hung on the proper choice of the route over the "Hump."

Yet, how well, after all, could judgment forecast the ultimate result? There were few facts on which we might base a decision. We knew, for example, from Amundsen's report, that the highest point of the pass of Axel Heiberg Glacier was 10,500 feet. We should know, in a very few minutes, after June had calculated the gasoline consumption, the weight of the plane. From that we could determine, according to the tables we had worked out and which were then before us, the approximate ceiling we should have. We should know, too, whether or not we should be able to complete the flight, other conditions being favorable.

These were the known elements. The unknown were burdened with equally important consequences. The structural nature of the head of the pass was of prime importance. We knew from Amundsen's descriptions, and from what we could see with our own eyes, that the pass on both sides was surrounded by towering peaks, much higher than the maximum ceiling of the heavily loaded plane. But whether the pass was wide or narrow; whether it would allow us room to maneuver in case we could not rise above it; whether it would be narrow and running with a torrent of down-pressing wind which would dash a plane, already hovering near its service ceiling, to the glacier floor—these were things, naturally, we could not possibly know until the issue was directly at hand.

I stood beside Balchen, carefully studying the looming fortress, still wondering by what means we should attempt to carry it. With a gesture of the hand Balchen pointed to fog vapor rising from the black rock of the foothills which were Nansen's high priests [14]—caused no doubt by the condensation of warm currents of air radiated from the sun-heated rocks. A thin layer of cloud seemed to cap Axel Heiberg's pass, and extended almost to Liv Glacier. But of this we were not certain. Perhaps it was the surface of the snow. If cloud, then our difficulties were already upon us. Even high clouds would be resting on the floor of the uplifted plateau.

There was, then, a gamble in the decision. Doubtless a flip of the coin would have served as well. In the end, we decided to choose Liv Glacier, the unknown pass to the right which Amundsen had seen far in the distance and named after Dr. Nansen's daughter. It seemed to be broader than Axel Heiberg, and the pass not quite so high.

A few minutes after 9 o'clock we passed near the intermediate base, which, of course, we could not see. Our altitude

[14] NANSEN'S HIGH PRIESTS—Vapor resembling incense given off by Mount Nansen, named after the arctic explorer, Dr. Nansen.

was then about 9000 feet. At 9:15 o'clock we had the eastern portal on our left, and were ready to tackle the "Hump." We had discussed the "Hump" so often, had anticipated and maligned it so much, that now that it was in front of us and waiting in the flesh—in rock-ribbed, glacierized reality—it was like meeting an old acquaintance. But we approached it warily and respectfully, climbing steadily all the while with maximum power, to get a better view of its none too friendly visage.

June, wholly unaffected by the immediate perplexities, went about his job of getting the plane in fighting trim. He ripped open the last of the fuel cans, and poured the contents into the main tank. The empty tins he dropped overboard, through the trap door. Every tin weighed two pounds; and every pound dropped was to our gain. June examined the gauges of the five wing tanks, then measured with a graduated stick the amount of fuel in the main tank. He jotted the figures on a pad, made a few calculations, and handed me the results. Consumption had thus far averaged between fifty-five and sixty gallons per hour. It had taken us longer to reach the mountains than we had expected, owing to head winds. However, the extra fuel taken aboard just before we left had absorbed this loss, and we actually had a credit balance. We had, then, enough gasoline to take us to the Pole and back.

With that doubt disposed of, we went at the "Hump" confidently.

We were still rising, and the engines were pulling wonderfully well. The wind was about abeam,[15] and, according to my calculations, not materially affecting the speed.

The glacier floor rose sharply in a series of ice falls and terraces, some of which were well above the (then) altitude of the plane. These glacial waterfalls, some of which were from 200 to 400 feet high, seemed more beautiful than any precipitous stream I have ever seen. Beautiful, yes, but how rudely and with what finality they would deal with steel and duralumin that crashed into them at 100 miles per hour.

Now the stream of air pouring down the pass roughened perceptibly. The great wing shivered and teetered as it balanced itself against the changing pressures. The wind from the left flowed against Fisher's[16] steep flanks, and the constant, hammering bumps made footing uncertain in the plane. But McKinley steadily trained his 50-pound camera on the mountains to the left. The uncertainties of load and ceiling were not his concern. His only concern was photographs—photographs over which students and geographers might pore in the calm quiet of their studies.

The altimeters showed a height of 9600 feet, but the figure was not necessarily exact. Nevertheless there were indications we were near the service ceiling of the plane.

The roughness of the air increased and became so violent that we were forced to swing slightly to the left, in search of calmer air. This brought us over a frightfully crevassed slope which ran up and toward Mount Nansen. We thus escaped the turbulent swirl about Fisher, but the down-surging currents here

[15] ABEAM—From the side.

[16] FISHER—A mountain.

damped our climb. To the left we had the "blind" mountain glacier of Nansen in full view; and when we looked ahead we saw the plateau—a smooth, level plain of snow between Nansen and Fisher. The pass rose up to meet it.

In the center of the pass was a massive outcropping of snow-covered rock, resembling an island, which protruded above and separated the descending stream of ice. Perhaps it was a peak or the highest eminence of a ridge connecting Fisher and Nansen which had managed through the ages to hold its head above the glacial torrent pouring down from the plateau. But its particular structure or relationship was of small moment then. I watched it only with reference to the climb of the plane; and realized, with some disgust and more consternation, that the nose of the plane, in spite of the fact that Balchen had steepened the angle of attack, did not rise materially above the outcropping. We were still climbing, but at a rapidly diminishing rate of speed. In the rarefied air the heavy plane responded to the controls with marked sluggishness. There is a vast difference between the plane of 1928 and the plane of 1937.

It was an awesome thing, creeping (so it seemed) through the narrow pass, with the black walls of Nansen and Fisher on either side, higher than the level of the wings, and watching the nose of the ship bob up and down across the face of that chunk of rock. It would move up, then slide down. Then move up, and fall off again. For perhaps a minute or two we deferred the decision; but there was no escaping it. If we were to risk a passage through the pass, we needed greater maneuverability than we had at that moment. Once we entered the pass, there would be no retreat. It offered no room for turn. If power was lost momentarily or if the air became excessively rough, we could only go ahead, or down. We had to climb, and there was only one way in which we could climb.

June, anticipating the command, already had his hand on the dump valve of the main tank. A pressure of the fingers —that was all that was necessary—and in two minutes 600 gallons of gasoline would gush out. I signaled to wait.

Balchen held to the climb almost to the edge of a stall. But it was clear to both of us that he could not hold it long enough. Balchen began to yell and gesticulate, and it was hard to catch the words in the roar of the engines echoing from the cliffs on either side. But the meaning was manifest. "Overboard—overboard—200 pounds!"

Which would it be—gasoline or food?

If gasoline, I thought, we might as well stop there and turn back. We could never get back to the base from the Pole. If food, the lives of all of us would be jeopardized in the event of a forced landing. Was that fair to McKinley, Balchen, and June? It really took only a moment to reach the decision. The Pole, after all, was our objective. I knew the character of the three men. McKinley, in fact, had already hauled one of the food bags to the trap door. It weighed 125 pounds.

The brown bag was pushed out and fell, spinning, to the glacier. The improvement in the flying qualities of the plane was noticeable. It took another breath and resumed the climb.

Now the down-currents over Nansen became stronger. The plane trembled and rose and fell, as if struck bodily. We veered a trifle to the right, searching for helpful rising eddies. Balchen was flying shrewdly. He maintained flight at a sufficient distance below the absolute ceiling of the plane to retain at all times enough maneuverability to make him master of the ship. But he was hard pressed by circumstances; and I realized that, unless the plane was further lightened, the final thrust might bring us perilously close to the end of our reserve.

"More," Bernt shouted. "Another bag."

McKinley shoved a second bag through the trap door, and this time we saw it hit the glacier and scatter in a soundless explosion. Two hundred and fifty pounds of food—enough to feed four men for a month—lay strewn on the barren ice.

The sacrifice swung the scales. The plane literally rose with a jump; the engines dug in, and we soon showed a gain in altitude of from 300 to 400 feet. It was what we wanted. We should clear the pass with about 500 feet to spare. Balchen gave a shout of joy. It was just as well. We could dump no more food. There was nothing left to dump except McKinley's camera. I am sure that, had he been asked to put it overboard, he would have done so instantly; and I am equally sure he would have followed the precious instrument with his own body.

The next few minutes dragged. We moved at a speed of 77 nautical miles per hour through the pass, with the black walls of Nansen on our left. The wing gradually lifted above them. The floor of the plateau stretched in a white immensity to the south. We were over the dreaded "Hump" at last. The Pole lay dead ahead over the horizon, less than 300 miles away. It was then about 9:45

o'clock. (I did not note the exact time. There were other things to think about.)

Gaining the plateau, we studied the situation a moment and then shifted course to the southward. Nansen's enormous towering ridge, lipped [17] by the plateau, shoved its heavily broken sides into the sky. A whole chain of mountains began to parade across the eastern horizon. How high they are I cannot say, but surely some of them must be around 14,000 feet, to stand so boldly above the rim of the 10,000 foot plateau. Peak on peak, ridge on ridge, draped in snow garments which brilliantly reflected the sun, they extended in a solid array to the southeast. But can one really say they ran in that direction? The lines of direction are so bent in this region that 150 miles farther on, even were they to continue in the same general straight line, they must run north of east. This is what happens near the Pole. We laid our line of flight on the 171st meridian.

Our altitude was then between 10,500 and 11,000 feet. We were "riding" the engines,[18] conscious of the fact that if one should fail we must come down. Once the starboard [19] engine did sputter a bit, and Balchen nosed down while June rushed to the fuel valves. But it was nothing; to conserve fuel, Balchen had "leaned" the mixture too much. A quick adjustment corrected the fault, and in a moment the engine took up its steady rhythm. Moments like this one make a pioneering flight anything but dull; one moment everything is lovely, and the next is full of forebodings.

The drift indicator showed a variable wind from the east. To compensate for it, we had to point the nose of the plane an average of about 12° to the east, in order to steer a straight course for the Pole. The influence of the drift on the course was always a bothersome element. It had to be watched carefully, and any change in the angle of drift detected at once, so as to make good a straight course south. Fitted in the floor of the plane was a drift indicator which McKinley used in connection with his photographic work, and during the flight he constantly checked the drift with me. Whenever I noted any change in the direction or strength of the wind, I would steady Balchen on his course with the sun compass, first shaking the trolley line to attract his attention, then waving him on to the new course.

The character of the plateau surface varied from time to time. There were stretches of smooth, soft snow, colonies of domed ice haycocks and arrow-headed sastrugi.[20] From the time we had first struck across the plateau its level appeared to slope gently toward the Pole; the altimeter showed that the *Floyd Bennett* was maintaining a fairly steady altitude at approximately 11,000 feet, and the plateau fell farther below. We had named the Ford after my gallant friend and companion on the North Pole flight.

While the mountains on the left were still in view, I attempted to shoot the sun with the sextant to get its altitude. This would give us a sun line which would cut our line of flight and at the point of in-

[17] LIPPED—Acting as a lip to the mountain from which the glacier flowed.

[18] "RIDING" THE ENGINES—Running them at top speed.

[19] STARBOARD—Right side.

[20] SASTRUGI—Ridges of hard snow formed by the wind.

tersection tell us what the sun had to say about our progress. The air, however, was fairly rough. The powerful center engine, laboring to keep the heavy load at an altitude of two miles, produced a weaving in the plane; and the most patient efforts failed to bring the sun and the bubble together long enough for a dependable sight. This was bothersome, but relatively unimportant at the time; we were quite confident as to the accuracy of the dead reckoning.[21]

From time to time June "spelled" Balchen at the controls; and Balchen would walk back to the cabin, flexing his cramped muscles. There was little thought of food in any of us—a beef sandwich, stiff as a board from frost, and tea and coffee from a thermos bottle. It was difficult to believe that two decades or so before, the most resolute men who had ever attempted to carry a remote objective, Scott and Shackleton,[22] had plodded over this same plateau, a few miles each day, with hunger, fierce, unrelenting hunger, stalking them every step of the way.

Between 11:30 and 12:30 o'clock the mountains to the eastward began to disappear, dropping imperceptibly out of view, one after another. Not long after 12:30 o'clock the whole range had retreated from vision, and the plateau met the horizon in an indefinite line. The mountains to the right had long since disappeared.

The air finally turned smooth. At 12:38 o'clock I shot the sun. It hung, a ball of fire, just beyond *south* to the east, 21° above the horizon. So it was quite low, and we stared it in the eye. The sight gave me an approximate line of latitude, which placed us very near our position as calculated by dead reckoning. That dead reckoning and astronomy should check so closely was very encouraging. The position line placed us at Lat. 89° 4½′ S., or 55½ miles from the Pole. A short time later we reached an altitude of 11,000 feet. According to Amundsen's records, the plateau, which had risen to 10,300 feet, descended here to 9600 feet. We were, therefore, about 1400 feet above the plateau.

So the Pole was actually in sight. But I could not yet spare it so much as a glance. Chronometers, drift indicators, and compasses are hard taskmasters.

Relieved by June, Balchen came aft and reported that visibility was not as good as it had been. Clouds were gathering on the horizon off the port bow; and a storm, Balchen thought, was in the air. A storm was the last thing we wanted to meet on the plateau on the way back. It would be difficult enough to pass the Queen Maud Range in bright sunlight; in thick weather it would be suicidal. Conditions, however, were merely unpromising: not really bad, simply not good. If worst came to worst, we decided we could out-race the clouds to the mountains.

At six minutes after one o'clock, a sight of the sun put us a few miles ahead of our dead reckoning position. We were quite close now. At 1:14 o'clock, Greenwich civil time,[23] our calculations showed that we were at the Pole.

[21] DEAD RECKONING—Estimate of progress on the basis of previous known distance covered.

[22] SCOTT AND SHACKLETON—Two explorers who reached the South Pole in 1909 and 1912.

[23] GREENWICH CIVIL TIME—World standard time as determined at Greenwich, England.

I opened the trap door and dropped over the calculated position of the Pole the small flag which was weighted with the stone from Bennett's grave. Stone and flag plunged down together. The flag had been advanced 1500 miles farther south than it had ever been advanced by any American or American expedition.

For a few seconds we stood over the spot where Amundsen had stood, December 14, 1911; and where Scott had also stood, thirty-four days later, reading the note which Amundsen had left for him. In their honor, the flags of their countries were again carried over the Pole. There was nothing now to mark that scene: only a white desolation and solitude disturbed by the sound of our engines. The Pole lay in the center of a limitless plain. To the right, which is to say to the eastward, the horizon was covered with clouds. If mountains lay there, as some geologists believe, they were concealed and we had no hint of them.

And that, in brief, is all there is to tell about the South Pole. One gets there, and that is about all there is for the telling. It is the effort to get there that counts.

We put the Pole behind us and raced for home.

◇◇◇◇◇◇◇◇◇◇◇◇◇◇◇◇◇◇◇◇◇◇◇◇◇◇◇◇◇◇◇◇◇

FOR DISCUSSION

1. Note the careful preparations made just before the take-off. Explain why extreme precaution was necessary in these circumstances.

2. How many men were in the *Floyd Bennett?* What job did each perform? Were there any unnecessary passengers?

3. In what objective of the expedition was McKinley especially interested?

4. What was the problem of getting over the "Hump"? How do you account for the plane's low ceiling? What measures were taken to insure success in the climb?

5. The pilot and navigator had to alter course once they reached the plateau. Why could they no longer take a direct bearing on the Pole?

6. When they reached the Pole, how did they recognize it? What did they do there?

7. What traits of character do you observe in each of the men? Are such traits necessary in men who brave such dangers?

FINDING KEY WORDS

In describing a flight like this one, a writer necessarily draws heavily on his supply of words expressing some fear about success. Find in the text five expressions showing this concern and point out the key word: for instance—"There was a *gamble* in the decision."

TO THINK ABOUT

1. Rear Admiral Byrd made several other expeditions to the South Pole. He was able to gather much valuable scientific information as a result of them. Explain why he says in this account of his 1929 expedition, "And that, in brief, is all there is to tell about the South Pole. One gets there, and that is about all there is for the telling. It is the effort to get there that counts." Do you think he would have said this about his later expeditions?

2. Have you ever felt that you have been successful at something you tried to do, even though you could show no tangible results? Did you have a feeling of success because "it was the effort that counted"? Tell the class about your experience.

RELATED READING

In the book *Alone,* Admiral Byrd relates his harrowing experience while isolated near the South Pole.

Probably the most noted detective in the world of fiction is Sherlock Holmes. With his ingenious solutions to crimes, he has baffled the best of London's famous Scotland Yard. Through the eyes of Dr. Watson, Holmes' friend who narrates the story, you will see this master detective at work as he solves the mystery in "The Adventure of the Norwood Builder."

Sir Arthur Conan Doyle has established a pattern of telling a mystery story in his creation of the Sherlock Holmes' tales. Compare this story with other detective stories you have read or seen portrayed in television or the movies.

THE ADVENTURE OF THE NORWOOD BUILDER

ARTHUR CONAN DOYLE

"From the point of view of the criminal expert," said Mr. Sherlock Holmes, "London has become a singularly uninteresting city since the death of the late lamented Professor Moriarty."

"I can hardly think that you would find many decent citizens to agree with you," I answered.

"Well, well, I must not be selfish," said he, with a smile, as he pushed back his chair from the breakfast table. "The community is certainly the gainer, and no one the loser, save the poor out-of-work specialist, whose occupation has gone. With that man in the field, one's morning paper presented infinite possibilities. Often it was only the smallest trace, Watson, the faintest indication, and yet it was enough to tell me that the great malignant brain was there, as the gentlest tremors of the edges of the web remind one of the foul spider which lurks in the center. Petty thefts, wanton assaults, purposeless outrage—to the man who held the clue all could be worked into one connected whole. To the scientific student of the higher criminal world, no capital in Europe offered the advantages which London then possessed. But now—" He shrugged his shoulders in humorous deprecation of the state of things which he had himself done so much to produce.

At the time of which I speak, Holmes had been back for some months, and I at his request had sold my practice and returned to share the old quarters in Baker Street. A young doctor, named Verner, had purchased my small Kensington practice, and given with astonishingly little demur the highest price that I ventured to ask—an incident which only explained itself some years later, when I found that Verner was a distant relation of Holmes, and that it was my friend who had really found the money.

Our months of partnership had not been so uneventful as he had stated, for I find, on looking over my notes, that this period includes the case of the papers of ex-President Murillo, and also the shocking affair of the Dutch steamship *Friesland*, which so nearly cost us both our lives. His cold and proud nature was always averse, however, from anything in the shape of public applause, and he bound me in the most stringent terms to say no further word of himself, his methods, or his successes—a prohibition which, as I have explained, has only now been removed.

Mr. Sherlock Holmes was leaning back in his chair after his whimsical protest, and was unfolding his morning paper in a leisurely fashion, when our attention was arrested by a tremendous ring at the bell, followed immediately by a hollow drumming sound, as if someone were beating on the outer door with his fist. As it opened there came a tumultuous rush into the hall, rapid feet clattered up the stair, and an instant later a wild-eyed and frantic young man, pale, disheveled, and palpitating, burst into the room. He looked from one to the other of us, and under our gaze of inquiry he became conscious that some apology was needed for this unceremonious entry.

"I'm sorry, Mr. Holmes," he cried. "You mustn't blame me. I am nearly mad. Mr. Holmes, I am the unhappy John Hector McFarlane."

He made the announcement as if the name alone would explain both his visit and its manner, but I could see, by my companion's unresponsive face, that it meant no more to him than to me.

"Have a cigarette, Mr. McFarlane," said he, pushing his case across. "I am sure that, with your symptoms, my friend Dr. Watson here would prescribe a sedative. The weather has been so very warm these last few days. Now, if you feel a little more composed, I should be glad if you would sit down in that chair, and tell us very slowly and quietly who you are, and what it is that you want. You mentioned your name, as if I should recognize it, but I assure you that, beyond the obvious facts that you are a bachelor, a solicitor,[1] a Freemason, and an asthmatic, I know nothing whatever about you."

Familiar as I was with my friend's methods, it was not difficult for me to follow his deductions, and to observe the untidiness of attire, the sheaf of legal papers, the watch-charm, and the breathing which had prompted them. Our client, however, stared in amazement.

"Yes, I am all that, Mr. Holmes; and, in addition, I am the most unfortunate man at this moment in London. For heaven's sake, don't abandon me, Mr. Holmes! If they come to arrest me before I have finished my story, make them give me time, so that I may tell you the whole truth. I could go to jail happy if I knew that you were working for me outside."

"Arrest you!" said Holmes. "This is really most grati—most interesting. On what charge do you expect to be arrested?"

"Upon the charge of murdering Mr. Jonas Oldacre, of Lower Norwood."

[1] SOLICITOR—A lawyer.

My companion's expressive face showed a sympathy which was not, I am afraid, entirely unmixed with satisfaction.

"Dear me," said he, "it was only this moment at breakfast that I was saying to my friend, Dr. Watson, that sensational cases had disappeared out of our papers."

Our visitor stretched forward a quivering hand and picked up the *Daily Telegraph,* which still lay upon Holmes's knee.

"If you had looked at it, sir, you would have seen at a glance what the errand is on which I have come to you this morning. I feel as if my name and my misfortune must be in every man's mouth." He turned it over to expose the central page. "Here it is, and with your permission I will read it to you. Listen to this, Mr. Holmes. The headlines are: 'Mysterious Affair at Lower Norwood. Disappearance of Well-Known Builder. Suspicion of Murder and Arson. A Clue to the Criminal.' That is the clue which they are already following, Mr. Holmes, and I know that it leads infallibly to me. I have been followed from London Bridge Station, and I am sure that they are only waiting for the warrant to arrest me. It will break my mother's heart—it will break her heart!" He wrung his hands in an agony of apprehension, and swayed backward and forward in his chair.

I looked with interest upon this man who was accused of being the perpetrator of a crime of violence. He was flaxen-haired and handsome, in a washed-out negative fashion, with frightened blue eyes, and a clean-shaven face, with a weak, sensitive mouth. His age may have been about twenty-seven, his dress and bearing that of a gentleman. From the pocket of his light summer overcoat protruded the bundle of indorsed papers which proclaimed his profession.

"We must use what time we have," said Holmes. "Watson, would you have the kindness to take the paper and to read the paragraph in question?"

Underneath the vigorous headlines which our client had quoted, I read the following suggestive narrative:

> "Late last night, or early this morning, an incident occurred at Lower Norwood which points, it is feared, to a serious crime. Mr. Jonas Oldacre is a well-known resident of that suburb, where he has carried on his business as a builder for many years. Mr. Oldacre is a bachelor, fifty-two years of age, and lives in Deep Dene House, at the Sydenham end of the road of that name. He has had the reputation of being a man of eccentric habits, secretive and retiring. For some years he has practically withdrawn from the business, in which he is said to have amassed considerable wealth. A small timber-yard still exists, however, at the back of the house, and last night, about twelve o'clock, an alarm was given that one of the stacks was on fire. The engines were soon upon the spot, but the dry wood burned with great fury, and it was impossible to arrest the conflagration until the stack had been entirely consumed. Up to this point the incident bore the appearance of an ordinary accident, but fresh indications seem to point to serious crime. Surprise was expressed at the absence of the master of the establishment from the scene of the fire, and an inquiry followed, which showed that he had disappeared from the house. An examination of his room revealed that the bed had not been slept in, that a safe which stood in it was opened, that a number of important papers were scattered about the room, and, finally, that there were signs

of a murderous struggle, slight traces of blood being found within the room, and an oaken walking-stick, which also showed stains of blood upon the handle. It is known that Mr. Jonas Oldacre had received a late visitor in his bedroom upon that night, and the stick found has been identified as the property of this person, who is a young London solicitor named John Hector McFarlane, junior partner of Graham and McFarlane, of 426 Gresham Buildings, E. C. The police believe that they have evidence in their possession which supplies a very convincing motive for the crime, and altogether it cannot be doubted that sensational developments will follow.

LATER.—It is rumored as we go to press that Mr. John Hector McFarlane has actually been arrested on the charge of the murder of Mr. Jonas Oldacre. It is at least certain that a warrant has been issued. There have been further and sinister developments in the investigation at Norwood. Besides the signs of a struggle in the room of the unfortunate builder it is now known that the French windows of his bedroom (which is on the ground floor) were found to be open, that there were marks as if some bulky object had been dragged across to the woodpile, and, finally, it is asserted that charred remains have been found among the charcoal ashes of the fire. The police theory is that a most sensational crime has been committed, that the victim was clubbed to death in his own bedroom, his papers rifled, and his dead body dragged across to the woodstack, which was then ignited so as to hide all traces of the crime. The conduct of the criminal investigation has been left in the experienced hands of Inspector Lestrade of Scotland Yard, who is following up the clues with his accustomed energy and sagacity."

Sherlock Holmes listened with closed eyes and finger tips together to this remarkable account.

"The case has certainly some points of interest," said he, in his languid fashion. "May I ask, in the first place, Mr. McFarlane, how it is that you are still at liberty, since there appears to be enough evidence for your arrest?"

"I live at Torrington Lodge, Blackheath, with my parents, Mr. Holmes, but last night, having to do business very late with Mr. Jonas Oldacre, I stayed at a hotel in Norwood, and came to my business from there. I knew nothing of this affair until I was in the train, when I read what you have just heard. I at once saw the horrible danger of my position, and I hurried to put the case in your hands. I have no doubt that I should have been arrested either at my city office or at my home. A man followed me from London Bridge Station, and I have no doubt—Great heaven! What is that?"

It was a clang of the bell, followed instantly by heavy steps upon the stair. A moment later, our old friend Lestrade appeared in the doorway. Over his shoulder I caught a glimpse of one or two uniformed policemen outside.

"Mr. John Hector McFarlane?" said Lestrade.

Our unfortunate client rose with a ghastly face.

"I arrest you for the willful murder of Mr. Jonas Oldacre, of Lower Norwood."

McFarlane turned to us with a gesture of despair, and sank into his chair once more like one who is crushed.

"One moment, Lestrade," said Holmes. "Half an hour more or less can make no difference to you, and the gentleman was about to give us an account of this very interesting affair, which might aid us in clearing it up."

"I think there will be no difficulty in clearing it up," said Lestrade, grimly.

"None the less, with your permission, I should be much interested to hear his account."

"Well, Mr. Holmes, it is difficult for me to refuse you anything for you have been of use to the force once or twice in the past and we owe you a good turn at Scotland Yard," said Lestrade. "At the same time I must remain with my prisoner, and I am bound to warn him that anything he may say will appear in evidence against him."

"I wish nothing better," said our client. "All I ask is that you should hear and recognize the absolute truth."

Lestrade looked at his watch. "I'll give you half an hour," said he.

"I must explain first," said McFarlane, "that I knew nothing of Mr. Jonas Oldacre. His name was familiar to me, for many years ago my parents were acquainted with him, but they drifted apart. I was very much surprised, therefore, when yesterday, about three o'clock in the afternoon, he walked into my office in the city. But I was still more astonished when he told me the object of his visit. He had in his hand several sheets of a notebook, covered with scribbled writing —here they are—and he laid them on my table.

" 'Here is my will,' said he. 'I want you, Mr. McFarlane, to cast it into proper legal shape. I will sit here while you do so.'

"I set myself to copy it, and you can imagine my astonishment when I found that, with some reservations, he had left all his property to me. He was a strange little ferret-like man, with white eyelashes, and when I looked up at him I found his keen gray eyes fixed upon me with an amused expression. I could hardly believe my own senses as I read the terms of the will; but he explained that he was a bachelor with hardly any living relation, that he had known my parents in his youth, and that he had always heard of me as a very deserving young man, and was assured that his money would be in worthy hands. Of course, I could only stammer out my thanks. The will was duly finished, signed, and witnessed by my clerk. This is it on the blue paper, and these slips, as I have explained, are the rough draft. Mr. Jonas Oldacre then informed me that there were a number of documents—building leases, title-deeds, mortgages, scrip,[2] and so forth—which it was necessary that I should see and understand. He said that his mind would not be easy until the whole thing was settled, and he begged me to come out to his house at Norwood that night, bringing the will with me, and to arrange matters. 'Remember, my boy, not one word to your parents about the affair until everything is settled. We will keep it as a little surprise for them.' He was very insistent upon this point, and made me promise it faithfully.

"You can imagine, Mr. Holmes, that I was not in a humor to refuse him anything that he might ask. He was my benefactor, and all my desire was to carry out his wishes in every particular. I sent a telegram home, therefore, to say that I had important business on hand, and that it was impossible for me to say how late I might be. Mr. Oldacre had told me that he would like me to have supper with him

[2] SCRIP—Receipts of money or stock.

at nine, as he might not be home before that hour. I had some difficulty in finding his house, however, and it was nearly half-past before I reached it. I found him—"

"One moment!" said Holmes. "Who opened the door?"

"A middle-aged woman, who was, I suppose, his housekeeper."

"And it was she, I presume, who mentioned your name?"

"Exactly," said McFarlane.

"Pray proceed."

McFarlane wiped his damp brow, and then continued his narrative:

"I was shown by this woman into a sitting-room, where a frugal supper was laid out. Afterwards, Mr. Jonas Oldacre led me into his bedroom, in which there stood a heavy safe. This he opened and took out a mass of documents, which we went over together. It was between eleven and twelve when we finished. He remarked that we must not disturb the housekeeper. He showed me out through his own French window, which had been open all this time."

"Was the blind down?" asked Holmes.

"I will not be sure, but I believe that it was only half down. Yes, I remember how he pulled it up in order to swing open the window. I could not find my stick, and he said, 'Never mind, my boy, I shall see a good deal of you now, I hope, and I will keep your stick until you come back to claim it.' I left him there, the safe open, and the papers made up in packets upon the table. It was so late that I could not get back to Blackheath, so I spent the night at the Anerley Arms, and I knew nothing more until I read of this horrible affair in the morning."

"Anything more that you would like to ask, Mr. Holmes?" said Lestrade, whose eyebrows had gone up once or twice during this remarkable explanation.

"Not until I have been to Blackheath."

"You mean to Norwood," said Lestrade.

"Oh, yes, no doubt that is what I must have meant," said Holmes, with his enigmatical smile. Lestrade had learned by more experiences than he would care to acknowledge that that razor-like brain could cut through that which was impenetrable to him. I saw him look at my companion.

"I think I should like to have a word with you presently, Mr. Sherlock Holmes," said he. "Now, Mr. McFarlane, two of my constables are at the door, and there is a four-wheeler waiting." The wretched young man arose, and with a last beseeching glance at us walked from the room. The officers conducted him to the cab, but Lestrade remained.

Holmes had picked up the pages which formed the rough draft of the will, and was looking at them with the keenest interest upon his face.

"There are some points about that document, Lestrade, are there not?" said he, pushing them over.

The official looked at them with a puzzled expression.

"I can read the first few lines, and these in the middle of the second page, and one or two at the end. Those are as clear as print," said he, "but the writing in between is very bad, and there are three places where I cannot read it at all."

"What do you make of that?" said Holmes.

"Well, what do *you* make of it?"

"That it was written in a train. The good writing represents stations, the bad writing movement, and the very bad writing passing over points.[3] A scientific expert would pronounce at once that this was drawn up on a surburban line, since nowhere save in the immediate vicinity of a great city could there be so quick a succession of points. Granting that his whole journey was occupied in drawing up the will, then the train was an express, only stopping once between Norwood and London Bridge."

Lestrade began to laugh.

"You are too many for me when you begin to get on your theories, Mr. Holmes," said he. "How does this bear on the case?"

"Well, it corroborates the young man's story to the extent that the will was drawn up by Jonas Oldacre in his journey yesterday. It is curious—is it not?—that a man should draw up so important a document in so haphazard a fashion. It suggests that he did not think it was going to be of much practical importance. If a man drew up a will which he did not intend ever to be effective, he might do it so."

"Well, he drew up his own death warrant at the same time," said Lestrade.

"Oh, you think so?"

"Don't you?"

"Well, it is quite possible, but the case is not clear to me yet."

"Not clear? Well, if that isn't clear, what *could* be clear? Here is a young man who learns suddenly that, if a certain older man dies, he will succeed to a fortune. What does he do? He says nothing to anyone, but he arranges that he shall go out on some pretext to see his client that night. He waits until the only other person in the house is in bed, and

[3] POINTS—Railroad switches.

then in the solitude of the man's room he murders him, burns his body in the wood-pile, and departs to a neighboring hotel. The bloodstains in the room and also on the stick are very slight. It is probable that he imagined his crime to be a bloodless one, and hoped that if the body were consumed it would hide all traces of the method of his death—traces which, for some reason, must have pointed to him. Is not all this obvious?"

"It strikes me, my good Lestrade, as being just a trifle too obvious," said Holmes. "You do not add imagination to your other great qualities, but if you could for one moment put yourself in the place of this young man, would you choose the very night after the will had been made to commit your crime? Would it not seem dangerous to you to make so very close a relation between the two incidents? Again, would you choose an occasion when you are known to be in the house, when a servant has let you in? And, finally, would you take great pains to conceal the body, and yet leave your own stick as a sign that you were the criminal? Confess, Lestrade, that all this is very unlikely."

"As to the stick, Mr. Holmes, you know as well as I do that a criminal is often flurried, and does such things, which a cool man would avoid. He was very likely afraid to go back to the room. Give me another theory that would fit the facts."

"I could very easily give you half a dozen," said Holmes. "Here, for example, is a very possible and even probable one. I make you a free present of it. The older man is showing documents which are of evident value. A passing tramp sees them through the window, the blind of which is only half down. Exit the solicitor. Enter the tramp! He seizes a stick, which he observes there, kills Oldacre, and departs after burning the body."

"Why should the tramp burn the body?"

"For the matter of that, why should McFarlane?"

"To hide some evidence."

"Possibly the tramp wanted to hide that any murder at all had been committed."

"And why did the tramp take nothing?"

"Because they were papers that he could not negotiate." [4]

Lestrade shook his head, though it seemed to me that his manner was less absolutely assured than before.

"Well, Mr. Sherlock Holmes, you may look for your tramp, and while you are finding him we will hold on to our man. The future will show which is right. Just notice this point, Mr. Holmes: that so far as we know, none of the papers were removed, and that the prisoner is the one man in the world who had no reason for removing them, since he was an heir-at-law, and would come into them in any case."

My friend seemed struck by this remark.

"I don't mean to deny that the evidence is in some ways very strongly in favor of your theory," said he. "I only wish to point out that there are other theories possible. As you say, the future will decide. Good morning! I dare say

[4] NEGOTIATE—Dispose of by selling or transferring ownership.

that in the course of the day, I shall drop in at Norwood and see how you are getting on."

When the detective departed, my friend rose and made his preparations for the day's work with the alert air of a man who has a congenial task before him.

"My first movement, Watson," said he, as he bustled into his frockcoat, "must, as I said, be in the direction of Blackheath."

"And why not Norwood?"

"Because we have in this case one singular incident coming close to the heels of another singular incident. The police are making the mistake of concentrating their attention upon the second, because it happens to be the one which is actually criminal. But it is evident to me that the logical way to approach the case is to begin by trying to throw some light upon the first incident—the curious will, so suddenly made, and to so unexpected an heir. It may do something to simplify what followed. No, my dear fellow, I don't think you can help me. There is no prospect of danger, or I should not dream of stirring out without you. I trust that when I see you in the evening, I will be able to report that I have been able to do something for this unfortunate youngster, who has thrown himself upon my protection."

It was late when my friend returned, and I could see, by a glance at his haggard and anxious face, that the high hopes with which he had started had not been fulfilled. For an hour he droned away upon his violin, endeavoring to soothe his own ruffled spirits. At last he flung down the instrument, and plunged into a detailed account of his misadventures.

"It's all going wrong, Watson—all as wrong as it can go. I kept a bold face before Lestrade, but, upon my soul, I believe that for once the fellow is on the right track and we are on the wrong. All my instincts are one way, and all the facts are the other, and I much fear that British juries have not yet attained that pitch of intelligence when they will give the preference to my theories over Lestrade's facts."

"Did you go to Blackheath?"

"Yes, Watson, I went there, and I found very quickly that the late lamented Oldacre was a pretty considerable blackguard.[5] The father was away in search of his son. The mother was at home—a little, fluffy, blue-eyed person, in a tremor of fear and indignation. Of course, she would not admit even the possibility of his guilt. But she would not express either surprise or regret over the fate of Oldacre. On the contrary, she spoke of him with such bitterness that she was unconsciously considerably strengthening the case of the police for, of course, if her son had heard her speak of the man in this fashion, it would predispose him toward hatred and violence. 'He was more like a malignant and cunning ape than a human being,' said she, 'and he always was, ever since he was a young man.'

" 'You knew him at that time?' said I.

" 'Yes, I knew him well, in fact, he was an old suitor of mine. Thank heaven, that I had the sense to turn away from him and to marry a better, if poorer, man. I was engaged to him, Mr. Holmes, when I heard a shocking story of how he had turned a cat loose in an aviary,[6] and I was

[5] BLACKGUARD—Scoundrel.

[6] AVIARY—A pen for keeping and raising birds.

so horrified at his brutal cruelty that I would have nothing more to do with him.' She rummaged in a bureau, and presently she produced a photograph of a woman, shamefully defaced and mutilated with a knife. 'That is my own photograph,' she said. 'He sent it to me in that state, with his curse, upon my wedding morning.'

" 'Well,' said I, 'at least he has forgiven you now, since he has left all his property to your son.'

" 'Neither my son nor I want anything from Jonas Oldacre, dead or alive!' she cried, with a proper spirit. 'There is a God in heaven, Mr. Holmes, and that same God who has punished that wicked man will show, in His own good time, that my son's hands are guiltless of his blood.'

"Well, I tried one or two leads, but could get at nothing which would help our hypothesis, and several points which would make against it. I gave it up at last, and off I went to Norwood.

"This place, Deep Dene House, is a big modern villa of staring brick, standing back in its own grounds, with a laurel-clumped lawn in front of it. To the right and some distance back from the road was the timber-yard which had been the scene of the fire. Here's a rough plan on a leaf of my notebook. This window on the left is the one which opens into Oldacre's room. You can look into it from the road, you see. That is about the only bit of consolation I have had today. Lestrade was not there, but his head constable did the honors. They had just found a great treasure-trove. They had spent the morning raking among the ashes of the burned woodpile, and besides the charred organic remains they had secured several discolored metal discs. I examined them with care, and there was no doubt that they were trouser buttons. I even distinguished that one of them was marked with the name of 'Hyams,' who was Oldacre's tailor. I then worked the lawn very carefully for signs and traces, but this drought has made everything as hard as iron. Nothing was to be seen save that some body or bundle had been dragged through a low privet hedge which is in a line with the woodpile. And that, of course, fits in with the official theory. I crawled about the lawn with an August sun on my back, but I got up at the end of an hour no wiser than before.

"Well, after this fiasco [7] I went into the bedroom and examined that also. The bloodstains were very slight, mere smears and discolorations, but undoubtedly fresh. The stick had been removed, but there also the marks were slight. There is no doubt about the stick belonging to our client. He admits it. Footmarks of both men could be made out on the carpet, but none of any third person, which again is a trick for the other side. They were piling up their score all the time, and we were at a standstill.

"Only one little gleam of hope did I get—and yet it amounted to nothing. I examined the contents of the safe, most of which had been taken out and left on the table. The papers had been made up into sealed envelopes, one or two of which had been opened by the police. They were not, so far as I could judge, of any great value, nor did the bank book show that Mr. Oldacre was in such very affluent circumstances. But it seemed to

[7] FIASCO—A complete failure.

me that all the papers were not there. There were some allusions to some deeds—possibly the more valuable—which I could not find. This, of course, if we could definitely prove it, would turn Lestrade's argument against himself; for who would steal a thing if he knew that he would shortly inherit it?

"Finally, having drawn every other cover and picked up no scent, I tried my luck with the housekeeper. Mrs. Lexington is her name—a little, dark, silent person, with suspicious and sidelong eyes. She could tell us something if she would—I am convinced of it. But she was as close as wax. Yes, she had let Mr. McFarlane in at half-past nine. She wished her hand had withered before she had done so. She had gone to bed at half-past ten. Her room was at the other end of the house, and she could hear nothing of what passed. Mr. McFarlane had left his hat, and to the best of her belief his stick, in the hall. She had been awakened by the alarm of fire. Her poor, dear master had certainly been murdered. Had he any enemies? Well, every man had enemies, but Mr. Oldacre kept himself very much to himself, and only met people in the way of business. She had seen the buttons, and was sure that they belonged to the clothes which he had worn last night. The woodpile was very dry, for it had not rained for a month. It burned like tinder, and by the time she reached the spot, nothing could be seen but flames. She and all the firemen smelled the burned flesh from inside it. She knew nothing of the papers, nor of Mr. Oldacre's private affairs.

"So, my dear Watson, there's my report of a failure. And yet—and yet—" he clenched his thin hands in a paroxysm of conviction—"I *know* it's all wrong. I feel it in my bones. There is something that has not come out, and the housekeeper knows it. There was a sort of sulky defiance in her eyes, which only goes with guilty knowledge. However, there's no good talking any more about it, Watson; but unless some lucky chance comes our way I fear that the Norwood Disappearance Case will not figure in that chronicle of our successes which I foresee that a patient public will sooner or later have to endure."

"Surely," said I, "the man's appearance would go far with any jury?"

"That is a dangerous argument, my dear Watson. You remember that terrible murderer, Bert Stevens, who wanted us to get him off in '87? Was there ever a more mild-mannered, Sunday-school young man?"

"It is true."

"Unless we succeed in establishing an alternative theory, this man is lost. You can hardly find a flaw in the case which can now be presented against him, and all further investigation has served to strengthen it. By the way, there is one curious little point about those papers which may serve us as the starting-point for an inquiry. On looking over the bank book I found that the low state of the balance was principally due to large checks which have been made out during the last year to a Mr. Cornelius. I confess that I should be interested to know who this Mr. Cornelius may be with whom a retired builder has such very large transactions. Is it possible that he has had a hand in the affair? Cornelius might be a broker, but we have found no scrip to correspond with these large payments. Failing any other indication, my researches must now take the direction of an inquiry at the bank for the gentleman who has cashed these checks. But I fear, my dear fellow, that our case will end ingloriously by Lestrade hanging our client, which will certainly be a triumph for Scotland Yard."

I do not know how far Sherlock Holmes took any sleep that night, but when I came down to breakfast I found him pale and harassed, his bright eyes the brighter for the dark shadows round them. The carpet round his chair was littered with cigarette-ends and with the early editions of the morning papers. An open telegram lay upon the table.

"What do you think of this, Watson?" he asked, tossing it across.

It was from Norwood, and ran as follows:—

IMPORTANT FRESH EVIDENCE TO HAND MCFARLANE'S GUILT DEFINITELY ESTABLISHED ADVISE YOU TO ABANDON CASE
LESTRADE

"This sounds serious," said I.

"It is Lestrade's little cock-a-doodle of victory," Holmes answered, with a bitter smile. "And yet it may be premature to abandon the case. After all, important fresh evidence is a two-edged thing, and may possibly cut in a very different direction to that which Lestrade imagines. Take your breakfast, Watson, and we will go out together and see what we can do. I feel as if I shall need your company and your moral support today."

My friend had no breakfast himself, for it was one of his peculiarities that in his more intense moments he would permit himself no food, and I have known him to presume upon his iron strength until he has fainted from pure inanition. "At present I cannot spare energy and nerve force for digestion," he would say in answer to my medical remonstrances. I was not surprised, therefore, when this morning he left his untouched meal behind him, and started with me for Norwood. A crowd of morbid sightseers were still gathered round Deep Dene House, which was just such a suburban villa as I had pictured. Within the gates Lestrade met us, his face flushed with victory, his manner grossly triumphant.

"Well, Mr. Holmes, have you proved us to be wrong yet? Have you found your tramp?" he cried.

"I have formed no conclusion whatever," my companion answered.

"But we formed ours yesterday, and now it proves to be correct so you must acknowledge that we have been a little in front of you this time, Mr. Holmes."

"You certainly have the air of something unusual having occurred," said Holmes.

Lestrade laughed loudly.

"You don't like being beaten any more than the rest of us do," said he. "A man can't expect always to have it his own way, can he, Dr. Watson? Step this way, if you please, gentlemen, and I think I can convince you once for all that it was John McFarlane who did this crime."

He led us through the passage and out into a dark hall beyond.

"This is where young McFarlane must have come out to get his hat after the crime was done," said he. "Now look at this." With dramatic suddenness he struck a match, and by its light exposed a stain of blood upon the whitewashed wall. As he held the match nearer, I saw that it was more than a stain. It was the well-marked print of a thumb.

"Look at that with your magnifying glass, Mr. Holmes."

"Yes, I am doing so."

"You are aware that no two thumb marks are alike?"

"I have heard something of the kind."

"Well, then, will you please compare that print with this wax impression of young McFarlane's right thumb, taken by my orders this morning?"

As he held the waxen print close to the bloodstain, it did not take a magnifying glass to see that the two were undoubtedly from the same thumb. It was evident to me that our unfortunate client was lost.

"That is final," said Lestrade.

"Yes, that is final," I voluntarily echoed.

"It is final," said Holmes.

Something in his tone caught my ear, and I turned to look at him. An extraordinary change had come over his face. It was writhing with inward merriment. His two eyes were shining like stars. It seemed to me that he was making desperate efforts to restrain a convulsive attack of laughter.

"Dear me! Dear me!" he said at last. "Well, now, who would have thought it? And how deceptive appearances may be, to be sure! Such a nice young man to look at! It is a lesson to us not to trust our own judgment, is it not, Lestrade?"

"Yes, some of us are a little too much inclined to be cocksure, Mr. Holmes," said Lestrade. The man's insolence was maddening, but we could not resent it.

"What a providential thing that this young man should press his thumb against the wall in taking his hat from the peg! Such a very natural action, too, if you come to think of it." Holmes was outwardly calm, but his whole body gave a wriggle of suppressed excitement as he spoke. "By the way, Lestrade, who made this remarkable discovery?"

"It was the housekeeper, Mrs. Lexington, who drew the night constable's attention to it."

"Where was the night constable?"

"He remained on guard in the bedroom where the crime was committed, so as to see that nothing was touched."

"But why didn't the police see this mark yesterday?"

"Well, we had no particular reason to make a careful examination of the hall. Besides, it's not in a very prominent place, as you see."

"No, no—of course not. I suppose there is no doubt that the mark was there yesterday?"

Lestrade looked at Holmes as if he thought he was going out of his mind. I confess that I was myself surprised both at his hilarious manner and at his rather wild observation.

"I don't know whether you think that McFarlane came out of the jail in the dead of the night in order to strengthen the evidence against himself," said Lestrade. "I leave it to any expert in the world whether that is not the mark of his thumb."

"It is unquestionably the mark of his thumb."

"There, that's enough," said Lestrade. "I am a practical man, Mr. Holmes, and when I have got my evidence I come to my conclusions. If you have anything to say, you will find me writing my report in the sitting-room."

Holmes had recovered his equanimity, though I still seemed to detect gleams of amusement in his expression.

"Dear me, this is a very sad development, Watson, is it not?" said he. "And yet there are singular points about it which hold out some hopes for our client."

"I am delighted to hear it," said I, heartily. "I was afraid it was all up with him."

"I would hardly go so far as to say that, my dear Watson. The fact is that there is one really serious flaw in this evidence to which our friend attaches so much importance."

"Indeed, Holmes! What is it?"

"Only this: that I *know* that that mark was not there when I examined the hall yesterday. And now, Watson, let us have a little stroll round in the sunshine."

With a confused brain, but with a heart into which some warmth of hope was returning, I accompanied my friend in a walk round the garden. Holmes took each face of the house in turn, and examined it with great interest. He then led the way inside and went over the whole building from basement to attic.

Most of the rooms were unfurnished, but none the less Holmes inspected them all minutely. Finally, on the top corridor, which ran outside three untenanted bedrooms, he again was seized with a spasm of merriment.

"There are really some very unique features about this case, Watson," said he. "I think it is time now that we took our friend Lestrade into our confidence. He has had his little smile at our expense, and perhaps we may do as much by him, if my reading of this problem proves to be correct. Yes, yes, I think I see how we should approach it."

The Scotland Yard inspector was still writing in the parlor when Holmes interrupted him.

"I understood that you were writing a report of this case," said he.

"So I am."

"Don't you think it may be a little premature? I can't help thinking that your evidence is not complete."

Lestrade knew my friend too well to disregard his words. He laid down his pen and looked curiously at him.

"What do you mean, Mr. Holmes?"

"Only that there is an important witness whom you have not seen."

"Can you produce him?"

"I think I can."

"Then do so."

"I will do my best. How many constables have you?"

"There are three within call."

"Excellent!" said Holmes. "May I ask if they are all large, able-bodied men with powerful voices?"

"I have no doubt they are, though I fail to see what their voices have to do with it."

"Perhaps I can help you to see that and one or two other things as well," said Holmes. "Kindly summon your men, and I will try."

Five minutes later, three policemen had assembled in the hall.

"In the outhouse you will find a considerable quantity of straw," said Holmes. "I will ask you to carry in two bundles of it. I think it will be of the greatest assistance in producing the witness whom I require. Thank you very much. I believe you have some matches in your pocket, Watson. Now, Mr. Lestrade, I will ask you all to accompany me to the top landing."

As I have said, there was a broad corridor there, which ran outside three empty bedrooms. At one end of the corridor we were all marshalled by Sherlock Holmes, the constables grinning and Lestrade staring at my friend with amazement, expectation, and derision chasing each other across his features. Holmes stood before us with the air of a conjurer who is performing a trick.

"Would you kindly send one of your constables for two buckets of water? Put the straw on the floor here, free from the wall on either side. Now I think that we are all ready."

Lestrade's face had begun to grow red and angry.

"I don't know whether you are playing a game with us, Mr. Sherlock Holmes," said he. "If you know anything, you can surely say it without all this tomfoolery."

"I assure you, my good Lestrade, that I have an excellent reason for everything that I do. You may possibly remember that you chaffed me a little, some hours ago, when the sun seemed on your side of the hedge, so you must not grudge me a little pomp and ceremony now. Might I ask you, Watson, to open that window, and then to put a match to the edge of the straw?"

I did so, and driven by the draught, a coil of gray smoke swirled down the corridor, while the dry straw crackled and flamed.

"Now we must see if we can find this witness for you, Lestrade. Might I ask you all to join in the cry of 'Fire!'? Now, then; one, two, three—"

"Fire!" we all yelled.

"Thank you. I will trouble you once again."

"Fire!"

"Just once more, gentlemen, and all together."

"Fire!" The shout must have rung over Norwood.

It had hardly died away when an amazing thing happened. A door suddenly flew open out of what appeared to be solid wall at the end of the corridor, and a little, wizened man darted out of it, like a rabbit out of its burrow.

"Capital!" said Holmes, calmly. "Watson, a bucket of water over the straw. That will do! Lestrade, allow me to present you with your principal missing witness, Mr. Jonas Oldacre."

The detective stared at the newcomer with blank amazement. The latter was blinking in the bright light of the corridor, and peering at us and at the smoldering fire. It was an odious face—crafty, vicious, malignant, with shifty, light-gray eyes and white lashes.

"What's this, then?" said Lestrade at last. "What have you been doing all this time, eh?"

Oldacre gave an uneasy laugh, shrinking back from the furious red face of the angry detective.

"I have done no harm."

"No harm? You have done your best to get an innocent man hanged. If it wasn't for this gentleman here, I am not sure that you would not have succeeded."

The wretched creature began to whimper.

"I am sure, sir, it was only my practical joke."

"Oh! a joke, was it? You won't find the laugh on your side, I promise you. Take him down, and keep him in the sitting-room until I come. Mr. Holmes," he continued, when they had gone, "I could not speak before the constables, but I don't mind saying, in the presence of Dr. Watson, that this is the brightest thing that you have done yet, though it is a mystery to me how you did it. You have saved an innocent man's life, and you have prevented a very grave scandal, which would have ruined my reputation in the Force."

Holmes smiled, and clapped Lestrade upon the shoulder.

"Instead of being ruined, my good sir, you will find that your reputation has been enormously enhanced. Just make a few alterations in that report which you were writing, and they will understand how hard it is to throw dust in the eyes of Inspector Lestrade."

"And you don't want your name to appear?"

"Not at all. The work is its own reward. Perhaps I shall get the credit also at some distant day, when I permit my zealous historian to lay out his foolscap once more—eh, Watson? Well, now, let us see where this rat has been lurking."

A lath-and-plaster partition had been run across the passage six feet from the end, with a door cunningly concealed in it. It was lit within by slits under the eaves. A few articles of furniture and a supply of food and water were within, together with a number of books and papers.

"There's the advantage of being a builder," said Holmes, as we came out. "He was able to fix up his own little hiding-place without any confederate—save, of course, that precious housekeeper of his, whom I should lose no time in adding to your bag, Lestrade."

"I'll take your advice. But how did you know of this place, Mr. Holmes?"

"I made up my mind that the fellow was in hiding in the house. When I paced one corridor and found it six feet shorter than the corresponding one below, it was pretty clear where he was. I thought he had not the nerve to lie quiet before an alarm of fire. We could, of course, have gone in and taken him, but it amused me to make him reveal himself; besides, I owed you a little mystification, Lestrade, for your chaff in the morning."

"Well, sir, you certainly got equal with me on that. But how in the world did you know that he was in the house at all?"

"The thumb mark, Lestrade. You said it was final; and so it was, in a very different sense. I knew it had not been there the day before. I pay a good deal of attention to matters of detail, as you may have observed, and I had examined the hall, and was sure that the wall was clear. Therefore, it had been put on during the night."

"But how?"

"Very simply. When those packets were sealed up, Jonas Oldacre got McFarlane to secure one of the seals by putting his thumb upon the soft wax. It would be done so quickly and so naturally, that I dare say the young man himself has no recollection of it. Very likely it just so happened, and Oldacre had himself no notion of the use he would put it to. Brooding over the case in that den of his, it suddenly struck him what absolutely damning evidence he could make against McFarlane by using that thumb mark. It was the simplest thing in the world for him to take a wax impression from the seal, to moisten it in as much blood as he could get from a pin-prick, and to put the mark upon the wall during the night, either with his own hand or with that of his housekeeper. If you examine among those documents which he took with him into his retreat, I will lay you a wager that you find the seal with the thumb mark upon it."

"Wonderful!" said Lestrade. "Wonderful! It's all as clear as crystal, as you put it. But what is the object of this deep deception, Mr. Holmes?"

It was amusing to me to see how the detective's overbearing manner had changed suddenly to that of a child asking questions of its teacher.

"Well, I don't think that is very hard to explain. A very deep, malicious, vindictive person is the gentleman who is now waiting us downstairs. You know that he was once refused by McFarlane's mother? You don't! I told you that you should go to Blackheath first and Norwood afterwards. Well, this injury, as he would consider it, has rankled in his wicked, scheming brain, and all his life he has longed for vengeance, but never seen his chance. During the last year or two, things have gone against him—secret speculation, I think—and he finds himself in a bad way. He determines to swindle his creditors, and for this purpose he pays large checks to a certain Mr. Cornelius, who is, I imagine, himself under another name. I have not traced these checks yet, but I have no doubt that they were banked under that name at some provincial town where Oldacre from time to time led a double existence. He intended to change his name altogether, draw this money, and vanish, starting life again elsewhere."

"Well, that's likely enough."

"It would strike him that in disappearing he might throw all pursuit off his track, and at the same time have an ample and crushing revenge upon his old sweetheart, if he could give the impression that he had been murdered by her only child. It was a masterpiece of villainy, and he carried it out like a master. The idea of the will, which would give an obvious motive for the crime, the secret visit unknown to his own parents, the retention of the stick, the blood, and the animal remains and buttons in the wood-pile, all were admirable. It was a net from which it seemed to me, a few hours ago, that there was no possible escape. But he had not that supreme gift of the artist, the knowledge of when to stop. He wished to improve that which was already perfect—to draw the rope tighter yet round the neck of his unfortunate victim—and so he ruined all. Let us descend, Lestrade. There are just one or two questions that I would ask him."

The malignant creature was seated in his own parlor, with a policeman upon each side of him.

"It was a joke, my good sir—a practical joke, nothing more," he whined incessantly. "I assure you, sir, that I simply concealed myself in order to see the effect of my disappearance, and I am sure that you would not be so unjust as to imagine that I would have allowed any harm to befall poor young Mr. McFarlane."

"That's for a jury to decide," said Lestrade. "Anyhow, we shall have you on a charge of conspiracy, if not for attempted murder."

"And you'll probably find that your creditors will impound the banking account of Mr. Cornelius," said Holmes.

The little man started, and turned his malignant eyes upon my friend.

"I have to thank you for a good deal," said he. "Perhaps I'll pay my debt some day."

Holmes smiled indulgently.

"I fancy that, for some few years, you will find your time very fully occupied," said he. "By the way, what was it you put into the woodpile besides your old trousers? A dead dog, or rabbits, or what? You won't tell? Dear me, how very unkind of you! Well, well, I dare say that a couple of rabbits would account both for the blood and for the charred ashes. If ever you write an account, Watson, you can make rabbits serve your turn."

◇◇◇◇◇◇◇◇◇◇◇◇◇◇◇◇◇◇◇◇◇◇◇◇◇◇◇◇◇◇◇◇◇◇◇

FOR DISCUSSION

1. As you have observed, Holmes came to conclusions by observing small details. What did Holmes learn about McFarlane without asking any questions?

2. Detective procedure seeks to establish the motive for committing crime. Did Holmes consider that McFarlane had a likely motive for murdering Jonas Oldacre? Does this explain Holmes's instinct that the facts were being wrongly interpreted? Would you say the relations between Holmes and Lestrade were cordial?

3. Why did Holmes begin his investigation at Blackheath rather than at the scene of the crime? What did he learn there which strengthened or weakened McFarlane's case?

4. Was Lestrade's fresh evidence a "two-edged thing"? What incident decisively established McFarlane's innocence?

5. What was Oldacre's double motive for contriving his disappearance in the circumstances related in the story?

6. A well-written detective story offers hints toward its solution long before the story is actually solved. Did you anticipate the solution? Reread the story and then list the clues which pointed all along to the guilt of Jonas Oldacre.

ARE YOU A GOOD WORD DETECTIVE?

1. You can discover the meanings of many unfamiliar words from clues given within the sentence or paragraph. This method of determining word meanings is called learning by *context*. Study carefully the italicized adjectives in the following sentences. What moods do they describe? How does the rest of the sentence reveal the meaning of each word?

a. ". . . a wild-eyed and *frantic* young man . . . burst into the room."

b. ". . . I could see, by a glance at his *haggard* and anxious face, that the high hopes with which he had started had not been fulfilled."

c. "It seemed to me that he was making desperate efforts to restrain a *convulsive* attack of laughter."

2. Can you discover the meanings of each of the following italicized words from the context of the sentence? Discuss in class how the sentence helped you with the meaning. Give a synonym for each italicized word:

a. "That is the clue which they are already following, and I know it leads *infallibly* to me."

b. "Lestrade had learned . . . that that

razor-like brain could cut through that which was *impenetrable* to him."

c. "He was more like a *malignant* and cunning ape than a human being."

d. "I tried one or two leads, but could get at nothing which would help our *hypothesis*."

e. "In his more intense moments he would permit himself no food, and I have known him to presume upon his iron strength until he has fainted from pure *inanition*."

BRITISH OR AMERICAN?

Though both speak the English language, the British and the Americans often use different words to mean the same thing. Conan Doyle, for instance, calls a railway switch a "point" and a lawyer a "solicitor." Similarly, note these common British equivalents for the following American words: automobile—*motor-car,* baggage—*luggage,* bill (money)—*bank note,* biscuit—*scone,* bus—*tram,* can—*tin,* elevator—*lift,* gasoline—*petrol,* grain—*corn,* janitor—*porter,* policeman—*constable* or *bobby,* pie—*tart,* radio—*wireless,* sidewalk—*path,* swim—*bathe.*

A much larger list could be made of such variations. Just for the fun of it, see whether you can discover the meanings of these English expressions: *blighty, cheerio, head-master, drawing-room, fillet, tea, homely,* and *cricket.* (For help see your dictionary. A very helpful and interesting reference is *The American Language,* by H. L. Mencken.)

Perhaps you can find other British expressions that vary with the American. List them on the board.

RELATED READING

Conan Doyle published several books relating the exploits of Sherlock Holmes. One title is *The Adventures of Sherlock Holmes.* Two of the best stories are "The Adventure of the Speckled Band" and "The Red-Headed League."

A fisherman's life is a hard one. Monotonous, back-breaking, dangerous, fishing nevertheless makes MEN. *St. Peter and most of the other Apostles were fishermen. The Sea of Galilee could become rough, but never so rough, nor so cold, nor so murderous as a winter sea in an easterly wind on the shoals of Georges—two hundred miles southeast of Boston. Staunch St. Peter might well be the patron of Georges fishermen.*

WINTER ON GEORGES BANK

JAMES B. CONNOLLY

Georges Bank! The shoals of Georges! Gloucestermen's [1] wives would lower their voices when they spoke of Georges Shoals in wintertime. Fishermen's children learned to dread the news from Georges Shoals before they were old enough to know where the shoals [2] were. A hundred and seventy fishermen were lost in a single night on Georges. Seventy Gloucester widows were made by that single night. Count the children clinging to their mothers' skirts when the news of that night was brought home! Fourteen vessels gone in one night—and with all hands. When they go down on Georges they go with all hands.

So in a single bad night; and the shoals of Georges has known many bad nights. As a fisherman's son growing up to an age when I was beginning to understand the talk going on around me, when anybody—my father or uncle—mentioned Georges Bank, I would visualize battered hulls and frozen men being swept from ice-shrouded decks to their doom. I used to picture Judgment Day, when the seas would dry up and men arise and stand before the Lord. What a mighty host would be there from Georges Bank!

On a winter's day after I had heard from Editor Burlingame, I went down to Gloucester. One of the Chisholm fleet, the *Horace B. Parker*, was ready to put out. Her skipper was Bill McDonald, frequently spoken of as Red Jacket Bill, because of his unstinted praise of a vessel of that name, of which he had once been skipper.

Bill stood to the wheel of the *Parker* until she was clear of the harbor, then set her stern to Eastern Point Light, laid her course, gave over the wheel to the first on watch with the words: "East-s'utheast she is and keep her so." East-southeast is the immemorial course from Gloucester to a safe clearing of the North Shoal of Georges. And so:

"East-s'utheast," repeated that first helmsman, and east-s'utheast was the

[1] GLOUCESTERMEN—(glŏs′tĕr·mĕn).

[2] SHOAL—A bank or bar of sand which makes the water shallow.

word from helmsman to helmsman all that afternoon and night.

East-southeast it still was when I made the deck in the morning. It had been a mild day and night for wind, and eight to nine knots [3] was the best the *Parker* could log.[4] She was no big sailer for a Gloucesterman. She was more on the able kind. As Bill put it: "She's no *Red Jacket* for loggin' the knots, but she's able, boy, able."

Bill gave safe clearance to the Georges North Shoal, then headed southwesterly for the good fishing in the shoal water there.

It is in the shoal water of Georges that so many fishermen had been lost, and would be lost—Bill McDonald himself and all his crew were lost there later, though not in the *Parker*. Easterly gales pinned vessels in on the shoal water to the westward, and then they had to beat their way out against the gale. I am speaking of the all-sail *Parker's* day, before the advent of power in the fishing fleet. Let the gale blow hard and long enough, and vessels of the fleet would be pinned in the shoal water for good.

There are spots on Georges so shoal that in a high gale they show only white water; which means that a vessel caught in such a shoal spot usually batters herself to pieces on bottom. The shoal bottom of Georges is floored with the planks and frames of battered fishing vessels.

And don't fishermen see the gale coming? Or are they poor judges of weather? As to that, they know weather, nobody better; but the good fishing is in there in shoal water, and they are out there to catch fish. When they can't bring home the fish, there's no living for them and their families. And so they hang on.

The *Parker* wasn't long on her southerly tack [5] when the wind hauled [6] into the east. Also the barometer was falling.[7]

Bill held on to twenty-five fathoms [8] of water—a good fishing spot, though a dangerous depth of water for a vessel in an easterly gale. Bill, however, did not stay overlong in twenty-five fathoms. When he felt a strong wind coming he worked the *Parker* off the bank, held her to it until she found herself on the edge of the warm Gulf Stream.[9]

The strong wind increased to a gale. It was a gale for a time, and then roared into what Gloucestermen call a living gale. Wind aplenty, that means. Our mainsail was taken off before it would be blown off. Next her jib was triced up; [10] and then her foresail double-reefed; [11] and there she lay, head to the sea, and pitching to it. Pitching plenty, but no great harm in that. As Old Bill said: "She mayn't be a *Red Jacket* for sailing, but she's cert'nly an able little vessel!"

That word "little" meant that she was of lesser tonnage than the *Red Jacket*, though actually she wasn't a little vessel

[3] KNOT—A measure of speed at sea—one nautical mile an hour.

[4] LOG—To enter in the log book, the record of a ship's progress.

[5] TACK—A maneuver by which a sailing vessel shifts direction to take advantage of a side wind.

[6] THE WIND HAULED—The wind shifted.

[7] BAROMETER WAS FALLING—A sign of an approaching storm.

[8] FATHOM—A sea measure equal to six feet.

[9] GULF STREAM—A warm current flowing up from the Gulf of Mexico through the Atlantic.

[10] TRICED UP—Raised, lashed up.

[11] DOUBLE-REEFED—Shortened; that is, sail reduced by folding part and tying it round.

by Gloucester standards. She was of medium tonnage and carried ten dories,[12] which meant a crew of twenty-two all told—twenty dory men, the skipper, and the cook. He was a good cook, Quinn by name, and a great one for pies, and fishermen at sea do love pie. They love any kind of sweets, but especially pie—any kind of pie.

That easterly went three days without slacking. I spent the first day of it being seasick—my first seasickness since I was seven years of age, that time of my first fishing trip in my school vacation. The Gloucester way to lick seasickness is to get up on deck where the fresh air is, keep walking the deck, and chewing a hard biscuit. Downing a mug or two of sea water also helps. I knew all that, and I tried walking the deck until I grew weary of running for the weather rigging to save being swept overboard, which would mean being lost. Even if a dory could be launched, no man could live long enough in that sea for a dory to reach him. "Why don't you go below?" said Captain Bill. "You ain't havin' to stand a watch, and I ain't for askin' men to go in a dory this day."

So I stowed myself for the next few hours in a wide cabin bunk, which I shared with "Scotty"—whose real name I never learned. Aft and forward, the men not standing watch were taking it easy in their bunks, fishermen being great ones for storing away sleep against the heavy heaving and hauling of trawls[13] and rowing of dories always ahead of them.

Lying in a bunk allowed me only a smothered conception of what was going on outside; but the picture wasn't all lost. By snugging up to the vessel's outside planking I could get my shoulder within three inches of the whirling waters under her hull. I could feel the premonitory heavings of oncoming seas. I had a windward[14] bunk. In advance of a sea, the side of the vessel at my shoulder would sag away. I would feel her hull beneath me lifting. It was lift, lift, lift! And then she would poise herself, waiting like for what next, with her timbers groaning under the strain of it: then to leeward[15] she would sag before the oncoming sea. Below decks we would hear and feel it coming. She being head to wind, the sea would board her forward quarter, and then over our heads we would hear a rumbling and a thumping, a swashing the length of her deck.

The seas were coming on so fast that by the time someone would finish saying: "Here's another jeesly one coming!" that other one would be roaring over our heads and gone by way of our lee quarter rail. The vessel would resist—fight to stay where she was. We could hear her groaning—her beam frames that would be, battling to hold her hull intact; we could feel her battling against it, but after the roaring sea she would be drawn. She was an able vessel, yes; but after all she was a little thing—eighty tons. She would be tossed before it, rolled down before it, and then—suddenly—she would come rushing back, and we would see her inclined cabin floor go level again—al-

[12] DORIES—Sharp-nosed, flat-bottomed rowboats.

[13] TRAWL—A trawl-line, a line anchored and buoyed bearing a great number of hooks.

[14] WINDWARD—The side of the ship toward the wind.

[15] LEEWARD—The side of the ship away from the wind.

most level—and we in our bunks would roll back to where we had been.

Regularly in my cabin bunk at night I would roll to leeward against Scotty, and he would roll too; but not to roll out onto the cabin floor. The bunk board would keep him from doing that.

All that day and all that night the boarding seas kept the *Parker* busy and her crew saying: "Well, if we ain't fishin', we're restin' up."

Seasickness, when a man has it beaten, leaves him feeling wonderfully fit. Next morning, after trying to make up for the two meals I had missed, I took to the deck, meaning to see the difference between seeing and listening to the way of wind and sea with a vessel.

It was still blowing, though not a high gale; but the seas, as often after the wind dies down, were running higher than before. And looking at the high seas rolling down on the vessel left a man—left me, at least—marveling that nothing was happening to the vessel. The seas looked to be masthead high, some of them. I have read the judgments of men—who have it that no seas ever ran as high as the masthead of a vessel. They may know whereof they speak. All I know is that after climbing the fore rigging to the masthead, I still couldn't see over the crests of the oncoming seas.

The seas came at us with deceptive speed. The men on watch would see one coming, gauge the time of its arrival aboard, and govern themselves accordingly. My bunkmate Scotty watched one coming, a little one it looked, and in his contempt of it he let go his two-handed grip of the weather fore rigging. The little one broke at our windward rail, and only the white collar of it came aboard; but there was weight enough and speed enough in that white edge to pick up Scotty and sweep him across the deck and lay him across the gunnel of the top windward dory. The dories had been nested bottom up and hauled inboard to the fore hatch. When Scotty had his breath back and spat out the salt water and found himself still aboard, he turned to me, saying: "Let that be a lesson to you. There's no trusting a single one of them!"—as if he had let himself get caught for my benefit.

The *Parker* was a buoyant craft—she had to be to withstand that battering; and because she was the buoyant kind she was being tossed about like an empty soapbox in the surf of a beach when a high wind is driving in from sea. She rode the seas—she'd better, of course—rode them high and rode them low. When high riding up the steep slopes she went, her bowsprit [16] would be pointing—well, not straight up, but almost; and when she went roller-coasting down the slopes, she would plunge her knightheads [17] well under. At times she would bury her windlass in the white smother.

The reefed foresail was to keep the vessel's head to wind; and mostly it was making a good job of it; but there were times when a sea would sideswipe the vessel and her head would fall off. Never for long, but for a little while. And then? Instead of coming aboard forward, a sea would strike her abeam.[18] And when they were big seas, they filled her rail to

[16] BOWSPRIT—A spar projecting forward from the bow or front of the vessel.

[17] KNIGHTHEADS—Two stout upright posts on either side of the bowsprit as support.

[18] ABEAM—From or on the side.

rail from her fo'c'sle[19] hatch to her wheel almost. Then it was the *Parker* would show what she was made of. We on deck—the two on watch and myself—would be into the rigging before an especially wicked-looking sea could strike aboard, and looking down from our perch could see the ship struggling to free herself of the immense weight on her back; and we would be rooting for her, hunching our shoulders to help her out. When up she would come, one of the watch was sure to shout: "What a great little one! An able vessel!" I was shouting it too before the day was out.

Along about midday we got rain, a heavy rain which beat the seas down some. When the watch thought it safe to stay down on deck, they rigged a square of canvas to the windward fore rigging just above the rail. Johnny LeCost they called it, and they stood their watches for the rest of the day in the lee of Johnny.

The men standing watch were bulky figures, with heavy flannels and outer clothing and a thick sweater under oilskins. They were wearing rubber boots, or knee-high leather boots called redjacks. Sou'westers[20] were buttoned under their chins, and woolen mitts were keeping their hands warm.

The seas let down some; but some able-looking fellows were still rolling down,

[19] FO'C'SLE (fōk's'l)—Short upper deck forward.

[20] SOU'WESTERS—Southwesters, a tarpaulin hat with broad brim behind.

lads with deep white collars. The watch kept a special lookout for the white-collar boys. When they saw one on the way, they hooked both elbows into the fore rigging, laid their shoulders snug up to Johnny LeCost, and hung on so till the high roller had passed on.

Through all this the heavy rain was sweeping the *Parker;* and between the rain and the seas and spray coming aboard, the deck and the cabin house and the rails of the *Parker* were shining clean and bright and beautiful.

When it isn't too cold, a winter northeaster on the banks usually brings snow. That night the cold air softened, and next morning came in with snow. It was a heavy damp snow which stuck like wet white plaster where it fell. The weight of it was doing the vessel no good, she was going logy, no longer lifting buoyantly to the seas, so the skipper added two men to every watch to keep the snow shoveled off.

We weren't the only vessel that had edged away from the bank—we sighted the lights of three others in the night—and so while the snow fell the foghorn was sounded once a minute.

The snow ceased falling, the gale blew itself out, and we ran back to the fishing spot the skipper had picked out for himself. It had gone colder again, and the men had to bait their trawls in a hold that was cold enough of itself on a winter morning; and twenty tons of ice to keep the fish fresh was making it colder. The men worked by candlelight, and the bait being frozen, and their hands half frozen, they beginning the day by the baiting of twelve hundred hooks for every two dory men—well, it took offshore bank fishermen to crack jokes while at the labor of it.

At the first peep of dawn the dories were put over the side. The vessel was under sail, the ten dories went one after another sliding past her quarter, with the skipper telling them where to set their trawls and how long to let them set before hauling.

A wind was blowing and the sea was choppy; what bank fishermen called choppy, though almost any other people would have called it a rough sea. The dories rode the sea, now high, now low, with one man rowing the dory, the other heaving the trawl, and neither paying any attention, apparently, to what might happen to the dory. From the deck of the vessel, a dory—any dory I spotted—would ride a sea, drop out of sight beyond it, and stay out of sight for just about long enough to set me thinking she wasn't coming up again. It was my first winter trawling trip, and a lot about winter fishing I still had to learn.

The wind wasn't heavy, but it was cold. The vessel was sailing in and out among the dories, the skipper to the wheel, and spray was splashing over our rail—no great amount of spray by now, but enough to allow some of it to stay aboard; and where it stayed it froze, making the deck like a skating rink to me whenever I went forward to cast away the jumbo sheet—my job when the vessel was under sail, the dories out, and the skipper tacking ship.

There was a long row to the vessel from some of the dories after they had hauled their trawls; and then came pitching the fish aboard, with the dories rolling high and low to the seaway. Out went the dories again, and so for four sets of the trawls that day. It was dark when the last dory was aboard for the night. It was dress fish and wash fish then, chop ice in the hold, and stow the fish in the pens. Those who hadn't a watch to stand were now free to turn in. That was the usual routine on the winter trawlers on the offshore banks. A hard and dangerous way to make a living, but never a sign from these men that they thought so. All they asked for was good fishing; and it was thank God with them when they got the good fishing.

Tough men, those dory men on the winter offshore banks; and before that first trip of mine ended, I was approving my intention of writing my next Gloucester stories around a sterner way of fishing life than pleasant summer seining.[21]

We got in three days of fair fishing, and then came a thick fog. Fog on Georges when so many vessels are fishing neighborly is a bad business. Let two vessels with any sort of headway on them come together, and down they go. And down with all hands! There won't be time to launch a single dory before they go under.

Riding lights or sailing lights are dim things in a thick o' fog on the offshore banks. It's a sharp lookout then, with a patent flare handy to stick in the hot fire of the cabin stove if another vessel is heard or seen bearing down.

Coasting steamers, and ocean liners too, would sometimes go off their course and bear in on the easterly edge of Georges. We were jogging clear of the bank on one of the foggy nights when the watch caught the sound of a horn. It was no fisherman's horn. It was a siren, which meant a steamer of some tonnage. The man on forward watch shouted a warning. The watch in the vessel's waist came scrambling aft and shouted it down the cabin companionway, so that the skipper would be sure to know. Again the siren. Wo-o-o-gh!—this one much nearer. The skipper grabbed a flare, always handy in the cabin, held it in the hot coals of the cabin stove till it blazed. It also smoked. He hustled up to the deck and held the blazing flare aloft. "If they have an eye in their heads they'll soon see this light. And if they're blind they'll be smellin' it."

Whatever it was made of, it smelled. And it smoked and blazed, and beneath it stood the skipper, Liberty, in yellow oilskins.

The siren went Woo-gh!—a short one, meaning close at hand. A matter to worry about now. The Woo-gh! was to our windward. Four men hurried to stand by the lee dories, to hoist them over the side if the steamer crashed us.

It was a quiet sea and wind, the usual thing in a thick o' fog. Now came the thrashing of the steamer's propellers. Not far off now. We got a glimpse of a red light. A pale light—a ship's port light—and to see it in a fog meant that the steamer was quite close.

Wh-gh! she went now—a short blast. All this time half our crew were yelling at her to sheer off. Her red light showed again—she was coming for us. Her red light sheered off a bit. So she was seeing our light. Well, about time, with us on deck yelling without a let-up and our foghorn sounding without stop! And there were our sailing lights for her watch

[21] SEINING (sān′ĭng)—Fishing with a net.

to see, if a watch she was keeping. There being no wind, we had to lay there and take what might come.

She passed close to our stern—a long shadow of a hulk—so close that our skipper felt he could talk to her bridge without his talk going astray. And he did so talk, still holding the blazing torch high over his head. It was Bill talking now. And he talked and shouted—a six-foot, 220-pound figure in yellow oilskins under the blazing torch. He blasted and double-blasted and double-double-blasted steamer people who didn't have navigation enough to find their way to north or south or east or west, to wherever they were bound, without running down honest fishermen. And so on and so on. Even when the steamer must have been a mile astern, the skipper was still sounding off.

Two days of a northwester followed. A safe wind, a northwester on Georges; no danger of being driven into the shoal water before it, but a cold wind always in winter; frequently a terribly cold wind, with spray freezing when it comes aboard, and in no thin film, but thickly on deck and rail and up the rigging if the sea is rough; and the spray freezing in the nests of the dories overnight so that they have to be pounded apart in the bitter morning. And filling the gangway between cabin house and rail solid with ice. And always it was dangerous footing on deck —men were liable to go sliding across the sloping deck before a boarding sea and over the lee rail before they knew what was happening.

But even on Georges in wintertime good days come along. We got in two more days of fishing, and the skipper said: "Dories inboard, bottom up, and double-gripe 'em!"

And after that was done, and while the crew were starting to dress the day's catch, the skipper was at the wheel and laying her course to clear the North Shoal and so to the Boston market.

That night the crew could relax, that night they took time to gossip. "Along about this time," said John Houghton—it was then ten o'clock—"we got our last sight of the *Commonwealth*."

I'd read about the *Commonwealth*, but here was a firsthand account of her.

The *Parker* and the *Commonwealth* left Georges together. The *Parker's* watchers could see the *Commonwealth's* sailing light for three hours after they left the bank. That midnight a northeaster set in. By morning it was a hurricane. The *Parker* took a beating before weathering the North Shoal and heading to the westward. The wind hauled ahead, and she took another beating. It was tack, tack, tack for every cable length she made. After four days she sighted Cape Cod Light. It took her another two days to make that last fifty miles home. The *Commonwealth* never got home. She was gone and all hands with her. She was undoubtedly driven back into the shoal water by the easterly hurricane. Driven there and smothered and battered to death.

And as she went, so did scores of fine vessels before her; and hundreds upon hundreds of gallant men with the fine vessels. The ablest schooners in the world they are, and the smartest schooner men in the world handling them, but so they go.

We made good going of it to clear the

North Shoal in my trip with the *Parker*. And then came a strong head wind. It was all head wind to Cape Cod. Then we caught a beam wind—no strong wind, but a fair enough sailing breeze. A-westerly we went then, scuppers well under. It was lovely sailing. A clear sky, a smooth sea, and into the setting sun we sailed.

At five o'clock in the afternoon we were off Boston Harbor. The loom of Boston lay ahead; and up the harbor went the *Parker* as though she owned it. Steamers were anchored in the harbor, which meant having to dodge many riding lights and avoid the hulls beneath them.

The skipper ran her close to the end of T Wharf before he jibed [22] her. Around she came and into the slip she shot, with her sails fluttering in the wind. It was dark then, but we could make out a man standing aft on a vessel already tied up. He caught our bowline and buttoned it to a cleat. The *Parker* ran ahead a bit, settled back, and there she was in port again, with 95,000 pounds of fresh fish.

It was seven o'clock when we slid into the T Wharf slip, and John Houghton and Scotty were already shaved and dressed to go ashore.

"Where bound, John?"

"There's a play—*Ben Hur*—and Scotty and me been told there's a chariot race in it with the drivers lashin' the chariot horses till you think they're going leaping through the side of the house. Man, they say it's the excitingest thing to watch!"

There was my kind of a bank fisherman to write about—the man who could see excitement, even danger, in what other men were doing ashore, but who took his own sea danger as a matter of course.

[22] JIBED—Shifted direction.

◇◇◇◇◇◇◇◇◇◇◇◇◇◇◇◇◇◇◇◇◇◇◇◇◇◇◇◇◇◇

FOR DISCUSSION

1. Georges Bank has a rugged reputation. List a few facts that lead you to believe that it is a dangerous spot.

2. Explain just why the shoals of Georges are so dangerous in an easterly wind. Why was the danger lessened with the introduction of power fishing boats?

3. What did the watch do when they saw a big wave coming up? Were there any near-accidents? How high were the waves?

4. Outline the things you would have to do if you were a dory man on the *Parker*. Do you think you could stand the work?

5. We sometimes complain, all of us, about the little jobs that we have to do. How did the fishermen of the *Parker* accept their hard life?

6. Fog! How great is the danger of fog in a small fishing vessel at sea? Was Captain Bill glad to see the steamer? Name three ways the *Parker* signaled her presence.

THE SAILOR'S VOCABULARY

1. Are you enough of a sailor to know the meaning of *shoal, stern, gale, dory?* Distinguish between: *gale, storm, breeze, squall, hurricane*.

2. Find examples of vivid usage as in the examples below. Discuss the effectiveness of each expression.

ice-*shrouded*	white *collar*
pinned vessels	*roller-coasting* down
floored with planks	white *smother*

FURTHER RESEARCH

Find in the Gospels the passages in which the Evangelists speak of fishing in Galilee. Compare the hardships there with those on Georges. Is there a difference in the manner of catching fish? Explain.

The Gospel references you will use are: Matthew 8:23–27; Matthew 14:24–33; Luke 5:1–7; and John 21:1–11.

Long ago there lived in Sherwood Forest a legendary outlaw who was loved by the common folk in England because he robbed the rich to give to the poor. The story below is the entertaining tale of how Little John joined Robin Hood's band of outlaws.

Robin Hood and Little John

ENGLISH BALLAD

When Robin Hood was about twenty years old,
With a hey down down and a down,
He happened to meet Little John,
A jolly brisk blade, right fit for the trade,
For he was a lusty young man. 5

Tho' he was called Little, his limbs they were large,
And his stature was seven foot high;
Wherever he came, they quaked at his name,
For soon he would make them to fly.

How they came acquainted, I'll tell you in brief, 10
If you will but listen awhile;
For this very jest, among all the rest,
I think it may cause you to smile.

Bold Robin Hood said to his jolly bowmen,
"Pray tarry you here in this grove; 15
And see that you all observe well my call,
While thorough the forest I rove.

"We have had no sport for these fourteen long days,
Therefore now abroad will I go;
Now should I be beat, and cannot retreat, 20
My horn I will presently blow."

4. BLADE—Sharp-witted, reckless fellow.
17. THOROUGH—Through.

Then did he shake hands with his merrymen all,
And bid them at present good b'w'ye;
Then, as near a brook his journey he took,
A stranger he chanced to espy. 25

They happened to meet on a long narrow bridge,
And neither of them would give way;
Quoth bold Robin Hood, and sturdily stood,
"I'll show you right Nottingham play."

With that from his quiver an arrow he drew, 30
A broad arrow with a goose-wing.
The stranger replied, "I'll liquor thy hide,
If thou offerst to touch the string."

Quoth bold Robin Hood, "Thou doest prate like an ass,
For were I to bend but my bow, 35
I could send a dart quite thro' thy proud heart,
Before thou couldst strike me one blow."

"Thou talkst like a coward," the stranger replied;
"Well armed with a long bow you stand,
To shoot at my breast, while I, I protest, 40
Have nought but a staff in my hand."

"The name of a coward," quoth Robin, "I scorn,
Wherefore my long bow I'll lay by;
And now, for thy sake, a staff will I take,
The truth of thy manhood to try." 45

Then Robin Hood stepped to a thicket of trees,
And chose him a staff of ground-oak;
Now this being done, away he did run
To the stranger, and merrily spoke:

"Lo! see my staff, it is lusty and tough, 50
Now here on the bridge we will play;
Whoever falls in, the other shall win
The battle, and so we'll away."

23. GOOD B'W'YE—"Good (or God) be with ye"; that is, good-bye.
29. RIGHT NOTTINGHAM PLAY—How we handle this situation in Nottingham.
32. LIQUOR THY HIDE—Draw your blood; that is, by giving you a beating.
34. PRATE—Chatter idly.

"With all my whole heart," the stranger replied;
"I scorn in the least to give out"; 55
This said, they fell to 't without more dispute,
And their staffs they did flourish about.

And first Robin he gave the stranger a bang,
So hard that it made his bones ring;
The stranger he said, "This must be repaid; 60
I'll give you as good as you bring.

"So long as I'm able to handle my staff,
To die in your debt, friend, I scorn."
Then to it each goes, and followed their blows,
As if they had been threshing of corn. 65

The stranger gave Robin a crack on the crown,
Which caused the blood to appear;
Then Robin, enraged, more fiercely engaged,
And followed his blows more severe.

So thick and so fast did he lay it on him, 70
With a passionate fury and ire,
At every stroke, he made him to smoke,
As if he had been all on fire.

O then into fury the stranger he grew,
And gave him a terrible look, 75
And with it a blow that laid him full low,
And tumbled him into the brook.

"I prithee, good fellow, O where art thou now?"
The stranger, in laughter, he cried;
Quoth bold Robin Hood, "Good faith, in the flood, 80
And floating along with the tide.

"I needs must acknowledge thou art a brave soul;
With thee I'll no longer contend;
For needs must I say, thou hast got the day,
Our battle shall be at an end." 85

Then unto the bank he did presently wade,
  And pulled himself out by a thorn;
Which done, at the last, he blew a loud blast
  Straightway on his fine bugle-horn.

The echo of which through the valley did fly, 90
  At which his stout bowmen appeared,
All clothed in green, most gay to be seen;
  So up to their master they steered.

"O what's the matter?" quoth William Stutely;
  "Good master, you are wet to the skin"; 95
"No matter," quoth he; "the lad which you see,
  In fighting, hath tumbled me in."

"He shall not go scot-free," the others replied;
  So straight they were seizing him there,
To duck him likewise; but Robin Hood cries, 100
  "He is a stout fellow, forbear.

87. THORN—Hawthorn or blackthorn tree.

"There's no one shall wrong thee, friend, be not afraid;
These bowmen upon me do wait;
There's threescore and nine; if thou wilt be mine,
Thou shalt have my livery straight. 105

"And other accouterments fit for a man;
Speak up, jolly blade, never fear;
I'll teach you also the use of the bow,
To shoot at the fat fallow deer."

"O here is my hand," the stranger replied, 110
"I'll serve you with all my whole heart;
My name is John Little, a man of good mettle;
Never doubt me, for I'll play my part."

"His name shall be altered," quoth William Stutely,
"And I will his godfather be; 115
Prepare then a feast, and none of the least,
For we will be merry," quoth he.

They presently fetched in a brace of fat does,
With humming strong liquor likewise;
They loved what was good; so, in the greenwood, 120
This pretty sweet babe they baptize.

He was, I must tell you, but seven foot high,
And, maybe, an ell in the waist,
A pretty sweet lad; much feasting they had;
Bold Robin the christening graced, 125

With all his bowmen, which stood in a ring,
And were of the Nottingham breed;
Brave Stutely comes then, with seven yeomen,
And did in this manner proceed:

"This infant was called John Little," quoth he, 130
"Which name shall be changed anon;
The words we'll transpose, so wherever he goes,
His name shall be called Little John."

104. THREESCORE—Sixty.
105. LIVERY—Uniform which Robin Hood gave to each of his men.
118. BRACE—A pair.
118. DOE—Female deer.
123. ELL—A measure of cloth. The English ell is 45 inches.

Then Robin he took the pretty sweet babe,
And clothed him from top to the toe 135
In garments of green, most gay to be seen,
And gave him a curious long bow.

"Thou shalt be an archer as well as the best,
And range in the greenwood with us;
Where we'll not want gold nor silver, behold, 140
While bishops have ought in their purse.

"We live here like squires, or lords of renown,
Without e'er a foot of free land;
We feast on good cheer, with wine, ale, and beer,
And ev'rything at our command." 145

Then music and dancing did finish the day;
At length, when the sun waxed low,
Then all the whole train the grove did refrain,
And unto their caves they did go.

And so ever after, as long as he lived, 150
Although he was proper and tall,
Yet nevertheless, the truth to express,
Still Little John they did him call.

137. CURIOUS—Excellent.

FOR DISCUSSION

1. Before going in search of "sport," what agreement did Robin make with his men?
2. What weapon did Robin threaten to use *first* against John Little? With what weapons did they finally fight?
3. Who started to bleed first? Who won the duel?
4. What three things did Robin promise John if the latter would join his band? Who performed the christening?
5. From whom did these merry men regularly "receive their allowance"?

PROJECTS

1. Since ballads are meant to be sung or chanted, it might be fun to prepare to read this ballad before the class. Volunteers may take the parts of individual characters (Robin Hood, John Little, William Stutely, and the narrator). Practice using the tone of voice and gestures which you think would have been used by the person whose part you are taking.
2. It is easy to find many of the Robin Hood ballads. Your teacher or librarian can help you. Perhaps several students will enjoy preparing readings of other Robin Hood ballads to present before the class.
3. What news story can you find in the daily paper which suggests to you an incident or series of incidents which might well be put into a ballad? Several students may work together writing a ballad based on these news stories. Prepare to read your ballad before the class.

RELATED READING

Besides this Robin Hood story there are many others. The best are "Robin Hood and Allan-A-Dale," "Robin Hood and the Monk," "The Bold Pedlar and Robin Hood," "Robin Hood and Guy of Gisborne," "Robin Hood and the Tanner," "Robin Hood Rescuing Will Stutely," and "Robin Hood's Death." The best-known prose account of this bandit of Sherwood Forest is Howard Pyle's *The Merry Adventures of Robin Hood*. One of the most popular versions among young people is *Bold Robin Hood and His Outlaw Band*, written and illustrated by Louis Rhead.

◇◇◇◇◇

Stalking the lion with beaters and guns is dangerous enough, but imagine the thrill of taking pictures of him as he charges you in a noble rage. Osa Johnson recounts many adventures that she and her husband Martin had in dealing with the lord of the jungle.

"SHOOTING" LIONS

OSA JOHNSON

Lions! For a year we lived with them in what Carl Akeley had called the "lions' den," that area some five hundred miles square in Tanganyika Territory [1] to which Carl had taken us shortly before the illness which was to end his life. We worked with lions; we ate and slept with their roars all round us. At times, and with good reason, we feared the great tawny cats, but in the end we grew, as Carl said we would, to respect and love them.

Our equipment consisted roughly of five tents, two water stills, ten motion picture cameras, eleven still cameras, one hundred thousand feet of film, medical stores, foodstuffs, a typewriter, and even a phonograph, and guns, of course. In all there was something like four tons of stuff; and our big touring car, together with four trucks, carried the lot.

I drove the touring car with four natives hanging on wherever they could. Martin took the wheel of one of the trucks which carried two tons of supplies and six black boys, while the next truck, equally overloaded, was driven by Urg, our newly acquired Swahili mechanic.

As we rolled into this vast and almost immeasurable domain that is the lion's "Happy Hunting Ground," I thought of Carl Akeley's resentment against the caging of these beautiful beasts. Here, the lion has an abundance for his every need, from food and air to freedom, and re-

[1] TANGANYIKA TERRITORY (tăn·găn·yē′kä)—A region of east Africa, south of the equator, under British control.

straint is probably the one thing he cannot comprehend. Yet, for thousands of years, he has been hunted and captured and caged to satisfy the vanity of man. I am deeply in sympathy with those enlightened zoos, such as that at San Diego, dedicated to education rather than to entertainment, which are willing to appropriate sufficient ground to give their lion prizes some of the liberty and color of their native home.

Although the lion has counted more than any other factor in man's dread of Africa, curiously enough, man is the only enemy the lion really fears. Hunters from the days of the ancient Ptolemies [2] and before have ranged the plains of Africa with all manner of weapons which were too much even for his magnificent strength and speed and cunning, and it has always surprised me that lions did not somehow remember and that they would trust us at all.

Government has now reduced the menace of the hunter as much as possible by high license fees and other protections, but there is still considerable wanton killing. Martin and I have always done all we could to encourage the setting aside of game preserves, and it was one of his special hopes to see the Serengetti Plains made into a protected area where lions could be hunted only with the camera, which now has finally become a fact under the direction of Game Warden Monty Moore and his splendid and heroic wife.

For the most part, the lion is a thoroughly agreeable personage. He lives a most leisurely existence, loafs and sleeps a great deal, has just as playful moods as a house cat and just as decided a personality. He minds his own business, is very fond of his family, and takes his duties as a family protector and provider very seriously. As a youngster he usually attaches himself to a pride or "gang" of young males and they roam about together, sometimes for years, having an hilarious time, sharing their food and their fun, until he finally settles down to domestic bliss and the raising of a family. When he becomes a grandfather and too old to keep up with his family and friends, he is ejected from the pride and left to roam about alone, and it is then that he often becomes a "rogue," probably a neurasthenic [3] condition not unfamiliar to humans.

Naturally, being of the cat family, he is carnivorous. He kills to eat. Except in self-defense, he seldom disturbs a living thing although I have known him to attack without provocation and have always been careful not to startle or annoy him. When attacked or wounded, he never retreats, but fights as long as there is a spark of life in his magnificent body.

Weighing anywhere between four hundred and five hundred pounds, this massive cat has great strength combined with feline suppleness. On short spurts he can overtake almost any other animal on the plains and a single blow of his huge clawed foot, or crunch of his jaw, is almost certain death. Many of my friends, expert shots and fine sportsmen and fully aware of the ways of the lion, have been killed or disabled or severely mauled in a moment of recklessness.

Sir Alfred Pease, the well-known game

[2] PTOLEMIES—Ancient Egyptian kings.

[3] NEURASTHENIC—Pertaining to nervous prostration.

hunter, made it a rule when hunting lions to keep at least two hundred yards between himself and the beast. His friend, George Grey—brother of Sir Edward Grey—hunting with him one day, failed to observe this rule and galloped to within ninety yards of a lion that had been slightly wounded. The animal charged. Sir Alfred tried heading it off, and pumped several shots into it at close range, but the maddened creature, though terribly wounded, leaped upon Mr. Grey, lacerating him so cruelly that he died shortly afterwards.

Theodore Roosevelt wrote: "The hunter should never go near a lion until it is dead; and even when it is on the point of death he should not stand near nor approach his head from the front."

Martin had the complacent look of a man who has just finished a large and thoroughly satisfactory meal. What he had just finished, however, was not a meal but an afternoon's photography in the midst of fourteen lions. The big beasts had been as indifferent to us as we, in turn, might have been to a couple of field mice; and while this attitude on their part gave us a comfortable enough feeling, I can't say it was exactly flattering.

My husband had exposed several magazines of film and was about to put still another into the camera.

"Well, my gracious," I said, "haven't you got about enough?"

Martin grinned at me a little sheepishly. "Oh, I guess so," he said, "but, golly, aren't they wonderful?"

He looked fondly off at the sleek, lovely animals. For hours they had boxed and mauled one another. When tired, they had slept, usually on their backs with their feet in the air and snoring mightily. They had been through this routine several times. There were perhaps eight or nine lionesses among them, but very little ill temper or jealousy was displayed, and, in fact, a better mannered or more amiable group—man or beast—could not be imagined.

"Of course they're wonderful," I replied, "but they've eaten nothing in hours. Suppose they suddenly decide they're hungry?"

I stepped on the starter and began backing away, whereupon one of the husky young males decided to challenge our departure. He bristled, his eyes sharpened with excitement and he started to follow us, measuring his sinewy, menacing stride exactly to the roll of our car. There was only one safe thing to do, and that was to stop, for a lion, like any other member of the cat family, finds a retreating object almost irresistible. Martin trained his gun on the animal's great head.

Looking up at us in mild surprise that we should have stopped, and a little disappointed, I think, at our taking the fun out of his little game of pursuit, the lion sniffed at our left front tire, then bit it gently. The taste of rubber was new to him, apparently, and he wrinkled his nose, not quite sure that he liked it. Then he tried again. Persuaded this time that it was nothing he cared particularly to eat, but that it might be worth playing with, he began mouthing and growling over it in the manner of a puppy with a rubber ball. The other lions moved up as if on cue, and stood lazily watching this performance.

My husband looked a little anxious. "A puncture wouldn't be a very healthy thing right now," he said, his voice lowered to a cautious key. The more he thought about this the less he liked it. "The explosion right in his teeth might make him mad, too," he added.

"How about racing the motor?" I offered.

Martin nodded. "Yes. Try it. It might distract him."

I did so. The lion forgot the tire, as we hoped he would and, cocking his head, listened attentively. So far, so good, I thought, and pushed a little harder on the accelerator. The racing engine now gave off a cloud of noxious fumes, and taking advantage of the astonished sniffs and distaste, which all the lions suddenly exhibited, I backed away, jockeyed out of sight around a huge rock and streaked off across the plain.

In order to obtain a really complete pictorial history of the lion, it became apparent that we must photograph his nocturnal as well as his daylight habits.

Fortunately, Martin had experimented at length and successfully with night camera-work and knew all the mechanical requirements. Contrary to his usual procedure, however, of rigging up the flashlights and cameras and letting the mechanical devices do the work, he decided that he would probably have better results with lion if we stationed ourselves in our car and he operated the camera himself.

The method followed was to set four flash lamps on firmly planted poles about six feet above the ground, then to fasten the cameras securely to solid platforms three feet in front of and below each lamp. These were connected with dry batteries and controlled by a long "firing" wire. The cameras, especially made for this purpose, took pictures automatically at a speed of one three-hundredths of a second when the light from the flash was at its maximum.

After setting up this apparatus, a much less pleasant task confronted us; the shooting of a zebra for bait. The guilty feeling we always had about this would have seemed ridiculous to anyone less concerned than ourselves, but the sight of the happy, rowdy little fellows always reminded Martin of his pony, Socks, and put me in a mood where I wanted to pet and certainly not to shoot them.

First, in this connection, of course, there was the ignominious business of sneaking away from camp. Assuredly, since we wouldn't admit to each other that we were sentimental about zebra, we weren't going to attempt to explain our actions to the black boys.

Our routine usually followed the same pattern. Having located a herd and moved within shooting distance of it, we would glance furtively at each other, and then, either Martin or I would yawn. I usually managed to get in ahead of my husband on this.

"Ho, hum," I would say. "You haven't done much shooting lately. It's about time you practiced up."

"Oh, as to that," he would reply carelessly, "as long as I'm only the cameraman around here and you're the one who holds the gun, I think you should keep in practice."

"Well," I would then say, "I don't feel like shooting today. I think my head aches."

"Oh, all right," my husband would growl, "but if I just wound one of the poor fellows, don't blame me."

With this he'd jerk his gun to his shoulder and pretend to take aim.

This was my cue to sigh. "Never mind," I'd say. "Let's pick out an old one or a lame one and get it over with."

Martin's look of relief at this always endeared him to me. Then we would stand for quite a long time, weighing the relative age or lameness of this zebra or that zebra. Finally one would be selected, I would shoot him, and in silence we would go back to camp. Our boys were then sent, of course, to fetch the victim of my gun and place him at a spot exactly fifteen feet from the cameras. Ouranga always directed this part of the flashlight operation and it was he, too, who, waiting until it was quite dark, cut the entrails from the carcass and dragged them about the site. He always added a mumbled incantation to this disagreeable business and took credit for the results—if good. Seated in our car at a discreet distance by this time, with gun and "firing" wire ready, we sent all the blacks, including the theatrical Ouranga, back to camp.

The wretched hyenas were invariably the first to find our zebra. Sometimes a well-aimed rock would disperse them, but when they came in packs and seemed on the point of eating all the bait, we were usually forced to shoot one or two to show them we were in earnest.

"If only the lions would eat the darned old hyenas," Martin grumbled, "everything would be fine."

"Shhh," I whispered. "I think I hear something."

"Oh, there won't be anything doing tonight," my husband said drowsily. "I wish I were in bed." This said, he promptly went to sleep.

The sky was overcast; there was no moon and the darkness was black and thick and cold. I remembered how quietly lions moved on their padded paws. I also derived what comfort I could from the fact that we had sat in open cars many times before, with lions all around us, and that so far we had not been eaten.

Then I heard a tearing sound, and a chewing and gulping and crunching and, along with this, a sort of purring growl.

I nudged Martin, but he was too fast asleep for gentle methods to have effect. I pinched him. He said "ouch"; the crunching accompanied only by a deep growl went steadily on.

"Golly!" my husband said. He turned on his electric torch and there, sitting right in front of us and wearing one of the finest manes I have ever seen, was surely the king himself; the king of all the Tanganyika lions. Lifting his great head slowly the big animal looked disdainfully straight into our light. A piece of zebra flesh, torn and dripping, dangled from his mouth, but not even this could detract from his majesty.

My husband now put our flashlights and cameras into operation. The lion dropped his piece of meat, bared his teeth and roared and then, with an abruptness that left me trembling and my gun still pointed at his head, he went back to his feast.

Others of his family joined him. Several of them were his wives, apparently, and the smaller ones might have been his half-grown sons. They were a fine looking lot and formed a perfect picture.

"Oh, that's great! that's great!" I heard Martin whispering to himself. He pressed the button. Nothing happened. Again he pressed it with all his might, and there was no sign of a flash. Frantically he pulled the wires from the button and touched them together, but still without result.

"Well," he said, "I guess there's nothing else to do."

He was looking straight out to where the lions were feeding.

I knew what he meant, but I wouldn't believe him. "What do you mean?" I demanded.

"I've got to get out there and fix it, that's all."

He was out of the car before I could stop him. I caught him by the collar.

"You're crazy," I said, half crying.

"Give me the sawed-off gun," was all he said.

So I drove the lions off the kill by throwing the powerful searchlight of our car in their faces, tooting the auto horn and yelling, covering Martin the while with my gun. The lions retreated about twenty yards and in a few brief minutes, which seemed like an eternity, my husband found the loose connection and returned to the car.

"Don't you ever do that again!" I said, practically in collapse.

Martin went straight to work, though I saw that he was shaking a little.

The lion king, having eaten his fill, apparently decided now to investigate the flashlights and cameras. He even gave one of the cameras an experimental bite.

"You let that camera alone!" my husband yelled, completely beside himself.

The majestic cat glanced our way indifferently, then began chewing at the base on which the camera was fastened. The whole thing went over.

Martin got out of the car again and began throwing rocks and anything else that came to hand. To add to the complication, one of the younger lions now decided to follow the cue of the older lion, and seizing one of the wires, tugged at it until he had torn it and several other wires from their fastenings.

We sat there throwing rocks, shooting our guns into the air, yelling until we were hoarse, but not until those two lions had pulled down every wire, battery, camera, and pole of our equipment were they satisfied. Then they strolled off, their tails waving proudly, and our night of flashlight photography was definitely at an end.

A few days later we came upon a large pride of young males resting under a cluster of trees and we stopped to watch. They were extremely curious and began edging up to look us over. They were so playful and frisky that Martin obtained some new and very valuable film. We decided to lunch there and climbed out through the aperture at the top of the truck and sat down to enjoy our sandwiches and to watch.

At the sight of our food, the lions came up close to the car and sat down like a bunch of hungry beggars. I threw them some partridge legs which they tasted and then licked their chops as much as to say, "Pretty high-toned food for a jungle lion."

For an hour they played about us, within a few feet of the car, bit at the tires and nipped at one another and had a rowdy time. We even called them by name (not for exact resemblance, of course): Roy Chapman Andrews, the most dapper of them; Lowell Thomas, the one who roared most; George Dryden, the one who bit the tires and seemed most interested in the rubber business; Merian Cooper, the wise and well-mannered one who kept his distance through most of the fracas. And the lions seemed satisfied with the comparisons.

Perhaps it was experiences of this sort that made us a little reckless; that had us thinking of the huge felines in terms of fireside tabbies. At any rate, we were on foot one very hot day, our camera and gun-bearers were with us, of course, when we turned a sort of corner past a jagged rock and there, not twenty yards from us was a sleeping lion.

The big creature was on his feet almost instantly and facing us. He drew his ears back, switched his tail, and snarled—three signs I didn't at all like. My husband proceeded busily, however, to set up his camera.

"I don't like his looks, Martin," I said cautiously. At the same time I signaled for my gun.

"Oh, he's all right," my husband said. "A little cranky, maybe, but just bluffing." He started to crank the camera.

Then, with a low growl, the lion started slowly toward us, his tail lashing from side to side. How at such a moment I could notice, and sharply at that, the ripple of his hard shoulder muscles under his shining yellow coat, I don't know.

"He's going to charge, Martin—I tell you he is!"

"I don't think so," my husband said, biting hard on his cigar.

The lion, crouching tensely now, stared at us in what seemed to be an all-consuming hatred. Then he charged.

Martin's hand continued mechanically to crank the camera.

The animal looked as large as a bull as

he leaped toward us—his mane flying, fangs bared. I seemed to be watching in a prolonged, timeless sort of daze and then, without really being aware of what I was doing, I shot. Afterwards I couldn't even recall taking aim.

The lion seemed to hesitate in mid-air and then fell just thirteen feet from the camera's tripod.

To give an adequate picture of our almost innumerable encounters with lions of the Tanganyika region, would require many weeks to tell. There were triumphs and disappointments. We worked long hours under the most discouraging conditions. We saw the leonine prototypes [4] of the entire human race; the clown, the outcast, the misfit, the arrogant, the tragic, the noble, the dictator, yes, and even the flirt, and we made photographic records of all of these in their natural habitat.[5]

Sometimes our adventures were exciting; other times they were plain drudgery. Much of the time we were happy and comfortable; some of the time as on all our *safaris*,[6] we went through almost unbearable hardships. It was the sum total that mattered to us both, however, and there was an immense satisfaction in being able to present the true picture of this noble animal to the millions of people who had thought of him as a vicious, treacherous, blood-thirsty beast.

[4] PROTOTYYPES—Primitive forms; originals.
[5] HABITAT—Region where a species dwells.
[6] *Safaris*—Hunting expeditions.

◇◇◇◇◇◇◇◇◇◇◇◇◇◇◇◇◇◇◇◇◇◇◇◇◇◇◇◇◇◇◇◇

FOR DISCUSSION

1. Summarize briefly Mrs. Johnson's characterization of the lion.

2. When the lion started to bite the tires of the car, what device did the Johnsons use to scare him off? Picture to yourself the look on the animal's face. Describe the retreat.

3. Did you enjoy the night "hunt"? Do you think Martin Johnson did a brave or a foolhardy thing in going out to fix the wires? Would you have done it?

4. "A retreating object has an almost irresistible fascination for a lion." Can you verify this statement from your own knowledge of the cat family?

5. Did you stay with the Johnsons when that last lion charged? What do you suppose made Johnson set up his camera in so obviously dangerous a situation?

DETERMINING WORD MEANINGS

1. ". . . there is still considerable *wanton* killing." What is the difference between *wanton, gratuitous,* and *uncalled-for?*

2. As you know, many of our English words have been derived from the Latin. Consider these Latin words:

caro, carnis—meat　　*omnis*—all
herba—vegetable　　*vorare*—to eat

Now decide whether you are *carnivorous* like the lion, or *herbivorous,* or *omnivorous.*

LEARNING TO KNOW THE ADVENTURER

Find out more about Osa and Martin Johnson. Do you think *I Married Adventure* an appropriate title for Osa Johnson's book?

In imagination, accompany them on one of their hunts. Then write a letter home telling about one of your experiences.

RELATED READING

You may enjoy reading about some other unusual experiences of the Johnsons: *Congorilla, Lion,* and *Over African Jungles* by Martin Johnson; *Four Years in Paradise* by Osa Johnson.

Here is a ballad of love and romance—of a daring elopement on the Scottish border long ago. As you read this poem, try to catch the rhythm of the lines, which suggest the galloping of the young lover's horse.

Lochinvar

WALTER SCOTT

Oh, young Lochinvar is come out of the west;
Through all the wide Border his steed was the best;
And save his good broadsword he weapons had none;
He rode all unarmed, and he rode all alone.
So faithful in love, and so dauntless in war, 5
There never was knight like the young Lochinvar.

He stayed not for brake, and he stopped not for stone;
He swam the Eske River where ford there was none;
But, ere he alighted at Netherby gate,
The bride had consented, the gallant came late: 10
For a laggard in love, and a dastard in war,
Was to wed the fair Ellen of brave Lochinvar.

So boldly he entered the Netherby hall,
'Mong bridesmen and kinsmen, and brothers and all:
Then spoke the bride's father, his hand on his sword 15
(For the poor craven bridegroom said never a word),
"Oh, come ye in peace here, or come ye in war,
Or to dance at our bridal, young Lord Lochinvar?"

"I long wooed your daughter, my suit you denied—
Love swells like the Solway, but ebbs like its tide; 20
And now am I come, with this lost love of mine
To lead but one measure, drink one cup of wine,
There are maidens in Scotland more lovely by far
That would gladly be bride to the young Lochinvar."

7. BRAKE—Brushwood.
20. SOLWAY—Narrow bay of the Irish Sea.

The bride kissed the goblet; the knight took it up: 25
He quaffed off the wine, and he threw down the cup.
She looked down to blush, and she looked up to sigh,
With a smile on her lips and a tear in her eye.
He took her soft hand ere her mother could bar—
"Now tread we a measure!" said young Lochinvar. 30

So stately his form, and so lovely her face,
That never a hall such a galliard did grace;
While her mother did fret, and her father did fume,
And the bridegroom stood dangling his bonnet and plume;
And the bridemaidens whispered, " 'T were better by far 35
To have matched our fair cousin with young Lochinvar."

One touch to her hand, and one word in her ear,
When they reached the hall door and the charger stood near;
So light to the croupe the fair lady he swung,
So light to the saddle before her he sprung! 40
"She is won! we are gone, over bank, bush, and scaur!
They'll have fleet steeds that follow!" quoth young Lochinvar.

There was mounting 'mong Graemes of the Netherby clan;
Forsters, Fenwick, and Musgraves, they rode and they ran;
There was racing and chasing on Cannobie Lee; 45
But the lost bride of Netherby ne'er did they see.
So daring in love, and so dauntless in war,
Have ye e'er heard of gallant like young Lochinvar?

32. GALLIARD—Old-fashioned dance.
41. SCAUR—Cliff.

FOR DISCUSSION

1. If Lochinvar had used a more direct method in reclaiming his sweetheart, do you think he would have succeeded in winning her? Why did Lochinvar mention the "maidens in Scotland"?

2. Does this story strike you as realistic? Would it be possible today to "lift" the bride from a bridal party with the eyes of all the guests upon you? Was it unlikely at the time Scott writes about? Why is it still a good story?

3. Which of Lochinvar's outstanding virtues are illustrated in the poem? Do you think Ellen will be happy with him? Discuss. Which lines are the bases for your answer?

A DIFFERENT STORY

If the bride's father had not permitted Lochinvar either to speak to Ellen or dance with her, the elopement might not have taken place. There would have been another story entirely. Write that story now. The characters remain the same; the setting remains the same; the action alone changes because Ellen's father refuses to allow Lochinvar even to remain in the hall. Your ending to the story may be either more realistic than the one in the poem, or even more fanciful.

Action, danger, suspense are at hand in a midnight adventure involving mistaken identity. You will see this story unfold as though you were watching it on your own television screen.

THE SIRE DE MALETROIT'S DOOR

ROBERT LOUIS STEVENSON

Denis de Beaulieu [1] was not yet two-and-twenty, but he counted himself a grown man, and a very accomplished cavalier into the bargain. Lads were early formed in that rough, warfaring epoch; and when one has been in a pitched battle and a dozen raids, has killed one's man in an honorable fashion, and knows a thing or two of strategy and mankind, a certain swagger in the gait is surely to be pardoned. He had put up his horse with due care, and supped with due deliberation; and then, in a very agreeable frame of mind, went out to pay a visit in the gray of the evening. It was not a very wise proceeding on the young man's part. He would have done better to remain beside the fire or go decently to bed. For the town was full of troops of Burgundy and England under a mixed command; and though Denis was there on safe-conduct, his safe-conduct was like to serve him little on a chance encounter.

It was September, 1429; the weather had fallen sharp; a flighty piping wind, laden with shower, beat about the township; and the dead leaves ran riot along the streets. Here and there a window was already lighted up; and the noise of men-at-arms making merry over supper within, came forth in fits and was swallowed up and carried away by the wind. The night fell swiftly; the flag of England, fluttering on the spire top, grew ever fainter and fainter against the flying clouds—a black speck like a swallow in the tumultuous, laden chaos of the sky. As the night fell the wind rose, and began to hoot under archways and roar amid the tree-tops in the valley below the town.

Denis de Beaulieu walked fast and was soon knocking at his friend's door; but though he promised himself to stay only a little while and make an early return, his welcome was so pleasant, and he found so much to delay him, that it was already long past midnight before he said good-bye upon the threshold. The wind had fallen again in the meanwhile; the night was as black as the grave; not a star, nor a glimmer of moonshine, slipped through the canopy of cloud. Denis was

[1] DENIS DE BEAULIEU—Pronounced dē·nē′ dē bō·lū′.

ill-acquainted with the intricate lanes of Château[2] Landon; even by daylight he had found some trouble in picking his way; and in this absolute darkness he soon lost it altogether. He was certain of one thing only—to keep mounting the hill; for his friend's house lay at the lower end, or tail, of Château Landon while the inn was up at the head, under the great church spire. With this clew to go upon he stumbled and groped forward, now breathing more freely in the open places where there was a good slice of sky overhead, now feeling along the wall in stifling closes. It is an eerie and mysterious position to be thus submerged in opaque blackness in an almost unknown town. The silence is terrifying in its possibilities. The touch of cold window bars to the exploring hand startles the man like a touch of a toad; the inequalities of the pavement shake his heart into his mouth; a piece of denser darkness threatens an ambuscade or a chasm in the pathway; and where the air is brighter, the houses put on strange and bewildering appearances, as if to lead him further from his way. For Denis, who had to regain his inn without attracting notice, there was real danger as well as mere discomfort in the walk; and he went warily and boldly at once, and at every corner paused to make an observation.

He had been for some time threading a lane so narrow that he could touch a wall with either hand, when it began to open out and go sharply downward. Plainly this lay no longer in the direction of his inn; but the hope of a little more light tempted him forward to reconnoiter. The lane ended in a terrace with a bartizan[3] wall, which gave an outlook between high houses, as out of an embrasure, into the valley lying dark and formless several hundred feet below. Denis looked down, and could discern a few tree-tops waving and a single speck of brightness where the river ran across a weir. The weather was clearing up, and the sky had lightened, so as to show the outline of the heavier clouds and the dark margin of the hills. By the uncertain glimmer, the house on his left hand should be a place of some pretensions; it was surmounted by several pinnacles and turret-tops; the round stern of a chapel, with a fringe of flying buttresses,[4] projected boldly from the main block; and the door was sheltered under a deep porch carved with figures and overhung by two long gargoyles. The windows of the chapel gleamed through their intricate tracery with a light as of many tapers, and threw out the buttresses and the peaked roof in a more intense blackness against the sky. It was plainly the hotel[5] of some great family of the neighborhood; and as it reminded Denis of a town house of his own at Bourges, he stood for some time gazing up at it and mentally gauging the skill of the architects and the consideration of the two families.

There seemed to be no issue to the terrace but the lane by which he had reached it; he could only retrace his steps, but he had gained some notion of his whereabouts, and hoped by this means to hit the main thoroughfare and speedily regain the inn. He was reckoning without

[2] CHÂTEAU—Pronounced shä·tō′.

[3] BARTIZAN—A turret, with loopholes for defense, jutting from the wall.

[4] FLYING BUTTRESSES—Columns of masonry supporting walls and projecting above them.

[5] HOTEL—French home of considerable size.

that chapter of accidents which was to make this night memorable above all others in his career; for he had not gone back above a hundred yards before he saw a light coming to meet him, and heard loud voices speaking together in the echoing narrows of the lane. It was a party of men-at-arms going the night round with torches. Denis assured himself that they had all been making free with the wine bowl, and were in no mood to be particular about safe-conduct or the niceties of chivalrous war. It was as like as not that they would kill him like a dog and leave him where he fell. The situation was inspiriting but nervous. Their own torches would conceal him from sight, he reflected; and he hoped that they would drown the noise of his footsteps with their own empty voices. If he were but fleet and silent, he might evade their notice altogether.

Unfortunately, as he turned to beat a retreat, his foot rolled upon a pebble; he fell against the wall with an ejaculation, and his sword rung loudly on the stones. Two or three voices demanded who went there—some in French, some in English; but Denis made no reply, and ran the faster down the lane. Once upon the terrace, he paused to look back. They still kept calling after him, and just then began to double the pace in pursuit, with a considerable clank in armor, and great tossing of the torchlight to and fro in the narrow jaws of the passage.

Denis cast a look around and darted into the porch. There he might escape observation, or—if that were too much to expect—was in a capital posture whether for parley or defense. So thinking, he drew his sword and tried to set his back against the door. To his surprise it yielded behind his weight; and though he turned in a moment, continued to swing back on oiled and noiseless hinges until it stood wide open on a black interior. When things fall out opportunely for the person concerned, he is not apt to be critical about the how or why, his own immediate personal convenience seeming a sufficient reason for the strangest oddities and revolutions in our sublunary[6] things; and so Denis, without a moment's hesitation, stepped within, and partly closed the door behind him to conceal his place of refuge. Nothing was further from his thoughts than to close it altogether; but for some inexplicable reason—perhaps by a spring or a weight—the ponderous mass of oak whipped itself out of his fingers and clanked to, with a formidable rumble and a noise like the falling of an automatic bar.

The round,[7] at that very moment, debouched upon the terrace and proceeded to summon him with shouts and curses. He heard them ferreting in the dark corners; the stock of a lance even rattled along the outer surface of the door behind which he stood; but these gentlemen were in too high a humor to be long delayed, and soon made off down a corkscrew pathway which had escaped Denis' observation, and passed out of sight and hearing along the battlements of the town.

Denis breathed again. He gave them a few minutes' grace for fear of accidents, and then groped about for some means of opening the door and slipping forth again. The inner surface was quite

[6] SUBLUNARY—Belonging to this world.
[7] ROUND—The group pursuing.

smooth, not a handle, not a molding, not a projection of any sort. He got his finger-nails round the edges and pulled, but the mass was immovable. He shook it, it was as firm as a rock. Denis de Beaulieu frowned and gave vent to a little noiseless whistle. What ailed the door he wondered. Why was it open? How came it to shut so easily and so effectually after him? There was something obscure and underhand about all this, that was little to the young man's fancy. It looked like a snare, and yet who could suppose a snare in such a quiet bystreet and in a house of so prosperous and even noble an exterior? And yet—snare or no snare, intentionally or unintentionally—here he was, prettily trapped; and for the life of him he could see no way out of it again. The darkness began to weigh about him. He gave ear; all was silent without, but within and close by he seemed to catch a faint sighing, a faint sobbing rustle, a little stealthy creak—as though many persons were at his side, holding themselves quite still, and governing even their respiration with the extreme of slyness. The idea went to his vitals with a shock, and he faced about suddenly as if to defend his life. Then, for the first time, he became aware of a light about the level of his eyes and at some distance in the interior of the house—a vertical thread of light, widening toward the bottom, such as might escape between two wings of arras over a doorway.

To see anything was a relief to Denis; it was like a piece of solid ground to a man laboring in a morass; his mind seized upon it with avidity; and he stood staring at it and trying to piece together some logical conception of his surroundings. Plainly there was a flight of steps ascending from his own level to that of this illuminated doorway, and indeed he thought he could make out another thread of light, as fine as a needle and as faint as phosphorescence, which might very well be reflected along the polished wood of a handrail. Since he had begun to suspect that he was not alone, his heart had continued to beat with smothering violence, and an intolerable desire for action of any sort had possessed itself of his spirit. He was in deadly peril, he believed. What could be more natural than to mount the staircase, lift the curtain, and confront his difficulty at once? At least he would be dealing with something tangible; at least he would be no longer in the dark. He stepped slowly forward with outstretched hands, until his foot struck the bottom step; then he rapidly scaled the stairs, stood for a moment to compose his expression, lifted the arras and went in.

He found himself in a large apartment of polished stone. There were three doors; one on each of three sides; all similarly curtained with tapestry. The fourth side was occupied by two large windows and a great stone chimney-piece, carved with the arms of the Maletroits.[8] Denis recognized the bearings,[9] and was gratified to find himself in such good hands. The room was strongly illuminated; but it contained little furniture except a heavy table and a chair or two; the hearth was innocent of fire, and the pavement was but sparsely strewn with rushes [10] clearly many days old.

On a high chair beside the chimney,

[8] MALETROITS—Pronounced măl·ĕ·twä′.
[9] BEARINGS—Heraldic devices.
[10] RUSHES—Soft grass used for floor-covering.

and directly facing Denis as he entered, sat a little old gentleman in a fur tippet.[11] He sat with his legs crossed and his hands folded, and a cup of spiced wine stood by his elbow on a bracket on the wall. His countenance had a strong masculine cast; not properly human, but such as we see in the bull, the goat, or the domestic boar; something equivocal and wheedling, something greedy, brutal, and dangerous. The upper lip was inordinately full, as though swollen by a blow or a toothache; and the smile, the peaked eyebrows, and the small, strong eyes were quaintly and almost comically evil in expression. Beautiful white hair hung straight all round his head, like a saint's, and fell in a single curl upon the tippet. His beard and mustache were the pink [12] of venerable sweetness. Age, probably in consequence of inordinate precautions, had left no mark upon his hands; and the Maletroit hand was famous. It would be difficult to imagine anything at once so fleshy and so delicate in design; the taper, sensual fingers were like those of one of Leonardo's [13] women; the fork of the thumb made a dimpled protuberance when closed; the nails were perfectly shaped, and of a dead, surprising whiteness. It rendered his aspect tenfold more redoubtable, that a man with hands like these should keep them devoutly folded like a virgin martyr—that a man with so intent and startling an expression of face would sit patiently on his seat and contemplate people with an unwinking stare, like a god, or a god's statue. His quiescence seemed ironical and treacherous, it fitted so poorly with his looks.

Such was Alain, Sire de Maletroit.

Denis and he looked silently at each other for a second or two.

"Pray step in," said the Sire de Male-

[11] TIPPET—A short fur cape.
[12] PINK—Here, it means perfection.
[13] LEONARDO—Leonardo da Vinci, an Italian painter and sculptor.

troit. "I have been expecting you all the evening."

He had not risen but he accompanied his words with a smile and a slight but courteous inclination of the head. Partly from the smile, partly from the strange musical murmur with which the sire prefaced his observation, Denis felt a strong shudder of disgust go through his marrow. And what with disgust and honest confusion of mind, he could scarcely get words together in reply.

"I fear," he said, "that this is a double accident. I am not the person you suppose me. It seems you were looking for a visit; but for my part, nothing was further from my thoughts—nothing could be more contrary to my wishes—than this intrusion."

"Well, well," replied the old gentleman indulgently, "here you are, which is the main point. Seat yourself, my friend, and put yourself entirely at your ease. We shall arrange our little affairs presently."

Denis perceived that the matter was still complicated with some misconception, and he hastened to continue his explanations.

"Your door," he began.

"About my door?" asked the other, raising his peaked eyebrows. "A little piece of ingenuity." And he shrugged his shoulders. "A hospitable fancy! By your own account, you were not desirous of making my acquaintance. We old people look for such reluctance now and then; when it touches our honor, we cast about until we find some way of overcoming it. You arrive uninvited, but believe me, very welcome."

"You persist in error, sir," said Denis. "There can be no question between you and me. I am a stranger in this countryside. My name is Denis, damoiseau [14] de Beaulieu. If you see me in your house it is only—"

"My young friend," interrupted the other, "you will permit me to have my own ideas on that subject. They probably differ from yours at the present moment," he added with a leer, "but time will show which of us is in the right."

Denis was convinced he had to do with a lunatic. He seated himself with a shrug, content to wait the upshot; and a pause ensued, during which he thought he could distinguish a hurried gabbling as of a prayer from behind the arras immediately opposite him. Sometimes there seemed to be but one person engaged, sometimes two; and the vehemence of the voice, low as it was, seemed to indicate either great haste or an agony of spirit. It occurred to him that this piece of tapestry covered the entrance to the chapel he had noticed from without.

The old gentleman fell into a fit of silent laughter, so prolonged and violent that he became quite red in the face. Denis got upon his feet at once, and put on his hat with a flourish.

"Sir," he said, "if you are in your wits, you have affronted me grossly. If you are out of them, I flatter myself I can find better employment for my brains than to talk with lunatics. My conscience is clear; you have made a fool of me from the first moment; you have refused to hear my explanations; and now there is no power under God will make me stay here any longer; and if I cannot make my way out in a more decent fashion, I will

[14] DAMOISEAU (dȧ·mwȧ·zō′)—A young man of the Beaulieu family; of noble rank.

hack your door to pieces with my sword."

The Sire de Maletroit raised his right hand and wagged it at Denis with the fore and little fingers extended.

"My dear nephew," he said, "sit down."

"Nephew!" retorted Denis, "you lie in your throat"; and he snapped his fingers in his face.

"Sit down, you rogue!" cried the old gentleman, in a sudden, harsh voice, like the barking of a dog. "Do you fancy," he went on, "that when I had made my little contrivance for the door I had stopped short with that? If you choose to remain a free young buck, agreeably conversing with an old gentleman—why, sit where you are in peace, and God be with you."

"Do you mean I am a prisoner?" demanded Denis.

"I state the facts," replied the other. "I would rather leave the conclusion to yourself."

Denis sat down again. Externally he managed to keep pretty calm, but within, he was now boiling with anger, now chilled with apprehension. He no longer felt convinced that he was dealing with a madman. And if the old gentleman was sane, what, in God's name, had he to look for? What absurd or tragical adventure had befallen him? What countenance was he to assume?

While he was thus unpleasantly reflecting, the arras that overhung the chapel door was raised, and a tall priest in his robes came forth, and, giving a long, keen stare at Denis, said something in an undertone to Sire de Maletroit.

"She is in a better frame of spirit?" asked the latter.

"She is more resigned, messire," replied the priest.

"Now, the Lord help her, she is hard to please!" sneered the old gentleman. "A likely stripling—not ill-born—and of her own choosing, too! Why, what more would the jade have?"

"The situation is not usual for a young damsel," said the other, "and somewhat trying to her blushes."

"She should have thought of that before she began the dance! It was none of my choosing, God knows that; but since she is in it, by our Lady, she shall carry it to the end." And then addressing Denis, "Monsieur de Beaulieu," he asked, "may I present you to my niece? She has been waiting your arrival, I may say, with even greater impatience than myself."

Denis had resigned himself with a good grace—all he desired was to know the worst of it as speedily as possible; so he rose at once, and bowed in acquiescence. The Sire de Maletroit followed his example and limped, with the assistance of the chaplain's arm, toward the chapel door. The priest pulled aside the arras, and all three entered. The building had considerable architectural pretensions. A light groining [15] sprang from six stout columns, and hung down in two rich pendants from the center of the vault. The place terminated behind the altar in a round end, embossed and honeycombed with a superfluity of ornament in relief, and pierced by many little windows shaped like stars, trefoils, or wheels. These windows were imperfectly glazed, so that the night air circulated freely in the chapel. The tapers, of which there must have been half a hundred burning on the altar, were unmercifully blown about; and the light

[15] GROINING—The line of intersection between overhead arches.

went through many different phases of brilliancy and semi-eclipse. On the steps in front of the altar knelt a young girl richly attired as a bride. A chill settled over Denis as he observed her costume; he fought with desperate energy against the conclusion that was being thrust upon his mind; it could not—it should not—be as he feared.

"Blanche," said the sire, in his most flute-like tones, "I have brought a friend to see you, my little girl; turn round and give him your pretty hand. It is good to be devout; but it is necessary to be polite, my niece."

The girl rose to her feet and turned toward the newcomers. She moved all of a piece; and shame and exhaustion were expressed in every line of her fresh young body; and she held her head down and kept her eyes upon the pavement, as she came slowly forward. In the course of her advance her eyes fell upon Denis de Beaulieu's feet—feet of which he was justly vain, be it remarked, and wore in the most elegant accouterment even while traveling. She paused—started, as if his yellow boots had conveyed some shocking meaning—and glanced suddenly up into the wearer's countenance. Their eyes met; shame gave place to horror and terror to her looks; the blood left her lips, with a piercing scream she covered her face with her hands and sank upon the chapel floor.

"That is not the man!" she cried. "My uncle, that is not the man!"

The Sire de Maletroit chirped agreeably. "Of course not," he said; "I expected as much. It was so unfortunate you could not remember his name."

"Indeed," she cried, "indeed, I have never seen this person till this moment—I have never so much as set eyes upon him—I never wish to see him again. Sir," she said, turning to Denis, "if you are a gentleman, you will bear me out. Have I ever seen you—have you ever seen me—before this accursed hour?"

"To speak for myself, I have never had that pleasure," answered the young man. "This is the first time, messire, that I have met with your engaging niece."

The old gentleman shrugged his shoulders.

"I am distressed to hear it," he said. "But it is never too late to begin. I had little more acquaintance with my own late lady ere I married her; which proves," he added, with a grimace, "that these impromptu marriages may often produce an excellent understanding in the long run. As the bridegroom is to have a voice in the matter, I will give him two hours to make up for lost time before we proceed with the ceremony." And he turned toward the door, followed by the clergyman.

The girl was on her feet in a moment. "My uncle, you cannot be in earnest," she said. "I declare before God I will stab myself rather than be forced on that young man. The heart rises at it; God forbids such marriages; you dishonor your white hair. Oh, my uncle, pity me! There is not a woman in all the world, but would prefer death to such a nuptial. Is it possible," she added, faltering—"is it possible that you do not believe me—that you still think this"—and she pointed at Denis with a tremor of anger and contempt—"that you think *this* to be the man?"

"Frankly," said the old gentleman, pausing on the threshold, "I do. But let me explain to you once for all, Blanche de Maletroit, my way of thinking about this affair. When you took it into your head to dishonor my family and the name that I have borne, in peace and war, for more than threescore years, you forfeited, not only the right to question my designs, but that of looking me in the face. If your father had been alive, he would have spat on you and turned you out of doors. His was the hand of iron. You may bless your God you have only to deal with the hand of velvet, mademoiselle. It was my duty to get you married without delay. Out of pure good will, I have tried to find your own gallant for you. And I believe I have succeeded. But before God and all the holy angels, Blanche de Maletroit, if I have not, I care not one jackstraw. So let me recommend you to be polite to our young friend; for, upon my word, your next groom may be less appetizing."

And with that he went out, with the chaplain at his heels; and the arras fell behind the pair.

The girl turned upon Denis with flashing eyes.

"And what, sir," she demanded, "may be the meaning of all this?"

"God knows," returned Denis, gloomily. "I am a prisoner in this house, which seems full of mad people. More I know not; and nothing do I understand."

"And pray how came you here?" she asked.

He told her as briefly as he could. "For the rest," he added, "perhaps you will follow my example, and tell me the answer to all these riddles, and what is like to be the end of it."

She stood silent for a little, and he could see her lips tremble and her tearless eyes burn with a feverish luster. Then she pressed her forehead in both hands.

"Alas, how my head aches!" she said, wearily—"to say nothing of my poor heart! But it is due to you to know my story, unmaidenly as it must seem. I am called Blanche de Maletroit; I have been without father or mother for—oh! for as long as I can recollect, and indeed I have been most unhappy all my life. Three months ago a young captain began to stand near me every day in church. I could see that I pleased him; I am much to blame, but I was so glad that anyone should love me; and when he passed me a letter, I took it home with me and read it with great pleasure. Since that time he has written many. He was so anxious to speak with me, poor fellow! and kept asking me to leave the door open some evening that we might have two words upon the stair. For he knew how much my uncle trusted me." She gave something like a sob at that, and it was a moment before she could go on. "My uncle is a hard man, but he is very shrewd," she said at last. "He has performed many feats in war, and was a great person at court, and much trusted by Queen Isabeau [16] in old days. How he came to suspect me I cannot tell; but it is hard to keep anything from his knowledge; and this morning, as we came from mass, he took my hand in his, forced it open, and read my little billet, walking by my side all the while.

"When he finished, he gave it back to me with great politeness. It contained another request to have the door left open; and this has been the ruin of us all. My uncle kept me strictly in my room

[16] ISABEAU—Pronounced ē·zȧ·bō′.

until evening, and then ordered me to dress myself as you see me—a hard mockery for a young girl, do you not think so? I suppose, when he could not prevail with me to tell him the young captain's name, he must have laid a trap for him; into which, alas! you have fallen in the anger of God. I looked for much confusion; for how could I tell whether he was willing to take me for his wife on these sharp terms? He might have been trifling with me from the first; or I might have made myself too cheap in his eyes. But truly I had not looked for such a shameful punishment as this! I could not think that God would let a girl be so disgraced before a young man. And now I tell you all; and I can scarcely hope that you will not despise me."

Denis made her a respectful inclination.

"Madam," he said, "you have honored me by your confidence. It remains for me to prove that I am not unworthy of the honor. Is Messire de Maletroit at hand?"

"I believe he is writing in the salle[17] without," she answered.

"May I lead you thither, madam?" asked Denis, offering his hand with his most courtly bearing.

She accepted; and the pair passed out of the chapel, Blanche in a very drooping and shamefast condition, but Denis strutting and ruffling in the consciousness of a mission, and the boyish certainty of accomplishing it with honor.

The Sire de Maletroit rose to meet them with an ironical obeisance.

"Sir," said Denis, with the grandest possible air, "I believe I am to have some say in the matter of this marriage; and let me tell you at once, I will be no party to forcing the inclination of this young lady. Had it been freely offered to me, I should have been proud to accept her hand, for I perceive she is as good as she is beautiful; but as things are, I have now the honor, messire, of refusing."

Blanche looked at him with gratitude in her eyes; but the old gentleman only smiled and smiled, until his smile grew positively sickening to Denis.

"I am afraid," he said, "Monsieur de Beaulieu, that you do not perfectly understand the choice I have offered you. Follow me, I beseech you, to this window." And he led the way to one of the large windows which stood open on the night. "You observe," he went on, "there is an iron ring in the upper masonry, and reeved through that, a very efficacious rope. Now, mark my words: if you should find your disinclination to my niece's person insurmountable, I shall have you hanged out of this window before sunrise. I shall only proceed to such an extremity with the greatest regret, you may believe me. For it is not at all your death that I desire, but my niece's establishment in life. At the same time, it must come to that if you prove obstinate. Your family, Monsieur de Beaulieu, is very well in its way, but if you sprung from Charlemagne, you should not refuse the hand of a Maletroit with impunity—not if she had been as common as the Paris road—not if she was as hideous as the gargoyle over my door. Neither my niece nor you, nor my own private feelings, move me at all in this matter. The honor of my house has been compromised; I believe you to be the guilty per-

[17] SALLE—Room, or hall.

son, at least you are now in the secret; and you can hardly wonder if I request you to wipe out the stain. If you will not, your blood be on your own head! It will be no great satisfaction to me to have your interesting relics kicking their heels in the breeze below my windows, but half a loaf is better than no bread and if I cannot cure the dishonor, I shall at least stop the scandal."

There was a pause.

"I believe there are other ways of settling such imbroglios [18] among gentlemen," said Denis. "You wear a sword, and I hear you have used it with distinction."

The Sire de Maletroit made a signal to the chaplain, who crossed the room with long silent strides and raised the arras over the third of the three doors. It was only a moment before he let it fall again; but Denis had time to see a dusky passage full of armed men.

"When I was a little younger, I should have been delighted to honor you, Monsieur de Beaulieu," said Sire Alain; "but I am now too old. Faithful retainers are the sinews of age, and I must employ the strength I have. This is one of the hardest things to swallow as a man grows up in years; but with a little patience, even this becomes habitual. You and the lady seem to prefer the salle for what remains of your two hours; and as I have no desire to cross your preference, I shall resign it to your use with all the pleasure in the world. No haste!" he added, holding up his hand, as he saw a dangerous look come into Denis de Beaulieu's face. "If your mind revolt against hanging, it will be time enough two hours hence to throw yourself out of the window or upon the pikes of my retainers. Two hours of life are always two hours. A great many things may turn up in even as little a while as that. And, besides, if I understand her appearance, my niece has something to say to you. You will not disfigure your last hours by a want of politeness to a lady?"

Denis looked at Blanche, and she made him an imploring gesture.

It is likely that the old gentleman was hugely pleased at this symptom of an understanding; for he smiled on both, and added sweetly: "If you will give me your word of honor, Monsieur de Beaulieu, to await my return at the end of the two hours before attempting anything desperate, I shall withdraw my retainers and let you speak in greater privacy with mademoiselle."

Denis again glanced at the girl, who seemed to beseech him to agree.

"I give you my word of honor," he said.

Messire de Maletroit bowed, and proceeded to limp about the apartment, clearing his throat the while with that odd musical chirp which had already grown so irritating in the ears of Denis de Beaulieu. He first possessed himself of some papers which lay upon the table; then he went to the mouth of the passage and appeared to give an order to the men behind the arras; and lastly he hobbled out through the door by which Denis had come in, turning upon the threshold to address a last smiling bow to the young couple, and followed by the chaplain with a hand-lamp.

No sooner were they alone than Blanche advanced toward Denis with her

[18] IMBROGLIO (ĭm·brōl′yō)—A misunderstanding attended by quarrels.

hands extended. Her face was flushed and excited, and her eyes shone with tears.

"You shall not die!" she cried, "You shall marry me after all."

"You seem to think, madam," replied Denis, "that I stand much in fear of death."

"Oh, no, no," she said, "I see you are no poltroon. It is for my own sake—I could not bear to have you slain for such a scruple."

"I am afraid," returned Denis, "that you underrate the difficulty, madam. What you may be too generous to refuse, I may be too proud to accept. In a moment of noble feeling toward me, you forget what you perhaps owe to others."

He had the decency to keep his eyes on the floor as he said this, and after he had finished, so as not to spy upon her confusion. She stood silent for a moment, then walked suddenly away, and falling on her uncle's chair, fairly burst out sobbing. Denis was in the acme of embarrassment. He looked round, as if to seek for inspiration, and, seeing a stool, plumped down upon it for something to do. There he sat, playing with the guard of his rapier, and wishing himself dead a thousand times over, and buried in the nastiest kitchen-heap in France. His eyes wandered round the apartment, but found nothing to arrest them. There were such wide spaces between the furniture, the light fell so badly and cheerlessly over all, the dark outside air looked in so coldly through the windows, that he thought he had never seen a church so vast, nor a tomb so melancholy. The regular sobs of Blanche de Maletroit measured out the time like the ticking of a clock. He read the device upon the shield over and over again, until his eyes became obscured; he stared into shadowy corners until he imagined they were swarming with horrible animals; and every now and again he awoke with a start, to remember that his last two hours were running, and death was on the march.

Oftener and oftener, as the time went on, did his glance settle on the girl herself. Her face was bowed forward and covered with her hands, and she was shaken at intervals by the convulsive hiccough of grief. Even thus she was not an unpleasant object to dwell upon, so plump and yet so fine, with a warm brown skin, and the most beautiful hair, Denis thought, in the whole world of womankind. Her hands were like her uncle's; but they were more in place at the end of her young arms, and looked infinitely soft and caressing. He remembered how her blue eyes had shone upon him, full of anger, pity, and innocence. And the more he dwelt on her perfections, the uglier death looked, and the more deeply was he smitten with penitence at her continued tears. Now he felt that no man could have the courage to leave a world which contained so beautiful a creature; and now he would have given forty minutes of his last hour to have unsaid his cruel speech.

Suddenly a hoarse and ragged peal of cockcrow rose to their ears from the dark valley below the windows. And this shattering noise in the silence of all around was like a light in a dark place, and shook them both out of their reflections.

"Alas, can I do nothing to help you?" she said, looking up.

"Madam," replied Denis, with a fine irrelevancy, "if I have said anything to wound you, believe me, it was for your own sake and not for mine."

She thanked him with a tearful look.

"I feel your position cruelly," he went on. "The world has been bitter hard on you. Your uncle is a disgrace to mankind. Believe me, madam, there is no young gentleman in all France but would be glad of my opportunity, to die in doing you a momentary service."

"I know already that you can be very brave and generous," she answered. "What I *want* to know is whether I can serve you—now or afterward," she added, with a quaver.

"Most certainly," he answered, with a smile. "Let me sit beside you as if I were a friend, instead of a foolish intruder; try to forget how awkwardly we are placed to one another; make my last moments go pleasantly; and you will do me the chief service possible."

"You are very gallant," she added, with a yet deeper sadness—"very gallant—and it somehow pains me. But draw nearer, if you please; and if you find anything to say to me, you will at least make certain of a very friendly listener. Ah! Monsieur de Beaulieu," she broke forth—"ah! Monsieur de Beaulieu, how can I look you in the face?" And she fell to weeping again with a renewed effusion.

"Madam," said Denis, taking her hand in both of his, "reflect on the little time I have before me, and the great bitterness into which I am cast by the sight of your distress. Spare me, in my last moments, the spectacle of what I cannot cure even with the sacrifice of my life."

"I am very selfish," answered Blanche. "I will be braver, Monsieur de Beaulieu, for your sake. But think if I can do you no kindness in the future—if you have no friends to whom I could carry your adieus. Charge me as heavily as you can; every burden will lighten, by so little, the invaluable gratitude I owe you. Put it in my power to do something more for you than weep."

"My mother is married again, and has a young family to care for. My brother Guichard will inherit my fiefs; [19] and if I am not in error, that will content him amply for my death. Life is a little vapor that passeth away, as we are told by those in holy orders. When a man is in a fair way and sees all his life open in front of him, he seems to himself to make a very important figure in the world. His horse whinnies to him; the trumpets blow and the girls look out of windows as he rides into town before his company; he receives many assurances of trust and regard—sometimes by express in a letter—sometimes face to face, with persons of great consequence falling on his neck. It is not wonderful if his head is turned for a time. But once he is dead, were he as brave as Hercules or as wise as Solomon, he is soon forgotten. It is not ten years since my father fell, with many other knights around him, in a very fierce encounter, and I do not think that any one of them, nor as much as the name of the fight, is now remembered. No, no, madam, the nearer you come to it, you see that death is a dark and dusty corner, where a man gets into his tomb and has the door shut after him till the judgment day. I have few friends just now, and once I am dead I shall have none."

[19] FIEFS—Feudal estates.

"Ah, Monsieur de Beaulieu!" she exclaimed, "you forget Blanche de Maletroit."

"You have a sweet nature, madam, and you are pleased to estimate a little service far beyond its worth."

"It is not that," she answered. "You mistake me if you think I am easily touched by my own concerns. I say so because you are the noblest man I have ever met; because I recognize in you a spirit that would have made even a common person famous in the land."

"And yet here I die in a mousetrap—with no more noise about it than my own squeaking," answered he.

A look of pain crossed her face and she was silent for a little while. Then a light came into her eyes, and with a smile she spoke again.

"I cannot have my champion think meanly of himself. Anyone who gives his life for another will be met in paradise by all the heralds and angels of the Lord God. And you have no such cause to hang your head. For— Pray, do you think me beautiful?" she asked, with a deep flush.

"Indeed, madam, I do," he said.

"I am glad of that," she answered heartily. "Do you think there are many men in France who have been asked in marriage by a beautiful maiden—with her own lips—and who have refused her to her face? I know you men would half despise such a triumph; but believe me, we women know more of what is precious in love. There is nothing that should set a person higher in his own esteem; and we women would prize nothing more dearly."

"You are very good," he said; "but you cannot make me forget that I was asked in pity and not for love."

"I am not so sure of that," she replied, holding down her head. "Hear me to an end, Monsieur de Beaulieu. I know how you must despise me; I feel you are right to do so; I am too poor a creature to occupy one thought of your mind, although, alas! you must die for me this morning. But when I asked you to marry me, indeed, and indeed, it was because I respected and admired you, and loved you with my whole soul, from the very moment that you took my part against my uncle. If you had seen yourself, and how noble you looked, you would pity rather than despise me. And now," she went on, hurriedly checking him with her hand, "although I have laid aside all reserve and told you so much, remember that I know your sentiments toward me already. I would not, believe me, being nobly born, weary you with importunities into consent. I too have a pride of my own; and I declare before the holy mother of God, if you should now go back from your word already given, I would no more marry you than I would marry my uncle's groom."

Denis smiled a little bitterly.

"It is a small love," he said, "that shies at a little pride."

She made no answer, although she probably had her own thoughts.

"Come hither to the window," he said with a sigh. "Here is the dawn."

And indeed the dawn was already beginning. The hollow of the sky was full of essential daylight, colorless and clean; and the valley underneath was flooded with a gray reflection. A few thin vapors clung in the coves of the forest or lay along the winding course of the river. The scene disengaged a surprising effect of stillness, which was hardly interrupted when the cocks began once more to crow among the steadings. Perhaps the same fellow who had made so horrid a clangor in the darkness not half an hour before, now sent up the merriest cheer to greet the coming day. A little wind went bustling and eddying among the tree-tops underneath the windows. And still the daylight kept flooding insensibly out of the east, which was soon to grow incandescent and cast up that red-hot cannonball, the rising sun.

Denis looked out over all this with a bit of a shiver. He had taken her hand, and retained it in his almost unconsciously.

"Has the day begun already?" she said; and then illogically enough: "The night has been so long! Alas! what shall we say to my uncle when he returns?"

"What you will," said Denis, and he pressed her fingers in his.

She was silent.

"Blanche," he said, with a swift, uncertain, passionate utterance, "you have seen whether I fear death. You must know well enough that I would as gladly leap out of that window into the empty air as to lay a finger on you without your free and full consent. But if you care for me at all do not let me lose my life in a misapprehension, for I love you better than the whole world; and though I will die for you blithely, it would be like all the joys of Paradise to live on and spend my life in your service."

As he stopped speaking, a bell began to ring loudly in the interior of the house; and a clatter of armor in the corridor showed that the retainers were returning to their post, and the two hours were at an end.

"After all that you have heard?" she

whispered, leaning toward him with her lips and eyes.

"I have heard nothing," he replied.

"The captain's name was Florimond de Champdivers," [20] she said in his ear.

"I did not hear it," he answered, taking her supple body in his arms, and covering her wet face with kisses.

A melodious chirping was audible behind, followed by a beautiful chuckle, and the voice of Messire de Maletroit wished his new nephew a good morning.

[20] FLORIMOND DE CHAMPDIVERS—Pronounced (flōr·ē-mōNd′ dē shäN·dē·vĕr′)—("N" indicates the peculiar French nasal sound.)

◇◇◇◇◇◇◇◇◇◇◇◇◇◇◇◇◇◇◇◇◇◇◇◇◇◇◇◇◇◇◇◇

FOR DISCUSSION

1. Stevenson projects an atmosphere of danger and foreboding into the story at its outset. Can you find in the first paragraphs descriptive details which further his purpose? What pictures did you see of the ill-lighted medieval town as night and the rain swept down? Out of what phrases did you paint the pictures?

2. Why was it unwise for Denis de Beaulieu to be abroad in town that night?

3. Describe the incident which led Denis to the house of the Sire de Maletroit. What one event enmeshed him in the plot of the Sire de Maletroit and in the fate of Blanche?

4. Denis' reaction to the demand of the Sire de Maletroit is natural enough in view of the threat of forced marriage with the unknown Blanche. What details reveal his youth and chivalric ideals of conduct?

5. Why did the coming of dawn provoke a shiver from Denis? Do you think the Sire de Maletroit was justified in taking the law into his own hands?

6. Stevenson described the Sire de Maletroit at length because his character explains the strange treatment of his niece. List ten words and phrases hinting at his cunning, dangerous nature.

FOR UNDERSTANDING

Your complete understanding of the following sentences depends on whether you know the meanings of the italicized words in each. Look up these words in a dictionary, if necessary, and then explain the sentences in your own way. You may substitute a synonym for each word if you wish.

a. "The night fell swiftly; the flag of England, fluttering on the spire top, grew ever fainter and fainter against the flying clouds—a black speck like a swallow in the *tumultuous,* laden *chaos* of the sky."

b. "It is an *eerie* and mysterious position to be thus *submerged* in *opaque* blackness in an almost unknown town."

c. ". . . he was boiling with anger, now chilled with *apprehension.*"

d. "What *countenance* was he to assume?"

e. ". . . so he rose at once, and bowed in *acquiescence.*"

RECALLING AN EXPERIENCE

Have you ever been in a disturbing situation paralleling the experience of Denis de Beaulieu in the first paragraphs of the story? It may have been when you were alone, with a storm coming up. Have you been afraid at night? Did you ever speak too hastily? From what embarrassing situation have you tried to escape? Think over the experience, focusing on your fears and recalling clear, sharp details of time and place. Put down the experience in a carefully written paragraph. Use vivid sense words of sight, feeling, and sound.

RELATED READING

A rather sinister story is Stevenson's *The Strange Case of Dr. Jekyll and Mr. Hyde.*

Captain Blood by Rafael Sabatini is set in seventeenth-century England.

Sir Walter Scott's *Quentin Durward* is a swift-moving novel of medieval adventure.

A native Texan shares with you his love of adventure in the old Southwest. For full enjoyment read this poem aloud. Start it off with a swashbuckling air! Then as the mood of the poem changes, read the lines more slowly and deliberately. Catch the change in the character of Jean Lafitte as he realizes there are things in life far more valuable than riches.

The Ballad of Jean Lafitte

LOIA C. CHEANEY

I'll sing the ballad of Jean Lafitte,
A right good man was he
For he was tall and brave and strong
And learned in gallantry.

In Louis' town in early days 5
He felt the wanderlust;
With his stern bright eyes as cold as steel
He picked his men of trust.

A hundred and twenty who sought romance
And craved life daring and free 10
Called Jean Lafitte their captain brave
And they lived right merrily.

He sailed the gulf and captured the ships
Of Mexico, England, and Spain,
And with the treasure, he as king 15
On Galveston island did reign.

Now on this island there were three trees,
Three trees alone were there,
He took the island from Indian braves
But he treated them good and square. 20

5. LOUIS' TOWN—New Orleans, early nineteenth century.

In a large Red House this pirate prince
Held court right royally
With all his men dressed up in gold—
They served him loyally.

Old Louis' regent sent a notice wide 25
That for Jean's own handsome head
He'd give a bounty of good red gold
To the one who would bring him dead.

But Jean, the daring and jovial knave,
Laughed at this with glee, 30
And he offered back the same reward
To the one who would make so free.

And many's the time he would lay his head
Against this self-same card
While he laughed and joked with the chief gendarme 35
And called the man his pard.

25. LOUIS' REGENT—French King Louis' deputy who governed the territory of Louisiana.
35. CHIEF GENDARME—Chief of police.
36. PARD—Partner. During the War of 1812 the British tried to enlist Lafitte's service in a raid on New Orleans, but they were refused. Later, however, after having fought admirably in the battle of New Orleans, Jean and his men were forgiven their outlawry.

But as time went on adventures palled,
He ordered his tribe to disband,
And with gloomy step and broken heart
He paced the glistening sand. 40

And three of his men from a sheltered nook
Heard as he paced, a groan,
"Under the trees, the three lone trees
Lies all my treasure alone."

With gluttonous greed they chose their tools 45
And quickly sped them there;
They dug the earth and found in the soil
The corpse of a maiden fair.

It was his wife—his fair young wife
And 'twas not Spanish gold, 50
They tremblingly cursed as they crossed themselves
In the damp night air and cold.

Then Jean Lafitte in a scarlet suit
Went sailing out in the bay,
His good ship *Pride* from Texas shore
Carried him far away. 56

But oft in the night of Galveston
His spirit is heard to moan,
"Under the trees—the three lone trees
Lies all my treasure alone." 60

51. CROSSED THEMSELVES—Made the sign of the cross in fear of punishment.

FOR DISCUSSION

1. One hundred and twenty men is no small crowd for a man to gather about him. What motive prompted the men to cast their lot with Jean? Notice the feeling of daring and camaraderie which characterizes the opening lines.

2. Briefly describe Galveston Island and Jean's life there.

3. How did Jean react when a price was placed on his head? Would you expect him to act this way? Why?

4. What loss destroyed Jean's love of money?

MEASURING VALUES

This ballad has a serious lesson you cannot afford to miss. Do you know what this lesson is? Does it have any significance today? Can you cite an experience of your own or that of a friend in which you have seen this truth revealed? Explain your conclusions to the class.

For Further Reading

The Story of Marco Polo by Noah Brooks is a fascinating account of the thirteenth century travels of Marco Polo in Asia.

Father Brown Omnibus by G. K. Chesterton contains short detective stories centering around Father Brown, England's most astute detective.

Black Ivory by Norman Collins is a sea story of the last days of the slave trade. The hero is a young farm lad, pressed into service on board the "Nero." When he discovers the evil deeds being done, he helps bring the criminals to final judgment.

Out of Gloucester by James B. Connolly. This book will appeal to anyone with a love of the sea. It is a collection of adventures of fishermen in the Atlantic Ocean.

Unlocking Adventure by Charles Courtney. The sensitivity of his fingers and his wide knowledge of locks led Mr. Courtney all over the world to open safes, strong boxes, and vaults.

Moonfleet by John Meade Falkner is an adventure tale of eighteenth century England, dealing with hidden treasure, smugglers' caves, and dangers at sea. Those who enjoyed *Treasure Island* will find this book an excellent second to Stevenson's adventure tales.

Backfield Comet by William Heyliger is an exciting football story for boys.

Prisoner of Zenda by Anthony Hope is a romantic adventure of the last century in Old World Ruritania. It is fast-moving, with much suspense and sword play.

Smoky, the Cowhorse by Will James features the range, the rodeo, and the round-up of the real West.

I Married Adventure by Osa Johnson is a true story. Mrs. Johnson writes of the adventures she experienced in Africa with her husband, a big game hunter.

The Trumpeter of Krakow by Eric Kelly is an historically accurate story of adventure and mystery in Poland.

Assignment in Brittany by Helen MacInnes is the gripping story of a British secret service agent who poses as a Frenchman; his troubles are made worse by the discovery that the Frenchman was a Nazi collaborator. This exciting tale of war intrigue in Nazi-occupied Brittany also contains a delightful love story.

Jim Davis by John Masefield. Jim tells about spying on a band of smugglers along the Gloucester coast.

Mutiny on the Bounty by Charles Nordhoff and James Hall. In this exciting adventure story Captain Bligh's harshness provokes a mutiny; his sailors take over the "Bounty" and set him adrift.

Secret Cargo by Howard Pease. A sea story, *Secret Cargo* has action, mystery, and good characterization.

Whispering Smith by Frank Spearman. Trouble-shooter Smith is pitted against vengeful Sinclair and his hard-riding, fast-shooting mountain outlaws. Railroading and range life in the West offer a lively background.

Storm Canvas by Armstrong Sperry. The author's knowledge of the sea, and his pictures, add a salty tang to this vigorous story of a fifteen-year-old boy aboard an American frigate during the War of 1812.

20,000 Leagues Under the Sea by Jules Verne. Written when undersea craft were yet unknown, this book still ranks first among the submarine stories.

Tales of Xavier by James H. Walsh, M.M., tells in fictional style of the incredible missionary feats of St. Francis Xavier.

Short Stories As You Like Them by William Wood and John Husband. These absorbing short stories are selected for their high interest content.

WITH A MERRY HEART

A merry heart is quick to banish gloom, the enemy of human nature in general, and of Christian men and women in particular. Through the centuries, the true Christian has habitually rated life in terms of joy; even his grief has been no more than superficial, like a bandage. Why is this so? Because ever since an angel told the Bethlehem shepherds, "I bring you tidings of great joy . . . for this day is born to you a Saviour," joy has been the Christian's tremendous secret. To be happy, in fact, is his *duty*, since our Lord came to earth expressly in order that "joy may be in you, and your joy may be made full."

It is good, then, to laugh, to meet the experiences of every day with a smile, to share one's sense of humor with one's friends. Fun and laughter are all about us—and especially in literature. Writers, too, know the "saving" quality of humor and often share with us their whimsical moods.

The stories found in this section of the book speak for themselves. You will meet nuns "laughing into the business end of a Japanese rifle" and getting a "terriffic kick out of starving, because they do not take it seriously"; you will watch a queer cremation under the Arctic midnight sun; you will go on a kidnaping spree in Alabama with a ten-year-old "who was only funning"; you will cast sidelong glances at a vulture, chamois, polar bear, and a tiger taking lessons in self-defense; you will be bullied by a bee; you will see the marvels of a crystal palace in Mogadore, with forty tipsy sailors; you will even gamble with the devil.

That is your schedule. If you are at all susceptible to laughs, some of this unhurried humor should stay with you the rest of your lives.

HERBERT LANKS—PIX

Japan had attacked Pearl Harbor. What would happen to the hundreds of missionary nuns laboring in the Far East? There was only one answer—they would stay at their posts. Saving souls was far more important than war or flight to them. The writer of this account was interned with them at the Los Baños prison camp. He tells how he came to appreciate them better than ever before. Making the best of extreme hardship requires a sense of humor. You'll be impressed along with the writer at the laughing and joking of these nuns who knew how important it was to face grim reality with a smile.

NUNS IN PRISON

JAMES B. REUTER, S.J.

"When I'm Mother General," said the little nun grimly, as she climbed into the Japanese truck at two in the morning, "I'm going to take the wires out of these bonnets."

Five hundred of us had been herded into the Santo Tomas gym, ready for shipment to a new prison camp—Los Baños.[1] At midnight, after a final roll call, we lay down on the wooden floor and slept. All save the Maryknoll Sisters. They could not sleep. They had wires in their wimples which stuck into them when they lay down.

We rolled in covered trucks through the silent streets of Manila, in the dead of night. The drivers picked their route cautiously, carefully, lest the Filipinos see the nuns in the hands of the Japanese and rise up in revolution.

Los Baños was a pen in the foothills of a beautiful mountain range, with a pretty blue lake beside it, two depths of barbed wire around it, three concentric waves of Japanese guarding it, and 2,154 miserable prisoners inside it. The nuns were jammed into a bamboo barracks like everybody else. Water was a terrible problem. One spigot for five hundred of us. The Sisters would stand in line all day for a drink. To wash your face was a luxury. The camp was muddy, hot, and the Sisters dress in immaculate white. Three weeks in the same clothes, and no chance to do any laundry! Every barracks had a wash room attached, but the faucets were as dry as mummies in Egypt. When you turned them on they coughed and cackled and laughed at you, but no water came.

Till one midnight. A Sister found a faucet dripping! The Japanese garrison used the water all day and at night the pressure rose. This time it had risen so high that the Sisters had the water! The little nun stole into the sleeping barracks

[1] LOS BAÑOS—Pronounced Lōs Bän′yōs.

"Nuns in Prison" by James B. Reuter. Reprinted by permission of Jesuit Missions.

and gathered up her laundry. Another woke, and followed. By three in the morning all the Sisters were laughing over the trough, washing clothes. The water sank to a trickle at dawn, then stopped. But the nuns wrung out their wash triumphantly and hung it on the line. Then to Mass, to breakfast, and to bed.

When Sister Rose ran out of shoes a sympathetic lady gave her a pair. They were red, with high heels and no toes. She would come modestly into chapel after that, her eyes cast down, hands folded, and the red shoes on. Her congregation renamed her: Sister Rose Immaculate of the Worldly Slippers.

One morning the hairy internee who had charge of camp sanitation called on the monitor of the nuns' barracks. She could tell it was a state occasion because he had his shirt on. "We've decided to take over sanitation for you, Sister," he said. "It's too tough a job for women. Too ugly. So a squad of men will . . ."

"They will not! Not while I'm monitor! We prefer the privacy!"

"But the job's too mean for you!"

"Oh, it isn't really. Conditions here are excellent! Did you ever see Korea?"

Eventually he wandered away, taking off his shirt, canceling the orders for a special squad. "Father," he asked a month later, "what did those nuns do in Korea?"

But when the rains came and we had built a box to store the water, one of the Korea veterans turned up on the Sisters' sanitation crew. She had served two hitches in the army, right through the first world war, before she became a nursing nun. One day I found her trudging away from the tank with a heavy bucket in each hand.

"Let me take those, Sister!" I begged her. "This work is too hard for you!"

"Hard?" She set down the buckets and wiped the sweat from her old Irish face. "Child, this is the easiest job I've had since I got out of the army. I'm dreading the day of armistice when I'll have to go back to work."

There was one demure little Sister with a pale, oval face. She looked so delicate! When she dipped her buckets into the rain barrel we groaned. But the way she

shipped them out again, brimful of water, gave us pause. She must have been a weight lifter!

Perhaps it is the long years of getting to bed on time, the hard work in a convent, the days of discipline, but Sisters are strong! When the Dutch nuns tilled their gardens they lifted their mattocks [2] high over their heads and brought them down hard, like a man. Once I took a bundle of wood from a Dutch Sister and it nearly broke my back. After that I would stand off and calculate the strength of a nun before I volunteered to help her. If she was Dutch it was always safer to have two men volunteer at once. The finest furniture in the camp was made out of boxwood by Sister Patricia Marie. When we amateur carpenters marveled at the smoothness and speed of her work she said casually, "It's only a knack. Before I entered Maryknoll I used to teach manual arts in the public schools of Philadelphia."

Before Los Baños I had the vague impression that nuns grew up like sweet lilies in secluded gardens, sheltered from the world, slipping into convents naturally, at the age of fifteen. I was disillusioned. When Mother Godfrey entered the Franciscan Missionaries of Mary, a New York paper carried the headline: "Brooklyn Belle Flies to Convent!"

Sister Vitalis was a terrific success at the Good Shepherd Press in Manila partly because for seven years before she entered the convent she had been private secretary to the president of a printing concern.

Sister Rose Marie, who is small and Irish, grew up with Father O'Callahan, the hero of the *U.S.S. Franklin*. She is his sister. A grand cook! She would take the boiled rice as it came to us—it looked like a pot of paste sprinkled with woolly worms—and over an open fire transfer it into glorious things! She is as courageous as her brother, but much better looking. He will admit this.

The French-Canadian Sisters were painters, poets, and singers. In the evening when they sang the divine office, hard-bitten old beachcombers would lie dreamily in the grass outside the chapel, listening to the voice of a lyric soprano. She sang the solos sweetly, beautifully, with a little French lilt. The camp entertainment committee came around to the nuns' barracks at noon one day when the Sister in question was reading at table. Her soft voice rose and fell in the background as her superior interviewed the committee just outside the barracks' door.

"No!" said the superior firmly. "Sister may not give a concert! . . . No, I do not think that my refusal to let her do so is being unpatriotic. . . . Besides, she is on retreat! . . . Well, yes. She will sing in the chapel on Christmas. . . . No! You may not advertise it!"

As the months rolled by it dawned on us that women who became nuns are not ordinary. After our rescue by the paratroopers two young ladies came to visit the Sisters in the recuperation camp. One was a professional actress who had played Roxane in *Cyrano de Bergerac*. The other was an army nurse named Daisy. I knew her name was Daisy because it was painted in white letters on the brim of her hat. Each morning as she tilted her blonde head to receive communion the sun would glisten on the

[2] MATTOCK—A flat-bladed pick-axe.

white letters and "Daisy" would flash from the communion rail, like a name in lights. Both Roxane and Daisy were postulants. A postulant is a girl who wants to become a nun, whose application has already been accepted.

As we began our fourth year of imprisonment we had run out of clothes; we had run out of food; we had run out of everything but Japanese.

If ever you had seen Sister Miriam Thomas, the head of the nuns' sewing circle, dancing from table to table in her workshop, making polo shirts out of rags, unraveling old socks for thread, you never would have known that she had a Ph.D. When my last pair of shorts were wearing out and cloth was unobtainable, when I was just on the verge of being confined to bed for the duration, Sister Miriam Thomas came to the rescue. She presented me with a new pair—black, light and strong. The cloth? Oh, she found it.

Days later, working out on the hills in the sun, felling a huge acacia tree with a two-handed saw, I was clad only in those black shorts. And the man who was sweating away on the other end of the saw told me the awful truth. "Do you know?" he said, panting, as we swept through the tree with long, even strokes, "This . . . is the first time . . . I ever worked with a guy . . . who was dressed . . . in a nun's veil!"

When we were down to seven ounces of rice a day the Mother Superior of one group of Sisters came to the Bishop with tears in her eyes. "I know that things are hard, Sister," he said weakly, trying to console her. "It is difficult to live on rice . . ."

"Oh, it isn't the rice!" she said. "It's the soap! We've run out of soap!"

On the night of January 15, 1945, five minutes after they laid Father Mulry on the operating table, Sister Isabel turned to Doctor Nance and said through her white mask: "He's dead."

Nance would not believe it. He put his hand through the incision and worked the heart with his fingers, trying to bring life back again, but Sister Isabel was right. She washed the body and dressed it, weeping, put the purple vestments on that grand priest, and combed his hair as he lay in the coffin. In the middle of the night we carried the casket, a bare plank box, out of the hospital, along the dark road, past the Japanese sentries, to the chapel. There Sister Isabel took the bandage from around his chin and Father Mulry's face fell into a natural smile.

"Look at that!" she said through her tears. "You can't stop him, even when he's dead! Don't you laugh, Father Mulry! You ought to be reverent, at least at your own funeral!"

A Sister died at Los Baños, very gently. She offered her last agony "especially for the scholastics" [3] because it pained her that so many young men destined for the priesthood should be forced to live under the brutal Japanese. The fact that she was dying under them did not seem to bother her at all. Nuns embrace pain as if it were a gift, and die like a child going to sleep. We buried her in the rain, in an unpainted coffin, putting on her grave a wooden cross and wild flowers.

At night, in the blackout, I would lie in my bunk and listen to the Sisters sing-

[3] SCHOLASTICS—Jesuit students for the priesthood.

ing in their barracks. They had a good time at Los Baños. They would have had a good time anywhere. It is a queer paradox. Having weighed this world and found it wanting, living only for heaven, they enjoyed everything that happened to them. They got a terrific kick out of starving, because they did not take it seriously! Once I saw Sister Frederica laughing into the business end of a Japanese rifle.

They had a staggering simplicity of approach. . . . In their attack on sinners they were about as subtle as a sandbag. "I just don't like to go to church anymore," said a girl from the women's barracks to a Good Shepherd Sister who had known her of old.

"The trouble with you," said the Sister vigorously, "is that you're not in the state of grace! How long since your confession?"

A priest would use diplomacy on a renegade for months, without effect. A nun would catch him in five scorching minutes. Next morning he would come blushing up to communion.

When Sister Marcella took Shanghai Lil under instruction she hesitated when she came to the ten commandments. That was pretty deep matter for her pupil. But she was convinced that Shanghai Lil would get to heaven! "In that girl's bag," she said, "with her jewelry and lipstick, she carries a little broken piece of rosary. She doesn't know how to say it, but she carries it. If in her last moment she turns to God with that in her hand and a crooked sign of the cross, He'll let her right in!"

The wonder of the nuns at Los Baños was not their innocence, in the sense of ignorance—in a hospital in Manila they had the scum of the seven seas gathered into one ward; in twenty-four hours a nursing nun sees more of sin and its effects than an ordinary girl sees in a lifetime—it was the beauty of their minds and lives despite the atmosphere they lived in. A nun in a prison camp is like a rose blossoming in a desert.

And she is easy on the nerves, like music! You can be with nuns for hours without ever feeling that you must entertain them. You can fall asleep and they will not mind. If the Japanese give out biscuits for lunch one will take yours and save it for you until you wake up. When there are shots outside she will not squeal and grab you by the shirt. If you carry her baggage for her, she will not gush. But she will remember it.

Nuns are perhaps the most appreciative people in the world. If you are a downtrodden playwright, belittled by producers, discouraged and disheartened, present your play in a convent. You will come away convinced that you are William Shakespeare. In camp they even liked this little ditty, when we sang it for them. You know the tune.

"There were three little Sisters, three little Sis-ters
Missionaries in the Philippines!
One taught in college, one taught in high school,
And one fed the infants Ovaltine!
Now the three little Sisters, they were protected
While they worked in the Philippines
By an army of soldiers, a fleetful of sailors,
And by a mob of big marines!
But when the boys marched away . . .
The schools broke down
The Sisters found
That the war was here to stay!

So the three little Sisters, the poor little Sisters,
They're living now on rice and greens,
Waiting for the soldiers, waiting for the sailors,
And waiting for the marines!"

One morning nine planes swept low over the camp and paratroopers stepped out. As the first parachute opened, the guerrillas came howling out of the hills, throwing hand grenades into the sentry boxes. Bullets whistled through the barracks.

Sister Frederica had a cup shot cleanly out of her hand. "Oh, dear!" she sighed. "The best piece of crockery in the camp!" Then she lay flat on the floor.

Betty Silen, a nineteen-year-old who lived with them, stood up and was shot through the stomach. With the bullets buzzing over them, the nuns cut away the clothes, stopped the flow of blood, ripped up their habits for bandages and dressed the wound.

Not many of the Sisters came home. They are real missionaries. When they go to a foreign country they stay there, war or no war. But recently I met a handful of repatriated Maryknollers begging for the missions at the front door of a church as the people came out of Mass. They were also hearing all the Sunday Masses, following them in their missals!

"Don't do that, Sister!" I whispered to one of them in the vestibule. "You're still sick and you'll wear out! Rest somewhere and just appear at the crises, when the Masses are over!"

"Young man," she said sternly, blinking with fatigue. "At Los Baños, I used to hear Mass after Mass, when I was dizzy with hunger, when all I could see in front of me was a platter!"

"A platter of what? Bacon and eggs?"

"No," she said, "strangely enough, it was noodles!" And she dashed into church for the consecration.

Ever since I was a little boy I knew that nuns were pure and good, but at Los Baños, I discovered something else: they're REAL!

◇◇◇◇◇◇◇◇◇◇◇◇◇◇◇◇◇◇◇◇◇◇◇◇◇◇◇◇◇◇

FOR DISCUSSION

1. How does the opening sentence set the tone for the whole piece? List three other tone-setting statements.

2. What, to his surprise and semi-sorrow, did the author learn of the strength of the apparently weak nuns?

3. What do you find here to confirm your belief that nuns are very capable people? List at least four skills mentioned here.

4. What are postulants? Do the two mentioned in this article strike you as helpless and unsuccessful women?

5. Name two or three incidents you enjoyed most which reflect the nuns' sense of humor. How was their sense of humor helpful at the time?

6. Put the main idea of the entire selection in one sentence to show that you have grasped it.

THE AUTHOR'S SKILL

In this story the author is particularly adept at using imaginative language in order to make you laugh with him. For instance:

". . . the faucets were as dry as mummies in Egypt."

". . . they coughed and cackled and laughed at you . . ."

". . . the vague impression that nuns grew up like lilies in secluded gardens."

a. Find other expressions that draw comparisons to help you see a picture clearly.

b. Write a one-paragraph essay relating an incident in your own experience which proved to you that nuns are real. Use one or two original comparisons to put humor into your story.

RELATED READING

Murder in a Nunnery by Eric Shepherd is a good mystery story. It also shows us what real people nuns are.

O. Henry is a master at short story writing. His stories are loved for their humor and realism. In this one he has used his favorite trick—a surprise ending. But you'll really find a surprise on almost every page.

THE RANSOM OF RED CHIEF

O. HENRY

It looked like a good thing; but wait till I tell you. We were down south, in Alabama—Bill Driscoll and myself—when this kidnaping idea struck us. It was, as Bill afterwards expressed it, "during a moment of temporary mental apparition," [1] but we didn't find that out till later.

There was a town down there, as flat as a flannel cake, and called Summit, of course. It contained inhabitants of as undeleterious [2] and self-satisfied a class of peasantry as ever clustered around a Maypole.

Bill and me had a joint capital of about six hundred dollars, and we needed just two thousand dollars more to pull off a town lot scheme in Western Illinois. We talked it over on the front steps of the hotel. Philoprogenitiveness,[3] says we, is strong in semi-rural communities; therefore, and for other reasons, a kidnaping project ought to do better there than in the radius of newspapers that send reporters out in plain clothes to stir up talk about such things. We knew that Summit couldn't get after us with anything stronger than constables and, maybe, some lackadaisical bloodhounds and a diatribe [4] or two in the *Weekly Farmers' Budget*. So it looked good.

We selected for our victim the only child of a prominent citizen named Ebenezer Dorset. The father was respectable and tight, a mortgage fancier and a stern, upright collection-plate passer and forecloser. The kid was a boy of ten, with

[1] APPARITION—A ghost; here deliberately mischosen for "aberration"—an error or mental wandering.

[2] UNDELETERIOUS—Harmless.

[3] PHILOPROGENITIVENESS—Instinctive love of parents for their children.

[4] DIATRIBE—Bitter criticism.

bas-relief[5] freckles, and hair the color of the cover of the magazine you buy at the newsstand when you want to catch a train. Bill and me figured that Ebenezer would melt down for a ransom of two thousand dollars to a cent. But wait till I tell you.

About two miles from Summit was a little mountain covered with a dense cedar brake.[6] On the rear elevation of this mountain was a cave. There we stored provisions.

One evening after sundown, we drove in a buggy past old Dorset's house. The kid was in the street, throwing rocks at a kitten on the opposite fence.

"Hey, little boy!" said Bill, "would you like to have a bag of candy and a ride?"

The boy catches Bill neatly in the eye with a piece of brick.

That boy put up a fight like a welterweight cinnamon bear; but, at last, we got him down in the bottom of the buggy and drove away. We took him up to the cave, and I hitched the horse in the cedar brake. After dark I drove the buggy to the little village, three miles away, where we had hired it, and walked back to the mountain.

Bill was pasting court-plaster over the scratches and bruises on his features. There was a fire burning behind the big rock at the entrance of the cave, and the boy was watching a pot of boiling coffee, with two buzzard tail feathers stuck in his red hair. He points a stick at me when I come up, and says:

[5] BAS-RELIEF (bä′rē·lēf′)—In a bas-relief the figures stand out slightly from the background.

[6] CEDAR BRAKE—A woods of cedar covered with dense underbrush.

"Ha! cursed paleface, do you dare to enter the camp of Red Chief, the terror of the plains?"

"He's all right now," says Bill, rolling up his trousers and examining some bruises on his shins. "We're playing Indian. We're making Buffalo Bill's show look like magic lantern views of Palestine in the town hall. I'm old Hank, the Trapper, Red Chief's captive, and I'm to be scalped at daybreak. By Geronimo! that kid can kick hard."

Yes, sir, that boy seemed to be having the time of his life. The fun of camping out in a cave had made him forget that he was a captive himself. He immediately christened me Snake-eye, the Spy, and announced that, when his braves returned from the warpath, I was to be broiled at the stake at the rising of the sun.

Then we had supper; and he filled his mouth full of bacon and bread and gravy, and began to talk. He made a during-dinner speech something like this:

"I like this fine. I never camped out before; but I had a pet 'possum once, and I was nine last birthday. I hate to go to school. Rats ate up sixteen of Jimmy Talbot's aunt's speckled hen's eggs. Are there any real Indians in these woods? I want some more gravy. Does the trees moving make the wind blow? We had five puppies. What makes your nose so red, Hank? My father has lots of money. Are the stars hot? I whipped Ed Walker twice, Saturday. I don't like girls. You dassent catch toads unless with a string. Do oxen make any noise? Why are oranges round? Have you got beds to sleep on in this cave? Amos Murray has got six toes. A parrot can talk, but a monkey or a fish can't. How many does it take to make twelve?"

Every few minutes he would remember that he was a pesky redskin, and pick up his stick rifle and tiptoe to the mouth of the cave to rubber for the scouts of the hated paleface. Now and then he would let out a war whoop that made Old Hank, the Trapper, shiver. That boy had Bill terrorized from the start.

"Red Chief," says I to the kid, "would you like to go home?"

"Aw, what for?" says he. "I don't have any fun at home. I hate to go to school. I like to camp out. You won't take me back home again, Snake-eye, will you?"

"Not right away," says I. "We'll stay here in the cave a while."

"All right!" says he. "That'll be fine. I never had such fun in all my life."

We went to bed about eleven o'clock. We spread down some wide blankets and quilts and put Red Chief between us. We weren't afraid he'd run away. He kept us awake for three hours, jumping up and reaching for his rifle and screeching: "Hist! pard!" in mine and Bill's ears, as the fancied crackle of a twig or the rustle of a leaf revealed to his young imagination the stealthy approach of the outlaw band. At last, I fell into a troubled sleep, and dreamed that I had been kidnaped and chained to a tree by a ferocious pirate with red hair.

Just at daybreak, I was awakened by a series of awful screams from Bill. They weren't yells, or howls, or shouts, or whoops, or yawps, such as you'd expect from a manly set of vocal organs—they were simply indecent, terrifying, humiliating screams, such as women emit when they see ghosts or caterpillars. It's an awful thing to hear a strong, desperate, fat man scream incontinently in a cave at daybreak.

I jumped up to see what the matter was. Red Chief was sitting on Bill's chest, with one hand twined in Bill's hair. In the other he had the sharp case knife we used for slicing bacon; and he was industriously and realistically trying to take Bill's scalp, according to the sentence that had been pronounced upon him the evening before.

I got the knife away from the kid and made him lie down again. But, from that moment, Bill's spirit was broken. He lay down on his side of the bed, but he never closed an eye again in sleep as long as that boy was with us. I dozed off for a while, but along toward sunup I remembered that Red Chief had said I was to be burned at the stake at the rising of the sun. I wasn't nervous or afraid; but I sat up and lit my pipe and leaned against a rock.

"What you getting up so soon for, Sam?" asked Bill.

"Me?" says I. "Oh, I got a kind of a pain in my shoulder. I thought sitting up would rest it."

"You're a liar!" says Bill. "You're afraid. You was to be burned at sunrise, and you was afraid he'd do it. And he would, too, if he could find a match. Ain't it awful, Sam? Do you think anybody will pay out money to get a little imp like that back home?"

"Sure," said I. "A rowdy kid like that is just the kind that parents dote on. Now, you and the Chief get up and cook breakfast, while I go up on the top of this mountain and reconnoiter."

I went up on the peak of the little mountain and ran my eye over the contiguous vicinity. Over toward Summit I expected to see the sturdy yeomanry of the village armed with scythes and pitchforks beating the countryside for the dastardly kidnapers. But what I saw was a peaceful landscape dotted with one man plowing with a dun mule. Nobody was dragging the creek, no couriers dashed hither and yon, bringing tidings of no news to the distracted parents. There was a sylvan attitude of somnolent sleepiness pervading that section of the external outward surface of Alabama that lay exposed to my view. "Perhaps," says I to myself, "it has not yet been discovered that the wolves have borne away the tender lambkin from the fold. Heaven help the wolves!" says I, and went down the mountain to breakfast.

When I got to the cave I found Bill backed up against the side of it, breathing hard, and the boy threatening to smash him with a rock half as big as a cocoanut. "He put a red-hot boiled potato down my back," explained Bill, "and then mashed it with his foot; and I boxed his ears. Have you got a gun about you, Sam?"

I took the rock away from the boy and kind of patched up the argument. "I'll fix you," says the kid to Bill. "No man ever yet struck the Red Chief but what he got paid for it. You better beware!"

After breakfast the kid takes a piece of leather with strings wrapped around it out of his pocket and goes outside the cave unwinding it.

"What's he up to now?" says Bill, anxiously. "You don't think he'll run away, do you, Sam?"

"No fear of it," says I. "He don't seem to be much of a home body. But we've got to fix up some plan about the ransom. There don't seem to be much excitement around Summit on account of his disappearance; but maybe they haven't realized yet that he's gone. His folks may think he's spending the night with Aunt Jane or one of the neighbors. Anyhow, he'll be missed today. Tonight we must get a message to his father demanding the two thousand dollars for his return."

Just then we heard a kind of war whoop, such as David might have emitted when he knocked out the champion Goliath. It was a sling that Red Chief had pulled out of his pocket, and he was whirling it around his head.

I dodged, and heard a heavy thud and a kind of a sigh from Bill, like one a horse gives out when you take his saddle off. A niggerhead rock the size of an egg had caught Bill just behind his left ear. He loosened himself all over and fell in the fire across the frying pan of hot water for washing the dishes. I dragged him out and poured cold water on his head for half an hour.

By and by, Bill sits up and feels behind his ear and says: "Sam, do you know who my favorite Biblical character is?"

"Take it easy," says I. "You'll come to your senses presently."

"King Herod," says he. "You won't go away and leave me here alone, will you, Sam?"

I went out and caught that boy and shook him until his freckles rattled.

"If you don't behave," says I, "I'll take you straight home. Now, are you going to be good, or not?"

"I was only funning," says he sullenly. "I didn't mean to hurt Old Hank. But what did he hit me for? I'll behave, Snake-eye, if you won't send me home, and if you'll let me play the Black Scout today."

"I don't know the game," says I. "That's for you and Mr. Bill to decide. He's your playmate for the day. I'm going away for a while, on business. Now, you come in and make friends with him and say you are sorry for hurting him, or home you go, at once."

I made him and Bill shake hands, and then I took Bill aside and told him I was going to Poplar Cove, a little village three miles from the cave, and find out what I could about how the kidnaping had been regarded in Summit. Also, I thought it best to send a peremptory letter to old man Dorset that day, demanding the ransom and dictating how it should be paid.

"You know, Sam," says Bill, "I've stood by you without batting an eye in earthquake, fire, and flood—in poker games, dynamite outrages, police raids, train robberies, and cyclones. I never lost my nerve yet till we kidnaped that two-legged skyrocket of a kid. He's got me going. You won't leave me long with him, will you, Sam?"

"I'll be back some time this afternoon," says I. "You must keep the boy amused and quiet till I return. And now we'll write the letter to old Dorset."

Bill and I got paper and pencil and worked on the letter while Red Chief, with a blanket wrapped around him, strutted up and down, guarding the mouth of the cave. Bill begged me tearfully to make the ransom fifteen hundred dollars instead of two thousand. "I ain't attempting," says he, "to decry the celebrated moral aspect of parental affection, but we're dealing with humans, and it ain't human for anybody to give up two thousand dollars for that forty-pound chunk of freckled wildcat. I'm willing to take a chance at fifteen hundred dollars. You can charge the difference up to me."

So, to relieve Bill, I acceded, and we collaborated a letter that ran this way:

EBENEZER DORSET, ESQ.:

We have your boy concealed in a place far from Summit. It is useless for you or the most skillful detectives to attempt to find him. Absolutely the only terms on which you can have him restored to you are these: We demand fifteen hundred dollars in large bills for his return; the money to be left at midnight tonight at the same spot and in the same box as your reply—as hereinafter described. If you agree to these terms, send your answer in writing by a solitary messenger tonight at half-past eight o'clock. After crossing Owl Creek, on the road to Poplar Cove, there are three large trees about a hundred yards apart, close to the fence of the wheat field on the right-hand side. At the bottom of the fence post, opposite the third tree, will be found a small pasteboard box.

The messenger will place the answer in this box and return immediately to Summit.

If you attempt any treachery or fail to comply with our demand as stated, you will never see your boy again.

If you pay the money as demanded, he will be returned to you safe and well within three hours. These terms are final, and if you do not accede to them, no further communication will be attempted.

TWO DESPERATE MEN.

I addressed this letter to Dorset, and put it in my pocket. As I was about to start, the kid comes up to me and says:

"Aw, Snake-eye, you said I could play the Black Scout while you was gone."

"Play it, of course," says I. "Mr. Bill will play with you. What kind of a game is it?"

"I'm the Black Scout," says Red Chief, "and I have to ride to the stockade to warn the settlers that the Indians are coming. I'm tired of playing Indian myself. I want to be the Black Scout."

"All right," says I. "It sounds harmless to me. I guess Mr. Bill will help you foil the pesky savages."

"What am I to do?" asks Bill, looking at the kid suspiciously.

"You are the hoss," says Black Scout. "Get down on your hands and knees. How can I ride to the stockade without a hoss?"

"You'd better keep him interested," said I, "till we get the scheme going. Loosen up."

Bill gets down on his all fours, and a look comes in his eye like a rabbit when you catch it in a trap.

"How far is it to the stockade, kid?" he asks in a husky manner of voice.

"Ninety miles," says the Black Scout. "And you have to hump yourself to get there on time. Whoa, now!"

The Black Scout jumps on Bill's back and digs his heels in his side.

"For Heaven's sake," says Bill, "hurry back, Sam, as soon as you can. I wish we hadn't made the ransom more than a thousand. Say, you quit kicking me, or I'll get up and warm you good."

I walked over to Poplar Cove and sat around the post office and store, talking with the chawbacons that come in to trade. One whiskerando says that he hears Summit is all upset on account of

Elder Ebenezer Dorset's boy having been lost or stolen. That was all I wanted to know. I bought some smoking tobacco, referred casually to the price of black-eyed peas, posted my letter surreptitiously [7] and came away. The postmaster said the mail carrier would come by in an hour to take the mail on to Summit.

When I got back to the cave Bill and the boy were not to be found. I explored the vicinity of the cave, and risked a yodel or two, but there was no response.

So I lighted my pipe and sat down on a mossy bank to await developments.

In about half an hour I heard the bushes rustle, and Bill wabbled out into the little glade in front of the cave. Behind him was the kid, stepping softly like a scout, with a broad grin on his face. Bill stopped, took off his hat and wiped his face with a red handkerchief. The kid stopped about eight feet behind him.

"Sam," says Bill, "I suppose you'll think I'm a renegade, but I couldn't help it. I'm a grown person with masculine proclivities [8] and habits of self-defense, but there is a time when all systems of egotism and predominance fail. The boy is gone. I have sent him home. All is off. There was martyrs in old times," goes on Bill, "that suffered death rather than give up the particular graft they enjoyed. None of 'em ever was subjugated to such supernatural tortures as I have been. I tried to be faithful to our articles of depredation; [9] but there came a limit."

"What's the trouble, Bill?" I asks him.

"I was rode," says Bill, "the ninety miles to the stockade, not barring an inch. Then when the settlers was rescued, I was given oats. Sand ain't a palatable substitute. And then, for an hour I had to try to explain why there was nothin' in holes, how a road can run both ways, and what makes the grass green. I tell you, Sam, a human can only stand so much. I takes him by the neck of his clothes and drags him down the mountain. On the way he kicks my legs black-an'-blue from the knees down; and I've got two or three bites on my thumb and hand cauterized.

"But he's gone,"—continues Bill—"gone home. I showed him the road to Summit and kicked him about eight feet nearer there at one kick. I'm sorry we lose the ransom; but it was either that or Bill Driscoll to the madhouse."

"Bill," says I, "there isn't any heart disease in your family, is there?"

"No," says Bill, "nothing chronic except malaria and accidents. Why?"

"Then you might turn around," says I, "and have a look behind you."

Bill turns and sees the boy, and loses his complexion and sits down plump on the ground and begins to pluck aimlessly at grass and little sticks. For an hour I was afraid for his mind. And then I told him that my scheme was to put the whole job through immediately and that we would get the ransom and be off with it by midnight if old Dorset fell in with our proposition. So Bill braced up enough to give the kid a weak sort of smile and a promise to play the Russian in a Japanese war with him as soon as he felt a little better.

I had a scheme for collecting that ransom without danger of being caught by counterplots that ought to commend itself to professional kidnapers. The tree

[7] SURREPTITIOUSLY—Quietly, secretly.
[8] PROCLIVITIES—Tendencies.
[9] DEPREDATION—Robbery, plundering.

under which the answer was to be left—and the money later on—was close to the road fence with big, bare fields on all sides. If a gang of constables should be watching for anyone to come for the note they could see him a long way off crossing the fields, or in the road. But no, siree! At half-past eight I was up in that tree as well hidden as a tree toad, waiting for the messenger to arrive.

Exactly on time, a half-grown boy rides up the road on a bicycle, locates the pasteboard box at the foot of the fence post, slips a folded piece of paper into it and pedals away again back toward Summit.

I waited an hour and then concluded the thing was square. I slid down the tree, got the note, slipped along the fence till I struck the woods, and was back at the cave in another half an hour. I opened the note, got near the lantern, and read it to Bill. It was written with a pen in a crabbed hand, and the sum and substance of it was this:

TWO DESPERATE MEN.

Gentlemen: I received your letter today by post, in regard to the ransom you ask for the return of my son. I think you are a little high in your demands, and I hereby make you a counterproposition, which I am inclined to believe you will accept. You bring Johnny home and pay me two hundred and fifty dollars in cash, and I agree to take him off your hands. You had better come at night, for the neighbors believe he is lost, and I couldn't be responsible for what they would do to anybody they saw bringing him back.

Very respectfully,

EBENEZER DORSET.

"Great pirates of Penzance!" says I, "of all the impudent—" But I glanced at Bill, and hesitated. He had the most appealing look in his eyes I ever saw on the face of a dumb or a talking brute.

"Sam," says he, "what's two hundred and fifty dollars, after all? We've got the money. One more night of this kid will send me to a bed in Bedlam.[10] Besides being a thorough gentleman, I think Mr. Dorset is a spendthrift for making us such a liberal offer. You ain't going to let the chance go, are you?"

"Tell you the truth, Bill," says I, "this little he ewe lamb has somewhat got on my nerves, too. We'll take him home, pay the ransom, and make our getaway."

We took him home that night. We got him to go by telling him that his father had bought a silver-mounted rifle and a pair of moccasins for him, and we were going to hunt bears the next day.

It was just twelve o'clock when we knocked at Ebenezer's front door. Just at the moment when I should have been abstracting the fifteen hundred dollars from the box under the tree, according to the original proposition, Bill was counting out two hundred and fifty dollars into Dorset's hand.

When the kid found out we were going to leave him at home he started up a howl like a calliope and fastened himself as tight as a leech to Bill's leg. His father peeled him away gradually, like a porous plaster.

"How long can you hold him?" asks Bill.

"I'm not as strong as I used to be," says old Dorset, "but I think I can promise you ten minutes."

"Enough," says Bill. "In ten minutes I shall cross the Central, Southern, and

[10] BEDLAM—A house for lunatics.

Middle Western States, and be legging it trippingly for the Canadian border."

And, as dark as it was, and as fat as Bill was, and as good a runner as I am, he was a good mile and a half out of Summit before I could catch up with him.

◇◇◇◇◇◇◇◇◇◇◇◇◇◇◇◇◇◇◇◇◇◇◇◇◇◇◇◇◇◇◇◇

FOR DISCUSSION

1. Why was the town of Summit an apt locality for performing the kidnaping of Red Chief? What contradiction is expressed in characterizing Ebenezer Dorset as "a stern, upright collection-plate passer and forecloser"?

2. What effect had the scalping incident on Bill Driscoll? Why did King Herod suddenly become Bill's favorite Biblical character?

3. Describe the posting of the ransom letter and the developments after Sam returned to camp.

4. Who paid the ransom of Red Chief?

5. Would the Dorsets' neighbors have been really glad to lose Red Chief or is O. Henry merely representing the way people talk about a nuisance?

6. Which surprise in the story is the biggest one to you?

7. Contrast the following sentences:

a. "The kid was a boy of ten, with bas-relief freckles, and hair the color of the magazine you buy at the newsstand when you want to catch a train."

b. The kid was a boy of ten, with big freckles and red hair.

O. Henry's style is readily apparent in the first of the two sentences. What other sentences can you select which show humorous exaggeration or picturesque comparison?

THE KIDNAPERS HAD A WORD FOR IT

1. Much of O. Henry's humor is in the way he uses language—in speaking high-sounding words in commonplace situations. In the paragraph on page 102 beginning: "I went up on the peak of the little mountain . . ." find examples of this ridiculous contrast between language and the situation in which it is used.

2. In the paragraph mentioned above look up the meanings of these words: *contiguous, yeomanry, dastardly, couriers, tidings, sylvan, somnolent, pervading.* Rewrite the paragraph, substituting more familiar words.

YOUR OWN STORY

Imagine that you were the half-grown boy commissioned to deliver the reply to the kidnapers. Describe the evening ride to the spot appointed on the lonely country road. In supplying details it will help to recall the geography of a country road you know. Tell what you *see, hear,* and *feel* as you ride to the rendezvous with "two desperate men."

RELATED READING

O. Henry wrote many books of short stories. Among the best of his mischievous, whimsical yarns are "The Gift of the Magi" from *The Four Million,* "A Retrieved Reformation" from *Roads of Destiny,* and "The Third Ingredient" from *Destiny.*

Eight years in the Yukon territory gave Robert W. Service plenty of material for his "secret tales" of "queer sights" that "make your blood run cold." This one is about the weird cremation of a frozen gold-prospector. Decide whether you think the author is a teller of "tall tales."

The Cremation of Sam McGee

ROBERT W. SERVICE

There are strange things done in the midnight sun
By the men who moil for gold;
The Arctic trails have their secret tales
That would make your blood run cold;
The Northern Lights have seen queer sights, 5
But the queerest they ever did see
Was that night on the marge of Lake Lebarge
I cremated Sam McGee.

Now Sam McGee was from Tennessee, where the cotton blooms and blows,
Why he left his home in the South to roam 'round the Pole, God only knows. 10
He was always cold, but the land of gold seemed to hold him like a spell;
Though he'd often say in his homely way that "he'd sooner live in hell."

On a Christmas Day we were mushing our way over the Dawson Trail.
Talk of your cold! through the parka's fold it stabbed like a driven nail.
If our eyes we'd close, then the lashes froze till sometimes we couldn't see; 15
It wasn't much fun, but the only one to whimper was Sam McGee.

And that very night, as we lay packed tight in our robes beneath the snow,
And the dogs were fed, and the stars o'erhead were dancing heel and toe,
He turned to me, and "Cap," says he, "I'll cash in this trip, I guess;
And if I do, I'm asking that you won't refuse my last request." 20

2. MOIL—Work hard.
7. MARGE—Edge.
7. LAKE LEBARGE—Alaskan lake.
13. DAWSON TRAIL—A trail in the Klondike.
19. CASH IN—Die.

Well, he seemed so low that I couldn't say no; then he says with a sort of moan:
"It's the cursèd cold and it's got right hold till I'm chilled clean through to the
bone.
Yet 'tain't being dead—it's my awful dread of the icy grave that pains;
So I want you to swear that, foul or fair, you'll cremate my last remains."

A pal's last need is a thing to heed, so I swore I would not fail; 25
And we started on at the streak of dawn; but ah! he looked ghastly pale.
He crouched on the sleigh, and he raved all day of his home in Tennessee;
And before nightfall a corpse was all that was left of Sam McGee.

There wasn't a breath in that land of death, and I hurried, horror-driven,
With a corpse half hid that I couldn't get rid, because of a promise given; 30
It was lashed to the sleigh, and it seemed to say: "You may tax your brawn and
brains,
But you promised true, and it's up to you to cremate those last remains."

Now a promise made is a debt unpaid, and the trail has its own stern code.
In the days to come, though my lips were dumb, in my heart how I cursed that
load.
In the long, long night, by the lone firelight, while the huskies, round in a ring, 35
Howled out their woes to the homeless snows—O man! how I loathed the thing.

And every day that quiet clay seemed to heavy and heavier grow;
And on I went, though the dogs were spent and the grub was getting low;
The trail was bad, and I felt half mad, but I swore I would not give in;
And I'd often sing to the hateful thing, and it hearkened with a grin. 40

Till I came to the marge of Lake Lebarge, and a derelict there lay;
It was jammed in the ice, but I saw in a trice it was called the "Alice May."
And I looked at it, and I thought a bit, and I looked at my frozen chum;
Then "Here," said I, with a sudden cry, "is my cre-ma-tor-e-um."

Some planks I tore from the cabin floor, and I lit the boiler fire; 45
Some coal I found that was lying around, and I heaped the fuel higher;
The flames just soared, and the furnace roared—such a blaze you seldom see;
And I burrowed a hole in the glowing coal, and I stuffed in Sam McGee.

24. CREMATE—To burn to ashes. The dead are sometimes cremated instead of being buried.
41. DERELICT—An abandoned ship.
44. CREMATOREUM—A furnace for burning corpses. A crematory.

Then I made a hike, for I didn't like to hear him sizzle so; 49
And the heavens scowled, and the huskies howled, and the wind began to blow.
It was icy cold, but the hot sweat rolled down my cheeks, and I don't know why;
And the greasy smoke in an inky cloak went streaking down the sky.

I do not know how long in the snow I wrestled with grisly fear;
But the stars came out and they danced about ere again I ventured near;
I was sick with dread, but I bravely said: "I'll just take a peep inside. 55
I guess he's cooked, and it's time I looked"; . . . then the door I opened wide.

And there sat Sam, looking cold and calm, in the heart of the furnace roar;
And he wore a smile you could see a mile, and he said: "Please close that door!
It's fine in here, but I greatly fear you'll let in the cold and storm—
Since I left Plumtree, down in Tennessee, it's the first time I've been warm." 60

There are strange things done in the midnight sun
By the men who moil for gold;
The Arctic trails have their secret tales
That would make your blood run cold;
The Northern Lights have seen queer sights, 65
But the queerest they ever did see
Was that night on the marge of Lake Lebarge
I cremated Sam McGee.

RHYMING STUNTS

Repetition of the same sound is one of the poet's best tricks. The name of this trick is *rhyme*. Sometimes the last sound of each line is repeated two or three times; sometimes two sounds in the same line are the same:

"There are strange things *done*
in the midnight *sun*."

The "rhyming stunt" adds to the enjoyment of this poem. To appreciate fully the rhymes in "The Cremation of Sam McGee," read the poem aloud. Then go through the poem, finding examples of repetition of similar sounds. How long a list of rhyming words can you compile?

A STRANGE NEWS STORY

If you were assigned to cover Alaskan news for the Associated Press, what details would you include in your article on the decease of Sam McGee? Write a headline to catch the eye of any reader. Then begin your story with the most astonishing facts first. Be sure to include the time and place that the events occurred. Do you think your story should include some items about McGee's origin and background? After the stories have been written, vote on the most interesting one in the class.

◇◇◇◇◇

When an ingenious Irishman matches his wits with the evil schemes of Satan, a clever story unfolds. The author has given his story a quaint Irish flavor, which adds the humorous touch. From beginning to end, you'll be struggling with Sam and cheering him on to his inevitable victory.

SATAN AND SAM SHAY

ROBERT ARTHUR

I am told that sin has somewhat declined since Satan met Sam Shay. I cannot vouch for this, but they say that production has definitely fallen off since that evening when Sam Shay won three wagers from the Devil. And this is the tale of it.

Sam Shay, you'll understand, was a bold rascal with Irish blood in his veins, though Yankee-born and bred. Six feet he stood, with wide shoulders and a grin and dark hair with a touch of curl to it. Looking at his hands and his brawn, you'd hardly have guessed he'd never done an honest day's labor in his life. But it was true. For Sam was a gambling man, and since he was a boy, matching coppers or playing odd and even with his fellows, every penny passing through his fingers had been the fruit of wagering. And he was now approaching his thirtieth year.

Do not think to his discredit, however, that Sam Shay was a flinty-hearted professional betting only on things that were

"Satan and Sam Shay" by Robert Arthur, as reprinted in *The Elks Magazine*. Reprinted by permission of Jacques Chambrun, Inc.

sure or at odds much tipped in his favor. He bet not mathematically but by intuition, and the betting was as important as the winning. Were you to have given him the money he would not have taken it; there would have been no savor to it. He must win it by his wits to enjoy it, and he could find fun in losing a good wager, too.

So it was a sad thing to Sam that the one girl of his heart, Shannon Malloy, should be dead set against gambling. But the late Malloy had squandered all his earnings in just such divertissements as Sam Shay enjoyed, and the Widow Malloy had brought her daughter up most strictly to abjure men who loved the sound of rolling dice, the riffle of the cards, or the quickening of the pulse that comes as the horses turn into the home stretch and stream for the finish line.

In the early days of their acquaintance, Shannon Malloy, who was small, with dark eyes that held a glow in their depths, had overlooked Sam's failing, feeling that Sam would mend his ways for love of her. And indeed Sam promised. But he could no more live without betting than he could without eating—less, for he could go a day without food undistressed, but in twenty years no sun had set without his making a wager of some kind, however small, just to keep his hand in.

Frequently, therefore, Sam Shay found himself in disgrace, while Shannon, more in sorrow than in anger, pleaded with him. And each time Sam once again promised to reform, knowing in his heart that once again he would fail. Inevitably, then, there came the time when Shannon, putting aside the veils that love cast upon her vision, saw with sad clarity that Sam Shay was Sam Shay and naught would alter him. She loved him, but her convictions were as adamant.[1] So she gave him back the ring she had accepted from him when his resolves had been less tarnished.

"I'm sorry, Sam," she had said, this very evening, and her words rang knell-like in Sam's ears now as he strode homeward through the soft evening dusk that lay across the park. "I'm sorry," and her voice had broken. "But today I heard your name spoken. By some men. And they were saying you are a born gambler who could make three bets with Satan and win them all. And if that is true, I can't marry you. Not feeling as I do. Not until you change."

And Sam, knowing that only some force far stronger than himself could turn him from his wagering, took the ring and went with only one backward glance. That glance showed him Shannon Malloy weeping but resolute, and he was as proud of her resolution as disconsolate that she should feel so strongly about his little weakness.

The ring was in his pocket and his fingers touched it sadly as he walked. It was a circlet cold to the touch, a metal zero that summed the total of his chances for having Shannon Malloy to wife. The twilight lay upon the park, and it was queerly hushed, as if something was impending. But, lost in his thoughts, he strode along taking no notice.

It was as he came abreast an ancient oak that the shadow of the tree, athwart the sidewalk, with great unexpectedness solidified into a pillar of blackness church-steeple high, which condensed swiftly

[1] ADAMANT (ăd'ă·mănt)—Hard stone.

into a smallish individual with flowing white locks and a benign countenance.

The individual who had so unconventionally placed himself in Sam's path was clad in garments of sober cut, an old-fashioned cape slung over his shoulders and a soft dark hat upon his white hair. He smiled with innocent engagingness at Samuel Shay, and spoke in a voice both mild and friendly.

"Good evening, Sam," he said, as one might to an acquaintance not seen in a great while. "I'll bet you don't know who I am."

But Sam Shay, his right hand gripping the stout thorn stick he liked to carry about with him, was not to be trapped. He had seen the shadow of an oak tree change into a man, and this, to say the least, was unusual.

"Why," he proclaimed boldly, "I have a hundred dollars in my pocket, and I'll lay it against one that you are Satan."

Satan—for Sam's intuition had not failed him—let an expression of displeasure cross the benign countenance he had assumed for this visit. For he too had heard the report Shannon Malloy had quoted to Sam—that he could make three bets with Satan and win them all. And, his curiosity aroused, the Devil had come to test Sam's prowess, for he was fond of gambling, though a bad loser.

But the expression was gone in an instant and the gentle smile resumed its place. The old gentleman reached beneath his cloak and brought out a wallet which bulged pleasingly, although it was of a leather whose appearance Sam did not care for.

"That may be, Sam," Satan replied genially. "And if I am, I owe you a dollar. But I have another hundred here says you can't prove it."

And he waited, well pleased, for this was a wager that had stumped many eminent philosophers in centuries past. But Sam Shay was a man of action, not of words.

"Taken," he agreed at once, and raised his thorn stick above his head. "I'll just bash you a time or two over the pate. If you're an honest citizen I'll take your wallet, and if you're Satan I'll win the wager. For you could not let a mortal man trounce you so and still look yourself in the eye—an accomplishment quite individually yours. So—"

And Sam brought the stick down in a whistling blow.

A sulphurous sheet of flame cracked out from the heart of the oak tree, and the thorn stick was riven into a thousand splinters that hissed away through the air. A strong pain shot up Sam's arm, a tingling, numbing sensation that extended to the shoulder. But, rubbing his wrist, he was well satisfied.

Not so Satan. In his anger the little old gentleman had shot upward until he loomed twelve feet high now, and looked far more terrifying than benign.

"You win, Sam Shay," Satan told him sourly. "But there's a third bet yet to come." Which Sam knew to be true, for on any such occasion as this when the Devil showed himself to a mortal, the unhappy man must win three wagers from him to go free. "And this time we'll increase the stakes. Your soul against the contents of this wallet that you can't win from me again."

Sam did not hesitate. For he must wager, whether he would or not.

"Taken," he answered. "But I must name the bet, since you named the others and it is my turn now."

Satan it was who hesitated, but right and logic were with Sam, so he nodded.

"Name it, then," he directed, and his voice was like grumbling thunder beyond the skyline.

"Why, as to that," Sam told him with an impudent grin, "I am betting you do not intend for me to win this wager."

Hardly were the words out of his mouth before Satan, in uncontrolled rage, had shot up to a tremendous height, his black cloak flowing from him like night itself draping over the city. For Sam had caught him neatly. If he responded that he did intend for Sam to win, then Sam perforce must go free. And if he responded that he had not so intended, then Sam won anyway.

Glaring down from his great height, Satan directed an awful gaze upon Sam Shay.

"This is an ill night's work you have done!" he cried, in a voice that shook with rage, so that the skyscrapers near by trembled a bit, and the next day's papers carried an item concerning a small earthquake. "Hear me well, Sam Shay! From this moment onward, never shall you win another wager! All the forces of hell will be marshalled to prevent you."

Then, while Sam still gaped upward in dismay, the great figure faded from sight. A vast blast of hot air fanned past Sam, singeing the leaves of the nearest trees. He heard a distant clanging sound, as of a metal gate closing. After that all was quiet as it had been before.

Sam Shay stood in thought for several minutes, and then realized he still was fingering the ring Shannon Malloy had returned to him. He laughed, in something of relief.

"Glory!" he said aloud. "I've been standing here dreaming, while my mind wandered. If I'm to have nightmares, I'd best have them in bed."

And he hurried homeward, stopping by the way only long enough to buy the next day's racing form.

By morning Sam had half forgotten his queer bemusement of the evening before. But that Shannon had dismissed him and returned his ring he remembered all too well. The bit of gold seemed heavy in his pocket as the weight that lay on his heart, so that he set about choosing his wagers for the day's racing with a gloomy mind.

It was perhaps this gloom that made it harder than was customary for him to make a choice. Usually his intuition made quick decision. But today he labored long, and was only half satisfied when he had finished marking down his picks.

Then, having breakfasted, with Shannon Malloy's face coming betwixt him and his coffee, he rode out to the track. Today he desired action, crowds, noise, excitement to take his mind off Shannon's rejection of him. So that the pushing throngs about the mutuel [2] windows, the crowd murmur that rose to a shrill ululation [3] as the horses burst from the barrier, the heart-tightening sensation as they turned into the home stretch all fitted well into his mood.

And he was feeling better when, his tickets tucked inside his pocket, he stood

[2] MUTUEL—Pari-mutuel; system of betting on horses. Window where bets are made.

[3] ULULATION (ūl′û·lā′shŭn)—Literally, howling; here, shouting and cheering.

with the rest and watched the leaders in the first swing 'round the turn. He was well pleased to note his choice to the fore by half a dozen lengths, when something happened. Perhaps the nag put its hoof into a pocket in the track. Perhaps it broke stride, or merely tired. At all events it faltered, slowed as though the Devil himself had it by the tail—now why had that precise comparison flashed across his mind then, Sam Shay wondered—and was beaten to the finish by a neck.

Sam tore up his tickets and scattered them to the breeze. He was not distressed. There were six races yet to come, and his pockets were well filled with money.

But when in the second his pick threw its jockey rounding the three-quarters pole and in the lead, and when in the third a saddle girth broke just as the jockey was lifting his mount for a winning surge, Sam Shay began to whistle a bit beneath his breath.

It was queer. It was decidedly queer, and he did not like it in the least. And when in the fourth, just as it was in the clear, his choice swerved and cut across the nag behind it, thus being disqualified, Sam's whistle grew more tuneless. He sniffed, and sniffed again. Yes, it was there—the faintest whiff of sulphur somewhere about. In a most meditative mood Sam purchased a single two-dollar ticket for the fifth.

The ticket, as he had been unhappily convinced would be the case, proved a poor investment, his horse throwing a shoe at the far turn and pulling up last, limping badly.

Sam's whistle dropped until it was quite inaudible. He made his way toward the paddock and stood close as they led the winded horses out. As his choice passed he sniffed, strongly. And this time there was the slightest touch of brimstone mixed with the smell of sulphur.

Walking with a slow pace that did not in any way reflect the churning of his thoughts, Sam Shay returned to the grandstand and in the minutes before the next race was run reflected fast and furiously. Already his pockets, so thickly lined but an hour before, were well-nigh empty. And apprehension was beginning to sit, a tiny cloud, on Sam's brow.

This time he bought no ticket. But he sought out an individual with whom he had had dealings, and stood beside him as the race was run. The ponies were streaming around the three-quarter pole and into the stretch, with forty lengths and half a dozen horses separating the first nag from the last, when Sam spoke suddenly.

"Ten dollars," said he to his acquaintance, "to a dime that Seven doesn't win."

The bookie[4] gave him an odd glance. For Seven was the trailer, forty lengths behind and losing distance steadily. Any mortal eye could see she couldn't win, and it came to him Sam might be daft.

"Twenty dollars!" said Samuel Shay. "To a five-cent piece!"

They were odds not to be resisted, and the bookie nodded.

"Taken!" he agreed, and the words were scarce out of his mouth before Seven put on a burst of speed. She seemed to rise into the air with the very rapidity of her motion. Her legs churned. And she

[4] BOOKIE—Person who makes a business of betting other people's money on horse races.

whisked forward so fast her astonished jockey was but an ace from being blown out of the saddle by the very rush of air. Closing the gap in a manner quite unbelievable, she came up to the leaders and, with a scant yard to the finish, shot ahead to win.

The crowd was too dazed even to roar. The judges gathered at once in frowning conference. But nothing amiss with Seven's equipment could be found—no electric batteries or other illegal contrivances—so at last her number was posted.

Sam Shay paid over the twenty dollars, while his acquaintance goggled at him. He would have asked questions, but Sam was in no mood for conversation. He moved away and sought a seat. There he pondered.

There could no longer be any doubt. His dream of the evening before had been no dream. It was Satan himself he had met face to face in the park, and Satan was having his vengeance for being bested. Sam could not call to mind the name of any other man in history who had outwitted the Devil without ruing it,[5] and it was plain he was not to be the exception.

Wagering was Sam's life and livelihood, as Satan had well known. And if Sam was never to win another bet— He swallowed hard at the thought. Not only would he have lost Shannon Malloy for naught, but he would even be forced to the indignity of earning his living by the strength of his hands, he who had lived by his wits so pleasantly for so long.

It was a sobering reflection. But for

[5] RUING IT—Regretting it.

the moment no helpful scheme would come. Just before the warning bell for the last race of the day, however, Sam rose with alacrity. He counted his money. Aside from carfare back to town, he had just fourteen dollars upon him. Seven two-dollar tickets—and in the last there was a field of seven!

Sam chuckled and bought seven tickets to win, one on each of the entries. Then, feeling somewhat set up, he found a position of vantage. Now, he said beneath his breath, let's see the Devil himself keep you from having a winning ticket this time, Samuel Shay! And complacently he watched his seven horses get off to a good start.

The race proceeded normally toward the half, and then to the three-quarters, with nothing untoward come about. Sam chuckled some more, for if he cashed a ticket on this race then Satan had been bested again, and his curse on Sam's wagering broken.

But the chuckle came too soon. As the seven turned into the stretch, into a sky that had been cerulean [6] blue leaped a storm cloud purple and black. From the cloud a bolt of lightning sped downward, in a blinding flash, to strike among the branches of an ancient elm which stood beside the grandstand near the finish line. A horrid thunderclap deafened the throng. The elm tottered. Then it toppled and fell across the track, so that the seven jockeys were just able to pull up their mounts in time to avoid plunging into it.

And as sudden as it had come, the storm cloud was gone.

[6] CERULEAN (sê·rōō′lê·ăn)—A deep, clear blue.

But obviously there could be no winner of the last race. The perplexed and shaken stewards hurriedly declared it no race, and announced that all bets would be refunded. Sam received his money back—but that was not winning. And with the bills thrust into his coat he gloomily returned to his lodgings to devote more thought to this matter. For it was plain the Devil had meant what he had said—Sam would never win another wager. And with all the myriad [7] hosts of hell arrayed against him, Sam did not see what he could do about it.

But the Shays were never a quitter stock. Though Beelzebub and all his myrmidons [8] opposed him, Sam was of no mind to turn to honest labor without giving the Devil a run for his money. So in the days that followed, Sam with dogged resolution, did not cease his efforts to make a wager he could win. And his endeavors were a source of some concern in hell.

It was on an afternoon two weeks perhaps after the fateful meeting between Satan and Sam Shay that the Devil recalled the matter to his mind and pressed a button summoning his chief lieutenant to make report. Whisking from his private laboratory, where he was engaged in a delicate experiment leading toward the creation of a brand new and improved form of sin, his head assistant covered seven million miles in no time at all and deposited himself in Satan's presence, still scorching from the speed at which he had come.

[7] MYRIAD—Numberless.

[8] MYRMIDONS (mûr′mĭ·dŏns)—Originally the name of people in Greece who followed Achilles in the Trojan War; faithful followers.

The Devil, seated behind a desk of basalt,[9] frowned upon him.

"I wish," he stated, "to know if my orders concerning the mortal y-clept [10] Sam Shay have been carried out."

"To the letter, Infernal Highness," his lieutenant replied, with a slight air of reserve.

"He has not won a wager since I pronounced my curse upon him?"

"Not of the most inconsequential kind."

"He is thoroughly miserable?"

"Completely so."

"He is in such despair he might even commit suicide, and so place himself in our hands?"

The other was silent. Satan's voice took on sharpness.

"He is *not* in despair?"

"He is in a very low frame of mind indeed," his chief assistant replied with reluctance. "But there is no notion of suicide in his mind. He is defiant. And troublesome in the extreme, I must add."

"Troublesome?" The three-billion-bulb chandelier overhead rattled. "How can a mere mortal be troublesome to the hosts of hell? Kindly explain yourself."

The tips of his lieutenant's bat wings quivered with inward nervousness, and absently he plucked a loose scale from his chest. But summoning his resolution, he answered.

"He is a persistent mortal, this Sam Shay," he replied humbly. "Although your infernal curse has been passed upon him, he refuses to be convinced he cannot evade it. He is constantly scheming to get around the fiat [11] by means of trickery and verbal quibbling. And I have had to assign a good many of my best and most resourceful workers to keep a twenty-four-hour watch on Sam Shay to see he does not succeed. Let me explain.

"Last week, having already tried some hundreds of wagers of various kinds, he offered to bet an acquaintance it would not rain before noon. The wager was the merest quibble of a bet, for it then lacked but ten seconds of the hour, the sun was shining in a cloudless sky, and in addition the Weather Bureau had actually predicted storm.

"Sam Shay, however, got his gamble accepted by promising to spend double his winnings, if he won, on strong drink for his companion. A completely specious [12] wager if ever one was made. Nevertheless, had it not rained before the hour of noon, technically he would have been the winner of a bet, and so the letter of your hellish curse would have been violated.

"So, upon the notice of merest seconds, I had to call two hundred and eighty workers away from urgent duty in Proselytizing,[13] to borrow on an instant's notice another hundred from Punishment, to take a score of my best laboratory technicians off Research, and rush them all to the spot. Between them they managed to divert a storm that was raging over Ohio and scheduled to cause a flood estimated to produce for us a job-lot of a hundred and eighty souls, whisking it to cover New England within the time-limit.

[9] BASALT—A black rock of volcanic origin.

[10] Y-CLEPT (archaic)—Called, known by the name of.

[11] FIAT (fī'ăt)—Decree.

[12] SPECIOUS—Having the appearance of rightness and truth.

[13] PROSELYTIZING—The making of converts; here, to Satan's cause.

"But the affair caused widespread comment, threw us off schedule and has disrupted my entire force, due to the necessity for keeping a large emergency squad upon twenty-four-hour duty in constant readiness for any other such calls. And there have been dozens of them. Simply dozens!"

A drop of sweat rolled down the unhappy demon's brow, dissolving in steam.

"That's only a sample," he said earnestly. "This Sam Shay has scores of such tricks up his sleeves. Only yesterday he was attempting to win a wager at the race track, and his efforts kept us busy the entire afternoon. In the fifth race he made such a complicated series of bets as to the relative positions in which the various horses would finish that my most trusted aide completely lost track of them. He had to call on me personally at the last moment, and since one of the wagers was that the race itself wouldn't be finished, the only solution I could hit upon in time was to have all the horses finish in a dead heat,[14] save for the one Sam Shay had bet upon to win.

"This one, in order to confound the fellow, I was forced to remove entirely from the race and set down in Australia, so that none of Shay's various stipulations concerning it could come true. But the talk caused by a seven-horse dead heat, together with the complete disappearance of one of the beasts and its jockey, caused a considerable stir.

"Taken in conjunction with the storm I had to arrange, and a number of similar matters, it has started a religious revival. People are flocking into the churches, undoing some of our best work. So, Your Infernal Highness, if only we could overlook one or two of Sam Shay's more difficult wagers, it would make things much easier to—"

The crash of Satan's hoofs upon the adamantine tiling cut him short.

"Never! I have put my curse upon this Shay! It must be carried out to the letter. 'Tend to it!"

"Yes, Prince of Evil," his head assistant squeaked, and being a prudent demon hurled himself away and across the seven million miles of space to his laboratory so swiftly that he struck with such force at the other end he was lame for a month. And never again did he dare mention the matter.

But of all this Sam Shay had no inkling. He was immersed in his own problems. Having failed in every wager he had made, however difficult to lose, he was in a depressed state of mind.

His resources were coming to an end. There were but a few dollars left in his pockets and none in his bank account. Shannon Malloy refused to see him. He had not won a wager since the night he had met the Devil, and he was so low in his mind that several times he had caught himself glancing through the Help Wanted sections of the papers.

Upon this particular day he was so sunk in despair that it was the middle of the afternoon, and he had not once tried the Devil's mettle to see if this time he could slip a winning wager past the demonic forces on watchful guard all about him. It was a day cut and tailored to his mood. The sky was lowering gray and rain whipped down out of the north as if

[14] DEAD HEAT—A single race in which all contestants reach the goal at the same instant, so that none wins.

each drop had personal anger against the earth upon which it struck. And Sam Shay sat in his room, staring out at the storm, as close to despair as it had ever been his misfortune to come.

At last he bestirred himself; it was not in the blood of a Shay to sit thus forever wrapped in gray gloom. He found his hat and ulster,[15] and with heavy step made his way out and down the street to a cozy bar and grill where perhaps a cheery companion might lighten his mood.

Ensconced in a corner where a fireplace glowed he found Tim Malloy, who was by way of being Shannon's brother, a round, merry little man who was the merrier because a mug of dark [16] stood upon the table before him. Tim Malloy greeted him with words of cheer and Sam sat himself down, answering as nearly in kind as he might. He ordered himself a mug of dark too, and made inquiry concerning Shannon.

"Why, as to that," Tim Malloy said, draining off half his mug, "sometimes of a night I hear her crying behind her locked door. And—" he drained off the rest of his dark—"she never did that before she gave you back your ring, Sam."

"Have another," Sam invited, feeling, suddenly, somewhat heartened. "Then mayhap she might take back the ring if I asked her, you think?" he asked, hope in his tone.

Tim Malloy accepted the dark, but after dipping into it shook his head, a mustache of foam on his lip.

"Never while you're a betting man, Sam, and that'll be forever," he said, "unless some wondrous force stronger than she is makes her do it. Not though she's unhappy the rest of her life from sending you away."

Sam sighed.

"Would it make any difference if she knew I lost all the wagers I make now?" he asked.

"Not so much as a pin-point of difference," Tim Malloy answered. "Not so much as a pin-point. To change the subject, how long will it keep raining, would you say?"

"All day, I suppose," Sam said, in a gloom again. "And all night too. I've no doubt. Though I could stop it raining in five minutes if I'd a mind to."

"Could you so?" Tim Malloy said, interested. "Let's see how it goes, Sam. Just for curiosity's sake."

Sam Shay shrugged.

"Bet me a dollar it'll stop raining within five minutes," he said. "And I'll bet the same it'll not. But since it'll be costing me a dollar to show, you must promise to spend it back again treating me."

"Fair's fair," Tim Malloy answered prompt. "And I promise. Then, Sam, I bet you a dollar it'll stop raining inside five minutes."

Lackadaisically Sam accepted and they laid their wagers out upon the table. And sure enough, within the five minutes the storm clouds overhead abruptly whisked away. The blue sky appeared, the sun shone, and it was as if the storm had never been.

"Now that's a curious thing, Sam," Tim Malloy said, eyes wide, as he ordered up more dark. "And if you could do that any time you wished, your fortune would be made."

[15] ULSTER—Overcoat. [16] DARK—Dark beer.

"Oh, I can do it," Sam sighed, disinterested. "Fair to storm and storm to fair, I need but wager on it to make it come the opposite of my bet. For that matter, any event I make a gamble on will come out the opposite, be it what it may. It's a curse laid upon me, Tim."

"Is it now?" said Tim Malloy, and his eyes grew wider. "And by whom would the curse be laid, Sam Shay?"

Sam leaned forward and whispered in his ear, and Tim Malloy's eyes bade fair to start from their sockets.

"Draw in a deep breath," Sam said, nodding. "Sniff hard, Tim. You'll see."

Tim Malloy sniffed long and deep, and awe crept upon his features.

"Sulphur!" he whispered. "Sulphur and brimstone!"

Sam but nodded and went on drinking his dark. Tim Malloy, though, stretched out a hand and put it upon his arm.

"Sam," he said, voice hoarse, "you have never heard that there's people willing to pay good money to insure the weather'll be as they want it upon a certain day? Have you never heard of insuring against storms, Sam, and against accidents, sickness, twins and such misfortunes? And insuring isn't really betting. It's but a business—a legitimate, money-making business."

Sam stopped drinking his dark. He put his mug upon the table with a bang, and upon his face there came a look.

"So it is," he said, struck by the sudden thought. "So it is!"

"Sam," Tim Malloy said, emotion in his tone, "let us take but a single example. This Sunday coming the Loyal Sons of Saint Patrick parade. Suppose, then, the Loyal Sons said to you, 'Sam, we want to insure it does not storm this Sunday coming. Here's twenty dollars insurance money against rain. If it storms, now, you must pay us five hundred, but if it's fair, you keep the twenty.'

"And then suppose, Sam, you came to me and, 'Tim,' you'd say, 'I want to make a bet. And the bet is one dollar against another dollar that this Sunday coming it will rain.' Whereupon I'd say to you, 'Sam, I accept the wager. One dollar to one dollar that it does not rain this Sunday coming.'

"And as you are doomed to lose your gamble, it does not rain; you keep the twenty dollars paid you by the Loyal Sons, and your profit, Sam, your fair profit on a straightforward business deal which no one could call gambling would be—"

"Nineteen dollars!" Sam said, much moved. "Nineteen dollars profit, Tim, and no wager involved. And you say there are many people wanting such insurance?"

"Thousands of them," said Tim Malloy. "Thousands upon thousands of them. And there's no reason why you shouldn't insure them against anything they wish—seeing as you're backed, one might say, by all the resources of a tremendous big firm."

Sam Shay stood up, and in his eyes there was a light.

"Tim," he said, in a voice that rang, "here is twenty dollars. Rent me an office and have a sign painted saying Samuel Shay, Insurance. The biggest sign that can be managed. And here, Tim, is a dollar. That dollar I bet you Shannon will not say 'yes' to me a moment hence when I call upon her. Do you take the wager?"

"I take it, Sam," agreed Tim Malloy, but already Sam was striding out, and in scarce a minute was standing in the Malloy living room, large and masterful, while Shannon, who had tried to hold the door shut against him, stared at him with blazing eyes.

"Sam Shay," she cried hotly, "I won't see you!"

"You cannot help seeing me," Sam replied with tenderness, "for I am standing here before you."

"Then I won't look at you!" cried Shannon, and shut her eyes.

"In that case you must take the consequences," said Sam, and stepping forward, kissed her so that Shannon's eyes flew open again.

"Sam Shay," she exclaimed, "I—"

"I'll bet a dollar," Sam interrupted her, "you're going to say you hate me."

It was indeed what Shannon had been about to say, but now some perverse demon seemed to seize her tongue.

"I'm not!" she denied. "I was going to say I love you." And having said it, she stared at Sam as if she could not believe her ears.

"Then, Shannon, darling," Sam Shay asked, "will you take back my ring and marry me? And I'll bet another dollar you're going to say no."

And "no" it was that Shannon tried to say. But once again it was as if a contrary devil had her tongue.

"Indeed I'm not," she declared, to her own consternation. "For I say yes, and I will."

With which Sam swept her into his arms and kissed her again, so soundly she had no more time to wonder at the way her tongue had twisted. Indeed, she was forced to believe it was some strange power in Sam himself that had drawn the words from her. And on this point Sam wisely refrained from ever correcting her.

Thus they were married, and at this moment Sam Shay's insurance business is prospering beyond belief. Money is flowing in from all sides, and being a prudent man Sam has arranged his affairs in excellent order. He has wagered with Tim Malloy, his junior partner, that he and Shannon will not live in good health to be ninety-nine each, while Tim has wagered they will. Sam has likewise bet that he and Shannon will be desperately unhappy, Tim gambling to the contrary. Finally Sam has gambled that they will not have ten fine, strapping children, six boys and four girls, and Tim has placed his money that they will.

So sin continues to decline as Sam's business grows, and Sam himself sleeps soundly of nights. And if there is sometimes the faintest smell of brimstone and sulphur about the house, as though from much coming and going of harassed demons, no one in the household minds it, not even Dion, youngest of the ten young Shays.

◇◇◇◇◇◇◇◇◇◇◇◇◇◇◇◇◇◇◇◇◇◇◇◇◇◇◇◇◇◇◇◇◇

FOR DISCUSSION

1. What was Sam Shay's great weakness? All things considered, do you blame Shannon Malloy for returning Sam's ring?

2. Describe Sam's meeting with Satan. Is Satan's innocent and friendly approach true to life?

3. What does the author mean on page 113 when he says that "for this was a wager

that had stumped many eminent philosophers in centuries past"?

4. What was the outcome of the three wagers Sam made with Satan? How did His Satanic Majesty avenge himself?

5. A smell of sulphur and brimstone persisted whenever Sam lost a bet. What did this indicate? How did Sam's series of wagers affect the good order of the infernal regions?

6. How did Sam solve his difficulties both with Satan and Shannon Malloy? In the final clause do you find the author indulging his sense of humor? At whose expense?

WORD FAMILIES

A *word-family* is a group of words having the same parent or root. There are hundreds of such word-families in our language. Many of them are derived from Latin. For example:

1. *Decline* (page 122), *incline, recline,* These words stem from the Latin root *clino,* which means to lean or bend.
   - *a.* decline—to lean *down* or *away* from. Accidents *decline* in frequency; one *declines* an invitation. Would you know why the *declensions* in your Latin grammar are so named?
   - *b.* incline—to lean *toward.* You might say, "John is *inclined* to be quick-tempered." What would *inclination* mean?
   - *c.* recline—to lean *back.* A hospital patient *reclines* in bed.

2. *Circumspect, inspect, respect, retrospect, suspect.* Here is a well-known family derived from the Latin root *spicere,* to look.
   - *a.* circumspect—to look *around.* A *circumspect* person looks about him before choosing a course of action; the adjective describes therefore a prudent or cautious individual.
   - *b.* inspect—to look *into.* You will know the meaning here. Make up a sentence to illustrate it.
   - *c.* retrospect—to look *back.* In *retrospect* the summer vacation seemed all too short.
   - *d.* respect—to look *back,* but in a more general sense than above. Tom did not *respect* his employer. (He did not look back to him with esteem.)
   - *e.* suspect—to look *under.* The derived meaning here is very near the word's literal force. I *suspected* that he was not telling the truth. (I looked under his words for the truth.)

EVIDENCE OF SATAN AT WORK

1. If you have read this story closely, you will have discovered many traces of Satan. The effects of his presence are always described as unpleasant and frequently destructive. You know Satan has been there! For instance, the author uses such details as these:

"A strong pain shot up Sam's arm, a tingling, numbing sensation that extended to the shoulder."

"A vast blast of hot air . . . singeing the leaves of the nearest tree . . ."

"At all events it faltered, slowed as though the Devil himself had it by the tail . . ."

Find as many details as you can which the author has used to show the characteristics of Satan.

2. In the selection just read, Satan tried to win Sam's soul through a wager. Satan lost. You will find a kind of parallel to this story in the opera *Faust.* Look up this opera and find the part Satan plays in tempting Faust and whether the latter saved or lost his soul.

RELATED READING

For a story with a similar theme, read Stephen Benét's play, "The Devil and Daniel Webster." In *The Screwtape Letters,* C. E. Lewis describes with rare insight Screwtape's attempts to educate his infernal nephew, Wormwood, in the destruction of souls.

To enjoy thoroughly the three following poems, read them aloud. The first one depends on a play on words for its humorous effect. "It's so true it's funny" expresses the reason why the second poem seems funnier with each new reading. To appreciate the dialogue in "Why Tigers Can't Climb," practice reading with much expression. Don't take any of these poems seriously. They are meant to give you a laugh.

Sage Counsel

ARTHUR T. QUILLER-COUCH

The lion is the beast to fight:
He leaps along the plain,
And if you run with all your might,
He runs with all his mane.
I'm glad I'm not a Hottentot,
But if I were, with outward *cal-lum*
I'd either faint upon the spot
Or hie me up a leafy *pal-lum.*

The chamois is the beast to hunt:
He's fleeter than the wind,
And when the chamois is in front
The hunter is behind.
The Tyrolese make famous cheese
And hunt the chamois o'er the *chaz-zums;*
I'd choose the former, if you please,
The precipices give me *spaz-zums.*

The polar bear will make a rug
Almost as white as snow:
But if he gets you in his hug,
He rarely lets you go.
And polar ice looks very nice,
With all the colors of a *pris-sum:*
But, if you'll follow my advice,
Stay home and learn your *catechis-sum.*

5. HOTTENTOT—African bushman.
6. *Cal-lum*—Calm.
8. *Pal-lum*—Palm.
9. CHAMOIS—Small goatlike antelope.
13. TYROLESE—Inhabitants of the Tyrol, a region in the Alps.
22. *Pris-sum*—Prism.

FOR DISCUSSION

Although this is a nonsense poem, it has at least a shred of sense. In this poem two different tricks make you laugh. What are they? One is in the fourth line; the other occurs twice in each stanza.

THE PUN

When words with the same sound but different meanings are used in place of each other, in order to get a laugh, you have a *pun*. In this poem the word *mane* is used as a pun. Another pun appears in this statement concerning the taking of the national census: "Everybody has a chance to become a national figure." In the next few days list the puns you hear or read. Decide which of those brought to class are the best.

YOUR OWN PLAY ON WORDS

Do you think you could add another bit of sage counsel to the poem? It shouldn't be too hard. For example, what advice would you give about bees, or dogs, or two-ton trucks? Try to use the two ways of getting laughs which are in this poem!

◇◇◇◇◇

The Vulture

HILAIRE BELLOC

The vulture eats between his meals,
And that's the reason why
He very, very rarely feels
As well as you or I.

His eye is dull, his head is bald,
His neck is growing thinner,
Oh, what a lesson for us all,
To only eat at dinner!

◇◇

FOR DISCUSSION

Besides its obvious humor, there *is* an idea in the poem. You have probably heard it time and time again. What is it? Do you think the poet wrote this piece because he wanted to express that idea, or because he wanted to have a little fun?

WORD MEANINGS CHANGE

The word *meal* (here's one word you *know!*) was originally an Anglo-Saxon word, *mael*, meaning *measure* or *appointed time*. What is the connection between this original meaning and the derived meaning it has today?

WRITING A POEM

How about trying to dash off a poem of your own—like this one? Take some piece of advice you've been hearing as far back as you can remember, like "Take your hat off when you enter the house," or "Say 'please' when you ask for anything." Next choose some animal that knows nothing about such rules of conduct. Piece the two together in eight lines. Presto! There she is! (If necessary, get a classmate to help.)

Why Tigers Can't Climb

ARTHUR GUITERMAN

This tale is of the Tiger and his Aunt, who is the Cat:
They dwelt among the jungles in the shade of Ararat,
The Cat was very clever, but the Tiger, he was slow;
He couldn't catch the Nilghau nor the heavy Buffalo;
His claws were long and pointed, but his wit was short and blunt; 5
He begged his Wise Relation to instruct him how to hunt.

The Cat on velvet pattens stole along the quiet hill:
"Now this," she whispered, "Nephew, is the way to stalk your Kill."
The Cat drew up her haunches on the mossy forest couch:
"And this," she said, "my Nephew, is the proper way to crouch." 10
She hurtled through the shadows like a missile from a sling:
"And that, my loving Nephew, is the only way to spring!"

Oh, hungry was the Nephew, and the Aunt was sleek and plump;
The Tiger at his Teacher made his first apprentice Jump;
He did it very ably, but the Cat, more quick than he, 15
Escaped his clutching talons and ran up a cedar tree,
And purred upon the Snarler from the bough on which she sat,
"How glad I am, my Nephew, that I didn't teach you that!"

And, since that Curtailed Lesson in the Rudiments of Crime,
The most ambitious Tiger hasn't learned the way to climb. 20

2. ARARAT (ăr′ȧ·răt)—A mountain in Turkey.
4. NILGHAU (nĭl′gô)—Large antelope of India.
7. PATTENS—Shoes.

FOR DISCUSSION

Were you surprised by the quick twist at the end of the story? How many of the stories which you've read this year have given you enjoyment because, among other good things, they had a surprise at the end?

WORD STUDY

1. Another word of interesting derivation is *missile*. It comes from the Latin verb *mitto, mittere, misi, missum*. On which of the Latin principal parts is the English word built? Figure out the English meaning

from your knowledge of Latin. Trace the meaning of each of the following English words to its Latin origin: *mission, missionary, missive.*

2. *Apprentice:* The meaning of this word reaches far back into history. Look the word up in the dictionary, and find out with what period of history it is associated.

3. Even in ancient Rome candidates for public office went about soliciting votes. This activity was given the name *ambitio, a going about. Ambitio* was derived from *ambire, to go about,* formed from *amb-* (about) and *ire* (to go). Since this activity indicated a desire for honor or power, the word *ambitio* came to mean the desire for official honors. This word was borrowed in France and England as *ambition,* and its meaning broadened to denote the *earnest desire for preferment or achievement.*

USE YOUR IMAGINATION

Hollywood cartoonists are clamoring for more material like this poem. Suppose that you have contracted to provide them with ten scenarios telling of ridiculous situations and clever animals. Choose one of the many suggestions offered by the class, and begin writing. Perhaps you have a duck teaching all her tricks of diet and flight to her friend, the chicken. But for some reason the chicken, when educated, tries to dominate the duck—who coolly *swims* out of danger, safe with the one trick the chicken hasn't learned. There are hundreds of ideas for stories, but limit yourself to one.

RELATED READING

While you're in the mood, read *The Laughing Muse* by the same author.

◇◇◇◇◇

Though usually identified as a writer of serious prose, Heywood Broun exhibits much charm when he unbends in a lighter vein. Here is an example.

STUNG!

HEYWOOD BROUN

I love nature, but I do think it can be overdone. There is so much sympathy for dumb animals along Hunting Ridge that human rights are neglected. Yesterday, for instance, I was stung by a bee and everybody around blamed me. There was much indignation when I killed him, even though I exhibited the bite and pleaded self-defense.

They all say that bees were never known to adopt aggressively hostile action. The theory was that I must have frightened him. Indeed, the community sentiment appeared to be that I had nagged and bullied the insect until he lashed out in righteous anger.

The truth of the matter is that I didn't do a thing to that bee up to the time I killed him. No honest witness can testify that there were sounds of an altercation before the blow was struck.

At the time of his attack I was sitting on a rock very quietly engaged in fishing. The bee persisted in bumping into me. Round about were acres and acres of land unoccupied by man or beast. Within twenty yards there lay a large field of clover. It is true that the bee seemed to be flying in that direction, but he could hardly have asserted with any justice that I had him completely stymied from his destination.

It would have been a simple matter for him to have flown around me or over my head. As far as I know, there is nothing in the tradition of bees which compels them invariably to fly in a straight line. It's crows who are committed to keeping faith with Euclid.[1] And as a matter of fact, even crows do turn heretical and circle around at times.

But this bee was bullheaded and nothing would do him except to fly straight through me, since I bisected the straight line which he planned to follow. I don't know whether he thought I would eventually part like the Red Sea or whether he purposed tunneling, but three times he flew bang against the upper righthand side of my chest.

Not until after the third collision did I speak to him at all, and then it was in the mildest sort of way which should not have caused him either anger or fear.

What I said was, "If I were you I wouldn't do that any more."

And at that he flew into a terrific rage or panic and stung me. Upon that instant, I confess, a primitive instinct overpowered me. I am not going to pretend that I didn't know my own strength or that I merely tried to wound him. I struck to kill and under the same circumstances I would do it again. A bee is all right as long as he behaves himself and I hope the issue will not arise again.

In order to avoid confusion in future, I shall have my chest tattooed in large and legible letters reading, "No Thoroughfare."

[1] EUCLID—An ancient Greek geometer (300 B.C.); reference here is to his statement that a straight line is the shortest distance between two points.

◇◇◇◇◇◇◇◇◇◇◇◇◇◇◇◇◇◇◇◇◇◇◇◇◇◇◇◇◇◇

FOR DISCUSSION

1. Why is the author's choice of subject and title good for a humorous essay?
2. Do you see any moral to be drawn from the piece? What is its purpose?

LATIN AIDS TO MEANING

1. "They all say . . . *aggressively* hostile action." How does *ag-gressive* differ in meaning from *re-gressive* and *pro-gressive?*
2. From the Latin word *hostis, enemy,* comes the adjective *hostile.* What word for *unfriendly* is derived from the other Latin word for *enemy, inimicus?*
3. *Bisect*—(Latin, *bi* and *secare, to cut*) —means to cut into two parts. What other words composed of the prefix *bi-* and a word root can you suggest? Do not confuse *bi-* with *bio-* the prefix meaning *life.*

HOW THE BEE TOLD IT

With Broun's mock seriousness try writing the same episode as told by the bee or the bee's surviving brother.

RELATED READING

Christopher Morley in his book, *Mince Pie,* has an amusing piece called "Bullied by the Birds."

Fantastic is the word for this poem. By the time its magic spell is cast, you can't tell whether you or the sailors have been drinking the grog.

Forty Singing Seamen

ALFRED NOYES

I

Across the seas of Wonderland to Mogadore we plodded,
Forty singing seamen in an old black barque,
And we landed in the twilight where a Polyphemus nodded
With his battered moon-eye winking red and yellow through the dark!
For his eye was growing mellow, 5
Rich and ripe and red and yellow,
As was time, since old Ulysses made him bellow in the dark!
Cho.—Since Ulysses bunged his eye up with a pine-torch in the dark!

II

Were they mountains in the gloaming or the giant's ugly shoulders
Just beneath the rolling eyeball, with its bleared and vinous glow, 10
Red and yellow o'er the purple of the pines among the boulders
And the shaggy horror brooding on the sullen slopes below,
Were they pines among the boulders
Or the hair upon his shoulders?
We were only simple seamen, so of course we didn't know. 15
Cho.—We were simple singing seamen, so of course we couldn't know.

III

But we crossed a plain of poppies, and we came upon a fountain
Not of water, but of jewels, like a spray of leaping fire;
And behind it, in an emerald glade, beneath a golden mountain,
There stood a crystal palace, for a sailor to admire; 20
For a troop of ghosts came round us,
Which with leaves of bay they crowned us,
Then with grog they well nigh drowned us, to the depth of our desire!
Cho.—And 'twas very friendly of them, as a sailor can admire!

1. MOGADORE—African seaport on the Atlantic coast. 3. POLYPHEMUS—A one-eyed giant.
7. ULYSSES—Grecian king and hero who gouged out the eye of a one-eyed giant with a burning stick, and so escaped being eaten.
10. VINOUS—Wine-like. 23. GROG—A sailor's term for any intoxicating drink.

IV

There was music all about us, we were growing quite forgetful 25
We were only singing seamen from the dirt of London-town,
Though the nectar that we swallowed seemed to vanish half regretful
As if we wasn't good enough to take such vittles down,
When we saw a sudden figure,
Tall and black as any digger, 30
Like the devil—only bigger—drawing near us with a frown!
Cho.—Like the devil—but much bigger—and he wore a golden crown!

V

And "What's all this?" he growls at us! With dignity we chaunted,
"Forty singing seamen, sir, as won't be put upon!"
"What? Englishmen?" he cries. "Well, if ye don't mind being haunted, 35
Faith, you're welcome to my palace; I'm the famous Prester John!
Will ye walk into my palace?
I don't bear 'ee any malice!
One and all ye shall be welcome in the halls of Prester John!"
Cho.—So we walked into the palace and the halls of Prester John! 40

VI

Now the door was one great diamond and the hall a hollow ruby—
Big as Beachy Head, my lads, nay bigger by a half!
And I sees the mate wi' mouth agape, a-staring like a booby,
And the skipper close behind him, with his tongue out like a calf!
Now the way to take it rightly 45
Was to walk along politely
Just as if you didn't notice—so I couldn't help but laugh!
Cho.—For they both forgot their manners and the crew was bound to laugh!

VII

But he took us through his palace and, my lads, as I'm a sinner,
We walked into an opal like a sunset-colored cloud. 50
"My dining-room," he says, and, quick as light we saw a dinner
Spread before us by the fingers of a hidden fairy crowd;
And the skipper, swaying gently
After dinner, murmurs faintly,
"I looks to-wards you, Prester John, you've done us very proud!" 55
Cho.—And we drank his health with honors, for he *done* us *very* proud!

36. PRESTER JOHN—A legendary medieval priest and king.
42. BEACHY HEAD—A headland in Sussex, England, 575 feet high, with a lighthouse 142 feet high erected at its base.

VIII

Then he walks us to his garden where we sees a feathered demon
  Very splendid and important on a sort of spicy tree!
"That's the Phoenix," whispers Prester, "which all eddicated seamen
  Knows the only one existent, and *he's* waiting for to flee! 60
    When his hundred years expire
    Then he'll set hisself a-fire
  And another from his ashes rise most beautiful to see!"
Cho.—With wings of rose and emerald most beautiful to see!

IX

Then he says, "In yonder forest there's a little silver river, 65
  And whosoever drinks of it, his youth shall never die!
The centuries go by, but Prester John endures forever
  With his music in the mountains and his magic on the sky!
    While *your* hearts are growing colder,
    While your world is growing older, 70
  There's a magic in the distance, where the sea-line meets the sky."
Cho.—It shall call to singing seamen till the fount o' song is dry!

59. PHOENIX—A mythical bird like an eagle, with red and gold plumage.

X

So we thought we'd up and seek it, but that forest fair defied us.
First a crimson leopard laughs at us most horrible to see.
Then a sea-green lion came and sniffed and licked his chops and eyed us, 75
While a red and yellow unicorn was dancing round a tree!
We was trying to look thinner
Which was hard, because our dinner
Must ha' made us very tempting to a cat o' high degree!
Cho.—Must ha' made us very tempting to the whole menarjeree! 80

XI

So we scuttled from that forest and across the poppy meadows
Where the awful shaggy horror brooded o'er us in the dark!
And we pushes out from shore again a-jumping at our shadows,
And pulls away most joyful to the old black barque!
And home again we plodded 85
While the Polyphemus nodded
With his battered moon-eye winking red and yellow through the dark,
Cho.—Oh, the moon above the mountains, red and yellow through the dark!

XII

Across the seas of Wonderland to London-town we blundered,
Forty singing seamen as was puzzled for to know 90
If the visions that we saw was caused by—here again we pondered—
A tipple in a vision forty thousand years ago.
Could the grog we *dreamt* we swallowed
Make us *dream* of all that followed?
We were only simple seamen, so of course we didn't know! 95
Cho.—We were simple singing seamen, so of course we could not know!

80. MENARJEREE—Menagerie, a collection of wild animals for exhibition.
92. TIPPLE—A stimulating non-alcoholic drink.

FOR DISCUSSION

1. The poet really let his imagination run wild in this poem. Can you cut away the trimmings, so that you have the plain story in a dozen sentences? For example, the basic idea of the first stanza would be: Forty sailors landed at evening on a strange shore.

2. Now that you know the story of the poem, reread it aloud to get its rhythm. To bear out its title, it should be read in a singsong fashion. The entire class should join in on the chorus. Various persons with light, medium, and heavy voices should read the other lines, as these voices fit the tone of the poem.

3. Decide to your own satisfaction the question in the last stanza.

4. Find the origin of the word "grog" by looking it up in a dictionary.

SPARKLING WORDS

Many of the lines in this poem sparkle

because the poet has used the names of precious stones to make a detail more colorful. With how many of these stones are you familiar? Distinguish their meanings carefully: *emerald, crystal, jewel, diamond, ruby, opal.* Discuss the images you see in the lines where these words are used.

SCENES FROM THE POEM

If you were to illustrate the most dramatic scenes in the poem, which would you choose? What caption would you put under each picture? Some students in class should try their hand at drawing the pictures which are suggested.

◇◇◇◇◇

The poem below is simply a picture painted with words. Read it with a lively imagination, so that all the words, especially the verbs, will make a vivid impression.

The Railway Train

EMILY DICKINSON

I like to see it lap the miles,
And lick the valleys up,
And stop to feed itself at tanks;
And then, prodigious, step

Around a pile of mountains, 5
And, supercilious, peer
In shanties by the sides of roads;
And then a quarry pare

To fit its sides, and crawl between,
Complaining all the while 10
In horrid, hooting stanza;
Then chase itself down hill

And neigh like Boanerges;
Then, punctual as a star,
Stop—docile and omnipotent— 15
At its own stable door.

13. BOANERGES (bō′ȧ·nûr′jēz)—A Hebrew name meaning "Sons of Thunder." The title was given to James and John. It is sometimes used to designate any loud-speaking orator.

FOR DISCUSSION

1. To what is the train compared? On what words is your answer based? The pictures are so vivid that you can follow the train right along and still see *the other thing,* too. Such picturesque comparisons as these are called either *similes* or *metaphors.* If the comparison is expressed with the words *like, as,* or *than,* it is called *simile;* otherwise

it is called *metaphor*. Which type of comparison is used more often in this poem? Which type of comparison is used in line 14 where the train is said to be "punctual as a star"?

2. From your experience with trains, does the description of this one seem true to life? Does a train ever seem to "lick the valleys up," "step around a pile of mountains," or "chase itself down hill"? If these descriptions strike you as inaccurate, suggest others more true to life and just as vivid. How does the word "complaining" fit in line 10?

THE STORY BEHIND THE WORD

An interesting story behind the word *supercilious* reveals that it literally means *eye-browish*. In Latin, *super* (*over*) and *cilium* (*eyelid*) formed *supercilium*, meaning *eyebrow*. Because raising the eyebrows is a habit of haughty people, *supercilium* came to mean *pride*, and the English *supercilious* has the meaning *proud*. Why is *supercilious* used to describe a *train?*

USING PICTURE VERBS

Can you see any likeness between an automobile and a mule? Between a bus and a greyhound? Try painting a picture with words, drawing a comparison between some mode of travel and an animal, as Emily Dickinson has done in her poem. When all in the class have finished reading their poems aloud, judge which has the most accurate and most picturesque description.

◇◇◇◇◇

Here is a tale you will read with interest and enjoyment. You cannot fail to appreciate its humor. But you cannot fail, either, to learn from it a simple truth about life. A story which is written to teach a lesson is called a fable or an allegory. Decide whether there is a lesson for you in Gawaine's experience with fighting the dragons.

THE FIFTY-FIRST DRAGON

HEYWOOD BROUN

Of all the pupils at the knight school Gawaine le Coeur-Hardy [1] was among the least promising. He was tall and sturdy, but his instructors soon discovered that he lacked spirit. He would hide in the woods when the jousting class was called, although his companions and members of the faculty sought to appeal to his better nature by shouting to him to come out and break his neck like a man. Even when they told him that the lances were padded, the horses no more than ponies, and the field unusually soft for late autumn, Gawaine refused to grow enthusiastic. The Headmaster and the Assistant

[1] GAWAINE LE COEUR-HARDY—Gawaine the Stout-Hearted.

Professor of Pleasaunce [2] were discussing the case one spring afternoon, and the Assistant Professor could see no remedy but expulsion.

"No," said the Headmaster, as he looked out at the purple hills which ringed the school, "I think I'll train him to slay dragons."

"He might be killed," objected the Assistant Professor.

"So he might," replied the Headmaster, brightly; "but," he added more soberly, "we must consider the greater good. We are responsible for the formation of this lad's character."

"Are the dragons particularly bad this year?" interrupted the Assistant Professor. This was characteristic. He always seemed restive when the head of the school began to talk ethics and the ideals of the institution.

"I've never known them worse," replied the Headmaster. "Up in the hills to the south last week they killed a number of peasants, two cows, and a prize pig. And if this dry spell holds there's no telling when they may start a forest fire simply by breathing around indiscriminately."

"Would any refund on the tuition fee be necessary in case of an accident to young Coeur-Hardy?"

"No," the principal answered judicially; "that's all covered in the contract. But as a matter of fact he won't be killed. Before I send him up in the hills I'm going to give him a magic word."

"That's a good idea," said the Professor. "Sometimes they work wonders."

From that day on Gawaine specialized in dragons. His course included both theory and practice. In the morning there were long lectures on the history, anatomy, manners, and customs of dragons. Gawaine did not distinguish himself in these studies. He had a marvelously versatile gift for forgetting things. In the afternoon he showed to better advantage, for then he would go down to the South Meadow and practice with a battle-axe. In this exercise he was truly impressive, for he had enormous strength as well as speed and grace. He even developed a deceptive display of ferocity. Old alumni say that it was a thrilling sight to see Gawaine charging across the field toward the dummy paper dragon which had been set up for his practice. As he ran he would brandish his axe and shout "A murrain on thee!" [3] or some other vivid bit of campus slang. It never took him more than one stroke to behead the dummy dragon.

Gradually his task was made more difficult. Paper gave way to papier-mâché [4] and finally to wood, but even the toughest of these dummy dragons had no terrors for Gawaine. One sweep of the axe always did the business. There were those who said that when the practice was protracted until dusk and the dragons threw long, fantastic shadows across the meadow, Gawaine did not charge so impetuously nor shout so loudly. It is possible there was malice in this charge. At any rate, the Headmaster decided by the end of June that it was time for the test. Only the night before, a dragon had come close to the school grounds and had eaten

[2] PLEASAUNCE—Literally, "pleasure," here, "sports."

[3] A MURRAIN ON THEE!—"A plague on thee," a reputed war-cry of the knights of old.

[4] PAPIER-MÂCHÉ (pȧ·pyā′ mä·shā′)—Pulped paper molded into shape while moist.

some of the lettuce from the garden. The faculty decided that Gawaine was ready. They gave him a diploma and a new battle-axe, and the Headmaster summoned him to a private conference.

"Sit down," said the Headmaster. "Have a cigarette."

Gawaine hesitated.

"Oh, I know it's against the rules," said the Headmaster; "but, after all, you have received your preliminary degree. You are no longer a boy. You are a man. Tomorrow you will go out into the world—the great world of achievement."

Gawaine took a cigarette. The Headmaster offered him a match, but he produced one of his own and began to puff away with a dexterity which quite amazed the principal.

"Here you have learned the theories of life," continued the Headmaster, resuming the thread of his discourse; "but, after all, life is not a matter of theories. Life is a matter of facts. It calls on the young and the old alike to face these facts, even though they are hard and sometimes unpleasant. Your problem, for example, is to slay dragons."

"They say that those dragons down in the south wood are five hundred feet long," ventured Gawaine, timorously.

"Stuff and nonsense!" said the Headmaster. "The curate saw one last week from the top of Arthur's Hill. The dragon was sunning himself down in the valley. The curate didn't have an opportunity to look at him very long because he felt it was his duty to hurry back to make a report to me. He said the monster—or shall I say, the big lizard?—wasn't an inch over two hundred feet. But the size has nothing at all to do with it. You'll find the big ones even easier than the little ones. They're far slower on their feet and less aggressive, I'm told. Besides, before you go I'm going to equip you in such fashion that you need have no fear of all the dragons in the world."

"I'd like an enchanted cap," said Gawaine.

"What's that?" answered the Headmaster, testily.

"A cap to make me disappear," explained Gawaine.

The Headmaster laughed indulgently. "You mustn't believe all those old wives' stories," he said. "There isn't any such thing. A cap to make you disappear, indeed! What would you do with it? You haven't even appeared yet. Why, my boy, you could walk from here to London, and nobody would so much as look at you. You're nobody. You couldn't be more invisible than that."

Gawaine seemed dangerously close to a relapse into his old habit of whimpering. The Headmaster reassured him: "Don't worry; I'll give you something much better than an enchanted cap. I'm going to give you a magic word. All you have to do is to repeat this magic charm once and no dragon can possibly harm a hair of your head. You can cut off his head at your leisure."

He took a heavy book from the shelf behind his desk and began to run through it. "Sometimes," he said, "the charm is a whole phrase or even a sentence. I might, for instance, give you 'To make the—' No, that might not do. I think a single word would be best for dragons."

"A short word," suggested Gawaine.

"It can't be too short or it wouldn't be potent. There isn't so much hurry as all that. Here's a splendid magic word: 'Rumplesnitz.' Do you think you can learn that?"

Gawaine tried and in an hour or so he seemed to have the word well in hand. Again and again he interrupted the lesson to inquire, "And if I say 'Rumplesnitz' the dragon can't possibly hurt me?" And always the Headmaster replied, "If you only say 'Rumplesnitz,' you are perfectly safe."

Toward morning Gawaine seemed resigned to his career. At daybreak the Headmaster saw him to the edge of the forest and pointed him to the direction in which he should proceed. About a mile away to the southwest a cloud of steam hovered over an open meadow in the woods, and the Headmaster assured Gawaine that under the steam he would find a dragon. Gawaine went forward slowly. He wondered whether it would be best to approach the dragon on the run, as he did in his practice in the South Meadow, or to walk toward him, shouting "Rumplesnitz" all the way.

The problem was decided for him. No sooner had he come to the fringe of the meadow than the dragon spied him and began to charge. It was a large dragon, and yet it seemed decidedly aggressive in spite of the Headmaster's statement to the contrary. As the dragon charged, it released huge clouds of hissing steam through its nostrils. It was almost as if a gigantic teapot had gone mad. The dragon came forward so fast, and Gawaine was so frightened, that he had time to say "Rumplesnitz" only once. As he said it he swung his battle-axe, and off popped the head of the dragon. Gawaine had to admit that it was even easier to kill a real dragon than a wooden one, if only you said "Rumplesnitz."

Gawaine brought the ears home and a small section of the tail. His schoolmates and the faculty made much of him and the Headmaster wisely kept him from being spoiled by insisting that he go on with his work. Every clear day Gawaine rose at dawn and went out to kill dragons. The Headmaster kept him at home when it rained, because he said the woods were damp and unhealthy at such times, and he didn't want the boy to run needless risks. Few good days passed in which Gawaine failed to get a dragon. On one particularly fortunate day he killed three, a husband and wife and a visiting relative. Gradually he developed a technique. Pupils who sometimes watched him from the hilltops a long way off said that he often allowed the dragon to come within a few feet before he said "Rumplesnitz." He came to say it with a mocking sneer. Occasionally he did stunts. Once when an excursion party from London was watching him he went into action with his right hand tied behind his back. The dragon's head came off just as easily.

As Gawaine's record of killings mounted higher, the Headmaster found it impossible to keep him completely in hand. He fell into the habit of stealing out at night and engaging in long drinking bouts at the village tavern. It was after such a debauch [5] that he rose a little before dawn one fine August morning and started out after his fiftieth dragon. His head was heavy and his mind sluggish. He was heavy in other respects as well, for he had adopted the somewhat

[5] DEBAUCH—Excessive indulgence in drink and pleasure.

vulgar practice of wearing his medals, ribbons and all, when he went out dragon-hunting. The decorations began on his chest and ran all the way down to his abdomen. They must have weighed at least eight pounds.

Gawaine found a dragon in the same meadow where he had killed the first one. It was a fair-sized dragon but evidently an old one. Its face was wrinkled and Gawaine thought he had never seen so hideous a countenance. Much to the lad's disgust the monster refused to charge, and Gawaine was obliged to walk toward him. He whistled as he went. The dragon regarded him hopelessly but craftily. Of course it had heard of Gawaine. Even when the lad raised his battle-axe, the dragon made no move. It knew that there was no salvation in the quickest thrust of the head, for it had been informed that this hunter was protected by an enchantment. It merely waited, hoping something would turn up. Gawaine raised the battle-axe and suddenly lowered it again. He had grown very pale, and he trembled violently. The dragon suspected a trick. "What's the matter?" it asked, with false solicitude.

"I've forgotten the magic word," stammered Gawaine.

"What a pity!" said the dragon. "So that was the secret. It doesn't seem quite sporting to me, all this magic stuff, you know. Not cricket,[6] as we used to say when I was a little dragon; but, after all, that's a matter of opinion."

Gawaine was so helpless with terror that the dragon's confidence rose immeasurably and it could not resist the temptation to show off a bit.

"Could I possibly be of any assistance?" it asked. "What's the first letter of the magic word?"

[6] CRICKET—Sportsmanlike.

"It begins with an 'R'," said Gawaine, weakly.

"Let's see," mused the dragon, "that doesn't tell us much, does it? What sort of a word is this? Is it an epithet, do you think?"

Gawaine could do no more than nod.

"Why, of course," exclaimed the dragon, "reactionary Republican."

Gawaine shook his head.

"Well, then," said the dragon, "we'd better get down to business. Will you surrender?"

With the suggestion of a compromise Gawaine mustered up enough courage to speak.

"What will you do if I surrender?"

"Why, I'll eat you," said the dragon.

"And if I don't surrender?"

"I'll eat you just the same."

"Then it doesn't make any difference, does it?" moaned Gawaine.

"It does to me," said the dragon, with a smile. "I'd rather you didn't surrender. You'd taste much better if you didn't."

The dragon waited for a long time for Gawaine to ask "Why?" but the boy was too frightened to speak. At last the dragon had to give the explanation without his cue line. "You see," he said, "if you don't surrender, you'll taste better because you'll die game."

This was an old and ancient trick of the dragons. By means of some such quip he was accustomed to paralyze his victims with laughter and then to destroy them. Gawaine was sufficiently paralyzed as it was, but laughter had no part in his helplessness. With the last word of the joke the dragon drew back and struck. In that second there flashed into the mind of Gawaine the magic word "Rumplesnitz" but there was no time to say it. There was time only to strike, and without a word Gawaine met the onrush of the dragon with a full swing. He put all his back and shoulders into it. The impact was terrific, and the head of the dragon flew away almost a hundred yards and landed in a thicket.

Gawaine did not remain frightened very long after the death of the dragon. His mood was one of wonder. He was enormously puzzled. He cut off the ears of the monster almost in a trance. Again and again he thought to himself, "I didn't say 'Rumplesnitz'!" He was sure of that, and yet there was no question that he had killed the dragon. In fact, he had never killed one so utterly. Never before had he driven a head for anything like the same distance. Twenty-five yards was perhaps his best previous record. All the way back to the knight school he kept rumbling about in his mind, seeking an explanation for what had occurred. He went to the Headmaster immediately and, after closing the door, told him what had happened. "I didn't say 'Rumplesnitz'," he explained with great earnestness.

The Headmaster laughed. "I'm glad you've found out," he said. "It makes you ever so much more of a hero. Don't you see that? Now you know that it was you who killed all these dragons, and not that foolish little word 'Rumplesnitz.' "

Gawaine frowned. "Then it wasn't a magic word, after all?" he asked.

"Of course not," said the Headmaster; "you ought to be too old for such foolishness. There isn't any such thing as a magic word."

"But you told me it was magic," protested Gawaine. "You said it was magic, and now you say it isn't."

"It wasn't magic in a literal sense," answered the Headmaster, "but it was much more wonderful than that. The word gave you confidence. It took away your fears. If I hadn't told you that, you might have been killed the very first time. It was your battle-axe did the trick."

Gawaine surprised the Headmaster by his attitude. He was obviously distressed by the explanation. He interrupted a long philosophic and ethical discourse by the Headmaster with, "If I hadn't of hit 'em all mighty hard and fast any one of 'em might have crushed me like a, like a—" He fumbled for a word.

"Eggshell," suggested the Headmaster.

"Like a eggshell," assented Gawaine and he said it many times. All through the evening meal people who sat near him heard him muttering, "Like a eggshell, like a eggshell."

The next day was clear, but Gawaine did not get up at dawn. Indeed, it was almost noon when the Headmaster found him cowering in bed, with the clothes pulled over his head. The principal called the Assistant Professor of Pleasaunce, and together they dragged the boy toward the forest.

"He'll be all right as soon as he gets a couple more dragons under his belt," explained the Headmaster.

The Assistant Professor of Pleasaunce agreed. "It would be a shame to stop such a fine run," he said. "Why, counting that one yesterday, he's killed fifty dragons."

They pushed the boy into a thicket above which hung a meager cloud of steam. It was obviously quite a small dragon. But Gawaine did not come back that night or the next. In fact, he never came back. Some weeks afterward, brave spirits from the school explored the thicket but they could find nothing to remind them of Gawaine except the metal parts of his medals. Even the ribbons had been devoured.

The Headmaster and the Assistant Professor of Pleasaunce agreed that it would be just as well not to tell the school how Gawaine had achieved his record, and still less how he came to die. They held that it might have a bad effect on school spirit. Accordingly Gawaine has lived in the memory of the school as its greatest hero. No visitor succeeds in leaving the building today without seeing a great shield which hangs on the wall of the dining hall. Fifty pairs of dragons' ears are mounted upon the shield, and underneath in gilt letters is "Gawaine le Coeur-Hardy," followed by the simple inscription, "He killed fifty dragons." The record has never been equaled.

FOR DISCUSSION

1. What was Gawaine's great fault? How did the Headmaster propose to cure him?

2. Describe Gawaine's first encounter with a live dragon.

3. How did the young knight's mounting success at dragon slaying influence him for good and bad?

4. What lesson might Gawaine have learned from the fact that he slew the fiftieth dragon without the magic word? Instead, how did the experience affect him? What happened when he met dragon fifty-one?

5. Beneath the humor, what serious

moral lesson do you think may be found in this fable?

THE HISTORY OF THE WORD

1. The word *jousting* has a picturesque past, dating back to the days of chivalry. Look up the word to learn its story and come to class prepared to describe the medieval custom with which jousting is associated.

2. The Latin word *poten(t)s* means *having power over*. From it is derived the word *potent*, meaning *strong* or *powerful;* hence, a powerful drug or strong alcoholic drink is termed potent. Whenever you see words built on the stem *poten*, you can be sure they refer to power. Some of these words are *potency, potentate, potential, impotent, omnipotent*. Use each of these words in a sentence.

YOU LEARNED A LESSON

Confidence growing from knowledge of one's abilities plays an important role in the lives of all of us. Do you remember a time when belief in yourself enabled you to do a difficult thing? When did timidity keep you from joining in a game or from meeting strangers? Most of us have had timid moments in which we have surrendered to or conquered fear. In a written paragraph describe one such experience of your own.

For Further Reading

Friends and Fiddlers by Catherine Bowen. Humor, music, and biography are mixed in a delightful way.

The Collected Works of Heywood Broun by Heywood Broun contains selections from the author's works ranging from his first contribution to journalism up to his death in 1939. It includes a discussion of many of the issues—both vital and trivial—of our times. His vigorous opinions combined with his literary skill make excellent reading.

Back to Treasure Island by Harold Calahan is a continuation of the well-loved story of Long John Silver and Jim Hawkins.

The Babe Ruth Story by Bob Considine. Considine has not only described Ruth's experiences as told by Ruth himself, but he has captured the team personality of the Yankees of the 1920's and 1930's with the lively stories he tells.

Belvedere by Gwen Davenport is the hilarious story of the eccentric Lynn Belvedere, who hired himself out as a "mother's helper." Since he wanted to write a book and hated small children, his management of the three King children is both masterful and laughable.

It Happens Every Spring by Valentine Davies is a fantastic story of a chemistry teacher who becomes a phenomenally successful baseball player. A sheer delight from beginning to end, the story has romance, sports, surprise, suspense, and humor.

Dictators of the Baton by David Ewen contains biographical, critical, and personal portraits of thirty orchestra conductors. It was written in terms the non-musician can understand and enjoy.

Cheaper by the Dozen by Frank B. Gilbreth and Ernestine Gilbreth Carey. Twelve children in one family can make life very complicated and very hilarious.

What a Life by Clifford Goldsmith. Henry Aldrich, under the direction of his assistant principal, decides to follow his own talents in his career rather than his father's choice. This is a humorous three-act play.

Al Smith: American by Frank Graham. This biography of the Democratic political leader is full of stories about that fascinating personality—some humorous, some very revealing, all interesting.

Happiness of Father Happé by Cecily Hallack. Father Happé finds his mission in spreading happiness even in the presence of death.

See Here, Private Hargrove by Marion Hargrove is a humorous account of the life of a private in World War II.

Uncle Remus Stories by Joel Chandler Harris. An old colored man tells a small lad delightful Negro folk tales.

Wings on My Feet by Sonja Henie. Here is a double treat: not only Miss Henie's autobiography, but also her course in ice skating.

Mush! You Malemutes by Bernard J. Hubbard, S.J. Danger and discovery mark this account of Alaskan exploration.

Young Geoffrey Chaucer by Regina Kelly. The story of the life of Geoffrey Chaucer from boyhood to young manhood is told here with a wealth of historical detail.

Manners Can Be Fun by Munro Leaf. Cartoons illustrate the text in this common-sense book on manners.

In Chimney Corners by Seumas MacManus is a collection of merry tales of Irish folklore.

Saints for Home and School by Thomas Melady is a collection of stories about the saints, told in fictional style. They emphasize action in the lives of the saints and the miracles which they performed.

Split Seconds by Jackson Scholz. These track and field stories were gathered by an Olympic champion runner.

Drawing People for Fun by Roger Vernam is a book on figure drawing, especially interesting to future artists.

MEETING THE CHALLENGE

"*Youth is not formed for pleasure, but for heroism.*"—Paul Claudel.

School is usually the first of those challenges which life hurls at all of us. It is the beginning of our career of personal achievement. It gives the initial push, after which we must go ahead under our own power.

That is one reason why hero-worship enters into everyone's life. Since we ourselves must become heroes, we naturally are curious about the heroism of others; we are attracted, we admire, we imitate. So universal is this appeal of personal bravery that stories by the wholesale can be found in which moral giants unmask liars, deflate bluffers, and establish Right on unconquerable ground.

Especially to Christians does bravery appeal, for Christianity is built on courage. Because Christ the Leader, although troubled in the Garden, was not troubled at the sight of the Cross, innumerable Christians have chosen to die for their Faith rather than live without it. "Let fire, cross, wild beasts, stabbing, ripping up the middle, racking of bones, mangling of limbs, crushing of my whole body, and the cruel torments of the Devil come upon me," said Saint Ignatius of Antioch, "it is nothing if only I attain unto Christ Jesus." Such heroism makes the martyrs of the Church a challenge to any standard of success which the world has erected.

The stories offered in this section show how various are the persons whom success has crowned. We see a poor lame boy become a physician who heals his whole county, a young diver overcome his terror of three thousand rooters, a giant in Nero's Circus saving his doomed queen, Hill-Billy Jim the victor at a fiddling contest, two girls of Carthage intimidating lions in the arena, and a simple Breton sailor saving the entire French fleet from destruction. Make these persons your friends.

NATIONAL GALLERY OF ART, CHESTER DALE COLLECTION

A. J. Cronin possesses an honest love of simple humanity. This quality has no doubt been the key to his success as a writer. The reader feels this author's keen appreciation of human nature—man's frailties and his ability to succeed if he so desires. The Doctor of Lennox was a person with courage; and, just as important, he had the ability to love others, even those who showed no affection for him. With these traits he was able to surmount difficulties—physical and emotional—which to the less courageous and self-confident would have spelled defeat.

THE DOCTOR OF LENNOX

A. J. CRONIN

The most unforgettable character I ever met? To my surprise I find myself thinking, not of some famous statesman, soldier or tycoon, but of a simple soul who had no wish to dominate an empire, but set out instead to conquer circumstance—and himself.

I first knew him as a boy, small, insignificant, and poor, who hung onto us, so to speak, by the skin of his teeth—barely accepted by the select band of adventurous youths of which I was one in my native Scottish town of Levenford.

If he were in any way remarkable, it was through his defects. He was quite comically lame, one leg being so much shorter than the other that he was obliged to wear a boot with a sole six inches thick. To see him run, saving his bad leg, his undersized form tense and limping, the sweat breaking out on his eager face, well—Chisholm, the minister's son, acknowledged wit of our band, hit the nail on the head when he dubbed him Dot-and-Carry.[1] It was shortened subsequently to Carry. "Look out," someone would shout, "here comes Carry. Let's get away before he tags onto us." And off we would dart to the swimming pool or the woods, with Carry, dotting along, cheerful and unprotesting, in our wake.

That was his quality, a shy, a smiling cheerfulness—and how we mocked it! To us, Carry was an oddity. His clothes, though carefully patched and mended, were terrible. Socially he was almost beyond the pale.[2] His mother, a gaunt little widow of a drunken loafer, supported herself and her son by scrubbing out sundry shops. Again Chisholm epitomized the jest with his classic epigram, "Carry's mother takes in stairs to wash."

Carry supplemented the family income

[1] DOT-AND-CARRY—From arithmetic; to set down, point, and carry figures; hence to go step by step; to limp.

[2] BEYOND THE PALE—Beyond limits.

by rising at five o'clock every morning to deliver milk. This long milk round sometimes made him late for school. Glancing down the arches of the years, I can still see a small lame boy, hot and trembling, in the middle of the classroom floor, while the master, a sadistic brute, drew titters with his shafts.

"Well, well . . . can it be possible ye're late again?"

"Y-y-yes, sir."

"And where has your lordship been? Taking breakfast with the provost [3] no doubt?"

"N-n-n-n"

At such moments of crisis Carry had a stammer which rose and tortured him. He could not articulate another syllable. And the class, reading permission in the master's grim smile, dissolved in roars of mirth.

If Carry had been clever, all might have been well for him. In Scotland everything is forgiven the brilliant "lad o' pairts." But though Carry did well enough at his books, oral examinations were to him the crack of doom.

There was heartburning in this fact for Carry's mother. She longed for her son to excel, and to excel in one especial field. Poor, humble, despised, she nourished in her fiercely religious soul a fervent ambition. She desired to see her son an ordained minister of the Church of Scotland. Sublime folly! But Carry's mother had sworn to achieve the miracle or die!

Carry much preferred the open countryside to a stuffy prayer meeting. He loved the woods and moors and the wild things that lived there—was never happier than when tending some sick or maimed creature picked up on his wanderings. He had a most uncanny knack of healing. In fact, Carry had a tremendous longing to be a doctor.

[3] PROVOST—The chief magistrate; mayor.

But obedience was inherent in his gentle nature, and when he left school it was to enter college as a student of divinity. Heaven knows how they managed. His mother scrimped and saved, her figure grew more gaunt, but in her deep-set eye there glowed unquenchable fire. Carry himself, though his heart was not in what he did, worked like a hero.

And it so happened, quicker than might have been imagined, that Carry was duly licensed at the age of twenty-four in the cure of souls according to the Kirk of Scotland. Locally there was great interest in the prodigy of the scrub-woman's son turned parson. He was proposed for the parish church assistantship and named to preach a trial sermon.

A full congregation assembled to see "what was in the young meenister." And Carry, who for weeks past had rehearsed his sermon, ascended the pulpit feeling himself word-perfect. He began to speak in an earnest voice and for a few moments he went well enough. Then all at once he became conscious of those rows and rows of upturned faces, of his mother dressed in her best in a front pew, her eyes fixed rapturously upon him. A paralyzing shiver of self-distrust swept over him. He hesitated, lost the thread of his ideas, and began to stammer. Once that frightful impotence of speech had gripped him he was lost. He labored on pitifully, but while he struggled for the words he saw the restlessness, the significant smiles; heard even a faint titter. And then again he saw his mother's face,

and broke down completely. There was a long and awful pause, then falteringly Carry drew the service to a close by announcing the hymn.

Within the hour, when Carry's mother reached home, she was mercifully taken by an apoplectic seizure.[4] She never spoke again.

The funeral over, Carry disappeared from Levenford. No one knew or cared where he went. He was stigmatized, branded contemptuously for life, a failure. When some years later news reached me that he was teaching in a wretched school in a mining district, I thought of him for a moment, with a kind of shamefaced sorrow, as a despairing soul, a man predestined for disaster. But I soon forgot him.

I was working in Edinburgh when Chisholm, now first assistant to the Regius Professor of Anatomy there, dropped into my rooms one evening. "You'll never guess," he grinned, "who's dissecting in my department. None other than our boyhood friend, Dot-and-Carry."

Carry it was. Carry, at nearly thirty years of age, starting out to be a doctor! A strange figure he made, with his shabby suit, his limp and stoop, among the gay young bucks who were his fellow students. No one ever spoke to him. He occupied a room in a poor district, cooked his own meals, husbanded the slender savings from his teacher's pittance. I saw something of his struggle for the next two years. His age, appearance, and traitorous stammer hampered him. But he went plodding indefatigably on, refusing to admit defeat, the old dogged cheerfulness and hopeful courage still in his eyes.

Time marched on. Five years and more. I found myself in London, and had long since again lost touch with Carry. But I saw much of Chisholm, whose good looks and glib tongue had destined him for political honors. He was now indeed a Member of Parliament and a junior minister into the bargain. In May of 1934 I went with him for a fishing holiday at Lennox in the Highlands. The food at our inn was vile and the landlady a scrawny shrew. It was

[4] APOPLECTIC SEIZURE—A stroke of paralysis.

something of a satisfaction when, two days after our arrival, she slipped on the taproom floor and damaged her kneecap. Perfunctorily, we two renegades from the healing art offered our assistance. But the dame would have none of us. No one would suit her but her own village doctor, of whose canny skill and notable achievements she drew an enthusiastic picture that made Chisholm glance at me and smile.

An hour later the practitioner arrived, black bag in hand, with all the quick assurance of a busy man. In no time he had silenced the patient with a reassuring word and reduced the dislocation with a sure, deft touch. Only then did he turn toward us.

"My God!" exclaimed Chisholm, under his breath. "Carry!"

Yes, Carry it was. But not the shy, shabby, stammering Carry of old. He had the quietly confident air of a man established and secure. In a flash of recognition he greeted us warmly, and pressed us to come to supper at his home. Meanwhile, he had an urgent case to attend.

It was with an odd expectancy, half excitement and half lingering misgiving, that we entered the village doctor's house that evening. What a shock to find that Carry had a wife! Yet it was so. She welcomed us, fresh and pretty as her own countryside. Since the doctor (she gave the title with a naïve reverence) was still engaged in his surgery, she took us upstairs to see the children. Two red-cheeked girls and a little boy, already asleep. Surprise made us mute.

Downstairs, Carry joined us with two other guests. Now, at his own table, he was a man poised and serene, holding his place as host with quiet dignity. His friends, both men of substance, treated him with deference. Less from what he said than what was said by others we gathered the facts. His practice was wide and scattered. His patients were country folk, canny, silent, hard to know. Yet somehow he had won them. Now as he went through a village the women would run to him, babes in arms, to consult him in the roadway. Such times he never bothered about fees. More than enough came his way, and at New Year's there was always a string of presents on his doorstep, a brace of ducks, a goose, a clutch of new-laid eggs, in handsome settlement for some quite forgotten service.

But there were other tales—of midnight vigils when in some humble home the battle for a human life was waged: a child choking with diphtheria, a plowman stricken with pneumonia, a shepherd's wife in painful labor, all to be sustained, comforted, exhorted, brought back haltingly, their hands in his, from the shadows.

The doctor was a force now, permeating the whole countryside, wise and gentle, blending the best of science and nature, unsparing, undemanding, loving this work he had been born to do, conscious of the place that he had won in the affections of the people, a man who had refused defeat and won through to victory at last.

Late that night as we left the doctor's house and trudged through the darkness, silence fell between Chisholm and myself. Then, as with an effort, he declared:

"It looks as though the little man has found himself at last."

Something patronizing in the remark jarred me. I could not resist a quick reply.

"Which would you rather be, Chisholm—yourself, or the doctor of Lennox?"

"Confound you," he muttered. "Don't you know?"

◇◇◇◇◇◇◇◇◇◇◇◇◇◇◇◇◇◇◇◇◇◇◇◇◇◇◇◇◇◇◇◇

FOR DISCUSSION

1. The boys conceived of Carry as "quite comically lame." Do you think this was deliberately cruel or just thoughtless?

2. What did Carry do when the boys tried to be rid of him? What does this attitude reveal about Carry's personality?

3. Do you think Carry really wanted to be a doctor? If so, why did he teach school for six years after his first great failure?

4. What admirable qualities do you find in Carry as he worked at the study of medicine?

5. Carry found his place—his vocation. Can you explain the last two sentences of the selection? If you can, you have learned a good lesson from the doctor of Lennox.

DETERMINING THE EXACT WORD

1. *Imitate, mimic, ape* are synonyms for *mock.* Though these words carry approximately the same meaning as *mock,* each varies in its shade of meaning. Decide whether you think any of these words would make a good substitute for the italicized word in this sentence: "That was his quality . . . a smiling cheerfulness . . . and how we *mocked* it." Explain your answer.

2. "Again Chisholm *epitomized* the jest . . ." What is a synonym for *epitomize?*

3. "He had a most *uncanny* knack of healing." What does *uncanny* say that *strange* does not? How is it different from *weird?*

4. "In no time he had reduced the dislocation with a sure, *deft* touch." What is the meaning of *deft?* Does *dexterous* have exactly the same meaning as *deft?* If not, what is the meaning? Can you use *dexterous* in a sentence of your own?

LEAPING THE HURDLES

In this story by A. J. Cronin you have met a very admirable person. List on a sheet of paper as many personality traits as you can which make Dot-and-Carry a person to be admired.

Now write a paragraph showing your appreciation of Dot-and-Carry. Be sure to begin your paragraph with a sentence which will show your attitude toward him. Perhaps you will wish to write, instead, a paragraph on the question and answer at the end of the story.

RELATED READING

To see what wonders can be done in the way of overcoming handicaps, read Helen Keller's autobiography, *The Education of Helen Keller.*

Art Weed was sure that Sunny Ray could win first place in diving at the conference meet. The coach wondered if Art was placing confidence in the right man. Read Art's account of what happened when he tried to make a champion of a diving fool.

THE DIVING FOOL

FRANKLIN M. RECK

I stumbled on to "Sunny" Ray one afternoon in the pool at the State College gym. I had just taken a dive—a front jackknife—and was hoisting myself over the edge of the tank when I caught a glimpse of a flashing white body bouncing off the end of the springboard and scooting up into the air. That was Sunny Ray, although I didn't know it then.

What caught my eyes was the surprising height of his dive. I craned my neck around to see the finish of it, meanwhile supporting myself foolishly half in and half out of water. What I saw gave me a warm thrill. At the very top of his dive, he bent easily at the hips and gracefully touched his extended toes with his fingers. He opened out effortlessly and was perfectly straight before he entered the water. The same dive I had just completed—only much better done.

A pleased glow crawled up the back of my neck as I climbed out of the pool and turned around to watch for the unknown diver to appear. I was puzzled. I know most of the divers in school. I'm the varsity diver myself. And nobody in school could do a front jackknife like the one I had just seen.

When the head finally bobbed up, over near the polished nickel ladder, I saw a mouth framed for a laugh, and a pair of alert chuckling eyes. A fun-loving face if there ever was one. Not mischievous—but radiating fun.

I stepped on the board, feeling elated, somehow, and without a moment's hesitation performed a fairly difficult dive—a forward one and a half. That's the one where you make a complete somersault and a half and enter the water headfirst. The moment I completed it, I thrashed quickly to the ladder, climbed out dripping, and looked around at the board. Fun-loving was just stepping forward, and in another instant he was flying like a bird for the ceiling. High up, he tucked, turned one and a half times and slanted for the water like an arrow.

Golly, but it was beautiful! There was a rollicking challenge in it, too. Grinning all over, I strode out to the end of the board and rose up on my toes with my back to the water. Let Fun-loving try this one! Gathering all my strength, I leaped backward and upward, at the same time pulling up my knees to start my body on its whirl. When the old sense

"The Diving Fool" by Franklin M. Reck. Reprinted by permission of the author and *The American Boy*.

of gravity gave me the order, I thrust out my hands backward and felt myself sliding into the water with a satisfying *suff!* A pretty good backward one and a half, I thought, as I scudded for the edge of the pool. And a blasted difficult dive!

I glanced quickly at the board. Sure enough, there was Fun-loving, poised with his back to the water and his arms extended for the jump—just as I had been, a moment before. Up into the air he went. His smooth, white body doubled into a knot, whirled too fast for the eye, and opened out into a perfect arch. In another instant his pointed toes had disappeared softly into the water.

The perfection of it choked me. Why in the dickens wasn't he out for the varsity? I walked over to him, as he vaulted, catlike, out of the pool.

"My name's Weed," I said, sticking out my hand. "Art Weed."

He gave me a firm grip and grinned at me. "Mine's Donald Ray—for no good reason."

"I just wanted to say," I told him, "that I know about three more hard dives, but something tells me they wouldn't stump you. Who'd you dive for last?"

"Nobody."

I was surprised. "You mean to say you've never done any diving in competition?"

Ray shook his head.

"Where in blazes did you learn?"

His face flushed at my abrupt question. "Oh, just—I don't know. At resorts and places."

"Freshman?"

"No. Second year. I came here from Simpson this fall."

"Why aren't you out for the varsity?"

"Why—I guess I never thought about it. Diving always seemed—well—fun. I've never taken it seriously."

"I think you ought to," I told him earnestly. "Why not be here tomorrow afternoon at three o'clock? That's when the varsity practices."

Ray's eyes lit up with pleasure. "Gosh —d'you think there's any use?"

I caught my chortle before it reached my lips, and shoved it back into its chortle-box. If he didn't know how good he was, I didn't intend to enlighten him. He'd find out soon enough.

"It won't hurt to try out, anyhow," I answered casually. "Will you be there?"

"Sure!" he came back, eagerly.

"Don't forget," I smiled back at him, as I started for the showers. He was looking at me, open-mouthed, face all alight. He didn't take his eyes off me until a group of fellows yelling "Sunny!" drew his attention.

"Sunny," I grinned. "Sunny Ray. . . . Just fits him. Gosh, I like him."

Thrills chased each other up and down my spine as I hurried through my dressing and hustled up to Coach Allen's office. Scotty Allen and I are good friends. I'd do a back jackknife off the Eiffel Tower [1] into a bathtub, if he asked me to. He's a good, hard driver with a well-concealed sense of sympathy and an unfailing sense of humor.

I opened the door to his office all keyed up, and as I always do when I'm keyed up, I tried to calm myself—stifle my feelings.

"Hello, Coach," I said, very casually, as though I had just dropped in to pass the time of day.

[1] EIFFEL TOWER (ī′fĕl)—Noted for its height.

"Hello yourself," answered Scotty, barely glancing up from the trial cards he was studying. "What are you so excited about? Has the United States declared war or something?"

"No," I replied, slightly disappointed. "Not since morning, anyway. I hate to disturb you, but I just dropped in to ask if you really wanted to win first at the Conference meet."

"I do have peculiar leanings that way," he smiled, still gazing at his trial cards. "But some of the other teams have the same silly idea—particularly Lawrence."

"Would first place in the dives help out any?"

"It would give us five points," he answered. "Why? Have you finally mastered that gainer one and a half? I always said you had it in you—"

"Not me, Coach!" I blurted, joyously. "I know my limit. I know that Kramer, of Lawrence, for one, can beat the tar out of me. But I've just discovered a kid who can spot Kramer ten points and then wallop him! Coach, he's—he's—"

Words failed me.

"He is, is he?" commented Scotty, indifferently. "Where'd you stumble on to him?"

Pent-up words rushed out of my mouth. "In the pool, just a half hour ago. Saw him do a front jack, a forward one and a half, and—gosh—Coach, his front jack would take him over a bar twelve feet above the pool. No kidding! And—"

"Does he keep his feet together?"

"Yes, sir! And his toes pointed. And he arches with his stomach instead of his chest—"

The coach began to look interested and respectful. I ran on.

"He's taller than I am, and slender, and graceful as a cat! He's a diving fool!"

I was just beaming, I guess, because Scotty smiled at me appreciatively. "When do I get a look at this phenom?" [2]

"At practice, tomorrow. He's eligible for the varsity, too, because he's had a year at Simpson! Wait until you see him!"

"I hope he's as good as you say he is," said Scotty, looking at me quizzically. Then he leaned my way confidentially. "I've just come from a meeting of the athletic council. We went over the plans for the new field house, and the council wants to build the pool with only five hundred seats."

"Holy smokes!" I ejaculated. "Is that all?"

"There ought to be two thousand seats!" exploded Scotty. His lips closed in a thin line and his eyes burned so hotly at me that I thought my shirt would catch fire. "I'd give my right eye to win that Conference—show 'em! And a first in the dives would be a godsend. The athletic council ought to wake up!"

"Sunny Ray's your man," I yelped gleefully. "Unless I'm blind as well as cock-eyed, there's no diver in this Conference can beat him."

"How about second place, too?" Scotty asked, looking at me intently.

I blushed. I'm only an ordinary diver, and the coach knows it. I just haven't the brilliance—the flash that Kramer of Lawrence has—or Sunny Ray.

"I'll knock off my usual fourth place."

[2] PHENOM—Short for *phenomenon.*

"Somebody ought to knock off your block!" he snorted.

I laughed. Scotty is always prodding me to be better than I can be, and I'm always trying. But it's like trying to make a silk ear out of a sow's purse—or whatever it is. It can't be done. I'll always be fairly good, but I'll never be sensational.

The next afternoon, at three, I undressed in record time and fairly flew down the steps leading to the pool. Frank Richardson and Jack Crandall, our two dash men, were already in the water, thrashing out their twenty laps. Several others of the squad were chatting and laughing near the springboard. These hailed me when I slid through the door on the wet tile. The coach wasn't down yet.

Over in the corner, sitting on a canvas chair and studying his curled-up toes, was Sunny Ray. I walked over to him.

"'Smatter, Ray," I grinned, "is your lunch doing handsprings?"

"No, I just—" he turned a slightly pale face upward, "I never did anything like this before."

"Don't worry," I reassured him. "It's just practice."

I knew what Sunny's feelings were. Fancy diving is the tensest, most nerve-racking kind of competitive sport. When you want to vent your energy strenuously, you've got to poise delicately—to make every move just so. And hovering over you, every minute, is the specter of a flop. Sunny, for the first time, was beginning to realize all this. I looked down and noticed him shivering almost imperceptibly.

"Better take a practice dive," I suggested, "to start the old circulation."

"I—I guess I'll wait a while."

Just then, Scotty came into the pool. I trotted over to him, brought him to the corner, and introduced Sunny.

"Just a minute," the coach smiled, "until I put this gang to work."

A few minutes later, after he had started the distance men on their long grind, Scotty turned to us.

"All right, Art," he called, "go through your dives. You follow him, Ray."

I slapped Sunny on the back. "Give it all you've got," I whispered, and then started for the board.

I completed my swan dive—it felt like a good one—and clambered out of the water to watch Sunny. He was standing halfway up the board, nervously rubbing his hands together. He dropped his hands to his side, clenched them involuntarily, and started. Three steps up the board, a short final leap, and Sunny was traveling skyward. His head was back, his arms outspread, and his body perfectly arched. But just at the top of his dive, he broke—bent at the hips—and dropped headfirst into the pool.

"Gosh, Coach," I murmured, "that'll happen to anybody. He tried to go too high and had to bend to get down."

Scotty nodded. I went nervously to the board for my second dive while Sunny was climbing out of the pool. I was terrifically anxious for him to make good—to dive as beautifully as he had yesterday.

But he didn't. I don't mean that he flopped completely. He just didn't go quite so high, didn't turn so swiftly, didn't enter the water so cleanly. He was intent, serious, and just a bit uncertain. His last dive was the back one and a half, and he splashed quite a bit of water on it. I turned to the coach. He looked entirely unconvinced.

"You wait," I said, earnestly. "You haven't seen anything."

"He'll make a pretty fair diver," Scotty said gently. "He's a bit green."

I felt like shouting: "Fair diver! You take my word for it, he's a natural-born champion!" But I knew there had been no evidence of it today.

In the next two practices—the last two before the dual meet at Lawrence—Sunny improved only slightly. He was trying desperately hard, but the realization that he was diving before critical eyes seemed to upset him. He couldn't call out the bounding, carefree brilliance that was somewhere inside of him. On Friday the team left for Lawrence, and Sunny Ray stayed behind.

We lost the Lawrence meet by a heartbreaking score—35 to 33. I placed second in the dives to Kramer. Kramer is a marvelously flashing performer—just like Sunny was the first time I saw him.

"Golly," I confided to the coach on the train going home, "I wish I could dive like Kramer! Isn't he beautiful? But—he's no better than Sunny. Not so good."

I said it challengingly, but I didn't get a rise out of Scotty. He just looked at me queerly. Made me want to duck my head.

During the next week, Scotty began driving the squad. The Conference meet was only three weeks away, and there was one more hard dual—with Tech. So far, we had lost only the one meet, and we had a fair chance for the big title. We worked like blazes and were happy. I had double duty—practicing dives and working out for the relay.

On the Thursday before the Tech meet I got down to practice early. Sunny was already in the pool.

" 'Lo early bird!" I yelped. "Found any worms?"

"Fat, woolly ones," retorted Ray. "They're all gone. You might as well trot back to your nest."

"You don't trot to a nest," I reproved him. "You fly. And here goes!"

I stepped on the board and did my swan dive.

"That wasn't high enough," chided Sunny. "You should fly like an iggle. This way."

High up into the air he soared, like a zooming sea gull. I whistled. *That* was something like!

"When an iggle has corns on his feet," grinned Sunny, vaulting out of the water, "he flies above a mounting and scratches 'em—like this."

Three slow steps, that predatory pounce on the end of the board, and he was again shooting for the ceiling. Away up there, he quickly jacked, touched his toes with his hands, and dropped. Straight as a plumb line. No splash.

I chuckled joyfully.

"What happens," I asked him with mock seriousness, "when an iggle has a cramp?"

"He makes for a cloud," Sunny replied lightly, "and doubles up. Poor iggle."

Again he sailed skyward. Unbelievably high up, he tucked, turned one and a half times and zipped for the water. I was seeing the real Sunny now!

"Don't mind me," I told him weakly. "I'm just a ground hog."

He made a couple of mysterious passes at me with his hands.

"Now," he announced in a deep, formal tone, "you're a naviator. A naviator hunting iggles. Chase me."

For a quarter of an hour we played our game. Sunny's face was all alight. He wasn't on inspection now—he was disporting himself naturally and joyously.

"What do you two think you are," grunted Frank Richardson, who had just come in, "a couple of bounding porpoises?"

"Porpoises!" I bellowed. "He called us porpoises! Tell him what we are, Sunny!"

"We're iggles," grinned Sunny.

"We live in igloos," I added.

"And spend all our time iggling."

Frank Richardson backed away from us slightly in awe.

I turned to Sunny. "He doesn't understand," I murmured. "He's an eel."

"And eels," finished Sunny, "can't speak igglish."

Chortling foolishly, he ran to the board and did another perfect one and a half. There was a lump in my throat, but it tasted sweet. I sensed that somebody was standing close to me, and I turned around to see Scotty looking keenly at the circular ripples that marked the end of Sunny's uncannily beautiful dive.

"I've been watching from the balcony," the coach said in my ear. "I'm beginning to understand."

"Wasn't that wonderful?" I gulped. "He's a diving fool, isn't he?"

Scotty didn't answer, but his eyes were shining.

I didn't sleep a lot that night. For about a half hour I lay in bed and thrilled over Sunny's performance. Then it occurred to me that he was the man to go

to Tech with the team tomorrow night. I wasn't particularly needed on the relay. Either Wilson or Harwood could take my place. And the coach couldn't take more than ten men.

"The ax," I grunted, half aloud, "will fall tomorrow."

"Shut up," growled a sleepy voice in the next bed. You just don't have any chance to be sorry for yourself in a fraternity house; so I turned over and shut my eyes.

The next morning, at breakfast, I decided not to wait for the ax to fall. At nine-fifty—between classes—I went up to Scotty's office. I knew he'd be in because he has swimming classes in the morning.

He was studying those blasted time cards of his.

"If you're trying to figure out why you should take two divers to Tech, you can quit," I told him. "I've got two exams next Monday, and I'd be just as well satisfied if you'd let me stay home."

The coach looked at me thoughtfully. "Don't you think you could win first at Tech?"

I had a good laugh. The same story.

"I *know* Sunny can win first. That boy—gosh—" Thinking of those dives he made yesterday left me speechless.

Scotty looked straight at the wall in front of him. I began to get fidgety—to feel that I had spoken out of turn. Tried to help him out with his job, and all that.

"I don't mean," I explained hastily, "that I don't want to go! I do—but—"

"Might as well break Sunny in," Scotty interrupted. "You'd better take a workout while we're gone."

I had a sudden glimpse of the rollicking squad of mermen cutting up on the train and me sitting around a fraternity house.

"I will," I replied, getting to my feet and walking unsteadily to the door. "I—I'll take a workout tomorrow afternoon."

That night, when I saw the gang off at the train, Sunny drew me aside.

"Gee whiz, Art," he blurted out, "this isn't right."

I grinned. "The best man wins, Sunny." I roughed him up a bit, to steer him away from anything sentimental.

"B-but," he said, holding me off, "I'm not sure I'm the best man."

"You've never seen yourself dive!" I chuckled.

That night, at the fraternity house, several of the brothers wanted to know why I wasn't out of town with the team.

"Trying out a new diver," I explained. "Sunny Ray."

"Is he good?"

"He's the coming Conference champion," I asserted, with conviction.

"Heck," mourned one of the fellows. "I thought we had the coming champ right here in the house!"

"Don't be funny," I grunted.

Saturday morning I had a couple of classes. In the afternoon I went down to the pool and punished the springboard savagely. In the evening I went to the movie and saw nothing on the screen except my mind's picture of the team battling Tech—of Sunny soaring upward. After the show I hurried to the *Campus Daily* office to get the results.

"We won, 40 to 28," Spike Hanlon, the sporting editor informed me, as he handed me the summary.

I scanned it eagerly to see how Sunny

had come out in the dives. Halfway down was this paragraph:

"Fancy dives: First, Marlowe, Tech, 108.6; second, Floyd, Tech, 102; *third, Ray, State College,* 96."

Sunny had flopped! I knew what had happened just as though I'd been there. I could almost feel the coldness that possessed Sunny's knees the first time he walked out to the board before a thousand rooters and three judges. Just like walking up to a blasted electric chair!

"Just the same," I murmured, "he's the greatest natural diver I've ever seen. And he's going to win first at the Conference!"

Monday afternoon, just as I went into the locker room to undress, the coach called me. He led me up to his office, where he drew up a second chair and motioned me to sit down in it.

For a couple of minutes he scribbled busily on a sheet of paper, and then he shoved it over to me.

"Barring upsets," he said, briefly, "that's how things will stack up at the Conference meet."

This is what he'd written on the sheet:

	LAW-RENCE	STATE COL.	OTHERS
200 yd. relay	5	3	3
50 yd. dash	3	5	3
100 yd. dash	3	5	3
150 yd. backstroke	3	2	6
200 yd. breast stroke	3	2	6
440 yd. swim	2	8	1
300 yd. medley relay	5	1	5
	24	26	27
Dives	—	—	—

"We'll take first in the fifty and hundred, and we'll sweep the four-forty," he said. "Lawrence will take the relay and push us in the dashes. We haven't got a chance in the medley—we may take a fourth. Which means that the dives will tell the story. You and Sunny—" he paused.

I knew how badly the coach wanted to win the Conference. The athletic council was disposed to regard swimming lightly. And now, with the plans for the new field house under consideration, swimming at State College was at the crossroads. I had two visions—one of a spacious pool, built to accommodate thousands of rooters; another of an ordinary pool, around which a narrow bank of spectators sat hemmed in by walls.

"I haven't said much to the athletic council," Scotty said, reading my thoughts, "because I wouldn't have been listened to. But if we win the Conference, I will talk—and I'll get a respectful hearing."

I cleared my throat huskily. "Looks like it's up to Sunny and me, doesn't it?"

My face must have been kind of pale and long, because the coach grinned. "It is—but don't take it too seriously. Just give me the best you've got. And see if you can't work that self-conscious fear out of Sunny. He was utterly lost at Tech. It was a new and terrible experience for him."

Sunny and I did hard labor the first week. We bounced and bounced off the end of the springboard until the bottoms of our feet were sore. On two occasions Sunny was his own buoyantly unconcerned self, and his glorious diving made us jubilant. But during the second week, when every practice brought the crisis closer, he seemed to lose his grip. He became uncertain—hesitant—fatal traits in diving! I plugged along at my usual mediocre level.

The coach looked on, urgently cheerful. But when I caught him off guard, his face was drawn and his eyes a bit worried. The day before we were due to leave for Lawrence, he called me aside. "You and Sunny," he grinned, "have about wrecked my composure. At times Sunny is a marvel—at other times he flops unaccountably. And you—well, if I didn't know you, I'd say you weren't trying as hard as you might."

He paused a moment and then went on: "We've *got* to have that first in the dives. I've decided to take both you liabilities to the meet, and I want you to talk Sunny into the title."

He waited a moment while I looked at him in blank amazement. Was the coach going nutty? His eyes didn't look a bit wild—just blazing with purpose. He went on—

"Talk him into it! Take his mind off the ordeal. Get that joyous look into his face."

"I—I'll try," I stammered.

The coach drew a long breath. "That's all I can ask. And if you *really try*—" he looked at me long and searchingly—"you'll win the Conference title for me."

I'd never seen three thousand rooters at a swimming meet before, and the sight almost unnerved me. We'd come through the preliminaries safely—Sunny and I—along with the dreadful Kramer of Lawrence, Marlowe of Tech, and three others, and we felt good—until we saw that crowd. Lawrence has an immense new field house and a tremendous pool, 150 feet long and 60 wide. Around it rise banks of seats almost to the high steel girders. They were jammed solid with spectators.

We sat down on a bench at the diving end of the pool, feeling awed and shriveled in our bathrobes.

"Thank the lord," chattered Sunny, "the d-divers don't come until next to the last."

I was too busy wondering how I could talk Sunny into his natural self to answer. At the moment, the job seemed utterly beyond me.

We had stayed in the locker room until the last minute, and the meet got under way almost immediately after we entered the pool. Before I knew it, the relay swimmers had thrown off their bathrobes and stepped up to the edge. They were lifting their feet gingerly and rubbing their arms.

I'll never forget that relay. One hoarse, unpunctuated roar accompanied the swimmers from the first lap to the last.

Lawrence led all the way. Frank Richardson, our last man—he's the fastest dash man in the Conference—made a heroic effort to overtake the purple swimmer and lost by inches. Lawrence 5, State 3. The other schools weren't going to count in this meet. It was a battle royal between Lawrence and State!

We took only a fourth in the next event—we haven't a good breast stroke man—and Lawrence took first. That made it 10 to 4. I shivered and blamed the cold. Attendants had opened most of the high windows, much to the comfort of the rooters and the discomfort of the swimmers.

Good old Frank Richardson took his expected first in the fifty, and Crandall took an unexpected fourth. Six points in one splash! Lawrence got only three. State 10, Lawrence 13.

The long 440 grind was all ours, because we have the best distance men in the Conference. First and second place put us ahead 18 to 15. I noticed that the tense lines around Scotty's mouth had relaxed a bit.

We were shut out of the 150-yard backstroke, while Lawrence pulled a second. That evened the score at 18-all. I felt almost exhausted with the tension. The crowd was hoarsely mad. I looked around at Sunny. His face was utterly blank, but his eyes told me he was having bad dreams. My throat was sticky and I didn't dare talk—but I had to. Only the hundred, now, and then the fancy dives. State College needed that big pool! Time for me to start talking Sunny into the championship!

I felt like saying to him: "Snap out of it, you lily-livered, palsied pup!" But I felt that way, too—lily-livered and palsied. I clenched my trembling fingers and squared my shoulders.

"Gotta be light-hearted—gay!" I gritted between my closed teeth.

"Wh-what?" queried Sunny.

I laughed aloud. I hadn't meant that remark to be heard.

"I was just saying," I gritted to Sunny, "that you and I are letting this thing get our goats. And that isn't right."

I laid a calm hand on his bare knee and felt the tremor of it. I was stronger, cooler, now, and some of my new-found composure must have passed to Sunny, because he smiled faintly. I nodded reassuringly to the coach, who was looking my way tensely.

The hundred was called. The squad leaped up and patted Frank Richardson on the back.

"Go to it!" we all muttered to him. I was tickled to see Sunny on his feet, too.

Frank won the hundred in 55.2, with the Lawrence man a body length behind, and the rest trailing. State 23, Lawrence 21! Lawrence would most certainly win first in the medley relay, and we wouldn't take more than one point. That would leave it 26 to 24, in favor of Lawrence—not counting the dives. We needed at least six points in the dives—Sunny's first and my fourth—to win!

"All out for the fancy dives!" bawled the announcer.

Sunny's face paled.

"Come on, Sunny," I said, calmly. "You need a bath—and it's Saturday night."

The squad milled around us, helping us off with our bathrobes and slapping us on the back. I hoped fervently that Sunny wasn't taking to heart their tense, eager expression. Every face said: "It's up to you!"

Diving is a terrific test of a man's nerves! When your muscles are crying out for vigorous action, you've got to restrain them. Thousands of eyes are glued on you, and you alone. You're the star performer, in a spotlight. And the slightest misstep, the least error in timing may cause your downfall!

Sunny's voice called me out of my nerve-racking thoughts.

"Are we going to t-take a practice dive?" he asked.

I squared my shoulders. I had a job to perform. *This meet was up to me!*

"No," I replied seriously. "I'm an iggle."

"Wh-what?"

"I'm an iggle," I repeated, "and an iggle never dives. He swoops. Swatch me."

Without looking back at Sunny, I walked up to the board and took my first practice dive—a swan. As I climbed out of the water, I noticed the coach looking at me with a confident smile. I walked back to where Sunny was standing, rubbing his thighs.

"I tried to swash that beam up there with my tail feathers," I told him, "but I missed it. Heck."

Sunny grinned at me for the first time that night. "No wonder," he said, starting for the board. "Your tail feathers have moulted."

My heart bounded. Sunny at least had a comeback! I watched him eagerly as he poised and started forward. He sailed up—not quite so high as I could have wished, but still, better than I had expected.

I racked my brains for my next line. As he came up to me, dripping, I smiled.

"You swished it," I said, "with a swooping swish. I'm going after it with a swipping swoop."

A little weak on that remark, I thought dolefully, as I strode up and took my second practice—a running half gainer. Streaming wet, I clambered out and walked back to Sunny, putting on an expression of mock disgust.

"I swipped too hard," I grunted, "and got all dusty."

"I swish I could swoop like that," he said, grinning.

I chuckled joyously. Kramer, the Lawrence diver, walking past us to the board, looked at us in dumb amazement. After Kramer, Sunny started up.

"If you get dusty, swoop down and swash," I cautioned him.

"All right," he chuckled. "Here goes for a swishing swoop."

"A swipping, soaring swoosh!" I encouraged him.

I could have wept out of pure joy. His one and a half was a thing of beauty, and I knew then that everything was all right. There'd be just one more crisis—when the clerk called Sunny for his first official dive. The nonsense chatter—silly as it seemed—was working on Sunny's naturally buoyant spirit.

"You fellows had enough practice?" an official near us inquired.

We nodded. I felt a tightening in my throat.

A man with a megaphone walked to the edge of the pool.

"The next event," he sang out to the crowd, "is the fancy dive. Each man is required to do four dives—the plain front, the plain back, the front jackknife, and the back jackknife. After that, he does four difficult dives of his own choosing! First man up, Kramer of Lawrence. The plain front!"

Kramer did a good dive—too good for comfort—and won a storm of applause.

"Ray! State College!" bellowed the announcer.

This, for me, was the critical point. Sunny's first dive!

"That beam, iggle," I whispered to him solicitously, "is still dusty."

"'Sawful," he whispered back, "I'll swish it."

Sunny went so high on that dive that I was afraid he'd have to break. But he didn't. At the very top of his dive, his feet rose gracefully toward the ceiling, his back perfectly arched every moment. And the smooth entry into the water! Golly!

He walked back to me with a light-hearted grin glistening through the water streaming from his hair.

"Did I get it?" he asked.

"Every speck," I gurgled. "I'll go up and polish it." I felt supremely confident now. Sunny, I felt sure, was going to come through!

And I was right. Every time he stepped on the board, he grew better. Not an uncertain step. No sudden hesitancy. And, all through it, we played our game. The crowd, the sober-faced judges with their pads, the loud applause meant nothing to us. We were too intent upon sweeping that skyward beam immaculately clean. Weren't we iggles? Iggles cannot be bothered with mundane things. They dust the mountain tops!

I looked over to where our squad was sitting, noticed the look of awe on Frank Richardson's face and the happy smile on Scotty's lean countenance. My heart leaped fiercely.

Sunny's last dive—that marvelously sinuous thing of flashing turns called the gainer one and a half—brought forth an unrestrained outburst from the crowd. Not another diver had done so well—I felt sure of it.

Dripping and content, our play of iggles ended, we walked back to the bench. The coach bounded forward to meet us.

"Fine work, Sunny," he said warmly. Then he turned to me.

"Art," he grinned, "I didn't think you had it in you."

"It worked," I bubbled happily. "Didn't it?"

The coach just looked at me, his face all alight. The rest of the squad pulled us to the bench, wrapped our bathrobes about us, and rubbed our legs and arms with towels, meanwhile babbling joyfully in our ears.

I didn't respond to their outburst because I was trying to dope the status of the meet. The results of the dives would not be announced until after the medley relay was finished—that was the last event. Sunny's first and my fourth—if I was that lucky—would give us six points. Kramer of Lawrence had most certainly won second. That would make the score 29 to 24 in our favor. Lawrence would win first in the medley. 29 to 29! We had to have a fourth in the medley!

But we didn't get it. We were shut out completely. I felt sick at heart. That glorious diving—for nothing. . . .

"While we're waiting for the results of the fancy dives," called an announcer, "I'll read you the status of the meet so far. Lawrence 26, State College 23—" As the announcer read off the other scores, a clerk walked up to him with a sheet of paper. I gripped Sunny's leg, hard. "Results of the fancy dives!" bawled the megaphone. "Ah-ha! You'd never guess!"

I felt exultant. That was Sunny!

"First—" came from the megaphone, "—Weed, State College, 108.4."

I almost fell off the bench. Me—me? A wave of hand clapping pelted the walls.

—"Second, Donald Ray, State College, 103.2—"

Another wave of handclapping. Unaware of what I was doing, I got to my feet.

"He's—he's cockeyed!" I yelled. Unfortunately, I had picked a dead calm in which to give utterance to my thoughts. The crowd tittered.

"I'm cockeyed!" the announcer singsonged. "I'll have to have my eyes examined. Third, Kramer, Lawrence, 99.8. Fourth, Marlowe, Tech, 94. Fifth, Hendricks, Cole, 91.5. Final results of the meet: State College, 31, Lawrence, 28—"

I didn't hear the rest of it, because about eight husky swimmers were trying to pull me apart. Still dazed, I jerked myself free and walked to the coach. It wasn't right, because I'm just not good enough to beat Sunny and Kramer!

"Sunny won those dives, Coach," I protested. But he just grinned at me. I felt the need of explaining myself.

"It worked out just as we planned," I elaborated painfully. "I did what you said—talked him into it—"

"*You talked yourself into it*, you diving fool, you," laughed Scotty. "Haven't I been telling you all season you had it in you?"

I just stared at him, and if I looked as dumb as I felt, I must have been a sight. *Me?* Conference champion?

"Nope," I said positively. "There's something wrong."

Sunny had his arm around my shoulder, and he tightened it, grinning.

"You've never seen yourself dive, iggle," he chuckled.

◇◇◇◇◇◇◇◇◇◇◇◇◇◇◇◇◇◇◇◇◇◇◇◇◇◇◇◇◇◇

FOR DISCUSSION

1. How did Art Weed meet Sunny Ray? In the first paragraphs find a description of Sunny which explains his nickname.

2. The ability to relax under stress of competition is the mark of the trained athlete. How does this thought apply to study and examinations? How did Sunny react to team practice and the first swimming meets? Why?

3. Did Art Weed's humble notion of his own diving ability influence the quality of his performance? Did the coach have this idea in mind? From various hints in the story, whom do you consider Scotty was counting on for the success of the conference meet—Sunny or Art Weed?

4. Why was Art Weed convinced that Sunny had won first place in the final meet? What had Scotty actually meant in saying to him, "I didn't think you had it in you" (page 161)?

5. What qualities about Art Weed did you like?

MAGIC IN WORDS

1. The word *chuckle* on page 154 describes a low, suppressed laugh. Like many words in our language, it originated because it imitated a sound—here, the sound of laughter. In the story, what are the meanings of *chortle, zipp, thrash, flop, whistle,* and *suff!* What sounds do these words imitate? Name three other words that imitate the sounds they name. The use of words that imitate their own meanings in sound is called *onomatopoeia* (ŏn·ô·măt·ô·pē'yȧ).

2. Nothing adds more life to narrative than sharp, specific *action* words. Examine the following words in their context and be prepared to illustrate the different kinds of action they describe:

hoist (p. 150) thrash (p. 153)
stride (p. 150) pounce (p. 154)
thrust (p. 151) zipped (p. 154)
scudded (p. 151) milled around (p. 159)
vaulted (p. 151) jerked (p. 162)
bounded forward (p. 161)

3. Sometimes a writer can draw an exact picture by describing one thing in terms of something else—by using comparison. When the comparison contains the word

like or *as*, it is called a *simile*. Franklin Reck uses the following similes:

"flying like a bird for the ceiling"
"graceful as a cat"
"Just like walking up to a blasted electric chair!"
"High up into the air he soared like a zooming sea gull."

What is the force of these comparisons? Do they help you to see the action? Explain why each simile is appropriate.

NOW YOU ARE THE MAGICIAN

If you are observant, you will be able to make comparisons of your own. Try your imagination with the following phrases. Remind yourself what the thing is like, what it acts or moves like; then complete the figure.

a. The wind cut through my thin clothing like . . .
b. The stars, glittering in the winter night, looked as big as . . .
c. Running low and hard, the halfback plunged through the line, swerving and spinning like . . .
d. He paced the room like . . .

RELATED READING

Read "The Freshman Fullback" by Ralph Paine. For sparkling biography there are *Lou Gehrig* by Frank Graham and Knute Rockne's *Autobiography*.

◇◇◇◇◇

In the First World War, Edith Cavell harbored scores of British, French, and Belgian soldiers and sent them on to Brussels. For her work she was tried as a spy by a German military court, condemned, and shot to death. But her death proved the signal that rallied thousands to her country's cause.

EDITH CAVELL

HERMANN HAGEDORN

She sits before her judges, a tall, slender woman, with the beauty of a noble spirit on the calm, high forehead, in the gray, unperturbed eyes. Behind her sits her attorney, but she may not speak to him. Behind her testify her accusers, but she may not turn to see who they are. She scarcely knows why she is in this great Hall of Deputies where the German authorities who rule in Brussels are holding their military court; but she hears herself called a "spy."

A spy! She, Edith Cavell! A smile comes to her sensitive, humorous lips at the thought. The idea that she who is direct and frank to a fault should be thought a spy would be superbly comical, if the Germans apparently did not take it seriously. She is nothing so clever or so heroic, she would tell you if you asked her. She is just a nurse and head of a

"Edith Cavell" from *The Book of Courage* by Hermann Hagedorn. Reprinted by permission of the author.

training school for nurses in Brussels, which, since the outbreak of war, had been turned into a Red Cross hospital; a very unimportant person, she will tell you.

She is not alone, facing the judges. At her right and at her left sit her friends, the Princess of Croy, the Countess of Belleville, and some two dozen others. No definite, formal indictment is brought against any of them, but it appears in the course of the proceedings that they are all accused of the same crime.

There is something very appealing in the story as it unfolds. After the swift German advance in the summer of 1914, a year before, especially after the battle of Mons in which the British troops were heavily engaged, English soldiers, cut off from their army, have hidden in the forests and fields of Hainaut and Brabant seeking to avoid discovery by the German patrols, which have a way of shooting on sight, and taking no prisoners.

The Princess of Croy, an elderly spinster, has turned her château near Mons into a Red Cross hospital, and from wounded soldiers, whom she helps to nurse, hears of these forsaken fugitives, living for months like hunted animals, knowing that to be found means to die. It seems to her and her neighbor and friend, the Countess of Belleville, no great crime to help these poor boys to make their way to Brussels where they stand a better chance with the German authorities than in the open where the patrols go.

They draw a number of others into their confidence and before long have organized an "underground railway" similar to the system once in operation in the United States for aiding fugitive slaves to escape into Canada. They send them to Brussels; what happens to them after they get there is a matter into which they do not inquire. The fact is that in Brussels, directly under the noses of the German authorities, others take the young men and send them on toward the Dutch border. At the border the "railway" has its terminus. Holland is a neutral country. If Holland, in defiance of international law, shuts one eye and lets them go on to England or France, that is Holland's business, not the business of the devoted little company which starts the fugitives on their journey.

Edith Cavell's hospital is a station on this "underground railway." She whose life work it is to alleviate suffering has it not in her, in the face of such pain and trouble, to pass by on the other side. She procures money for the fugitives and guides, does it naturally as a part of the day's work. She nurses the German wounded as tenderly as she nurses the English, the French, or the Belgian, but she feels under no obligation to respect the authority of the German invaders.

Somehow the Germans hear of what she is doing; how, no one, perhaps, will ever know. A nurse, gossiping, perhaps. "It is no small prudence to keep silence in an evil time," Edith Cavell remarks a little wistfully as the net closes upon her.

It is August. The Germans put her in prison. They are not unkind to her and she bears them no resentment. She finds herself, in fact, almost grateful to them. Her life has been filled with work from morning till night, from one year's end to the other; but here in prison she cannot work. She has time to meditate, to examine the record of her experience, to think quietly of life and death and love and duty. She is deeply religious, with a Puritan conscience. She reproaches herself that she has been too stern with others, not stern enough with herself. The days pass into weeks; a month passes, two months. For her it is a period of purification. . . . Hitherto life has been "so hurried"; now she is at peace. She can afford to be patient.

Meanwhile, she has not been forgotten. She has friends. Everyone who knows her in Brussels admires her, loves her. Word of her imprisonment reaches the American minister, Brand Whitlock, who is in charge of British interests, and he instantly writes Baron von der Lancken, head of the Political Department of the German military government in Brussels, asking for particulars.

He receives no reply.

A month later he writes again. Two days later he has his answer. "Miss Cavell," writes His Excellency, "is in the prison of St. Giles. She has admitted having hidden English and French soldiers in her home, admitted giving them money and guides. She is in solitary confinement. No one may see her."

A month thereafter she is in the Chamber of Deputies, facing the German court. It is a military court, not a law court. Here there are no safeguards to protect the accused from injustice. As far as those hard-faced judges in their field-gray uniforms are concerned, everything "goes." They are not brutal men in their personal relations, those judges, no harder, no more selfish probably than other men. But they are not individuals where they sit, behind the long table on the platform. They are parts of a machine, a machine that knows no human feeling, that is conscious of its power and uses it blindly according to certain printed rules. It has crushed and beaten Germans for years, crushed them mercilessly, crushed the fine flower of their freedom, their wisdom, their pure lightheartedness, made them stupid little cogs in its great machine. Now it has gone forth to crush Germany's neighbors. The machine is in the Chamber of Deputies not to see justice done, but to protect the German army. Let the accused protect themselves.

Edith Cavell has no instinct for self-protection. She denies nothing, evades nothing; if anything, she takes a certain modest pride in what she has done. She is entirely calm and self-possessed.

"You admit aiding English soldiers left behind after the battle of Mons?"

"Yes. They were English, and I am English, and I will help my own."

The judges become a little human; they are clearly impressed by her fearless words. One of them leans forward. "You will admit that you helped as many as twenty?"

"Yes," she answers. "More than twenty. Two hundred."

"English?"

"No, not all English. French and Belgians too."

"But the French and Belgians are not of your nationality," one judge points out.

"You were foolish to help the English," interposes another. "The English are ungrateful."

"No," she answers. "The English are not ungrateful."

"How do you know?"

"Because some of them have written to me from England to thank me."

It is a fatal admission. She has been charged hitherto merely with aiding men to reach a neutral country, but now she has admitted that she has helped them to reach England, and the English army. The officers of the court look solemn. Her friends are horrified. But that is Edith Cavell, honest, frank, direct, unafraid.

The trial begins on Thursday, and lasts two days. What is the judgment? No one knows. The court is weighing the evidence, but the American Minister hears rumors which disquiet him. He communicates with Baron von der Lancken's office, and is told that no decision has been reached. "Will the Baron please inform Mr. Whitlock when the sentence has been pronounced?"

"Of course, Your Excellence," is the reply. "At once. Without question."

Sunday. There is no news except a rumor that the judges are not in agreement.

Monday. Baron von der Lancken's office, in answer to repeated inquiries, states that the judgment has not been pronounced, and will not be pronounced until the following day. But the American Legation is anxious and restless. A sense of foreboding hangs over it.

The weather is wet and chill. Leaves are falling; autumn is here. And Imperial Germany is stronger than ever, with all Belgium under her heel, and power of life and death in the hands of her servants.

Tomorrow, judgment is to be pronounced.

Tomorrow?

At nine o'clock that night, two nurses, frightened and in tears, come to the Legation. The court-martial, they declare, has given its decision. Miss Cavell has been condemned to death and is to be executed at six o'clock the next morning. They have it on the best authority.

Whitlock is horror-stricken. He is ill; he cannot leave the house. He sends his aide and the legal adviser of the Legation, a Belgian, to find von der Lancken. The Spanish Minister, Villalabar, joins him. The Baron is at the theater. He is annoyed at being disturbed, and refuses to come to them until the play is over. When he meets them at last he declares that he has heard of no judgment. The story is absurd, impossible. The German Governor-General would not think of executing a woman on such short notice. He is angry at the thought that the Americans should imagine such a thing of the German authorities.

"All right," says Whitlock's aide. "Suppose you call up the prison?"

The Baron goes to the telephone and comes back flushed and a little embarrassed. The story is true.

The American and the Spaniard argue with him, plead, beg for time, ask him to see the Governor-General, point out what the world will say. Von der Lancken is impressed, and goes to the Governor of the city. But the Governor is obdurate. He will not listen. He will not even receive the appeal for mercy. The Machine never admits a mistake. The judgment stands.

And Edith Cavell? She is in her cell writing letters, quite calm. She has not expected a sentence of death, certainly not expected execution to follow so swiftly on the heels of the judgment, but she is wasting no time in lamentations. She has letters to write to her mother and to some friends in England, advice to give to the nurses in her training school, a last word to send to a poor girl who is struggling with the drug habit.

The British chaplain comes to her cell. They are old friends.

"I am glad you came," she says quietly. "I want my friends to know that I gladly give my life for my country. I have no fear nor shrinking. I have seen death so often that it is not strange or fearful to me. They have been very kind to me here, and this period of rest before the end has been a great mercy. I have had a chance to meditate on many things. And I have learned this: standing as I do in view of God and eternity, I realize that patriotism is not enough. I must have no hatred or bitterness toward anyone."

They partake of the Holy Communion together, and when he repeats the verses of "Abide with Me," she joins softly in the end.

It is time for the chaplain to go. "Good-by," he says.

She smiles gently as she clasps his hand. "We shall meet again."

And now she is alone, waiting. And now the German chaplain, gentle and courteous, is with her. And now the officer comes to lead her to her execution.

The corridors of the prison are dark and silent. Here and there they pass a guard in the shadows. There is something appallingly furtive about this thing that is about to happen, that even now is happening, this slipping down dark halls, dark stairs, in the dim light of an October dawn. Why this blind haste? Is the Military Machine afraid that mercy might somehow get her hand through that iron ring? She is a woman, a frail, slender woman, and the great Machine is so afraid of her that she must be done away with before reason shall have time to discomfit the judges, or an indignant world shall have an opportunity to voice its protest.

The very walls seem to cry, "Look at her, gentlemen, you with your spiked helmets! Can this woman plot? Can this woman deceive? And would your own wives and daughters not do what she has done for their countrymen if the occasion came? And would you not be proud of them if they did? Keep this woman in prison if you must, but execute her in cold blood? What can she do to you? Living, what can she do? And *dead*, what can she *not* do?"

The footsteps ring hard and metallic on the cement floor. Now she is in the black van rushing to the place of execution. Now she is in the yard with the firing squad before her. She speaks a word to the German chaplain. Her voice is unwavering, her face is bright. She is tied loosely to a pillar.

"The grace of our Lord Jesus Christ, and the love of God and the fellowship of the Holy Ghost be with thee now and forever."

It is the chaplain who is trembling. She herself is quite calm. But the soldier who places the bandage over her eyes notes that they are full of tears.

Seconds pass. They seem endless. Then the sharp word of command cuts the appalling silence. Twelve rifles ring out in one clap of thunder. She sinks to the ground. She is dead.

The rain has ceased, the air is soft and warm, the sunlight shines through an autumn haze. Edith Cavell is dead; Edith Cavell, the unknown nurse, the head of an unimportant training school is dead; her work is done. But another Edith Cavell has risen from her grave to do a work so vastly more important that the other fades into insignificance beside it. The world has her name, the world has her story. Was the Military Machine afraid of the living woman? What will they say of her now that they have struck her down? Dead? Yes. Buried, too. And yet all over the world, she speaks! What are orators, with all their eloquence beside her? What are flaring posters? What are books, cartoons, pamphlets? Just the repetition of her name tells more than any fiery words could. She is a cry in every heart, a picture burned into every brain in England, France, Belgium, America. Recruiting in England instantly jumps ten thousand a day; British soldiers shout *For Edith Cavell!* as they climb out of the trenches and charge. Through America runs a shudder, and those who were neither hot nor cold toward the forces fighting in Europe awake with sudden comprehension to what it is which has made itself strong in Belgium and northern France. The Kaiser, himself, they say, is displeased, and hastens to commute the sentences of the Princess of Croy and the Countess of Belleville and their friends. Even he recognizes that the Great Machine he has built up may be too ruthless, too stupid, too blind.

It is not the German people which has done this thing. It is not even the ruler of the German people which has done it. A Machine has acted. It has struck in hysterical fury at the enemy, but it has inflicted a deeper wound upon the German people and the German cause.

For Edith Cavell, living, could help a few wounded or starving boys into Holland, that is all. But Edith Cavell, dead, is an angel with a flaming sword sweeping through the consciences of mankind, and calling the world to battle.

FOR DISCUSSION

1. How does the author arouse your sympathy for Edith Cavell in the first two paragraphs? Do you have a feeling that the results of this trial will be very important? Why? For whom?

2. We read much of the French and Belgian underground during World War II. How does that of World War I, as we see it here, seem to compare with it?

3. List four expressions which the author uses to give color to our impression of the German court martial.

4. Does the Baron von der Lancken belong to the "Machine"? Give reasons for your answer.

5. Do you think the judges would have been justified in sending Edith Cavell to prison? Defend your answer.

6. "The blood of martyrs is the seed of the Church." Apply this saying to the situation in this story. What are the points of similarity?

FOR BETTER UNDERSTANDING

What characters or situations in the story do you think the following words fit? Use each word in a sentence involving its situation or character to show its suitability: *superb, alleviate, wistful, meditate.*

A DEFENSE OF EDITH CAVELL

Write a brief, earnest defense of Edith Cavell. Show that she was helping her countrymen and that her work could have been stopped without condemning her to death. Make much of the fact that her death might stir the world against Germany and that her life might save other lives.

RELATED READING

In *Joan of Arc,* Hilaire Belloc has described the life of another heroine whose name is written in the hearts of her people.

Hillbilly Jim treats his fiddle as though it were a living thing. As he describes his native hills and talks to his fiddle, which he calls whippoorwill, he reveals things about himself that make him well worth knowing.

The Mountain Whippoorwill

STEPHEN VINCENT BENÉT

Up in the mountains, it's lonesome all the time,
(Sof' win' slewin' thu' the sweet-potato vine).

Up in the mountains, it's lonesome for a child,
(Whippoorwills a-callin' when the sap runs wild).

Up in the mountains, mountains in the fog, 5
Everythin's as lazy as an old houn' dog.

Born in the mountains, never raised a pet,
Don't want nuthin' an' never got it yet.

Born in the mountains, lonesome-born,
Raised runnin' ragged thu' the cockleburrs and corn. 10

Never knew my pappy, mebbe never should.
Think he was a fiddle made of mountain laurel-wood.

Never had a mammy to teach me pretty-please.
Think she was a whippoorwill, a-skitin' thu' the trees.

Never had a brother ner a whole pair of pants, 15
But when I start to fiddle, why, you got to start to dance!

Listen to my fiddle—Kingdom Come—Kingdom Come!
Hear the frogs a-chunkin' "Jug o' rum, Jug o' rum!"

2. SOF' WIN' SLEWIN' THU'—Soft wind twisting through.
14. A-SKITIN'—Gliding quickly.
18. A-CHUNKIN'—The sound is like the "chunk" of a heavy object hitting the water.

Hear that mountain-whippoorwill be lonesome in the air,
And I'll tell yuh how I traveled to the Essex County Fair. 20

Essex County has a mighty pretty fair,
All the smarty fiddlers from the South come there.

Elbows flyin' as they rosin up the bow
For the First Prize Contest in the Georgia Fiddlers' Show.

Old Dan Wheeling, with his whiskers in his ears, 25
King-pin fiddler for nearly twenty years.

Big Tom Sargent, with his blue wall-eye,
An' Little Jimmy Weezer that can make a fiddle cry.

All sittin' roun', spittin' high an' struttin' proud,
(Listen, little whippoorwill, yuh better bug yore eyes!) 30
Tun-a-tun-a-tunin' while the jedges told the crowd
Them that got the mostest claps'd win the bestest prize.

Everybody waitin' for the first tweedle-dee,
When in comes a-stumblin'—hill-billy me!

Bowed right pretty to the judges an' the rest, 35
Took a silver dollar from a hole inside my vest,

Plunked it on the table an' said, "There's my callin' card!
An' anyone that licks me—well, he's got to fiddle hard!"

Old Dan Wheeling, he was laughin' fit to holler,
Little Jimmy Weezer said, "There's one dead dollar!" 40

Big Tom Sargent had a yaller-toothy grin,
But I tucked my little whippoorwill spang underneath my chin,
An' petted it an' tuned it till the jedges said, "Begin!"

Big Tom Sargent was the first in line;
He could fiddle all the bugs off a sweet-potato vine. 45
He could fiddle down a possum from a mile-high tree.
He could fiddle up a whale from the bottom of the sea.

27. WALL-EYE—A large staring eye, as of a fish.
40. THERE'S ONE DEAD DOLLAR—You've lost before you even begin.

Yuh could hear hands spankin' till they spanked each other raw,
When he finished variations on "Turkey in the Straw."

Little Jimmy Weezer was the next to play; 50
He could fiddle all night, he could fiddle all day.

He could fiddle chills, he could fiddle fever,
He could make a fiddle rustle like a lowland river.

He could make a fiddle croon like a lovin' woman.
And they clapped like thunder when he'd finished strummin'. 55

Then came the ruck of the bob-tailed fiddlers,
The let's-go-easies, the fair-to-middlers.

They got their claps an' they lost their bicker,
An' settled back for some more corn-licker.

An' the crowd was tired of their no-count squealing, 60
When out in the center steps Old Dan Wheeling.

He fiddled high and he fiddled low,
(Listen, little whippoorwill; you got to spread yore wings!)
He fiddled with a cherrywood bow.
(Old Dan Wheeling's got bee-honey in his strings.) 65

He fiddled the wind by the lonesome moon,
He fiddled a most almighty tune.

He started fiddling like a ghost.
He ended fiddling like a host.

He fiddled north an' he fiddled south, 70
He fiddled the heart right out of your mouth.

He fiddled here an' he fiddled there.
He fiddled salvation everywhere.

When he was finished, the crowd cut loose,
(Whippoorwill, they's rain on yore breast.) 75
An' I sat there wonderin', "What's the use?"
(Whippoorwill, fly home to yore nest.)

56. RUCK OF THE BOB-TAILED FIDDLERS—The ordinary crowd of unskilled fiddlers.
58. BICKER—Contest.

But I stood up pert an' I took my bow,
An' my fiddle went to my shoulder, so.

An'—they wasn't no crowd to get me fazed— 80
But I was alone where I was raised.

Up in the mountains, so still it makes yuh skeered.
Where God lies sleepin' in his big white beard.

An' I heard the sound of the squirrel in the pine,
An' I heard the earth a-breathin' thu' the long nighttime. 85

They've fiddled the rose, an' they've fiddled the thorn,
But they haven't fiddled the mountain-corn.

They've fiddled sinful an' fiddled moral,
But they haven't fiddled the breshwood-laurel.

They've fiddled loud, an' they've fiddled still, 90
But they haven't fiddled the whippoorwill.

80. FAZED—Worried.

I started off with a *dump-diddle-dump,*
(*Oh, hell's broke loose in Georgia!*)
Skunk-cabbage growin' by the bee-gum stump,
(*Whippoorwill, yo're singin' now!*) 95

Oh Georgia booze is mighty fine booze,
The best yuh ever poured yuh,
But it eats the soles right offen yore shoes,
For Hell's broke loose in Georgia.

My mother was a whippoorwill pert, 100
My father, he was lazy,
But I'm Hell broke loose in a new store shirt
To fiddle all Georgia crazy.

Swing yore partners—up an' down the middle!
Sashay now—oh, listen to that fiddle! 105
Flapjacks flippin' on a red-hot griddle,
An' hell broke loose,

Hell broke loose,
Fire on the mountains—snakes in the grass.
Satan's here a-bilin'—oh, Lordy, let him pass! 110
Go down Moses, set my people free,
Pop goes the weasel thu' the old Red Sea!
Jonah sittin' on a hickory-bough,
Up jumps a whale—an' where's yore prophet now?
Rabbit in the pea-patch, possum in the pot, 115
Try an' stop my fiddle, now my fiddle's gettin' hot!
Whippoorwill, singin' thu' the mountain hush,
Whippoorwill, shoutin' from the burnin' bush,
Whippoorwill, cryin' in the stable door,
Sing tonight as yuh never sang before! 120

Hell's broke loose like a stompin' mountain-shoat,
Sing till yuh bust the gold in yore throat!
Hell's broke loose for forty miles aroun'
Bound to stop yore music if yuh don't sing it down.

105. SWING . . . SASHAY NOW—Calls in the old square dances.
121. MOUNTAIN-SHOAT—A mountain hog.

Sing on the mountains, little whippoorwill, 125
Sing to the valleys, an' slap 'em with a hill,
For I'm struttin' high as an eagle's quill,
An' Hell's broke loose,
Hell's broke loose,
Hell's broke loose in Georgia! 130

They wasn't a sound when I stopped bowin',
(*Whippoorwill, yuh can sing no more.*)

But, somewhere or other, the dawn was growin',
(*Oh, mountain whippoorwill!*)

An' I thought, "I've fiddled all night an' lost. 135
Yo're a good hill-billy, but yuh've been bossed."

So I went to congratulate old man Dan,
—But he put his fiddle into my han'
An' then the noise of the crowd began.

136. BOSSED—Defeated.

FOR DISCUSSION

1. Where did Jim make his first public appearance? Who were on the program with him?

2. Before the contest what did the crowd think of Jim's musical ability?

3. What name had Jim given his fiddle? Explain why this name was a natural choice for him to make.

4. Just before his part in the contest, what did Jim do to put himself in the proper mood? Do you think it was a wise thing to do?

5. In how many ways does the poet repeat the idea, "Hell broke loose"? Did Jim play many or few selections? How can you tell?

6. What was the *immediate* reaction of the crowd when Jim stopped playing? Read the line which indicates this. What was the tribute Dan Wheeling paid to Jim?

7. The following lines are charged with emotion and suggest a great deal more than they say. Find the places in the poem where they occur, and see whether you can interpret the full meaning of each line.

a. "Up in the mountains, it's lonesome for a child."
b. "Think she was a whippoorwill a-skitin' thu' the trees."
c. "When in comes a-stumblin'—hill-billy me!"
d. "(Listen, little whippoorwill; yuh got to spread yore wings!)"
e. "An' then the noise of the crowd began."

8. Discuss in class the following topics. Find lines in the story to support your opinions.

a. Jim's loneliness as a boy
b. Jim's sense of pride in accomplishment
c. Jim's self-confidence
d. Jim's just appraisal of the ability of others
e. Jim's pleasure in fiddling

9. What do you think of Jim's achievement? Did he have much competition?

Explain to the class whether Jim was modest or "cocky." Is there a difference between modesty and timidity? Between self-confidence and arrogance? Is self-confidence a necessary attribute? Can it be combined with modesty? What do we learn about Jim's character from his conduct throughout the contest and after it was over?

ONOMATOPOEIA

Stephen Vincent Benét is a master artist in producing sound effects with words. You may remember that the name of this effect is a long word—*onomatopoeia*. But the thing itself is easy to enjoy. For example, the second line of the poem actually sounds like the wind blowing through the sweet potato vine. See if it doesn't!

"Sof' win' slewin' thu' the sweet potato vine."

Another example is ". . . runnin' ragged thu' the cockleburrs and corn." You can actually hear what it sounds like when someone runs through the crisp and dry cornfield. One more example: "Hear the frogs a-chunkin' 'Jug o' rum, jug o' rum.' " What do you hear? Now see how many more examples *you* can find. You may find *single* words like "a-chunkin' " or longer expressions like the lines quoted above. Don't overlook any examples, even though they add up to dozens!

RHYTHM IN POETRY

1. Reading this poem aloud will emphasize its rhythm, important for real appreciation. Decide how your class or a group from your class would like to present the poem in a choral reading. One suggestion might be to appoint one person as soloist to read the italicized lines. The meaning in the lines themselves will determine whether you should read them slowly or rapidly, softly or loudly. When Jim cuts loose near the end, cut loose right with him!

2. Discover some of the other ways your pleasure in this story has been increased by the fact that it is written in verse instead of prose. It will help you to know that among the musical devices available to the poet, two of the best are rhythm and the repetition of sounds. Point out specific examples of the poem-pleasure you are describing.

◇◇◇◇◇

In the middle 1500's Christian Europe was an embattled fortress. Riddled by the Protestant Revolt that swept the North and England from the fold of the Church, she faced almost in despair yet another threat—the mounting attack of a centuries-old enemy, the Turk.

Like an angry sea not to be denied, the Turkish menace licked and growled at the frontiers. On the eastern flank in 1529, a Moslem army stormed up from prostrate Hungary, to be turned back only at the gates of Vienna. Increasingly, Turkish pirates boldly raided the shores of Spain and Italy, going so far as to sack Ostia, the port of Rome. In 1570, the Turks barbarously conquered all Cyprus except for the city of Famagosta where the Venetians grimly held on. Cyprus in their hands, the Moslems would sweep the Mediterranean with their powerful fleet, thus exposing southern Europe, especially Italy, to invasion.

It took the faith of a great saint—Pope St. Pius V—to kindle anew Europe's crusading spirit. The odds seemed hopeless. North and south Europe were split apart; William of Orange in Holland had actually intrigued with the Turks to invade Spain; jealous France held aloof from a common effort with Philip II of Spain. But Pius V refused to believe that the Moslem could not be defeated at sea, or that the Crusaders' faith was dead. Early in 1571 he appealed to Philip for help.

Philip, although his armies were at the other end of Europe and his treasury bare, wholeheartedly responded, naming his young half-brother, Don Juan, to command the united Papal, Spanish, and Venetian fleets. And so, as a mighty Turkish fleet converged on beleaguered Famagosta in early summer of 1571, the Christian armada grew apace at Messina, Sicily, readying to strike a great crusader's blow in the historic Battle of Lepanto off the west coast of Greece.

THE BATTLE OF LEPANTO

WILLIAM THOMAS WALSH

"Who is she that cometh forth as the morning rising, fair as the moon, bright as the sun, terrible as an army set in array?"

The Turkish fleet, about that time, was setting out from Constantinople, with instructions to find and destroy the Christian navies and to complete the conquest of Cyprus. Before Ali Pasha left the Bosphorus [1] with forty great galleys, four Christian prisoners were crucified, and others skinned alive, as sacrifices to Mohammed for victory. While an army of 70,000 began the siege of Dolcino, on the coast of Albania,[2] the fleet proceeded to Chios [3] (April eighth) where it was joined by forty more vessels under Mohammed-Bey, governor of Negroponte. A second armada was preparing to follow from Constantinople, and Aluch Ali was cruising from Algiers with twenty more. Before the end of April the Grand Turk had almost 300 heavy warships, with a huge army of crack Janizaries [4] and Spahis [5] on board, on the way to Cyprus, where, on May nineteenth, Mustaphá resumed the siege of Famagosta, which had

[1] BOSPHORUS (bŏs′fô·rŭs)—Strait near Constantinople; Bosporus.

[2] ALBANIA—A country in southeastern Europe on the Adriatic Sea.

[3] CHIOS (kī′ŏs)—Island in the Aegean Sea.

[4] JANIZARIES—The bodyguard of the Turkish Sultan.

[5] SPAHIS—Turkish corps of irregular cavalry.

held out heroically for nearly a year under the Venetian general Bragadino.

Mustaphá loosed all his fury upon this city for three months. The Italian women fought in the breaches with their men. The children carried dirt and ammunition. Hunger at last got the better of them, and, in August, Bragadino agreed to surrender, if the Turks would spare their lives. Mustaphá agreed; but as soon as the Christians had laid down their arms, he had them tortured and butchered, women and children with the men. The valiant Bragadino was skinned alive. There were other atrocities too horrible to mention. Mustaphá went sailing off to range the Mediterranean in quest of the Christian fleet, with the stuffed skin of Bragadino swinging from his yardarm.

It seems incredible that with such dangers hanging over their other eastern possessions, and even their own shores, the Venetians should have haggled over the details of the League [6] treaty for fully two months after the Pope had signed it. . . .

At last, however, the treaty was signed, on May twentieth. The news reached Madrid on the Feast of Corpus Christi, and the nuncio hastened to San Lorenzo, to notify the King. Philip was attending a solemn procession in honor of the Blessed Sacrament. It was a day he had long anticipated, for the monastery portion of the Escorial [7] was finished, and he was formally handing it over to the Jeronymite friars he had chosen as its custodians. He would not grant Castagna [8] an audience until the next day; but he had the Cardinal of Siguenza tell him of his pleasure over the good news, and say that Don Juan would start at once. Philip was waiting for confirmation of the news from his own commissioners. This arrived on the morning of June sixth. He then gave his orders. The Prince left Madrid at three o'clock the same afternoon, reaching Guadalajara,[9] thirty-five miles away, the same night. He was at Barcelona on the fifteenth. Don Juan of Austria was riding to the sea at last. . . .

The Pope was pleased with what he heard of his Generalissimo, and wanted him to come to Rome. King Philip refused to allow this. Pope Pius was compelled, therefore, to send the banner of the Crusade and the Admiral's truncheon,[10] which he blessed, to Naples, where, on August second, an immense crowd gathered to hear Mass, and to see Don Juan seated in a throne on the steps of the high altar in Santa Chiara, a noble figure in steel armor, spangled with gold, his shoulders draped with the decoration of the Golden Fleece, even his hair golden in the soft multicolored light of the old church. After Mass, Cardinal Granvelle, as viceroy of Naples and a Prince of the Church, presented to him the truncheon and the azure banner on which was emblazoned the figure of Christ Crucified, with the arms of the Pope, King Philip, Venice, and Don Juan at His feet.

"Take, O illustrious Prince," said Granvelle, "the insignia of the true Word Made Flesh. Take the living symbol of the holy Faith whose defender you will be in this enterprise. He gives you glorious

[6] THE LEAGUE—An association of the Pope, Spain, and Venice joined to fight the Turk.

[7] ESCORIAL—Philip II's magnificent palace.

[8] CASTAGNA (cäs·stän′yä)—The Papal Nuncio to Spain.

[9] GUADALAJARA (gwä·dä·lä·hä′rä).

[10] TRUNCHEON—Officer's baton.

victory over the impious enemy, and by your hand shall his pride be laid in the dust." "Amen!" A mighty shout like that of Clermont [11] burst from the people. "Amen!"

On August twenty-third, when Don Juan arrived at Messina, the harbor was a cluttered forest of masts, the ancient town swarming with men of all nations. By September first, when the whole fleet was assembled, there were 208 galleys in all, 90 of Spain and her dependencies, 106 of Venice and 12 of the Pope; besides nearly 100 brigantines, frigates, and transports, mostly furnished by Spain; with some 50,000 sailors and galley slaves, and 31,000 soldiers: 19,000 of them paid by King Philip (including Germans and Italians), 8,000 Venetians, 2,000 Papal troops, and 2,000 volunteers, chiefly from Spain.

The Spanish galleys were by far the best built, best equipped, and best handled, and would bear the brunt of any fighting. The Venetian ships showed up so badly in a review that Don Juan inspected some of them, and found, to his disgust, that they were not even sufficiently manned. Some had hardly any crews. Others lacked fighting men. He distributed among the worst of them about 4,000 of the famous Spanish and Italian infantry. Then he held a Council of War, attended by seventy officers. Some favored a merely defensive campaign, since the Turks evidently outnumbered them, and the risk would be great, especially as the time for autumn tempests was at hand. Others said that if the Turk galleys were more numerous, they were not so efficient; and "something always had to be left to luck." Don Juan himself apparently hesitated, thinking of the King's instructions.[12]

The Papal influence was all in favor of fighting, whatever the odds. The invincible spirit of the old saint in the Vatican was perhaps the decisive factor. When Bishop Odescalchi, his nuncio, came to bless the fleet and to give a large portion of the True Cross for distribution among the crews, each vessel having a grain of the Precious Wood, he also brought to Don Juan the solemn assurance of Pope Pius V that, if he offered battle, God would give him the victory. If they were defeated, the Pope promised "to go to war himself with his gray hairs, to put idle youth to shame." But with courage they could not fail. Had not several revelations, including two prophecies by Saint Isidore of Sevilla, described such a battle and victory as seemed imminent, won by a youth closely resembling Don Juan?

At the Holy Father's suggestion, Don Juan adopted a *modus operandi* [13] seldom if ever taught in naval academies. No women were allowed aboard the ships. Blasphemy was to be punished with death. While waiting for a good wind and the return of his scouting squadron with news of where the Turks were, the Generalissimo fasted for three days. All his officers and crews did likewise. Contemporary accounts agree that not one of the 81,000 sailors and soldiers failed to confess and to receive Holy Communion. Even the galley slaves were unshackled from their long benches and led in droves

[11] CLERMONT—The place where Pope Urban II announced the First Crusade.

[12] KING'S INSTRUCTIONS—Not to risk battle without the unanimous consent of Philip's envoy, Requesens, and admirals Doria and Santa Cruz.

[13] *Modus operandi*—Mode of operating.

ashore, to confess to the numerous priests who toiled day and night at the Jesuit College helping the chaplains of the galleys. . . .

When the last of the Venetians had arrived, the Armada began to put to sea, September fifteenth, in the order agreed upon. Doria led the vanguard with 54 galleys of the right wing, flying green banners. Don Juan followed next morning with the *batalla*[14] or center, under azure banners, with the blue standard of Our Lady of Guadalupe over the *Real*.[15] (The Pope's Standard of the League was reserved for battle.) Marcantonio Colonna, on the flagship of the Pope, was on his right. Veniero, a cantankerous old Venetian sea-dog, at his left. The third squadron of the Venetian Barbarigo followed, with yellow banners; and the Marqúes of Santa Cruz (Don Álvaro de Bazan) brought up the rear with thirty Spanish galleys and some of Italy, all under white flags.

It was a sight to remember—the papal nuncio, a flaming figure in scarlet from head to foot, standing on the mole[16] with hand uplifted to bless each ship as it passed, the crusaders kneeling on the decks, the knights and men-at-arms glittering with steel, the sailors in red suits and caps, the rowers with dark naked backs glistening with sweat, the brown sails bellying out to catch the first breeze; and on the lofty prow of the flagship, Don Juan in golden armor, like an avenging angel under the outflung blue banner of her who had trodden on the serpent's head. Thus they passed into the open Mediterranean and formed in ranks, two by two. The six great Venetian *galeasses*,[17] each a bristling fort with 44 heavy guns, led the way into the sapphire-studded morning light. The galeasses kept a full mile ahead, to open the fray with a heavy bombardment. Two by two the whole Armada followed, almost in battle order, according to a plan carefully worked out by old paralyzed Don Garcia de Toledo. The plan was somewhat modified, apparently, to leave spaces between the squadrons, so that Santa Cruz could intervene where his help might be needed. . . .

Don Juan left Corfu on September twenty-eighth. While the Turkish fleet was skirting the southern shore of Aetolia,[18] making for the Gulf of Corinth (or Lepanto) the Christian Armada, using oars because the wind was contrary, nosed through the waters of the Ionian Sea,[19] with the Albanian shore off the port bows, past Nicopolis and that stretch of sea lying off Actium where the spirit of the East had fled from the spirit of the West in the jaded galleys of Antony and Cleopatra, and around the coast of Santa Maura to Cephalonia,[20] with the narrow isle of Ithaca[21] hugged under its lee shore, still fragrant with the memory of Penelope and the unconquerable fortitude of Odysseus.

It was October fifth when the fleet cast

[14] *Batalla*—Pronounced bä·tī′yä.
[15] *Real*—Pronounced rā·äl′.
[16] MOLE—A jetty or breakwater partially enclosing a harbor.

[17] *Galeasses*—Large armed galleys, with three masts, and at least fifteen oars on each side.
[18] AETOLIA—A district in western Greece.
[19] IONIAN SEA—The part of the Mediterranean between Greece and southern Italy.
[20] CEPHALONIA—Islands in the Mediterranean Sea.
[21] ITHACA—For a story of Ithaca, Penelope (pḗ·nĕl′ṓ·pē), and Odysseus (ṓ·dĭs′ūs) see page 373 of this book.

anchor among the Curzolares.[22] That day a brigantine from Candia came by with news of the fall of Famagosta, and the horrible atrocities perpetrated by Mustaphá upon the helpless Christians who had surrendered. A quiver of rage passed through the floating city of armed men. Nothing could have been better timed to make them fight like holy madmen.

The wind was east, the sky overcast, the sea gray with fog. All day Saturday and well into the night, the fleet remained inactive, not knowing that the wind which kept them there had brought the Turkish fleet across the Gulf of Patras to the Albanian shore, and that Aluch Ali, with all his Algerian galleys, was still with them. With the falling of the starless night a dead silence settled over the sea.

About two o'clock in the morning of Sunday, the seventh, there came up a fresh steady wind from the west, across the Ionian Sea, sweeping the stars and the wide bay clear of the wraiths of fog. Don Juan, lying sleepless in the cabin of his *Real*, saw that he was in the middle of what seemed a huge lake, flooded with moonlight. He gave the word, the great anchors were weighed and the sails unfurled, the whips cracked over the straining backs of the galley slaves, the great ships hove through the choppy waters, as if racing the dawn to the Albanian coast. When the sun came flaming up over the Gulf of Lepanto, Doria's lookout, in the vanguard, sighted a squadron of the enemy about twelve miles away, returning from a scouting trip to Santa Maura. The signal flag agreed upon was on the masthead of the royal frigate, where Doria was on watch.

"We must conquer or die here," said Don Juan, exultantly, and ordered a green banner displayed as a sign for all to get in battle array. The multiple banks of oars on the six great Venetian galeasses plunged into the sea, driving the massive hulks to their positions, two of them a mile in front of each of the three sections of the battle line.

The Venetian Barbarigo, with sixty-four galleys, veered as closely as possible to the Aetolian shore, to prevent an encircling movement by the enemy on the north. Don Juan commanded the center or *batalla* of sixty-three galleys, with Colonna and Veniero on either side of him, and Requesens in the ship behind him. Doria's squadron of sixty took the right wing, nearest the open sea, the most dangerous post of all. Thirty-five vessels were held in reserve in the rear under the Marqúes of Santa Cruz, with orders to give help wherever it might be needed. Thus the great fleet advanced into the Gulf of Patras, in a long arc extending over a league-and-a-half of sea and gradually stiffening into a straighter line as the enemy came in sight.

The Turks, having a total of 286 galleys (for Hascen Bey had just arrived with 22 extra ones from Tripoli) against 208, had decided to fight, and were clearing their decks for action. Mohammed Siroco with 55 galleys opposed Barbarigo. Ali Pasha and Pertew with 96 faced the *batalla* of Don Juan. Aluch Ali with 73 took the side nearest the open sea, opposite Gianandrea Doria. There was also a squadron of reserve in the rear. The wind had shifted to the east, bringing on

[22] CURZOLARES—A group of islands in the eastern Adriatic Sea.

the Turks with bellied sails, while the Christians had to use their oars. Toward noon it almost died away. Four hours passed while both fleets made their preparations for combat.

Doria meanwhile came back in a swift frigate to consult with Don Juan and the others. According to one account he was averse, at the start, to giving battle to an enemy with so large a preponderance of heavy ships. He wanted a council of war, at least. But Don Juan cried, "It is time to fight now, not to talk"; and so it was agreed. Cabrera says Doria not only drew up the final battle order of the fleet, but suggested that the Generalissimo have the *espolones* cut away from the bows of his galleys. These were sharp spurs, fourteen feet long which could crash through the side of an enemy ship, doing great damage when propelled by the arms of a hundred galley slaves. It was obvious that in fighting at close quarters, hand-to-hand, ship locked to ship, they would be useless. Without them, too, Don Juan could place his bow guns lower, and hit the Turkish hulks nearer the water line. The plan was adopted. One after another down the long line the *espolones* splashed into the calm sea.

The young Admiral, now in his golden armor, went in a fast frigate from ship to ship, holding up an iron crucifix for all to see. "Hey, valorous soldiers!" he cried. "Here's the chance you wanted. I have done my part. Do you now humble the pride of the enemy and win glory in this holy fight. Live or die, be conquerors; if you die, you go to Heaven." The sight of the gallant young figure and the sound of his fresh voice had an extraordinary effect. A mighty shout answered him from each ship. There passed across the sparkling sea a long broken cheer as the Pope's banner of the League, with the image of Christ Crucified catching the glint of the high sun, rose above the *Real* beside the blue flag of Our Lady of Guadalupe. On the forward mast of his flagship Don Juan had hung a crucifix which alone of all his effects survived the fire in his house of Alcalá.

As the Turks advanced in a great half-moon he knelt on the prow and in a loud voice begged the blessing of God on the Christian arms, while priests and monks throughout the fleet held up crucifixes before the kneeling sailors and soldiers. The sun was now directly overhead. The clear water, almost unrippled, flashed back a tremulous replica in vivid colors of a thousand standards, streamers, pennons and gonfalons, the cold brilliant glitter of weapons and armor, the gold and silver of armaments, all wavering kaleidoscopically between the blue sea and the dazzling sky. A hush like that which comes just before the consecration of the Mass fell over the whole Armada. The Turkish side replied with the usual blood-curdling chorus of screams, hoots, jibes and groans, the clashing of cimeters on shields, the blaring of horns and trumpets. The Christians waited in silence.

At that moment the wind, which had thus far favored the Turks, shifted to the west and sped the Christian galleys on to the shock. Ali Pasha, in the Moslem center, opened the battle with a cannon shot. Don Juan answered, with another. As the Turkish oarsmen churned the sea, the six great galeasses of Venice opened fire with their 264 guns. This bombardment was not as devastating as had been expected, but it had the effect of breaking the enemy's line. The Turkish right was racing now to gain the open water between the Venetians and the Aetolian shore. Five ships closed upon the galley of Barbarigo, while the Moorish archers let fly clouds of poisoned arrows, which they preferred to firearms and used with more deadly effect. Ship to ship they were lashed now, fighting hand-to-hand. Huge Barbarigo fought like a lion, until, taking his shield from his face to shout an order, he was pierced through the eye with an arrow.

It was the Christian right that stood the heaviest attack. Doria was held in fear and respect by the Moslems. Moreover, he occupied the most dangerous post, where strategy and good sailing counted. If there was a match for him among the mariners of the Mediterranean, it was Aluch Ali, the Italian apostate.[23] As the Turkish left tried to gain the open sea, to attack by poop and prow, Doria extended his line farther to the right, leaving a space between his squadron and the *batalla.* Aluch Ali swiftly changed his course and came crashing through the open space with his best ships, while his slower sailing galleys took the Genoese on the side toward the open sea. Doria, heavily outnumbered, fought a magnificent engagement. On ten of his vessels, nearly all the soldiers were killed in the first hour of the conflict. The handful of survivors fought on, desperately holding their ships in the hope of succor.

Santa Cruz' reserve, however, had gone to the aid of some of the Venetians on the left, and the whole *batalla* was locked in mortal conflict with the Turkish center. As soon as Ali Pasha saw where the holy flags flew over the galley of Don Juan, he drove straight for it. The two enormous hulks crashed prow to prow. Ali's ship was higher and heavier, and manned with 500 picked Janizaries.

The wisdom of Doria's advice to cut away the *espolones* was now apparent; while the Turk's artillery fired through the rigging of the *Real,* Don Juan's poured death into the ranks of the Janizaries as the ships grappled. Hand-to-hand they fought from one deck to the other, for two hours. Seven Turkish ships stood by to help the *Sultana.* As fast as the Janizaries fell on the decks, they were replaced by others from the hulks of reserve. Twice the horde of yelling Turks penetrated the *Real* to the mainmast, and twice the Spaniards thrust them back. But Don Juan, with heavy losses, had only two ships of reserves. Fighting gallantly in a little ring of chosen Spanish cavaliers, he was wounded in the foot. His situation was extremely perilous, in fact, when Santa Cruz, having saved the Venetians, came to his aid and rushed 200 reserves aboard.

Heartened by this fresh blood, the Spanish threw themselves on Ali and his Janizaries so furiously that they hurled them back into their own ship. Three times the Christians charged, and three times the Turks cast them out over decks now red and slippery with blood, piled with heaps of dead men, ghastly mangled trunks, severed arms and legs still quivering. The two fleets were locked in the embrace of death, ships lashed by twos and threes in water already streaked with

[23] APOSTATE—A deserter from a cause; as from faith or religion.

crimson from floating bodies and limbs. The din of musketry, screams of rage and pain, clash of steel on steel, thunder of artillery, falling of spars and lashing of bloody waters between rocking timbers resounded horribly all through the Sunday afternoon. Splendid and terrible deeds were done. Old Veniero, seventy years old, fought sword in hand at the head of his men. Cervantes arose from his bed of fever to fight and to lose his left hand. Young Alexander of Parma boarded a Turkish galley alone, and survived the experience. The moment was critical, and the issue still in doubt, when the magnificent Ali Pasha, defending his ship from the last Christian onslaught, was laid low by a ball from a Spanish arquebus.[24] His body was dragged to the feet of Don Juan. A Spanish soldier triumphantly pounced upon it and shore away the head. One version says that Don Juan reproved him for this brutality. Another, more likely, says that the Prince impaled the head on the end of a long pike and held it up for all to see. Hoarse shouts of victory burst from the Christians on the *Real*, as they brushed the disheartened Turks into the sea and hoisted the banner of Christ Crucified to the enemy masthead. There was not a single hole in this flag, though the spars and masts were riddled, and the mainmast bristled with arrows like a porcupine. From ship to ship the shout of triumph was taken up, with the word that Ali was dead and the Christians had won. A panic seized the enemy, and he took to flight.

As the sun sank over Cephalonia, Doria's right wing was still furiously engaged with the Algerians. Gianandrea was red from head to foot with blood, but escaped without a scratch. When Aluch Ali saw that the Moslem fleet was getting

[24] ARQUEBUS (är′kwê·bŭs)—An ancient firearm, predecessor of the musket.

the worse of it, he skillfully withdrew between the right and the center of the Christians. In the rear of Doria's fleet he came upon a galley of the Knights of Malta, whom he especially hated. He pounced upon it from the stern, slew all the knights and the crew, and took possession of the vessel; but when Santa Cruz attacked him, he abandoned his prize and fled with 40 of his best ships toward the open sea and the crimson sunset. Doria's fleet pursued him until night and the coming of a storm forced him to desist.

The Christians took refuge in the port of Petala, and there counted their casualties, which were comparatively light, and their booty, which was exceedingly rich. They had lost 8,000 slain, including 2,000 Spanish, 800 of the Pope's men, and 5,200 Venetians. The Turks had lost 224 vessels, 130 captured and more than 90 sunk or burned; 25,000 of their men had been slain, and 5,000 captured; 10,000 of their Christian captives were set free.

Don Juan at once sent ten galleys to Spain to inform the King, and dispatched the Count of Priego to Rome. But Pius V had speedier means of communication than galleys. On the afternoon of Sunday, October seventh, he was walking in the Vatican with his treasurer, Donata Cesis. The evening before he had sent out orders to all convents in Rome and nearby to double their prayers for the victory of the Christian fleet, but now he was listening to a recital of some of his financial difficulties. Suddenly he stepped aside, opened a window, and stood watching the sky as if astonished. Then, turning with a radiant face to the treasurer, he said,

"Go with God. This is not the time for business, but to give thanks to Jesus Christ, for our fleet has just conquered."

He then hurried to his chapel to prostrate himself in thanksgiving. Afterwards he went out, and everybody noticed his youthful step and joyous countenance.

The first news of the battle, through human agencies, reached Rome by way of Venice on the night of October twenty-first, just two weeks after the event. Saint Pius went to St. Peter's in a procession, singing the *Te Deum Laudamus.* There was great joy in Rome. The Holy Father commemorated the victory by designating October seventh as the Feast of the Holy Rosary, and by adding "Help of Christians" to the titles of Our Lady in the Litany of Loreto.

◇◇◇◇◇◇◇◇◇◇◇◇◇◇◇◇◇◇◇◇◇◇◇◇◇◇◇◇◇◇

FOR DISCUSSION

1. How was your interest aroused at the very beginning of the selection? What impression do you gain of Mustaphá?

2. Cite at least four occasions on which the intense Catholicity of the expedition was manifested. Was this expedition and battle before or after the Protestant Revolt?

3. Get a Mediterranean map and trace for yourself the fleet's course. Do you know from your ancient history whether any other famous battle had taken place near Lepanto?

4. Compare the original fleet sizes with the losses suffered by each. Was it a real Christian victory or did the Turks just retreat to prepare for another battle?

5. How did Pope Pius V get word of the Christian success? What was his reaction? What do you know about Pius V which makes you think he was a holy man?

6. What marks of the true Christian do you observe in Don Juan? What other ad-

mirable qualities of character or ability do you note in him?

PICTURE WORDS

Note the author's use of words that *fit*. For example, he does not say that Mustaphá sailed the Mediterranean; he says he *ranged* the Mediterranean. Show why such words as *crack, haggled, cluttered, brunt, glittering, skirting, nosed, pounced* are effective in their sentences.

PROJECTS

1. You will be interested in learning about other occasions on which the Mohammedans nearly conquered Christian Europe. See what you can find out about the Battle of Tours; about the immortal Polish king, John Sobieski and about his people's heroic defense of the Faith's eastern boundaries. Make a report to the class on the information you have gathered.

2. Write an account of the Battle of Lepanto as a news reporter would have done in the year 1571.

3. Write an editorial about the victory of the Christians as an editor of a pro-Christian paper might have written in 1571.

RELATED READING

A pulsating account of the battle of Lepanto is G. K. Chesterton's poem, "Lepanto."

Translated into English, "Guilielmus Rex" (gwĭl·ē·ĕl′mŭs rĕks) means "King William." This poem is a portrait of a man who never actually wore a crown. As you read, you will recognize why he is referred to as a king.

Guilielmus Rex

THOMAS BAILEY ALDRICH

The folk who lived in Shakespeare's day
And saw that gentle figure pass
By London Bridge, his frequent way—
They little knew what man he was.

The pointed beard, the courteous mien,
The equal port to high and low,
All this they saw or might have seen—
But not the light behind the brow!

The doublet's modest gray or brown,
The slender sword-hilt's plain device,
What sign had these for prince or clown?
Few turned, or none, to scan him twice.

Yet 'twas the king of England's kings!
The rest with all their pomps and trains
Are moulded, half-remembered things—
'Tis he alone that lives and reigns!

5. MIEN—Manner.
6. EQUAL PORT—Same treatment.
9. DOUBLET—Close-fitting jacket.
10. DEVICE—Emblem.

FOR DISCUSSION

1. What did bystanders notice about the "gentle figure" passing London Bridge? What did they *fail* to see?
2. Who was the man? Of what realm was he king?
3. Even though Shakespeare was a successful playwright during his lifetime, why does the author insist that the general public of 16th century England did not recognize his true greatness?
4. Do you agree with the last three lines of the poem? Discuss.

WORD STUDY

Modestus is a Latin word from *modus,* meaning *measure.* We get our English word *modest* from it. Find the English word in the dictionary and notice how closely its first and second meanings are related to the original Latin.

What relationship is there between the derivations of *rex, rich,* and *king?*

FOR DEEPER MEANING

The clue to the meaning in this poem is hidden in the first four lines and repeated variously in each successive set of four lines. In preparation for doing one of the following projects, write a sentence or two in your own words, telling the meaning of this poem. Then choose one of these activities:

1. Name a woman or man (living or dead) about whom this same truth can be said. Write a paragraph telling why you think the person you have named can be called a king or queen.
2. Have you ever felt that others have overlooked your ability in sports or studies or in some other realm? Have you ignored the skills that someone else has? Write a short character sketch of a person whom you appreciate but whose qualities you feel are overlooked by others.

Can you imagine what it would be to see two frail girls martyred? Reading these lines is like having such an experience or like watching a grim news reel. Read thoughtfully, so that every word will carry its full meaning.

Two Carthaginian Girls

ALFRED BARRETT, S.J.

Walking at night-fall where the pink
And red hibiscus trimly furls,
I watch two petals blow to the grass,
Two crimson stains to make me think
Upon those Carthaginian girls, 5
Perpetua, Felicitas,
Whose very names our missals link
In perpetual felicity.

Blurred centuries dissolved. I see
A martyr walking to her crown, 10
Pale as her ungirded gown,
The tall, serene, patrician
Perpetua. . . . Felicitas,
Of humbler origin, a slave,
Nurses her dungeon-born with tears, 15
Her babe of two brief days. Some man
Derides her travail pain and sneers,
"How against beasts will you be brave?"
To whom the martyr makes reply,
"I suffer now, but when I die 20
Christ suffers in me then, not I."

7. OUR MISSALS LINK—Prayers after the Elevation of the chalice during Mass mention their names together.
8. PERPETUAL FELICITY—An exact translation of the Latin names of the two martyrs.
12. PATRICIAN—Aristocratic.

They wait unseeing side by side,
When over the arena sands
Races a tawny, snarling tide,
A surf of lions circling round, 25
Lions that cringe and paw the ground—
For suddenly no spear can prod
Them on to where Perpetua stands
Like a lighthouse shining out to God
With the white beams of extended hands.
Careless of death, its when and how, 31
Perpetua, Felicitas,
The mistress and the serving lass,
Encircle one another's necks,
Embracing, till a goaded cow 35
Is loosed to match and mock their sex.
Perpetua is tossed. She falls
Piteously. The heifer mauls
With violating horns. But she
Arises, mangled, smoothes her dress 40
And drapes that riven tunic, less
Mindful of pain than modesty.
Then gathering her streaming hair
In the pathos of her womanly pride,
Begs for some clasp. With skill and care
Both arms sweep in fluent curves 46

41. RIVEN—Torn.
44. PATHOS—Suffering.

To her head, that, though her robes be
torn,
His eyes whom she dying serves
May deem her vain as any bride
And not as one who seems to mourn. . . .
Two Carthaginian girls, they kneel, 51
Perpetua, Felicitas,
Upon their lifted throats to feel
The sacrificial *coup-de-grace,*
The stroke of consecrating steel. 55

So far away and long ago
These girls were born and loved and died,
It daily sets my heart aglow
To see—like petals side by side—
Perpetua, Felicitas 60
Pressed in the canon of the Mass!

54. *Coup-de-grace*—The death-dealing blow given in mercy to end the suffering of a victim.
61. CANON—Main part.

FOR DISCUSSION

1. What starts the poet thinking about these two early Christian martyrs?
2. What was Perpetua to Felicitas and Felicitas to Perpetua? Why are their names still joined after many centuries? What was the source of their great courage?
3. Do you think Catholic girls of today would act in the same way if placed in the same circumstances? Give reasons for your answer.

WORD STUDY

1. The poet speaks of Felicitas' humble origin. *Humble* comes from the Latin word *humilis,* meaning *on the ground* or *low.* Hence we know that Felicitas was of lower origin. What is the meaning of *humble* today?
2. Perpetua is described as *serene.* This word also is originally Latin—*serenus,* meaning *bright* or *clear.* What is the modern meaning of *serene?*

A PROJECT

Bring to class the *Roman Martyrology,* which is a list of the martyrs. Under the date, March 7, find what is told about these two Carthaginian girls. Then reread the poem, noticing how much the poet has added to the story from his own sources. Do you marvel at the magic of the poet's imagination? While you have the *Martyrology* in class, see if you can find your own saint's day.

RELATED READING

Mint by Night has more poems by the same author.

The story you are about to read is an excerpt from the novel QUO VADIS. This novel by the brilliant Polish author, Henryk Sienkiewicz, deals with the history of Rome in the time of Nero. Born in 37 A.D. Nero, often called Caesar, ruled as Emperor of Rome from 54 to 68 A.D. QUO VADIS thus recalls the first days of the Church, the love and courage of the early Christians, the burning of Rome, and that first savage thunderblast of the Empire against the Church—Nero's persecution. Against this spectacular backdrop moves the dramatic story—the romance between Vinicius, a young Roman tribune, and a Christian hostage of noble blood, Lygia.

At the outset of the story, Vinicius and Lygia meet at the home of her guardians. Lygia is attracted to the manly pagan, a veteran of the Armenian war. Struck by her young beauty, Vinicius falls passionately in love. Without scruple, he employs his prestige to withdraw the lovely, innocent girl from the protection of her Christian home. At Nero's command, Lygia is thrust for a moment into the sultry, poison-laden air of the imperial household. When she is being brought like a plaything to the palace of Vinicius, the Roman Christians unexpectedly rescue Lygia in a night foray, and hide her in the sprawling slums of the city.

In fury, the young Roman attempts to find Lygia. When he discovers her, Lygia is under Saint Peter's protection. A rash kidnaping venture by Vinicius fails, owing to the giant strength of the Christian barbarian, Ursus; Vinicius' life is saved only by Lygia's intervention. In Lygia and in the Christians he glimpses for the first time a noble goodness completely foreign to his pagan, self-seeking nature. Vinicius humbly determines to search out the truths of the unknown and hitherto despised Christian religion.

As we take up the story, the young tribune is a changed man. He has been baptized by Saint Peter, and his love for Lygia has been purified in his new-found love for Our Lord. But the persecution of the Christians in the wake of the great fire of Rome thrusts itself inexorably between the two young people. Lygia is captured, and mad Nero, knowing the story of their love, cruelly plans her death before the eyes of Vinicius. The news spreads over the city that this event in the great Roman arena will climax the bloody holocaust of the martyrs.

It is night in the imperial city. The stars are out, and under their majestic canopy the approaches and banks of the arena glitter with light cast *by hundreds of flaming torches. The shadowy amphitheater has come to life under its burden of noisy thousands. In the imperial boxes are Nero and his laughing retinue, and among the latter at Nero's command, sits Vinicius, grim and almost helpless.*

THE SAVING OF LYGIA

HENRYK SIENKIEWICZ

Evening exhibitions, rare up to that period and given only exceptionally, became common in Nero's time, both in the Circus and amphitheater. The Augustians [1] liked them, frequently because they were followed by feasts and drinking-bouts which lasted till daylight. Though the people were sated already with blood-spilling, still, when the news went forth that the end of the games was approaching, and that the last of the Christians were to die at an evening spectacle, a countless audience assembled in the amphitheater. The Augustians came to a man, for they understood that it would not be a common spectacle; they knew that Caesar had determined to make for himself a tragedy out of the suffering of Vinicius. Tigellinus had kept secret the kind of punishment intended for the betrothed of the young tribune; but that merely roused general curiosity. Those who had seen Lygia at the house of Plautius told wonders of her beauty. Others were occupied above all with the question, would they see her really in the arena that day; for many of those who had heard the answer given Petronius [2] and Nerva by Caesar explained it in two ways: some supposed simply that Nero would give or perhaps had given the maiden to Vinicius; they remembered that she was a hostage, hence free to worship whatever divinities she liked, and that the law of nations did not permit her punishment.

Uncertainty, waiting, and curiosity had mastered all spectators. Caesar arrived earlier than usual; and immediately at his coming people whispered that something uncommon would happen, for besides Tigellinus and Vatinius, Caesar had with him Cassius, a centurion [3] of enormous size and gigantic strength, whom he summoned only when he wished to have a defender at his side,—for example, when he desired night expeditions to the Suburra,[4] where he arranged the amusement called "sagatio," which consisted in tossing on a

[1] AUGUSTIANS—The circle of patricians who enjoyed Nero's favor.

[2] PETRONIUS—A Roman noble, the uncle of Vinicius.

[3] CENTURION—A captain in the Roman army, in command of a century (100 soldiers).

[4] SUBURRA—A slum section of Rome.

soldier's cloak maidens met on the way. It was noted also that certain precautions had been taken in the amphitheater itself. The pretorian[5] guards were increased; command over them was held, not by a centurion, but by the tribune Subrius Flavius, known hitherto for blind attachment to Nero. It was understood, then, that Caesar wished in every case to secure himself against an outburst of despair from Vinicius, and curiosity rose all the more.

Every eye was turned with strained gaze to the place where the unfortunate lover was sitting. He was exceedingly pale, and his forehead was covered with drops of sweat; he was in as much doubt as were other spectators, but alarmed to the lowest depth of his soul. Petronius knew not what would happen; he was silent, except that, while turning from Nerva, he asked Vinicius whether he was ready for everything, and next, whether he would remain at the spectacle. To both questions Vinicius answered "Yes," but a shudder passed through his whole body; he divined that Petronius did not ask without reason. For some time he had lived with only half his life,—he had sunk in death, and reconciled himself to Lygia's death, since for both it was to be liberation and a marriage; but he learned now that it was one thing to think of the last moment when it was distant as of a quiet dropping asleep, and another to look at the torment of a person dearer to one than life. All sufferings endured formerly rose in him anew. Despair, which had been set at rest, began again to cry in his soul; the former desire to save Lygia at any price seized him anew. Beginning with the morning, he had tried to go to the cunicula[6] to be sure that she was there; but the pretorians watched every entrance, and orders were so strict that the soldiers, even those whom he knew, would not be softened by prayers or gold. It seemed to the tribune that uncertainty would kill him before he should see the spectacle. Somewhere at the bottom of his heart the hope was still throbbing, that perhaps Lygia was not in the amphitheater, that his fears were groundless. At times he seized on this hope with all his strength. He said in his soul that Christ might take her to himself out of the prison, but could not permit her torture in the Circus. Formerly he was resigned to the divine will in everything; now, when repulsed from the doors of the cunicula, he returned to his place in the amphitheater, and when he learned, from the curious glances turned on him, that the most dreadful suppositions might be true, he began to implore in his soul with passionateness almost approaching a threat. "Thou canst!" repeated he, clenching his fists convulsively. "Thou canst!" Hitherto he had not supposed that that moment when present would be so terrible. Now, without clear consciousness of what was happening in his mind, he had the feeling that if he should see Lygia tortured, his love for God would be turned to hatred, and his faith to despair. But he was amazed at the feeling, for he feared to offend Christ, whom he was imploring for mercy and miracles. He implored no longer for her life; he wished merely that she should die before they brought her to the arena, and from the abyss of his pain he repeated in spirit:

[5] PRETORIAN—Caesar's bodyguard.

[6] CUNICULA—The dungeons under the arena.

"Do not refuse even this, and I will love Thee still more than hitherto." And then his thoughts raged as a sea torn by a whirlwind. A desire for blood and vengeance was roused in him. He was seized by a mad wish to rush at Nero and stifle him there in presence of all the spectators; but he felt that desire to be a new offense against Christ, and a breach of His command. At times flashes of hope flew to his head that everything before which his soul was trembling would be turned away by an almighty and merciful hand; but they were quenched at once, as if in measureless sorrow that He who could destroy that Circus with one word and save Lygia had abandoned her, though she trusted in Him and loved Him with all the strength of her pure heart. And he thought, moreover, that she was lying there in that dark place, weak, defenseless, deserted, abandoned to the whim or disfavor of brutal guards, drawing her last breath, perhaps, while he had to wait, helpless, in that dreadful amphitheater, without knowing what torture was prepared for her, or what he would witness in a moment. Finally, as a man falling over a precipice grasps at everything which grows on the edge of it, so did he grasp with both hands at the thought that faith alone could save her. That one method remained! Peter had said that faith could move the earth to its foundations.

Hence he rallied; he crushed doubt in himself, he compressed his whole being into the sentence, "I believe," and he looked for a miracle.

But as an overdrawn cord may break, so exertion broke him. The pallor of death covered his face, and his body relaxed. He thought then that his prayer had been heard, for he was dying. It seemed to him that Lygia must surely die too, and that Christ would take them to himself in that way. The arena, the white togas,[7] the countless spectators, the light of thousands of lamps and torches, all vanished from his vision.

But his weakness did not last long. After a while he roused himself, or rather the stamping of the impatient multitude roused him.

"Thou art ill," said Petronius; "give command to bear thee home."

And without regard to what Caesar would say, he rose to support Vinicius and go out with him. His heart was filled with pity, and, moreover, he was irritated beyond endurance because Caesar was looking through the emerald[8] at Vinicius, studying his pain with satisfaction to describe it afterward, perhaps, in pathetic strophes,[9] and win the applause of hearers.

Vinicius shook his head. He might die in that amphitheater, but he could not go out of it. Moreover the spectacle might begin at any moment.

In fact, at that very instant almost, the prefect of the city waved a red handkerchief; the hinges opposite Caesar's podium[10] creaked, and out of the dark gully came Ursus into the brightly lighted arena.

The giant blinked, dazed evidently by the glitter of the arena; then he pushed

[7] TOGA—The outer cloak worn by Roman citizens.

[8] EMERALD—A transparent gem cut to serve as an eye-glass; Nero was shortsighted.

[9] STROPHES (strō′fēs)—Lines characteristic of ancient dramatic poetry and recited on stage by a chorus; Nero fancied himself a great poet.

[10] PODIUM (pō′dĭ·ŭm)—Caesar's special box.

into the center, gazing around as if to see what he had to meet. It was known to all the Augustians and to most of the spectators that he was the man who had stifled Croton;[11] hence at sight of him a murmur passed along every bench. In Rome there was no lack of gladiators larger by far than the common measure of man, but Roman eyes had never seen the like of Ursus. Cassius, standing in Caesar's podium, seemed puny compared with that Lygian. Senators, vestals,[12] Caesar, the Augustians, and the people gazed with delight of experts at his mighty limbs as large as tree-trunks, at his breast as large as two shields joined together, and his arms of a Hercules.[13] The murmur rose to shouts, and eager questions were put: Where did the people live who could produce such a giant? He stood there, in the middle of the amphitheater, naked, more like a stone colossus[14] than a man, with a collected expression, and at the same time the sad look of a barbarian; and while surveying the empty arena, he gazed wonderingly with his blue childlike eyes, now at the spectators, now at Caesar, now at the grating of the cunicula, whence, as he thought, his executioners would come.

At the moment when he stepped into the arena his simple heart was beating for the last time with the hope that perhaps a cross was waiting for him; but when he saw neither the cross nor the hole in which it might be put, he thought that he was unworthy of such favor,—that he would find death in another way, and surely from wild beasts. He was unarmed, and had determined to die as became a confessor of the "Lamb," peacefully and patiently. Meanwhile he wished to pray once more to the Saviour; so he knelt on the arena, joined his hands, and raised his eyes toward the stars which were glittering in the lofty opening of the amphitheater.

That act displeased the crowd. They had had enough of those Christians who died like sheep. They understood that if the giant would not defend himself the spectacle would be a failure. Here and there hisses were heard. Some began to cry for scourgers, whose office it was to lash combatants unwilling to fight. But soon all had grown silent, for no one knew what was waiting for the giant, nor whether he would not be ready to struggle when he met death eye to eye.

In fact, they had not long to wait. Suddenly the shrill sound of brazen trumpets was heard, and at that signal a grating opposite Caesar's podium was opened, and into the arena rushed, amid shouts of beast-keepers, an enormous German aurochs,[15] bearing on his head the naked body of a woman.

"Lygia! Lygia!" cried Vinicius.

Then he seized his hair near the temples, squirmed like a man who feels a sharp dart in his body, and began to repeat in hoarse accents,—

"I believe! I believe! O Christ, a miracle!"

And he did not even feel that Petronius covered his head that moment with the toga. It seemed to him that death or

[11] CROTON—A gladiator of tremendous strength. Ursus broke Croton's back in an earlier incident to prevent the kidnaping of Lygia.

[12] VESTALS—Roman maidens who served the sacred fires of Vesta.

[13] HERCULES—A mythical Greek hero.

[14] COLOSSUS—A gigantic bronze statue of Apollo; hence, any strikingly large person.

[15] AUROCHS—A wild European buffalo.

pain had closed his eyes. He did not look, he did not see. The feeling of some awful emptiness possessed him. In his head there remained not a thought; his lips merely repeated, as if in madness,—

"I believe! I believe! I believe!"

This time the amphitheater was silent. The Augustians rose in their places, as one man, for in the arena something uncommon had happened. That Lygian, obedient and ready to die, when he saw his queen on the horns of the wild beast, sprang up, as if touched by living fire, and bending forward he ran at the raging animal.

From all breasts a sudden cry of amazement was heard, after which came deep silence.

The Lygian fell on the raging bull in a twinkle, and seized him by the horns.

"Look!" cried Petronius, snatching the toga from the head of Vinicius.

The latter rose and bent back his head; his face was as pale as linen, and he looked into the arena with a glassy, vacant stare.

All breasts ceased to breathe. In the amphitheater a fly might be heard on the wing. People could not believe their own eyes. Since Rome was Rome, no one had seen such a spectacle.

The Lygian held the wild beast by the horns. The man's feet sank in the sand to his ankles, his back was bent like a drawn bow, his head was hidden between his shoulders, on his arms the muscles came out so that the skin almost burst from their pressure; but he had stopped the bull in his tracks. And the man and the beast remained so still that the spectators thought themselves looking at a picture showing a deed of Hercules or Theseus,[16] or a group hewn from stone. But in that apparent repose there was a tremendous exertion of two struggling forces. The bull sank his feet as well as did the man in the sand, and his dark, shaggy body was curved so that it seemed a gigantic ball. Which of the two would fail first, which would fall first,—that was the question for those spectators enamored of such struggles; a question which at that moment meant more for them than their own fate, than all Rome and its lordship over the world. That Lygian was in their eyes then a demigod[17] worthy of honor and statues. Caesar himself stood up as well as others. He and Tigellinus, hearing of the man's strength, had arranged this spectacle purposely, and said to each other with a jeer, "Let that slayer of Croton kill the bull we choose for him"; so they looked now with amazement at that picture, as if not believing that it could be real.

In the amphitheater were men who had raised their arms and remained in that posture. Sweat covered the faces of others, as if they themselves were struggling with the beast. In the Circus nothing was heard save the sound of flame in the lamps, and the crackle of bits of coal as they dropped from the torches. Their voices died on the lips of the spectators, but their hearts were beating in their breasts as if to split them. It seemed to all that the struggle was lasting for ages. But the man and the beast continued on in their monstrous exertion; one might have said that they were planted in the earth.

Meanwhile a dull roar resembling a

[16] THESEUS—A legendary Greek hero who fought against the Amazons and Centaurs.

[17] DEMIGOD—A man with divine attributes.

groan was heard from the arena, after which a brief shout was wrested from every breast, and again there was silence. People thought themselves dreaming till the enormous head of the bull began to turn in the iron hands of the barbarian. The face, neck, and arms of the Lygian grew purple; his back bent still more. It was clear that he was rallying the remnant of his superhuman strength, but that he could not last long.

Duller and duller, hoarser and hoarser, more and more painful grew the groan of the bull as it mingled with the whistling breath from the breast of the giant. The head of the beast turned more and more, and from his jaws came a long, foaming tongue.

A moment more, and to the ears of spectators sitting nearer came as it were the crack of breaking bones; then the beast rolled on the earth with his neck twisted in death.

The giant removed in a twinkle the ropes from the horns of the bull, and raising the maiden, began to breathe hurriedly. His face became pale, his hair stuck together from sweat, his shoulders and arms seemed flooded with water. For a moment he stood as if only half conscious; then he raised his eyes and looked at the spectators.

The amphitheater had gone wild.

The walls of the building were trembling from the roar of tens of thousands of people. Since the beginning of spectacles there was no memory of such excitement. Those who were sitting on the highest rows came down, crowding in the passages between benches to look more nearly at the strong man. Everywhere were heard cries for mercy, passionate and persistent, which soon turned into one unbroken thunder. That giant had become dear to those people enamored of physical strength; he was the first personage in Rome.

He understood that the multitude were striving to grant him his life and restore him his freedom, but clearly his thought was not on himself alone. He looked around awhile; then approached Caesar's podium, and, holding the body of the maiden on his outstretched arms, raised his eyes with entreaty, as if to say,—

"Have mercy on her! Save the maiden. I did that for her sake!"

The spectators understood perfectly what he wanted. At sight of the unconscious maiden, who near the enormous Lygian seemed a child, emotion seized the multitude of Senators and knights. Her slender form, as white as if chiseled from alabaster, her fainting, the dreadful danger from which the giant had freed her, and finally her beauty and attachment had moved every heart. Some thought the man a father begging mercy for his child. Pity burst forth suddenly, like a flame. They had had blood, death, and torture in sufficiency. Voices choked with tears began to entreat mercy for both.

Meanwhile Ursus, holding the girl in his arms, moved around the arena, and with his eyes and with motions begged her life for her. Now Vinicius started up from his seat, sprang over the barrier which separated the front places from the arena, and running to Lygia, covered her naked body with his toga.

Then he tore apart the tunic on his breast, laid bare the scars left by wounds received in the Armenian war, and stretched out his hands to the audience.

Then the enthusiasm of the multitude passed everything seen in a Circus before. The crowd stamped and howled. Voices calling for mercy grew simply terrible. People not only took the part of the athlete, but rose in defense of the soldier, the maiden, their love. Thousands of spectators turned to Caesar with flashes of anger in their eyes and with clinched fists.

But Caesar halted and hesitated. Against Vinicius he had no hatred indeed, and the death of Lygia did not concern him; but he preferred to see the body of the maiden rent by the horns of the bull or torn by the claws of the beast. His cruelty, his deformed imagination, and deformed desires found a kind of delight in such spectacles. And now the people wanted to rob him. Hence anger appeared on his bloated face. Self-love also would not let him yield to the wish of the multitude, and still he did not dare to oppose it, through his inborn cowardice.

So he gazed around to see if among the Augustians at least, he could not find fingers turned down in sign of death.[18] But Petronius held up his hand, and looked almost challengingly into Nero's face. Vestinius, superstitious but inclined to enthusiasm, a man who feared ghosts but not the living, gave a sign for mercy also. So did Scevinus, the Senator; so did Nerva, so did Tullius Senecio, so did the famous leader, Ostorius Scapula, and Antistius, and Piso, and Vetus, and Crispi-

[18] SIGN OF DEATH—A gladiator victorious in the arena placed his dagger at the throat of the fallen foe. The spectators signaled for mercy with thumbs up. Thumbs down signaled the victim was to die.

nus, and Minucius Thermus, and Pontius Telesinus, and the most important of all, one honored by the people, Thrasea.

In view of this, Caesar took the emerald from his eye with an expression of contempt and offense; when Tigellinus, whose desire was to spite Petronius, turned to him and said,—

"Yield not, divinity; we have the pretorians."

Then Nero turned to the place where command over the pretorians was held by the stern Subrius Flavius, hitherto devoted with whole soul to him, and saw something unusual. The face of the old tribune was stern, but covered with tears, and he was holding his hand up in sign of mercy.

Now rage began to possess the multitude. Dust rose from beneath the stamping feet, and filled the amphitheater. In the midst of shouts were heard cries: "Ahenobarbus![19] Matricide! Incendiary!"

Nero was alarmed. The people were absolute lords in the Circus. Former Caesars, and especially Caligula, had permitted themselves sometimes to go against popular desire; this, however, called forth disturbance always, going sometimes to bloodshed. But Nero was in a different position. First, as a comedian and a singer he needed the people's favor; second, he wanted it on his side against the Senate and the patricians, and especially after the burning of Rome he strove by all means to win it, and turn their anger against the Christians. He understood, besides, that to oppose longer was simply dangerous. A disturbance begun in the Circus might seize the whole city, and have results incalculable.

He looked once more at Subrius Flavius, at Scevinus the centurion, a relative of the Senator, at the soldiers; and seeing everywhere frowning brows, moved faces, and eyes fixed on him, he gave the sign for mercy.

Then a thunder of applause was heard from the highest seats to the lowest. The people were sure of the lives of the condemned, for from that moment they went under their protection, and even Caesar would not have dared to pursue them any longer with his vengeance.

[19] AHENOBARBUS—"Red-beard"; Nero had murdered his mother and the populace suspected him of setting the great fire of Rome.

◇◇◇◇◇◇◇◇◇◇◇◇◇◇◇◇◇◇◇◇◇◇◇◇◇◇◇◇◇

FOR DISCUSSION

1. Saint Paul described the pagans as "full of envy . . . irreverent, proud, haughty, plotters of evil . . . foolish, dissolute, without affection, without fidelity, without mercy." What insight into the character of the Romans does their eager delight at the torture of the Christians give you?

2. Why had Caesar strengthened his bodyguard the evening of the spectacle?

3. Vinicius was a convert to Christianity. To whom did he appeal to save Lygia? Why did he have such a struggle within himself to understand why Christ did not perform a miracle to save Lygia? How can you as a Christian explain to others the commandment of love and forgive your enemies?

4. How did the Roman crowd react to Ursus' prayer in the arena? Why was Nero compelled to reckon with the demands of the crowd? Describe the circumstances under which Nero finally gave the sign of mercy.

WORDS

No less than one-half of the words in present-day English are derived from Latin.

Extensive borrowing from the Latin came very early through the coming to Britain of the Roman missionaries under St. Augustine, in 597. English scholars of the Renaissance likewise introduced many Latin words into our language. Another source of Latin influence was the imposition of French—itself a Romance or Latin language—through the Norman invasion of 1066.

1. Using your dictionary, find the Latin root of these English words: *homicide, benediction, malediction, inventor, fortitude, proximate, altitude, animate, fidelity, utility, virtue.*

2. The Anglo-Saxon vocabulary was made up of short words as *love, hate, fight, work, die, hot, bold.* With the adoption of Latin words, the English language was enriched. The addition of new words enabled people to make clear different shades of meaning. For instance, the word *lift* usually implies effort to raise a weight; *elevate,* from the Latin, is used in place of *lift* when one wants to say that something has been exalted or raised to a higher rank. Opposite each of the Anglo-Saxon words below is a Latin derivative. When would you use the shorter English word? When would you use the word derived from the Latin? Write a sentence with each word in the list.

get—obtain	same—identical
break—fracture	love—adore
cold—frigid	show—exhibit

RELATED READING

You will find another story of a Roman soldier and a Christian girl in *The Robe,* a novel by Lloyd C. Douglas.

When you have something to do that is going to take all your courage, how do you feel inside? The poet here gives a description of that feeling.

Courage

HELEN FRAZEE-BOWER

You asked me, "What is courage?" And I took
The dictionary down and spelled it out.
For such a little boy, the heavy book
Was ponderous. You twisted it about;
You said, "It's being brave—and what is that?"
You said, "It's not to fear—am I afraid?
Does courage arch its back up like our cat,
And spit at everything it meets?" you said.

Perplexed, we closed the book and took a walk,
  And came where fire had worked untimely death;
The woods were gone. But on a slender stalk
  A flower inched for life. I caught my breath.
"Courage," I said, and took you by the hand,
"Is one white flower in a fire-swept land."

FOR DISCUSSION

1. Which of the three definitions of *courage* given in this poem do you prefer? Why?

2. Just how important is courage as a part of character? Can a person live up to his ideals without practicing courage? Why is a person happiest when he lives up to his best self? Why does the poet call courage such a delicate thing as a flower?

3. "A flower *inched for life*." Why is the use of the verb *inched* especially good? What does it mean?

DO YOU AGREE?

A brave modern author writes that "Courage is the basic virtue, and the man with the courage of his convictions will always command respect." Write in your own words what you think this statement means. Tell whether or not you agree with it and why.

Early in World War II the British Army in Europe was pushed back and almost surrounded by the German Army at Dunkirk (Dunkerque) on the French shore of the English Channel. When complete disaster seemed inevitable, all the boats and sailors, amateur and professional, were summoned by the English leaders to rescue the helpless soldiers from the Dunkirk beach. The response resulted in one of the most dramatic incidents of the war. The small English boats picked up the soldiers who waded out into the shallow water and took them to the larger ships in deeper water. Despite heavy bombardment and machine gun fire from the air, the evacuation of the troops was successful.

In this poem Robert Nathan tells about an English boy and girl who joined the rescue fleet in their small sailboat, the SARAH P.

Dunkirk

ROBERT NATHAN

Will came back from school that day,
And he had little to say.
But he stood a long time looking down
To where the gray-green Channel water
Slapped at the foot of the little town, 5
And to where his boat, the *Sarah P*,
Bobbed at the tide on an even keel,
With her one old sail, patched at the leech,
Furled like a slattern down at heel.

He stood for a while above the beach; 10
He saw how the wind and current caught her.
He looked a long time out to sea.
There was steady wind and the sky was pale
And a haze in the east that looked like smoke.

9. SLATTERN—A bedraggled, untidy woman.

Will went back to the house to dress. 15
He was halfway through when his sister Bess,
Who was near fourteen and younger than he
By just two years, came home from play.
She asked him, "Where are you going, Will?"
He said, "For a good long sail." 20
"Can I come along?"

"No, Bess," he spoke.
"I may be gone for a night and a day."
Bess looked at him. She kept very still.
She had heard the news of the Flanders rout,
How the English were trapped above Dunkirk, 25
And the fleet had gone to get them out—
But everyone thought that it wouldn't work.
There was too much fear, there was too much doubt.
She looked at him and he looked at her.
They were English children, born and bred. 30
He frowned her down, but she wouldn't stir.
She shook her proud young head.
"You'll need a crew," she said.

They raised the sail on the *Sarah P*,
Like a penoncel on a young knight's lance, 35
And headed the *Sarah* out to sea,
To bring their soldiers home from France.

There was no command, there was no set plan,
But six hundred boats went out with them
On the gray-green waters, sailing fast, 40
River excursion and fisherman,
Tug and schooner and racing M,
And the little boats came following last.

From every harbor and town they went
Who had sailed their craft in the sun and rain, 45
From the South Downs, from the cliffs of Kent,
From the village street, from the country lane.

24. FLANDERS ROUT—A reference to the battle of Flanders in World War II in which the German Army crushed Dutch and Belgian resistance and moved on toward France.
35. PENONCEL (pěn′ŭn·sěl)—A flag or streamer attached to the lance of a knight.

There are twenty miles of rolling sea
From coast to coast, by the sea gull's flight,
But the tides were fair and the wind was free, 50
And they raised Dunkirk by the fall of night.
They raised Dunkirk with its harbor torn
By the blasted stern and the sunken prow;
They had raced for fun on an English tide,
They were English children bred and born, 55
And whether they lived or whether they died,
They raced for England now.

Bess was as white as the *Sarah's* sail,
She set her teeth and smiled at Will.
He held his course for the smoky veil 60
Where the harbor narrowed thin and long.
The British ships were firing strong.

He took the *Sarah* into his hands,
He drove her in through fire and death
To the wet men waiting on the sands. 65
He got his load and he got his breath,
And she came about, and the wind fought her.

He shut his eyes and he tried to pray.
He saw his England where she lay,
The wind's green home, the sea's proud daughter, 70
Still in the moonlight, dreaming deep,
The English cliffs and the English loam—
He had fourteen men to get away,
And the moon was clear and the night like day
For planes to see where the white sails creep 75
Over the black water.

He closed his eyes and he prayed for her;
He prayed to the men who had made her great,
Who had built her land of forest and park,
Who had made the seas an English lake; 80
He prayed for a fog to bring the dark;
He prayed to get home for England's sake.
And the fog came down on the rolling sea,
And covered the ships with English mist.
The diving planes were baffled and blind. 85

51. RAISED DUNKIRK—Came into view of Dunkirk. 67. SHE . . . HER—The boat.

For Nelson was there in the *Victory*,
With his one good eye, and his sullen twist,
And the guns were out on *The Golden Hind*,
Their shot flashed over the *Sarah P.*
He could hear them cheer as he came about. 90

By burning wharves, by battered slips,
Galleon, frigate, and brigantine,
The old dead Captains fought their ships,
And the great dead Admirals led the line.
It was England's night, it was England's sea. 95

The fog rolled over the harbor key.
Bess held to the stays and conned him out.
And all through the dark, while the *Sarah's* wake
Hissed behind him, and vanished in foam,
There at his side sat Francis Drake, 100
And held him true and steered him home.

86. NELSON, HORATIO (1758–1805)—English naval hero. He was killed in the battle of Trafalgar during the Napoleonic Wars. In previous battles he had lost an eye and an arm.
88. *The Golden Hind*—The ship of Sir Francis Drake.
97. STAYS—Guy ropes on cables that hold the mast in place.
97. CONNED—Directed his steering.

FOR DISCUSSION

1. The British are noted for being restrained in their speech and calm in the face of danger. How did the conversations of Will and Bess and their actions throughout the poem show those characteristics?

2. Does it seem possible to you that a boy of fifteen and a girl of thirteen could successfully sail a small boat across the English Channel? What previous experience had they had with boats? How were they aided in navigation?

3. Admiral Nelson, the hero of Trafalgar, and Sir Francis Drake, the commander of *The Golden Hind*, lived and died long before Dunkirk. In what sense were they present to aid Will and Bess and the other rescuers? How much do you think the two young people were inspired to do what they did by other great captains and admirals of British naval history?

4. What reasons can you give for the success of the English in evacuating the soldiers from Dunkirk?

THE POET'S CRAFT

1. In the first stanza, notice how the poet creates a somber mood in keeping with the seriousness of the situation. He calls attention to the fact that the boy is quiet and thoughtful, the water is gray-green, and the little boat is shabby. The verbs *slapped* and *bobbed* as they are used here suggest aimless, futile motion. The simile, or poetic comparison, in the last two lines produces a forlorn or dejected image. Now examine the two stanzas beginning with line 34. How is the mood of these two stanzas different from that of the first one? What specific details help create a picture in keeping with the mood? What contrast is there between the picture of the sail in line 35 and that in the first stanza?

2. Point out other vivid passages and effective comparisons in the poem.

A highly successful and deeply cultured college professor in France, Father Chabanel, came to the Huron Indian missions in Canada, to failure and savagery. When his heart and soul revolted, he took a vow to stay till death. He did.

This short biography of St. Noël Chabanel is from a great Catholic novel, Shadows on the Rock. *Its narrator is Father Hector Saint-Cyr. In telling Euclide Auclair the story of Noël's heroic life, Father Hector explains his own decision to remain in Canada as a missionary.*

NOËL CHABANEL

WILLA CATHER

"There was among the early missionaries, among the martyrs, one whom I have selected for my especial reverence. I mean Noël Chabanel,[1] Euclide. He was not so great a figure as Brébeuf or Jogues or Lalemant,[2] but I feel a peculiar sympathy for him. He perished, you remember, in the great Iroquois raid of '49. But his martyrdom was his life, not his death.

"He was a little different from all the others,—equal to them in desire, but not in fitness. He was only thirty years of age when he came, and was from Toulouse, that gracious city.

"Chabanel had been a professor of rhetoric like me, and like me he was fond of the decencies, the elegancies of life. From the beginning his life in Canada was one long humiliation and disappointment. Strange to say, he was utterly unable to learn the Huron language, though he was a master of Greek and Hebrew and spoke both Italian and Spanish. After five years of devoted study he was still unable to converse or to preach in any Indian tongue. He was sent out to the mission of Saint Jean in the Tobacco nation,[3] as helper to Father Charles Garnier. Father Garnier, though not at all Chabanel's equal in scholarship, had learned the Huron language so thoroughly that the Indians said there was nothing more to teach him,—he spoke like one of themselves.

"His humiliating inability to learn the language was only one of poor Chabanel's mortifications. He had no love for his converts. Everything about the savages and their mode of life was utterly repulsive and horrible to him; their filth, their indecency, their cruelty. The very smell of their bodies revolted him to nausea.

[1] NOËL CHABANEL—Pronounced nō·ĕl′ shä·bȧ·nĕl′.

[2] BRÉBEUF, JOGUES, LALEMANT—Fellow missionaries and martyrs along with Chabanel.

[3] TOBACCO NATION—A branch of the great Huron tribe.

He could never feel toward them that long-suffering love which has been the consolation of our missionaries. He never became hardened to any of the privations of his life, not even to the vermin and mosquitoes that preyed upon his body, nor to the smoke and smells in the savage wigwams. In his struggle to learn the language he went and lived with the Indians, sleeping in their bark shelters, crowded with dogs and dirty savages. Often Father Chabanel would lie out in the snow until he was in danger of a death self-inflicted, and only then creep inside the wigwam. The food was so hateful to him that one might say he lived upon fasting. The flesh of dogs he could never eat without becoming ill, and even cornmeal boiled in dirty water and dirty kettles brought on vomiting; so that he used to beg the women to give him a little uncooked meal in his hand, and upon that he subsisted.

"The Huron converts were more brutal to him than to Father Garnier. They were contemptuous of his backwardness in their language, and they must have divined his excessive sensibility, for they took every occasion to outrage it. In the wigwam they tirelessly perpetrated indecencies to wound him. Once when a hunting party returned after a long famine, they invited him to a feast of flesh. After he had swallowed the portion in his bowl, they pulled a human hand out of the kettle to show him that he had eaten of an Iroquois prisoner. He became ill at once, and they followed him into the forest to make merry over his retchings.

"But through all these physical sufferings, which remained as sharp as on the first day, the greatest of his sufferings was an almost continual sense of the withdrawal of God. All missionaries have that anguish at times, but with Chabanel it was continual. For long months, for a whole winter, he would exist in the forest, every human sense outraged, and with no assurance of the nearness of God. In those seasons of despair he was constantly beset by temptation in the form of homesickness. He longed to leave the mission to priests who were better suited to its hardships, to return to France and teach the young, and to find again that peace of soul, that cleanliness and order, which made him the master of his mind and its powers. Everything that he had lost was awaiting him in France, and the Director of Missions in Quebec had suggested his return.

"On Corpus Christi Day, in the fifth year of his labors in Canada and the thirty-fifth of his age, he cut short this struggle and overcame his temptation. At the mission of Saint Matthias, in the presence of the Blessed Sacrament exposed, he made a vow of perpetual stability[4] (*perpetuam stabilitatem*) in the Huron missions. This vow he recorded in writing, and he sent copies of it to his brethren in Kebec.[5]

"Having made up his mind to die in the wilderness, he had not long to wait. Two years later he perished when the mission of Saint Jean was destroyed by the Iroquois,—though whether he died of cold in his flight through the forest, or was murdered by a faithless convert for the sake of the poor belongings he carried on his back, was not surely known. No

[4] PERPETUAL STABILITY—Referring to the vow to remain until death in a determined locality.

[5] KEBEC—Quebec.

man ever gave up more for Christ than Noël Chabanel; many gave all, but few had so much to give."

◇◇◇◇◇◇◇◇◇◇◇◇◇◇◇◇◇◇◇◇◇◇◇◇◇◇◇◇◇◇

FOR DISCUSSION

1. Name some of the physical sufferings which St. Noël endured. What did Father Hector consider Noël's greatest suffering?

2. What is a vow? What is meant by a vow of perpetual stability? How can you explain Father Chabanel's taking such a vow in the face of his terrible sufferings?

3. Can you explain: "But his martyrdom was his life, not his death"?

4. Explain the last statement in the story.

YOUR VOCABULARY

It is said that we all have three vocabularies: a speaking vocabulary, a listening vocabulary, a reading vocabulary. Many of the words which you read you understand because of their context in a sentence or paragraph. However, you are often unable to use these same words in conversation because you are not sure enough of their meanings. Are these words in your speaking vocabulary: *subsist, repulsive, mortification?* Look up the ones which are in your reading vocabulary only. Then try to use the words in sentences of your own.

A PROJECT

Suppose that you have been five years a missionary in Canada and have found your experiences in the wilderness almost beyond endurance. Write a letter to your Superior, telling of the terrible temptation to give up. At the end ask permission to stay with the Indians until death.

RELATED READING

The Champlain Road by Franklin McDowell pictures the heroic lives of the North American martyr-saints.

◇◇◇◇◇

Has anyone ever told you that you hold the key to your own success? Notice how the poet expresses that idea.

One Ship Drives East

ELLA WHEELER WILCOX

One ship drives east and another drives
west,
With the selfsame winds that blow.
'Tis the set of the sails
And not the gales
That determines the way they go. 5

Like the winds of the sea are the winds of
fate,
As we voyage along through life.
'Tis the set of the soul
That decides the goal
And not the calm or the strife. 10

8. SET OF THE SOUL—Your attitude toward things, your personal ideals, your capacity for making the most of every experience.

FOR DISCUSSION

1. If you have ever operated a sailboat, you should be able to explain how two sailboats can go in opposite directions simultaneously using the same wind. How does this nautical fact explain the first four lines of the poem?

2. In the last half of the poem life is compared to a sailboat. To what are the *calm* and the *strife* compared? What idea does the poem give you about the importance of personal ideals?

3. Can you apply the lesson in this poem to an incident in your own life? How did you meet a difficult situation—a quarrel with your family or a friend, a bad report card, losing an important contest?

HISTORY OF WORDS

Have you ever heard the history of the simple word, *journey?* Latin *dies* means *day,* and *diurnus* means *belonging to the day.* This is the origin of the Old French *jorn* (*a day*) and *jornée* (*a day's work or travel*). Middle English borrowed this as *journée* (*a day's travel*). *Journey,* now refers to *travel* without any reference to the time consumed.

Perhaps you can find the history of these words. Each one has an interesting story:

achieve ambition calm opportunity

◇◇◇◇◇

In our nation's capital, the Tomb of the Unknown Soldier is a tribute to those soldiers whose full sacrifice for their country has had to stand unrecorded and otherwise unhonored. The following poem is a tribute to a young Breton sailor whose service to France was in no way memorialized by his own countrymen.

Hervé Riel

ROBERT BROWNING

On the sea and at the Hogue, sixteen hundred ninety-two,
　Did the English fight the French—woe to France!
And, the thirty-first of May, helter-skelter thro' the blue,
Like a crowd of frightened porpoises a shoal of sharks pursue,
　Came crowding ship on ship to St. Malo on the Rance, 　5
With the English fleet in view.

1. HOGUE—A protected harbor on the east side of the peninsula of Cotenin in France, but not Cape de la Hague.

2. FIGHT—A naval battle instigated by Louis XIV of France against the English and Dutch, in an attempt to reinstate King James II, whom the English had dethroned and expelled from their land.

5. ST. MALO—A fortified seaport of Normandy, at the mouth of the river Rance.

'Twas the squadron that escaped, with the victor in full chase;
First and foremost of the drove, in his great ship, Damfreville;
Close on him fled, great and small,
Twenty-two good ships in all; 10
And they signaled to the place
"Help the winners of a race!
Give us guidance, give us harbor, take us quick—or, quicker still,
Here's the English can and will!"

Then the pilots of the place put out brisk and leapt on board; 15
"Why, what hope or chance have ships like these to pass?" laughed they:
"Rocks to starboard, rocks to port, all the passage scarred and scored,
Shall the *Formidable* here with her twelve and eighty guns
Think to make the river mouth by the single narrow way,
Trust to enter where 'tis ticklish for a craft of twenty tons, 20
And with flow at full beside?
Now, 'tis slackest ebb of tide.
Reach the mooring? Rather say,
While the rock stands or water runs,
Not a ship will leave the bay!" 25

Then was called a council straight.
Brief and bitter the debate:
"Here's the English at our heels; would you have them take in tow
All that's left us of the fleet, linked together stern and bow,
For a prize to Plymouth Sound? 30
Better run the ships aground!"
(Ended Damfreville his speech.)
"Not a minute more to wait!
Let the Captains all and each
Shove ashore, then blow up, burn the vessels on the beach! 35
France must undergo her fate.

"Give the word!" But no such word
Was ever spoke or heard;
For up stood, for out stepped, for in struck amid all these
—A Captain? A Lieutenant? A Mate—first, second, third? 40
No such man of mark, and meet

8. DAMFREVILLE—Marquis d'Amfreville—A French naval officer who commanded the vanguard at La Hogue.
18. *Formidable*—The name of the ship which was leading the fleet.
21. FLOW AT FULL—High tide.
30. PLYMOUTH SOUND—An important English naval station.

With his betters to compete!
But a simple Breton sailor pressed by Tourville for the fleet,
A poor coasting pilot he, Hervé Riel, the Croisickese.

And, "What mockery or malice, have we here?" cries Hervé Riel: 45
"Are you mad, you Malouins? Are you cowards, fools, or rogues?
Talk to me of rocks and shoals, me who took the soundings, tell
On my fingers every bank, every shallow, every swell
'Twixt the offing here and Grève where the river disembogues?
Are you bought by English gold? Is it love the lying's for? 50
Morn and eve, night and day,
Have I piloted your bay,
Entered free and anchored fast at foot of Solidor.
Burn the fleet and ruin France? That were worse than fifty Hogues!
Sirs, they know I speak the truth! Sirs, believe me there's a way! 55
Only let me lead the line,
Have the biggest ship to steer,
Get this *Formidable* clear,
Make the others follow mine,
And I lead them, most and least, by a passage I know well, 60
Right to Solidor past Grève,
And there lay them safe and sound;
And if one ship misbehave,
Keel so much as grate the ground,
Why, I've nothing but my life—here's my head!" cries Hervé Riel. 65

Not a minute more to wait.
"Steer us in, then, small and great!
Take the helm, lead the line, save the squadron!" cried its chief.
Captains, give the sailor place!
He is Admiral, in brief. 70
Still the north wind, by God's grace!
See the noble fellow's face
As the big ship, with a bound,
Clears the entry like a hound,

43. PRESSED—Drafted, forced to serve.
43. TOURVILLE—Admiral of the fleet, and Damfreville's superior.
44. CROISICKESE—A native of Le Croisic, a seaport town.
46. MALOUINS—People or citizens of St. Malo.
47. SOUNDINGS—Measurements of the depth of water.
49. OFFING—Water offshore just beyond anchorage depth.
49. GRÈVE—A small village at the mouth of the Rance.
49. DISEMBOGUES—Discharges, empties.
53. SOLIDOR—A feudal fort built on the mainland.

Keeps the passage as its inch of way were the wide seas profound! 75
  See, safe through shoal and rock,
  How they follow in a flock,
Not a ship that misbehaves, not a keel that grates the ground,
  Not a spar that comes to grief!
The peril, see, is past, 80
All are harbored to the last,
And just as Hervé Riel hollas "Anchor!" sure as fate,
Up the English come—too late!

So, the storm subsides to calm:
  They see the green trees wave 85
  On the heights o'erlooking Grève.
Hearts that bled are stanched with balm,
"Just our rapture to enhance,
  Let the English rake the bay,
Gnash their teeth and glare askance 90
  As they cannonade away!

75. KEEPS . . . PROFOUND—As if its narrow passage were as wide and deep as the ocean.
89. RAKE—Bombard.

'Neath rampired Solidor pleasant riding on the Rance!"
How hope succeeds despair on each Captain's countenance!
Out burst all with one accord,
"This is Paradise for Hell!
Let France, let France's King 95
Thank the man that did the thing!"
What a shout, and all one word,
"Hervé Riel!"
As he stepped in front once more,
Not a symptom of surprise 100
In the frank blue Breton eyes,
Just the same man as before.

Then said Damfreville, "My friend,
I must speak out at the end,
Though I find the speaking hard. 105
Praise is deeper than the lips:
You have saved the King his ships,
You must name your own reward.
'Faith, our sun was near eclipse!
Demand whate'er you will, 110
France remains your debtor still.
Ask to heart's content and have! or my name's not Damfreville."

Then a beam of fun outbroke
On the bearded mouth that spoke,
As the honest heart laughed through 115
Those frank eyes of Breton blue:
"Since I needs must say my say,
Since on board the duty's done,
And from Malo Roads to Croisic Point, what is it but a run?—
Since 'tis ask and have, I may— 120
Since the others go ashore—
Come! a good whole holiday!
Leave to go and see my wife, whom I call the Belle Aurore!"
That he asked and that he got—nothing more. 125

92. RAMPIRED—An old form for "ramparted" which means that the fort was banked up around the outside.
120. FROM MALO ROADS TO CROISIC POINT—About one hundred miles.
124. BELLE AURORE—*Belle* in French means *beautiful*. *Aurore* means *dawn*.

Name and deed alike are lost:
Not a pillar nor a post
  In his Croisic keeps alive the feat as it befell;
Not a head in white and black
On a single fishing smack, 130
In memory of the man but for whom had gone to wrack
  All that France saved from the fight whence England bore the bell.
Go to Paris: rank on rank
  Search the heroes flung pell-mell
On the Louvre, face and flank! 135
  You shall look long enough ere you come to Hervé Riel.
So, for better and for worse,
Hervé Riel, accept my verse!
In my verse, Hervé Riel, do thou once more
Save the squadron, honor France, love thy wife, the Belle Aurore! 140

129. HEAD IN WHITE AND BLACK—A figurehead.
132. BORE THE BELL—Won the prize.
135. LOUVRE—That is, the pictures of heroes on the walls of the Louvre, which is the great national museum and art gallery at Paris.

FOR DISCUSSION

1. The French fleet was in a tight spot when Damfreville signaled the pilots on shore for help. What advice did they give him?

2. What did Hervé Riel contribute to the council? Why did the others listen to this simple sailor who was not even a third-class mate, much less a lieutenant or captain?

3. Everyone admires a man who can take success without conceit. Was Hervé a hero in the true sense of the word even after his heroic performance? Explain your answer.

A THEME ASSIGNMENT

1. In your experience in an athletic game or a competitive contest of some kind, have you ever seen anyone, who, because of his keen observation, ingenuity, and self-confidence, was able to guide a discouraged and confused team to victory? Write an account of this experience.

2. What news stories clipped from the daily paper have the makings of a metrical tale as lively as "Hervé Riel"? Bring the clippings to class for discussion and save the best for some future theme assignment.

For Further Reading

Bring 'Em Back Alive by Frank and Anthony Buck tells of the suspense and excitement in trapping wild animals in forests and jungles in order to bring them back alive.

Test Pilot by James Collins portrays courage and responsibility in the sky.

Microbe Hunters by Paul de Kruif. A distinguished writer tells of outstanding bacteriologists—Pasteur, Koch, Theobald Smith, Walter Reed, and others—of how they battled with dangerous microbes to make the world safer for man.

White Fire by Edward Edwards tells in excellent language and description the work of an American community among Philippine lepers.

Men Under the Sea by Edward Ellsberg describes the exciting rescues in the S-51 and S-4 disasters.

Men Without Fear by John Joseph Floherty. This book contains dramatic stories of the men who work in some of the world's most hazardous occupations. The reader can see these men at work, share their risks, and appreciate their skill.

Lou Gehrig by Frank Graham is a biography of the famous baseball hero.

Guerilla Padre by Edward Haggerty, S. J. The Jesuit rector of the College of Cagayan aids the fighting Filipinos in their guerilla warfare of World War II.

Columbus Sails by Walter Hodges is a colorful story of Columbus' life told supposedly by four men close to him.

Famous American Athletes of Today by Harold Kaese and others. This is a series of books on the backgrounds and achievements of the latest stars in basketball, hockey, football, track, ice skating, golf, and baseball.

The Story of My Life by Helen Keller is the story of a courageous girl blind and deaf from infancy. Here she reveals her personality and personality training.

Men of Maryknoll by James G. Keller, M.M., is a collection of stories of generous American Catholic boys who labor for God in the Orient and South America.

Captains Courageous by Rudyard Kipling is a dramatic sea story of the rescue of a wealthy man's son and the development of his manhood.

Listen! the Wind by Anne Morrow Lindbergh tells the story of a survey flight around the North Atlantic Ocean to study air routes between Europe and America.

The Crusade and the Cup by Elizabeth Meigs is a novel about two Irish brothers who go with Richard of England on a crusade to the Holy Land.

These Are Your Sons by Timothy Mulvey. Father Mulvey assembled these stories of the "unsung heroes" of the war in Korea in order to tell the people at home how their sons were facing up to the situation.

Heroes and Hazards by Margaret Norris. Here are short sketches of men whose daily work is an adventure—deep sea divers, riveters, iron workers, and firemen.

Men of Iron by Howard Pyle. Henry IV, Prince Hal, and the English court are presented in this picture of the days of Chivalry.

The Wright Brothers by Quentin Reynolds is the life story of the famous Wright Brothers. This book has much appeal for the air-minded person.

How They Carried the Mail by Joseph Walker contains sixteen stories showing how young men throughout the ages dared danger in order to deliver their messages safely.

Up from Slavery by Booker T. Washington is the autobiography of a man, born in slavery, who became the founder of a school for his race.

They Were Expendable by William L. White reads like an adventure story but is the true tale of the experiences of the crews of P. T. boats in the Pacific area in World War II.

SO MUCH MAJESTY

Though he lives in a marvelous world, man seldom marvels at it. When he notices it at all, he usually sees only the surface. But once in a while somebody penetrates beyond the surface and sees things to which the rest of men have been blind. Such seers want to share with you the treasures they have found. Some of them look beyond the physical world to an invisible world.

The task of finding words to describe one's vision is not easy. The radiance and fullness of light, the awesome panorama of a sea now green and now purple, the perfume of flowers and shadowy woods, the varied plumage and song of birds, the countless beasts—this universe trembling with God's own beauty has made many a writer struggle with despair at trying to find means to describe it.

Some men have succeeded in showing what Saints have always known—that nothing is mean in God's creation. All is magnificent. It is as though God had smiled when He set each beautiful feature in the universe. Like a parent wrapping Christmas presents for his child, He was thinking of the day when you would open His gift, gaze upon the marvels of creation, and lift your mind and heart to Him.

Can you appreciate beauty in the first streaks of morning light as it breaks through a darkness of nothingness? in misty stars marching up the hill of heaven over spicy pines? in the silent wonder of God's mountains, sea, and sky? in sea-gulls cruising over the ocean spray? in valleys brimful of radiant mist? in the gorgeous realm of fluttering life and shadow on the pale sand of the ocean floor? You can find such experiences of beauty in your reading. The insight of others will enrich your own appreciation.

EWING GALLOWAY

"The old-time Negro preacher is rapidly passing, and I have here tried sincerely to fix something of him." Thus the author has explained why he wrote his collection of Negro sermons, from which "The Creation" is taken. Though there is no Negro dialect in this poem, the style is that used by many Negro preachers. Try to read it with the sincerity and depth of feeling that must have been in the preacher's voice when he delivered this sermon to his congregation. Make your reading realistic; above all do not make it funny.

The Creation

JAMES WELDON JOHNSON

And God stepped out on space,
And He looked around and said:
I'm lonely—
I'll make me a world.

And far as the eye of God could see 5
Darkness covered everything,
Blacker than a hundred midnights
Down in a cypress swamp.

Then God smiled,
And the light broke, 10
And the darkness rolled up on one side,
And the light stood shining on the other,
And God said: That's good!

Then God reached out and took the light
 in His hands,
And God rolled the light around in His
 hands 15
Until He made the sun;
And He set that sun a-blazing in the
 heavens.
And the light that was left from making
 the sun
God gathered it up in a shining ball
And flung it against the darkness, 20
Spangling the night with the moon and
 stars.
Then down between
The darkness and the light
He hurled the world;
And God said: That's good! 25

Then God himself stepped down—
And the sun was on His right hand,
And the moon was on His left;
The stars were clustered about His head,
And the earth was under His feet. 30
And God walked, and where He trod
His footsteps hollowed the valleys out
And bulged the mountains up.

Then He stopped and looked and saw
That the earth was hot and barren. 35
So God stepped over to the edge of the world
And He spat out the seven seas—
He batted His eyes, and the lightnings flashed—
He clapped His hands, and the thunders rolled—
And the waters above the earth came down, 40
The cooling waters came down.

Then the green grass sprouted,
And the little red flowers blossomed,
The pine tree pointed his finger to the sky,
And the oak spread out his arms, 45
The lakes cuddled down in the hollows of the ground,
And the rivers ran down to the sea;
And God smiled again,
And the rainbow appeared, 49
And curled itself around His shoulder.

Then God raised His arm and He waved His hand
Over the sea and over the land,
And He said: Bring forth! Bring forth!
And quicker than God could drop His hand,
Fishes and fowls 55
And beasts and birds
Swam the rivers and the seas,
Roamed the forests and the woods,
And split the air with their wings.
And God said: That's good! 60

Then God walked around,
And God looked around
On all that He had made.
He looked at His sun,
And He looked at His moon, 65
And He looked at His little stars;
He looked on His world
With all its living things,
And God said: I'm lonely still.

Then God sat down— 70
On the side of a hill where He could think;
By a deep, wide river He sat down;
With His head in His hands,
God thought and thought, 74
Till He thought: I'll make me a man!

Up from the bed of the river
God scooped the clay;
And by the bank of the river
He kneeled Him down;
And there the great God Almighty 80
Who lit the sun and fixed it in the sky,
Who flung the stars to the most far corner of the night,
Who rounded the earth in the middle of His hand;
This Great God,
Like a mammy bending over her baby,
Kneeled down in the dust 86
Toiling over a lump of clay
Till He shaped it in His own image;

Then into it He blew the breath of life,
And man became a living soul. 90
Amen. Amen.

◇◇◇◇◇◇◇◇◇◇◇◇◇◇◇◇◇◇◇◇◇◇◇◇◇◇◇◇◇◇

FOR DISCUSSION

1. Is the poem based on fact? To find out how closely the poet follows the historical version, compare these lines with the story found in the first book of the Bible.

2. The steps of the Creation you have heard before; but the poem expresses many of them in brand-new phrases. Make a list of these. Which ones do you especially like? Why?

3. Make a list of all the beautiful things mentioned in the poem. How many more beautiful things created by God can you add to the list? Write down at least five.

FOR APPRECIATION

If you have read these lines reverently and imaginatively, you have looked in on a moving picture of the creation of the world. Mr. Johnson has tried to produce images which even a child can grasp. This he has done through using descriptive words which appeal directly to the senses of sight, hearing, smell, taste, and touch. Find as many words or phrases as you can which appeal to these senses. Here are two to get you started: *stepped out in space*—sight; *the earth was hot and barren*—feeling and sight.

WRITING A STORY

Suppose that you are an author preparing an edition of Bible stories written in simple language that high school people will understand immediately. You have a few stories ready to submit to a publisher. Which one will you show him as your best example? Will it be your story about Adam and Eve? about Cain and Abel? about Noah and the flood? about the tower of Babel? Choose a story you would like to tell in your own words and write it for your teen-agers' anthology. Remember that the words should be right out of your own vocabulary, in language your associates can easily understand.

RELATED READING

If you liked "The Creation," you will enjoy other poems from the same book, *God's Trombones*.

In every line of this poem the poet has stressed her personal enjoyment in observing the stars. In every stanza she has sketched a picture. Read the poem slowly, so that each word will make its separate impression.

Stars

SARA TEASDALE

Alone in the night
  On a dark hill
With pines around me
  Spicy and still,

And a heaven full of stars
  Over my head,
White and topaz
  And misty red,

Myriads with beating
  Hearts of fire
That aeons
  Cannot vex or tire;

Up the dome of heaven
  Like a great hill,
I watch them marching
  Stately and still,

And I know that I
  Am honored to be
Witness
  Of so much majesty.

9. MYRIADS—Thousands.
11. AEONS—Immeasurably long periods of time.

"Stars" from *Collected Poems* by Sara Teasdale. Reprinted by permission of The Macmillan Company.

THE POET'S CRAFT

1. *Personification* is the name given to presenting non-living things as if they had human characteristics. What examples of personification do you find in this poem? Read aloud the lines you like especially well.

2. Which lines in the poem suggest the beauty of the heavens at night? Which lines express the power in nature? Which lines suggest mystery?

3. Everyone has some chance to enjoy beauty; it is not created solely for poets. For example, have you ever on an autumn day walked down a street lined with fiery leaves—some rustling overhead, some smoldering along the curb beneath columns of blue, aromatic smoke? Choose any similar scene which you remember for its beauty, and describe what you saw in a few short phrases or sentences. Try to give the rest of the class the same impression you received.

Cowboy stories and tales of the western plains are constant reminders of the frontier and the expanding grandeur of America. In "Riding the Rim Rock" you will share a thrilling experience riding herd on thirst-crazed, stampeding cattle. You will taste the frontier flavor of western desert, heat, and alkali dust.

RIDING THE RIM ROCK

DALLAS LORE SHARP

From P Ranch to Winnemucca is a seventeen-day drive through a desert of rim rock[1] and greasewood and sage which, under the most favorable of conditions, is beset with difficulty, but which, in dry season and with a herd of anything like four thousand, becomes an unbroken hazard. More than anything else on such a drive is feared the wild herd spirit, the quick black temper of the cattle which by one sign or another ever threatens to break the spell of the rider's power and sweep the maddened or terrorized herd to destruction. The handling of the herd to keep this spirit sleeping is very frequently a thrilling experience.

Some time before my visit to P Ranch in Harney County, southeastern Oregon, in the summer of 1912, the riders had taken a herd of four thousand steers out on what proved to be one of the most difficult drives ever made to Winnemucca, the shipping station in northern Nevada.

For the first two days on the trail the cattle were strange to each other, having been gathered from widely distant grazing-grounds,—from the Double O and the Home ranches,—and were somewhat clannish and restive under the driving. At the beginning of the third day signs of real ugliness appeared. The hot weather and a shortage of water began to tell on the temper of the herd.

The third day was long and exceedingly hot. The line started forward at dawn and all day long kept moving, with the sun cooking the bitter smell of sage into the air, and with the sixteen thousand hoofs kicking up a still bitterer smell of alkali dust that inflamed eyes and coated the very lungs of the cattle. The fierce desert thirst was upon the herd long before it reached the creek where it was to bed for the night, according to plan.

The heat and dust had made slow work of the driving, and it was late when they reached the creek—only to find it dry.

This was bad. The men were tired. But worse, the cattle were thirsty and Wade, the "Boss of the buckaroos,"

[1] RIM ROCK—Rock bounding a plateau, usually at a drop-off.

pushed the herd on toward the next rim rock, hoping to get down to the plain below to water before the end of the slow desert twilight. Anything for the night but a dry camp.

They had hardly started on when a whole flank of the herd, suddenly breaking away and dividing about two of the riders, tore off through the brush as if by pre-arrangement. The horses were as tired as the men, and before the chase was over the twilight was gray in the sage. It was necessary to halt at once and make camp where they were. They would have to go without water.

The runaways were brought up and the herd closed in till it formed a circle nearly a mile around. This was as close as it could be drawn, for the cattle would not bed—lie down. They wanted water more than they wanted rest. Their eyes were red, their tongues raspy with thirst. The situation was a serious one.

But camp was made. Two of the riders were sent back along the trail to bring up the "drags" [2] while Wade with his other men circled the uneasy cattle, closing them in, quieting them, and doing everything possible to make them bed.

But they were thirsty and, instead of bedding, the herd began to growl—a distant mutter of throats, low, rumbling, ominous, as when faint thunder rolls behind the hills. Every plainsman fears the growl, for it usually is a prelude to the milling. It proved to be so now. The vast herd began to stir—slowly, singly, and without discretion—till at length it moved together, round and round, a great compact circle of clicking hoofs, of clashing horns. The chafing sides were like the sound of rushing rain across a field of corn.

Nothing could be worse for the cattle. The cooler twilight was falling but, mingling with it, the choking dust from their feet rose and thickened and spread. Soon it covered them and shut out all but the dark wall of the herd from sight.

Slowly, evenly swung the wall, round and round without a break. Only one who has watched a milling herd can know its suppressed excitement. To keep that excitement in check was the problem of Wade and his men. And the night had not yet begun.

When the riders had brought in the drags, and the chuck wagon had lumbered up with supper, Wade set the first watch.

Along with the wagon had come the fresh horses—and Peroxide Jim, a supple, powerful, clean-limbed buckskin that had, I think, as fine and intelligent an animal face as any I ever saw. And why should he not have been saved fresh for just such a need as this? Are there not superior horses to match superior men—a Peroxide Jim to join a Wade and so combine as to make a real centaur,[3] noble physical power controlled by noble intelligence? At any rate, the horse understood the situation, and though there was nothing like sentiment about the boss of the P Ranch riders, his faith in Peroxide Jim was complete.

The other night horses were saddled and tied to the wheels of the wagon. It was Wade's custom to take his turn with

[2] "DRAGS"—Young, lame, or sick cattle that fall behind.

[3] CENTAUR—A mythical monster with the body of a horse and the neck and head of a man.

the second watch, but, shifting his saddle to Peroxide Jim, he rode out with the four of the first watch. Evenly spaced, they quietly circled the herd.

The night, for this part of the desert, was unusually warm; it was close, silent, and without a sky. The near thick darkness blotted out the stars. There is usually a breeze at night over these highest rim-rock plains that, no matter how hot the day has been, crowds the cattle together for warmth. Tonight as Wade wound in and out among the bushes, the hot dust stinging his eyes and caking rough on his skin, not a breath stirred the sage.

Round and round moved the weaving shifting forms, out of the dark and into the dark, a gray, spectral line like a procession of ghosts or some slow dance of the desert's sheeted dead. But it was not a line, it was a sea of forms; not a procession, but the even surging of a maelstrom of hoofs a mile around.

Wade galloped out on the plain for a breath of air and a look at the sky. A quick cold rain would quiet them, but there was no feel of rain in the air. There was only the powdery taste of bitter sage.

The desert where the herd had camped was one of the highest of a series of tablelands, or benches, that lay as level as a floor. It was rimmed by a sheer wall of rock over which there was a drop to the bench of sage below. The herd had been headed for a pass, and was now halted within a mile of a rim rock on the east where there was a perpendicular fall of about three hundred feet.

It was the last place an experienced plainsman would have chosen for a camp. Every time Wade circled the herd and came in between the cattle and the rim, he felt the nearness of the drop. The darkness helped to bring it near. The height of his horse brought it near—he seemed to look down from his saddle over it, into its dark depths. The herd in its milling was surely warping [4] slowly in the direction of the precipice. But this was all fancy, the trick of the dark and of nerves—if a plainsman has nerves.

At twelve o'clock the first guard came in and woke the second watch. Wade had been in his saddle since dawn, but this was his regular watch. More than that his trained ear had timed the milling hoofs. The movement of the herd had quickened.

If now he could keep them going and could prevent their taking any sudden fright! They must not stop until they stopped from utter weariness. Safety lay in their continued motion. So Wade, with fresh riders, flanked them closely, paced them, and urged them quietly on. They must be kept milling, and they must be kept from fright.

In the taut silence of the starless desert night, with the tension of the cattle at the snapping-point, any quick unwonted sight or sound would stampede the herd. The sneezing of a horse or the flare of a match would be enough to send all four thousand headlong—blind, frenzied, tramping—till they were spent and scattered over the plain.

And so, as he rode, Wade began to sing. The rider ahead of him took up the air and passed it on until above the stepping stir of the hoofs rose the faint voices of men. All the herd was bound about by the slow, plaintive measure of some

[4] WARPING—Bending, moving.

old song. It was not to soothe their savage breasts that the riders sang to the cattle, but to prevent the shock of any loud or sudden noise.

So they sang, and rode, and the night wore on to one o'clock. Then Wade, coming up on the rim-rock side, felt a cool breeze of fresh, moist wind with the taste of water in it.

He checked his horse instantly, listening as the wind swept past him over the cattle. But they must already have smelled it, for they had ceased their milling. The whole herd stood motionless. He could see, in the dark, the indistinct forms nearest him with their bald faces lifted to drink the sweet wet breath that came over the rim. Then they started again, but faster and with a rumbling from their hoarse throats that immediately tightened Wade's grip on his reins.

The sound seemed to come out of the earth—a low, rumbling mumble as deep as the night and as wide as the plain—a thick, inarticulate bellow that stood every rider stiff in his stirrups.

The breeze caught the dust and carried it back from the gray-coated ghostly shapes. Wade saw that they were still moving in a circle. If only he could keep them going! He touched his horse to ride on with them. Then across the black sky flashed a vivid streak of lightning.

There was a snort from the steers, a quick clap of horns and hoofs from within the herd, a tremor of the plain, a roar, a surging mass—and Wade was riding the flank of a wild stampede. Before him, behind him, beside him, pressing hard upon his horse galloped frenzied steers. Beyond them was the multitude, borne on, and bearing him on, by the heave of their galloping.

Wade was riding for his life. He knew it. His horse knew it. He was riding to turn the herd back from the rim, too, as the horse also knew. The cattle were after water—they were water-mad—and would go over the precipice to get it, carrying horse and rider with them.

Wade was the only rider between the herd and the rim. It was black as death. He could see nothing in the sage, could scarcely discern the pounding, panting shadows at his side; but he knew by the swish of the brush and the plunging of the horse that the ground was growing stonier, that they were nearing the rocks.

To outrun the cattle seemed his only chance. If he could come up with the leaders he might yet head them off upon the plain and save the herd. There were cattle still ahead of him—how many, what part of the herd, he could not tell. But the horse knew. The reins hung on his straight neck while Wade, yelling and firing in the air, gave him the race to win, to lose.

Suddenly they veered and went high in the air, as a steer plunged headlong into a draw [5] almost beneath his feet. They cleared the narrow ravine, landed on bare rock, and reeled on.

They were riding the rim. Close on their left bore down the flank of the herd, and on their right, under their very feet, was the precipice, so close that they felt its blackness, its three hundred feet of fall.

A piercing, half-human bawl of terror told where a steer had been crowded over.

[5] DRAW—A washed-out creek bed leading to a canyon.

Would the next leap crowd them over, too? Then Wade found himself racing neck and neck with a big white steer which the horse, with marvelous instinct, seemed to pick from a bunch and to cling to, forcing him gradually ahead till, cutting him free from the bunch entirely, he bore him off into the sage.

The group coming on behind followed the leader, and after them swung others. The tide was turning. Within a short time the whole herd had veered and, bearing off from the cliffs, was pounding over the open plains.

Whose race was it? It was Peroxide Jim's, according to Wade, for not by word or by touch of hand or knee had he been directed in the run. From the flash of lightning the horse had taken the bit, had covered an indescribably perilous path at top speed, had outrun the herd and turned it back away from the edge of the rim rock without a false step or a shaken nerve.

Bred on the desert, broken in at the roundup, trained to think as the rider thinks, the horse knew as swiftly, as clearly as did his rider the work before him. But that he kept himself from fright, that none of the wild herd madness passed into him, is a thing for great wonder. He was as thirsty as any of the herd; he knew his own peril, I believe, as none of the herd had ever known anything. And yet such coolness, courage, wisdom, and power!

Was it training? superior intelligence? more intimate association with the man on his back? Or was it all suggestion, was that superior intelligence above him riding not only the flesh but the spirit?

Not all suggestion, I believe. Perhaps a herd of horses could not be stampeded so easily as these P Ranch cattle. In this race nothing of the wild herd spirit touched the horse. Had the cattle been horses, would Peroxide Jim have been able to keep himself outside of the herd?

FOR DISCUSSION

1. What factors affected the temper of the herd? What disappointment met men and cattle at the end of the day?

2. How did you first suspect that Peroxide Jim was to play a considerable part in the story? Describe Peroxide Jim.

3. Once the milling had started, Wade made every effort to keep the cattle moving. Why? Why did he begin to sing? What do you think he sang?

4. What caused the herd to stop milling? What started the cattle stampeding?

5. What trick did man and horse use to avert disaster? The author asks whether it was superior intelligence on the part of the horse that caused him to turn the herd. What do you think?

6. How would you answer the last question in the story?

SOUND WORDS

Onomatopoeia describes the use of a word which, when pronounced, makes the sound it represents. We have in "Riding the Rim Rock" the word *mutter*. *Mutter* pronounced slowly reminds you of the sound made by a man muttering. *Roar* is another onomatopoetic word. Name five more.

WESTERN COLOR

1. Find the paragraph or the sentences which you think particularly colorful because they best represent the West. Read these lines to the class. How many chose the same paragraphs?

2. There was much action in this story, and the author allowed us to see it because of his choice of action words. List the ten words which you feel were most effective.

3. Such mood words as *wild, black, ugliness, raspy* lend an atmosphere of suspense. Find other mood words.

RELATED READING

If you have a taste for cowboy stories, Stewart Edward White's "The Drive," appearing in *Arizona Nights*, will please you.

Rudyard Kipling spent many years in India, both in his early childhood and in later life. From his ayah, or native nurse, he heard countless Hindu fables, Mohammedan hero tales, and stories from Indian folklore. He made good use of his first-hand knowledge of the country in his writings. "Rikki-Tikki-Tavi" is from THE JUNGLE BOOK, *his famous collection of stories about the strange animals of India.*

RIKKI-TIKKI-TAVI

RUDYARD KIPLING

At the hole where he went in
Red-Eye called to Wrinkle-Skin.
Hear what little Red-Eye saith:
"Nag, come up and dance with death!"

Eye to eye and head to head,
(*Keep the measure, Nag.*)
This shall end when one is dead;
(*At thy pleasure, Nag.*)

Turn for turn and twist for twist—
(*Run and hide thee, Nag.*)
Hah! The hooded Death has missed!
(*Woe betide thee, Nag!*)

This is the story of the great war that Rikki-tikki-tavi fought singlehanded, through the bathrooms of the big bungalow in Segowlee cantonment. Darzee, the tailorbird, helped him, and Chuchundra, the muskrat, who never comes out into the middle of the floor, but always creeps round by the wall, gave him advice; but Rikki-tikki did the real fighting.

He was a mongoose,[1] rather like a little cat in his fur and his tail, but quite like a weasel in his head and his habits. His eyes and the end of his restless nose were pink; he could scratch himself anywhere he pleased, with any leg, front or back, that he chose to use; he could fluff up his tail till it looked like a bottle brush, and his war cry as he scuttled through the long grass was: "rikk-tikk-tikki-tikki-tchk!"

One day a high summer flood washed him out of the burrow where he lived with his father and mother, and carried him, kicking and clucking, down a roadside ditch. He found a little wisp of grass floating there and clung to it till he lost his senses. When he revived, he was lying in the hot sun on the middle of a garden path, very draggled indeed, and a small boy was saying: "Here's a dead mongoose. Let's have a funeral."

"No," said his mother; "let's take him in and dry him. Perhaps he isn't really dead."

They took him into the house, and a big man picked him up between his finger and thumb and said he was not dead but

[1] MONGOOSE (mŏng′gōōs)—A small animal noted for its ability to kill mice and rats and the most poisonous of snakes.

half choked; so they wrapped him in cotton wool[2] and warmed him, and he opened his eyes and sneezed.

"Now," said the big man (he was an Englishman who had just moved into the bungalow), "don't frighten him, and we'll see what he'll do."

It is the hardest thing in the world to frighten a mongoose, because he is eaten up from nose to tail with curiosity. The motto of all the mongoose family is "Run and find out"; and Rikki-tikki was a true mongoose. He looked at the cotton wool, decided that it was not good to eat, ran all round the table, sat up and put his fur in order, scratched himself, and jumped on the small boy's shoulder.

"Don't be frightened, Teddy," said his father. "That's his way of making friends."

"Ouch! He's tickling under my chin," said Teddy.

Rikki-tikki looked down between the boy's collar and neck, sniffed at his ear, and climbed down to the floor, where he sat rubbing his nose.

"Good gracious," said Teddy's mother, "and that's a wild creature! I suppose he's so tame because we've been kind to him."

"All mongooses are like that," said her husband. "If Teddy doesn't pick him up by the tail, or try to put him in a cage, he'll run in and out of the house all day long. Let's give him something to eat."

They gave him a little piece of raw meat. Rikki-tikki liked it immensely, and when it was finished he went out into the veranda and sat in the sunshine and fluffed up his fur to make it dry to the roots. Then he felt better.

[2] COTTON WOOL—Raw cotton.

"There are more things to find out about in this house," he said to himself, "than all my family could find out in all their lives. I shall certainly stay and find out."

He spent all that day roaming over the house. He nearly drowned himself in the bathtubs, put his nose into the ink on a writing table, and burned it on the end of the big man's cigar, for he climbed up in the big man's lap to see how writing was done. At nightfall he ran into Teddy's nursery to watch how kerosene lamps were lighted, and when Teddy went to bed Rikki-tikki climbed up too; but he was a restless companion, because he had to get up and attend to every noise all through the night and find out what made it. Teddy's mother and father came in, the last thing, to look at their boy, and Rikki-tikki was awake on the pillow. "I don't like that," said Teddy's mother, "he may bite the child." "He'll do no such thing," said the father. "Teddy's safer with that little beast than if he had a bloodhound to watch him. If a snake came into the nursery now—"

But Teddy's mother wouldn't think of anything so awful.

Early in the morning Rikki-tikki came to early breakfast in the veranda riding on Teddy's shoulder, and they gave him banana and some boiled egg; and he sat on all their laps one after the other, because every well-brought-up mongoose always hopes to be a house-mongoose some day and have rooms to run about in, and Rikki-tikki's mother (she used to live in the General's house at Segowlee) had carefully told Rikki what to do if ever he came across white men.

Then Rikki-tikki went out into the garden to see what was to be seen. It was a large garden, only half cultivated, with bushes as big as summerhouses of Marshal Niel roses, lime and orange trees, clumps of bamboo, and thickets of high grass. Rikki-tikki licked his lips. "This is a splendid hunting ground," he said, and his tail grew bottle-brushy at the thought of it, and he scuttled up and down the garden, snuffing here and there till he heard very sorrowful voices in a thorn-bush.

It was Darzee, the tailorbird, and his wife. They had made a beautiful nest by pulling two big leaves together and stitching them up the edges with fibers, and had filled the hollow with cotton and downy fluff. The nest swayed to and fro, as they sat on the rim and cried.

"What is the matter?" asked Rikki-tikki.

"We are very miserable," said Darzee. "One of our babies fell out of the nest yesterday and Nag ate him."

"H'm!" said Rikki-tikki, "that is very sad—but I am a stranger here. Who is Nag?"

Darzee and his wife only cowered down in the nest without answering, for from the thick grass at the foot of the bush there came a low hiss—a horrid cold sound that made Rikki-tikki jump back two clear feet. Then inch by inch out of the grass rose up the head and spread hood [3] of Nag, the big black cobra, and he was five feet long from tongue to tail. When he had lifted one-third of himself clear of the ground, he stayed balancing to and fro exactly as a dandelion tuft balances in the wind, and he looked at Rikki-tikki with the wicked snake's eyes that never change their expression whatever the snake may be thinking of.

"Who is Nag?" he said. "*I* am Nag. The great god Brahm put his mark upon all our people when the first cobra spread his hood to keep the sun off Brahm as he slept. Look, and be afraid!"

He spread out his hood more than ever, and Rikki-tikki saw the spectacle-mark on the back of it that looks exactly like the eye part of a hook-and-eye fastening. He was afraid for the minute; but it is impossible for a mongoose to stay frightened for any length of time, and though Rikki-tikki had never met a live cobra before, his mother had fed him on dead ones, and he knew that all a grown mongoose's business in life was to fight and eat snakes. Nag knew that too, and at the bottom of his cold heart he was afraid.

"Well," said Rikki-tikki, and his tail began to fluff up again, "marks or no marks, do you think it is right for you to eat fledglings out of a nest?"

Nag was thinking to himself, and watching the least little movement in the grass behind Rikki-tikki. He knew that mongooses in the garden meant death sooner or later for him and his family; but he wanted to get Rikki-tikki off his guard. So he dropped his head a little and put it on one side.

"Let us talk," he said. "You eat eggs. Why should not I eat birds?"

"Behind you! Look behind you!" said Darzee.

Rikki-tikki knew better than to waste time in staring. He jumped up in the air as high as he could go, and just under him whizzed by the head of Nagaina, Nag's wicked wife. She had crept up be-

[3] HOOD—The skin of the neck which, when the reptile is excited, expands into the shape of a hood.

hind him as he was talking, to make an end of him; and he heard her savage hiss as the stroke missed. He came down almost across her back, and if he had been an old mongoose he would have known that then was the time to break her back with one bite; but he was afraid of the terrible lashing return-stroke of the cobra. He bit, indeed, but did not bite long enough, and he jumped clear of the whisking tail, leaving Nagaina torn and angry.

"Wicked, wicked Darzee!" said Nag, lashing up as high as he could reach toward the nest in the thornbush; but Darzee had built it out of reach of snakes, and it only swayed to and fro.

Rikki-tikki felt his eyes growing red and hot (when a mongoose's eyes grow red, he is angry), and he sat back on his tail and hind legs like a little kangaroo, and looked all around him, and chattered with rage. But Nag and Nagaina had disappeared into the grass. When a snake misses its stroke, it never says anything or gives any sign of what it means to do next. Rikki-tikki did not care to follow them, for he did not feel sure that he could manage two snakes at once. So he trotted off to the gravel path near the house and sat down to think. It was a serious matter for him.

If you read the old books of natural history, you will find they say that when the mongoose fights the snake and happens to get bitten, he runs off and eats some herb that cures him. That is not true. The victory is only a matter of quickness of eye and quickness of foot—snake's blow against mongoose's jump—and as no eye can follow the motion of a snake's head when it strikes, that makes things much more wonderful than any magic herb. Rikki-tikki knew he was a young mongoose, and it made him all the more pleased to think that he had managed to escape a blow from behind. It gave him confidence in himself, and when Teddy came running down the path, Rikki-tikki was ready to be petted.

But just as Teddy was stooping, something flinched a little in the dust, and a tiny voice said: "Be careful. I am death!" It was Karait, the dusty brown snakeling that lies for choice on the dusty earth; and his bite is as dangerous as the cobra's. But he is so small that nobody thinks of him, and so he does the more harm to people.

Rikki-tikki's eyes grew red again, and he danced up to Karait with the peculiar rocking, swaying motion that he had inherited from his family. It looks very funny, but it is so perfectly balanced a gait that you can fly off from it at any angle you please; and in dealing with snakes this is an advantage. If Rikki-tikki had only known, he was doing a much more dangerous thing than fighting Nag, for Karait is so small, and can turn so quickly, that unless Rikki bit him close to the back of the head, he would get the return-stroke in his eye or lip. But Rikki did not know; his eyes were all red, and he rocked back and forth, looking for a good place to hold. Karait struck out. Rikki jumped sideways and tried to run in, but the wicked little dusty gray head lashed within a fraction of his shoulder, and he had to jump over the body, and the head followed his heels close.

Teddy shouted to the house: "Oh, look here! Our mongoose is killing a snake"; and Rikki-tikki heard a scream from Teddy's mother. His father ran out with a stick, but by the time he came up, Karait had lunged out once too far, and Rikki-tikki had sprung, jumped on the snake's back, dropped his head far between his forelegs, bitten as high up the back as he could get hold, and rolled away. That bite paralyzed Karait, and Rikki-tikki was just going to eat him up from the tail, after the custom of his family at dinner, when he remembered that a full meal makes a slow mongoose, and if he wanted all his strength and quickness ready he must keep thin.

He went away for a dust-bath under the castor-oil bushes, while Teddy's father beat the dead Karait. "What is the use of that?" thought Rikki-tikki. "I have settled it all"; and then Teddy's mother picked him up from the dust and hugged him, crying that he had saved Teddy from death, and Teddy's father said that he was a providence, and Teddy looked on with big scared eyes. Rikki-tikki was rather amused at all the fuss, which, of course, he did not understand. Teddy's mother might just as well have petted Teddy for playing in the dust. Rikki was thoroughly enjoying himself.

That night, at dinner, walking to and fro among the wineglasses on the table, he could have stuffed himself three times over with nice things; but he remembered Nag and Nagaina, and though it was very pleasant to be patted and petted by Teddy's mother, and to sit on Teddy's shoulder, his eyes would get red from time to time, and he would go off into his long war cry of "*rikk-tikk-tikki-tikki-tchk!*"

Teddy carried him off to bed and insisted on Rikki-tikki sleeping under his chin. Rikki-tikki was too well bred to bite or scratch, but as soon as Teddy was asleep he went off for his nightly walk around the house, and in the dark he ran up against Chuchundra, the muskrat, creeping round by the wall. Chuchundra is a broken-hearted little beast. He whimpers and cheeps all the night, trying to make up his mind to run into the middle of the room, but he never gets there.

"Don't kill me," said Chuchundra, almost weeping. "Rikki-tikki, don't kill me."

"Do you think a snake-killer kills muskrats?" said Rikki-tikki scornfully.

"Those who kill snakes get killed by snakes," said Chuchundra, more sorrowfully than ever. "And how am I to be sure that Nag won't mistake me for you some dark night?"

"There's not the least danger," said Rikki-tikki, "but Nag is in the garden, and I know you don't go there."

"My cousin Chua, the rat, told me—" said Chuchundra, and then he stopped.

"Told you what?"

"H'sh! Nag is everywhere, Rikki-tikki. You should have talked to Chua in the garden."

"I didn't—so you must tell me. Quick, Chuchundra, or I'll bite you!"

Chuchundra sat down and cried till the tears rolled off his whiskers. "I am a very poor man," he sobbed. "I never had spirit enough to run out into the middle of the room. H'sh! I mustn't tell you anything. Can't you *hear*, Rikki-tikki?"

Rikki-tikki listened. The house was as still as still, but he thought he could just catch the faintest *scratch-scratch* in the world—a noise as faint as that of a wasp walking on a windowpane—the dry scratch of a snake's scales on brickwork.

"That's Nag or Nagaina," he said to himself, "and he is crawling into the bathroom sluice. You're right, Chuchundra; I should have talked to Chua."

He stole off to Teddy's bathroom, but there was nothing there, and then to Teddy's mother's bathroom. At the bottom of the smooth plaster wall there was a brick pulled out to make a sluice for the bath water, and as Rikki-tikki stole in by the masonry curb where the bath is put, he heard Nag and Nagaina whispering together outside in the moonlight.

"When the house is emptied of people," said Nagaina to her husband, "*he* will have to go away, and then the garden will be our own again. Go in quietly, and remember that the big man who killed Karait is the first one to bite. Then come out and tell me, and we will hunt for Rikki-tikki together."

"But are you sure that there is anything to be gained by killing the people?" said Nag.

"Everything. When there were no people in the bungalow, did we have any mongoose in the garden? So long as the bungalow is empty, we are king and queen of the garden; and remember that as soon as our eggs in the melon bed hatch (as they may tomorrow), our children will need room and quiet."

"I had not thought of that," said Nag. "I will go, but there is no need that we should hunt for Rikki-tikki afterward. I will kill the big man and his wife, and the child if I can, and come away quietly. Then the bungalow will be empty, and Rikki-tikki will go."

Rikki-tikki tingled all over with rage and hatred at this, and then Nag's head came through the sluice, and his five feet of cold body followed it. Angry as he was, Rikki-tikki was very frightened as he saw the size of the big cobra. Nag coiled himself up, raised his head, and looked into the bathroom in the dark, and Rikki could see his eyes glitter.

"Now, if I kill him here, Nagaina will know; and if I fight him on the open floor, the odds are in his favor. What am I to do?" said Rikki-tikki-tavi.

Nag waved to and fro, and then Rikki-tikki heard him drinking from the biggest water jar that was used to fill the bath.

"That is good," said the snake. "Now, when Karait was killed, the big man had a stick. He may have that stick still, but when he comes in to bathe in the morning he will not have a stick. I shall wait here till he comes. Nagaina—do you hear me?—I shall wait here in the cool till daytime."

There was no answer from outside, so Rikki-tikki knew Nagaina had gone away. Nag coiled himself down, coil by coil, round the bulge at the bottom of the water jar, and Rikki-tikki stayed still as death. After an hour he began to move, muscle by muscle, toward the jar. Nag was asleep, and Rikki-tikki looked at his big back, wondering which would be the best place for a good hold. "If I don't break his back at the first jump," said Rikki, "he can still fight; and if he fights —O Rikki!" He looked at the thickness of the neck below the hood, but that was too much for him; and a bite near the tail would only make Nag savage.

"It must be the head," he said at last, "the head above the hood; and, when I am once there, I must not let go."

Then he jumped. The head was lying a little clear of the water jar under the curve of it; and, as his teeth met, Rikki braced his back against the bulge of the red earthenware to hold down the head. This gave him just one second's purchase,[4] and he made the most of it. Then he was battered to and fro as a rat is shaken by a dog—to and fro on the floor, up and down and round in great circles; but his eyes were red, and he held on as the body cartwhipped over the floor, upsetting the tin dipper and the soap dish and the flesh brush, and banged against the tin side of the bath. As he held he closed his jaws tighter and tighter, for he made sure he would be banged to death, and, for the honor of his family, he preferred to be found with his teeth locked. He was dizzy, aching, and felt shaken to pieces when something went off like a thunderclap just behind him; a hot wind knocked him senseless and red fire singed his fur. The big man had been wakened by the noise and had fired both barrels of a shotgun into Nag just behind the hood.

Rikki-tikki held on with his eyes shut, for now he was quite sure he was dead; but the head did not move, and the big man picked him up and said, "It's the mongoose again, Alice; the little chap has saved *our* lives now." Then Teddy's mother came in with a very white face and saw what was left of Nag, and Rikki-tikki dragged himself to Teddy's bedroom and spent half the rest of the night shaking himself tenderly to find out whether he really was broken into forty pieces, as he fancied. When morning came he was very stiff, but well pleased with his doings. "Now I have Nagaina to settle with, and she will be worse than five Nags, and there's no knowing when the eggs she spoke of will hatch. Goodness! I must go and see Darzee," he said.

[4] PURCHASE—Leverage; a position of advantage for exerting force.

Without waiting for breakfast, Rikki-tikki ran to the thornbush where Darzee was singing a song of triumph at the top of his voice. The news of Nag's death was all over the garden, for the sweeper had thrown the body on the rubbish heap.

"Oh, you stupid tuft of feathers!" said Rikki-tikki, angrily. "Is this the time to sing?"

"Nag is dead—is dead—is dead!" said Darzee. "The valiant Rikki-tikki caught him by the head and held fast. The big man brought the bangstick and Nag fell in two pieces! He will never eat my babies again."

"All that's true enough; but where's Nagaina?" said Rikki-tikki, looking carefully round him.

"Nagaina came to the bathroom sluice and called for Nag," Darzee went on, "and Nag came out on the end of a stick; the sweeper picked him up on the end of a stick and threw him upon the rubbish heap. Let us sing about the great, the red-eyed Rikki-tikki!" and Darzee filled his throat and sang.

"If I could get up to your nest, I'd roll all your babies out!" said Rikki-tikki. "You don't know when to do the right thing at the right time. You're safe enough in your nest there, but it's war for me down here. Stop singing a minute, Darzee."

"For the great, the beautiful Rikki-tikki I will stop," said Darzee. "What is it, O Killer of the terrible Nag?"

"Where is Nagaina, for the third time?"

"On the rubbish heap by the stables, mourning for Nag. Great is Rikki-tikki with the white teeth."

"Bother my white teeth! Have you ever heard where she keeps her eggs?"

"In the melon bed, on the end nearest the wall, where the sun strikes nearly all day. She had them there weeks ago."

"And you never thought it worth while to tell me? The end nearest the wall, you said?"

"Rikki-tikki, you are not going to eat her eggs?"

"Not eat exactly; no. Darzee, if you have a grain of sense you will fly off to the stables and pretend that your wing is broken and let Nagaina chase you away to this bush! I must get to the melon bed, and if I went there now she'd see me."

Darzee was a feather-brained little fellow who could never hold more than one idea at a time in his head; and just because he knew that Nagaina's children were born in eggs like his own, he didn't think at first that it was fair to kill them. But his wife was a sensible bird, and she knew that cobra's eggs meant young cobras later on; so she flew off from the nest, and left Darzee to keep the babies warm, and continue his song about the death of Nag. Darzee was very like a man in some ways.

She fluttered in front of Nagaina by the rubbish heap and cried out, "Oh, my wing is broken! The boy in the house threw a stone at me and broke it." Then she fluttered more desperately than ever.

Nagaina lifted up her head and hissed, "You warned Rikki-tikki when I would have killed him. Indeed and truly, you've chosen a bad place to be lame in." And she moved toward Darzee's wife, slipping along over the dust.

"The boy broke it with a stone!" shrieked Darzee's wife.

"Well! It may be some consolation to you when you're dead to know that I shall settle accounts with the boy. My husband lies on the rubbish heap this morning, but before night the boy in the house will lie very still. What is the use of running away? I am sure to catch you. Little fool, look at me!"

Darzee's wife knew better than to do *that*, for a bird who looks at a snake's eyes gets so frightened that she cannot move. Darzee's wife fluttered on, piping sorrowfully, and never leaving the ground, and Nagaina quickened her pace.

Rikki-tikki heard them going up the path from the stables, and he raced for the end of the melon patch near the wall. There, in the warm litter about the melons, very cunningly hidden, he found twenty-five eggs, about the size of a bantam's eggs, but with whitish skin instead of shell.

"I was not a day too soon," he said; for he could see the baby cobras curled up inside the skin, and he knew that the minute they were hatched they could each kill a man or a mongoose. He bit off the tops of the eggs as fast as he could, taking care to crush the young cobras, and turned over the litter from time to time to see whether he had missed any. At last there were only three eggs left, and Rikki-tikki began to chuckle to himself, when he heard Darzee's wife screaming:

"Rikki-tikki, I led Nagaina toward the house, and she has gone into the veranda, and—oh, come quickly—she means killing!"

Rikki-tikki smashed two eggs and tumbled backward down the melon bed with the third egg in his mouth, and scuttled to the veranda as hard as he could put foot to the ground. Teddy and his mother and father were there at early breakfast; but Rikki-tikki saw they were not eating anything. They sat stone-still, and their faces were white. Nagaina was coiled up on the matting by Teddy's chair, within easy striking distance of Teddy's bare leg, and she was swaying to and fro singing a song of triumph.

"Son of the big man that killed Nag," she hissed, "stay still. I am not ready yet. Wait a little. Keep very still, all you three. If you move I strike, and if you do not move I strike. Oh, foolish people, who killed my Nag!"

Teddy's eyes were fixed on his father, and all his father could do was to whisper, "Sit still, Teddy. You mustn't move. Teddy, keep still."

Then Rikki-tikki came up and cried: "Turn round, Nagaina; turn and fight!"

"All in good time," said she, without moving her eyes. "I will settle my account with *you* presently. Look at your friends, Rikki-tikki. They are still and white; they are afraid. They dare not move, and if you come a step nearer I strike."

"Look at your eggs," said Rikki-tikki, "in the melon bed near the wall. Go and look, Nagaina."

The big snake turned half round, and saw the egg on the veranda. "Ah-h! Give it to me," she said.

Rikki-tikki put his paws one on each side of the egg, and his eyes were blood-red. "What price for a snake's egg? For a young cobra? For a young king cobra? For the last—the very last of the brood?

The ants are eating all the others down by the melon bed."

Nagaina spun clear round, forgetting everything for the sake of the one egg; and Rikki-tikki saw Teddy's father shoot out a big hand, catch Teddy by the shoulder and drag him across the little table with the teacups, safe and out of reach of Nagaina.

"Tricked! Tricked! Tricked! *Rikk-tck-tck!*" chuckled Rikki-tikki. "The boy is safe, and it was I—I—I that caught Nag by the hood last night in the bathroom." Then he began to jump up and down, all four feet together, his head close to the floor. "He threw me to and fro, but he could not shake me off. He was dead before the big man blew him in two. I did it. *Rikki-tikki-tck-tck!* Come then, Nagaina. Come and fight with me. You shall not be a widow long."

Nagaina saw that she had lost her chance of killing Teddy, and the egg lay between Rikki-tikki's paws. "Give me the egg, Rikki-tikki. Give me the last of my eggs, and I will go away and never come back," she said, lowering her hood.

"Yes, you will go away, and you will never come back; for you will go to the rubbish heap with Nag. Fight, widow! The big man has gone for his gun! Fight."

Rikki-tikki was bounding all round Nagaina, keeping just out of the reach of her stroke, his little eyes like hot coals. Nagaina gathered herself together, and flung out at him. Rikki-tikki jumped up and backward. Again and again and again she struck, and each time her head came with a whack on the matting of the veranda and she gathered herself together like a watch spring. Then Rikki-tikki danced in a circle to get behind her, and Nagaina spun round to keep her head to his head, so that the rustle of her tail on the matting sounded like dry leaves blown along by the wind.

He had forgotten the egg. It still lay on the veranda, and Nagaina came nearer and nearer to it, till at last, while Rikki-tikki was drawing breath, she caught it in her mouth, turned to the veranda steps, and flew like an arrow down the path, with Rikki-tikki behind her. When the cobra runs for her life, she goes like a whiplash flicked across a horse's neck.

Rikki-tikki knew that he must catch her, or all the trouble would begin again. She headed straight for the long grass by the thornbush, and as he was running Rikki-tikki heard Darzee still singing his foolish little song of triumph. But Darzee's wife was wiser. She flew off her nest as Nagaina came along and flapped her wings about Nagaina's head. If Darzee had helped they might have turned her; but Nagaina only lowered her hood and went on. Still, the instant's delay brought Rikki-tikki up to her, and as she plunged into the rathole where she and Nag used to live, his little white teeth were clenched on her tail, and he went down with her—and very few mongooses, however wise and old they may be, care to follow a cobra into its hole. It was dark in the hole; and Rikki-tikki never knew when it might open out and give Nagaina room to turn and strike at him. He held on savagely and stuck out his feet to act as brakes on the dark slope of the hot, moist earth.

Then the grass by the mouth of the hole stopped waving, and Darzee said:

"It is all over with Rikki-tikki! We must sing his death song. Valiant Rikki-tikki is dead! For Nagaina will surely kill him underground."

So he sang a very mournful song that he made up all on the spur of the minute, and just as he got to the most touching part the grass quivered again, and Rikki-tikki, covered with dirt, dragged himself out of the hole leg by leg, licking his whiskers. Darzee stopped with a little shout. Rikki-tikki shook some of the dust out of his fur and sneezed. "It is all over," he said. "The widow will never come out again." And the red ants that live between the grass stems heard him and began to troop down one after another to see if he had spoken the truth.

Rikki-tikki curled himself up in the grass and slept where he was—slept and slept till it was late in the afternoon, for he had done a hard day's work.

"Now," he said, when he awoke, "I will go back to the house. Tell the coppersmith, Darzee, and he will tell the garden that Nagaina is dead."

The coppersmith is a bird who makes a noise exactly like the beating of a little hammer on a copper pot; and the reason he is always making it is because he is the town crier to every Indian garden, and tells all the news to everybody who cares to listen. As Rikki-tikki went up the path, he heard his "attention" notes like a tiny dinner gong; and then the steady "*Ding-dong-tock!* Nag is dead—*dong!* Nagaina is dead! *Ding-dong-tock!*" That set all the birds in the garden singing, and the frogs croaking; for Nag and Nagaina used to eat frogs as well as little birds.

When Rikki got to the house, Teddy and Teddy's mother (she looked very white still, for she had been fainting) and Teddy's father came out and almost cried over him; and that night he ate all that was given to him till he could eat no more, and went to bed on Teddy's shoulder, where Teddy's mother saw him when she came to look late at night.

"He saved our lives and Teddy's life," she said to her husband. "Just think, he saved all our lives."

Rikki-tikki woke up with a jump, for all mongooses are light sleepers.

"Oh, it's you," said he. "What are you bothering for? All the cobras are dead; and if they weren't, I'm here."

Rikki-tikki had a right to be proud of himself; but he did not grow too proud, and he kept that garden as a mongoose should keep it, with tooth and jump and spring and bite, till never a cobra dared show its head inside the walls.

FOR DISCUSSION

1. The stories in *The Jungle Book* are written from the point of view of the animals. With "Rikki-Tikki-Tavi" in mind tell what you think Kipling accomplished by using this method. What does the dialogue of the animal characters add to the story? What would the story have lost had the author told only what was seen or understood by one of the humans?

2. In many ways Rikki-tikki-tavi talks and acts like a person. Name some of the things he does that show such human traits as curiosity, self-confidence, pride, and cleverness.

3. Indirectly, Kipling gives us considerable information about the jungle creatures of India. What have you learned from this story about the habits of the mongoose, the cobra, and other animals?

4. Now that you have read the story, reread the introductory poem. Who are Red-Eye and Wrinkle-Skin? What action is described? In the last stanza, what is meant by "the hooded Death"?

CAN YOU HEAR THESE ANIMALS?

Good writers are not only keenly sensitive to the sights and sounds around them, but they are also able to use language skillfully to communicate what they see and hear. Notice how Kipling chose words and made comparisons to help us hear the animal sounds he knew.

1. ". . . from the thick grass at the foot of the bush there came a low *hiss*—a horrid cold sound . . ."; "he *whimpers* and *cheeps* all night . . ."; "'*Rikk-tck-tck!*' chuckled Rikki-tikki." The italicized words imitate the voices of the animals. From this story make a list of other sound words for animal voices.

2. ". . . the rustle of her tail on the matting sounded like dry leaves blown along by the wind." The author uses two methods to help us hear the snake move. The sound is suggested by the sound of the word *rustle* and is made more vivid by a comparison with something all of us have heard. Try to find in the story or recall other sound words for animal movements. See if you can find or compose another good comparison which would help a reader to hear an animal move.

3. "The coppersmith is a bird who makes a noise exactly like the beating of a little hammer on a copper pot." Choose a bird sound with which you are very familiar and see how well you can use language to convey the sound to someone who had never heard it.

◇◇◇◇◇

With masculine and ardent strokes this poet paints a portrait of our Lady, using the world of nature as his palette. His poem is remarkable for its vigor and richness.

Mary

ROBERT FARREN

Thou art God's sky,
in which the Sun arose:
Thou art His moon,
the window of His light.
Thou art God's earth,
God in thee taking root;
God's seed: He was thy tree;
God's tree . . . thy fruit.
Thou art God's spring
jetting out Life;
God's river-bed
through which His torrent rushed;

God's sea
in which He spawned His sacred fish;
God's oyster
secreting the pearl of Christ.
God's lake His cloud rose from
to rain on earth;
God's cloud:
by Him from thee was lightning struck;
God's lightning
blazing the encumbered Heaven;
God's Heaven,
for Heaven's where's God.

◇◇

FOR DISCUSSION

1. The author praises Mary through a litany of picture words. Choose the picture in the poem which most appeals to you and defend your choice.

2. Comparison is one of the poet's most effective ways of communicating meaning. When the comparison is direct, the word *like* or *as* is used: "My heart is like a singing bird." This kind of comparison is called a *simile*. When the comparison is implied, without the use of *like* or *as*, it is called a *metaphor*. Robert Farren has used many metaphors in his poem, "Mary." Discuss in class which metaphors you believe best explain why the Church honors Mary above all other creatures.

3. The Litany of our Lady also praises Mary in a series of metaphors like "House of Gold." Try your hand at making a litany of the poet's series, adding "pray for us" after each metaphor. Say, for instance, "Mary, God's sky, in which the Sun arose, pray for us."

4. Can you add to the poet's series a metaphor of your own that is in tune with those he chose, saying, "Thou art God's . . ."?

5. Explain these lines:

> "Thou art God's spring
> jetting out Life."

6. How does a torrent differ from a stream? Do you think the word *stream* would be a good substitute for *torrent* in line 12? Would it strengthen or weaken the meaning? Explain your answer.

7. Explain the meaning of *spawned*, line 14. In line 22, what is the meaning of *encumbered?* Explain the meaning of the line.

Man is not the only creature made in the image of God. The world of nature also mirrors its Creator. In this poem the poet's appreciation of the beauty of nature and his deep devotion to Christ fuse together. This is a poem from a man's heart. Read it as such.

I See His Blood upon the Rose

JOSEPH M. PLUNKETT

I see His blood upon the rose
And in the stars the glory of His eyes,
His body gleams amid eternal snows,
His tears fall from the skies.

I see His face in every flower;
The thunder and the singing of the birds
Are but His voice—and carven by His power,
Rocks are His written words.

All pathways by His feet are worn,
His strong heart stirs the ever-beating sea,
His crown of thorns is twined with every thorn,
His cross is every tree.

FOR DISCUSSION

1. What lines make Christ seem distant from man in His majesty and power? What lines make Him seem near in His gentleness and love?

2. Do you think that the poet's comparisons are too far-fetched? What reason can you give for your answer? Which line has the most meaning for you? Why?

3. In this poem the poet looks at the beauty of the world sacramentally. In what sense can we say that the beauty of nature is like a sacrament?

4. Read the brief story of Plunkett's life included in this book. In view of what you know about Plunkett's life, does the last line take on added meaning?

PROJECT

At some time in your life you may have looked upon some scene of outdoor beauty which was so moving that it reminded you of God, His might, His purity, or His beauty. Describe it and tell how you felt.

RELATED READING

If religious poetry has a particular appeal for you, read *The Golden Book of Catholic Poetry* edited by Alfred Noyes.

Have you ever been away from home long enough really to miss the many beauties and blessings which you had always taken for granted? If you have, you have experienced homesickness, and you will understand the feeling that the author of this poem is expressing. Hers is a homesickness for the country she loves because its beauties have become a part of her.

Irish Skies

WINIFRED M. LETTS

In London here the streets are gray, and gray the sky above;
I wish I were in Ireland to see the skies I love—
Pearl cloud, buff cloud, the color of a dove.

All day I travel English streets, but in my dreams I tread
The far Glencullen road and see the soft sky overhead, 5
Gray clouds, white clouds, the wind has shepherded.

At night the London lamps shine bright, but what are they to me?
I've seen the moonlight in Glendhu, the stars above Glenchree—
The lamps of Heaven give light enough for me.

The city in the wintertime puts on a shroud of smoke, 10
But the sky above the Three rock was blue as Mary's cloak,
Ruffled like doves' wings when the wind awoke.

I dream I see the Wicklow hills by evening sunlight kissed,
And every glen and valley there brimful of radiant mist—
The jeweled sky topaz and amethyst. 15

I wake to see the London streets, the somber sky above;
God's blessing on the far-off roads, and on the skies I love,—
Pearl feather, gray feather, wings of a dove.

FOR DISCUSSION

1. The poet here repeats one idea five times. What is it?

2. Notice the many picturesque details the author has written into her poem. List five which tell clearly what she misses when she is away from Ireland.

3. The poet contrasts the "radiant mist" of the Irish hills with the somber sky of London. By reading the last six lines of the poem can you tell what this phrase means.

PROJECT

Can you think of any place you have ever visited or a scene you have viewed which you would very much like to see again? Can you recall the details of that place? Jot down as many details as you can in vivid words and phrases. Then, if you are so inclined, put them into a poem; each line might be a picture in itself. Or if you do not like to write poetry, perhaps you could compose a paragraph, putting the details together so that they form a picture for all the class to see.

RELATED READING

Don't miss reading Robert Browning's poem, "Home Thoughts from Abroad," in which he expresses his homesickness for England.

◇◇◇◇◇

Homesick with longing for a ship, a star, and seagulls, the poet has here written of a life he loves.

Sea-Fever

JOHN MASEFIELD

I must down to the seas again, to the lonely sea and the sky,
And all I ask is a tall ship and a star to steer her by,
And the wheel's kick and the wind's song and the white sail's shaking,
And a grey mist on the sea's face and a grey dawn breaking.

I must down to the seas again, for the call of the running tide 5
Is a wild call and a clear call that may not be denied;
And all I ask is a windy day with the white clouds flying,
And the flung spray and the blown spume, and the sea-gulls crying.

I must down to the seas again, to the vagrant gypsy life,
To the gull's way and the whale's way where the wind's like a whetted knife; 10
And all I ask is a merry yarn from a laughing fellow-rover,
And quiet sleep and a sweet dream when the long trick's over.

12. TRICK—A sailor's turn of duty.

FOR APPRECIATION

1. The poet has expressed three moods of the sea. What are they?
2. To make clear pictures the poet has used these words and phrases: *wheel's kick, wind's song, running tide, blown spume, whale's way, long trick's over.* What is the literal meaning of each of these? Which do you prefer, the picture words or the literal substitutes?

A WORD PICTURE

From your own experience, either at the lake, in the mountains, or on city streets, construct a short essay stressing the different moods of the place you are describing.

◇◇◇◇◇

Beauty is not always on parade, but it is never far away either. According to Father Tabb, you have only to look beneath the surface of things in order to view divine realities.

Faith

JOHN BANNISTER TABB

In every seed to breathe the flower,
  In every drop of dew
To reverence a cloistered star
  Within the distant blue;
To wait the promise of the bow,
  Despite the cloud between,
Is Faith—the fervid evidence
  Of loveliness unseen.

5. BOW—Rainbow.

FOR DISCUSSION

1. The first line seems to be nonsense. How can anyone "breathe the flower" in a seed?
2. Explain lines 2–4. What does the poet see in a drop of dew?
3. What is the "promise of the bow"? Tell the whole story about the origin of the rainbow.
4. Of what "evidence" does the poet speak? What does the "evidence" prove?
5. Can you think of any other things in God's creation that might also be called "fervid evidence"? How can the rain, snow, wind, cold, be "evidence"? Write out your findings, and bring them to read in class.

FOR WORD MEANING

The word *cloistered* can be traced back to an old Latin word, *claustrum,* meaning *bolt* or *bar.* Look in your dictionary to find out how close the modern meaning of *cloister* is to its original Latin meaning. Define *cloistral* and *cloistress.*

Midwinter on the Yukon. Seventy-five degrees below zero—so cold that the breath froze in tinkling crystals in the air. It was no time to be mushing alone on the open trail. But the prospector set out, warmed by the thought that nightfall would find him by the roaring fire at Henderson Creek.

TO BUILD A FIRE

JACK LONDON

Day had broken cold and gray, exceedingly cold and gray, when the man turned aside from the main Yukon trail and climbed the high earth bank, where a dim and little-traveled trail led eastward through the fat spruce timberland. It was a steep bank, and he paused for breath at the top, excusing the act to himself by looking at his watch. It was nine o'clock. There was no sun nor hint of sun,[1] though there was not a cloud in the sky. It was a clear day, and yet there seemed an intangible pall over the face of things, a subtle gloom that made the day dark, and that was due to the absence of sun. This fact did not worry the man. He was used to the lack of sun. It had been days since he had seen the sun, and he knew that a few more days must pass before that cheerful orb, due south, would just peep above the sky line and dip immediately from view.

The man flung a look back along the way he had come. The Yukon lay a mile wide and hidden under three feet of ice. On top of this ice were as many feet of snow. It was all pure white, rolling in gentle undulations where the ice jams of the freeze-up had formed. North and south, as far as his eye could see, it was unbroken white, save for a dark hairline that curved and twisted from around the spruce-covered island to the south, and that curved and twisted away into the north, where it disappeared behind another spruce-covered island. This dark hairline was the trail—the main trail—that led south five hundred miles to the Chilcoot Pass, Dyea, and salt water; and that led north seventy miles to Dawson, and still on to the north a thousand miles to Nulato, and finally to St. Michael on Bering Sea, a thousand miles and half a thousand more.

But all this—the mysterious, far-reaching hairline trail, the absence of sun from the sky, the tremendous cold, and the strangeness and weirdness of it all—made no impression on the man. It was not because he was long used to it. He was a newcomer in the land, a *chechaquo*, and this was his first winter. The trouble with him was that he was without imagination. He was quick and alert in the

[1] SUN—In midwinter the sun is not visible in the latitude of Alaska.

things of life, but only in the things, and not in the significances. Fifty degrees below zero meant eighty-odd degrees of frost. Such fact impressed him as being cold and uncomfortable, and that was all. It did not lead him to meditate upon his frailty as a creature of temperature, and upon man's frailty in general, able only to live within certain narrow limits of heat and cold, and from there on it did not lead him to the conjectural field of immortality and man's place in the universe. Fifty degrees below zero stood for a bite of frost that hurt and that must be guarded against by the use of mittens, ear flaps, warm moccasins, and thick socks. Fifty degrees below zero was to him just precisely fifty degrees below zero. That there should be anything more to it than that was a thought that never entered his head.

As he turned to go on, he spat speculatively. There was a sharp, explosive crackle that startled him. He spat again. And again, in the air, before it could fall to the snow, the spittle crackled. He knew that at fifty below spittle crackled on the snow, but this spittle had crackled in the air. Undoubtedly it was colder than fifty below—how much colder he did not know. But the temperature did not matter. He was bound for the old claim on the left fork of Henderson Creek, where the boys were already. They had come over across the divide from the Indian Creek country, while he had come the roundabout way to take a look at the possibilities of getting out logs in the spring from the islands in the Yukon. He would be in to camp by six o'clock; a bit after dark, it was true, but the boys would be there, a fire would be going, and a hot supper would be ready. As for lunch, he passed his hand against the protruding bundle under his jacket. It was also under his shirt, wrapped up in a handkerchief and lying against the naked skin. It was the only way to keep the biscuits from freezing. He smiled agreeably to himself as he thought of those biscuits, each cut open and sopped in bacon grease, and each inclosing a generous slice of fried bacon.

He plunged in among the big spruce trees. The trail was faint. A foot of snow had fallen since the last sled had passed over, and he was glad he was without a sled, traveling light. In fact, he carried nothing but the lunch wrapped in the handkerchief. He was surprised, however, at the cold. It certainly was cold, he concluded, as he rubbed his numb nose and cheek bones with his mittened hand. He was a warm-whiskered man, but the hair on his face did not protect the high cheek bones and the eager nose that thrust itself aggressively into the frosty air.

At the man's heels trotted a dog, a big native husky, the proper wolf dog, gray-coated and without any visible or temperamental difference from its brother, the wild wolf. The animal was depressed by the tremendous cold. It knew that it was no time for traveling. Its instinct told it a truer tale than was told to the man by the man's judgment. In reality, it was not merely colder than fifty below zero; it was colder than sixty below, than seventy below. It was seventy-five below zero. Since the freezing point is thirty-two above zero, it meant that one hundred and seven degrees of frost obtained. The dog did not know anything about thermometers. Possibly in the brain there was no sharp consciousness of a condition of very cold such as was in the man's brain. But the brute had its instinct. It experienced a vague but menacing apprehension that subdued it and made it slink along at the man's heels, and that made it question eagerly every unwonted [2] movement of the man, as if expecting him to go into camp or to seek shelter somewhere and build a fire. The dog had learned fire, and it wanted fire, or else to burrow under the snow and cuddle its warmth away from the air.

The frozen moisture of its breathing had settled on its fur in a fine powder of frost, and especially were its jowls, muzzle, and eyelashes whitened by its crystaled breath. The man's red beard and mustache were likewise frosted, but more solidly, the deposit taking the form of ice and increasing with every warm, moist breath he exhaled. Also the man was chewing tobacco, and the muzzle of ice held his lips so rigidly that he was unable to clean his chin when he expelled the juice. The result was that a crystal beard of the color and solidity of amber was increasing its length on his chin. If he fell down it would shatter itself, like glass, into brittle fragments. But he did not mind the appendage. It was the penalty all tobacco-chewers paid in that country, and he had been out before in two cold snaps. They had not been so cold as this, he knew, but by the spirit thermometer [3] at Sixty Mile he knew they had been registered at fifty below and at fifty-five.

[2] UNWONTED—Unusual.
[3] SPIRIT THERMOMETER—An alcoholic thermometer used to measure extreme cold.

He held on through the level stretch of woods for several miles, crossed a wide flat of boulders, and dropped down a bank to the frozen bed of a small stream. This was Henderson Creek, and he knew he was ten miles from the forks. He looked at his watch. It was ten o'clock. He was making four miles an hour, and he calculated that he would arrive at the forks at half-past twelve. He decided to celebrate that event by eating his lunch there.

The dog dropped in again at his heels, with a tail drooping discouragement, as the man swung along the creek bed. The furrow of the old sled trail was plainly visible, but a dozen inches of snow covered the marks of the last runners. In a month no man had come up or down that silent creek. The man held steadily on. He was not much given to thinking, and just then particularly he had nothing to think about save that he would eat lunch at the forks and that at six o'clock he would be in camp with the boys. There was nobody to talk to; and, had there been, speech would have been impossible because of the ice muzzle on his mouth. So he continued monotonously to chew tobacco and to increase the length of his amber beard.

Once in a while the thought reiterated itself that it was very cold and that he had never experienced such cold. As he walked along he rubbed his cheek bones and nose with the back of his mittened hand. He did this automatically, now and again changing hands. But rub as he would, the instant he stopped his cheek bones went numb, and the following instant the end of his nose went numb. He was sure to frost his cheeks;

he knew that, and experienced a pang of regret that he had not devised a nose strap of the sort Bud wore in cold snaps. Such a strap passed across the cheeks, as well, and saved them. But it didn't matter much, after all. What were frosted cheeks? A bit painful, that was all; they were never serious.

Empty as the man's mind was of thoughts, he was keenly observant, and he noticed the changes in the creek, the curves and bends and timber jams, and always he sharply noted where he placed his feet. Once, coming around a bend, he shied abruptly, like a startled horse, curved away from the place where he had been walking, and retreated several paces back along the trail. The creek, he knew, was frozen clear to the bottom,—no creek could contain water in that arctic winter,—but he knew also that there were springs that bubbled out from the hillsides and ran along under the snow and on top of the ice of the creek. He knew that the coldest snaps never froze these springs, and he knew likewise their danger. They were traps. They hid pools of water under the snow that might be three inches deep, or three feet. Sometimes a skin of ice half an inch thick covered them, and in turn was covered by the snow. Sometimes there were alternate layers of water and ice skin, so that when one broke through he kept on breaking through for a while, sometimes wetting himself to the waist.

That was why he had shied in such panic. He had felt the give under his feet and heard the crackle of a snow-hidden ice skin. And to get his feet wet in such a temperature meant trouble and danger. At the very least it meant delay, for he would be forced to stop and build a fire, and under its protection to bare his feet while he dried his socks and moccasins. He stood and studied the creek bed and its banks, and decided that the flow of water came from the right. He reflected a while, rubbing his nose and cheeks, then skirted to the left, stepping gingerly and testing the footing for each step. Once clear of the danger, he took a fresh chew of tobacco and swung along at his four-mile gait.

In the course of the next two hours he came upon several similar traps. Usually the snow above the hidden pools had a sunken candied appearance that advertised the danger. Once again, however, he had a close call; and once, suspecting danger, he compelled the dog to go on in front. The dog did not want to go. It hung back until the man shoved it forward, and then it went quickly across the white, unbroken surface. Suddenly it broke through, floundered to one side, and got away to firmer footing. It had wet its forefeet and legs, and almost immediately the water that clung to it turned to ice. It made quick efforts to lick the ice off its legs, then dropped down in the snow and began to bite out the ice that had formed between the toes. This was a matter of instinct. To permit the ice to remain would mean sore feet. It did not know this. It merely obeyed the mysterious prompting that arose from the deep crypts of its being. But the man knew, having achieved a judgment on the subject, and he removed the mitten from his right hand and helped tear out the ice particles. He did not expose his fingers more than a minute, and was astonished at the swift numbness that smote them. It certainly was cold. He pulled on the mitten hastily, and beat the hand savagely across his chest.

At twelve o'clock the day was at its brightest. Yet the sun was too far south on its winter journey to clear the horizon. The bulge of the earth intervened between it and Henderson Creek, where the man walked under a clear sky at noon and cast no shadow. At half-past twelve, to the minute, he arrived at the forks of the creek. He was pleased at the speed he had made. If he kept it up, he would certainly be with the boys by six. He unbuttoned his jacket and shirt and drew forth his lunch. The action consumed no more than a quarter of a minute, yet in that brief moment the numbness laid hold of the exposed fingers. He did not put the mitten on, but, instead, struck the fingers a dozen sharp smashes against his leg. Then he sat down on a snow-covered log to eat. The sting that followed upon the striking of his fingers against his leg ceased so quickly that he was startled. He had had no chance to take a bite of biscuit. He struck the fingers repeatedly and returned them to the mitten, baring the other hand for the purpose of eating. He tried to take a mouthful, but the ice muzzle prevented. He had forgotten to build a fire and thaw out. He chuckled at his foolishness, and as he chuckled he noted the numbness creeping into the exposed fingers. Also he noted that the stinging which had first come to his toes when he sat down was already passing away. He wondered whether the toes were warm or numb. He moved them inside the moccasins and decided that they were numb.

He pulled the mitten on hurriedly and stood up. He was a bit frightened. He stamped up and down until the stinging returned into the feet. It certainly was cold, was his thought. That man from Sulphur Creek had spoken the truth when telling how cold it sometimes got in the country. And he had laughed at him at the time! That showed one must not be too sure of things.

There was no mistake about it, it *was* cold. He strode up and down, stamping his feet and threshing his arms, until reassured by the returning warmth. Then he got out matches and proceeded to make a fire. From the undergrowth, where high water of the previous spring had lodged a supply of seasoned twigs, he got his firewood. Working carefully from a small beginning, he soon had a roaring fire, over which he thawed the ice from his face and in the protection of which he ate his biscuits. For the moment the cold of space was outwitted. The dog took satisfaction in the fire, stretching out close enough for warmth and far enough away to escape being singed.

When the man had finished, he filled his pipe and took his comfortable time over a smoke. Then he pulled on his mittens, settled the ear flaps of his cap firmly about his ears, and took the creek trail up the left fork. The dog was disappointed and yearned back toward the fire. The man did not know cold. Possibly all the generations of his ancestry had been ignorant of cold, of real cold, of cold one hundred and seven degrees below freezing point. But the dog knew; all its ancestry knew, and it had inherited the knowledge. And it knew that it was not good to walk abroad in such fearful cold. It was the time to lie snug in a hole in the snow and wait for a curtain of cloud to be drawn across the face of outer space whence this cold came. On the other hand, there was no keen intimacy between the dog and the man. The one was the toil-slave of the other, and the only caresses it had ever received were the caresses of the whiplash and of harsh and menacing throat sounds that threatened the whiplash. So the dog made no effort to communicate its apprehension to the man. It was not concerned in the welfare of the man; it was for its own sake that it yearned back toward the fire. But the man whistled, and spoke to it with the sound of whiplashes, and the dog swung in at the man's heels and followed after.

The man took a chew of tobacco and proceeded to start a new amber beard. Also, his moist breath quickly powdered with white his mustache, eyebrows, and lashes. There did not seem to be so many springs on the left fork of the Henderson, and for half an hour the man saw no signs of any. And then it happened. At a place where there were no signs, where the soft, unbroken snow seemed to advertise solidity beneath, the man broke through. It was not deep. He wet himself halfway to the knees before he floundered out to the firm crust.

He was angry, and cursed his luck aloud. He had hoped to get into camp with the boys at six o'clock, and this would delay him an hour, for he would have to build a fire and dry out his footgear. This was imperative at that low temperature—he knew that much; and he turned aside to the bank, which he climbed. On top, tangled in the underbrush about the trunks of several small spruce trees, was a high-water deposit of dry firewood—sticks and twigs, principally, but also larger portions of seasoned branches and fine, dry, last year's grasses. He threw down several large pieces on top of the snow. This served for a foundation and prevented the young flame from drowning itself in the snow it otherwise would melt. The flame he got by touching a match to a small shred of birchbark that he took from his pocket. This burned even more readily than paper. Placing it on the foundation, he fed the young flame with wisps of dry grass and with the tiniest dry twigs.

He worked slowly and carefully, keenly aware of his danger. Gradually, as the flame grew stronger, he increased the size of the twigs with which he fed it. He squatted in the snow, pulling the twigs out from their entanglement in the brush and feeding directly to the flame. He knew there must be no failure. When it is seventy-five below zero a man must not fail in his first attempt to build a fire—that is, if his feet are wet. If his feet are dry, and he fails, he can run along the trail for half a mile and restore his circulation. But the circulation of wet and freezing feet cannot be restored by running when it is seventy-five below. No matter how fast he runs, the wet feet will freeze the harder.

All this the man knew. The old-timer on Sulphur Creek had told him about it the previous fall, and now he was appreciating the advice. Already all sensation had gone out of his feet. To build the fire, he had been forced to remove his mittens, and the fingers had quickly gone numb. His pace of four miles an hour had kept his heart pumping blood to the surface of his body and to all the extremities. But the instant he stopped, the action of the pump eased down. The cold of space smote the unprotected tip of the planet, and he, being on that unprotected tip, received the full force of the blow. The blood of his body recoiled before it. The blood was alive, like the dog, and like the dog it wanted to hide away and cover itself up from the fearful cold. So long as he walked four miles an hour, he pumped that blood, willy-nilly, to the surface; but now it ebbed away and sank down into the recesses of his body. The extremities were the first to feel its absence. His wet feet froze the faster, and his exposed fingers numbed the faster, though they had not yet begun to freeze. Nose and cheeks were already freezing, while the skin of all his body chilled as it lost its blood.

But he was safe. Toes and nose and cheeks would be only touched by the frost, for the fire was beginning to burn with strength. He was feeding it with twigs the size of his finger. In another minute he would be able to feed it with branches the size of his wrist, and then he could remove his wet footgear, and, while it dried, he could keep his naked feet warm by the fire, rubbing them at first, of course, with snow. The fire was a success. He was safe. He remembered the advice of the old-timer on Sulphur Creek, and smiled. The old-timer had been very serious in laying down the law that no man must travel alone in the Klondike[4] after fifty below. Well, here he was; he had had the accident; he was alone; and he had saved himself. Those old-timers were rather womanish, some of them, he thought. All a man had to do was to keep his head, and he was all right. Any man who was a man could travel alone. But it was surprising the rapidity with which his cheeks and nose were freezing. And he had not thought his fingers could go lifeless in so short a time. Lifeless they were, for he could scarcely make them move together to grip a twig, and they seemed remote from his body and from him. When he touched a twig he had to look and see whether or not he had hold of it. The wires were pretty well down between him and his finger ends.

All of which counted for little. There was the fire, snapping and crackling and promising life with every dancing flame. He started to untie his moccasins. They were coated with ice; the thick German socks were like sheaths of iron halfway to the knees; and the moccasin strings were like rods of steel all twisted and knotted as by some conflagration. For a moment he tugged with his numb fingers, then, realizing the folly of it, he drew his sheath knife.

But before he could cut the strings, it happened. It was his own fault, or, rather, his mistake. He should not have built the fire under the spruce tree. He should have built it in the open. But it had been easier to pull the twigs from the brush and drop them directly on the fire. Now the tree under which he had done this carried a weight of snow on its boughs. No wind had blown for weeks, and each bough was fully freighted. Each time he had pulled a twig he had communicated a slight agitation to the

[4] KLONDIKE—A region of upper Alaska, the scene of the gold rush of 1897.

tree—an imperceptible agitation, so far as he was concerned, but an agitation sufficient to bring about the disaster. High up in the tree one bough capsized its load of snow. This fell on the boughs beneath, capsizing them. This process continued, spreading out and involving the whole tree. It grew like an avalanche, and it descended without warning upon the man and the fire, and the fire was blotted out! Where it had burned was a mantle of fresh and disordered snow.

The man was shocked. It was as though he had just heard his own sentence of death. For a moment he sat and stared at the spot where the fire had been. Then he grew very calm. Perhaps the old-timer on Sulphur Creek was right. If he had only had a trail mate he would have been in no danger now. The trail mate could have built the fire. Well, it was up to him to build the fire over again, and this second time there must be no failure. Even if he succeeded, he would most likely lose some toes. His feet must be badly frozen by now, and there would be some time before the second fire was ready.

Such were his thoughts, but he did not sit and think them. He was busy all the time they were passing through his mind. He made a new foundation for a fire, this time in the open, where no treacherous tree could blot it out. Next he gathered dry grasses and tiny twigs from the high-water flotsam.[5] He could not bring his fingers together to pull them out, but he was able to gather them by the handful. In this way he got many rotten twigs and bits of green moss that were undesirable, but it was the best he could do. He worked methodically, even collecting an armful of the larger branches to be used later when the fire gathered strength. And all the while the dog sat and watched him, a certain yearning wistfulness in its eyes, for it looked upon him as the fire-provider, and the fire was slow in coming.

When all was ready, the man reached in his pocket for a second piece of birch-bark. He knew the bark was there, and, though he could not feel it with his fingers, he could hear its crisp rustling as he fumbled for it. Try as he would, he could not clutch hold of it. And all the time, in his consciousness, was the knowledge that each instant his feet were freezing. This thought tended to put him in a panic, but he fought against it and kept calm. He pulled on his mittens with his teeth, and threshed his arms back and forth, beating his hands with all his might against his sides. He did this sitting down, and he stood up to do it; and all the while the dog sat in the snow, its wolf brush of a tail curled around warmly over its forefeet, its sharp wolf ears pricked forward intently as it watched the man. And the man, as he beat and threshed his arms and hands, felt a great surge of envy as he regarded the creature that was warm and secure in its natural covering.

After a while he was aware of the first faraway signals of sensation in his beaten fingers. The faint tingling grew stronger till it evolved into a stinging ache that was excruciating, but which the man hailed with satisfaction. He stripped the mitten from his right hand and fetched

[5] FLOTSAM—Driftwood, floating debris cast up by the water.

forth the birchbark. The exposed fingers were quickly going numb again. Next he brought out his bunch of sulphur matches. But the tremendous cold had already driven the life out of his fingers. In his effort to separate one match from the others, the whole bunch fell in the snow. He tried to pick it up out of the snow, but failed. The dead fingers could neither touch nor clutch. He was very careful. He drove the thought of his freezing feet, and nose, and cheeks, out of his mind, devoting his whole soul to the matches. He watched, using the sense of vision in place of that of touch, and when he saw his fingers on each side the bunch, he closed them—that is, he willed to close them, for the wires were down, and the fingers did not obey. He pulled the mitten on the right hand, and beat it fiercely against his knee. Then, with both mittened hands, he scooped the bunch of matches, along with much snow, into his lap. Yet he was no better off.

After some manipulation he managed to get the bunch between the heels of his mittened hands. In this fashion he carried it to his mouth. The ice crackled and snapped when by a violent effort he opened his mouth. He drew the lower jaw in, curled the upper lip out of the way, and scraped the bunch with his upper teeth in order to separate a match. He succeeded in getting one, which he dropped on his lap. He was no better off. He could not pick it up. Then he devised a way. He picked it up in his teeth and scratched it on his leg. Twenty times he scratched before he succeeded in lighting it. As it flamed he held it with his teeth to the birchbark. But the burning brimstone went up his nostrils and into his lungs, causing him to cough spasmodically. The match fell into the snow and went out.

The old-timer on Sulphur Creek was right, he thought in the moment of controlled despair that ensued: after fifty below, a man should travel with a partner. He beat his hands, but failed in exciting any sensation. Suddenly he bared both hands, removing the mittens with his teeth. He caught the whole bunch between the heels of his hands. His arm muscles, not being frozen, enabled him to press the hand heels tightly against the matches. Then he scratched the bunch along his leg. It flared into flame, seventy sulphur matches at once! There was no wind to blow them out. He kept his head to one side to escape the strangling fumes, and held the blazing bunch to the birchbark. As he so held it, he became aware of sensation in his hands. His flesh was burning. He could smell it. Deep down below the surface he could feel it. The sensation developed into pain that grew acute. And still he endured it, holding the flame of the matches clumsily to the bark that would not light readily because his own burning hands were in the way, absorbing most of the flame.

At last, when he could endure no more, he jerked his hands apart. The blazing matches fell sizzling into the snow, but the birchbark was alight. He began laying dry grasses and the tiniest twigs on the flame. He could not pick and choose, for he had to lift the fuel between the heels of his hands. Small pieces of rotten wood and green moss clung to the twigs, and he bit them off as well as he

could with his teeth. He cherished the flame carefully and awkwardly. It meant life, and it must not perish. The withdrawal of blood from the surface of his body now made him begin to shiver, and he grew more awkward. A large piece of green moss fell squarely on the little fire. He tried to poke it out with his fingers, but his shivering frame made him poke too far, and he disrupted the nucleus of the little fire, the burning grasses and tiny twigs separating and scattering. He tried to poke them together again, but, in spite of the tenseness of the effort, his shivering got away with him, and the twigs were hopelessly scattered. Each twig gushed a puff of smoke and went out. The fire-provider had failed. As he looked apathetically about him, his eyes chanced on the dog, sitting across the ruins of the fire from him, in the snow, making restless, hunching movements, slightly lifting one forefoot and then the other, shifting its weight back and forth on them with wistful eagerness.

The sight of the dog put a wild idea into his head. He remembered the tale of the man, caught in a blizzard, who killed a steer and crawled inside the carcass, and so was saved. He would kill the dog and bury his hands in the warm body until the numbness went out of them. Then he could build another fire. He spoke to the dog, calling it to him; but in his voice was a strange note of fear that frightened the animal, who had never known the man to speak in such way before. Something was the matter, and its suspicious nature sensed danger—it knew not what danger, but somewhere, somehow, in its brain arose an apprehension of the man. It flattened its ears down at the sound of the man's voice, and its restless, hunching movements, and the liftings and shiftings of its forefeet became more pronounced; but it would not come to the man. He got on his hands and knees and crawled toward the dog. This unusual posture again excited suspicion, and the animal sidled mincingly away.

The man sat up in the snow for a moment and struggled for calmness. Then he pulled on his mittens, by means of his teeth, and got upon his feet. He glanced down at first in order to assure himself that he was really standing up, for the absence of sensation in his feet left him unrelated to the earth. His erect position in itself started to drive the webs of suspicion from the dog's mind; and when he spoke peremptorily with the sound of whiplashes in his voice, the dog rendered its customary allegiance and came to him. As it came within reaching distance, the man lost control. His arms flashed out to the dog, and he experienced genuine surprise when he discovered that his hands could not clutch, that there was neither bend nor feeling in the fingers. He had forgotten for the moment that they were frozen and that they were freezing more and more. All this happened quickly, and before the animal could get away, he encircled its body with his arms. He sat down in the snow, and in this fashion held the dog, while it snarled and whined and struggled.

But it was all he could do, hold its body encircled in his arms and sit there. He realized that he could not kill the dog. There was no way to do it. With his helpless hands he could neither draw nor hold his sheath knife nor throttle the animal. He released it, and it plunged wildly away, with tail between its legs, and still snarling. It halted forty feet away and surveyed him curiously, with ears sharply pricked forward. The man looked down at his hands in order to locate them, and found them hanging on the ends of his arms. It struck him as curious that one should have to use his eyes in order to find out where his hands were. He began threshing his arms back and forth, beating the mittened hands against his sides. He did this for five minutes, violently, and his heart pumped enough blood up to the surface to put a stop to his shivering. But no sensation was aroused in the hands. He had an impression that they hung like weights on the ends of his arms, but when he tried to run the impression down, he could not find it.

A certain fear of death, dull and oppressive, came to him. This fear quickly became poignant [6] as he realized that it was no longer a mere matter of freezing his fingers and toes, or of losing his hands and feet, but that it was a matter of life and death, with the chances against him. This threw him into a panic, and he turned and ran up the creek bed along the old dim trail. The dog joined in behind and kept up with him. He ran blindly, without intention, in fear such as he had never known in his life. Slowly, as he plowed and floundered through the snow, he began to see things again,—the banks of the creek, the old timber jams, the leafless aspens, and the sky. The running made him feel better. He did not shiver. Maybe, if he ran on, his feet would thaw out; and, anyway, if he ran

[6] POIGNANT (poin′yănt)—Sharp and keenly piercing.

far enough he would reach the camp and the boys. Without doubt he would lose some fingers and toes and some of his face; but the boys would take care of him, and save the rest of him when he got there. And at the same time there was another thought in his mind that said he would never get to the camp and the boys; that it was too many miles away, that the freezing had too great a start on him, and that he would soon be stiff and dead. This thought he kept in the background and refused to consider. Sometimes it pushed itself forward and demanded to be heard, but he thrust it back and strove to think of other things.

It struck him as curious that he could run at all on feet so frozen that he could not feel them when they struck the earth and took the weight of his body. He seemed to himself to skim along above the surface, and to have no connection with the earth. Somewhere he had once seen a winged Mercury,[7] and he wondered if Mercury felt as he felt when skimming over the earth.

His theory of running until he reached camp and the boys had one flaw in it: he lacked the endurance. Several times he stumbled, and finally he tottered, crumpled up, and fell. When he tried to rise, he failed. He must sit and rest, he decided, and next time he would merely walk and keep on going. As he sat and regained his breath, he noted that he was feeling quite warm and comfortable. He was not shivering, and it even seemed that a warm glow had come to his chest and trunk. And yet, when he touched his nose or cheeks, there was no sensation. Running would not thaw them out. Nor would it thaw out his hands and feet.

Then the thought came to him that the frozen portions of his body must be extending. He tried to keep this thought down, to forget it, to think of something else; he was aware of the panicky feeling that it caused, and he was afraid of the panic. But the thought asserted itself, and persisted, until it produced a vision of his body totally frozen. This was too much, and he made another wild run along the trail. Once he slowed down to a walk, but the thought of the freezing extending itself made him run again.

And all the time the dog ran with him, at his heels. When he fell down a second time, it curled its tail over its forefeet and sat in front of him, facing him, curiously eager and intent. The warmth and security of the animal angered him, and he cursed it till it flattened down its ears appeasingly. This time the shivering came more quickly upon the man. He was losing in his battle with the frost. It was creeping into his body from all sides. The thought of it drove him on, but he ran no more than a hundred feet, when he staggered and pitched headlong. It was his last panic. When he had recovered his breath and control, he sat up and entertained in his mind the conception of meeting death with dignity. However, the conception did not come to him in such terms. His idea of it was that he had been making a fool of himself, running around like a chicken with its head cut off—such was the simile[8] that occurred to him. Well, he was bound to freeze anyway, and he might as

[7] MERCURY—The wing-footed messenger of the mythical Greek gods.

[8] SIMILE (sĭm′ĭ·lē)—Likeness.

well take it decently. With this new-found peace of mind came the first glimmerings of drowsiness. A good idea, he thought, to sleep off to death. It was like taking an anesthetic. Freezing was not so bad as people thought. There were lots worse ways to die.

He pictured the boys finding his body next day. Suddenly he found himself with them, coming along the trail and looking for himself. And, still with them, he came around a turn in the trail and found himself lying in the snow. He did not belong with himself any more, for even then he was out of himself standing with the boys and looking at himself in the snow. It certainly was cold, was his thought. When he got back to the States, he could tell the folks what real cold was. He drifted on from this to a vision of the old-timer on Sulphur Creek. He could see him quite clearly, warm and comfortable, and smoking a pipe.

"You were right, old hoss; you were right," the man mumbled to the old-timer of Sulphur Creek.

Then the man drowsed off into what seemed to him the most comfortable and satisfying sleep he had ever known. The dog sat facing him and waiting. The brief day drew to a close in a long, slow twilight. There were no signs of a fire to be made, and, besides, never in the dog's experience had it known a man to sit like that in the snow and make no fire. As the twilight drew on, its eager yearning for the fire mastered it, and with a great lifting and shifting of forefeet, it whined softly, then flattened its ear down in anticipation of being chidden by the man. But the man remained silent. Later, the dog whined loudly. And still later it crept close to the man and caught the scent of death. This made the animal bristle and back away. A little longer it delayed, howling under the stars that leaped and danced and shone brightly in the cold sky. Then it turned and trotted up the trail in the direction of the camp it knew, where were other food-providers and fire-providers.

◇◇◇◇◇◇◇◇◇◇◇◇◇◇◇◇◇◇◇◇◇◇◇◇◇◇◇◇◇◇

FOR DISCUSSION

1. "To Build a Fire" is a tragic story. Did you feel a chill of foreboding as you read the first paragraphs? How did Jack London achieve this effect? Note his selection of grim details—the day cold and gray, the dim trail, the lonely winter scene, the sinister crackle of the ice.

2. What faculty did the prospector lack which would have warned him of danger in venturing forth into the cold? For what kind of trap was he watching as he followed the creek bed? Describe the first incident that occasioned fear.

3. Is the husky pictured as the loyal, devoted friend of the man on the trail? What actions of the prospector partly explain the timorous, sullen character of the dog? From this story what characteristics of the husky can you list?

4. How did disaster overtake the traveler? What mistake did he make in building the fire?

5. In the man's peril, speed of action was an utmost necessity. What circumstances made his movements agonizingly slow and clumsy? How did he tackle the problem? With what success?

6. Describe the prospector's final steps to avoid death by freezing. Has your foot at any time "gone to sleep"? Would such numbness describe his sensations as the cold crept relentlessly through his body? Do you find any trace of Christian dispositions in the man as he realized his death was inevitable?

7. Does Jack London appear to write from personal experience of the Yukon country? Explain.

DESCRIPTIVE WORDS

1. Jack London achieved a remarkable impression of the cold and gloominess of a winter day on the Yukon trail by repetition of descriptive details. In the first four paragraphs list as many different nouns and adjectives as you can find which suggest *coldness*. Which words in the first paragraph suggest *darkness?*

2. *Dip, twist, plunge, slink, burrow under, droop, shy, skirt, flounder, ebb, capsize, thresh, hunch, sidle away, skim,* and *totter* all describe movement; yet each has a special shade of meaning. Come to class prepared to describe or illustrate the kinds of movement represented in these words.

WRITING PROJECTS

1. From details in the story, write a short account telling how to build a fire on the Yukon trail.

2. Compare the style of Jack London with that of Richard E. Byrd in "Flight to the South Pole" on page 18. Which is the grimmer tale? What different view of life in the two authors do you detect?

RELATED READING

Jack London wrote many tales of swift and vivid action, of adventure in the Far North, the West, and the South Seas. Another characteristic story of his is *The Call of the Wild,* picturing the Klondike gold rush. For a different view of the North, read Father Bernard J. Hubbard's *Mush, You Malemutes!* or *Dogsled Apostles* by Alma H. Savage.

Have you ever seen lambs grazing in a field or flocking down a road? This poet did, and for her the picture was one of religious significance.

Sheep and Lambs

KATHARINE TYNAN HINKSON

All in the April evening,
  April airs were abroad;
The sheep with their little lambs
  Passed me by on the road.

The sheep with their little lambs 5
  Passed me by on the road;
All in an April evening,
  I thought on the Lamb of God.

The lambs were weary, and crying
  With a weak, human cry. 10
I thought on the Lamb of God
  Going meekly to die.

Up in the blue, blue mountains
  Dewy pastures are sweet;
Rest for the little bodies, 15
  Rest for the little feet.

But for the Lamb of God
  Up on the hilltop green,
Only a Cross of shame,
  Two stark crosses between. 20

All in the April evening,
  April airs were abroad;
I saw the sheep with their lambs,
  And thought on the Lamb of God.

FOR DISCUSSION

1. The poet passed some lambs on the road and was reminded of our Lord. Can you name the one way in which the lambs resembled Him? The one way in which they did not?

2. Was the feeling which the poem left with you one of sadness or gladness? Can you determine the reasons why? Which lines best express the mood of the poem?

3. To explore the meaning of the word *meekly* is to increase your understanding of our Lord and of life. Can you guess its meaning from its use in the poem, "Going *meekly* to die"? Name three occasions on which you might be said to have acted *meekly*. Find out from your dictionary how the words *gentle*, *mild*, and *meek* differ.

MEANINGS IN NATURE

To be reminded of supernatural things by looking at natural objects is a good habit that should be developed. "I See His Blood upon the Rose," "Stars," and "Faith" are three selections in each of which the author has mirrored a deep spiritual feeling. Can you think of something you have seen which reminded you of a heavenly thing? Sometimes the blue sky reminds people of Mary's protection; sometimes a tiny new-born bird reminds people of the Creator's infinite tenderness. Try to recall at least three different things you have seen in nature which lift your thoughts to supernatural truths. When all in the class have finished their lists, pass the papers around so that each can benefit from everyone else's work.

You have noticed the candles burning beside the tabernacle during Mass. So has the author of this poem. The sight of them inspired him to write a short history of candles.

Candles

CLIFFORD LAUBE

Wondrous stalks are these that bear
Petals mystical and fair.

I have seen their fiery bloom
Kindle witchcraft in a room.

I have watched their frolic light
Tagging shadows in the night;

Seen their cheery signals pour
Welcome through a tavern door.

2. MYSTICAL—Having a spiritual meaning.
4. WITCHCRAFT—Irresistible influence or charm.

These, from winged spark to spark,
Guided Learning through the dark.

These from crypt and catacomb
Were the flares that conquered Rome.

Childhood near an altar knows
How a flame can be a rose.

FOR DISCUSSION

1. Have you ever seen so many descriptions of candles? Find at least eight different descriptions. Which one seems most vivid to you?

2. What is the meaning of the last two lines?

WORD MEANING

The word *crypt* traces its origin back to a Greek word meaning *to hide*. What this meaning has to do with its modern meaning, *a vault partly or wholly underground*, is not hard to see. But there are other members of this *crypto*-family that are not so easily recognized, other words springing from the same Greek root with meanings a dictionary may have to supply: *cryptic, cryptogram, cryptograph, cryptography, cryptographer, cryptonym.* Discuss these words in class. With which ones are you most familiar? Use two in sentences of your own.

Have you ever watched fog settle over the hills and valley or perhaps the top of a mountain? Here is Carl Sandburg's impression as he watches fog.

Fog

CARL SANDBURG

The fog comes
on little cat feet.

It sits looking
over harbor and city
on silent haunches
and then moves on.

FOR DISCUSSION

Is there any reason why the poet should compare fog to a cat rather than to any other animal? How do you account for the feeling of soft drifting motion in the first two lines? Is the impression true to life? How would you describe a very foggy day?

MORE OF SANDBURG

Perhaps you can get from your library an anthology of Carl Sandburg's poems. Choose one you like and read it to the class.

◇◇◇◇◇

Not everyone is a Saint Francis of Assisi, who felt in the strength of cliffs the strength of his Creator, and who saw His beautiful tenderness in a morning flower or in the trustfulness of a little bird. But anyone in a thoughtful mood can understand St. Francis' song of gratitude to God for the assurance of salvation. The first of these lines were written after he had heard a voice from heaven assuring him that "the Kingdom of God belongs to you." In all things created by God, St. Francis could see the image of the Creator.

The Song of the Creatures

ST. FRANCIS OF ASSISI

O most high, almighty, good Lord God, to Thee belong praise, glory, honor, and all blessing!

Praised be my Lord God with all His creatures, and especially our brother the sun, who brings us the day and who brings us the light; fair is he and shines with very great splendor; O Lord, he signifies to us Thee!

Praised be my Lord for our sister the moon, and for the stars, the which He has set clear and lovely in heaven.

Praised be my Lord for our brother the wind, and for air and cloud, calms and all weather by which Thou upholdest life in all creatures.

Praised be my Lord for all those who pardon one another, for His love's sake, and who endure weakness and tribulation; blessed are they who peaceably shall endure. For Thou, O Most Highest, shalt give them a crown!

Praised be my Lord for our sister, the death of the body, from which no man escapeth. Woe to him who dieth in mortal sin! Blessed are they who are found walking by Thy most holy will, for the second death shall have no power to do them harm.

Praise ye and bless the Lord, and give thanks unto Him and serve Him with great humility.

6. SECOND DEATH—Death of the soul, because of mortal sin.

FOR DISCUSSION

1. For what things created by God is the poet grateful? Do you consider them benefits, too? Why?

2. What people does the author praise? How do their actions remind you of our Lord's Sermon on the Mount? What Beatitudes do they resemble?

3. St. Francis added the last lines on death when he himself was dying. What do these lines teach about how a person should face death? How can he be prepared to face death in this attitude?

4. Read the "Benedicite," the hymn of thanksgiving recited by the priest after Mass, and the "Nunc Dimittis." Compare them with this poem.

Sometimes a prominent feature of the landscape makes a deep impression on the people who live close to it. The forest, the prairie, a river, or a waterfall may take on an almost human personality. Here Hamlin Garland tells how the mountains appeared to him.

The Mountains Are a Lonely Folk

HAMLIN GARLAND

The mountains they are silent folk,
They stand afar—alone,
And the clouds that kiss their brows at night
Hear neither sigh nor groan.
Each bears him in his ordered place
As soldiers do, and bold and high
They fold their forests round their feet
And bolster up the sky.

FOR DISCUSSION

1. In order to convey his feelings for the mountains, as well as to suggest how they looked, the poet does more than compare them to people in a general way. He gives them personality by suggesting specific character traits in his comparisons. In addition to silence, what quality do the people possess who "neither sigh nor groan"? In what respect are the mountains like soldiers? Why are the mountains lonely?

2. How does the poet help you to visualize the mountains as he saw them? For example, what do you see as you read the third line? How do the last two lines suggest the height and grandeur of the mountains?

Are you looking for new worlds to study? William Beebe, the naturalist and writer, has explored one of beauty and constant surprise. But it would not be an easy world for the rest of us to observe firsthand, so let us listen to Mr. Beebe as he tells of some of the strange things to be found in the world under the sea.

BROTHERING FISH

WILLIAM BEEBE

You are standing on a metal ladder in water up to your neck. Something round and heavy is slipped gently over your head, and a metal helmet rests upon your shoulders. Thus were the knights of old helmed by their squires for the grim business of war. Instead of a slotted vizor, however, you find two large frames of glass before your eyes. Turning your head, you see emerald waves breaking upon the distant beach of ivory, backed by feathery palms waving in the sunlight against a sky of pure azure.

You wave good-by to your grinning friend at the pump, and slowly descend, climbing down step by step. For a brief space of time the palms and the beach show intermittently through waves which are now breaking over your very face. Then the world changes. There is no more harsh sunlight, but delicate blue-greens with a fluttering of shadows everywhere. Huge pink and orange growths rise on all sides—you know they are living corals, just as you know that the perfect clouds in the sky visible in the earliest light of dawn from Darjeeling[1] are not clouds, but the snow peaks of the distant Himalayas. The first little people of this strange realm greet you—a quartet of swimming rainbows—four gorgeously tinted fish who rush up and peer in at you. You reach out for them, and they vanish.

Now your feet touch ground and you walk slowly about on the cleanest white sand in the world. An ostrich feather of a sea-plume as tall as yourself sweeps against you; it is royal-purple and might well be some weird fern from Mars. On a mound of sand you gently seat yourself, sand-colored crabs and small fish skittering just out of the way. You lean against a fretwork of purest marble while at your elbow is a rounded table of lapis lazuli[2] on which are blossoming three flowers—flowers unearthly and which lean toward you of their own free will. Their petals are resplendent in hues of gold and malachite,[3] and are fluted and

[1] DARJEELING (där·jē′lĭng)—A town in northern India.

[2] LAPIS LAZULI (lā′pĭs lăz′ū·lī)—A semi-precious stone of deep rich blue; also, as here, used for the color alone.

[3] MALACHITE—A green carbonate of copper.

fringed like some rare and unknown orchid. You reach forward to pluck one, and, faster than the eye can follow, the blossoms disappear beneath the fur of lapis velvet from which they seemed to sprout.

Dozens of fishes, all strange, all graceful and beautiful, play about you, nibbling at the coral, rushing toward the sponge which you have lifted from its place, hoping for some disturbed titbit. When you sit quietly, they gather closer and peer in through the glass at you again and again. Their absurd mouths forever open and close, and if you are a good lip-reader, you cannot fail to decipher the syllables which seem to issue in watery waves. They say, "Oh! Oh! Brother! Brother! Oh! Oh!" And you answer them in kind, speaking from the safe, dry, airy room of your helmet. They are so friendly, so curious, so utterly unlike the nervous, useless-lived inmates of our aquariums.

Your attention swings from wonders to marvels and back again. You begin to say things to yourself, gasps of surprise, inarticulate sounds of awe; you are troubled with a terrible sense of loss that (as the case may be) twenty, thirty, or fifty years of your life have passed and gone without your knowing of the ease of entry into this new world. *Are* you under water? There is no sense of wetness; the air you breathe is, if anything, better than that in the motorboat rocking overhead. You hold up your hand and see little washer-woman's wrinkles on the soles of your fingers, and you realize you are where you are. A great blue enameled

fish glides past, then suddenly stands straight upon his head and mumbles something; a skein of fairy lace drifts against your helmet; to your friends in the boat it is merely a school of jellyfish.

Only a moment has passed since you left the world overhead, or was it many hours? A gentle tug comes along the hose, and you resent this reminder of an existence which you had almost forgotten. But you rise and half walk, half float to the swaying ladder, and regretfully mount it. You find that you have been down forty minutes and another impatient adventurer is waiting to take your place. You had planned to tell the others all about it, but you suddenly find yourself wordless. You exclaim something bromidic[4] which sounds like Marvelous! Great! Wonderful! then relapse futilely into silence and look helplessly into the distance where the emerald waves still break and the palms wave as if fairyland had not intervened in your life since you saw them last.

All I ask of each reader is this— Don't die without having borrowed, stolen, purchased, or made a helmet of sorts, to glimpse for yourself this new world. Books, aquaria, and glass-bottomed boats are, to such an experience, only what a time-table is to an actual tour, or what a dried, dusty bit of coral in the whatnot of the best parlor is to this unsuspected realm of gorgeous life and color existing with us today on the self-same planet Earth.

[4] BROMIDIC (brô·mĭd′ĭk)—Commonplace, obvious.

◇◇◇◇◇◇◇◇◇◇◇◇◇◇◇◇◇◇◇◇◇◇◇◇◇◇◇◇◇◇

FOR DISCUSSION

1. In what part of the world would you judge Mr. Beebe did his underwater sightseeing? Give reasons for your answer.

2. What plea does the author make of each reader? Why wouldn't a trip to the aquarium or a careful reading of Mr. Beebe's own writings be just as good as a firsthand experience? Be specific in your answers.

PICTURES UNDER THE WATER

Mr. Beebe has drawn many word-picture comparisons. Make a list of under-water objects to which he gives names of land-objects, like the *school of jelly fish* which he called "a skein of fairy lace."

USE YOUR IMAGINATION

We know now what Mr. Beebe thought of the fish. There remains one question: What did the fish think of Mr. Beebe? Suppose you are a fish. As you face this strange, iron-headed creature, what do you think of him? Write your impressions in a paragraph.

RELATED READING

For a further study of life under the sea read *Under Sea with Helmet and Camera* by A. Felix Dupont.

"Requiem" is the opening word of a Mass for the dead; it means "rest." Here the poet tells where he wants to rest after death.

Requiem

ROBERT LOUIS STEVENSON

Under the wide and starry sky,
Dig the grave and let me lie.
Glad did I live and gladly die,
And I laid me down with a will.

This be the verse you grave for me:
Here he lies where he longed to be,
Home is the sailor, home from the sea,
And the hunter home from the hill.

5. GRAVE—Engrave.

FOR DISCUSSION

1. Do you think the author of this poem had a happy life? What makes you think so?

2. He calls himself a "sailor home from the sea," and a "hunter home from the hill." Can you think of any reasons why these names are appropriate? Tell them to the class.

3. Despite the poet's evident admiration of the beauty of the universe, he says that "he longed to be" in another place, which he calls "home . . . home . . . home." Explain in your own words this seeming contradiction.

UNDERSTANDING THE AUTHOR

Robert Louis Stevenson's life is one which everyone should know about. One or two volunteers should give reports about Stevenson. Then the whole class can discuss whether his wish, as expressed in his poem, was carried out. In the third line he says, "Glad did I live." Do you think this statement true? Explain your answer.

For Further Reading

Quest in the Desert by Roy Andrews. Wolf, the dog, could scent danger. He was always on the alert, ready to fight an enemy; and there are enemies aplenty when Wolf goes with his master on a scientific expedition into the Gobi Desert.

Half-Mile Down by William Beebe describes hair-raising undersea adventures in Bermuda.

Beyond Time and Space by August Derleth is a collection of science fiction short stories whose authors range from Plato to Jules Verne and H. G. Wells—reminding the reader that science fiction is not an invention of the 20th century.

Kon-tiki by Thor Heyerdahl. The author and five companions take a journey across the Pacific Ocean on a primitive raft in order to prove a theory.

Hunter by J. A. Hunter. A veteran hunter here shares a lifetime of adventure, most of it spent in Africa. He paints a vivid and saddening picture of Africa as it will never be again.

Nunamint by Helge Ingstad. The author, a Norwegian arctic expert, found these primitive people in inland Alaska. He recorded their legends and superstitions and participated in their activities.

Wildwood Wisdom by Ellsworth Jaeger is a manual for the woodsman or camper. It not only tells the modern camper how to make his way in the woods, but also has many drawings which show how the American Indians and the pioneers made their way in the woods.

Sun, Sea, and Sky by Krick. This is a combination of science and literature about the weather by a meteorologist.

Primer for Stargazers by Henry M. Neely is a beginner's book on astronomy which can help anyone to locate various constellations. It is written in the simplest of terms and is full of legendary material which brightens the text.

Singing in the Wilderness: A Salute to John James Audubon by Donald Peattie is a fictional biography of the great naturalist.

Bambi by Felix Salten is the life story of a forest deer, from fawn to full-grown stag. The story of Bambi's life in the forest and of all his relations is entrancing and will appeal to all who love animals and nature.

Animal Treasure by Ivan T. Sanderson is an exciting account of jungle wild life by a collector of museum specimens.

The Larks of Umbria by Albert Schimberg is a biography of St. Francis of Assisi, poetical enough to catch the unique spirit of brotherhood with all of God's creatures that was characteristic of the Friar "who preached with his heart and argued with his life."

The Watcher in the Woods by Dallas Lore Sharp. This account of wild life in the woods is full of nature lore and interesting observation.

The White Deer by James Thurber is a delightful fairy tale with the customary enchantments and dangers.

The Perfect Joy of St. Francis by Felix Timmermans. This story of the life of St. Francis of Assisi, told in devout and simple terms, will touch the reader who wishes to learn more about this most gentle saint.

South American Zoo by Victor W. Von Hagen is an entertaining account of the strange bird and animal life of the southern continent. It contains some excellent illustrations.

SWORD OF SORROW

> " . . . *In the world you have affliction.*
> *But take courage, I have overcome the world.*"
>
> ST. JOHN 16: 33

All men wish for happiness, but sorrow is part of man's experience on earth. Some people are able to overcome grief more easily than others. In this unit you can read about persons who have faced hardship: a priest who died for his faith; a dancing Negro with a broken heart; a woman whose vanity led her astray. Some, you will see, came through.

Christianity has through the ages pointed to Jesus bowed with anguish in the Garden and stretched in desolation on Calvary. Even the God-man did not conceal His tears. But Christians must remember that Christ was victorious over sorrow and death.

Life is a mixture of joy and sorrow. By walking with our Lord, we are better able to meet hardships and face life with gladness.

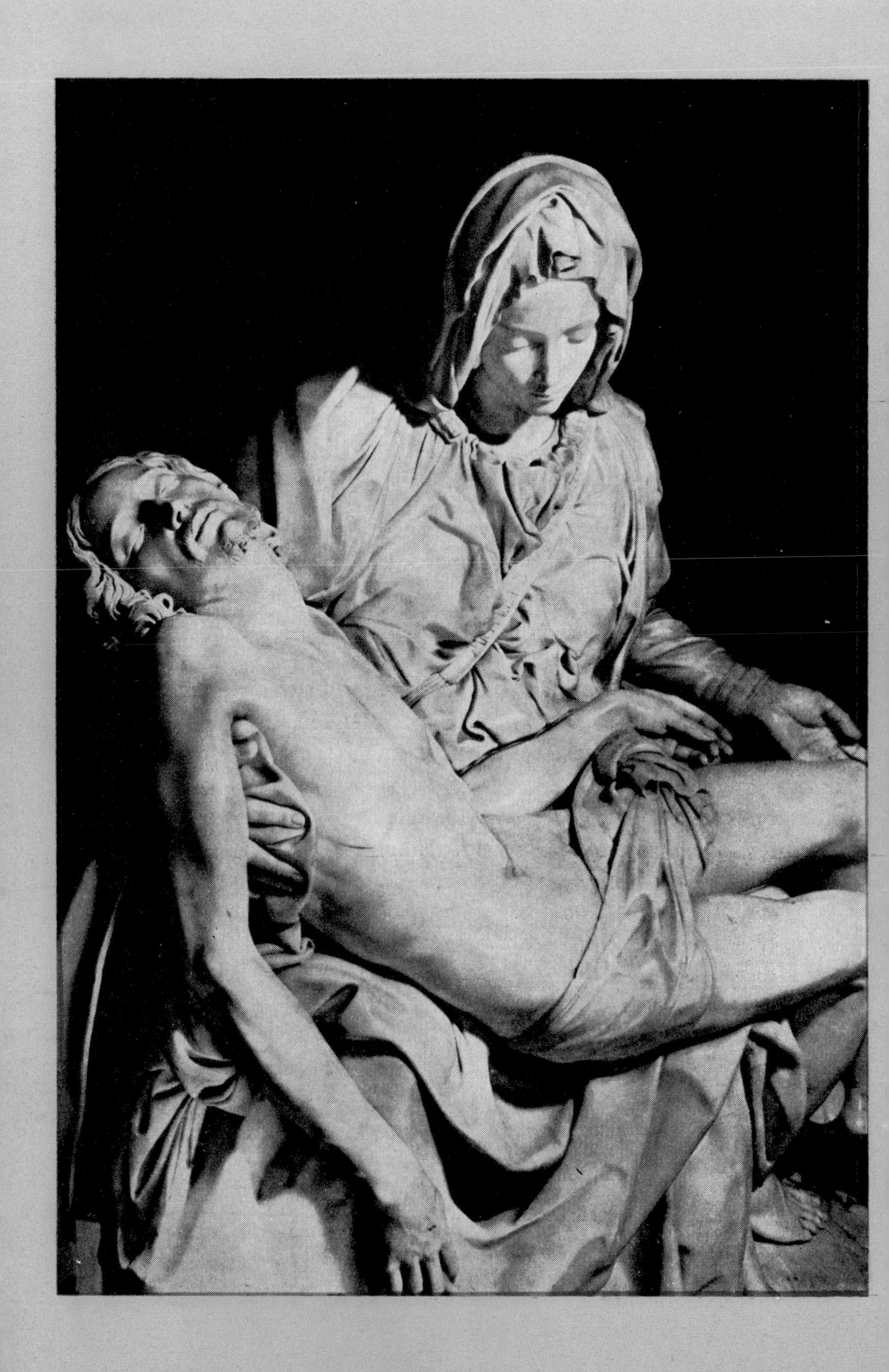

No two human beings could feel more loyalty and affection for one another than did Pierre, the milkman, and Joseph, his horse. They had a secret—something that must remain just between the two of them. Not even the folks on Prince Edward Street or Pierre's fellow employees from the milk company could share it with them. This, then, is the pathetic and tender story of the friendship between an old man and his horse.

A SECRET FOR TWO

QUENTIN REYNOLDS

Montreal is a very large city, but, like all large cities, it has some very small streets. Streets, for instance, like Prince Edward Street, which is only four blocks long, ending in a *cul de sac*.[1] No one knew Prince Edward Street as well as did Pierre Dupin,[2] for Pierre had delivered milk to the families on the street for thirty years now.

During the past fifteen years the horse which drew the milk wagon used by Pierre was a large white horse named Joseph. In Montreal, especially in that part of Montreal which is very French, the animals, like children, are often given the names of saints. When the big white horse first came to the Provinçale[3] Milk Company he didn't have a name. They told Pierre that he could use the white horse henceforth. Pierre stroked the softness of the horse's neck; he stroked the sheen of its splendid belly and he looked into the eyes of the horse.

"This is a kind horse, a gentle and a faithful horse," Pierre said, "and I can see a beautiful spirit shining out of the eyes of the horse. I will name him after good St. Joseph, who was also kind and gentle and faithful and a beautiful spirit."

Within a year Joseph knew the milk route as well as Pierre. Pierre used to boast that he didn't need reins—he never touched them. Each morning Pierre arrived at the stables of the Provinçale Milk Company at five o'clock. The wagon would be loaded and Joseph hitched to it. Pierre would call "*Bon jour, vieil ami,*"[4] as he climbed into his seat and Joseph would turn his head and the other drivers would say that the horse would smile at Pierre. Then Jacques,[5] the foreman, would say, "All right, Pierre, go on," and Pierre would call softly to Joseph, "*Avance, mon ami,*"[6] and this splendid combination would stalk proudly down the street.

[1] *Cul de sac* (kü'd'·sȧk')—A dead end street. Literally, the French means "the bottom of a bag."

[2] DUPIN—Pronounced dū·păN'.

[3] PROVINÇALE—Pronounced prō·văn·säl'.

[4] *Bon jour, vieil ami* (bôn zhōōr', vē·ā' ä·mē')—"Good morning, old friend."

[5] JACQUES—Pronounced zhȧk.

[6] *Avance, mon ami* (ä·väNs', mōN ä·mē')—"Forward, my friend."

The wagon, without any direction from Pierre, would roll three blocks down St. Catherine Street, then turn right two blocks along Roslyn Avenue; then left, for that was Prince Edward Street. The horse would stop at the first house, allow Pierre perhaps thirty seconds to get down from his seat and put a bottle of milk at the front door and would then go on, skipping two houses and stopping at the third. So down the length of the street. Then Joseph, still without any direction from Pierre, would turn around and come back along the other side. Yes, Joseph was a smart horse.

Pierre would boast at the stable of Joseph's skill, "I never touch the reins. He knows just where to stop. Why, a blind man could handle my route with Joseph pulling the wagon."

So it went for years—always the same. Pierre and Joseph both grew old together, but gradually, not suddenly. Pierre's huge walrus mustache was pure white now and Joseph didn't lift his knees so high or raise his head quite as much. Jacques, the foreman of the stables, never noticed that they were both getting old until Pierre appeared one morning carrying a heavy walking stick.

"Hey, Pierre," Jacques laughed. "Maybe you got the gout, hey?"

"*Mais oui, Jacques,*" [7] Pierre said a bit uncertainly. "One grows old. One's legs get tired."

"You should teach that horse to carry the milk to the front door for you," Jacques told him. "He does everything else."

He knew every one of the forty families he served on Prince Edward Street. The cooks knew that Pierre could neither read nor write, so instead of following the usual custom of leaving a note in an empty bottle if an additional quart of milk was needed they would sing out when they heard the rumble of his wagon wheels over the cobbled street, "Bring an extra quart this morning, Pierre."

"So you have company for dinner tonight," he would call back gaily.

Pierre had a remarkable memory. When he arrived back at the stable he'd always remember to tell Jacques, "The Paquins took an extra quart this morning; the Lemoines bought a pint of cream."

Jacques would note these things in a little book he always carried. Most of the drivers had to make out the weekly bills and collect the money, but Jacques, liking Pierre, had always excused him from the task. All Pierre had to do was to arrive at five in the morning, walk to his wagon, which was always in the same spot at the curb, and deliver his milk. He returned some two hours later, got down stiffly from his seat, called a cheery "*Au 'voir*" [8] to Jacques, and then limped slowly down the street.

One morning the president of the Provinçale Milk Company came to inspect the early morning deliveries. Jacques pointed Pierre out to him and said: "Watch how he talks to that horse. See how the horse listens and how he turns his head toward Pierre? See the look in that horse's eyes? You know, I think those two share a secret. I have

[7] *Mais oui, Jacques* (mā wē′, zhäk)—"Yes, Jim"; "But of course, Jim."

[8] *Au 'voir* (ō·vwär′)—The short form of *au revoir*: "Good-by"; "Till we meet again."

often noticed it. It is as though they both sometimes chuckle at us as they go off on their route. Pierre is a good man, Monsieur[9] President, but he gets old. Would it be too bold of me to suggest that he be retired and be given perhaps a small pension?" he added anxiously.

"But of course," the president laughed. "I know his record. He has been on this route now for thirty years and never once has there been a complaint. Tell him it is time he rested. His salary will go on just the same."

But Pierre refused to retire. He was panic-stricken at the thought of not driving Joseph every day. "We are two old men," he said to Jacques. "Let us wear out together. When Joseph is ready to retire—then I, too, will quit."

[9] MONSIEUR—Pronounced mẽ·syû′.

Jacques, who was a kind man, understood. There was something about Pierre and Joseph which made a man smile tenderly. It was as though each drew some hidden strength from the other. When Pierre was sitting in his seat, and when Joseph was hitched to the wagon, neither seemed old. But when they finished their work, then Pierre would limp down the street slowly, seeming very old indeed, and the horse's head would drop and he would walk very wearily back to his stall.

Then one morning Jacques had dreadful news for Pierre when he arrived. It was a cold morning and still pitch-dark. The air was like iced wine that morning and the snow which had fallen during the night glistened like a million diamonds piled together.

Jacques said, "Pierre, your horse, Joseph, did not wake up this morning. He was very old, Pierre; he was twenty-five and that is like being seventy-five for a man."

"Yes," Pierre said, slowly. "Yes, I am seventy-five. And I cannot see Joseph again."

"Of course you can," Jacques soothed. "He is over in his stall, looking very peaceful. Go over and see him."

Pierre took one step forward, then turned. "No . . . no . . . you don't understand, Jacques."

Jacques clapped him on the shoulder. "We'll find another horse just as good as Joseph. Why, in a month you'll teach him to know your route as well as Joseph did. We'll . . ."

The look in Pierre's eyes stopped him. For years Pierre had worn a heavy cap, the peak of which came low over his eyes, keeping the bitter morning wind out of them. Now Jacques looked into Pierre's eyes and he saw something which startled him. He saw a dead, lifeless look in them. The eyes were mirroring the grief that was in Pierre's heart and his soul. It was as though his heart and soul had died.

"Take today off, Pierre," Jacques said, but already Pierre was hobbling off down the street, and had one been near one would have seen tears streaming down his cheeks and have heard half-smothered sobs. Pierre walked to the corner and stepped into the street. There was a warning yell from the driver of a huge truck that was coming fast and there was the scream of brakes, but Pierre apparently heard neither.

Five minutes later an ambulance driver said, "He's dead. Was killed instantly."

Jacques and several of the milk-wagon drivers had arrived and they looked down at the still figure.

"I couldn't help it," the driver of the truck protested; "he walked right into my truck. He never saw it, I guess. Why, he walked into it as though he were blind."

The ambulance doctor bent down. "Blind? Of course the man was blind. Look at his eyes. See those cataracts? This man has been blind for five years." He turned to Jacques, "You say he worked for you? Didn't you know he was blind?"

"No. . . no. . . ," Jacques said softly. "None of us knew. Only one knew—a friend of his named Joseph. . . . It was a secret, I think, just between those two."

FOR DISCUSSION

1. When did you first become aware of Pierre's blindness? What details in the story hint at the fact he is blind?

2. Joseph seemed to appreciate Pierre. How did Pierre's associates regard him?

3. What evidences are there in the story that Pierre enjoyed his work? Do you think Joseph enjoyed his work, too? Give details to prove your answer.

4. Have you ever known of a similar situation as this which existed between Joseph and Pierre? Tell the class about it.

FROM THE FRENCH

1. *Jacques* is the French for "James." What are the English equivalents for *Jean, François, Pierre, Marie, Guillaume, Henri, Laurent, Edouard?*

2. Pay special attention to the pronunciation of *monsieur* (mẽ·syû′). It is the French form of "Mister." Notice that the pronunciation is not much like the spelling. This word will probably come up often in your reading.

CHOOSING A NAME

Suppose that you are invited to suggest a saint's name for a baby sister or brother. Make your choice and tell why you so chose. At the back of some dictionaries you will find a list of Christian names with their origins and meanings; the list may help you choose wisely. In the *Roman Martyrology* and in *Lives of the Saints* you will find a still further abundance of names with a brief history of each saint's career.

RELATED READING

Stories you are sure to enjoy are *The Yearling* by Margaret K. Rawlings and *Lad, A Dog* by Albert P. Terhune.

A minstrel show is a long line of smiling black faces, with the lads on the ends doing a little "extra-smiling." Interlocutor, end-men, and singers all join to create an impression of gaiety. In this poem the minstrel man speaks, to tell that there is not always happiness behind that smile. Read this poem with the deep feeling which must be in the minstrel's voice.

Minstrel Man

LANGSTON HUGHES

Because my mouth
Is wide with laughter
And my throat
Is deep with song,
You do not think 5
I suffer after
I have held my pain so long?
Because my mouth is wide with laughter
You do not hear my inner cry?
Because my feet are gay with dancing 10
You do not know I die?

FOR DISCUSSION

1. Have you ever felt as the minstrel man does? In that moment did you feel that you were being a hero? Tell about your experience.

2. What words emphasize the contrast between gaiety and sadness in this poem?

3. Read the brief sketch of Langston Hughes' life on page 635 of this book. Do you think he might have been thinking of the whole Negro race when he wrote this poem? Explain your answer. What line or lines seem to hold the deepest meaning?

READING POETRY FOR MEANING AND ENJOYMENT

To achieve complete enjoyment of poetry, the reader must not be a slave to line-by-line reading. As in prose, punctuation is used for meaning in poetry. A pause at the end of a line is usually indicated by some mark of punctuation. A thoughtless reader might make this out of the first three lines of "Minstrel Man":

Because my mouth.
Is wide with laughter.
And my throat.

A thoughtful reader, however, would think about the meaning of the lines; and, watching the punctuation as he reads, he would know that the author really says: "Because my mouth is wide with laughter and my throat is deep with song, you do not think I suffer after I have held my pain so long?"

Now read the complete poem aloud, putting feeling into it. Then select another poem with which you are familiar, and practice reading it aloud for meaning and enjoyment.

A PROJECT

A long time ago there was a popular song called "Laugh, Clown, Laugh." It was very similar to "The Minstrel Man" in its meaning. But it was a little different in the way it urged the clown to "go on make-believing" even though "inside his heart was grieving." It told him not to let his "heart get too mellow," but just "be a good Punchinello fellow." Why is such a theme popular? Sometimes you hear people say, "Well, that's life!" What do they mean? Does this expression explain the popularity of the theme of "Minstrel Man"? Explain.

Get a copy of "Laugh, Clown, Laugh," if you can. Play it during class and have everybody sing it. After singing, try to reconstruct the story behind the song (or you may use "The Minstrel Man" for this exercise if you prefer). It will be a story with some sadness in it and with some happiness that bucks up against hardship.

◇◇◇◇◇

In the sixteenth century when the Protestant Revolt broke in thunder over Europe, the white horsemen of Christ fought gallantly to save the faith. On enemy terrain they charged against great odds. By executioner's axe and hangman's rope, they went bravely to death, gladly giving all for God and for His Church. In the number of these white horsemen was the English priest, Edmund Campion.

On a June night in 1580, Edmund stole quietly across the English Channel into Elizabeth's England. He was back in his homeland after eight years on the continent—years in which the young Englishman had been reconciled with the Church, had joined the young Company of Jesus, had been ordained priest. Once Elizabeth had marked Campion for a high place in her church. In 1560, at Oxford, the brilliant young scholar had wavered and taken the oath to the Church of England, then finally fled across the sea. He was in England now, sent by the Holy Father and his Jesuit superior to minister in secret to his ruined and persecuted countrymen. This order was his passport to martyrdom.

For one year, disguising himself to avoid recognition, Campion traveled up and down the country. Rarely did he stop more than a night anywhere, pausing only to hear confessions, celebrate the Holy Sacrifice, and speak a heartening word to the brave faithful who stole to him in the dead of night. Then Campion rode off, striving to keep ahead of the Queen's men who quickly closed in on his trail.

One day in July, 1581, what was bound to happen did happen. At Lyford, in Berkshire, Campion stopped at the home of a Mr. Yate. Some forty of the faithful were on hand to hear Mass, and in their number was a renegade Catholic and professional priest-hunter, George Eliot. Eliot had then in his pocket a commission from the Queen's ministers to track down missing priests. Having received Holy Communion from Father Campion, he hurried away to summon help.

A cordon of soldiers was thrown about the house and an entry forced. At the first alarm, however, Campion and two other priests took refuge in a secret room, and so for a while the search was fruitless. The soldiers were on the point of giving up, when in the hiding place "someone stumbled." The priests' refuge was broken into. Campion was taken and led away under heavy guard to the infamous Tower of London.

The charges against him and the account of his trial are depicted in the following, the third act of the play, WHO RIDE ON WHITE HORSES.

THE TRIAL OF EDMUND CAMPION

RICHARD BREEN AND HARRY SCHNIBBE

CHARACTERS

EDMUND CAMPION, S.J.
QUEEN ELIZABETH
EARL OF LEICESTER (*Robert Dudley*)
STEPHEN SLEDD, *a witness at the trial*
MR. ANDERSON, *Queen's counsel*
CHIEF JUSTICE WRAY
SIR PHILIP SIDNEY
DUKE OF ANJOU

Associate Judges, Clerks, Defendants, Witnesses, and Guards

VOICE OF CAMPION. Eliot came back! It was the day appointed and I was ready. I was hardly surprised when someone stumbled and our hiding place was quickly discovered. That was four days ago. And now I am in the Tower of London, the great gates closed behind me.

"The Trial of Edmund Campion" from *Who Ride on White Horses* by Richard Breen and Harry Schnibbe. Reprinted by permission of Longmans, Green and Co., Inc.

How clear the past seems now. I know that Eliot and Elizabeth alone are not our captors. They are the instruments of our misfortune but not the reason for it. Villains change but villainy does not. If it were not Sledd,[1] Eliot, and Elizabeth . . . then someone else—the grosser mortals of another hour.

I am being taken from my cell . . . to be rowed upstream to the house of the Earl of Leicester:[2] Leicester, once my patron, now one of the first Lords of England . . .

SCENE I

SETTING: *The great hall of Leicester house—suggested briefly by a great window in the space between the towers—pennants, on the walls.*

In a throne chair down left is ELIZABETH, *attended by* LEICESTER. *Somewhere chimes strike the hours.*

ELIZABETH (*impatiently gesturing with small mask in her hand*). Well—well—is he here? Is it not enough that I come here secretly to see him? How much longer—

LEICESTER. The barge has just arrived, Your Majesty—

ELIZABETH. Oh . . . then he is here. (*Pause.*) Well—what shall I say to him, Leicester? Tell me—

LEICESTER. It shouldn't be difficult, Your Majesty. You usually know what to say to . . . men.

ELIZABETH. Yes, but this is a brilliant one. And I asked to see him. I don't usually ask to see prisoners, so—

LEICESTER. Why did you ask to see this one?

ELIZABETH. Hmm. (*Pause.*) What do you think?

LEICESTER. Does it matter? Of course, if Your Majesty wishes to marry the Duke of Anjou,[3] you will naturally take every opportunity to offer Campion a chance to recant[4] . . .

ELIZABETH. Enough! (*Pause.*) . . . besides, you don't want me to marry the Duke of Anjou, do you?

LEICESTER. Does any man wish to see the Queen of his heart marry anyone else?

ELIZABETH. You are very quick, Lord Leicester. Almost as quick as Anjou. But I'm warning you: do not try to read my mind. Just tell me what to say to him if he is too quick for me. Tell me . . .

[*Two* GUARDS *enter with* CAMPION. QUEEN *immediately puts mask to her face.* GUARDS *salute and depart.*]

CAMPION (*with a slight bow to* ELIZABETH). Your Majesty— (*Then to* LEICESTER.) My Lord—

ELIZABETH (*lowering mask*). You have not changed, Master Campion, from the day we first met in Oxford—fifteen years ago.

CAMPION. People don't change, Your Majesty. It is the air about them that changes.

LEICESTER. Then I wish the air were different today, Campion. I little thought when I singled you out in Oxford that I should one day charge you with treason. It makes me a little sad. You have failed us and I am sorry.

[1] SLEDD—A renegade Catholic in the pay of Elizabeth.

[2] LEICESTER (lĕs′tẽr)—Elizabeth's favorite.

[3] ANJOU (ăn·jōō′)—French Catholic prince, son of Catherine of Medici; his projected marriage to Elizabeth was then under negotiation.

[4] RECANT—Deny, disavow the Faith.

CAMPION. England has failed me. That's sorrow too.

ELIZABETH. Master Campion!

CAMPION. Oh, I know. I am only a prisoner—but you are prisoner too. (*Pointing to the* QUEEN.) The difference is, I am a prisoner in the Tower. But you are a prisoner in your own mind, an uncertain mind that worries over phantoms and shadows and . . .

ELIZABETH. Stop—stop—I command you.

LEICESTER. Please—Master Campion—let me say that I did not particularly wish to arrest you for treason. But when a subject is not loyal to his Queen . . .

CAMPION. I have always been a loyal subject.

ELIZABETH. Yet you preach against the Crown?

CAMPION. I do not preach against the Crown.

LEICESTER. But the effect of your preaching is to imply that the Crown is in error.

CAMPION. Then the Crown is in error—that is all.

ELIZABETH. The Crown cannot be in error.

CAMPION. I'll say this much: the Crown should not be in error.

ELIZABETH. You seem very sure that what you preach is true.

CAMPION. No surer than most of England was until . . .

ELIZABETH. Please—what was true yesterday concerns us but little. What is true today may be false tomorrow—and either the people believe what the Queen believes—

CAMPION. Yes—that is what your father believed. That is what the Church of England believes. But men should not have to take their beliefs from kings and queens. Belief is seated in the heart.

ELIZABETH (*angrily to* LEICESTER). Take him away— Take him away at once . . . No. Stay. (*Pause.*) Leave me with Master Campion a moment.

[*The quick change of mood is as much a surprise to* LEICESTER *as it is to* CAMPION.]

LEICESTER. Alone, Your Majesty?

ELIZABETH. Alone. (LEICESTER *bows and goes out. Chimes off—silence for a second.*) Master Campion—

CAMPION. Yes, Your Majesty?

ELIZABETH. I offered you advancement, once.

CAMPION. Yes, I remember.

ELIZABETH (*Pause*). I offer it to you again.

CAMPION. I am sorry, Your Majesty—

ELIZABETH. I do not even ask that you defend my Church. I merely propose that you do not destroy it.

CAMPION. Your Majesty—

ELIZABETH. Wait—(*Pause.*) Put yourself in my place. If you were Queen of England, what would you do with Edmund Campion?

CAMPION. I think I should hang him!

ELIZABETH. Master Campion!

CAMPION. What else could I do? According to your rules anyone who is against the Crown in anything is some kind of a traitor.

ELIZABETH. Humph. But the Papists [5] are against me in everything. They are always against the Crown.

CAMPION. Only because you force

[5] PAPISTS—Catholics, those loyal to the Pope.

them to conspire against it. Conspiracy and necessity are English bedfellows.

ELIZABETH. Do you really believe that a man can be a good Catholic and a good Englishman too?

CAMPION. Yes, I think so.

ELIZABETH. Even with a Protestant on the Throne of England?

CAMPION. Even with a Protestant on the Throne of England!

ELIZABETH. And is that the opinion of every priest now in England?

CAMPION. I can obviously speak only for myself, Your Majesty.

ELIZABETH. You say you are a good Catholic and a loyal Englishman. Then, how do you stand as between your Pope and your Queen?

CAMPION. Must I stand somewhere?

ELIZABETH. Don't fence with me. I am a Protestant. I have been excommunicated [6] from your Church. I have been deposed by your Pope . . . (*Pause.*) . . . Well, do you acknowledge the deposition or do you deny it? . . .

CAMPION (*with difficulty*). I'm sorry, I cannot answer that question.

ELIZABETH (*Pause*). I thought so. Then you do say the Pope had the right to depose me.

CAMPION. No. I neither affirm it, nor do I deny it.

ELIZABETH. If you do not deny it, you do affirm it.

CAMPION. That does not follow. I

[6] EXCOMMUNICATED—Cut off from membership in the Church. Pope St. Pius V pronounced the sentence in 1570,

simply say as one who loves his God *and* his country; it is not for me to act the part of an umpire between the Holy Father and Your Majesty.

ELIZABETH. Your silence convicts you then. You are no more than a spy for a sovereign power. But you have a chance. Retract now . . .

CAMPION. No. Be content with this kind of victory. You've won this time. You might not win again.

ELIZABETH (*vigorously*). Ah, then we shall see—(*Rings a bell.*)—Call the guard!

CAMPION. Call the Lords in Council, if you like. (*Pause.*) You only appeal to force and I appeal to reason.

ELIZABETH. You are a fool, Master Campion. (*Scribbling at papers.*) I could have given you anything in England.

CAMPION. Except the sovereignty of my own heart.

ELIZABETH. Heart? Hearts are not in this age. They are something out of the past and small matter in England today.

[LEICESTER *returns with* GUARD—*The* QUEEN *gives him the indictment.*]

LEICESTER. Your Majesty?

ELIZABETH. Here is the indictment, my Lord. Take him to the Tower.

LEICESTER. Campion!

CAMPION. Sorry, my Lord, I found it hard to meet treason with treason.

ELIZABETH. Not for the wealth of a kingdom, even!

CAMPION. I have a kingdom. I have a kingdom here—in my heart—that you will not touch this side of Heaven.

[CAMPION *goes out with* GUARD. LEICESTER *turns to* QUEEN, *who holds her poise a moment, then breaks.*]

LEICESTER. Well, Your Majesty?

ELIZABETH (*at window—in fury*). Break him, rack him! Invent the evidence, buy his betrayal, but hang him! (QUEEN *turns around abruptly. The fury dwindles as swiftly as it came. At* LEICESTER'S *silence.*) Do you hear, do you hear? He will remember this.

LEICESTER (*folding the indictment*). Yes. This is dedicated to remembrance.

[QUEEN *walks uncertainly to a chair, stumbles into it.*]

ELIZABETH. Why—why didn't you tell me what to say to him?

LEICESTER. Your Majesty, he—he is guilty, isn't he?

ELIZABETH. I wish I knew. (*Slowly and with terrible uncertainty.*) I wish I knew.

BLACK OUT

VOICE OF CAMPION (*from Leicester to Trial*). How do I stand between the Pope and the Queen? I hear the question a thousand times in my dreams, until it seems that my whole destiny is bound up in an answer to that question. I have appealed to reason and on three different occasions I have disputed publicly with scholars and clergymen. But little comes of it, save a few distorted notes for history books. You cannot reason with those who do not love reason. In the Tower I hear rumors about Edmund Campion . . . some say that he has deserted the Pope . . . some say that he has deserted the Church . . . the Crown is very busy . . . while I am on the rack. . . . Sometimes I find it hard to pray . . . at times I seem to have no feeling . . . no memory . . . only an intention. The day for trial has come now

. . . and I must try to rouse myself . . . it seems so useless . . . until someone whispers that Persons [7] and Brother Ralph are safe! Seven of us must go to trial but they are free . . . free to carry on. Trial?—it is a trial in name only. And it is not a proud page in the history of English jurisprudence when we turn to the calendar of the Westminster Bar on the 20th of November, 1581. They have insisted on trying us all together, which is ridiculous: some of us have never met until this morning. And they will have it that because some Catholics might plot to overthrow the Queen, therefore all Catholics must, and especially all priests. (VOICE *rises strong and firm.*) Everyone talks of treason. No one defines it. It is all things to all men. But whatever it is, they are determined to make us guilty of it . . . and as the trial moves forward . . .

SCENE II

SETTING: *Bar at Westminster: Suggested briefly by shrewd use of the two towers, the velvet curtain hung between them as background for the judges' dais.*[8]

Three JUDGES *occupy the judges' dais: the inevitable clerks on the steps below them. Defendants are seated down center, backs to audience. The jury, we imagine, is on the audience side of the footlights.*

SLEDD, *across from* CAMPION, *on the prosecutor's side, is in witness box testifying.* ANDERSON, *the prosecutor, is examining him.*

ANDERSON (*to* SLEDD). You were in Rome at the same time as the defendant Campion?

SLEDD. I was.

ANDERSON. Were you familiar with the clergy and their plots?

SLEDD. I was. I worked for them.

ANDERSON. Do you recall any particular occasions when—

SLEDD. Yes. I recall the time a holy vow was made between the Pope and two hundred English priests for the restoration of Catholicism in England. I also heard that Sir Ralph Shelley was appointed by the Vatican to lead an invading fleet against England.

ANDERSON. And what did Shelley do?

SLEDD. He refused.

[ANDERSON *with a gesture to* CAMPION—*indicating he may ask questions.*]

CAMPION (*tired but commanding in a lean—gaunt—way*). So you remember me, Mr. Sledd?

SLEDD (*uneasily*). Yes, I remember you.

CAMPION. It's your business to remember people, isn't it?

SLEDD. Why, yes.

CAMPION. Of course. You're paid to, aren't you? You're a paid informer!

[ANDERSON *jumps up with an objection. There is a hum in court—the* CHIEF JUSTICE *raps table with gavel.*]

CHIEF JUSTICE. The objection is sustained.

CAMPION. Well, Mr. Sledd—about this plot of the Pope—who told you about it?

SLEDD. I—I don't remember exactly.

CAMPION. You weren't present at this meeting yourself?

SLEDD. No, I—I just heard about it.

CAMPION. I see. You weren't there.

[7] PERSONS (pur′sons)—An English Jesuit and Campion's superior; Brother Ralph, a Jesuit lay-brother and Campion's companion.
[8] DAIS (dā′is)—A raised platform.

You just heard about it. And you don't remember who told you. But you do remember the exact number of priests involved, eh?

SLEDD. Well—

CAMPION. I submit to Your Honors—(*turning to the bench*) that the evidence of this man is worthless. Suppose for just a moment that some priests did take an oath and suppose that oath did amount to treason—though neither supposition is true—does it follow that any of the seven defendants here today were among that two hundred?

ANDERSON (*quickly*). I submit, Your Honors, the testimony is merely offered to show the condition of affairs in Rome, of the conniving of the Pope and his plan to foster a God upon England.

CAMPION. Really, Master Anderson? I had assumed that it was we seven who were being tried here, not God Almighty and the Pope!

[*There is a demonstration in court among the witnesses and the defendants and the* CHIEF JUSTICE raps for *order.*]

CHIEF JUSTICE. Please, gentlemen, this court has allowed considerable latitude in the examination of witnesses upon rebuttal, and if there is nothing more—

ANDERSON. I have a question or two, Your Honor, for Father Campion—(*Then to* CAMPION.) Now isn't it a fact that many Papists have plotted to overthrow the Crown?

CAMPION. It is not a fact to my knowledge. I do not consort with [9] people who plot against the Crown.

ANDERSON. Master Campion, are you acquainted with Dr. Allen?

CAMPION. I am.

ANDERSON. Aren't you aware that Dr. Allen [10] would like to see the Queen deposed?

CAMPION. I have never discussed the matter with Dr. Allen, nor has he with me.

ANDERSON. Didn't you have a private conversation with Dr. Allen of Douai at Rheims? [11]

CAMPION. Yes, but why is any private conversation private? Because it is not public. Any time people talk together, their conversation is private.

ANDERSON. Didn't you talk about encouraging the Irish rebellion?

CAMPION. We did not. The Irish need no encouragement in the matter of rebellions!

ANDERSON. What did you talk about?

CAMPION. Unimportant things . . . school days at Oxford . . . a few friends we had not seen for a while . . .

ANDERSON. Anything else?

CAMPION. Yes.

ANDERSON. Ahaha! What?

CAMPION. A recipe for Italian wine!

[*Laughter in the court*—JUDGE *raps for order,* ANDERSON *turns angrily to the bench.*]

ANDERSON. Your Honors, there is no use in proceeding further. The man Campion, like all Jesuits, is evasive. And since the line of distinction is apparently so thin as between Papists who do plot and Papists who don't plot—

CHIEF JUSTICE. Just a moment, gentlemen. Before the case is submitted to the

[9] CONSORT WITH—Mix, associate with.

[10] DR. ALLEN—Founder, in 1568, of the English seminary at Douai in northern France.

[11] RHEIMS (rēmz)—Cathedral city in northern France.

jury, perhaps a good deal of confusion can be cleared up by a few simple questions to the defendant Campion.

CAMPION. I am ready to answer any questions, Your Honor—

[CAMPION *steps into the witness box at one side.*]

CHIEF JUSTICE (*impressively*). Now, Master Campion, the witness Eliot said on direct examination that in a sermon at Lyford you spoke of a "Great Day"? Was that great day to be one of rebellion?

CAMPION. Of course not. It had reference to Judgment Day. It concerned itself with the King of Heaven and not with the Queen of England.

CHIEF JUSTICE. I see. Now as to testimony that you have stopped at houses where treason may have been discussed. Do you wish us to understand that you have never heard the subject of a possible invasion of England discussed?

CAMPION. Of course I heard it discussed, discussed and denied, ridiculed and debated—just like any other topic of the day.

ANDERSON (*interrupting quickly*). And you never reported it to the authorities?

CAMPION. Certainly not.

ANDERSON. Then I submit, Your Honors, that by his silence he is guilty of treason.

CAMPION. Nonsense. Is a man a traitor to England because he hears idle chatter and does not report it? If that were so, how many men in England would be innocent of treason? Every man on this jury—every man in this court—yea, even the judges on the bench—would be guilty. Only a deaf man would be free of guilt.

[*Tremendous demonstration in the court room:* ANDERSON *shouts angrily and the* JUSTICE *pounds with gavel after a hurried conversation with his colleagues.*]

CHIEF JUSTICE. Now, Master Campion, you have maintained that much of the Crown testimony is irrelevant [12] and that a great deal of it is perjured.[13] But now let us consider your testimony.

CAMPION. Yes, My Lord.

CHIEF JUSTICE. You have said not once but many times that you do not stand as an umpire between the Pope and the Queen's conscience. Just what do you mean by that?

CAMPION. Just what I say, My Lord. Just that and no more.

CHIEF JUSTICE. Please, Master Campion, we are trying to give you every opportunity to explain yourself. As the Queen's counsel has said, the line of distinction between Catholics who plot and Catholics who do not plot is *rather* thin.

CAMPION. Thin or not, it is a real line, My Lord.

ANDERSON. Then why not define it? Why not explain why you cannot take a position as between the Pope and the Queen?

CHIEF JUSTICE. Yes, Master Campion, the point seems quite clear. It is, in fact, the crux [14] of the case. Your life depends on it. Now the Pope has excommunicated Her Majesty and has attempted to depose her. And you have taken an oath of spiritual allegiance to that Pope. Yet you say you are not against the Queen.

[12] IRRELEVANT—Not pertaining to the question.

[13] PERJURED—Lying, falsely witnessed to while under oath.

[14] CRUX—Central question.

CAMPION. That is correct, My Lord. I am not against the Queen.

CHIEF JUSTICE. But, Master Campion, I ask you: in this situation can you be for the Pope and the Queen at one and the same time?

CAMPION. I find it quite possible, My Lord.

CHIEF JUSTICE. Then how do you stand on the deposing power of the Pope? Do you agree that Elizabeth should be deposed?

CAMPION. That is just my point, My Lord. It is not for me to say whether she should or should not be deposed.

CHIEF JUSTICE. You must, Master Campion. You must, or stand suspected of some hidden reason as grave as the major charge itself.

CAMPION. I cannot and I will not choose between the Pope and Queen—

CHIEF JUSTICE. Why? Why, Master Campion?

ANDERSON. Is it because the line of distinction between those who plot and those who do not is not so thin where some of your friends are concerned, Master Campion? Friends such as—Father Persons?

CHIEF JUSTICE. Yes, what about Father Persons? How would *he* choose as between the Pope and the Queen?

CAMPION. I can speak for Father Persons no more than for a dead Caesar. I can only say—

CHIEF JUSTICE. There is only one thing you can say that will clear you of this charge, Master Campion. Do you, or do you not—depose the Queen?

CAMPION. I am sorry, My Lord. It is not a question that can be answered yes-or-no.

CHIEF JUSTICE. Then some good, some valid reason why you will not attempt to answer the question?

CAMPION. My reason, My Lord, my reason is my conscience. I cannot choose and I will not.

[*There is a tremendous demonstration in the court.* CHIEF JUSTICE, *worried, inclined to give the defendant every liberty, is ready to send the case to the jury.*

CAMPION, *aware of the crisis presented by the exact nature of the court's question, is distraught, but has not lost heart.*]

CHIEF JUSTICE (*rapping with gavel*). Very well then. There is nothing more to be said. And unless the Queen's Counsel has something to add at this point—

(QUEEN'S COUNSEL *is satisfied and shakes his head.*) You may sum up for the jury.

[CAMPION *bows to bench and turns partly toward the audience. The lights begin to dim half way through* CAMPION'S *speech.*]

CAMPION. My lords and jury: a great deal has been said today about plots and treason, and most of it from the mouths of professional informers. Much too about Catholics who plot and Catholics who don't plot. And the inference has been left with you that because I will not choose as between the Pope and the Queen, that I—and my companions—are against the Crown in all things. Let me say without equivocation that I have never encouraged nor tolerated conspiracy against the Crown. I have said and I do say that the Queen errs in matters of

Faith, but is it treason in this land of ours to say that the Queen is mistaken? If so, then our lives belong to the headsman, because we do say that the Queen errs. But we say something else too. We say that we love England, as much as man can love a country without despising its God—(*Voice fades away.*)

[*Lights out complete—then we pick up two flash scenes at stage right and left or in the doorways of the towers, if these have been prepared for use as shadow areas.*

FLASH: *In the shadows we come in on* SIR PHILIP SIDNEY *and* LORD LEICESTER. *They speak tensely—in whispers. Chimes are striking in solemn fashion.*]

LEICESTER (*impatiently*). Well, Sidney, how much longer are they going to take? The Council won't wait forever.

SIDNEY. Please, Leicester, you don't have to be so—so calculating about it, do you?

LEICESTER. Don't be so squeamish, Sidney. What has to be done will be done.

SIDNEY. It had just gone to the jury when I left. There is always the chance, I suppose—

LEICESTER. Chance? That jury is going to convict him. That's its job and the sooner it gets it over with, the better! I'm exhausted. (*Pause.*) Trials are so tiring.

FLASH: [*Fade-out—and then pick up* ELIZABETH *and* ANJOU*—standing at a balcony railing in the shadows; off scene a little music.*]

ANJOU. And what about us, Your Majesty?—What happens to us now?

ELIZABETH. I don't know, Anjou, I don't know. I was almost becoming fond of you too. Imagine that!

ANJOU. Of course even if the jury convicts him, you could always reprieve Campion or send him to prison? Then you and I—

ELIZABETH. No. No. You don't know England. Once the jury convicts him, every Puritan in England will cry for his blood. It is no use. The man is a shadow between us forever.

ANJOU (*significantly*). And over us.

[*Fade-out: Then a second later lights up on full court scene as before—* CAMPION *is standing down center before the bench and the* CHIEF JUSTICE *has the jury's verdict in his hand.*]

CHIEF JUSTICE (*droning on*). —and the verdict of the jury, gentlemen, is—GUILTY AS CHARGED—for all seven defendants!

[*There is a demonstration in the court among witnesses and the defendants —who with guards are standing near* CAMPION. *Court raps for order.*]

Is there any reason why the court shall not pass sentence of death? Is there any statement to be heard before—

CAMPION (*clearly—facing the* JUDGES.)[15] My Lords and Judges, it was not our deaths that we feared. Rather it was our lives, for we were not lords of our own lives. And all that we have to say now is that if our religion makes us traitors, we are worthy to be condemned; but otherwise we are, and have been, faithful subjects of the Queen. (*Turning to face audience—jury—directly.*) In condemning us you condemn all your own ancestors, all the ancient priests,

[15] Words taken from Campion's last speech.

bishops, and kings—all that once was the glory of England, the island of saints and the most devoted child of the See of Rome. For whatever we taught, that also was taught by these saints before us. To be condemned with them is to be rewarded for eternity.

I have no more to say but to recommend your case, My Lords, and ours to Almighty God, and to pray He may send us Grace and set us at accord before the day of payment, to the end that we may at last be friends in Heaven, when all injuries shall be forgotten.

[*Silence—complete silence in the court for a fleeting second—then the rapping of the gavel by the* JUDGE.]

CHIEF JUSTICE. Edmund Campion—You must go to the place from whence you came, there to remain until you shall be drawn through the open city of London upon hurdles to the place of execution, and there be hanged and let down alive . . . and then your head to be cut off and your body divided into four parts, to be disposed of at Her Majesty's pleasure, and may God have mercy on your soul.

[*Another demonstration in court—several raps of the* JUDGE'S *gavel—* GUARDS *start out with the defendants.*]

CAMPION (*beginning the Te Deum*[16]). *Te Deum Laudamus—*

DEFENDANTS (*together*). *Te Dominum confitemur—*

[*The defendants have picked up the hymn quickly and as they go out, the soft responses come up steadily like the chant of a triumphant army. Lights begin to fade:* CHIEF JUSTICE *comes down from bench accompanied by a brother* JUSTICE.]

CHIEF JUSTICE. Hello? What's that they are singing?

JUSTICE. Why, it's a *Te Deum.* Strange people . . . these martyrs.

CHIEF JUSTICE. Yes—very strange. (*Fingering papers.*) Not in all my cases have I . . . hello . . . this is strange too; . . . look—my finger's bleeding![17]

JUSTICE (*as they start out*). You probably scratched it with a pen.

[JUSTICE *goes on ahead of him, leaving* CHIEF JUSTICE *full in spot, rest of stage dark.*]

CHIEF JUSTICE. But I didn't scratch it. I had a glove on, and it's bleeding—*bleeding!*

[*He hurries off after his colleague. In the distance the Te Deum rises steadily.*]

BLACK OUT

EPILOGUE

SETTING: *On the curtains: the little white cross.*

In the background the Te Deum—then roll of thunder and drums—and softly—very softly—the voice of CAMPION *—alone—*

VOICE OF CAMPION. "There will never want in England men that will have care of their own salvation, nor such as shall advance other men's; neither shall this Church ever fail so long as priests and pastors shall be found for their sheep, rage man or devil ever so much."

[*Te Deum comes in briefly. The Cross begins to fade.*]

[16] *Te Deum*—A solemn hymn of praise and thanksgiving, traditional in the Church.

[17] Chronicles of the period report this incident as actually occurring.

FOR DISCUSSION

SCENE I

1. At the meeting in Leicester House, who was at a disadvantage—Elizabeth or Campion? Why? What offer did the Queen make to Campion? Can you surmise what career lay open to Campion, had he accepted her offer? Explain your answer.

2. Anything ". . . except the sovereignty of my heart." How does this phrase reveal Campion's reason for choosing dishonor and death?

SCENE II

1. Campion was racked three times and his fingernails torn out to secure evidence against him. In the trial scene what description suggests his worn and beaten condition?

2. Who was Sledd? Did his testimony really bear on the charges against the defendants?

3. Was treason the actual issue at the trial, or was it the religious faith of the defendants? Was it possible, as Campion insisted, to give spiritual allegiance to the Pope and yet remain a loyal subject of the Queen? Is there a parallel situation in the United States?

4. What was the verdict of the jury? Can you suggest why, after the sentence, Campion and the other condemned men sang the glad strains, "We praise Thee, O God; we confess Thee, O Lord . . ."?

FINDING SYNONYMS

These words occurred in the selection you have just read: *phantom, conspire, depose, rack, distort, ridicule, valid, tolerate.* Find a synonym for each in this list: *remove from office, twist, make fun of, ghost, torture, sound, allow, plot.*

A RESEARCH PROJECT

Oxford, the Tower of London, and Tyburn Hill each had a place in the story of Blessed Edmund Campion. Using an encyclopedia or a large dictionary, identify each of these places. Add any details you can discover about them which bear on Campion's life.

RELATED READING

Read the full three-act play, *Who Ride on White Horses,* by Breen and Schnibbe.

A father, lately arrived from Italy, tries to tell, in the best English he knows how, his experience as he watched helplessly at the bedside of his dying son. Read the poem slowly. Try to catch the way the dialect should be spoken so that you get the full meaning of the poem.

Da Leetla Boy

T. A. DALY

Da spreeng ees com'; but oh, da joy
  Eet ees too late!
He was so cold, my leetla boy,
  He no could wait.

I no can count how manny week, 5
How manny day, dat he ees seeck;
How manny night I seet an' hold
Da leetla hand dat was so cold.
He was so patience, oh, so sweet!
Eet hurts my throat for theenk of eet;
An' all he evra ask ees w'en
Ees gona com' da spreeng agen.
Wan day, wan brighta sunny day,
He see, across da alleyway,
Da leetla girl dat's livin' dere 15
Ees raise her window for da air,
An' put outside a leetla pot
Of—w'at-you-call?—forgat-me-not.
So smalla flower, so leetla theeng!
But steell eet mak' hees hearta seeng; 20
"Oh, now, at las', ees com' da spreeng!
Da leetla plant ees glad for know
Da sun ees com' for mak' eet grow.
So, too, I am grow warm and strong."
So lika dat he seeng hees song. 25
But, ah! da night com' down an' den
Da weenter ees sneak back agen,
An' een da alley all da night
Ees fall da snow, so cold, so white,
An' cover up da leetla pot 30
Of—w'at-you-call?—forgat-me-not.
All night da leetla hand I hold
Ees grow so cold, so cold, so cold!

Da spreeng ees com'; but oh, da joy
  Eet ees too late! 35
He was so cold, my leetla boy,
  He no could wait.

FOR DISCUSSION

1. Once you have accustomed yourself to the so-called Italian dialect, the simple story of "Da Leetla Boy" is easy to follow. Summarize the story in not more than three sentences. Use your own words.

2. From the way the father speaks about his little son, do you think he is a good father? Is his sorrow over the death of his son genuine? Why did he feel so helpless?

3. What was your feeling after reading the poem? Do you feel you might have been able to help? In what way?

WRITING YOUR OWN VERSION

If you are the type of reader who expects everything he reads to be clear as a simple problem in addition, you are probably criticizing the author of this poem for not providing answers to various questions in your mind: What sickness caused the boy's death? Why didn't the father get a doctor? Why did the dying boy yearn for the spring? Where was his mother?

Write your own version of the story, clearing up these points and any others that occur to you. Which of the stories written by class members has the most satisfying answers?

◇◇◇◇◇

Nine-year-old Selina was an only child. Her mother was dead, and her father was an English officer—away in India. Perhaps it was just loneliness then that made her the spoiled young lady she was. One day a new governess —wise, firm Miss Brown—took charge of the "problem" child, and a new and finer Selina began growing up from that date.

One of Selina's lessons in growing up is told in this selection from the book ALL ABOUT SELINA. *It happened that Selina came down with a cold. The cold quickly turned into pneumonia, and it looked as though she might die and go to Heaven. Selina didn't want to go to Heaven—she didn't think she would like God—until Miss Brown told her what Heaven was going to be like.*

LIKE GOING HOME

CECILY HALLACK

Things, thought Selina drowsily and painfully, had happened so differently from what had been expected. She had caught this chill, and then it had turned into being very hot and having this pain in her side and feeling all heavy and . . . too tired to think much. It had gone on and on until at last today it had seemed that all her chest was a terribly hot painful kind of wood. . . . The doctor had just gone; Miss Brown was just going downstairs with him. He had talked in a rather loud cheerful way, and had made her feel very tired. So tired that she could only lie still and just look at the shaded lamp on the table near the end of her bed where Miss Brown's work-basket was. So she lay still there, half-drowsing, until Miss Brown came back.

"Come and sit by me, please," said Selina in a tiny voice. She had become very polite lately. You do get polite

"Like Going Home" from *All About Selina* by Cecily Hallack. Reprinted by permission of Miss M. T. Horvil.

when you feel so small and wooden.

Miss Brown came and sat down beside her, and taking the hot hand held out to her, caressed it, pulling down the sleeve of the white jacket Selina was wearing.

"Am I better yet?" Selina asked tiredly.

"No, darling, you're not better," said Miss Brown. "Not even though we said those prayers to Our Lady of Lourdes this morning. I wonder what Our Lord means?"

"Do you think He means to make me worse?" asked Selina.

"He might do, my bird."

"Why?"

"Either to take you home to have you all to Himself, or else to cure you in such a way as to show that it was He who cured you and not the doctor."

"Oh, I don't want to die," said Selina. "D'you think I must? I don't want to leave you, darlingest. I don't know anything about dying, and I'm too tired. No, I'll stay with you, please," she said in her hoarse little voice.

"Please God you will," said Miss Brown, and her voice was just a bit funny. "But nobody's too tired to go to God. He's the greatest Rest, because He's so gentle and so near that you don't feel lonely. Selina, shall I ring up Father Kilpatrick and ask him to bring you Our Lord tonight, so that Our Lord and the holy oil can make you better if it is Our Lord's Will, and if He wants to take you home to Heaven with Him, He'll make you ready and go all the way very tight with you?"

It was a moment before Selina answered.

"Yes, I think so," she said. "Only I am so tired."

"Very well, smallest. Just one minute and I'll tell Rumbold to telephone and give my message."

She was back very soon, and then she drew her chair very close to Selina, and took the one hot hand in her own again.

"Rumbold is getting the altar all ready," she said, soothingly, "so what will you have your Miss Brown do for you, sweetheart? Tell you a story?"

"Thanks," said Selina in such a tiny voice that only Miss Brown could have heard what she said. "Yes, please. I don't think I mind whether I get well or I go to Heaven. Both of them sound pretty tiring to me. And I cawn't do anything tiring just now."

"Well, nothing will be tiring, my pretty."

"Well, you'd better tell me a story about Heaven," said Selina. "What'll it be like?"

"It'll be like going home to a home that you loved and loved, but somehow had a dream and forgot for a moment," said Miss Brown, stooping to turn Selina's pillow and settle her more comfortably, and then sitting down and stroking the thin little wrist firmly and comfortingly up towards the arm. "It'll be nicer and happier than I can possibly tell you, because something happy and surprising and secure will be happening all the time."

"But I don't want to be without you," said Selina. "I've got so used to you, and I talk about things with you and you laugh at me just right and you explain things."

"Well," said Miss Brown, and her voice was just a bit funny again, "if you go to Heaven, you'll discover that you

don't have to wait for me to come, somehow, because there's no such thing as time—it's just eternity, and all the happiest things come true at once."

"But what about perg'try?"

"Oh, you cuddle up tight to God because He's so good and ask Him to take away anything that isn't good in you and that's all you need bother about purgatory. It's only holding on to anything that God knows isn't good for us that makes purgatory."

"If God's very old—and He must be—I mayn't like Him," said Selina.

"He's only old in the way that He is very wise and understands everything," said Miss Brown. "He's the God who gives the spring all its youngness and who makes the lambs prance about and makes you rush about and the primroses smell so new and the daffodils be so beautifully stiff."

"Well, tell me a story about Heaven," said Selina.

"Once upon a time," began Miss Brown, "Selina went to Heaven. She arrived at the door and she could see St. Peter's sitting-room window with the pot of red geraniums that he always keeps there because it looks so cheerful. And she had no sooner knocked at the door than she suddenly felt the most fearful wanting to see God. She felt lonely for Him, homesick for Him, and she knew nobody else would do to comfort her.

"St. Peter came to the door. She knew

him at once, because he was bald and his hair was white and he had his big key.

" 'Why,' he said, 'here's little Missy at last. Well, you have been away a long time.' He picked her up and kissed her, but she wriggled, saying: 'Oh, I am so fearfully glad to be home but I cawn't wait a moment to see God, please St. Peter.'

"So he set her down, saying: 'Run along with you!' Selina felt someone was standing beside her, and turning she saw someone whose face seemed so familiar that Selina thought she must have seen it every day of her life. She knew it was her angel. She thought she ought to thank him for all his care of her and for bringing her safe to Heaven, but he read her thoughts and said: 'Don't stop a moment; run straight to God!'

"So Selina set off as fast as she could, tearing up the golden streets, past the houses where people looked out of the windows and waved to her—people she seemed to know as well as she knew these golden streets with the river running down the middle, and the trees that were full of fruit and fragrant flowers. Straight to the King's palace she ran, in at the great open doors, till suddenly a voice cried: 'Come, Selina!' and there was Our Lady. And Our Lady caught up her blue robes, and catching Selina's hand, they ran together into the throne room that was the very center of Heaven, with a pavement of stars and the four winds for walls, and music and a light gentler and more marvelous than sunlight —and Selina ran into the arms of God, and He lifted her on to His lap, and she tucked her head against Him and knew that nothing sad or lonely, and no pain or fear would ever happen again. She could feel His arms round her, and His hands—one of them holding her bare feet, and He was listening to her and telling her that she was His precious, and that Heaven was Heaven all over again to Him because He had His Selina safe home.

"And after a while—it might have been quite a short while, or a thousand years—Selina couldn't have told you, because she was so happy and because there is no tiresome time in Heaven, only a kind of happiness of which you can have as much as you want—well, after a while, Selina saw Our Lady looking at her over God's shoulder, and then she had to go to Our Lady to be welcomed and kissed. And Our Lady said to her:

" 'What would you like for tea, my bird?'

"And Selina said:

" 'I should like a rosy apple and some bread and honey.'

"So Our Lady said:

" 'I believe that I have just got that rosy apple sitting on a shelf in my store cupboard, and we'll call in on St. Bernard on our way to your own little house, and he'll give us some honey, and St. Zita will give you a little newly-baked loaf and a pat of golden butter with a rose patterned on it.'

"Taking Our Lady's hand, Selina skipped along. She kept having to wave to saints who waved to her from their crystal windows. There was St. Thomas Aquinas, writing in his window, and he waved his pen at her. There was St. Francis, standing in the street playing the fiddle for some children to dance to—and as soon as he saw her, he played such a merry tune that she couldn't help dancing, and so she danced on her way. When they knocked at St. Bernard's door, he opened it, and his habit was very white. He called Selina his little pippin, and gave her some honey in a crystal jar as round as a bubble. St. Zita —well, you could smell her baking down the street, and when she came to the door all smiling and kind, she said that as soon as she had heard Selina was coming, she had baked her a special little loaf.

" 'How did you hear I was coming?' asked Selina.

" 'The angels bring us good news every morning,' said St. Zita.

"Then they called in at Our Lady's house—going in at the back door that leads to Our Lady's storeroom, and which is always open, so that the boys and girls can come in for a piece of gingerbread or an apple if they feel hungry in the middle of the morning.

"The red apple for Selina was sitting and waiting for her on its shelf, and just then Selina's Angel Guardian looked in and asked if he could carry the honey and the loaf. He said somebody was waiting for Selina. So Our Lady bade them go along quickly to Selina's house. Off they went. They met St. Aloysius dashing along on horseback, and he waved his plumed hat to Selina.

" 'He's a nice boy,' said Selina. 'Do you think he will teach me to ride?'

" 'Of course he will,' said Selina's Angel. 'He's your elder brother, you know, and so very glad you've come.'

" '*Oh!*' said Selina, stopping short. 'Oh, *do* look at that darling house with a veranda and wallflowers in the garden and a swing and the white doves and the pear tree and the fountain . . . oh, it's the most beautiful house of all!'

" 'Don't you realize,' said her Angel, putting his arm round her and bending down, 'that if you like it best of all it must be yours? Who's that just come to the door?'

" 'Why,' said Selina, 'it's my Miss Brown!'

"Her Angel gave her a little push, and she simply flew up the street and through the gate and up the path and into Miss Brown's arms, and Miss Brown held her very tight and kissed her on the top of her head. And that is the story of Heaven for Selina."

Miss Brown felt Selina's hand snuggle very tight into hers.

"Will it really be as cosy as that?" Selina asked.

"It will be what you want most, and lovely surprises on top of that, and surprises inside surprises, only everything will be very near and dear and secure as well."

"Oh," said Selina. "That's good, isn't it? But will it really be like that?"

"It will be far better," said Miss Brown. "But that's the only way I can give you any idea of how complete it will be. I have to use the words that you understand, just as Our Lord did in telling human beings about the Infinite God."

"Oh, I see," said Selina. "That's pretty good."

There was a knock at the door. It was Rumbold. She looked very solemn and very gentle, and she brought in a table with a white cloth on it and two candlesticks and some other things. It was put near Selina's bed, and then Rose came in with two vases of violets, and went out again rather quickly.

Selina felt drowsy, and she lay still, holding Miss Brown's hand, and thinking about Heaven.

After a while, someone spoke to her, and it was Father Kilpatrick. He was telling her that he could not let her try and make her confession because she was so tired, but she should make a good act of contrition and kiss the crucifix and then he would give her Holy Communion.

Miss Brown was kneeling beside her. Selina was propped up on a big pillow, and she folded her hands and was suddenly very glad that Our Lord was in the Blessed Sacrament as well as in Heaven. She received Him, and then Miss Brown let her lie down again, and folded her hands across her heart to hold Our Lord tight. Selina was too tired to think, but she just lay there loving Him. And He said nothing to her, but just loved her and was nearer to her than her own heart.

And she thought He asked her if she would like to come with Him to Heaven, or be made well to live in this world and grow up. She answered in her heart that she'd rather He chose, but that she hadn't done very much to deserve Heaven yet—she hadn't made many people happy or done brave things for God. But He didn't seem to answer. He just loved her some more, and being very loved and very secure and very happy makes you sleepy if you are ill, so Selina fell asleep.

It was dark when she woke up, except for a soft light that came from somewhere. Someone was very near to her. She thought it was Our Lady, but quite suddenly she knew it was Miss Brown in her silk dressing-gown and that the feverishness had gone.

"I'm better!" she said. "Our Lord made me better. So I shan't be going to Heaven after all. It is disappointing."

"It's very disappointing," said Miss Brown. "But thank God my little pigeon is going to get well."

"Yes," said Selina, "because you'd have had to have waited, wouldn't you, darling? Can I have some orange juice, please? I'm not hot any more, am I? Oo-ow, I am feeling thin. Is it the middle of the night?"

"It is three o'clock in the morning," said Miss Brown. "Now drink this, and then I must go and tell Rumbold and Rose and Cook that you are better."

Selina drank her orange juice, and before Miss Brown came back from the top of the stairs, she was fast asleep again, and dreaming that St. Aloysius was giving her a riding lesson and that St. Francis was laughing at them.

FOR DISCUSSION

1. "Like Going Home" tells some things about Heaven that are true and other things that are fanciful. Can you decide, as you reread the selection, which descriptions are true ones? Why, for example, is going to Heaven like going home? In what sense is God old? Why will Heaven be "happy and surprising and secure"?

2. Will Heaven have "golden streets with the river running down the middle, and . . . trees . . . full of fruit and fragrant flowers"? In the selection find Miss Brown's hint as to the reason why we use such descriptions of Heaven. Give a brief oral description of Heaven as you imagine it to be.

3. If you are very tired or do not feel well when you receive Holy Communion, what can you learn from Selina's way of receiving Our Lord?

ABOUT PRONUNCIATION

Selina's pronunciation of "perg'try" and "cawn't" might sound affected to us. To the English, however, such pronunciation is both correct and natural. Pronunciations are determined by the part of the country in which we live. In America there are at least three acceptable dialects or types of pronunciation—Eastern, Midwestern, and Southern. The Midwestern pronunciation—in general use over the radio and in the movies—is used by some 90,000,000 Americans through a broad expanse of the United States.

In speaking, watch your own pronunciations carefully. Thumb your dictionary for the correct way of saying the new words you meet. Listen attentively to radio or television broadcasts as a check on your own speech habits. In this way, you can correct errors of pronunciation.

How, for example, do you pronounce these words: *idea, penny, fire, cow, dog,* and *new?* If you make them sound like ide-er, pinny, far, ca-ow, dawg, and noo, you are not pronouncing them correctly.

FOR UNDERSTANDING

Look up the lives of St. Thomas Aquinas, St. Francis of Assisi, and St. Zita. Come to class prepared to explain why Miss Brown described these saints as she did.

RELATED READING

Another book by Cecily Hallack is *The Sword Blade of Michael.*

◇◇◇◇◇

The Crucifixion is not a new story, but here is a legend which gives the old story a new poignancy.

Why the Robin's Breast Is Red

JAMES RYDER RANDALL

The Saviour, bowed beneath His Cross, climbed up the dreary hill,
And from the agonizing wreath ran many a crimson rill;
The cruel Roman thrust Him on with unrelenting hand,
Till, staggering slowly 'mid the crowd, He fell upon the sand.

A little bird that warbled near, that memorable day,
Flitted around and strove to wrench one single thorn away;
The cruel spike impaled his breast,—and thus 'tis sweetly said,
The robin has his silver vest incarnadined with red.

Ah, Jesu! Jesu! Son of man! my dolor and my sighs
Reveal the lesson taught by this winged Ishmael of the skies;
I, in the palace of delight or cavern of despair,
Have plucked no thorns from Thy dear brow, but planted thousands there!

10. ISHMAEL—An outcast.

FOR DISCUSSION

1. Is the poem historically true, or is it only a legend? Point out the clause in the poem which is the reason for your answer.

2. What heroic act did the robin try to perform? With what result?

3. What is the lesson the poet brings home to you and me in the last two lines of the poem? Do you like stories which teach lessons or convey truths? Some of the greatest stories in the world (the parables of Jesus, for instance) are frankly told to teach profoundly important truths which may add to your wisdom and to your joy in life. Tell one of these parables in your own words.

4. Note any lines that impress you especially and be prepared to say why.

WORD ORIGINS

1. *Dolor* is one word which has kept the meaning given it over twenty centuries ago. It comes from the Latin noun *dolor*, derived from the verb *dolere*. What does *dolor* mean? Use the related words *doleful* and *dolorous* in sentences.

2. It is strange that a word meaning *anguish and intolerable pain* should have originated in a sports event; yet that is true of *agony*, from which we get the word *agonizing*, used in line 2. In ancient Greece, *agon* was a public assembly, especially one for athletic contests. *Agonia* was the contest or struggle for the prize. From the meaning, *a struggle for victory in the games*, *agonia* gradually came to mean any physical struggle or activity engaged in with difficulty, pain, and mental anguish. Use each word, *agony* and *agonizing*, in a sentence.

ILLUSTRATING A TRUTH

The Sacred Heart of Jesus is ever ready to forgive a heart that is ashamed because it has offended Him. The Sacred Heart helps the soul to bear such sorrow for sin, uses that very pain for healing purposes, and unites the soul's sufferings with His own. Show how the person who tries to prove his love for the Sacred Heart (such a person is typified by the robin in the poem) by uniting his sufferings with His, is invariably rewarded. You may make the story original, or retell stories which history gives you of men and women who have overcome hardships through union with the Sacred Heart of Jesus.

Have you ever felt that to have a good time at a party you needed to wear a particular style of skirt or shirt? Have you ever stayed home because you could not afford to dress as your other friends did? Did you finally discover that the clothes you wore really had little to do with the fun and sociability you experienced?

Here is a story of a woman who coveted the clothes and jewelry that she could not afford to own. Try to identify yourself with her in order to appreciate fully her feelings to the very last word of the narrative.

THE NECKLACE

GUY DE MAUPASSANT

She was one of those pretty and charming girls who, as if by a mistake of destiny, are born in a family of employees. She had no dowry, no expectations, no means of becoming known, understood, loved, wedded by any rich and distinguished man; and so she let herself be married to a petty clerk in the Bureau of Public Instruction.

She was simple in her dress because she could not be elaborate, but she was as unhappy as if she had fallen from a higher rank, for with women there is no inherited distinction of higher and lower. Their beauty, their grace, and their natural charm fill the place of birth and family. Natural delicacy, instinctive elegance, a lively wit, are the ruling forces in the social realm, and these make the daughters of the common people the equals of the finest ladies.

She suffered intensely, feeling herself born for all the refinements and luxuries of life. She suffered from the poverty of her home as she looked at the dirty walls, the worn-out chairs, the ugly curtains. All those things of which another woman of her station would have been quite unconscious tortured her and made her indignant. The sight of the country girl who was maid of all work in her humble household filled her almost with desperation. She dreamed of echoing halls hung with Oriental draperies and lighted by tall bronze candelabra, while two tall footmen in knee breeches drowsed in great armchairs by reason of the heating stove's oppressive warmth. She dreamed of splendid parlors furnished in rare old silks, of carved cabinets loaded with priceless bric-a-brac, and of entrancing little boudoirs just right for afternoon chats with bosom friends—men famous and sought after, the envy and the desire of all the other women.

When she sat down to dinner at a little table covered with a cloth three days old, and looked across at her husband as he uncovered the soup and exclaimed with an air of rapture, "Oh, the delicious stew! I know nothing better than that," she dreamed of dainty dinners, of shining silverware, of tapestries which peopled the walls with antique figures and strange birds in fairy forests; she dreamed of delicious viands [1] served in wonderful dishes, of whispered gallantries heard with a sphinx-like smile as you eat the pink flesh of a trout or the wing of a quail.

She had no dresses, no jewels, nothing; and she loved nothing else. She felt made for that alone. She was filled with a desire to please, to be envied, to be bewitching and sought after. She had a rich friend, a former schoolmate at the convent, whom she no longer wished to visit because she suffered so much when she came home. For whole days at a time she wept without ceasing in bitterness and hopeless misery.

Now, one evening her husband came home with a triumphant air, holding in his hand a large envelope.

"There," said he, "there is something for you."

She quickly tore open the paper and drew out a printed card, bearing these words:—

> The Minister of Public Instruction and Mme. Georges Rampouneau [2] request the honor of M. and Mme. Loisel's [3] company at the palace of the Ministry, Monday evening, January 18th.

Instead of being overcome with delight, as her husband expected, she threw the invitation on the table with disdain, murmuring:

"What do you wish me to do with that?"

"Why, my dear, I thought you would be pleased. You never go out, and this is such a fine opportunity! I had awful trouble in getting it. Everyone wants to go; it is very select, and they are not giving many invitations to clerks. You will see all the official world."

She looked at him with irritation, and said, impatiently:

"What do you expect me to put on my back if I go?"

He had not thought of that. He stammered:

"Why, the dress you go to the theater in. It seems all right to me."

He stopped, stupefied, distracted, on seeing that his wife was crying. Two great tears descended slowly from the corners of her eyes toward the corners of her mouth. He stuttered:

"What's the matter? What's the matter?"

By a violent effort she subdued her feelings and replied in a calm voice, as she wiped her wet cheeks:

"Nothing. Only I have no dress and consequently I cannot go to this ball. Give your invitation to some friend whose wife has better clothes than I."

He was in despair, but began again:

"Let us see, Mathilde. How much would it cost, a suitable dress, which you could wear again on future occasions, something very simple?"

She reflected for some seconds, computing the cost, and also wondering what sum she could ask without bringing down upon herself an immediate refusal and

[1] VIANDS—Foods.
[2] GEORGES RAMPOUNEAU—Pronounced zhōrzh răm·pōō·nō′.
[3] LOISEL—Pronounced lwä·zĕl′.

an astonished exclamation from the economical clerk.

At last she answered hesitatingly:

"I don't know exactly, but it seems to me that with four hundred francs I could manage."

He turned a trifle pale, for he had been saving just that sum to buy a gun and treat himself to a little hunting trip the following summer, in the country near Nanterre, with a few friends who went there to shoot larks on Sundays.

However, he said:

"Well, I think I can give you four hundred francs. But see that you have a pretty dress."

The day of the ball drew near, and Madame Loisel seemed sad, restless, anxious. Her dress was ready, however. Her husband said to her one evening:

"What is the matter? Come, now, you've been looking queer these last three days."

And she replied:

"It worries me that I have no jewels, not a single stone, nothing to put on. I shall look wretched enough. I would almost rather not go to this party."

He answered:

"You might wear natural flowers. They are very fashionable this season. For ten francs you can get two or three magnificent roses."

She was not convinced.

"No; there is nothing more humiliating than to look poor among a lot of rich women."

But her husband cried:

"How stupid you are! Go and find your friend Madame Forestier[4] and ask her to lend you some jewels. You are in timate enough with her for that."

She uttered a cry of joy.

"Of course. I had not thought o that."

The next day she went to her friend' house and told her distress.

Madame Forestier went to her hand some wardrobe, took out a large casket brought it back, opened it, and said t Madame Loisel:

"Choose, my dear."

She saw first of all some bracelets, the a pearl necklace, then a Venetian cross o gold set with precious stones of wonder ful workmanship. She tried on the orna ments before the glass, hesitated, coul not make up her mind to part with them to give them back. She kept asking:

"You have nothing else?"

"Why, yes. But I do not know wha will please you."

All at once she discovered, in a black satin box, a splendid diamond necklace and her heart began to beat with bound less desire. Her hands trembled as sh took it. She fastened it around he throat, over her high-necked dress, and stood lost in ecstasy as she looked at her self.

Then she asked, hesitating, full of anx iety:

"Would you lend me that,—only that?"

"Why, yes, certainly."

She sprang upon the neck of her friend, embraced her rapturously, then fled with her treasure.

The day of the ball arrived. Madame Loisel was a success. She was prettier than all the others, elegant, gracious, smil-

[4] FORESTIER—Pronounced fô·rĕs·tyā′.

ing, and crazy with joy. All the men stared at her, asked her name, tried to be introduced. All the cabinet officials wished to waltz with her. The minister noticed her.

She danced with delight, with passion, intoxicated with pleasure, forgetting all in the triumph of her beauty, in the glory of her success, in a sort of mist of happiness, the result of all this homage, all this admiration, all these awakened desires, this victory so complete and so sweet to the heart of woman.

She left about four o'clock in the morning. Her husband had been dozing since midnight in a little deserted anteroom with three other gentlemen, whose wives were having a good time.

He threw about her shoulders the wraps which he had bought for her to go out in, the modest wraps of common life, whose poverty contrasted sharply with the elegance of the ball dress. She felt this and wished to escape, that she might not be noticed by the other women who were wrapping themselves in costly furs.

Loisel held her back.

"Wait here, you will catch cold outside. I will find a cab."

But she would not listen to him, and rapidly descended the stairs. When they were at last in the street, they could find no carriage, and began to look for one, hailing the cabmen they saw passing at a distance.

They walked down toward the Seine in despair, shivering with the cold. At last they found on the quay one of those ancient nocturnal cabs that one sees in Paris only after dark, as if they were ashamed to display their wretchedness during the day.

They were put down at their door in the Rue des Martyrs, and sadly mounted the steps to their apartment. It was all over, for her. And as for him, he reflected that he must be at his office at ten o'clock.

She took off the wraps which covered her shoulders, before the mirror, so as to take a final look at herself in all her glory. But suddenly she uttered a cry. She no longer had the necklace about her neck!

Her husband, already half undressed, inquired:

"What is the matter?"

She turned madly toward him.

"I have—I have—I no longer have Madame Forestier's necklace."

He stood up, distracted.

"What!—how!—it is impossible!"

They looked in the folds of her dress, in the folds of her cloak, in the pockets, everywhere. They could not find a trace of it.

He asked:

"You are sure you still had it when you left the ball?"

"Yes. I felt it on me in the vestibule at the palace."

"But if you had lost it in the street we should have heard it fall. It must be in the cab."

"Yes. That's probable. Did you take the number?"

"No. And you, you did not notice it?"

"No."

They looked at each other thunderstruck. At last Loisel put on his clothes again.

"I am going back," said he, "over every foot of the way we came, to see if I cannot find it."

So he started. She remained in her ball dress without strength to go to bed, sitting on a chair, with no fire, her mind a blank.

Her husband returned about seven o'clock. He had found nothing. He went to police headquarters, to the newspapers to offer a reward, to the cab companies, everywhere, in short, where a trace of hope led him.

She watched all day, in the same state of blank despair before this frightful disaster.

Loisel returned in the evening with cheeks hollow and pale; he had found nothing.

"You must write to your friend," said he, "that you have broken the clasp of her necklace and that you are having it repaired. It will give us time to turn around."

She wrote as he dictated.

At the end of a week they had lost all hope.

And Loisel, looking five years older, declared:

"We must consider how to replace the necklace."

The next day they took the box which had contained it, and went to the place of the jeweler whose name they found inside. He consulted his books.

"It was not I, Madame, who sold the necklace; I must simply have furnished the casket."

They went from jeweler to jeweler,

looking for an ornament like the other, consulting their memories, both sick with grief and anguish. They found, in a shop at the Palais Royal, a string of diamonds which seemed to them exactly what they were looking for. It was worth forty thousand francs. They could have it for thirty-six thousand. So they begged the jeweler not to sell it for three days. And they made an arrangement that he should take it back for thirty-four thousand francs if the other were found before the end of February.

Loisel had eighteen thousand francs which his father had left him. He would borrow the rest.

He did borrow, asking a thousand francs of one, five hundred of another, five louis here, three louis there. He gave notes, made ruinous engagements, dealt with usurers, with all the tribe of money-lenders. He compromised the rest of his life, risked his signature without knowing if he might not be involving his honor, and, terrified by the anguish yet to come, by the black misery about to fall upon him, by the prospect of every physical privation and every mental torture, he went to get the new necklace, and laid down on the dealer's counter thirty-six thousand francs.

When Madame Loisel took the necklace back to Madame Forestier, the latter said coldly:

"You should have returned it sooner, for I might have needed it."

She did not open the case, to the relief of her friend. If she had detected the substitution, what would she have thought? What would she have said? Would she have taken her friend for a thief?

Madame Loisel now knew the horrible life of the needy. But she took her part heroically. They must pay this frightful debt. She would pay it. They dismissed their maid; they gave up their room; they rented another, under the roof.

She came to know the drudgery of housework, the odious labors of the kitchen. She washed the dishes, staining her rosy nails on the greasy pots and the bottoms of the saucepans. She washed the dirty linen, the shirts, and the dishcloths, which she hung to dry on a line; she carried the garbage down to the street every morning, and carried up the water, stopping at each landing to rest. And, dressed like a woman of the people, she went to the fruiterer's, the grocer's, the butcher's, her basket on her arm, bargaining, abusing, defending sou [5] by sou of her miserable money.

Each month they had to pay some notes, renew others, obtain more time.

Her husband worked every evening, neatly footing up the account books of some tradesman, and often far into the night he sat copying manuscript at five sous a page.

And this life lasted ten years.

At the end of ten years they had paid everything,—everything, with the exactions of usury and the accumulations of compound interest.

Madame Loisel seemed aged now. She had become the woman of impoverished households,—strong and hard and tough. With hair half combed, with skirts awry, and reddened hands, she talked loud as she washed the floor with great swishes of water. But sometimes, when her hus-

[5] sou (sōō)—The French penny.

band was at the office, she sat down near the window and thought of that evening at the ball so long ago, when she had been so beautiful and so admired.

What would have happened if she had not lost that necklace? Who knows, who knows? How strange life is, how changeful! How little a thing is needed for us to be lost or to be saved!

But one Sunday, as she was going for a walk in the Champs Élysées to refresh herself after the labors of the week, all at once she saw a woman walking with a child. It was Madame Forestier, still young, still beautiful, still charming.

Madame Loisel was agitated. Should she speak to her? Why, of course. And now that she had paid, she would tell her all. Why not?

She drew near.

"Good morning, Jeanne."

The other, astonished to be addressed so familiarly by this woman of the people, did not recognize her. She stammered:

"But—madame—I do not know you. You must have made a mistake."

"No, I am Mathilde Loisel."

Her friend uttered a cry.

"Oh! my poor Mathilde, how changed you are!"

"Yes, I have had days hard enough since I saw you, days wretched enough—and all because of you!"

"Me? How so?"

"You remember that necklace of diamonds that you lent me to wear to the ministerial ball?"

"Yes. Well?"

"Well, I lost it."

"How can that be? You returned it to me."

"I returned to you another exactly like it. These ten years we've been paying for it. You know it was not easy for us, who had nothing. At last it is over, and I am very glad."

Madame Forestier was stunned.

"You say that you bought a diamond necklace to replace mine?"

"Yes; you did not notice it, then? They were just alike."

And she smiled with a proud and naïve pleasure.

Madame Forestier, deeply moved, took both her hands.

"Oh, my poor Mathilde! Why, my necklace was paste. It was worth five hundred francs at most."

FOR DISCUSSION

1. In what country and city is the scene of the story laid? Had Mademoiselle lived in America, would her birth in a family of employees have limited her "expectations"? Why or why not?

2. How did Madame Loisel prepare for the ball? Describe the immediate sequel to the dance.

3. Why did the Loisels decide to conceal the loss of the necklace? Was this a reasonable course in view of the sacrifices this decision carried with it?

4. What ironic circumstance disclosed at the end makes the tragedy of the lost necklace more touching?

WORD STUDY

1. List the different words—especially the adjectives—used by De Maupassant in the opening paragraphs to impress Madame's poverty and sadness on the reader.

2. The word *magnificent* occurred in the following sentence: "For ten francs you can get two or three *magnificent* roses."

The meaning of this word is very likely familiar to you. It belongs to an interesting word family:

Verb	Nouns	Adjectives
magnify	magnificence	magnificent
	magnitude	magnanimous
	magnate	magniloquent

Come to class prepared (a) to give the common root and meaning of each word, and (b) to tell when Mary speaks or sings the "Magnificat."

A LESSON YOU LEARNED

Have you ever tried to conceal from your parents the fact that you lost the grocery money or broke the neighbor's window? How did it turn out? Tell about it.

Perhaps you can imagine yourself as one of these men coming in from the field. You hear your own mother singing this lullaby to a baby sister or brother. Listen to the sad news she is telling.

A Cradle Song

PADRAIC COLUM

O, men from the fields!
Come gently within.
Tread softly, softly,
O! men come in.

Mavourneen is going
From me and from you.
Where Mary will fold him
With mantle of blue!

From reek of the smoke
And cold of the floor,
And the peering of things
Across the half door.

O, men from the fields!
Soft, softly come through—
Mary puts round him
Her mantle of blue.

5. MAVOURNEEN (mȧ·vo͝or′nēn)— My darling.

FOR DISCUSSION

1. What line convinces you that the mother is not singing an ordinary lullaby?
2. What lines in the poem indicate that the family is poor?
3. Who are the men mentioned in the poem? What work do they do?

FOR MEANING

What do you think is the meaning of each of the italicized words in the following lines:

a. "*Tread* softly, softly."
b. "With *mantle* of blue."
c. "And the *peering* of things."

For Further Reading

Dark Symphony by Elizabeth Adams is a warm biography of a Negro girl who struggles through prejudice and racial barriers to find spiritual truth.

Come Rack! Come Rope! by Robert Hugh Benson. An historical novel of the persecution of the English martyrs presents historical fact in a most vivid way.

Sorrow Built a Bridge by Katherine Burton. Rose Hawthorne Lathrop drops a promising literary career to nurse cancerous patients. She later becomes Mother Alphonsa, a Dominican nun.

Oliver Twist by Charles Dickens. Escaped from an English workhouse, Oliver falls into the hands of pickpockets and thieves.

The Survivors by Ralph Hammond-Innes is a novel of the shipwreck and hardship of an antarctic whaling expedition. The solving of the problem of the mysterious death of an officer shares the interest with the account of the disasters caused by ice and storms.

Pilots Also Pray by Thomas D. Harmon tells of the war experiences of pilot Tom Harmon, of college football fame. It includes his crash landing in the Brazilian jungle and his month-long struggle, alone, back to civilization.

Song at the Scaffold by Gertrud von Le Fort tells the story of a young Carmelite nun who fled when condemned to the guillotine during the French Revolution. She later overcame her fear and returned to die with her sister nuns.

Lily of the Marshes by Alfred MacConastair tells the story of twelve-year-old Maria Goretti who perished in order to preserve her purity. Readers will long remember the characters in this simply written book.

The Rose Unpetaled by Blanche Morteveille is a delightful biography based on the autobiography of St. Thérèse of Lisieux.

God Goes to Murderer's Row by M. Raymond. The central character, Tom Penny, was raised from the depths of crime to the heights of love. The reader won't be able to put the book down until it is read through.

Man of Molokai by Ann Roos gives a dramatic account of Father Damien's life and death on Molokai.

The Queen of the Seven Swords by Fulton J. Sheen contains inspiring reflections on Mary, Mother of Sorrows.

Saint Among Savages by Francis X. Talbot, S.J., is a complete biography of St. Isaac Jogues, martyr of the Iroquois Indians' cruelty.

The Raft by Robert Trumbull is the day-by-day account of the experiences of three American fliers who drifted in an eight-by-four rubber raft for thirty-four days in the Pacific. Told in the first person as the leader of the three told it to the author, this is a true story worth remembering.

FIRE FROM HEAVEN

We know the value of fire to man—how it serves him with light and heat and power. There is another kind of fire which man needs for his *soul*. Sanctifying grace is a light, heat, and power that can permeate and transform his spirit. With the light of grace in his heart, man recognizes God; with its supernatural heat, he loves Him; and with its divine power, he dares to do things which only saints can do.

Without this soul-fire, man cannot see the happy eternity beyond a troublesome present. He does not even suspect the glory of *human* life.

The heroes and heroines of this section illustrate the working of God's grace. You shall be judge of how intensely it burns. An acrobat substitutes tumbling for vocal prayer; trustful children pause between bombs at a wayside shrine; the man-breaker, Cratylus, resolves to serve only a person stronger than himself; two little brown boys kneel in prayer before Him Who loves all men. Wherever men are or whatever their occupation, with His grace in their souls, they are precious to Him. What sight is to the eye and hearing to the ear, His fire is to their souls—and *yours*.

EWING GALLOWAY

No legend is more beloved in all countries of the Western world than this anonymous medieval tale of the simple tumbler and his artless love for the Blessed Virgin. The story has been heard on the stage and radio; it has been featured in the movies; perhaps you have seen the televised version of it. Its tenderly stated truth is that God esteems not the value of the gift, but the love we bring with even our humblest offerings.

OUR LADY'S TUMBLER

A LEGEND TRANSLATED BY EDWARD MASON

Amongst the lives of the ancient Fathers, wherein may be found much profitable matter, this story is told for a true example. I do not say that you may not often have heard a fairer story, but at least this is not to be despised, and is well worth the telling. Now therefore will I say and narrate what chanced to this minstrel.

He erred [1] up and down, to and fro, so often and in so many places, that he took the whole world in despite,[2] and sought rest in a certain Holy Order. Horses and raiment and money, yea, all that he had, he straightway put from him, and seeking shelter from the world, was firmly set never to put foot within it more. For this cause he took refuge in this Holy Order, amongst the monks of Clairvaux.[3] Now, though this dancer was comely of face and shapely of person, yet when he had once entered the monastery he found that he was master of no craft practised therein. In the world he had gained his bread by tumbling and dancing and feats of address.[4] To leap, to spring, such matters he knew well, but of greater things he knew nothing, for he had never spelled from book—nor Paternoster, nor canticle, nor creed, nor Hail Mary, nor aught concerning his soul's salvation.

When the minstrel had joined himself to the Order, he marked how the tonsured monks spoke amongst themselves by signs, no words coming from their lips, so he thought within himself that they were dumb. But when he learned that truly it was by way of penance that speech was forbidden to their mouths, and that for holy obedience were they silent, then considered he that silence became him also; and he refrained his tongue from words, so discreetly and for so long a space, that day in, day out, he spake never, save by commandment; so

[1] ERRED—Wandered.

[2] IN DESPITE—He grew weary of the world.

[3] CLAIRVAUX (clâr·vō′)—A celebrated Cistercian monastery founded by St. Bernard.

[4] ADDRESS—Skill or cleverness, in juggling for example.

"Our Lady's Tumbler" from *Aucassin & Nicolette & Other Medieval Romances & Legends*, translated by Edward Mason, Everyman's Library. Reprinted by permission of E. P. Dutton & Co., Inc., and J. M. Dent & Sons, Ltd., London.

that the cloister often rang with the brothers' mirth. The tumbler moved amongst his fellows like a man ashamed, for he had neither part nor lot in all the business of the monastery, and for this he was right sad and sorrowful. He saw the monks and the penitents about him, each serving God, in this place and that, according to his office and degree. He marked the priests at their ritual before the altars; the deacons at the Gospels; the subdeacons at the Epistles; and the ministers about the vigils. This one repeats the Introit; this other the Lesson; cantors chant from the psalter; penitents spell out the Miserere—for thus are all things sweetly ordered—yea, and the most ignorant amongst them yet can pray his Paternoster. Wherever he went, here or there, in office or cloister, in every quiet corner and nook, there he found five, or three, or two, or at least one.

He gazes earnestly, if so he is able, upon each. Such an one laments; this other is in tears; yet another grieves and sighs. He marvels at their sorrow. Then he said, "Holy Mary, what bitter grief have all these men that they smite the breast so grievously! Too sad of heart, meseems, are they who make such bitter dole [5] together. Ah, St. Mary, alas, what words are these I say! These men are calling on the mercy of God, but I—what do I here? Here there is none so mean or vile but who serves God in his office and degree, save only me, for I work not, neither can I preach. Caitiff [6] and shamed was I when I thrust myself herein, seeing that I can do nothing well, either in labor or in prayer. I see my brothers upon their errands, one behind the other; but I do naught but fill my belly with the meat that they provide. If they perceive this thing, certainly shall I be in an evil case, for they will cast me out amongst the dogs, and none will take pity on the glutton and the idle man. Truly am I a caitiff, set in the high place for a sign." Then he wept for very woe, and would that he was quiet in the grave. "Mary, Mother," quoth he, "pray now your Heavenly Father that He keep me in His pleasure, and give me such good counsel that I may truly serve both Him and you; yea, and may deserve that meat which now is bitter in my mouth."

Driven mad with thoughts such as these, he wandered about the abbey until he found himself within the crypt, and took sanctuary by the altar, crouching close as he was able. Above the altar was carved the statue of Madame St. Mary. Truly his steps had not erred when he sought that refuge; nay, but rather, God who knows His own had led him thither by the hand. When he heard the bells ring for Mass he sprang to his feet all dismayed. "Ha!" said he; "now am I betrayed. Each adds his mite to the great offering, save only me. Like a tethered ox, naught I do but chew the cud, and waste good victuals on a useless man. Shall I speak my thought? Shall I work my will? By the Mother of God, thus am I set to do. None is here to blame. I will do that which I can, and honor with my craft the Mother of God in her monastery. Since others honor her with chant,[7] then I will serve with tumbling."

He takes off his cowl, and removes his garments, placing them near the altar,

[5] DOLE—Sorrow.
[6] CAITIFF—Vile, of no account.
[7] CHANT—The singing of the Divine Office.

but so that his body be not naked he dons a tunic, very thin and fine, of scarce more substance than a shirt. So, light and comely of body, with gown girt closely about his loins, he comes before the Image right humbly.

Then raising his eyes, "Lady," said he, "to your fair charge I give my body and my soul. Sweet Queen, sweet Lady, scorn not the thing I know, for with the help of God I will essay to serve you in good faith, even as I may. I cannot read your Hours nor chant your praise, but at least I can set before you what art I have. Now will I be as the lamb that plays and skips before his mother. Oh, Lady, who art nowise bitter to those who serve you with a good intent, that which thy servant is, that he is for you."

Then commenced he his merry play, leaping low and small, tall and high, over and under. Then once more he knelt upon his knees before the statue, and meekly bowed his head. "Ha!" said he, "most gracious Queen, of your pity and your charity scorn not this my service." Again he leaped and played, and for holiday and festival, made the somersault of Metz. Again he bowed before the Image, did reverence, and paid it all the honor that he might. Afterwards he did the French vault, then the vaults of Champagne, then the Spanish vault, then the vaults they love in Brittany, then the vault of Lorraine, and all these feats he did as best he was able. Afterwards he did the Roman vault, and then, with hands before his brow, danced daintily before the altar, gazing with a humble heart at the statue of God's Mother. "Lady," said he, "I set before you a fair play. This travail I do for you alone; so help me God, for you, Lady, and your Son. Think not I tumble for my own delight; but I serve you, and look for no other guerdon [8] on my carpet. My brothers serve you, yea, and so do I. Lady, scorn not your villein,[9] for he toils for your good pleasure; and, Lady, you are my delight and the sweetness of the world." Then he walked on his two hands, with his feet in the air, and his head near the ground. He twirled with his feet, and wept with his eyes. "Lady," said he, "I worship you with heart, with body, feet, and hands, for this I can neither add to nor take away. Now am I your very minstrel. Others may chant your praises in the church, but here in the crypt will I tumble for your delight. Lady, lead me truly in your way, and for the love of God hold me not in utter despite." Then he smote upon his breast, he sighed and wept most tenderly, since he knew no better prayer than tears. Then he turned him about, and leaped once again. "Lady," said he, "as God is my Saviour, never have I turned this somersault before. Never has tumbler done such a feat, and, certes, it is not bad. Lady, what delight is his who may harbor with you in your glorious manor. For God's love, Lady, grant me such fair hostelry, since I am yours, and am nothing of my own." Once again he did the vault of Metz; again he danced and tumbled. Then when the chants rose louder from the choir, he, too, forced the note, and put forward all his skill. So long as the priest was about that Mass, so long his flesh endured to dance and leap and spring, till at the last, nigh fainting, he

[8] GUERDON (gûr′dŭn)—Reward.
[9] VILLEIN—A servant of humble degree.

could stand no longer upon his feet, but fell for weariness on the ground. From head to heel sweat stood upon him, drop by drop, as blood falls from meat turning upon the hearth. "Lady," said he, "I can no more, but truly will I seek you again." Fire consumed him utterly. He took his habit once more, and when he was wrapped close therein, he rose to his feet, and bending low before the statue, went his way. "Farewell," said he, "gentlest Friend. For God's love take it not to heart, for so I may I will soon return. Not one Hour[10] shall pass but that I will serve you with right good will, so I may come, and so my service is pleasing in your sight." Thus he went from the crypt, yet gazing on his Lady. "Lady," said he, "my heart is sore that I cannot read your Hours. How would I love them for love of you, most gentle Lady! Into your care I commend my soul and my body."

In this fashion passed many days, for at every Hour he sought the crypt to do service, and pay homage before the Image. His service was so much to his mind that never once was he too weary to set out his most cunning feats to distract the Mother of God, nor did he ever wish for other play than this. Now, doubtless, the monks knew well enough that day by day he sought the crypt, but no man on earth —save God alone—was aware of aught that passed there; neither would he, for

[10] HOUR—A division of the Divine Office.

all the wealth of the world, have let his goings on be seen, save by the Lord his God alone. For truly he believed that were his secret once espied he would be hunted from the cloister, and flung once more into the foul, sinful world, and for his part he was more fain to fall on death than to suffer any taint of sin. But God considering his simplicity, his sorrow for all he had wrought amiss, and the love which moved him to this deed, would that this toil should be known; and the Lord willed that the work of His friend should be made plain to men, for the glory of the Mother whom he worshiped, and so that all men should know and hear and perceive that God refuses none who seeks His face in love, however low his degree, save only he love God and strive to do His will.

Now think you that the Lord would have accepted this service, had it not been done for love of Him? Verily and truly, no, however much this juggler tumbled; but God called him friend, because he loved Him much. Toil and labor, keep fast and vigil, sigh and weep, watch and pray, ply the sharp scourge, be diligent at Matins [11] and at Mass, owe no man anything, give alms of all you have—and yet, if you love not God with all your heart, all these good deeds are so much loss—mark well my words—and profit you naught for the saving of your soul. Without charity and love, works avail a man nothing. God asks not gold, neither for silver, but only for love unfeigned in His people's hearts, and since the tumbler loved Him beyond measure, for this reason God was willing to accept his service.

[11] MATINS—The first Hour of the Divine Office.

Thus things went well with this good man for a great space. For more years than I know the count of, he lived greatly at his ease, but the time came when the good man was sorely vexed, for a certain monk thought upon him, and blamed him in his heart that he was never set in choir for Matins. The monk marveled much at his absence, and said within himself that he would never rest till it was clear what manner of man this was, and how he spent the Hours, and for what service the convent gave him bread. So he spied and pried and followed, till he marked him plainly, sweating at his craft in just such fashion as you have heard. "By my faith," said he, "this is a merry jest, and a fairer festival than we observe altogether. Whilst others are at prayers, and about the business of the House, this tumbler dances daintily, as though one had given him a hundred silver marks. He prides himself on being so nimble of foot, and thus he repays us what he owes. Truly it is this for that; we chant for him, and he tumbles for us. We throw him largesse: [12] he doles us alms. We weep his sins, and he dries our eyes. Would that the monastery could see him, as I do, with their very eyes; willingly therefore would I fast till Vespers.[13] Not one could refrain from mirth at the sight of this simple fool doing himself to death with his tumbling, for on himself he has no pity. Since his folly is free from malice, may God grant it to him as penance. Certainly I will not impute it to him as sin, for in all simplicity and good faith, I firmly believe, he does this thing, so that he may deserve his bread." So the monk

[12] LARGESSE—Gifts.

[13] VESPERS—The final Hour of the Office, sung in early evening.

saw with his very eyes how the tumbler did service at all the Hours, without pause or rest, and he laughed with pure mirth and delight, for in his heart was joy and pity.

The monk went straight to the Abbot and told him the thing from beginning to end, just as you have heard. The Abbot got him on his feet and said to the monk, "By holy obedience I bid you hold your peace, and tell not this tale abroad against your brother. I lay on you my strict command to speak of this matter to none, save me. Come now, we will go forthwith to see what this can be, and let us pray the Heavenly King, and His very sweet, dear Mother, so precious and so bright, that in her gentleness she will plead with her Son, her Father, and her Lord, that I may look on this work—if thus it pleases Him—so that the good man be not wrongly blamed, and that God may be the more beloved, yet so that thus is His good pleasure." Then they secretly sought the crypt, and found a privy [14] place near the altar, where they could see, and yet not be seen. From there the Abbot and his monk marked the business of the penitent. They saw the vaults he varied so cunningly, his nimble leaping and his dancing, his salutations of Our Lady, and his springing and his bounding, till he was nigh to faint. So weak was he that he sank on the ground, all outworn, and the sweat fell from his body upon the pavement of the crypt. But presently, in this his need, came she, his refuge, to his aid. Well she knew that guileless heart.

Whilst the Abbot looked, forthwith there came down from the vault a Dame [15] so glorious that certainly no man had seen one so precious, nor so richly crowned. She was more beautiful than the daughters of men, and her vesture was heavy with gold and gleaming stones. In her train came the hosts of Heaven, angel and archangel also; and these pressed close about the minstrel, and solaced and refreshed him. When their shining ranks drew near, peace fell upon his heart; for they contended to do him service, and were the servants of the servitor of that Dame who is the rarest Jewel of God. Then the sweet and courteous Queen herself took a white napkin in her hand, and with it gently fanned her minstrel before the altar. Courteous and debonair, the Lady refreshed his neck, his body, and his brow. Meekly she served him as a handmaid in his need. But these things were hidden from the good man, for he neither saw nor knew that about him stood so fair a company.

The holy angels honor him greatly, but they can no longer stay, for their Lady turns to go. She blesses her minstrel with the sign of God, and the holy angels throng about her, still gazing back with delight upon their companion, for they await the hour when God shall release him from the burden of the world, and they possess his soul.

This marvel the Abbot and his monk saw at least four times, and thus at each Hour came the Mother of God with aid and succor for her man. Great joy had the Abbot that this thing was made plain to him. But the monk was filled with shame, since God had shown His pleasure in the service of His poor fool. His con-

[14] PRIVY—Hidden.

[15] DAME—Lady.

fusion burnt him like fire. "*Domine*,"[16] said he to the Abbot, "grant me grace. Certainly this is a holy man, and since I have judged him amiss, it is very right that my body should smart. Give me now fast or vigil or the scourge, for without question he is a saint. We are witnesses to the whole matter, nor is it possible that we can be deceived." But the Abbot replied, "You speak truly, for God has made us to know that He has bound him with the cords of love. So I lay my commandment upon you, in virtue of obedience, and under pain of your person, that you tell no word to any man of that you have seen, save to God alone and me." "Lord," said he, "thus will I do." On these words they turned them, and hastened from the crypt; and the good man, having brought his tumbling to an end, presently clothed himself in his habit, and joyously went his way to the monastery.

Thus time went and returned, till it chanced that in a little while the Abbot sent for him who was so filled with virtue. When he heard that he was bidden of the Abbot, his heart was sore with grief, for he could think of nothing profitable to say. "Alas!" said he, "I am undone; not a day of my days but I shall know misery and sorrow and shame, for well I trow that my service is not pleasing to God. Alas! plainly doth He show that it displeases Him since He causes the truth to be made clear. Could I believe that such work and play as mine could give delight to the mighty God? He had no pleasure therein, and all my toil was thrown away. Ah me, what shall I do? what shall I say? Fair, gentle God, what portion will be mine? Either shall I die in shame, or else shall I be banished from this place, and set up as a mark to the world and all the evil thereof. Sweet Lady, St. Mary, since I am all bewildered, and since there is none to give me counsel, Lady, come thou to my aid. Fair, gentle God, help me in my need. Stay not, neither tarry, but come quickly with Your Mother. For God's love, come not without her, but hasten both to me in my peril, for truly I know not what to plead. Before one word can pass my lips, surely will they bid me 'Begone.' Wretched that I am, what reply is he to make who has no advocate? Yet, why this dole, since go I must?" He came before the Abbot, with the tears yet wet upon his cheeks, and he was still weeping when he knelt upon the ground. "Lord," prayed he, "for the love of God deal not harshly with me. Would you send me from your door? Tell me what you would have me do, and thus it shall be done." Then replied the Abbot, "Answer me truly. Winter and summer have you lived here for a great space; now, tell me what service you have given, and how have you deserved your bread?" "Alas!" said the tumbler, "well I knew that quickly I should be put upon the street when once this business was heard of you, and that you would keep me no more. Lord," said he, "I take my leave. Miserable I am, and miserable shall I ever be. Never yet have I made a penny for all my juggling." But the Abbot answered, "Not so said I; but I ask and require of you—nay, more, by virtue of holy obedience I command you—to seek within your conscience and tell me truly by what craft you have furthered the business of our monastery." "Lord,"

[16] *Domine*—Lord, Master.

cried he, "now have you slain me, for this commandment is a sword." Then he laid bare before the Abbot the story of his days, from the first thing to the last, whatsoever pain it cost him; not a word did he leave out, but he told it all without a pause, just as I have told you the tale. He told it with clasped hands, and with tears, and at the close he kissed the Abbot's feet, and sighed.

The holy Abbot leaned above him, and, all in tears, raised him up, kissing both his eyes. "Brother," said he, "hold your peace now, for I make with you this true covenant, that you shall ever be of our monastery. God grant, rather, that we may be of yours, for all the worship you have brought to ours. I and you will call each other friend. Fair, sweet brother, pray you for me, and I for my part will pray for you. And now I pray you, my sweet friend, and lay this bidding upon you, without pretense, that you continue to do your service, even as you were wont heretofore—yea, and with greater craft yet, if you so may." "Lord," said he, "truly is this so?" "Yea," said the Abbot, "and verily." So he charged him, under peril of discipline, to put all doubts from his mind; for which reason the good man rejoiced so greatly that, as telleth the rhyme, he was all bemused, so that the blood left his cheeks, and his knees failed beneath him. When his courage came back, his very heart thrilled with joy; but so perilous was that quickening that therefrom he shortly died. But theretofore with a good heart he went about his service without rest, and Matins and Vespers, night and day, he missed no Hour till he became too sick to perform his office. So sore was his sickness upon him that he might not rise from his bed. Marvelous was the shame he proved when no more was he able to pay his rent. This was the grief that lay the heaviest upon him, for of his sickness he spake never a word, but he feared greatly lest he should fall from grace since he travailed no longer at his craft. He reckoned himself an idle man, and prayed God to take him to Himself before the sluggard might come to blame. For it was bitter to him to consider that all about him knew his case, so bitter that the burden was heavier than his heart could bear, yet there without remedy he must lie. The holy Abbot does him all honor; he and his monks chant the Hours about his bed, and in these praises of God he felt such delight that not for them would he have taken the province of Poitou,[17] so great was his happiness therein. Fair and contrite was his confession, but still he was not at peace; yet why say more of this, for the hour had struck, and he must rise and go.

The Abbot was in that cell with all his monks: there, too, was company of many a priest and many a canon. These all humbly watched the dying man, and saw with open eyes this wonder happen. Clear to their very sight, about that lowly bed, stood the Mother of God, with angel and archangel, to wait the passing of his soul. Over against them were set, like wild beasts, devils and the Adversary,[18] so that they might snatch his spirit. I speak not to you in parable. But little profit had they for all their coming, their waiting, and their straining on the leash. Never might they have part in such a soul

[17] POITOU (pwȧ·to͞o′)—An ancient province of Western France.
[18] ADVERSARY—Satan.

as his. When the soul took leave of his body, it fell not in their hands at all, for the Mother of God gathered it to her bosom, and the holy angels thronging round, quired [19] for joy, as the bright train swept to Heaven with its burthen,[20] according to the will of God. To these things the whole of the monastery was witness, besides such others as were there. So knew they and perceived that God sought no more to hide the love He bore to His poor servant, but rather would that his virtues should be plain to each man in that place; and very wonderful and joyful seemed this deed to them. Then with meet reverence, they bore the body on its bier within the abbey church, and with high pomp commended their brother to the care of God; nor was there monk who did not chant or read his portion that day within the choir of the mighty church.

Thus with great honor they laid him to his rest, and kept his holy body amongst them as a relic. At that time spake the Abbot plainly to their ears, telling them the story of this tumbler and of all his life, just as you have heard, and of all that he himself beheld within the crypt. No brother but kept awake during that sermon. "Certes," said they, "easy is it to give credence to such a tale; nor should any doubt your words, seeing that the truth bears testimony to itself, and witness comes with need; yea, without any doubt have we full assurance that his discipline is done." Great joy amongst themselves have all within that place.

Thus endeth the story of the minstrel. Fair was his tumbling, fair was his service, for thereby gained he such high honor as is above all earthly gain. So the holy Fathers narrate that in such fashion these things chanced to this minstrel. Now, therefore, let us pray to God—He who is above all other—that He may grant us so to do such faithful service that we may win the guerdon of His love.

Here endeth the Tumbler of Our Lady.

[19] QUIRED—Sang.
[20] BURTHEN—Same as burden.

FOR DISCUSSION

1. Why did the tumbler come to Clairvaux? Why did he feel unfit for the duties of monastery life?
2. Describe the tumbler's first attempts to take part in the works and spirit of his new life. What was the result? Is it true to say that our tumbler did not know how to pray? Explain your answer.
3. In what manner did the tumbler determine to honor the Mother of God? Where did he offer his homage? How did he reason that his service would please her?
4. How was the tumbler's manner of prayer discovered? Did the inquisitive monk rightly value the tumbler's efforts?
5. How did Our Lady convince the Abbot that all was pleasing to her? What effect had this proof on the monk?
6. Explain the fears of the tumbler when the Abbot summoned him. What was the result of the interview? Can you explain why the tumbler should be sad that the Abbot and all the monks paid him honor?
7. What final proof did Our Lady give of her love for the tumbler? What do you consider is the moral of the tale?

WORD STUDY

The Norman Conquest of England in 1066 introduced many French words into the English language. For several centuries after the conquest, French was the exclusive language of the higher classes. Can you guess why this was true?

In "Our Lady's Tumbler" the medieval setting is emphasized by the many English words of French origin: *travail, guerdon, largesse, debonair,* and *succor.* Find these words and tell what they mean.

To retain a medieval English flavor, the translator of this legend used many older forms of English words and phrases. For instance, *I trow, meseems,* and *certes* are now considered archaic. Can you tell what the modern English equivalents are?

The words below will look very familiar to you, but their meanings have been altered since medieval days. Find these words in the story and discuss the change in meaning for each. What modern English word would you substitute in the story?

fairer (p. 307) *dole* (p. 308)
erred (p. 307) *save* (p. 307)

Can you find other words which have altered in meaning? Discuss them in class.

OUR LADY

1. List the titles by which Our Lady's tumbler addressed his heavenly Mother.

2. In 1531 Our Lady appeared to Juan Diego, a poor Indian, at Guadalupe, Mexico; in 1858, to Bernadette Soubirous at Lourdes; in 1917, to the three children of Fatima, Portugal. If you are not familiar with the story of one of these apparitions, look up in the library Frances Parkinson Keyes' *The Grace of Guadalupe* or William T. Walsh's *Our Lady of Fatima,* or read "The Lesson of Bernadette" in this book.

3. Compare briefly the education, simplicity, and faith of the tumbler with that of Juan or Bernadette. Describe the appearance and dress of Our Lady as given in one of these accounts.

RELATED READING

Other versions of the selection just read are Arthur Stringer's "The Tumbler" and Alexander Woollcott's "Our Lady's Juggler." These appeared in issues of the *Reader's Digest* for December, 1938, and October, 1941.

◇◇◇◇◇

Like a movie, this picture of children in a town torn by war is vivid in its description, dramatic in its action. After you have read it once, you may wish to act it out in order to get its full significance.

Evening Prayer

AMELIA JOSEPHINE BURR

You say there's only evil in this war—
That bullets drive out Christ? If you had been
In Furnes with me that night . . . what would you say,
I wonder?

3. FURNES (fürn)—A Belgian city.

It was ruin past all words,
Horror where joyous comfort used to be, 5
And not clean quiet death, for all day long
The great shells tore the little that remained
Like vultures on a body that still breathes.
They stopped as it grew dark. I looked about
The ghastly wilderness that once had been 10
A village street, and saw no other life
Except a Belgian soldier, shadowy
Among the shadows, and a little group
Of children creeping from a cellar school
And hurrying home. One older than the rest— 15
So little older!—mothered them along
Till all at once a stray belated shell
Whined suddenly out of the gloom, and burst
Near by. The babies wailed and clung together,
Helpless with fear. In vain the little mother 20
Encouraged them— "But no! you mustn't cry,
That isn't brave, that isn't French!" At last
She led her frightened brood across the way
To where there stood a roadside Calvary
Bearing its sad, indomitable Christ— 25
Strange how the shells will spare just that! I saw
So many . . . There they knelt, poor innocents,
Hands folded and eyes closed. I stole across
And stood behind them. "We will say our prayer—
Our Father which art in heaven," she began, 30
And all the little sobbing voices piped,
"Hallowed be Thy Name." From down the road
The Belgian soldier had come near. I felt
Him standing there beside me in the dusk.
"Thy kingdom come—"
"Thy will be done on earth 35
As it is in heaven." The irony of it
Cut me like steel. If one could name this earth
In the same breath with heaven—what is hell?
Only a little child could pray like that.
"Give us this day our daily bread—" A pause. 40
There was no answer. She repeated it
Urgently. Silence yet. She opened wide
Reproachful eyes at them. Their eyes were open

24. ROADSIDE CALVARY—Small shrine by the road.

Also, and staring at the shadowy shapes
Of ruin all around them. Now that prayer 45
Had grown too hard even for little children.
"I know—I know—but we must say the prayer,"
She faltered. "Give us this day our daily bread,
And—and forgive—" she stopped.
"Our trespasses
As we forgive them who have trespassed against us." 50
The children turned amazed, to see who spoke
The words they could not. I too turned to him,
The soldier there beside me—and I looked
Into King Albert's face . . . I have no words
To tell you what I saw . . . only I thought 55
That while a man's breast held a heart like that,
Christ was not—even here—so far away.

54. KING ALBERT—King of Belgium during World War I.

FOR DISCUSSION

1. The poet here is sometimes more realistic than most of us find comfortable. Find the lines which create for you the most realistic pictures.

2. Why is Christ called *indomitable?*

3. What was the hardest part of the prayer to say? Why was it hardest? Who finally said these lines? Why is it significant to know who said the words?

4. Read the lines which contain the moral of the whole poem.

5. The following lines are charged with much more emotion and meaning than they indicate at first reading.

a. ". . . But no! you mustn't cry, That isn't brave, that isn't French!"

b. ". . . If one could name this earth In the same breath with heaven—what is hell?"

Find the place in the poem where each occurs, and see whether you can explain its full import.

WORD STUDY

The prefix *in-* in the word *indomitable* means *not.* The second part of the word comes from the Latin *domare* (*to tame*). Thus, *indomitable* means *unconquerable.* In many other words, the prefix *in-* means *not;* for example, *inexpensive, inexperienced, inactive.* Can you list a dozen more such words? Tell what they mean.

PROJECT

Look in the diocesan paper for a news item which you could develop into a story similar to this one. Bring it to class and write your story.

Racial prejudice is still one of our worst social evils. The poet wishes to emphasize the cruelty of rejecting a person because of the color of his skin. Here he draws a sharp comparison—two victims of racial intolerance against the background of Christ on the cross.

On Seeing Two Brown Boys in a Catholic Church

FRANK HORNE

It is fitting that you be here
Little brown boys
With Christ-like eyes
And curling hair.

Look you on yon crucifix 5
Where He hangs nailed and pierced
With head hung low
And eyes a'blind with blood that drips
From a thorny crown . . .
Look you well, 10
You shall know this thing.

Judas' kiss shall burn your cheek
And you shall be denied
By your Peter—
And Gethsemane . . . 15
You shall know full well Gethsemane . . .
You, too, will suffer under Pontius Pilate
And feel the rugged cut of rough hewn
cross

Upon your surging shoulder— 20
They will spit in your face
And laugh . . .
They will nail you up twixt thieves
And gamble for your little garments.

And in this you will exceed God 25
For on this earth
You shall know Hell—

O little brown boys
With Christ-like eyes
And curling hair 30
It is fitting that you be here.

FOR DISCUSSION

1. Through whose eyes does the poet see the two little boys?

2. Is the Negro the only one who suffers from racial prejudice in this country?

3. The Judas kiss, Peter, and Gethsem-

ane are figurative ways of telling the boys that they will suffer. What experiences will they most likely have to suffer?

4. What does the poet mean when he says "you will exceed God"?

5. Can you name any recent movies or television programs that tried to influence the public to deal intelligently and sympathetically with the race problem? Describe briefly how it was done.

ON RACIAL PREJUDICE

1. Imagine or recall some example of racial injustice and then write what would be a temperate protest from a good American Catholic to your local newspaper.

2. Coin a slogan against racial prejudice that might be used as a spot announcement on radio or television. Try to make it short and catching.

RELATED READING

A Saint in the Slave Trade by Arnold Lunn is the story of how a Christ-minded man answered this great problem and won Heaven.

◇◇◇◇◇

Soldier, traveler, monk, and hermit—Charles de Foucauld was a nobleman in whom were combined qualities of fearlessness, compassion, and a sincere desire to live a God-like life. In this unusual story about an unusual man, you will discover his secret of coming close to God, a secret simple enough for anyone to apply—that of praying.

THE VERY NOBLE THE VISCOUNT CHARLES DE FOUCAULD

JOHN GIBBONS

It is one of the most marvelous stories in the world, and now I know a little about it. And let us begin with 15 September, 1858, and the birth of Charles Eugène de Foucauld.[1] That was at Strasbourg,[2] but the family really came from the south. Genealogists have worked the pedigree out back to the time of the Crusades. It was a noble family with generation after generation of fighting

[1] FOUCAULD—Pronounced fōō·cō′.

[2] STRASBOURG—A city in France near the German border.

"The Very Noble the Viscount Charles de Foucauld" by John Gibbons from *Great Catholics,* edited by Claude Williamson, reprinted by permission of The Macmillan Company and Ivor Nicholson & Watson, Ltd., London.

men, and his father was the Vicomte [3] which young Charles became at the age of six. Actually the Republic, of course, grants no titles; but it does recognize the patents of the old nobility as being part of their surnames, and it is still something to be a Vicomte of France. Charles was a wealthy one at that, and, of course, he had to follow the family tradition and go into the army. He was a young officer of Hussars,[4] and a very dashing young officer. St. Cyr [5] military college means nothing particular to me, because I have never been there; but I was interested when I read that he had passed through Saumur,[6] where I have been. It is the cavalry riding-school of the French army, and one has to be rather a picked man to be sent there; it's the place that turns out the sort of teams which we see at international horseshows, those men who apparently ride up the side of a house. When one has been at Saumur, in fact, one does not hold on by one's horse's ears!

Then Lieutenant Charles was not a very virtuous young officer, and perhaps he had come into too much money too young. Would he in the '70's be an "exquisite" or a "dandy"? He had to have his own brand of cigars especially imported for him, and it was the same with everything else. There was too much card-playing, too many (shall we say?) lady-friends. Even in the hussars one can be over-dashing, and his military superiors were not pleased with him; in fact, the famous Père [7] de Foucauld of the future was quite often under officers' arrest, and the champagne parties had to be held in his own quarters. There was worse, with a serious scandal when the young hussar was openly flaunting one special lady much too publicly for even the not particularly squeamish etiquette of the army; and would he kindly get rid of the lady, or would he in short be "broke"? [8] And the grave seniors of his family with centuries of soldiers' honors behind them shook their heads; wild oats should have a limit, and the wise and prudent French Law was appealed to for the appointment of a guardian. "It is true that you have so many thousands a year," they said, "but it had better pass through the account of the family solicitor; he will know how to check these bills for diamond bracelets and the like." And so life became a little more serious.

Next there was Africa, and the young gentleman's particular hussars had now somehow turned into the famous Chasseurs d'Afrique,[9] those people with the wonderful horses and with the *musique* with the pride and the glory of the kettledrums. But now there was no more extravagance and folly; this was soldiering, and soon there was the desert. This North Africa must have been to the France of the earliest 1880's something like the Cecil Rhodes Africa to our England of the '90's, and here was a whole new world of Empire to be reached out for by the strong of heart. And now the ex-dandy of the scandals of the garrison-towns is leading real men in an expedi-

[3] VICOMTE (vē·kôNt′)—A viscount; a nobleman.

[4] HUSSARS—Light-horse troopers, brilliantly uniformed; originally applied to the Hungarian cavalry.

[5] ST. CYR—Pronounced săN·sēr′.

[6] SAUMUR—Pronounced sō·mür′.

[7] PÈRE—Father.

[8] BROKE—Degraded in rank; dismissed.

[9] CHASSEURS D'AFRIQUE (shä·sûr′ dȧ·frēk′)—African light cavalry.

tion down in the then uncharted *Sud*.[10] This was what an army was for, and here were the burning sands of the wilderness and nights of a gigantic silence that terrified and appealed at the same time. This Africa which he was seeing now, with its solitudes and its unbelievable hardships, was something which was to color the whole future life of the young officer. It is queer, but in one of his letters he refers to the men whom he was leading, rough troopers who would go anywhere and put up with anything; and they might, he says, in their discipline and self-sacrifice have been monks.

Very soon, however, he was an ex-officer. The expedition was successfully over, and it was inconceivable to think of a return to garrison life. What about going through Morocco, the unknown parts where nobody had ever been before, and making a survey of it? What about, say, a year's officer's leave, and he would pay his own expenses? But France said "No"; and probably his early record wasn't much recommendation. In that case if there was no more fighting for the moment, he would throw in his commission and be a civilian and still serve France. And Charles de Foucauld started off on one of the very great journeys of modern exploration-history.

What he actually did and exactly where he went comes in all the learned books on North Africa, and this and that Geographical Society voted their highest honors and their gold medals for the business. Take it here that he went through the unexplored part of Morocco when it was still the Forbidden Empire of the 1880's and when a European Christian if caught would have been tortured to death. In his planning of the journey he was helped by an extraordinary old Irishman called Oscar MacCarthy whom he found in Algiers. MacCarthy had spent nearly all his life in North Africa, he knew more than any other white man about the Moors, he had himself been to extraordinary places, and this particular journey through still more extraordinary places had been a dream of his for years. But he had never done it; he had not had the money or the strength. Now here was a young man with both; let him share the old man's knowledge. The two settled down together to plot out the details of that incredible journey. In the end, De Foucauld went through as a Jew. He had to have his skin dyed and to be instructed in all sorts of customs of eating and drinking and everything else; he had to be dressed in filthy rags of the proper color prescribed for a Jew to wear, he had to take his shoes off to walk through a Moslem village, he had to be prepared to be spat on by any Moor[11] who met him and he had to learn to cringe convincingly. . . . And then with it all, De Foucauld did exactly as he planned and went precisely where he had intended to go. Eleven months and three days that journey took, with one man's courage and endurance and resource matched against a barbarous and bitterly hostile nation; and for every single minute of all that time he was in danger of mutilation and death. He did it rather on the lines of the man in our Kipling's *Kim*, making his secret survey-notes at night for the

[10] *Sud*—The South; that is, the Sahara Desert directly south of French Algeria.

[11] MOOR—Native of North Africa or neighboring North African states.

better guidance and glory of his France, and his *Reconnaissance au Maroc* stands out as one of the geographical landmarks of his age. Even the Moors, the very people whose country he had penetrated, had their word about him as at least a man in a million for bravery. Years later and when the explorer had changed into something like the Saint, there came a Moor's letter to the Algiers garrison with an address misspelt to "*L'Officier Foukou.*" There were those, it seemed, who had not forgotten that trip.

But is not this volume titled *Great Catholics,* and when is there any Catholic part? So far there had not been much! That boy had been brought up by a good Catholic mother, and in fact in earliest childhood had shown signs of a more than usual piety. But the signs had vanished, and with youth and young manhood there had succeeded a blank nothingness. It was not that he just neglected ever to go to church; it was that he believed in nothing. There was Glory, perhaps, and of course France; but for the rest De Foucauld was a professed infidel. And then something happened. Perhaps it was due to his mother's prayers; perhaps the seeds of Catholic childhood were not quite withered after all. Or was it an effect of that awful trip through Morocco, and De Foucauld mentions it himself. He had been so "alone," he puts it. The Mohammedans had their religion, and the humble Hebrews were spat at for having theirs and then still kept it; and he who was liable to torture and death as a Christian had nothing at all. In this sort of short summary it is probably impossible to go too deeply into spiritual motives. Better put it, perhaps, that Something Happened. Put it that Charles de Foucauld returned to the Practice of the Faith which he had so long and so grievously neglected. Say simply, if you like, that he "Got Religion."

He got it very thoroughly! Here is an old French priest, and here is a man in his confessional but not kneeling down; he has not come to confess, he says, but to be told how To Believe. "Kneel down," the priest says, and the man protests; that is not what he had come for, and can he not be first instructed? "Kneel," says the priest; and he wins. Then we find a Jesuit Father as Director, and at another period there is Solesmes [12] Abbey and an effort to test a Benedictine Vocation. He tried three great Orders, and it is significant that the silence of the Trappists came nearest to his soul's ideal. Hard to please, wasn't he, the gay young man turned suddenly pious and wanting to pick and choose his own way of salvation! But it wasn't really so at all. His great biographer gives up scores of pages and many chapters to reports and letters written about him by this great Abbot or that famous Superior, and they all say much about the same thing. Here is a man of exceptional grace and of positively heroic humility and obedience. He himself is only too painfully anxious to be told what to do, and it is his Superiors who are in doubt. This man is plainly marked out by God Almighty for some great duty, he is clearly set apart for some special path. Only what path? And could it be the Holy Land? De Foucauld had visited it between his explorations of Morocco and of Religion, and had found a consolation in it; for it had the solitudes

[12] SOLESMES—Pronounced sô·lām′.

and silences of his beloved Africa, and it was, besides, a land which was Holy. And now as Brother Marie-Albéric of the Trappist Obedience, monk but not priest, professed but not yet under permanent vows, he is begging for permission to be sent out there again. There is a Trappist House in Syria, and can he be transferred? He is transferred.

Now he is leaving the Trappists altogether, and how do I get it on paper without giving all the wrong impression? This is not the discontented would-be Religious, trying Rule after Rule and satisfied by none. This is a rare soul, almost a soul apart, and recognized as such by Trappists, Jesuits, Franciscans, and everybody else he comes in contact with. Everyone is anxious to help. Here is a wonderful instrument for God in the forging. If only his humility can be overcome. They are discussing him in Rome itself, and there is a report of a Trappist Superior. Fifty years professed, he has never yet "met with a soul so entirely given to God." Now before the irrevocable life-vows are taken, the man leaves the Trappists and he is back in Palestine again as a layman. There is a silence and a sanctity in the Holy Land; this man wants to be quiet and to think. He wants to be alone, but he is never going to be lonely as he once had been; for he wants to be alone with God and learn His Will. He has ideas of his own; can he use his private fortune, untouched for so long, to purchase from the Turkish Government the Mount of Beatitudes and erect an oratory on it? It would be a kind of lighthouse of salvation; perhaps he himself might be a hermit-priest to serve the altar. Always the idea of the Hermit! Always the Solitude and the Hidden Life! But, of course, his ideas must be guided by God; that plan was impossible, and so God had meant "No." Now he is living as servant to the Poor Clares at Nazareth, an odd-job man mending walls, feeding chickens, running errands. There is an old shed for him at the bottom of the field, and M.[13] le Vicomte is beginning to be happy; Nazareth is a very holy place, and he has the freedom of the nuns' chapel and time to think.

Now the great decision is made. He is a priest at last, and has permission, extra-special exceptional permission from Rome, to be a very extra-special sort of priest, a Solitary in the Sahara. Here is an extract from one of the many high-ecclesiastical letters about him, and in a way it sums up the old life and points to the glories of the new.—"Monsieur le Vicomte Charles de Foucauld, long a lieutenant in the African Army, then an intrepid and skillful traveler in Morocco, then a novice with the Trappist Fathers in Syria, afterwards devoted to the service of the Poor Clares of Nazareth, lastly received Holy Orders and the priesthood. You will find in him heroic self-sacrifice, unlimited self-endurance, a vocation to influence the Mussulman world.—Never have I seen such prodigies of penance, humility, poverty, and of the Love of God."

Now he is back in his Africa at last. . . .

May we for a moment consider the Grand Sahara, three thousand miles from east to west and, say, a thousand miles from north to south. There are cases, of

[13] M.—Monsieur (mē·syû′).

course, where the roots of almost shadeless palm trees can tap the moisture of some underground stream; but for the most part it is desert, an infinity of either sand or of sand with patches of black rock. It is an uncannily queer country, with sand-dunes that are often hundreds of feet high standing up against the intolerable blue of the African sky; and with the wind those miniature mountains can move. The moistureless and overheated air gives a clarity of view in which it is possible to see for many miles, though with odd distortions; but for many miles there is nothing to see, neither road nor tree nor anything at all to break that terrifying monotone of sheer space. Somewhere in the furthest distance of that arid awfulness might seem to be some stream or pond; but really it is only the sun reflecting unevenly from burnished and almost red-hot rock. There is no water. The traveler caught unprepared would just die. The sun would be dangerous to a European by perhaps ten o'clock in the morning, and by high noon it would mean death; to get anywhere at all he must start his journey by possibly five in the morning. There are, however, no European travelers in the ordinary way; one cannot enter the Sahara except by permission of the French military authorities, and permission will not be readily given. It is too expensive; the traveler will probably break down, and aeroplanes or cavalry will have to be sent to his rescue. Let the traveler deposit so many thousands of francs in advance to make an insurance that will help pay for the rescue party. He may quite likely need a military escort, too, and the garrison headquarters will radio so many scores of native irregular horsemen to stand ready to protect his route. Against whom? Against Arabs. One is never sure with that desert; it looks so empty, but there may be fifty men hidden behind those rocks. Every Arab will have a rifle. The soldiers may not be able to find the rifles; they may perhaps be buried in the dry sand. But they are there somewhere, and the Arabs will know where to find them.

But, of course, I have only seen the fringe of the circumference of the desert, and perhaps it was only a hundred kilometers or say sixty miles that I was taken by very special permission and under very careful escort. The Père de Foucauld country was five hundred miles deeper into the Sahara! And he had no escort. Indeed there was no communication at all when he first went there, though France later on set up a monthly courier; the ultimate boast was that official telegrams could be delivered within twenty-two days. Tamanrasset is where Father Charles went, and it is fairly remote! It is in the Tuareg country. The Tuaregs are the "Veiled Men" of the romances, and there are all kinds of legends about them. Probably, however, nobody really quite knows who they are. They are not Arabs or Moors; they are possibly the descendants of the pre-Arab aboriginals of North Africa driven down here to their last strong-point. They are nominal Mohammedans, but with their distinctive customs. They are a slave-owning people, of course, but with their own system of slave-tribes; which means anybody whom they are able to conquer. Their slavery is probably the most horrible in the world, and even amongst the Arabs, themselves not a particularly humanitarian people, the Tuaregs are known as "The Merciless," and their treatment of the boys and young women of the conquered tribes cannot possibly be set down in English print. There are comparatively few travel-books with any genuine account of a race so remote and so dangerous, but Mr. W. B. Seabrook, the American travel-author, says that the most dreadful and unspeakable thing in the whole modern world is the slave trade which works some salt mines somewhere down in the Sahara. Those are, of course, Tuareg slaves. In a short summary it seems impossible and unnecessary to say more about them, except perhaps that another native name for them is the "Abandoned of God." And except that these were the people amongst whom Père de Foucauld chose to make his home.

Now this part of the story is hardest to write, and probably nobody but a religious could properly explain it at all. Père de Foucauld had no idea of being a missionary in the ordinary way; there were the Père Blancs for that, the White Fathers of Africa doing their own wonderful work. Father Charles was different; he was not to teach or preach in the ordinary sense of those words. He was less to do something than to be something, a Solitary leading a certain life which would open the door to an Inner Life with God; and God would do the rest. His "parish," he said, had 100,000 souls; and actually with the oases there are far more people in the Sahara than the old maps showed. Prayer was something that literally worked, every Mass was a spiritual dynamo. Come, let us light up the dark places! Who served the Mass, then? Inconceivable as it sounds, there nearly always was somebody. He was learning the Tuareg language, and was beginning to make converts without asking for them. There were soldiers, odd men in odd outposts. That is not the Foreign Legion of the films, and really there are plenty of decent men in it. There are practising Catholics even in the Legion, and there are more men who are nominal Catholics. Could not one try to remember the Responses to Mass which one learned as a boy and before life went wrong? This ex-officer, ex-nobleman, living on starvation diet and putting up with worse than any legionary for the sake of his God, mightn't one make an effort to oblige him and serve him Mass? It was a miracle, but almost always even in the desert there was somebody.

If ever there was a proof of the force of example, Père de Foucauld lived that proof. Seven francs a month he allowed himself to live on; at pre-war rate, say five-and-three-pence. What need of more than bread and water and a few dates? His Lord of the Blessed Sacrament of the Altar (for which he had special authority for Reservation), had He lived sumptuously? And when the Legion officers so to speak sent the hat round that an ex-comrade might at least have enough to eat, he smilingly acknowledged the money and would be grateful for more. It came in beautifully for buying slaves from the Tuaregs; perhaps they turned into catechumens, or at worst the poor creatures were a little happier. Wasn't life wonderful? His personal fortune, however, he wouldn't touch, and really

he disposed of most of it to relations. Our Lady of Nazareth, had she any private income to draw on? Only once in all those years did Father Charles touch his own money. That was years later when he visited France and took with him the son of a Tuareg chief. Then the man who had lived on fifteen pence a week must travel first-class and with all that money could buy; it must be *de luxe*, and he must stop at the château of this and that old friend. For here is a soul which will be able to influence other souls; this African must be impressed by the glories of the country of the Christians.

Meantime here was Père de Foucauld in his desert, gorgeously happy at last. He was living a kind of strict monastic Rule, only all by himself, sleeping on the earth and starting his prayers in the middle of the night. And it was working! The Tuaregs were coming in! Yes, one knows the usual scoff; that the slightly insane, the "Afflicted of God," are treated with respect. But it wasn't so. They were calling him the Christian Marabout, the "Good Man"; they came to his tiny home-made church to see what kind of a God could fashion a man like that. By and by that church even boasts a real bell. Back on Oran quay over a thousand miles away is a huge barrel consigned to Père de Foucauld down in the desert, and of course it must be altar-wine. What a pity! With the heat of the interminable journey it will all go sour. And from rail-head for hundreds of desert miles the Legion outposts, the Devil-May-Cares of Hollywood Heroics, are sparing a little of their precious water to damp that cask and keep it cool. Then it isn't wine, but a bell sent by some admirer in France. Father Charles is getting famous.

Even in Tuareg social circles he was becoming a notable! He knew more than any other white man of the language and customs. He was translating the Holy Scriptures; for light recreation he was compiling a Tuareg dictionary. Those people had their princes of a sort, and he knew them and himself ranked as a kind of chief and adviser. He even found and translated such Tuareg poetry as there was; but it must never be published in Paris under his name. Had Our Lord written books for publicity? Very well, then! And when the troops advanced so many more leagues and built a new *poste* and meant to call it "Fort de Foucauld," Father Charles with his terrible and uncompromising Latin logic forbade that too.

France recognized him, of course, and the great people were his friends. There was Marshal Lyautey as his staunch admirer; he could have a cavalry escort any time from this place to that. But no! That one needs no escort; he can walk alone where a regiment could never go. There was Colonel Laperrine, one of the tremendous figures of the *Sud*, and as a cadet he had been at the Academy with Father Charles; he never followed him into religion, but he was his lifelong friend. That was the man who tried the first aeroplane flight across the desert; the thing crashed and drove his ribs through his pulped body. They were trying to bring him back, carrying him by day and camping every night. The army of Africa has a discipline, and each night the colonel punctiliously drew his ration of water; but when it was dark he put it back into the common supply, for he knew himself a dying man. That was the man who was the great friend of Father Charles. There was a camel he once sent him, and the priest was most grateful; it was the very thing wanted to carry some altar furniture to a new oratory in the still more remote desert. What a fine chance, too, for a little joyous penance for sins of a lifetime back. Some of those camels can go quite fast, and of course a man can always run behind the beast.

Did Père de Foucauld ever stop belonging to the African army in his spirit? And one suspects that at the back of the human part of his mind he always remained a soldier. Here in his "parish" were those hundred-thousand souls to be recruited for the standard of Christ the Captain; the Sahara was Satan's citadel, something to be stormed with many Masses, besieged with infinite prayer. Certainly he was a soldiers' priest, almost a soldiers' idol. There was his famous ride to Taghit, and down in Africa the story has passed almost into legend. That place is a *poste*, the first fort in the real desert. Over the gateway is a stone, and it says that—Here the Undermentioned, so many men of such-and-such a company under Captain So-and-So, such-and-such another company and so forth, they held out for four days against six thousand armed Moors. There were four hundred and seventy of that garrison. At the start. Then when the news reached Beni-Abbes, nothing would serve Père de Foucauld but that he must borrow a horse and go to Taghit at once. It is seventy-five miles; but desert miles. And he was off on the instant without an escort. It took twenty-three hours, and he was in time to find forty-nine wounded still alive. He remained twenty-five days in that fort and was given an officer's room and never once slept in it. The place of the chaplain of the Sahara was with his wounded.

That, by the way, was in 1903; and in 1935 I was visited in London by an old man carrying a brown-paper parcel. As a young man he had served in the Legion, he said, and he had tried to write out some of his memories; could I look at the manuscript and advise him how to get it printed? He had seen things. Yes, he had even seen Père de Foucauld. He had been one of the wounded in Taghit Fort when that one came riding in from his twenty-three hours' ride. That was at nine o'clock in the morning, and he did not take one single minute for rest or food or even drink. It was straight off his horse and in with the wounded. The old man was proud he had seen Père de Foucauld; it was something to remember. Certainly Father Charles was a soldiers' priest!

Certainly, too, he never stopped being a Frenchman. Indeed we are not sure that he did not die for being a Frenchman, for when his earthly story came to an end in 1916 he was murdered by unknown natives at his chapel in the Sahara. Now why? He had next to nothing to steal; he had no local enemies. But it was war-time; this man had more influence over the tribes than any other white man, and his influence was French. And one suggestion is that he was assassinated by hired agents of an enemy power. We do not know. An odd thing, however, is that while his two native catechumens were found later as skeletons, the body of Father Charles was said to be mummified. "Incorrupt" is a word which we must not at present use of that body, but other people are wondering the same thing! The Saint of the Sahara, and will he one day be canonized?

There is one thing more to say. All those years in the desert, he had prayed for helpers; can we possibly say that he wanted a "Community" of Solitaries, men vowed to God? He had his Rule drawn up and approved, but there was nobody to share it. One man came out as a sort of disciple, an ex-zouave[14] of the African army; zouaves are strong men, but that one failed to stand the severity of the life and had to go back and find another vocation. Father Charles was still alone. He had even prayed for Sisters, and outlined the marvelous work they might do under God. But of course it was impossible. No woman could go out there. It was all a glorious dream, and had Père de Foucauld failed? He had done his life-work, and a marvelous work it had been. Was it now to die with him?

And years later those prayers are answered. The miracle has come. There is an Order of "Brothers of the Solitude" and they are in the desert and living the Rule. There are even the Sisters, too, of the many prayers, not at present in the desert but praying and planning for the desert from a "Solitude" in France. Père de Foucauld's work is not dead but alive; the Legion of the Lord is arming for the conquest of the Sahara.

[14] ZOUAVE—A French infantryman recruited in Algeria.

FOR DISCUSSION

1. Give a brief description of Charles de Foucauld's youth. What great feat did he first perform?

2. God has various ways of indicating a vocation. Trace the steps by which Père Charles' vocation developed. Why did this wealthy, cultured Frenchman embrace a life in the great Sahara Desert with all its terrors for the white man?

3. On what occasion did Père de Foucauld "lapse" into luxury? Was the lapse justified? What was its purpose?

4. What do you know of the heroic priest's death? Why are we uncertain of all the details?

5. Why does the author say that Père de Foucauld's work did not die with him?

WORDS THAT GIVE MEANING TO THE NARRATIVE

1. In speaking of the Arabs, the author says, "They are *nominal* Mohammedans, but with their distinctive customs." The word *nominal* is derived from *nomen*, the Latin word for *name*. What is the meaning, then, of the sentence quoted above? List as many words as you can which are derived from *nomen*. Use each one in a sentence.

2. Below are some quotations from the story. Give a synonym for each of the italicized words to show that you understand the meaning of each sentence.

a. "They settled down together to plot out the details of that *incredible* journey."

b. ". . . he had to learn to *cringe* convincingly."

c. ". . . one man's courage and endurance and resource matched against a *barbarous* and bitterly *hostile* nation . . ."

d. ". . . but for the rest De Foucauld was a professed *infidel*."

e. "Now before the *irrevocable* life-vows are taken, the man leaves the Trappists. . . ."

f. ". . . but for the most part it is desert, an *infinity* of either sand or of sand with patches of black rock."

A PROJECT

Père de Foucauld was a Trappist for a while. To see the heroic lives these religious lead, gather some information on that strict order. There are several communities of Trappists in the United States; perhaps the most famous is that at Gethsemane in Kentucky.

RELATED READING

William Stanton by William Kane is the biography of a modern American hero of God.

Cratylus, "Breaker of Men," had determined to serve only one who was stronger than he and who showed no weakness. With this philosophy, he easily became a victim of the Power of Evil. It was a revolting discovery for him that he was really a slave, not merely a servant, to his master, the devil. Later when it was revealed to him that the Cross was strongest of all and that even Satan cowered under its power, he determined that Christ should be his master. How he became the patron-saint of travelers and was named St. Christopher is an interesting story.

THE LEGEND OF SAINT CHRISTOPHER, BREAKER OF MEN

C. C. MARTINDALE, S.J.

It was while Cratylus was at school that he got his nickname, Breaker of Men. This was not because he was a bully, or brutal, or hurt for the pleasure of hurting. No doubt he had his fights, a good many of them; and always conquered in the sense that he was never frightened however big his enemy might be, and never gave in simply because he was hard hit. (And to tell the truth it was not long before everyone was quite content to do without fighting Cratylus.) But it was because the old schoolmaster had traveled a little, and was ready to teach Greek, even, to those whose parents would let them learn; and the *Iliad* so fascinated Cratylus that Homer[1] became the fashion.

How Cratylus adored Achilles! Achilles the man-breaker, the lion-souled! He could see him distinctly in imagination, upon the famous day when, raging at the death of Patroclus, the hero came out from his tent, armorless, just as he was, glorious like a sun. He could picture him standing there, settling himself, legs well apart, back hollow, hand to mouth, and then shouting! . . . And, at that shout, the despicable Trojans scuttling like so many wretched hares! He looked a young Achilles himself that day, though his hair was dark, not yellow, as he stood reading out the Homer; his boy's white cloak, wrapped over his shirt, could not hide how splendidly he was built, how easily and firmly he stood: as he unrolled

[1] HOMER—Great Greek poet. See page 373 of this book for a translation of some of his most interesting work. Achilles (ȧ·kĭl′ēz) was the great and strong hero of Homer's *Iliad*.

"The Legend of Saint Christopher, Breaker of Men" by C. C. Martindale, reprinted by permission of Burns Oates & Washbourne, Ltd., London.

and rolled the papyrus, you could see the muscles running clearly up and down his arm. The class saw it, and kicked applause with their heels against the benches. "Rhexénor! Rhexénor!" they murmured; "Breaker of Men!"

The old schoolmaster sighed. He was a Christian; and so, in name at least, was Cratylus. But father and mother were dead; and grandmother and schoolmaster and ignorant parish priest had no slightest influence over him. No doubt he had heard of God and Christ and devil; but life was so full of splendid and vigorous things to do, of pleasant things to look at and listen to, that he never troubled his head about what you could neither see nor hear. Not that he practised evil: sheer life and its opportunities of successful effort were quite enough for him.

People were inclined to wonder, at first, why Cratylus apprenticed himself to the larger of the two village smithies, instead of going soldiering at once, as he always said he meant to do. Possibly it was because he felt he was not wholly king here yet—in this little Armenian hamlet that must first be subdued before he went for larger fields. And certainly he succeeded: he became, as was inevitable, unlimitedly popular on account of his strength, his immense good humor, and his good looks. He succeeded, too, in another way. Not only in athletics and in the smithy, nothing could conquer him, but *people* too seemed to become useless when he was there; he could afford to neglect them; they could just pack up and go. Folks guessed this when the smaller smithy was closed. There was no call in the village for two smiths, when Cratylus worked for one of them. And the poor old craftsman, grown gray in Zandruanda, had, quite inevitably, to seek new trade elsewhere. Cratylus was sorry; but could he help it? Was he to work badly for a poorer workman's sake? Clearly not. The Breaker of Men became truer to his name: he set definitely before himself these two principles—"I will only serve a master who is stronger than myself"; and, "I will serve no one whom I shall see afraid." Given this resolve, his days in Zandruanda were numbered: for as to strength, in the whole countryside none equalled him: as to fear, he saw, one day, his master panic-stricken.

It was when the great bull broke loose, and plunged bellowing down the narrow street, scattering the inhabitants like sheep. The smith, too, took to his heels; but Cratylus, as the bull thundered towards him, was aware only of a sudden sheet of flame, which seemed to flood his thighs and sides and neck, and of the uncontrollable impulse which flung him at the brute, and which drove his hands at its horns. He twisted its huge head suddenly down and sideways, forcing the beast's body of its own tremendous impetus to hurtle forward, snapping the spine. The bull died with a roar, and over it stood Cratylus, laughing. It was unbelievable; a feat of giants, of Titans! The story grew; details were added, or modified; it became a myth. The bull, people told, had been colossal in size and weight; had snorted fire; had had hoofs of iron; Cratylus with one blow had felled him; or had swung him aloft like a puppy and dashed him to the ground. But to the hero of all this, one only fact stood out. The smith had fled; his master was a coward. "I have had enough of this," said Cratylus. "Next chance I get, I go."

That very evening the chance came.

A battalion of soldiers marched through the village, at their head a Roman centurion. For a helmet-buckle to be mended, they made for the forge; and there, framed in the doorway, limbs crimson in the firelight, stood Cratylus, swinging his great hammer. In the strong glow, the splendid muscles of chest and shoulders and rhythmically swinging arms and planted legs showed indomitable.

"Gods! what a man for the War-god!" shouted the centurion. "Will you come with us, lad? Will you join us?"

For answer, Cratylus flung down his hammer.

"I've done with *that!*" said he.

And so that was the end of his boyhood and life at Zandruanda; for in spite of his old grandmother's prayers, he left next day with the centurion. "Stay with me, dear lad," the old woman had asked, "and take care of me. There are only a very few months left. Else I shall be all alone. I have no one at all but you."

"Cheer up, old mother," he had cried. "Abroad I shall get gold in quantities, and you shall have it, and instead of this hut you shall have a stone house, and live like a queen for the rest of your days. If I stay here what can I do for you?"

Suddenly the air of Zandruanda had seemed to have grown suffocating; village life was flat—meaningless—in fact, no life at all. How had he stood it for so long?

"I shall die in this home, my darling," said the old woman. "But go, if go you must; and Jesus be your strength."

With a laugh and a parting cheer Cratylus rode off, helmeted and sworded already; all Armenia, with its mountains, lay before him, and the mysterious East beyond; or Thessaly, perhaps, where Achilles came from; and eternal Rome, even, where the Emperor lived!

He rode off; and it was incredible how few of the inhabitants, who all of them turned out to wave their hero a farewell, were really sorry that he went.

Only, in her poor plaster cabin, the old woman who loved him wept bitterly; and while she wept, and afterwards, prayed earnestly for Cratylus.

> And make me feel it was my sin,
> As though no other sin there were,
> That was to Him who bore the world
> A load that He could scarcely bear.
>
> *Faber*

During the next few years Cratylus traveled far, seeing many lands, serving many masters, all of whom, one after the other, proved weaker than himself, or showed themselves to be afraid. Then Cratylus would leave them, feeling himself humiliated by their weakness; and in this way very soon there was no country nor prince for whom he had not a certain contempt; love for his own home (if it had ever really existed) had died out, long ago, when with such fatal ease he had made himself its lord. He passed through that home, however, when he set out at last on his eastward journey. Rome he had seen, and had scorned that degenerate Empire. Of what use to him were its high posts, which money bought, —which were mere soft sinecures [2] for the idle noble who should win them? Thessaly, rich plain ringed with high mountains, had long ago forgotten Achilles,

[2] SINECURES (sī′nē·kūrs)—Offices with rewards but few duties.

and even its famous breed of horses was effete. So he set his face towards the East: who knew what fate awaited him in Bactria, in Sogdiana, or India itself? And, as he crossed Armenia, he passed through Zandruanda. It was long before he even recognized its neighborhood, so shrunken had it all become to his man's eyes; so decrepit, unpopulated, seemed the village. It was his birthplace, a flatterer reminded him. Making an effort, he recalled those old boyhood days. How had he existed, he asked himself, in that cramped life? Wondering thus, he forgot to look for the forge; and he could not identify the cottage where his old grandmother had lived three lonely months, upon the neighbors' alms, after his departure. Indeed, he wholly forgot her too, and forgot to ask to see her grave. Nor, indeed, could he have seen it (had he found a guide who could remember where it was), so overgrown was it with nettles.

During these twenty years his strength had increased, at first, and had then grown set; his body had become hard and rugged, and its beauty diminished. The expression of his face changed only towards anger or contempt, sometimes to disgust, when the stale days of reaction after some marked triumph had to be lived through. He had had enough triumphs now to find the sweetness gone even from them; but tasteless indeed were the hours when no effort was being made, no hard enterprise pursued. The old popularity was long ago departed. He loved no one, and was hated by many, whom, in his serenely unconscious power, he had trampled out of existence. His life had been more than once attempted, but he had always broken his man.

At last, on the furthest limit of the mysterious East, he thought he had found his heart's desire. The King there lived in a high fortress, all of a piece, it seemed, with the naked jumble of iron-colored crags on which it stood, so sheer did the precipice sweep upward into walls, so tiny the windows which pierced square-topped towers rising abruptly like the broken peaks of that high mountain. Only from the north could the fortress be approached; and the winding causeway was throughout commanded by smooth black bastions and guarded battlements. On east and south and west an immense view stretched, range upon range of mountains, jagged as the teeth of saws, fainter and fainter, one behind the other, down to the horizon.

Cratylus became the King's right-hand man; winning all but the supreme power, which was vigorously guarded by the tyrant. In his square, stone room (at the top of a corner tower, and absolutely bare save for a pile of fleeces for a bed, a large stone pitcher of water, and racks of armor) Cratylus thought out the plans which should reduce into an even more absolute obedience the vast kingdom; and wholly without ruth or pity did the King have them carried out. On embassies, Cratylus could cow the haughtiest of foreign princes into submission. His rule seemed like the very mountains, made of iron and stone.

And yet this, too, had its finishing.

With an almost unreasoning severity, as it seemed, the King waged war against the complicated witchcrafts and magic rites which he knew existed among his people. Even to that far country Christianity had, in perverted forms, penetrated; and Devil-worship and hideous travesties of the sacrament[3] were mingled with the abominable practices of pagan superstitions.

One evening the King and Cratylus and some half-dozen men-at-arms were at supper in the great hall. Through the high row of westward windows the setting sun flamed in, making great red-hot squares of light on the wall opposite and leaving the high vault dark. Only over the King an oil lamp spluttered, and in the middle of the hall stood a high brazier.[4] Suddenly the door crashed open. A body of soldiers, evidently guarding a prisoner in their midst, burst in; they rushed up to the dais, dragging the wretched creature with them, and a storm of execration arose. At last it could be seen that they held in their grasp a very old woman. She was a magician, they cried. Only yesterday, on being refused alms by a poor woman with a baby at her breast, she had taken the child in her arms and dandled it, and kissed it, and that very night it had fallen into convulsions, and today it was dead. They had brought her to the King: let him punish her—make an example of her!

Furious at being defied by an old woman, the King demanded nothing more. The old crone remained silent, but he would ask no questions, seek no defense.

"To the brazier with her!" he shouted. "Let us see whether she will like the kiss of coal! Let us see whether she, too, has blood that fire can drink!"

[3] TRAVESTIES OF THE SACRAMENT—Impious imitations of the Holy Eucharist.

[4] BRAZIER (brā′zhẽr)—An open pan for holding live coals.

Silence for a moment, and then the sudden crackle of burning flesh, as a red coal, held in tongs, was pressed upon the old woman's lips. And then a shriek; and then, from that flayed mouth, a stream of blasphemy.

"Curse you," she screamed; "the devil curse you—may the devil curse you! He that has made of the world a pestilence, curse you body and soul, flesh and brain and soul for the hurt you are doing me. . . ."

And as she shrieked on the devil she shrivelled suddenly and fell. The frame of the very old cannot resist much agony; and as the soldiers, with iron pincers, put coal after coal to her, she died.

They carried her away, and there was silence again.

The King sat, bent completely double, his face on his knees, his hands clasping his head. But his fingers, Cratylus saw, glistened with sweat, and his hair was matted.

Cratylus leaned over him.

"Gods!" he cried. "Has she bewitched you too? Are you dying? Lift your face."

The King lifted a face pale and full of shadows. His eyes moved restlessly with a hunted look, and his lips could not stay still.

Cratylus knew that look. It was terror.

"Are you afraid?" he asked, incredulous.

"Of the devil!" said the King. "She cursed me by the devil! It has been the terror of my life. O, have mercy upon me! The whole world is his, and she his favorite. . . . What will the devil do to me?"

Without a word Cratylus left the hall,

and the King sank completely to the floor, where he lay shuddering violently and sobbing.

Alone in his tower-chamber, Cratylus cursed his fate. Another failure, or futile triumph! Another coward! Another of these mighty potentates trembling and aghast when *he* stayed wholly fearless. How he despised them all, these high monarchs of the earth, of whom he had just seen the highest fall to tears and sweat at the curse of an old woman! He looked out over the sea of tumbled mountains and valleys, all gloom and glow alternately beneath a sky still red-hot with sunset, but darkening rapidly. The immense outlook lashed his despondency. Oh to meet the One who could really rule all that! Who should fear nothing in it—know no law but his own sovereign will! how Cratylus would fall down and adore him! And the kingdoms of the world and the glory of them rolled out into a great vision before him, there in the conflagration of the sunset so soon to sink to ashes. To meet with their real master! to serve him, whomsoever he might be, even were he that devil at thought of whom the King had trembled.

The sun dipped, and the last mountain blackened. An extraordinary silence grew rapidly, and suddenly Cratylus was aware of the silence. Not a sound within the castle, or in its courts; not a noise of dog that barked, nor even the whirr of beetle's wing or bat's; nor even the sigh of the wind. He sat there numbed, and the silence grew in the darkness, all round him, and within him.

Then, in the black and horrible stillness, he knew distinctly that he was not alone. There was a presence in the room, close to him. Though it had now grown absolutely dark, surer was he than if his eyes had seen it, that a dreadful thing was there; a *person*, someone who was as vividly aware of him as he was of his awful visitor, whose will was compelling his own, and forcing him to submission. It made him fall on his knees; it made him listen as if for words, and be ready for an extraordinary conversation. But a bewilderingly contradictory impression mingled with all this: he felt that this appalling Force would prove to be—could he really grasp it, get at its essence—something weak. And for a moment he actually saw, in the dense gloom, a white and sickly face, smiling with foolish lips into his eyes. An impression of utter corruption came upon him; the extreme of loathsomeness, a very filth of rottenness, was here: and yet it had its fascination; it commanded him; he felt, as he crouched, face on the stones, as if his whole self was streaming out of his keeping into it; and, as he gave himself, through and through, over and over, into its power, he knew for certain *that this was the devil, the Prince of Evil whom he had accepted for his master*; and he felt on his cheek as it were a sickening kiss, and in the very roots of his heart a chain that bound him, for all time, to sin. He consented.

The next few years in the life of Cratylus were too horrible for us to speak much of. He did not leave the King, as of course he had resolved on doing; yet it was not as the King's servant that he remained. For the supreme authority which, in the old days, had remained in the monarch's hands, now passed over, in all but the barest theory, to Cratylus.

For never before had strength, both of body and of will-power, seemed so extraordinary in the Armenian; though this was not really wonderful, since so tightly was he bound to his new master that all that master's power and will seemed to have passed into him, and what the devil willed, Cratylus could do, nay *must* do. And the panic which the King had always felt for the Evil one, he now felt in regard to Cratylus, so completely did he identify (and rightly) master and man.

And so for hideous sin and crime there never had been such a time as that. Never so many unjust wars that drenched the country in the blood of the fallen and the tears of the survivors. Never such oppression of the poor, bringing sweat and sickness and starvation to the people, and sleepless nights to the rich who lived in agonies of fear concerning the gold they had got, and agonies of greed for gains still to be extorted. Never such false judgments in the courts, widow and orphan perishing before unjust judges. Never such mad and brutal pleasures, drunkenness and sin rotting men's brains and limbs after they had drugged the soul to death. And in this matter of souls was it that Cratylus seemed another man, and did truly devil's work. Hitherto he had been content to quell men's bodies; to break into an external obedience the men and women who resisted him. Of interior submission he had recked not at all. Now it was the whole man, body and soul, that he longed to smash; soul above all, since it was there that Christian faith, especially, established citadels which his terrorizing had failed to carry. Grind men's bodies as he would to powder, there had been impregnable fortresses of patience, and forgiveness, and purity left intact. Now by most loathsome trickeries and cajoleries (since he made use of arts to which he never, before, would have stooped) no less than by sheer cruelties he sought his ends, and never rested till everywhere he had lit the fires of fury and vengeance in the hearts of young men; crushed maidens under shame more dreadful than any death; driven the aged to despair. Hell's kingdom filled fast.

And all this while there kept growing within him a double mood. He hated more and more the abominable master whom he served, and whom he felt always at his side, prompting, suggesting, congratulating. He loathed that master, and he loathed himself, feeling himself the slave, not merely the servant, of that tyrant-force.

And yet that it was master, and himself a slave, he never doubted for a moment. In fact he saw, with horror, that in no way could he ever break, even should he wish it, from that slavery. But to wish to break away was just what he could not do: "He is too strong for me," he said in despair. "The Devil is my master for always; I shall go on doing his work for always. *It is too strong for me: I cannot help myself.*"

And so at the time of his greatest worldly strength, Cratylus felt himself most weak; when most powerful for evil, he was most a slave; everywhere he did devil's work; everywhere *it was too strong for him.*

And yet the devil was not strongest of all.

There was a hermit who lived some leagues away beside a river, and, by holding up his lantern at night, showed the ford to travelers. Cratylus would make an end of that; nothing of good was too trivial for him to prevent; nothing too high for him to fear. So that lantern, he determined, should be extinguished; that little act of charity suppressed. And as for the old saint himself, might not he too be conquered, his high virtue spoiled?

He set out for the river, which he could see winding in the valley, suddenly broad after spouting from the mountains through a chasm only a few feet wide. He mused on how he should approach the hermit, and as he mused, a shrinking made itself felt within him, a reluctance to go at all. He wrestled against it, and dragged his feet along the path, exhausted more and more every moment, struggling as in a nightmare.

Suddenly he realized that it was the masterful presence that was near him; that was tugging at him to come back . . . must he not obey? And then once more he was conscious, not only of its power but of that bewildering *weakness* he had guessed at before. And now—could it be?—it was cowering, shuddering backwards because of *fear!* Cratylus set his teeth. He would go forward. He planted his feet and bowed his body towards the hermit's hut, only a yard or two away, now. The huge power, like great arms about his waist, strained at him, tearing him backwards. Never had he experienced so vigorous a wrestle. Whence came his power to resist?

Suddenly the hermit appeared at the door, holding up a large wooden Cross.

The hermit advanced a step.

"Back, Satan!" he said. "In this sign I conquer."

Abruptly, as though a chain had snapped, Cratylus was loosed. He fell violently forward at the foot of the Cross, his head striking a stone. He remained for a space unconscious.

When he revived he was lying on a pile of ferns, and the hermit was bathing his forehead.

Thoroughly ashamed of this position, Cratylus sat up, but fell back dizzy.

"What has happened?" said he.

"You are a free man," answered the hermit. "Your master left you."

Cratylus began to remember.

"He was afraid of the Cross," went on the other. "He was not so strong as the Cross."

Cratylus recalled everything—the years of slavery, the sudden snapping of the chain, the Cross high over him as he fell.

"Henceforward," said he in a strong voice, "I will be the servant of the Cross."

Later, as his dazedness passed away, he began to make his plans.

"I will fight, father," he began. "I am strong. I will fight the King, and upset his wicked judges, and break the prisons, and rebuild all I have destroyed."

The hermit laughed quietly.

"All that may come," said he. "You have other work to do first."

Cratylus had a troubled recollection that pious Christians prayed and fasted and scourged themselves even. . . .

"Must I pray, father?" he asked.

"You shall pray in good time," said the old man, still smiling. "For the present, work; and I will pray."

"Tell me what to do, father," said the Breaker of Men, "and I will do it."

"It is not hard," said the other. "You will live with me, and you shall carry on your shoulders all travelers who wish to cross the ford. That shall be your work."

And Cratylus labored long at this simple task, making himself servant of the wayfarers who came to the river. It was a strange career, full of humiliations wholly unexpected—as when those whom of old he had commanded, or evicted from their homes, or in any other way oppressed, now came to speak insolently to him, and jeer at him, or kick him as he carried them. For the rumor had spread that Cratylus had gone crazed; that the blow on his head had made a fool of him; and in proportion as he had been hated, so was he now contemned. Even this was not so painful to him as the terror shown by many—women especially and children—who did not understand the change. They could realize nothing but that here was their persecutor of yore—what cruelty, subtle and refined, was he not planning that he was fain to carry them over rivers? What diabolical craft was this? And they fled from him.

Cratylus in time ceased to wax furious at the insults, though never to suffer at the fear the women and children showed when they saw him. Only in both cases he repeated to himself, "For Thee, Crucified," and went on with his labor. That was his only prayer. He still felt bewildered, not least by the strangeness of his appointed task. He knew nothing of Christ, but did what he was told was His work, and gradually his heart was changed.

In the idle spaces when no travelers passed, he would watch the hermit praying, and thus became familiar with long passages of the psalms and of the Church's liturgy; at other times he explored the mountains, which fell, just there, in an immense black precipice, sheer to the plain where the river flowed. The water itself he tracked, once, into its ravine. This chasm was thought to be a gate to hell, and the country folk never dared to approach it. Cratylus, who was determined now to fear not even the devil, waded against the mighty current into the very heart of the mountain, and there, clambering over boulders, he could see in the dim light which filtered from the tiny strip of sky, far above, that the water gushed out, in tremendous force, from beneath the base of a kind of rock funnel in which the fissure terminated. This huge volume of water, forced upwards, it was clear, by some subterranean stream, welled up at first silent and black like sliding ebony; then, flinging itself against the narrow walls of the chasm, it foamed, booming through the echoing rocks, until it suddenly spread itself out over the pebbly ford.

In the spring the work was made infinitely harder by the melting snows and sudden storms, which sent the river up in great floods. One night Cratylus, having labored all day against the swollen current, was heavily asleep in the hut when he felt himself shaken briskly by the shoulder. He looked up and saw at his side the hermit, with a strangely glad look upon his face.

"Up," said the hermit, "you are being called."

Cratylus could not believe it. An appalling storm was raging, with thunder and wind and torrential rain. The ford would be impassable, and who could be abroad on such a night?

"Up," repeated the old man, a little sternly, "to the work!"

Cratylus arose and quitted the house. The wind tore the door from his hand and crashed it shut behind him. The very footpath leading down to the river had become a rivulet of rain. Over the shingly ford the river escaped, hissing and rushing with a curiously shrill sound; but in the chasm, as it flung itself violently from side to side in the blackness, it sent up the most terrible bellowing, even louder than the thunder.

In spite of thunder, though, and stream, Cratylus heard a wailing voice, inexpressibly sad and fearful, calling for help.

"Carry me across!" it cried. "Help me! Fetch me across."

There was a sudden sheet of dazzling lightning in which every detail of the further bank showed clear in black and white. And on it stood a little boy, very thin and weak looking; he was dressed only in a shirt, and his hair and linen were streaming with the rain. And his hands were clasped tight to his breast as he stooped a little and cried to be fetched across.

Cratylus, without waiting to wonder at this extraordinary spectacle, plunged into the river and was soon at the other side.

"Right!" shouted Cratylus. "Where are you?"

In the next flash he saw the little boy. He was still standing by the brink of the water, soaked and shivering, but silent now.

"Right!" cried Cratylus again, shocked at the boy's thinness. "We shall be across in no time, and there's a fire waiting for you. Up with you! Arms round my neck tight; don't be afraid of hurting me. Good."

The boy, with astonishing agility, climbed on to the strong man's shoulder and sat there with one hand round his neck. He was so light that Cratylus scarcely knew when he was up.

"Now for it," he said. "Sit tight."

And he turned and went down into the stream.

The storm had not ceased, and the flood, flung violently forward from the bellowing chasm, swept even higher than before about his knees; the cold of the rain, after the warm hut, seemed to freeze his blood. Almost at once he stumbled, and only saved himself from slipping back by bending double over his huge staff. To raise himself required effort; his knees grew weak, and his shoulders bowed beneath the impact of the wind, of the weight of which he had now grown all too sensible. For as he drew himself once more upright he seemed crushed; a tremendous strain made itself felt all through him as he went forward, step by painful step. And though the storm howled in the ravine, and the waters roared and hissed loud as ever, all that suddenly seemed to be happening at an immense distance; within himself he was immediately conscious only of grinding exhaustion and intolerable fatigue. Then, in that silence of his soul he seemed to be aware of all the whole world. The storm and river and ravine had grown so unimportant, because he seemed to feel at one and the same time, all the masses of all the mountains of that land, ponderous piles of rock, titanic boulders beating against the sky—all the huge oceans that swung terrifically against its coasts, and against the coasts of all the lands he had ever traveled through—and in a moment he had, as it were, a vision of the whole gigantic Earth, the overwhelming globe of seas and islands and continents, and all looming down on him, all posed upon his shoulders. And more than that: infinite tracts of clouds swathed that hugeness; and through these clouds other huge worlds swung round or hung, infinitely vast, and all to be held by him. For, unless he supported it, what should prevent its ruin? On whom else did it depend, all that universe of matter and of motion? Not on that Enemy whom he had served! He was the destroyer, the universal antagonist! Not on the paltry race of humans, so pitiably weak, whom he himself had crushed and broken like gnats! Satan hated that universe; men were mere phantoms in it. It rested on *his* shoulders; could *he* uphold it? And he saw himself, stronger than his fellow men, no doubt; yet, compared to that sum of all things now massed upon him, he too was weak like a ghost or dream. What was the world to do? What could *he* do? "O God Almighty," he panted, "have mercy on me."

He moved a few steps easily. Then a second time the terrific weight pressed down on his shoulders, and he moved through the water, crouching almost double. And this time an added horror broke him. For in the vast globe of all the universe he saw that there was *sin*. The pitiable race of human people, of which he was one—(he saw that, now; he was just one of many, equally responsible, unprivileged—nay, more responsible in that he was stronger than his fellows, though certainly not greater just because of that)—this weak race rose up, and in the face of the Power which kept them and their whole world in being, declared for their own will and supremacy. Cratylus stood in a sudden panic. Surely the Power, in scorn of all that insolence, would let go of the world; would simply let the universe, with the miserable revolutionaries in it, roll back into the nothingness whence it originally had come? And he seemed to feel the world left more and more to himself to bear; felt, too, more and more his own incredible dependence on that great Power; realized what had been *his* share in that appalling arrogance and revolt. "O God, most Merciful," he gasped, "be merciful to me, a sinner."

The bank was in sight already, but even as he pressed forward to cross the remaining water, there came down upon his bowed shoulders a new and wholly unconquerable load. Raised upon that sinful world, which he was struggling to carry, was a Cross, and on the Cross was lifted all the sin and all the sorrow of that world from its beginning to its distant end. It was all summed up in that hanging figure, and Cratylus felt it. And with it the pressure of the infinite Love which had brought the Son of God so to take upon himself that sin, and by that sorrow to atone for it. And beneath the triple burden of his new humility and repentance and love, Cratylus at last fell forward, crying as he fell, "I cannot bear it; Jesus, Thou knowest that I love Thee; save me, or I perish."

Cratylus fell, but found that his hands struck the further bank, and he was safe. The little boy slipped from his shoulder, and held out his hand. Cratylus took it, and stepped on to dry land, and looked into the Child's eyes. He knelt down, still looking, and then bowed till his face touched the ground. He had watched the wonderful change come over the Child's form and features, and, though he had never seen Him before, knew Him.

"I am Jesus," said the Child. "I am He through whom all the world was made and is preserved. In carrying Me, you carried the whole world. And I am He who, in My own body, carried your sins and all the sins of the world; and of their weight I suffered you to feel as it were the shadow. And now you know that it is I who carry you, and ever have carried, and ever shall."

"Lord," said Cratylus, speaking like a little child, "how was it, long ago, that I did not perish; that you did not, for my service of Satan and my oppression of your elect, long ago condemn me?"

"Because," answered the Child, "there never has been the time when you were not being rescued by the prayers of those whom you persecuted; of the very weak, like your old grandmother in the village; of your old schoolmaster; of all whom you strove to break; they were too strong for you; and in the end My heart obeyed them, and I have saved you."

"Lord," said the Breaker of Men, "may I be your servant?"

"You shall be my friend," answered Jesus; "and your new name shall be Christopher; for you have carried Christ on your shoulder, and henceforward you shall always carry Him in your heart."

When the hermit came down to the

river at sunrise, he found Christopher still kneeling, and the glorious light, now that the storm was over, made a halo all about him.

◇◇◇◇◇◇◇◇◇◇◇◇◇◇◇◇◇◇◇◇◇◇◇◇◇◇◇◇◇◇◇◇

FOR DISCUSSION

1. Why would Achilles naturally be an early hero of Cratylus? What kind of man did Cratylus want to be? What changes took place in him in the twenty years after he left home?

2. How did Cratylus find himself in the service of Satan? How was he freed?

3. How did the Cross prove to be stronger than the supreme power in the land which the devil had given him?

4. Why was his work at the ford particularly humiliating to Cratylus?

5. What kind of cry seemed to help Cratylus as he fought to ford the river with the Child on his back? What did such a cry show?

6. What reason did the Child give for having put up with Cratylus so long?

7. Why did Cratylus feel that Christ was even stronger than he?

INCREASING YOUR VOCABULARY

Following are listed eight words used in this legend. Do you know their meanings? Write a synonym for each and after it a sentence using the word correctly.

hamlet	impregnable
panic	contemn
hurtle	inevitable
subtle	incredible

A MEANINGFUL EXPERIENCE

Have you ever had an experience which made you feel very deeply the protection of St. Christopher? Perhaps there was the medal in your family car, or maybe you were wearing it at some time when you miraculously escaped an accident. Tell how you felt. Did you immediately associate the St. Christopher medal with your good fortune? Why?

RELATED READING

Read the story of another giant of God in *Saint Among Savages*, a life of Isaac Jogues and his companions, first American martyrs. Father Francis Talbot is the author.

This story is one of a popular series written by an Italian anti-Communist humorist and cartoonist about the standing feud between Don Camillo, burly parish priest, and Peppone, the Communist mayor of a village in northern Italy, somewhere in the valley of the Po River. In this particular story there is hardly more than a hint of this hard-hitting feud. For some of the more rough-and-tumble bouts, read other stories in DON CAMILLO AND HIS FLOCK *and in* THE LITTLE WORLD OF DON CAMILLO. *You will find the inimitable padre taking some hard thumpings but always paying back harder than he receives. Only Christ speaking to him from the big crucifix in the parish church can do much with this hard-headed pastor, and even He finds it sometimes difficult, always slow, going.*

THE UGLY MADONNA

GIOVANNI GUARESCHI

Don Camillo had a thorn in the flesh, one that had annoyed him intensely for a very long time. Once a year it was particularly painful, and that was during the procession in honor of the Assumption. For three hundred and sixty-four days the dim, shadowy chapel afforded concealment, but under the pitiless sun of August fifteenth the true state of affairs was visible to everybody. And it was a serious matter.

She was known as the "ugly Madonna," a phrase which smacked of collective blasphemy. But actually no disrespect toward the Mother of God was intended; this was merely an accurate description of the statue which was the cause of Don Camillo's pain. The statue was a six-foot-tall terra-cotta [1] affair, as heavy as lead, and painted in colors so offensive as to give anyone an eye ache. The sculptor—God rest his soul!—must have been one of the most miserable cheats the world has ever known. If an ignorant but honest man had done the job, no one would have called it ugly. Ignorance is not detrimental to a work of art, because a simple-minded craftsman may put his heart and soul into it and these count for infinitely more than his technical ability. But in this case the sculptor was obviously able and had turned all his skill to the creation of something ugly.

On that day long ago when Don Camillo had set foot in the church for the first time, he was shocked by the statue's ugliness and he determined then and there to replace it with some more fitting

[1] TERRA COTTA—Hard-baked clay.

image of God's Mother. He declared this intention on the spot, and was told to forget it. It was pointed out to him that the statue dated from 1693, and there was a date on the pedestal to prove it.

"I don't care about the date," Don Camillo objected. "It's downright ugly."

"Ugly, but venerably antique," they insisted.

"Venerably antique, but ugly," retorted Don Camillo.

"Historical, Father," they said, insisting upon having the last word.

For several years Don Camillo struggled in vain. If the statue had such historical importance, then it could be sent to a museum and replaced by one with a decent face. Or, if this wouldn't do, it could be moved into the sacristy and thus make way for a more suitable successor. Of course the purchase of another statue would require money. When Don Camillo started to make the rounds with fund-raising in view, he came upon more opposition.

"Replace the ugly Madonna? That statue is historical, and nothing can take its place. It wouldn't be right. Who ever heard of crowding out history?"

Don Camillo gave the project up, but the statue remained a thorn in his flesh, and every now and then he exploded to Christ at the main altar about it.

"Lord, why don't You help me? Aren't You personally offended by the sight of Your Mother in such an unworthy guise? How can You bear for people to call her the 'ugly Madonna'?"

"Don Camillo," Christ answered, "true beauty does not reside in the face. That, as we all know, must one day return to the dust from which it sprang. True beauty is eternal and does not die with the flesh. And the beauty of the Mother of God is in her soul and hence incorruptible. Why should I take offense because someone has carved a woman with an ugly face and set her up as a Madonna? Those who kneel before her aren't praying to a statue but to the Mother of God in Heaven."

"Amen," said Don Camillo.

There was no other answer, but it still troubled him to hear people refer to the "ugly Madonna." He became accustomed to the thorn in his flesh, but every August fifteenth, when the statue was taken down and carried in the procession, the pain was more than he could bear. Once removed from the kindly shadows of the chapel and exposed to the sunlight, the face stood out all too clearly. It was not only an ugly face but an evil one as well; the features were heavy and vulgar, and the eyes expressionless rather than ecstatic. And the Infant Jesus in the Madonna's arms was just a bundle of rags with an empty doll's head sticking out of them. Don Camillo had tried to mask the ugliness of the statue with a crown and necklace and veil, but these had served only to accentuate it. Finally he removed all extraneous ornaments and let the vile coloring show for exactly what it was.

Then war came to the river valley, leaving in its wake death and destruction. Bombs fell upon churches and thieving, sacrilegious hands plundered their altars as they passed by. Don Camillo didn't dare admit it but he secretly hoped that someone would "liberate" him from the "ugly Madonna." When foreign soldiers first appeared upon the scene Don Camillo hurried to the proper authorities to say:

"Our ugly Madonna is a masterpiece dating from 1693, an object of both historical and artistic importance. Shouldn't it be evacuated to a safe place of storage for the duration?"

But they told him to set his mind at rest. Historically and artistically important as the Madonna might be, the fact remained that she was ugly, and this was her best defense. If she hadn't been ugly, she would never have stayed in place for so many years.

The war came to an end, and the first post-war years went by, and then a time came when the thorn in Don Camillo's flesh bothered him most acutely. He had painted the church walls, varnished the imitation marble columns and the wooden railings and gilded the candlesticks on the various altars. As a result, the "ugly Madonna" simply didn't belong. A dark spot on a gray background is not too conspicuous, but on a white one it stands out like a black eye.

"Lord," said Don Camillo, on his knees before Christ. "This time You simply must help me. I've spent all the money I had and some I didn't have on fixing up the church. In order to pay my debts, I've rationed my food and given up cigars. And I rejoice not so much in the beauty of the church as in the God-given strength to sacrifice a few of my comforts. Now, won't You deliver me of the thorn in my flesh? Won't You do something to stop people from calling Don Camillo's church the 'Church of the Ugly Madonna'?"

"Don Camillo, do I have to tell you the same thing over and over?" Christ answered. "Do I have to tell you again that true beauty does not reside in the face, that true beauty cannot be seen, because it is a thing of the spirit, which defies the erosion of time and does not return to the dust whence the body sprang?"

Don Camillo lowered his head without answering. And this was a bad sign.

The feast of the Assumption was drawing near, and one day Don Camillo summoned those who would carry the statue in the procession.

"This year the route followed by the procession will be longer than usual," he told them, "because we must go as far as the newly built houses along the south road."

It was a steaming hot August, and the idea of walking an extra mile over a freshly gravelled road was enough to make even a strong man flinch.

"We might carry the statue in two shifts," suggested old Giarola, who was in charge of arrangements.

"That's dangerous," said Don Camillo. "The sun beats down and the bearers' hands get sweaty and may slip just at the moment of changing. No, I think we might rig up Rebecci's small truck. As a matter of fact, that would add to the dignity of the whole thing, and I don't see any real objections."

In a way the bearers were half sorry, but when they thought of the length of the route and the heat of the sun, they felt relieved and gave their assent. Rebecci was glad to lend his truck, and the next day he brought it to the shed back of the rectory. Don Camillo insisted on decorating it in person, and for a whole week he worked so hard that all over the village they could hear the sound of his hammer. He had built a platform on the back of the truck and then covered it with draperies and flowers, producing a truly magnificent effect. When Sunday came, the "ugly Madonna" was brought out of the church and hoisted up on to the platform. The pedestal was tied down with strong ropes, and these were covered with garlands of flowers.

"You don't have to worry about the driving," Don Camillo said to Rebecci. "Even if you go fifty miles an hour, I guarantee that it will hold fast."

"With all those decorations the Madonna is very nearly beautiful," people said when the truck started.

The procession began to wind its way toward the south road, with the truck moving at the speed of a man's walk. The freshly laid gravel was bumpy and the clutch suddenly got something wrong with it, which jolted the truck so hard that if Don Camillo hadn't tied the pedestal securely to the platform, the "ugly Madonna" would have been out of luck. Don Camillo saw that something was wrong and knew that Rebecci must be worried about it, so when they reached the south road he decided to change the route.

"The truck can't go so slowly over the gravel," he said, "so we'll cut across the fields to the highway. Rebecci will drive back at normal speed and wait for us at the bridge. There we'll re-form the procession and march on a smooth surface all the way back to the center of the village."

Rebecci went dutifully back, and the "ugly Madonna" made the most uncomfortable trip of her long life. The procession re-formed at the bridge and moved smoothly along the paved road, although occasionally Rebecci's clutch caused the truck to leap forward as if someone had given a kick from behind. The village was all decked out, especially the main street, with the arcades on either side, where every house was covered with streamers and people threw handfuls of flowers out the windows. Unfortunately this street was paved with cobblestones, and because the truck had hard tires as well as a broken clutch, it bounced up and down as if it had St. Vitus' dance. But the "ugly Madonna" seemed to be glued to the platform, through Don Camillo's particular merit. Halfway down the main street, however, there was an especially rough bit of paving, punctuated by holes left from the construction of a sewer running below it.

"Once they're over that, there's no more danger," people said. Although they had complete faith in Don Camillo, they left a considerable space between themselves and the bouncing truck.

But the "ugly Madonna" did not get through the danger zone. She didn't fall, because Don Camillo's ropes held her fast, but on a particularly rough bump she just crumbled into pieces. The statue was not made out of terra cotta after all; it was some infernal mixture of brick dust or plaster or who knows what, and after two or three thousand death-dealing blows such as it had just received an inevitable fate overtook it. But the shout which rose from the bystanders was not occasioned by the crumbling of the "ugly Madonna." It was a salute to the "fair

Madonna," which as if by a miracle took its place.

On the pedestal, which was still roped securely to the truck, there emerged, like a butterfly coming out of its cocoon, a somewhat smaller statue of solid silver. Don Camillo stared at it in astonishment, and into his mind came Christ's words: "True beauty does not reside in the face. . . . True beauty cannot be seen, because it is a thing of the spirit, which defies the erosion of time and does not return to the dust whence the body sprang. . . ." Then he turned around, because an old woman was shouting:

"A miracle! A miracle!"

He shouted her down and then stooped over to pick up a fragment of the "ugly Madonna," a piece of one of the expressionless eyes which had once so annoyed him.

"We'll put you together again, piece by piece," he said in a loud voice, "even if it takes us ten years; yes, I'll do it myself, you poor 'ugly Madonna' who concealed and saved this silver statue from one of the many barbarian invasions of the last three hundred years. Whoever hurriedly threw you together to cloak the Silver Madonna made you ugly on purpose, so as not to attract an invader already on the march against this village or some distant city from which you may have originally come. When we have put you together, piece by piece, you shall stand side by side with your silver sister. Quite involuntarily, I brought you to this miserable end."

Don Camillo was telling the most shameless lie of his life. But he could not, in the face of his assembled parish, explain that he had chosen a round-about and rocky route for the procession, blown up the truck tires to the bursting-point, sabotaged the clutch and even abetted the destructive power of holes and gravel by driving a pointed tool into the terra cotta and starting to crack it open, which last effort he had abandoned when he had seen that the material of which the ugly statue was made would crumble of its own accord. He meant to confess it to Christ, Who of course already knew about it. Meanwhile he went on with his peroration.

"Poor 'ugly Madonna,' you saved the silver statue from one of the many waves of barbarian invaders. But who will save the Silver Madonna from the barbarians of today as they press at our frontiers and eye with hatred the citadel of Christ? Is your appearance an omen? Does it mean that the new barbarians will not invade our valleys, or that if they do, our strong faith and powerful arms will defend you? . . ."

Peppone, who was standing in the front row, in order to "observe the phenomenon more closely," turned to his lieutenant, Smilzo: "What's he mean by the 'new barbarians'?" he asked him.

Smilzo shrugged his shoulders. "Just a bit of unbridled clerical imagination."

There was a moment of silence and then the procession continued.

◇◇◇◇◇◇◇◇◇◇◇◇◇◇◇◇◇◇◇◇◇◇◇◇◇◇◇◇◇◇

FOR DISCUSSION

1. What are some of the things you find likeable about Don Camillo?
2. Uncover what evidence you can to show that his people appreciated their pastor.
3. What do you think of the familiar way in which Christ and Don Camillo speak to each other?
4. How do you explain Don Camillo's rejoicing more in the "God-given strength to sacrifice a few of my comforts" than in having beautified God's church?
5. How much truth is there in the author's remark that "ignorance is not detrimental to a work of art"?
6. Whom did Don Camillo mean by "the barbarians of today"?

UNDERSTANDING WORD MEANINGS

1. What does it mean to say that a phrase "*smacked* of collective *blasphemy*"? Why speak of it as *collective* blasphemy?
2. In the dictionary investigate the root meaning of *terra cotta.* At the same time have a look at *terra firma* and *terra incognita,* and use the phrases in sentences.
3. What kinds of ornaments are "*extraneous* ornaments"?
4. What is the meaning of the root word common to *pedestal, pedal,* and *pedestrian?*
5. What is an "infernal mixture"?
6. "Meanwhile he went on with his peroration." What is a *peroration?*

TWO PROJECTS

1. For a non-Catholic friend write a brief, possibly humorous, Don Camillo–type explanation of the place of statues in Catholic devotional life. Before attempting the essay, you might ask that friend what objection a non-Catholic has to the use of statues, so that you may clearly understand his position.
2. Let the class select, and perhaps adapt, one of the Don Camillo stories for use in a speech contest.

RELATED READING

If you enjoyed this story, you will probably want to read more about Don Camillo and Peppone in *Don Camillo's Dilemma.*

A chariot drawn by fiery horses swung to earth and swept up Elijah to heaven in a whirlwind. That's the story in the Bible which the Negro imagination transformed into this famous spiritual. The vision of this redeeming chariot which will sweep every just man's soul to heaven keeps the singer clinging to his personal ideals. Read this spiritual leisurely, spreading out the vowels so that you will get the full effect of the melody.

Swing Low, Sweet Chariot

NEGRO SPIRITUAL

Swing low, sweet chariot,
  Comin' for to carry me home,
Swing low, sweet chariot,
  Comin' for to carry me home.

I looked over Jordan, an' what did I see,
  Comin' for to carry me home?
A band of angels comin' after me,
  Comin' for to carry me home.

If you get-a dere befo' I do,
  Comin' for to carry me home,
Tell all my friends I'm comin' too,
  Comin' for to carry me home.

I'm sometimes up and sometimes down,
  Comin' for to carry me home,
But still my soul feels heavenly bound,
  Comin' for to carry me home.

Swing low, sweet chariot,
  Comin' for to carry me home,
Swing low, sweet chariot,
  Comin' for to carry me home.

FOR DISCUSSION

This Negro singer isn't the only one who has been "sometimes up and sometimes down." You and I have been that way, too; we do not always live up to our best selves. What would you say is the tone of this poem: exaltation, sorrow, indifference, hope? Discuss.

APPRECIATING THE SPIRITUALS

List the titles of as many spirituals as you know. Now look at the simple but descriptive words used in these titles. Which do you think are the most beautiful?

Bring to class, if possible, recordings of Negro spirituals, especially those made by Negro singers. Play them and discuss them in class. Your discussion will be more interesting if one or two volunteers can give oral reports about the history of spirituals. A good source is "History of Spirituals" in *An Anthology of American Negro Literature*, edited by Sylvester C. Watkins.

RELATED READING

There are many more poems as enjoyable as this in J. W. and Rosamond Johnson's collection, *American Negro Spirituals. Singing Cowboy* by M. Larkin and H. Black will give you the same kind of enjoyment. Both music and words are provided.

◇◇◇◇◇

Many men who rise to positions of great importance tend to lose their sense of values and therefore to lose their sense of humor, too. This was not so, you will see, with St. Thomas More.

GOD'S JOKESTER

ALOYSIUS CROFT

Thomas More, Chancellor of England, was hearing Mass. He knelt toward the front of the chapel, his head bowed low in adoration as the priest raised the Sacred Host. The little altar bell tinkled and More poured out his soul in fervent prayer. In the rear there was a scuffling noise, and tiptoed steps came toward the silent figure of the chancellor. A courtier leaned over and whispered to him: "My Lord, His Majesty the king wishes you to come to him at once."

The chancellor looked up somewhat annoyed: "I cannot come now. As soon as Mass is finished I will go to His Majesty."

The messenger nodded and left. More resumed his prayers. It was not five minutes, however, before the same courtier was nudging him respectfully again. "My Lord, the king would have you come *now.*"

Sir Thomas More was silent a moment; then: "Say to the king for me that I am paying court to a greater King than he. My duty to the Greater done, I shall await upon His Majesty at once." The courtier stood amazed—who was this new chancellor—the first chancellor that England had ever had who was not a cardinal or at least an archbishop—who dared send such a message to the king? Sir Thomas noticed the man's hesitation. "Go," he whispered, "and give my message to the king. Remember that it is *my* message—I am responsible." The man left and the chancellor prayed devoutly until the end of Mass.

As More entered the council chamber, the king was studying some reports. His Majesty smiled and held out his hand as More bowed. "So, my Lord Chancellor, you were paying court to a greater King, were you?" More flushed as he answered: "Ay, my Lord, a greater King than any on earth." His Majesty arose and came around the table to lay his

"God's Jokester" from *Twenty-One Saints* by Aloysius Croft. Reprinted by permission of The Bruce Publishing Company.

hand upon the shoulder of his officer. "Good man. And if you but show me the same loyalty which you show our Lord and Master Christ, I will be satisfied. Mayhap Wolsey[1] would have still been living, had he done so. But come, I have business for you."

The king, indeed, was pleased with his new chancellor, and well he might be. More, at that time, was one of the best-known men in Europe. He had been a lawyer first as his father had been before him, and then a sheriff of London, a member of Parliament and of the king's council. Now the king of England, Henry VIII, had made him Lord Chancellor. His reputation, though, did not depend upon his political jobs. His writings alone were enough to make him famous, and he was a friend and teacher to every learned man of Europe.

But his close friends knew other things about him: how he loved to tease and joke—how he loved fun and music and laughter; how kind he was to his family, and how he had taken poorer relatives to live with him even when he had none too much money for his own family. His friends knew also that at one time he had thought of becoming a priest, and that, while studying law, he had lived for four years in a monastery so that he could see just how the monks lived: and that he had been advised by his confessor to give up the idea of the priesthood, marry, and live a good life in the world.

This advice Thomas had taken very seriously. He had married, and had tried to make use of his keen mind for all good causes. His piety and his love for the priesthood he had never given up. He treated his body as though it belonged to someone he did not like—very often his splendid court dress hid a hair shirt, and very often, too, he was hungry because of his strict fasts. But it was only his very closest friends who knew these things—for no one else could tell but what Thomas More was simply a very good man who was living as other wealthy men. Everyone could see, of course, that he was very regular at the sacraments, that he heard Mass every morning—he often sang in the choir, too, and sang none too well—and that Henry VIII, still a Catholic, still a firm defender of the Pope, had taken a great liking to the smiling More. It was not rare to see the king's beautifully decorated barge come down the Thames to stop before the house of More at Chelsea near London. The king and More often walked in the garden, talking over affairs of state, and laughing heartily at some joke of the chancellor's. More's son-in-law once spoke to Sir Thomas about this, and said that he must be very happy that the king was so friendly to him. More, however, knew Henry even better than Henry knew himself. His answer to his son-in-law showed that he was not as we should say "kidding himself" about this: "Son Roper," he said, "I am glad to find that the king is a very good master indeed. But do not be deceived. If my head would win him a castle in France, it would not fail to go."

More knew that trouble was ahead. The king had become tired of his wife Catharine, and had for some time been trying to get the Pope to grant a divorce

[1] WOLSEY—Cardinal Wolsey, chancellor of England immediately before St. Thomas.

so that he might marry a waiting maid, Anne Boleyn.[2] The Pope naturally would not consent, and it was this very quarrel that had caused Henry to dismiss Wolsey, the former chancellor. The bickering between the king and the Pope had gone on, but More was not called upon to take part in it. He could see, though, that things were slowly coming to a head, and knowing Henry as he did, he feared for what might happen.

His worst fears came true. The king was tired of waiting. If the Pope would not grant a divorce, the Pope would pay for it. The king had a law passed by a weak-spined Parliament making him head of the Church in England, and demanding that the bishops and priests take an oath recognizing him as their superior. More knew that it would be only a short time before he too would be called upon to take the oath—he could not take it and be true to his conscience, and so he resigned his office as chancellor.

More, when he gave up his office, knew that he would not be let alone and yet hoped that he might be. He had been a fairly wealthy man while chancellor, but most of his money had been spent in keeping up his household and given away in alms. Now he had nothing. Some of his servants he dismissed; in every way possible he tried to cut down expenses but even now he was happy. Money

[2] ANNE BOLEYN—Henry VIII's second wife and mother of Queen Elizabeth I.

meant nothing to him except that with it he could do a certain amount of good that he could not do without it. The king, however, and those who were counseling him could not allow More to go without taking the oath, for many men took their views from him and while More opposed it they would not take it. An attempt was made to convict him of treason—but he proved the charges to be so foolish that he was released. Time went by—Easter of 1534 passed, and on the Sunday following a summons was given him to appear before the court at Lambeth to take the oath.

On the next morning More left home for the last time. He went to Communion and as soon as Mass was over, set out for Lambeth. The court was ready for him. The oaths were read and he was asked if he would sign his name. "Could he read them himself?" He could. He did and then answered that he would sign the first which had nothing to do with religion directly, but the second—that which declared Henry head of the Church in England—he could not take. Why not? The bishops and priests [3] had. That, said More, was their business—*his* conscience would not allow him to take that oath. More argument, and when the court found that he could not be forced to take the oath, he was hustled off a prisoner to the home of the Abbot of Westminster.

Another day and More was called again. Would he take the oath now? He could not—his conscience would not let him. The judges suggested that maybe a little torture might make his conscience less difficult to deal with. More became angry: "These, my lords, are stories to scare children with. Don't threaten me. I am not afraid of your torture."

To the tower of London went More. He had always thought he might like to be a monk—the prison was bare enough and cold enough to make a good monastery. The jailer apologized for the poor food and bed. More laughed. He didn't mind it so much, he said. "But Master jailer," he went on, "if at any time you find me displeased with your hospitality, just put me out."

There were more questionings, and each time More was more certain that he could not take the oath. At last he was brought to trial for treason. The trial was a farce: false witnesses were brought in and testimony given that made even the judges smile. More himself answered the questions in such a way as to put the judges on trial rather than himself—they feared him and his knowledge of the law—but when it was all over they pronounced him guilty.

For More himself the trial was a relief. At no time had he flattered himself that he was strong enough to be a martyr. He had prayed for light to know what was right and for strength to follow it, but he was never cocksure. Now that he had gone this far, he felt that with God's help he could go the rest of the way.

The morning of his execution came. More dressed himself carefully in a fine suit of silk that had been given him. The jailer protested, and reminded him that the headsman—"that rascal" he called

[3] PRIESTS—St. John Cardinal Fisher, Bishop of Rochester, and a number of monks—Carthusians, Briggitines, and Franciscans—suffered martyrdom at this time because they also refused to take the oath.

him—would get the suit. "What!" said More, "should I call him a rascal who today will do me such a great favor?" He was led out of the prison and came before the scaffold. The steps leading up to it were shaky and More was weak from his long imprisonment. He turned to the guard and asked him for his hand: "I pray thee, sir, see me safe up. For my coming down, I will shift for myself."

The headsman was trembling. More noticed it. "Pluck up thy spirits, man," he said smilingly, "and be not afraid to do thy duty. My neck is very short: Be careful, then, that your stroke is straight or your reputation will be lost." He prayed for a while, then bound a cloth about his own eyes, and laid his head upon the block. He moved his beard so that it would not be cut: he did this, as he told the headsman, because the beard "had never committed treason."

The ax came down with a thud, and More, the greatest man of his time, was dead. It was said then and has been said many times since that in killing More, Henry had killed holiness and learning in Europe.

St. Thomas More is a saint because he thought straight and because he was brave enough to follow his thought. Others might take the oath which declared Henry head of the Church: More had nothing to say about them—that was their business. His conscience told him that he should not take the oath, and he followed his conscience. In other words, More did not believe that a thing was right just because "everybody else" did it.

FOR DISCUSSION

1. Why did Thomas More refuse to go to the king when the messenger disturbed him during Mass? When later he gave his reason to the king, what was Henry's reaction?

2. List qualities in Thomas More that show you he was a wise and lovable man.

3. Was St. Thomas fooled by the king's friendship? How do you know? What was the cause, finally, of the grievous trouble between them?

4. Was St. Thomas unpatriotic in refusing to take Henry's oath? Why did the king demand *he* especially take the oath?

5. More was a very witty man. Examine the sayings which the author has included in the selection and choose the one you think most humorous.

CONTEXT DETERMINES MEANING

1. "In the rear there was a *scuffling* noise . . ." Can you illustrate how a *scuffling* noise differs from a *shuffling, scraping,* or *rasping* noise?

2. "The *bickering* between the king and the Pope had gone on . . ." List five synonyms for the word *bickering.* Would any of them fit into the sentence as well as *bickering?* Explain your answer.

A PROJECT

At the end of the selection, the author praises St. Thomas "because he thought straight and because he was brave enough to follow his thought." Examine your own experience for an instance in which some person you know dared, like St. Thomas, to be different because he knew he was in the right. In a brief composition describe the incident. What was your personal reaction to the person's conduct in this instance? Would you have done the same thing?

RELATED READING

You will enjoy acquaintance with other personalities in Aloysius Croft's *Twenty-One Saints.*

The lesson of Bernadette Soubirous is the greatness of humility. Poor, illiterate, and suffering, Bernadette was chosen by Mary, humble Virgin of Nazareth, to spread her name and glory throughout the modern world. Read here the secret of the life and sanctity of Bernadette Soubirous, peasant and saint.

THE LESSON OF BERNADETTE OF LOURDES

SISTER M. ELEANORE, C.S.C.

We live in a purse-proud age. We talk glibly of democracy, and yet comparatively few of us judge others by the standard of personal worth. The external trappings of the man receive far more consideration than does his character. Because of our tendency to social judgments I am certain that if a vote were taken to determine the consensus of opinion concerning the greatest woman of the past century, lowly Bernadette of Lourdes [1] would receive not even a respectable minority. The size of this minority would, however, depend absolutely on the diffusion of knowledge of Bernadette among those who love the Blessed Virgin Mary. Anyone who loves the Queen of Heaven and who knows the story of Bernadette would perforce grant the greatness of this humble peasant girl of Lourdes.

The reasons of Bernadette's greatness are many, and one of the most important of them is her profound humility. Humility was a conspicuous virtue of our Blessed Lady, who so honored this little French girl. On the occasion of the Visitation to Elizabeth, the Virgin Mary did not merely compose poetry when she sang in her Magnificat: "My soul doth magnify the Lord, . . . because He hath regarded the humility of His handmaid." She really announced a cause and its effect, which were to be repeated often in ages to come. Every saint is entitled in some measure to say that God has regarded the humility of His servant; and no saint, perhaps, can say it with better right than this most favored child of our Heavenly Queen, Bernadette of Lourdes. Few of us moderns would select a child so poor, so illiterate, so unhealthy as Bernadette to do any task for us, and yet she was chosen by the Queen of angels and saints to accomplish a mission second only to that of the apostles. Lourdes is the living contradiction of infidelity.

[1] LOURDES—Pronounced lo͞ord.

Lourdes gives daily testimony to the power of God's mother and the faith of God's children. Lourdes is in many ways the most remarkable fact in the world today.

The scientific world went on its knees in homage to Madame Curie, because of the benefits conferred on mankind by her discovery of radium. Many are grateful to her for cure of cancer or other diseases through the radium treatments. But what homage is not due to the little peasant girl who, at the bidding of our Lady, scratched the earth with her hand to release a stream of water which is to flow always for the instant healing of thousands diseased in body and soul and for the benediction and conversion of an unbelieving multitude! The achievement of this child in the face of tremendous opposition is something to shake the foundations of incredulity, to awaken the admiration of the mightiest of the mighty, and to startle the ramparts of materialistic reasoning. This achievement is tremendous; and yet it was made humanly possible in consequence of her humble simplicity. This simplicity, in itself of course a result of grace, seems to have been more effective than were the first miracles at Lourdes in defeating those who opposed Bernadette's mission. By her guilelessness and unfaltering adherence to truth she refuted the arguments of savants [2] who sought to trap her. By her simple unconcern as she walked in the midst of thousands, some of whom doubted her sanity, some of whom worshiped her as one favored of God, others of whom despised her as an impostor, she proved unmistakably the divinity of her mission.

There is no more dramatic event in modern history than the one which occurred on Thursday, February 11, 1858, an event which was to teach the world the power of the Mother of God. This event occurred near the town of Lourdes in France on the bank of the river Gave, and its immediate setting was Massabielle, which in the simple *patois* [3] of the countryside means "Old Rocks." On that day High Heaven looked down on the most glorious scene of many centuries. There were two persons in this scene, and they were surrounded by a wild and solitary setting. A mill stream tumbled and frothed over its stony bed till it lost itself in the more placid river, shortly after it had passed the rocks of Massabielle. Just where these huge rocks reared their sullen heads highest into the air, three irregular caverns pierced their structure. The largest cavern was at the base and the two smaller ones were superimposed on this cavern. The three caverns were joined by canals. At the base of the larger of the two upper caverns a wild rose trailed itself along the rock.

Kneeling on the bank of the churning stream was a little peasant girl of fourteen years, clad in a patched black dress, with a white *capulet* or mantle covering her head and falling back over her shoulders. On her little feet she wore the coarse *sabots* [4] and stockings of the peasant. Between her clasped hands was a rosary, the beads of which were slipped along as she prayed. Her delicate face was transfig-

[2] SAVANTS (så·vänz′)—Scholars.

[3] *Patois* (på·twä′)—The local dialect of a language.

[4] *Sabots* (så·bō′)—Wooden shoes.

ured. Her wide brown eyes glowed with unearthly light as they gazed at the other person in the scene.

In the larger of the upper caverns of the rock, with her feet just above the trailing rose, stood the most beautiful of women, the Virgin Mary. Ineffable light floated about her—not the glaring light of the sun but the cool radiance of the morning star. She was of medium height, of human flesh like ours, but flesh lustrous, beautiful beyond dreams. Graceful in immortal youth she stood. On her face could be read the innocence of childhood, the purity of young virginity, the tender seriousness of motherhood, the wisdom of ages, all in sweet harmony. Her robe, long and graceful, was woven of some unimaginable fabric. It fell in folds of light to the small white feet on the dark rock. On each foot was a golden rose from which streamed a mystic light. A wide blue girdle around her slender waist was knotted loosely in front and fell to the edge of her robe. On her head was a white mantle which hovered like a moon-kissed cloud over her slim virginal shoulders. In her clasped hands was a milk-white rosary, the beads of which were slipped through her fingers as the little girl before her prayed. She wore no jewels, no diadem; and yet in the blessing of her smile and in the enraptured eyes of the little girl could be read the full measure of this peerless Woman's queenliness over Heaven and earth. The sum of all earthly beauty stood graciously in that little niche in the rock, and High Heaven hovered about the ragged child into whose eyes the Queen of Heaven was smiling.

Why were there in this glorious picture two such contrasting figures? We, in our poor foolish way, would have sought the world over to find a beautiful, cultured woman to represent us on the occasion

of Mary's visit to France. We would have furnished a palace for her entertainment, and a thousand ladies-in-waiting. Why did our Lady come to this child in this out-of-the-way place? The answer to this question furnishes the reason for the greatness of Bernadette. Our Lady chose Bernadette for the very same reasons, albeit in lesser measures, as those which brought the angel Gabriel to Mary herself, her innocence and her humility.

Eighteen times did our Lady come from Heaven to stand there in that cavern in the rock and to hold communion with the little girl who could not write or read. Every time she came a larger throng of people was in waiting. They could not see Mary, but they were well content to gaze on the enraptured face of the child who was privileged to converse with her. Monsieur Estrade, who went to Lourdes, as he said, to laugh and enjoy himself thoroughly, "expecting to see a kind of farce or some grotesque absurdities and wondering at the simplicity of so many blockheads," had, after a few minutes' contemplation of the child in ecstasy, "the certitude, the irresistible intuition that a mysterious being was there."

Thousands of eager eyes watched Bernadette when, during the ninth apparition on February 25, she opened the earth for the miraculous fountain of Lourdes, an event which has been and still is of such tremendous consequence. The little girl was entrusted, at the beginning of this apparition, with the third of her secrets. After she had learned this secret there was a brief silence on the part of our Lady. Then her lovely voice again ravished Bernadette's ears.

"Go and drink from the fountain and wash yourself in it and eat of the herb which is growing at its side."

At the word "fountain" Bernadette gazed about her in bewilderment. There was no fountain and there had never been one near the Grotto. She got up from her knees and walked toward the river, but she was stopped by a word from our Lady.

"Do not go there," said Mary, "I have not spoken of drinking from the Gave. Go to the fountain. It is here."

She pointed toward the parched corner of the Grotto, to which, on the preceding morning, she had made Bernadette ascend on her knees. The little girl climbed again to it on her knees. Then, perhaps at some sign from her Queen, she scratched the earth and scooped out a handful. Immediately the hole was filled with water. Bernadette three times lifted the muddy water to her lips in the hollow of her hand before she could force herself to swallow it. Finally she did so, and then bathed her face in the water. She then ate a blade of grass growing beside the hole. Suddenly the water leaped over the brim of the hole and flowed like a thread of silver toward the curious crowd below. At the same moment our Lady disappeared. Bernadette turned to face the crowd. There were streaks of mud on her face. Some of the people jeered. Some cried pitifully: "Bernadette is no longer herself; the poor child has gone mad." Most of them, however, bowed in admiration to the little girl who passed modestly through the crowd and went home.

After the vision and Bernadette's departure, the people examined the ground. It was dry all about, except in the place where Bernadette had dug it with her hand. There the tiny streamlet trickled in increasing volume. Today the output of water from that fountain is eighteen gallons a minute. Thus came the miraculous water which has given sight to the blind, hearing to the deaf, health to the sick, hope to the hopeless, courage to the despairing, and faith to the unbelieving. The waters of Lourdes have carried their healing power to the four corners of the earth. Little Bernadette drank of them often, but they never brought her physical health. She was chosen for the high favor of suffering, as the Son of Mary singles out His special friends who are brave enough to become martyrs for His sake. Little Bernadette was told by our Lady that she should receive her happiness only when she should come to Heaven. Bernadette understood our Lady well. Eyes that have looked on Mary can never be satisfied with the joys of earth. A heart that loves Mary is glad to suffer for her Son.

On April 4, 1864, the first of the processions at Lourdes was held, in accordance with our Lady's command given through Bernadette to the Church officials. About fifty thousand persons marched in this procession, people from every walk of life. It was a magnificent demonstration, a triumphal ceremony which marked the close of innumerable difficulties on the part of Bernadette and of those who believed in her mission. The name of the favored child was acclaimed by the multitude, and her story was told from pulpits near and far. The Queen of Heaven, however, feared for the humility of her little handmaid, and so Bernadette was not present to witness her dream come true. Instead, she lay on the humble pallet of public charity in the hospital, her frail body wracked with pain.

The story of Bernadette did not end with the eighteenth apparition of our Lady; it is a continued story whose full meaning will never be known in this world. Three secrets were entrusted to her by our Lady. They were not revealed in the succeeding years during which she lived her simple and laborious life as the daughter of a peasant. They were not revealed in the years during which she lived as a Sister of Charity, serving well the poor and sick. They were not revealed in the thirty years in which her body lay incorrupt in its humble tomb. They were not revealed when that body was given again to the veneration of the public. They were not revealed when the Church hailed her Blessed. The full measure of Bernadette's greatness, may, perhaps, be hidden in those secrets. She doubtless perfers it so, because she suffered much when forced to receive adulation. It is the way of those who receive gifts from an earthly sovereign to boast of them. Those who receive gifts from God, however, are prone to hide them in the depths of their own humility.

When Sister Mary Bernard, as Bernadette was called in religion, was once asked whether she did not sometimes feel the temptation to self-esteem in having been thus honored by Mary, she answered: "What a strange idea you have of me! As if I did not know that if the Holy Virgin made choice of me it was because I was the most ignorant of creatures. If she could have discovered another more ignorant she would have chosen her in my place." On another occasion she said that our Lady made use of her just as a woman makes use of a broom. After the woman sweeps she puts the broom into a corner. So, too, said Bernadette: "Our Blessed Lady made use of me, and when my work was done she put me away in a corner. It is the proper place for me. I am happy in it and there I shall stay."

Bernadette did indeed stay in her corner. Her efforts to avoid those who sought her that they might pay her homage were at times almost laughable. No pompous person ever made more heroic efforts to be in the foreground than this humble Sister made to keep herself in the background. She was conspicuous only by her unfailing charity, touching many of the sick unto healing. She who so studiously avoided interviews with persons of wealth or of rank was happy when the sick clamored for her attentions. Bernadette's sense of values had been perfected by that loveliest of women, who stood on the bleak rock and spoke these heartstirring words, "I am the Immaculate Conception."

This, then, is the lesson of Bernadette—the lesson of humility. Humility is the truth that sees things as they are and measures their values correctly. The lesson of clear-sighted humility is needed today more than any other lesson; and it is a lesson that Bernadette is perhaps better qualified than anyone else to teach. Humility is the safeguard of innocence, a quality of soul so much endangered by the false standards of today. It should be the prayer of us who know Bernadette that she may intercede for the sin-darkened world, that her glorified hands, no longer limited by time or space, may scoop up the healing waters which once flowed at her touch and scatter them in benediction over the nations. Wherever these drops of water fall, there will surely spring up the flowers of humility and purity and faith.

◇◇◇◇◇◇◇◇◇◇◇◇◇◇◇◇◇◇◇◇◇◇◇◇◇◇◇◇◇◇

FOR DISCUSSION

1. What is given as the keynote of Bernadette's "success"? Was she the first one to follow this path to greatness?
2. What do you mean by humility? Can a person have talent, know that he or she has it, and still be humble? Be specific in your answer.
3. Pick out every word denoting a color to describe the Blessed Virgin as she appeared to Bernadette. How many colors do you find?
4. Retell the story of the discovery of the fountain. What part did the waters of this fountain come to play in the drama of Lourdes?
5. Where and how did Bernadette spend the rest of her life? What characteristic was most noticeable about her in her later life?

RELATED WORDS

What does the word *literate* mean? What word means the opposite of *literate?* You can tell by looking at the words *literacy* and *literature* that they are related to *literate.* What is their relationship in meaning? The root of these words is in the Latin word *littera,* meaning "letter." What other words can you find that are from the same root? Explain their meanings.

RELATED READING

The Song of Bernadette by Franz Werfel is a long book but one very much worth reading. Learn the story behind its writing.

For Further Reading

Blessed Friend of Youth by Neil Boyton, S.J., is a biography of St. John Bosco. Here is an example of truth being more thrilling than fiction.

Blackrobe by Charles Corcoran, S.J. The charm of Father Marquette is radiated in this narrative of his life and travels.

Twenty-One Saints by Aloysius Croft is a collection of dramatic tales of the lives of the saints every boy and girl loves.

A Modern Galahad by Albert S. Foley, S.J., is the life of St. John Berchmans, patron of youth, and a study of his times and the men who helped to make him a saint.

Secrets of the Saints by Henri Ghéon. Here are short, warm biographies of the Curé d'Ars, the Little Flower, St. Margaret Mary, and St. John Bosco.

The Adventures of an Amethyst by Cecily Hallack. A prelate, lifelong family friend, instructs the four children of recent converts in the truths of the Faith with charm and clarity.

A Catholic Quiz Book by Herbert A. Kenny and Geoffrey P. Keane contains ideal quiz questions for a Catholic party. The questions are arranged according to various topics.

The Grace of Guadalupe by Frances P. Keyes. In this engaging story the Virgin of Guadalupe appears to the simple shepherd, Juan Diego.

Jesus of Nazareth by Mother M. Loyola is the story of the life of Our Lord written in simple and beautiful language.

Christ's Cadets by C. C. Martindale, S.J., tells the inspiring story of the growth of sanctity in three young saints, Aloysius Gonzaga, Stanislaus Kostka, and John Berchmans.

Too Small a World by Theodore Maynard. St. Frances X. Cabrini, first United States citizen enrolled in the list of saints, traveled about America, building hospitals, orphanages, and schools.

The Red Hat by Covelle Newcomb is an extremely interesting biography of Cardinal Newman for young people.

All Stars of Christ by Robert North, S.J. These are fifteen short biographies of God's heroes, most of them soldiers, and all of them lay leaders.

The Greatest Story Ever Told by Fulton Oursler is the life story of Jesus. Fulton Oursler follows closely and reverently the chronicles of Matthew, Mark, Luke, and John.

The Girl in the White Armor by Albert B. Paine. Joan of Arc comes to life in this fine study by a non-Catholic admirer.

The Virgin Mother by Sister Mary Paula is the life of Mary; it is an account by a supposed eyewitness of the most important events of Her life.

The Man Who Got Even with God by M. Raymond, O.C.S.O., is the life of an American Trappist monk. A boisterous ex-cowboy enters the Order and proves that an American cowboy can dedicate himself to a life of spiritual meditation, and that a fiery Southerner can be an excellent Trappist.

The City Set on a Hill—the Story of the Vatican by James A. Vander Velt, O.F.M. The reader is taken on an informal stroll through the Vatican City, seeing the buildings, gardens, libraries, and museums.

Our Lady of Fatima by William T. Walsh is the dramatic story of the six appearances of Our Blessed Lady to three Portuguese children.

Lad of Lima by Mary Windeatt is a successful effort to tell American boys and girls about the little-known Dominican saint, Blessed Martin de Porres. It is written for boys and girls who are interested in little brothers and sisters anywhere, who like to read of people in distant lands, or who enjoy tales of the impossible come true.

Fabiola by Nicholas Cardinal Wiseman is an historical story of early Christian martyrs.

UNDER ONE ROOF

How many rooms make a home? You know the answer. Rooms have little or nothing to do with a home. It is human hearts united by flesh and blood under a common roof, human wills blended in sympathy and mutual interest that make a home. God Himself planted in man the instinct to live in a family. He knew that the human race could not realize complete development intellectually, spiritually, and morally, if each man lived independently of all others. So God told the children of men: "Honor thy father and thy mother."

But more emphatic than words were the God-Man's thirty years of hidden life at Nazareth. Better than anything else they prove that home life is the *real* life. For in the family circle, man's social instinct is first exercised; in the family circle is the foundation of all future social relations. Other natural societies have for their purpose the family's protection and support. In them as in the family, the rule of life is simply that law of charity which the Holy Ghost is accustomed to write in the hearts of men.

The glimpses of home life offered in this section are realistic and varied. In the first selection you will feel the deep love of a boy for his father; then you will glimpse the pride of a mother and father for their maturing son. In the legend of ancient Greece you will relive a homecoming and the emotional experience of a man reunited with his family after years of wandering. Perhaps it will be easy to identify yourself with Clarence Day, Jr. in his verbal struggles with his father whose name and initials he shares. Finally you will meet the innkeeper whose stable sheltered Mary, Joseph, and the Child on the first Christmas.

Like a song at the right time and place, these stories will make you feel that you have a part in the chorus of joy which swells from happy family life.

H. ARMSTRONG ROBERTS

All his life the boy in this poem carried in his mind a snapshot of his father's love. As you read the poem, you will see how that one picture became so indelibly printed on his memory.

The Secret Heart

ROBERT P. TRISTRAM COFFIN

Across the years he could recall
His father one way best of all.

In the stillest hour of night
The boy awakened to a light.

Half in dreams, he saw his sire 5
With his great hands full of fire.

The man had struck a match to see
If his son slept peacefully.

He held his palms each side the spark
His love had kindled in the dark. 10

His two hands were curved apart
In the semblance of a heart.

He wore, it seemed to his small son,
A bare heart on his hidden one,

A heart that gave out such a glow 15
No son awake could bear to know.

It showed a look upon a face
Too tender for the day to trace.

One instant, it lit all about,
And then the secret heart went out. 20

But it shone long enough for one
To know that hands held up the sun.

FOR DISCUSSION

1. Why would it look to the small boy as though his father's hands were full of fire? Show the position of the father's hands as he held the match.
2. How was the expression on the father's face different from what the boy was accustomed to seeing during the day? Can you explain the difference?
3. How do you interpret the last stanza of the poem? What feeling did the boy experience from this glimpse of his father's affection?

RELATED READING

Give This Man Place by Hugh F. Blunt is the story of St. Joseph's life and character, especially his role as foster father and teacher of the Child Jesus.

Like many other American fathers, Howard Vincent O'Brien saw his son go away to World War II. The day his son left, hurried goodbyes were said and a car whirled the boy away. Father and mother walked slowly back into the house. A few days later, in a column in the Chicago DAILY NEWS, *Howard O'Brien put down the thoughts that came that evening as he wandered through the house listening to the soft voices of memory. His column touched the nation. As dramatized for radio by Malcolm Meacham, it was broadcast over a nationwide network from more than six hundred radio stations in the United States.*

SO LONG, SON

HOWARD VINCENT O'BRIEN

My son has gone to war. He came home from school one day, burst in the front door . . . [*Effect of front door opening and banging shut.*] . . . and threw his bag on the floor. I could hear him talking to his mother downstairs. I could hear her worried voice and his joshing laughter:

MOTHER. (*In distance.*) Why, for goodness sakes, son—is something the matter?

SON. Hello, Mums—no, I just thought I'd come home for a day or so—that's all.

[*Orchestra plays a staccato scale in rhythm with the sound of footsteps running upstairs.*]

Then he came bounding up the stairs three at a time, clomped down the hall and banged into my study.

[*Sound of door opened quickly and banged slightly . . . music fades.*]

SON. (*Coming in.*) Hello, Dad! Busy? Or can I come in for a minute?

FATHER. Hello, son. What're you doing home from school? Get the sack [1] or something?

SON. (*Laughing.*) No such luck! (*Then seriously.*) No . . . no, I came home because I wanted to talk to you.

"Talk to me . . . ?" Strange the havoc those words can create in a parent's mind. A thousand questions, a hundred unformed fears leap into being and clutch at your heart. Usually, you're pretty casual about it. You say:

FATHER. All right, son. What's on your mind?

SON. Wait until I get my pipe lit.

[*Sound of his drawing on pipe.*]

I sat and waited and watched him. He's a fine looking lad. I felt myself get-

[1] GET THE SACK—To be expelled from school; or to be dismissed from a job.

"So Long, Son" by Howard V. O'Brien, as adapted by William A. Bacher and Malcolm Meacham for *The Treasury Star Parade* (U. S. Savings Bonds Division of Treasury Department, Washington, D. C.), used by permission of Mrs. Howard V. O'Brien and Messrs. Bacher and Meacham.

ting kind of funny inside—proud of him, yet somehow a little frightened, too: you have them, you accept them—they're yours: then suddenly they're grown up and mysteriously not yours any more—not anyone's: they belong only to themselves.

When the pipe began to draw, this son of mine—and yet not mine—sprawled his frame out on the couch and blew a huge smoke ring to the ceiling. Watching him, I couldn't help smiling. There was a moment's silence and then—

SON. Dad, I want to enlist.

FATHER. What!

I couldn't believe my ears. Maybe I didn't want to believe them. Back in my mind, of course, I had known it had to happen some day. But there were still two years before he would be old enough to be drafted, or even to register. I'd closed my mind to the possibility that it could happen before then. Enlist! Why, he was only nineteen. Oh, no! I tried not to show what I was feeling. I tried to be casual and easy about it but when I finally could answer him, my voice sounded strange in my own ears. "Enlist, son?" I said.

SON. Yes, Dad.

FATHER. Don't you think you might wait until you finish college?—or at least until you're old enough to register? If it were a question of your being drafted . . .

Suddenly he was leaning forward, talking. The pipe in his hand, unheeded, went out. He talked about things of which I'd never realized he'd even thought: things like peace and democracy and the rights of free men . . .

SON. (*Intensely.*) Don't you see . . . I've got to go—now! I want peace, Dad—the kind of peace we've always had here in America—peace and freedom. Without that, what good is there in living?

There was finality in the way he said it, finality at once grim and gentle. I said no more about waiting. His mother took it better than I. She stood quite still for a moment when he told her, and then answered:

MOTHER. Of course, if you feel you should, then you must. You must do what you think is right, son.

That was all. No tears, no fuss. I wondered for a moment—women are strange: they get at the heart of things so much quicker and more surely than men.

My son went down and enlisted and I went with him to give him the go sign. Then he went back to school to wait. It wasn't long before he was home again. The house was the scene of furious activity for two days. At last we found ourselves, just the three of us, alone in the front room. [*Sound of car honking off.*] A car drove up outside and honked. There was no band, no ceremonial. It wasn't even dramatic. He said:

SON. Well, I guess that's for me.

And picked up his bag. His mother said:

MOTHER. You haven't forgotten your gloves?

SON. No, Mums—they're in my pocket.

Then he kissed her and held out his hand to me.

SON. So long, Dad.

FATHER. Good luck.

[*Slight pause; four quick footsteps and the opening and slamming of the front door.*]

SON. (*Distant, fading.*) Hyah, Bill—I didn't mean to keep you waiting.

[*Car in distance starts and fades away. Orchestra softly in for background mood.*]

That was all—another boy gone off to war. After the door had closed behind him, his mother turned quickly and went into the kitchen. I—? Well, I went upstairs to what had been his room. It was in worse chaos than usual. His dancing pumps; a tennis racket; his phonograph records; letters, invitations to parties he now would not attend; a packed steamer trunk marked, "Not to be opened"; his clothes in the closet, left for his mother to put into mothballs; on the closet floor, his prep school shoes . . . maybe you remember? . . . with their curled up toes—the more they curled, the better!—these turned up as far as he could curl them. On the shelf, there was a policeman's hat—the lord knows where it came from or how he got it! Hanging on a hook, there was a Kanaka bathing suit, which he had bought when we were in Hawaii on vacation—and next to it his prep school sweater with his letter on it. I turned towards his desk where stood two of his dearest treasures—a miniature suit of armor and a pair of dress epaulets, gold and shining, from the Seventh Regiment of the National Guards, New York City. I pulled out the desk drawer and found his prep school graduation dancing cards. I moved his pipe rack and tobacco jar and they left a ring of dust where they had stood. There was a scrapbook which he had started when he was six or seven—nothing but cowboy pictures cut out of magazines. Beside it in the corner was something I suppose every boy has—a box of abandoned cigarette lighters, none of which work. Thrown carelessly into the corner of the drawer were his dress studs which, of course, he wouldn't need in the army! I turned around slowly. It seemed to me that there were girls' pictures all over the walls. I realized then that his mother had come upstairs and was standing in the doorway watching me. "Funny," I said, "funny how a boy will plaster his walls with these things, isn't it?" And she said:

MOTHER. (*Smiling.*) There aren't really so many—only five or six. Now you go on back to your study and let me clean up in here.

I turned and went out the door, down the hall to my own room. I stood there a minute, looking at a framed photograph on the wall. It was of a little boy with a toothless grin, his face framed in curls. The same boy who had just taken my hand and said, "Well, so long." Not much time, I thought, between the taking of that picture and the slamming of the front door.

[*Orchestra in softly in mood with each of the whispering voices in the sequence.*]

Then suddenly a queer thing happened. Objects came alive and whispered to me. They led me all over the house. The rooms were full of soft voices. I tried to listen to them, to tell what they were saying . . .

POLICEMAN'S HAT. (*On filter*[2]. . . *Irish.*) Faith, an' I know what ye're thinking. Ye're wonderin' where in tarnation the lad picked up a policeman's hat! (*Impishly.*) Well, never mind, now, that's quite a story—quite a story! Maybe some day we'll be after tellin' it to you.

[*Now there is a faint clink-clank of the armor.*]

ARMOR. Hold, sirrah! Do you not know who I am? I am the symbol of chivalry, of days of old when knights were bold and boldly caparisoned, dauntlessly set forth to destroy evil and right the wrongs of the world!

[*The orchestra picks up a martial strain; there is a sound of marching feet.*]

EPAULETS. Squad—halt! (*Sound of stops.*) Epaulets, eh? A soldier's dress epaulets, all gold braid and glittering fringe—symbols, too: symbols of the bravery and courage and glory of manhood and the high ideals of all free men.

[*The music changes to a romantic dance melody.*]

GIRL. (*Fading in with a ripple of laughter.*) Hello! You don't know me—I'm just a picture on the wall. But like his mother, I kissed him good-bye and told him to go—because I knew he *had* to go . . .

[*The music changes again . . . this time to a soft Hawaiian theme with effect of surf.*]

BATHING SUIT. (*Soft laugh.*) A Kanaka bathing suit. I was his favorite. Remember? We were all there together. Such fun! The peaceful blue skies; the warm sunshine; the turquoise, tropical waters; the laughter, the careless laughter and light-heartedness of Honolulu; the

[2] *Filter*—A microphone giving the voice a remote, mechanical quality.

towering mass of Diamond Head and the dull drone of peaceful planes and the majestic beauty of the big ships in the great harbor—remember? Yes, and so does he!

[*There is a sharp chord that fades out into a theme as of soft whispered voices.*]

Oh, yes—yes, indeed, I did remember! I remember so much and yet, somehow, know so little about this boy of mine. The locked trunk, a symbol, too, of the inviolability of the human heart and mind. It tells a story as old as the world. I have never really known this boy's personality; I can never know it. The mystery of life and being are locked inside him and not even his parents can ever really know what lies there. It's the symbols that they and the rest of the world must go by. Somehow, I liked the voices and the symbols my son had left behind him. They seemed to me to be good voices, good symbols. Their whispering led me up the stairs into the attic. There I found a box of tin soldiers. [*There is a toy bugle call in the orchestra and a few muted bars of echoed march music.*] Gaudy little figures, these, that he had used to drill and march all up and down his room, now rusted, with the paint chipped off and faded, and piled carelessly into a box; prophetic symbols! Beside the box, there was a football helmet, very small. [*Orchestra mood changes to college tune.*] He played football only when he was very young because somehow he never managed to grow to regulation football size. Downstairs in my desk, however, there lay a scrapbook filled with items clipped from our local and his school papers telling a glowing story of his management of his football team. [*Music changes and grows soft and still.*] There were also, scattered around the attic, a home-made guitar, a stamp album, a penny bank with the lid pried off, each whispering of its memory in its own voice. [*We hear the voices in the orchestra chattering softly again.*] There were other voices which led me on to a folder stuffed with letters, papers, report cards, among them the wail of an exasperated teacher:

TEACHER. (*On filter.*) Though he looks like an angel, I can assure you . . . ! (*Fades.*)

I found his baptismal certificate, a ribbon won in a track meet and a photograph taken on the memorable first day of long pants. "How do you like them?" I'd inquired, watching him as he examined himself in the mirror.

BOY. I—I dunno. I guess they're all right.

[*Orchestra softly out.*]

His face beamed but his voice was shy, his heart a little frightened at this threat of approaching manhood. He didn't know, but he *thought* it was all right. His first long pants! Why, it was only yesterday when I had held him in my arms. That somehow made me remember all the scoldings I had given him, the preachments, the exhortations to a virtue and wisdom I did not myself possess. I thought, what fools we are with our children, always plotting their futures, always intent on what they may become, never accepting what they are. Before we know it, they grow to manhood and womanhood and the responsibilities of a world fall heavily upon their shoulders, shoulders we would have thought too young, too inexperienced to carry such burdens. When we would delay them, save them for a few days or weeks or months, that quiet smile, that firm voice:

SON. (*Slightly off mike.*) No, Dad. I've made up my mind. I want peace, Dad—the kind of peace we've always had here in America—peace and freedom. Without them, what good is there in living?

[*Orchestra in softly.*]

They are singularly unafraid, these young men and young women. It seems to me that they look straight ahead into the future, seeing there the kind of world they'd like, seeing also the present threat to the very existence of that world, knowing what they must do to keep it whole and make it better. These carefree young men and women who yesterday were boys and girls and tomorrow must have their hearts broken, their souls tested and their strength tried almost beyond human endurance—they are our children. We here in America have tried but often we have been weak or lazy, vacillating or afraid, avaricious or careless. Consequently, in great measure, we have failed. We aren't giving these young men and women the beautiful world they have expected and deserved. Somehow, though, I'm sure that they realize that we in America at least have tried. Where we have failed of accomplishment, at least we have passed on to them the symbols of manhood and womanhood, of liberty and freedom,—of America. We know that they have found these symbols good—good enough to be worth working for, fighting for; if necessary, dying for.

[*Orchestra slowly fades.*]

While I stood there in the attic, my brain full of the voices that had come alive out of my son's past, I could hear other voices, strange, fanatic voices, crying from across the sea:

VOICES. (*On filter.*)

"America is soft. America is degenerate."

"Democracy is outmoded and outworn."

"The youth of America have no ideals, no enthusiasms. They will not act."

"The youth of America is soft and degenerate."

[*Voices slowly fade; orchestra comes in for background.*]

America and the youth of America "degenerate"?—"soft"? Democracy and the things it implies, freedom, equal opportunities, the unalienable rights of man, outmoded, outworn? No! I have looked into my son's eyes, I have heard his voice—"Without peace and freedom, what good is there in living?" Quietly, without drama, in vindication of his ideals, he has gone away, another boy off to the war.

All of these voices which rise up whispering out of the past tell the story of American boys and girls. In my quiet attic their words ring stronger and more clearly than all of the shouted fanaticism, the screaming nationalism, the whine of planes and the roar of guns and the churning of great ships in the sea. These voices in my attic are quiet voices, quietly saying good-bye. That is as it should be. There is a grimness about them as they speak, there is a sureness in their going, there is a determination in their silence that will not be swerved nor changed until they have achieved their goal. The enemy was trained for war and victory;

our children were trained for peace, but theirs is the great strength, the greater courage, because it grows out of themselves and their realization of the task before them. When these others fail, when they find that they are not invincible, it will be because the strength of men who want peace is the greater strength, the quiet whispering of their voices in ten million homes is the biggest sound in all the earth. (*Orchestra builds under.*) My son has gone to war. Well, curly-head, you're a man now. I hated to see you go but I would not have halted you if I could. I cannot pretend I am not sad but I am proud, too. So long, son.

[*Orchestra up to triumphant finish.*]

◇◇◇◇◇◇◇◇◇◇◇◇◇◇◇◇◇◇◇◇◇◇◇◇◇◇◇◇◇◇

FOR DISCUSSION

1. Why had the son come home from school? Beneath the father's casual question, "What's on your mind, son?" was there a current of worried anticipation? How does the father describe a boy's transition to independent manhood?

2. Have you ever had a sudden shock, or seen another person deeply moved? Can you suggest why the father's voice sounded strange in his own ears, as he answered his son's declaration, "I want to enlist"?

3. What do you think of the son's reason for enlisting? Some think of war as a lark, as a great adventure. Was this the boy's spirit, or did his purpose spring from weighty, more serious ideals; for example, from acceptance of responsibility? Is the latter a prime difference between the spirit of youth and that of manhood?

4. How did the mother receive the news? What contrast did the father point out between her reactions and his own?

5. What things typical of a boy did the father linger over in his son's room? What did he hear as he sat alone in his study? Did he seem really to regret the scoldings of the past, or would you consider this a first emotional reaction to loneliness?

6. How does the father answer the charge, "America is soft . . . degenerate . . . the youth of America have no ideals, no enthusiasms"?

THE MEANING OF DEMOCRACY

Democracy as a word is important because of the principles it embodies, the things it stands for. It can be defined as "rule"—not by a race, class, group, or individual but—"by the people." Lincoln's definition was, "government of, by, and for the people." In the radio script you found a list of the things democracy implies. What are they?

RELATED READING

Of the many newspapermen who so brilliantly reported the events of World War II, America will long remember Ernie Pyle and his dispatches from across the seas. Mr. Pyle died near Okinawa. His book, *Here Is Your War*, contains the best things he wrote from the North African theater of battle.

More than two thousand years ago a blind poet, Homer, wrote the adventures of a legendary Greek hero, Odysseus. His poem has been translated many times; below is a translation told with much of the warmly human style of the original.

The story of Odysseus, king of Ithaka, begins with the Trojan War, a bitter conflict between the Greeks and the city of Troy in Asia Minor. After the fall of Troy, Odysseus set sail for home with his warriors. There, ten years before, he had bid good-bye to his wife, Penelope, and infant son, Telemachus. But Neptune, god of the sea, beset the returning fleet with storms and contrary winds, and for ten years his voyage home was delayed. He was beset by many hardships.

Meanwhile, during the years of her husband's wanderings, Penelope came to mourn him for dead. The young lords of the island thronged to his palace home to woo Penelope, dealing insolently with her and all the while eating up Odysseus' substance. Secretly, they planned the death of young Telemachus. For four years Penelope put off the wooers, but now in obedience to her parents she sorrowfully prepares to choose a husband.

It is at this point that Odysseus lands on the shores of Ithaka. Athene, his goddess protector, tells him of the evil wooers and, for his protection, makes him appear as an aged beggar. On the way to the city Odysseus meets Telemachus. Revealing himself, Odysseus sends his son ahead under charge to keep his arrival secret. In the company of an old swineherd, Odysseus draws near his palace, scheming to wreak swift vengeance on the wooers.

THE RETURN OF ODYSSEUS

ADAPTED FROM *The Odyssey*

BY PADRAIC COLUM

Just at that time Odysseus [1] and Eumaeus [2] were journeying towards the City. Odysseus, in the guise of a beggar, had a ragged bag across his shoulders and he carried a staff that the swineherd had given him to help him over the slippery ground. They went by a rugged path

[1] ODYSSEUS—Pronounced ȏ·dĭs′ūs.
[2] EUMAEUS—Pronounced ȗ·mē′ŭs.

"The Return of Odysseus" from *Adventures of Odysseus and The Tale of Troy* by Padraic Colum, reprinted by permission of the author.

and they came to a place where a spring flowed into a basin made for its water, and where there was an altar to the Nymphs, at which men made offerings.

As Eumaeus and Odysseus were resting at the spring, a servant from Odysseus' house came along. He was a goatherd, and Melanthius was his name. He was leading a flock of goats for the wooers to kill, and when he saw the swineherd with the seeming beggar he cried out:

"Now we see the vile leading the vile. Say, swineherd, whither art thou leading this wretch? It is easy to see the sort of fellow he is! He is the sort to rub shoulders against many doorposts, begging for scraps. Nothing else is he good for. But if thou wouldst give him to me, swineherd, I would make him watch my fields, and sweep out my stalls, and carry fresh water to the kids. He'd have his dish of whey from me. But a fellow like this doesn't want an honest job—he wants to lounge through the country, filling his belly, without doing anything for the people who feed him up. If he goes to the house of Odysseus, I pray that he be pelted from the door."

He said all this as he came up to them with his flock of goats. And as he went by he gave a kick to Odysseus.

Odysseus took thought whether he should strike the fellow with his staff or fling him upon the ground. But in the end he hardened his heart to endure the insult, and let the goatherd go on his way. But turning to the altar that was by the spring, he prayed:

"Nymphs of the Well! If ever Odysseus made offerings to you, fulfil for me this wish—that he—even Odysseus—may come to his own home, and have power to chastise the insolence that gathers around his house."

They journeyed on, and when they came near they heard the sound of the lyre within the house. The wooers were now feasting, and Phemius the minstrel was singing to them. And when Odysseus came before his own house, he caught the swineherd by the hand suddenly and with a hard grip, and he said:

"Lo now, I who have wandered in many lands and have walked in pain through many Cities have come at last to the house of Odysseus. There it is, standing as of old, with building beyond building; with its walls and its battlements; its courts and its doors. The house of Odysseus, verily! And lo! unwelcome men keep revel within it, and the smoke of their feast rises up and the sound of the lyre is heard playing for them."

Said Eumaeus, "What wilt thou have me do for thee, friend? Shall I bring thee into the hall and before the company of wooers, whilst I remain here, or wouldst thou have me go in before thee?"

"I would have thee go in before me," Odysseus said.

Now as they went through the courtyard a thing happened that dashed Odysseus' eyes with tears. A hound lay in the dirt of the yard, a hound that was very old. All uncared for he lay in the dirt, old and feeble. But he had been a famous hound, and Odysseus himself had trained him before he went to the wars of Troy. Argos was his name. Now as Odysseus came near, the hound Argos knew him, and stood up before him and whined and dropped his ears, but had no strength to come near him. Odysseus knew the hound and stopped and gazed at him. "A good hound lies there," said he to Eumaeus. "Once, I think, he was so swift that no beast in the deep places of the wood could flee from him." Then he went on, and the hound Argos lay down in the dirt of the yard, and that same day the life passed from him.

Behind Eumaeus, the swineherd, he came into his own hall, in the appearance of a beggar, wretchedly clad and leaning on an old man's staff. Odysseus looked upon the young lords who wooed his wife, and then he sat down upon the threshold and went no further into the hall.

Telemachus[3] was there. Seeing Eumaeus he called to him and gave the swineherd bread and meat, and said, "Take these, and give them to the stranger at the doorway, and tell him that he may go amongst the company and crave an alms from each."

Odysseus ate whilst the minstrel was finishing his song. When it was finished he rose up, and went into the hall, craving an alms from each of the wooers.

Seeing him, Antinous,[4] the most insolent of the wooers, cried out, "O notorious swineherd, why didst thou bring this fellow here? Have we not enough vagabonds? Is it nothing to thee that worthless fellows come here and devour thy master's substance?"

Hearing such a speech from Antinous, Telemachus had to say, "Antinous, I see that thou hast good care for me and mine. I marvel that thou hast such good care. But wouldst thou have me drive a stranger from the door? The gods forbid that I should do such a thing. Nay, Antinous. Give the stranger something for the sake of the house."

"If all the company gives him as much as I, he will have something to keep him from beggary for a three months' space," said Antinous, meaning by that he would work some hurt upon the beggar.

Odysseus came before him. "They say that thou art the noblest of all the wooers," he said, "and for that reason thou shouldst give me a better thing than any of the others have given me. Look upon me. I too had a house of mine own, and was accounted wealthy amongst men, and I had servants to wait upon me. And many a time would I make welcome the wanderer and give him something from my store."

"Stand far away from my table, thou wretched fellow," said Antinous.

Then said Odysseus, "Thou hast beauty, lord Antinous, but thou hast not wisdom. Out of thine own house thou wouldst not give a grain of salt to a suppliant. And even whilst thou dost sit at another man's table thou dost not find it in thy heart to give something out of the plenty that is before thee."

So Odysseus spoke and Antinous became terribly angered. He caught up a footstool, and with it he struck Odysseus in the back, at the base of the right shoulder. Such a blow would have knocked another man over, but Odysseus stood steadfast under it. He gave one look at Antinous, and then without a word he went over and sat down again upon the threshold.

Telemachus had in his heart a mighty rage for the stroke that had been given his father. But he let no tear fall from his eyes and he sat very still, brooding in his

[3] TELEMACHUS—Pronounced tē·lĕm′ȧ·kŭs.
[4] ANTINOUS—Pronounced ăn·tĭn′ō·ŭs.

heart evil for the wooers. Odysseus, after a while, lifted his head and spoke:

"Wooers of the renowned queen," he said, "hear what the spirit within me bids me say to you. There is neither pain nor shame in the blow that a man may get in battle. But in the blow that Antinous has given me—a blow aimed at a beggar—there is pain and there is shame. And now I call upon that god who is the avenger of the insult to the poor, to bring, not a wedding to Antinous, but the issue of death."

"Sit there and eat thy meat in quiet," Antinous called out, "or else thou wilt be dragged through the house by thy heels, and the flesh will be stripped off thy bones."

And now the lady Penelope [5] had come into the hall. Hearing that a stranger was there, she sent for Eumaeus and bade the swineherd bring him to her, that she might question him as to what he had heard about Odysseus. Eumaeus came and told him of Penelope's request. But Odysseus said, "Eumaeus, right willing am I to tell the truth about Odysseus to the fair and wise Penelope. But now I may not speak to her. Go to her and tell her that when the wooers have gone I will speak to her. And ask her to give me a seat near the fire, that I may sit and warm myself as I speak, for the clothes I wear are comfortless."

As Eumaeus gave the message to the lady Penelope, one who was there, Theoclymenus,[6] the guest who had come in Telemachus' ship, said, "O wife of the renowned Odysseus, be sure that thy lord will return to his house. As I came here on the ship of Telemachus, thy son, I saw a happening that is an omen of the return of Odysseus. A bird flew out on the right, a hawk. In his talons he held a dove, and plucked her and shed the feathers down on the ship. By that omen I know that the lord of this high house will return, and strike here in his anger."

Penelope left the hall and went back to her own chamber. Next Eumaeus went away to look after his swine. But still the wooers continued to feast, and still Odysseus sat in the guise of a beggar on the threshold of his own house.

. . . While these things were happening, the wife of Odysseus, the lady Penelope, called to Eurycleia,[7] and said, "This evening I will go into the hall of our house and speak to my son, Telemachus. Bid my two handmaidens make ready to come with me, for I shrink from going amongst the wooers alone."

Eurycleia went to tell the handmaidens and Penelope washed off her cheeks the traces of the tears that she had wept that day. Then she sat down to wait for the handmaidens to come to her. As she waited she fell into a deep sleep. And as she slept, the goddess Pallas Athene [8] bathed her face in the Water of Beauty and took all weariness away from her body, and restored all her youthfulness to her. The sound of the handmaidens' voices as they came in awakened her, and Penelope rose up to go into the hall.

Now when she came amongst them with her two handmaidens, one standing each side of her, the wooers were amazed,

[5] PENELOPE—Pronounced pê·nĕl′ô·pê.
[6] THEOCLYMENUS—Pronounced thê·ō·clỹm′-ĕn·ŭs.
[7] EURYCLEIA—Pronounced ū′rĭ·klē′yȧ.
[8] PALLAS ATHENE (păl′ȧs ȧ·thē′nē)—Goddess of wisdom.

or they had never seen one so beautiful. The hearts of all were enchanted with love for her, and each prayed that he might have her for his wife.

Penelope did not look on any of the wooers, but she went to her son, Telemachus, and spoke to him.

"Telemachus," she said, "I have heard that a stranger has been ill-treated in this house. How, my child, didst thou permit such a thing to happen?"

Telemachus said, "My lady mother, thou hast no right to be angered at what took place in this hall."

So they spoke to one another, mother and son. Now one of the wooers, Eurymachus [9] by name, spoke to Penelope, saying:

"Lady, if any more than we beheld thee in the beauty thou hast now, by so many more wouldst thou have wooers tomorrow."

"Speak not so to me, lord Eurymachus," said Penelope, "speak not of my beauty, which departed in the grief I felt when my lord went to the wars of Troy."

Odysseus stood up, and gazed upon his wife who was standing amongst her wooers. Eurymachus noted him and going to him, said, "Stranger, wouldst thou be my hireling? If thou wouldst work on my upland farm, I should give thee food and clothes. But I think thou art practised only in shifts and dodges, and that thou wouldst prefer to go begging thy way through the country."

Odysseus, standing there, said to that proud wooer, "Lord Eurymachus, if there might be a trial of labour between us two, I know which of us would come out the better man. I would that we two stood together, a scythe in the hands of each, and a good swath of meadow to be mown —then would I match with thee, fasting from dawn until evening's dark. Or would that we were set ploughing together. Then thou shouldst see who would plough the longest and the best furrow! Or would that we two were in the ways of war! Then shouldst thou see who would be in the front rank of battle. Thou dost think thyself a great man. But if Odysseus should return, that door, wide as it is, would be too narrow for thy flight."

So angry was Eurymachus at this speech that he would have struck Odysseus if Telemachus had not come amongst the wooers, saying, "That man must not be struck again in this hall. Sirs, if you have finished feasting, and if the time has come for you, go to your own homes, go in peace I pray you."

All were astonished that Telemachus should speak so boldly. No one answered him back, for one said to the other, "What he has said is proper. We have nothing to say against it. To misuse a stranger in the house of Odysseus is a shame. Now let us pour out a libation of wine to the gods, and then let each man go to his home."

The wine was poured out and the wooers departed. Then Penelope and her handmaidens went to her own chamber and Telemachus was left with his father, Odysseus.

To Telemachus Odysseus said, "My son, we must now get the weapons out of the hall. Take them down from the walls." Telemachus and his father took down the helmets and shields and sharp-

[9] EURYMACHUS—Pronounced ū·rĭm′ȧ·kŭs.

pointed spears. Then said Odysseus as they carried them out, "Tomorrow, when the wooers miss the weapons and say, 'Why have they been taken?' answer them, saying, 'The smoke of the fire dulled them, and they no longer looked the weapons that my father left behind him when he went to the wars of Troy. Besides, I am fearful lest some day the company in the hall come to a quarrel, one with the other, and snatch the weapons in anger. Strife has come here already. And iron draws iron, men say.' "

Telemachus carried the armour and weapons out of the hall and hid them in the women's apartment. Then when the hall was cleared he went to his own chamber.

It was then that Penelope came back to the hall to speak to the stranger. One of her handmaidens, Melantho by name, was there, and she was speaking angrily to him. Now this Melantho was proud and hard of heart because Antinous often conversed with her. As Penelope came near she was saying:

"Stranger, art thou still here, prying things out and spying on the servants? Be thankful for the supper thou hast gotten and betake thyself out of this."

Odysseus, looking fiercely at her, said, "Why shouldst thou speak to me in such a way? If I go in ragged clothes and beg through the land it is because of my necessity. Once I had a house with servants and with much substance, and the stranger who came there was not abused."

The lady Penelope called to the handmaiden and said, "Thou, Melantho, didst hear it from mine own lips that I was minded to speak to this stranger and ask him if he had tidings of my lord. Therefore, it does not become thee to revil him." She spoke to the old nurse who had come with her, and said, "Eurycleia bring to the fire a bench, with a fleece upon it, that this stranger may sit and tell me his story."

Eurycleia brought over the bench, and Odysseus sat down near the fire. Then said the lady Penelope, "First, stranger wilt thou tell me who thou art, and what is thy name, and thy race and thy country?"

Said Odysseus, "Ask me all thou wilt lady, but inquire not concerning my name, or race, or country, lest thou shouldst fill my heart with more pains than I am able to endure. Verily I am a man of grief. But hast thou no tale to tell me? We know of thee, Penelope, for thy fame goes up to heaven, and no one of mortal men can find fault with thee."

Then said Penelope, "What excellence I had of face or form departed from me when my lord Odysseus went from this hall to the wars of Troy. And since he went a host of ills has beset me. Ah, would that he were here to watch over my life! The lords of all the islands around—Dulichium and Same and Zacynthus; and the lords of the land of Ithaka, have come here and are wooing me against my will. They devour the substance of this house and my son is being impoverished.

"Long ago a god put into my mind a device to keep marriage with any of them away from me. I set up a great web upon my loom and I spoke to the wooers saying, 'Odysseus is assuredly dead, but I crave that you be not eager to speed on his marriage with me. Wait until I finish the web I am weaving. It is a shroud or Odysseus' father, and I make it gainst the day when death shall come to im. There will be no woman to care for aertes[10] when I have left his son's ouse, and I would not have such a hero ie without a shroud, lest the women of ur land should blame me for neglect f my husband's father in his last lays.'

"So I spoke, and they agreed to wait ntil the web was woven. In the dayime I wove it, but at night I unravelled he web. So three years passed away. Then the fourth year came, and my vooers were hard to deal with. My reacherous handmaidens brought them ipon me as I was unravelling the web. And now I cannot devise any other plan o keep the marriage away from me. My arents command me to marry one of ny wooers. My son cannot long endure o see the substance of his house and ield being wasted, and the wealth that hould be his destroyed. He too would vish that I should marry. And there s no reason why I should not be wed again, for surely Odysseus, my lord, is lead."

Said Odysseus, "Thy lord was known to me. On his way to Troy he came to my land, for the wind blew him out of his course, sending him wandering past Malea.[11] For twelve days he stayed in my city, and I gave him good entertainment, and saw that he lacked for nothing in cattle, or wine, or barley meal."

When Odysseus was spoken of, the heart of Penelope melted, and tears ran down her cheeks. Odysseus had pity for his wife when he saw her weeping for the man who was even then sitting by her. Tears would have run down his own cheeks only that he was strong enough to hold them back.

Said Penelope, "Stranger, I cannot help but question thee about Odysseus. What raiment had he on when thou didst see him? And what men were with him?"

Said Odysseus, "Lady, it is hard for one so long parted from him to tell thee what thou hast asked. It is now twenty years since I saw Odysseus. He wore a purple mantle that was fastened with a brooch. And this brooch had on it the image of a hound holding a fawn between its forepaws. All the people marvelled at this brooch, for it was of gold, and the fawn and the hound were done to the life. And I remember that there was a henchman with Odysseus—he was a man somewhat older than his master, roundshouldered and black-skinned and curlyheaded. His name was Eurybates,[12] and Odysseus honoured him above the rest of his company."

When he spoke, giving such tokens of Odysseus, Penelope wept again. And when she had wept for a long time she said:

"Stranger, thou wert made welcome, but now thou shalt be honoured in this hall. Thou dost speak of the garments that Odysseus wore. It was I who gave him these garments, folding them myself and bringing them out of the chamber. And it was I who gave him the brooch that thou hast described. Ah, it was an

[10] LAERTES (lâ·ûr′tēz)—Father of Odysseus, once King of Ithaka.

[11] MALEA (mä·lē′ä)—Southernmost headland of Greece.

[12] EURYBATES—Pronounced ū·rĭb′ȧ·tēz.

evil fate that took him from me, bringing him to Troy, that place too evil to be named by me."

Odysseus leaned towards her, and said, "Do not waste thy heart with endless weeping, lady. Cease from lamentation, and lay up in thy mind the word I give thee. Odysseus is near. He has lost all his companions, and he knows not how to come into this house, whether openly or by stealth. I swear it. By the hearth of Odysseus to which I am come, I swear that Odysseus himself will stand up here before the old moon wanes and the new moon is born."

"Ah, no," said Penelope. "Often before have wanderers told me such comfortable things, and I believed them. I know now that thy word cannot be accomplished. But it is time for thee to rest thyself, stranger. My handmaidens will make a bed for thee in the vestibule, and then come to thee and bathe thy feet."

Said Odysseus, "Thy handmaidens would be loath to touch the feet of a wanderer such as I. But if there is in the house some old wife who has borne such troubles as I have borne, I would have my feet bathed by her."

Said Penelope, "Here is an ancient woman who nursed and tended that hapless man, Odysseus. She took him in her arms in the very hour he was born. Eurycleia, wash the feet of this man, who knew thy lord and mine."

Thereupon the nurse, old Eurycleia, fetched water, both hot and cold, and brought the bath to the hearth. And standing before Odysseus in the flickering light of the fire, she said, "I will wash thy feet, both for Penelope's sake and for thine own. The heart within me is moved at the sight of thee. Many strangers have come into this hall, but I have never seen one that was so like as thou art to Odysseus."

Said Odysseus, "Many people have said that Odysseus and I favour each other."

His feet were in the water, and she put her hand upon one of them. As she did so, Odysseus turned his face away to the darkness, for it suddenly came into his mind that his nurse, old Eurycleia, might recognize the scar that was upon that foot.

How came it there, that scar? It had been made long ago when a boar's tusk had ripped up the flesh of his foot. Odysseus was then a youth, and he had gone to the mountain Parnassus to visit there his mother's father.

One morning, with his uncles, young Odysseus went up the slope of the mountain Parnassus, to hunt with hounds. In a thick lair a mighty boar was lying. When the sound of the men's trampling came near him, he sprang up with gleaming eyes and stood before them all. Odysseus, holding his spear in his hands, rushed upon him. But before he could strike him, the boar charged, ripping deep into his flesh with his tusk. Then Odysseus speared him through the shoulder and the boar was slain. His uncles staunched the wound and he stayed with them on the mountain Parnassus, in his grandfather's house, until the wound was healed.

And now, as Eurycleia, his old nurse, passed her hands along the leg, she let his foot drop suddenly. His knee struck against the bath, and the vessel of water was overturned. The nurse touched the

shin of Odysseus and she said, "Thou art Odysseus."

She looked to where Penelope was sitting, so that she might make a sign to her. But Penelope had her eyes turned away. Odysseus put his hand on Eurycleia's mouth, and with the other hand he drew her to him.

"Woman," he whispered. "Say nothing. Be silent, lest mine enemies learn what thou knowest now."

"Silent I'll be," said the nurse Eurycleia. "Thou knowest me. Firm and unyielding I am, and by no sign will I let anyone know that thou hast come under this roof."

So saying she went out of the hall to fetch water in the place of that which had been spilt. She came back and finished bathing his feet. Then Odysseus arranged the rags around his leg to hide the scar, and he drew the bench closer to the fire.

Penelope turned to him again. "Wise thou art, my guest," she said, "and it may be that thou art just such a man as can interpret a dream that comes to me constantly. I have twenty geese in the yard outside. In my dream I see them, and then a great eagle flies down from the mountains, and breaks their necks and kills them all, and lays them in a heap in this hall. I weep and lament for my geese, but then the eagle comes back, and perching on a beam of the roof speaks to me in the voice of a man. 'Take heart, O wife of Odysseus,' the eagle says, 'this is no dream but a true vision. For the geese that thou hast seen are thy wooers, and I, that appeared as an eagle, am thy husband who will swiftly bring death to the wooers.' Then the dream goes, and I waken and look out on the daylight and see my geese in the courtyard pecking at the wheat in the trough. Canst thou interpret this dream?"

"Lady," said Odysseus, "the dream interprets itself. All will come about as thou hast dreamed."

"Ah," said Penelope, "but it cannot now, for the day of my woe is at hand. I am being forced by my parents to choose a husband from the wooers, and depart from the house of Odysseus."

"And how wilt thou choose from amongst them?" said Odysseus.

"In this way will I make choice," said Penelope. "My husband's great bow is still in the house. The one who can bend that bow, and shoot an arrow through the holes in the backs of twelve axes set one behind the other—him will I choose for my husband."

Said Odysseus, "Thy device is good, Penelope, and some god hath instructed thee to do this. But delay no longer the contest of the bow. Let it be tomorrow."

"Is that thy counsel, O stranger?" said Penelope.

"It is my counsel," said Odysseus.

"I thank thee for thy counsel," she said. "And now farewell, for I must go to my rest. And do thou lie down in the vestibule, in the bed that has been made for thee."

So Penelope spoke, and then she went to her chamber with her handmaidens. And in her bed she thought over all the stranger had told her of Odysseus, and she wept again for him.

All night Odysseus lay awake, tossing this side and that, as he pondered on how he might slay the wooers, and save his house from them. As soon as the dawn came, he went into the open air and lifting up his hands, prayed to Zeus,[13] the greatest of the gods, that he might be shown some sign, as to whether he would win victory or meet with defeat.

And then, as he was going within the house, he heard the voice of a woman who ground barley-meal between stones. She was one of twelve, but the other women had fallen asleep by the quern stones.[14] She was an ancient, wretched woman, covered all over with the dust of the grain, and, as Odysseus came near her, she lifted up her hands and prayed in a weak voice:

"O Zeus, even for miserable men, fulfil a prayer! May this be the last day that the wooers make their feast in the house of Odysseus! They have loosened my knees with the cruel toil they have made me undergo, grinding for them the barley for the bread they eat. O Zeus, may they today sup their last!"

Thus the quern-woman spoke, as Odysseus crossed his threshold. He was glad of her speech, for it seemed to him her words were an omen from Zeus, and that vengeance would soon be wrought upon the proud and hard-hearted men who wasted the goods of the house and oppressed the servants.

And now the maids came into the hall from the women's apartment, and some cleaned the tables and others took pitchers and went to the well for water. Then

[13] ZEUS—Pronounced zūs.

[14] QUERN-STONES—Stones used for grinding grain in a handmill called a quern.

men-servants came in and split the fagots for the fire. Other servants came into the courtyard—Eumaeus the swineherd, driving fatted swine, the best of his drove, and Philoetius [15] the cattle-herd bringing a calf. The goatherd Melanthius, him whom Odysseus and Eumaeus had met on the road the day before, also came, bringing the best goats of his flock to be killed for the wooers' feast.

When the cattle-herd, Philoetius, saw a stranger in the guise of a beggar, he called out as he tethered the calf in the yard, "Hail, stranger friend! My eyes fill with tears as I look on thee. For even now, clad as thou art in rags, thou dost make me think of my master Odysseus, who may be a wanderer such as thou in friendless lands. Ah, that he might return and make a scattering of the wooers in his hall." Eumaeus the swineherd came up to Philoetius and made the same prayer. These two, and the ancient woman at the quern, were the only ones of his servants whom he heard pray for his return.

And now the wooers came into the hall. Philoetius the cattle-herd, and Melanthius the evil goatherd, went amongst them, handing them bread and meat and wine. Odysseus stood outside the hall until Telemachus went to him and brought him within.

Now there was amongst the wooers a man named Ctesippus,[16] and he was the rudest and the roughest of them all. When he saw Telemachus bringing Odysseus within he shouted out, "Here is a guest of Telemachus to whom some gift is due from us. It will be unseemly if he should get nothing today. Therefore I will bestow this upon him as a token."

Saying this, Ctesippus took up the foot of a slaughtered ox and flung it full at Odysseus. Odysseus drew back, and the ox's foot struck the wall. Then did Odysseus smile grimly upon the wooers.

Said Telemachus, "Verily, Ctesippus, the cast turned out happily for thyself. For if thou shouldst have struck my guest, there would have been a funeral feast instead of a wedding banquet in thy father's house. Assuredly I should have driven my spear through thee."

All the wooers were silent when Telemachus spoke these bold words. But soon they fell laughing at something one of their number said. The guest from Telemachus' ship, Theoclymenus, was there, and he started up and went to leave the hall.

"Why dost thou go, my guest?" said Telemachus.

"I see the walls and the beams of the roof sprinkled with blood," said Theoclymenus, the second-sighted [17] man. "I hear the voice of wailing. I see cheeks wet with tears. The men before me have shrouds upon them. The courtyard is filled with ghosts."

So Theoclymenus spoke, and all the wooers laughed at the second-sighted man, for he stumbled about the hall as if it were in darkness. Then said one of the wooers, "Lead that man out of the house, for surely he cannot tell day from night."

"I will go from the place," said Theoclymenus. "I see death approaching.

[15] PHILOETIUS—Pronounced fĭ·lē′tĭ·ŭs.
[16] CTESIPPUS—Pronounced tē·sĭp′pŭs.

[17] SECOND-SIGHTED—Able to foresee the future.

Not one of all the company before me will be able to avoid it."

So saying, the second-sighted man went out of the hall. The wooers looking at each other laughed again, and one of them said:

"Telemachus has no luck in his guests. One is a dirty beggar, who thinks of nothing but what he can put from his hand into his mouth, and the other wants to stand up here and play the seer." So the wooers spake in mockery, but neither Telemachus nor Odysseus paid heed to their words, for their minds were bent upon the time when they should take vengeance upon them.

In the treasure-chamber of the house Odysseus' great bow was kept. That bow had been given to him by a hero named Iphitus [18] long ago. Odysseus had not taken it with him when he went to the wars of Troy.

To the treasure-chamber Penelope went. She carried in her hand the great key that opened the doors—a key all of bronze with a handle of ivory. Now as she thrust the key into the locks, the doors groaned as a bull groans. She went within, and saw the great bow upon its peg. She took it down and laid it upon her knees, and thought long upon the man who had bent it.

Beside the bow was its quiver full of bronze-weighted arrows. The servant took the quiver and Penelope took the bow, and they went from the treasure-chamber and into the hall where the wooers were.

When she came in she spoke to the company and said: "Lords of Ithaka and of the islands around: You have come here, each desiring that I should wed him. Now the time has come for me to make my choice of a man from amongst you. Here is how I shall make choice.

"This is the bow of Odysseus, my lord who is no more. Whosoever amongst you who can bend this bow and shoot an arrow from it through the holes in the backs of twelve axes which I shall have set up, him will I wed, and to his house I will go, forsaking the house of my wedlock, this house so filled with treasure and substance, this house which I shall remember in my dreams."

As she spoke Telemachus took the twelve axes and set them upright in an even line, so that one could shoot an arrow through the hole that was in the back of each axe-head. Then Eumaeus, the old swineherd, took the bow of Odysseus, and laid it before the wooers.

One of the wooers took up the bow and tried to bend it. But he could not bend it, and he laid it down at the doorway with the arrow beside it. The others took up the bow, and warmed it at the fire, and rubbed it with lard to make it more pliable. As they were doing this, Eumaeus, the swineherd, and Philoetius, the cattle-herd, passed out of the hall.

Odysseus followed them into the courtyard. He laid a hand on each and said, "Swineherd and cattle-herd, I have a word to say to you. But will you keep it to yourselves, the word I say? And first, what would you do to help Odysseus if he should return? Would you stand on his side, or on the side of the wooers? Answer me now from your hearts."

Said Philoetius the cattle-herd, "May Zeus fulfil my wish and bring Odysseus

[18] IPHITUS—Pronounced ĭf′ĭ·tŭs.

back! Then thou shouldst know on whose side I should stand." And Eumaeus said, "If Odysseus should return I would be on his side, and that with all the strength that is in me."

When they said this, Odysseus declared himself. Lifting up his hand to heaven he said, "I am your master, Odysseus. After twenty years I have come back to my own country, and I find that of all my servants, by you two alone is my homecoming desired. If you need see a token that I am indeed Odysseus, look down on my foot. See there the mark that the wild boar left on me in the days of my youth."

Straightway he drew the rags from the scar, and the swineherd and the cattle-herd saw it and marked it well. Knowing that it was indeed Odysseus who stood before them, they cast their arms around him and kissed him on the head and shoulders. And Odysseus was moved by their tears, and he kissed their heads and their hands.

As they went back to the hall, he told Eumaeus to bring the bow to him as he was bearing it through the hall. He told him, too, to order Eurycleia, the faithful nurse, to bar the doors of the women's apartment at the end of the hall, and to bid the women, even if they heard a groaning and a din, not to come into the hall. And he charged the cattle-herd Philoetius to bar the gates of the courtyard.

As he went into the hall, one of the wooers, Eurymachus, was striving to bend the bow. As he struggled to do so he groaned aloud:

"Not because I may not marry Penelope do I groan, but because we youths of today are shown to be weaklings beside Odysseus, whose bow we can in no way bend."

Then Antinous, the proudest of the wooers, made answer and said, "Why should we strive to bend the bow today? Nay, lay the bow aside, Eurymachus, and let the wine-bearers pour us out a cupful each. In the morning let us make sacrifice to the Archer-god, and pray that the bow be fitted to some of our hands."

Then Odysseus came forward and said, "Sirs, you do well to lay the bow aside for today. But will you not put the bow into my hands, that I may try to bend it, and judge for myself whether I have any of the strength that once was mine?"

All the wooers were angry that a seeming beggar should attempt to bend the bow that none of their company were able to bend; Antinous spoke to him sharply and said:

"Thou wretched beggar! Is it not enough that thou art let into this high hall to pick up scraps, but thou must listen to our speech and join in our conversation? If thou shouldst bend that bow we will make short shrift of thee, I promise. We will put thee on a ship and send thee over to King Echetus,[19] who will cut thee to pieces and give thy flesh to his hounds."

Old Eumaeus had taken up the bow. As he went with it to Odysseus some of them shouted to him, "Where art thou going with the bow, thou crazy fellow? Put it down." Eumaeus was confused by their shouts and he put down the bow.

Then Telemachus spoke to him and said, "Eumaeus, beware of being the man who served many masters." Eumaeus,

[19] ECHETUS—Pronounced ĕk′ĕ·tŭs.

hearing these words, took it up again and brought it to Odysseus, and put the bow into his hands.

As Odysseus stood in the doorway of the hall, the bow in his hands, and with the arrows scattered at his feet, Eumaeus went to Eurycleia, and told her to bar the door of the women's apartment at the back. Then Philoetius, the cattle-herd, went out of the hall and barred the gates leading out of the courtyard.

For long Odysseus stood with the bow in his hands, handling it as a minstrel handles a lyre when he stretches a cord or tightens a peg. Then he bent the great bow; he bent it without an effort, and at his touch the bowstring made a sound that was like the cry of a swallow. The wooers seeing him bend that mighty bow felt, every man of them, a sharp pain at the heart. They saw Odysseus take up an arrow and fit it to the string. He held the notch, and he drew the string, and he shot the bronze-weighted arrow straight through the holes in the back of the axe-heads.

Then as Eumaeus took up the axes, and brought them outside, he said, "Thou seest, lord Telemachus, that thy guest does not shame thee through foolish boasting. I have bent the bow of Odysseus, and I have shot the arrow aright. But now it is time to provide the feast for the lords who woo thy lady mother. While it is yet light, the feast must be served to them, and with the feast they must have music and the dance."

Saying this he nodded to Telemachus, bending his terrible brows. Telemachus instantly girt his sword upon him and took his spear in his hand. Outside was heard the thunder of Zeus. And now Odysseus had stripped his rags from him and was standing upright, looking a master of men. The mighty bow was in his hands, and at his feet were scattered many bronze-weighted arrows.

"It is ended," Odysseus said, "my trial is ended. Now will I have another mark." Saying this, he put the bronze-weighted arrow against the string of the bow and shot at the first of his enemies.

It was at Antinous he pointed the arrow—at Antinous who was even then lifting up a golden cup filled with wine, and who was smiling, with death far from his thoughts. Odysseus aimed at him, and smote him with the arrow in the throat and the point passed out clean through his neck. The wine cup fell from his hands and Antinous fell dead across the table. Then did all the wooers raise a shout, threatening Odysseus for sending an arrow astray. It did not come into their minds that this stranger-beggar had aimed to kill Antinous.

But Odysseus shouted back to them, "Ye dogs, ye that said in your hearts that Odysseus would never return to his home, ye that wasted my substance, and troubled my wife, and injured my servants; ye who showed no fear of heaven, nor of the just judgments of men; behold Odysseus returned, and know what death is being loosed on you!"

Then Eurymachus shouted, "Friends, this man will not hold his hands, nor cease from shooting with the bow, until all of us are slain. Now must we enter into the battle with him. Draw your swords and hold up the tables before you for shields and advance upon him."

But even as he spoke Odysseus, with a terrible cry, loosed an arrow at him and shot Eurymachus through the breast. He let the sword fall from his hand, and he too fell dead upon the floor.

One of the band rushed straight at Odysseus with his sword in hand. But Telemachus was at hand, and he drove his spear through this man's shoulders. Then Telemachus ran quickly to a chamber where there were weapons and armour lying. The swineherd and the cattle-herd joined him, and all three put armour upon them. Odysseus, as long as he had arrows to defend himself, kept shooting at and smiting the wooers. When all the arrows were gone, he put the helmet on his head and took up the shield that Telemachus had brought, and the two great spears.

But now Melanthius, the goatherd—he who was the enemy of Odysseus, got into the chamber where the arms were kept, and brought out spears and shields and helmets, and gave them to the wooers. Seeing the goatherd go back for more arms, Telemachus and Eumaeus dashed into the chamber, and caught him and bound him with a rope, and dragged him up near the roofbeams, and left him hanging there. Then they closed and bolted the door, and stood on guard.

Many of the wooers lay dead upon the floor of the hall. Now one who was called Agelaus [20] stood forward, and directed the wooers to cast spears at Odysseus. But not one of the spears they cast struck him, for Odysseus was able to avoid them all.

And now he directed Telemachus and Eumaeus and Philoetius to cast their spears. When they cast them with Odysseus, each one struck a man, and four of the wooers fell down. And again Odysseus directed his following to cast their spears, and again they cast them, and slew their men. They drove those who remained from one end of the hall to the other, and slew them all.

Straightway the doors of the women's apartment were flung open, and Eurycleia appeared. She saw Odysseus amongst the bodies of the dead, all stained with blood. She would have cried out in triumph if Odysseus had not restrained her. "Rejoice within thine own heart," he said, "but do not cry aloud, for it is an unholy thing to triumph over men lying dead. These men the gods themselves have overcome, because of their own hard and unjust hearts."

As he spoke the women came out of their chambers, carrying torches in their hands. They fell upon Odysseus and embraced him and clasped and kissed his hands. A longing came over him to weep, for he remembered them from of old—every one of the servants who were there.

Eurycleia, the old nurse, went to the upper chamber where Penelope lay in her bed. She bent over her and called out, "Awake, Penelope, dear child. Come down and see with thine own eyes what hath happened. The wooers are overthrown. And he whom thou hast ever longed to see hath come back. Odysseus, thy husband, hath returned. He hath slain the proud wooers who have troubled thee for so long."

But Penelope only looked at the nurse,

[20] AGELAUS—Pronounced ăj·ē·lā′ŭs.

for she thought that her brain had been turned.

Still Eurycleia kept on saying, "In very deed Odysseus is here. He is that guest whom all the wooers dishonour in the hall."

Then hearing Eurycleia say these words, Penelope sprang out of bed and put her arms round the nurse's neck. "O tell me—if what thou dost say be true—tell me how this stranger slew the wooers, who were so many."

"I did not see the slaying," Eurycleia said, "but I heard the groaning of the men as they were slain. And then I found Odysseus standing amongst many dead men, and it comforted my heart to see him standing there like a lion aroused. Come with me now, lady, that you may both enter into your heart's delight—you that have suffered so much of affliction. Thy lord hath come alive to his own hearth, and he hath found his wife and his son alive and well."

"Ah no!" said Penelope, "ah no, Odysseus hath not returned. He who hath slain the wooers is one of the deathless gods, come down to punish them for their injustice and their hard-heartedness. Odysseus long ago lost the way of his returning, and he is lying dead in some far-off land."

"No, no," said Eurycleia. "I can show thee that it is Odysseus indeed who is in the hall. On his foot is the scar that the tusk of a boar gave him in the old days. I spied it when I was washing his feet last night, and I would have told thee of it, but he clapped a hand across my mouth to stop my speech. Lo, I stake my life that it is Odysseus, and none other who is in the hall below."

Saying this she took Penelope by the hand and led her from the upper chamber into the hall. Odysseus was standing by a tall pillar. He waited there for his wife to come and speak to him. But Penelope stood still, and gazed long upon him, and made no step towards him.

Then said Telemachus, "Mother, can it be that thy heart is so hard? Here is my father, and thou wilt not go to him nor question him at all."

Said Penelope, "My mind is amazed and I have no strength to speak, nor to ask him aught, nor even to look on him face to face. If this is indeed Odysseus who hath come home, a place has to be prepared for him."

Then Odysseus spoke to Telemachus and said, "Go now to the bath, and make thyself clean of the stains of battle. I will stay and speak with thy lady mother."

"Strange lady," said he to Penelope, "is thy heart indeed so hard? No other woman in the world, I think, would stand so aloof from her husband who, after so much toil and so many trials, has come back after twenty years to his own hearth. Is there no place for me here, and must I again sleep in the stranger's bed?"

Said Penelope, "In no stranger's bed wilt thou lie, my lord. Come, Eurycleia. Set up for him his own bedstead outside his bedchamber."

Then Odysseus said to her, speaking in anger: "How comes it that my bed can be moved to this place and that? Not a bed of that kind was the bed I built for myself. Knowest thou not how I built my bed? First, there grew up in the courtyard an olive tree. Round that olive tree I built a chamber, and I roofed it well and I set doors to it. Then I sheared off all the light wood on the growing olive tree, and I rough-hewed the trunk with the adze, and I made the tree into a bedpost. Beginning with this bed-post I wrought a bedstead, and when I finished it, I inlaid it with silver and ivory. Such was the bed I built for my-self, and such a bed could not be moved to this place or that."

Then did Penelope know assuredly that the man who stood before her was indeed her husband, the steadfast Odysseus—none other knew of where the bed was placed, and how it had been built. Pe-nelope fell a-weeping and she put her arms round his neck.

"O Odysseus, my lord," she said, "be not angry with thy wife. Always the fear was in my heart that some guileful stranger should come here professing to be Odysseus, and that I should take him to me as my husband. How terrible such a thing would be! But now my heart is freed from all doubts. Be not angry with me, Odysseus, for not throwing myself on thy neck, as the women of the house did."

Then husband and wife wept together, and Penelope said, "It was the gods did this to us, Odysseus—the gods who grudged that we should have joy of the days of our youth."

Next they told each other of things that happened in the twenty years they were apart; Odysseus speaking of his own toils and sorrows, and Penelope telling what she had endured at the hands of the wooers. And as they told tales, one to the other, slumber came upon them, and the dawn found them sleeping side by side.

FOR DISCUSSION

1. What incident at the well of the Nymphs provokes Odysseus to wish "to chastise the insolence that gathers around his house"?

2. Identify Argos. Did Argos recognize Odysseus? How do you know?

3. Why did Odysseus wish to remain in disguise?

4. Why is Odysseus unrecognized in his own house? Do you detect irony in these words of Antinous: "Is it nothing to thee that worthless fellows come here to devour thy master's substance?"

5. Why did Penelope desire to meet the strange beggar? What indicates that Penel-ope grieves for her husband?

6. By what device did Penelope delay her re-marriage? How was her stratagem betrayed?

7. What circumstance revealed Odys-seus to Eurycleia?

8. Describe the test by which Penelope meant to choose a husband.

9. Describe the scene in which the wooers and Odysseus make trial to bend the great bow.

10. To whose will did Odysseus ascribe the bloody fate of the wooers?

11. Describe the meeting between Odys-seus and Penelope after the slaying. What final proof convinced Penelope that the stranger was Odysseus?

12. Why did Telemachus regard his mother's heart as "hard" when she would not recognize Odysseus?

13. What is the meaning of the word "omen"? Tell some of the omens de-scribed in this story. What do they tell you about these ancient people?

14. Although the incidents related in the story of Odysseus are legendary, some of the descriptions of ancient Greek life and customs are true. From the selection just read, indicate incidents which reveal in these barbaric people: reverence toward the gods; respect for parents; hospitality toward strangers and the needy; respect for the dead.

A GREEK WORD FAMILY

The word *meter* is the parent of an interesting word family. *Meter* comes from the Greek word *metron*, measure, and is found in many words with which you are familiar: *thermometer*, *speedometer*, *kilometer*. Do you know what is meant by the *metric* system? *Chronometer* and *pedometer* are other words built on this root. Can you guess what they mean? If not, look them up in your dictionary.

READING FURTHER ADVENTURES OF ODYSSEUS

The slaying of the wooers and Odysseus' re-establishment as king of Ithaka are final incidents in his dramatic story. The full account of Odysseus' voyage and return is told in twenty-four chapters or "books." In the first part of this epic Odysseus had twelve adventures, among which three are especially interesting: those on the island of the enchantress Circe (Book X); those concerning the nymph-goddess Calypso (Book XIII); and those dealing with the princess Nausicäa and King Alcinous, to whom Odysseus related his escape from the Cyclops (Books VI–VIII). Using any translation of Homer's *Odyssey* which you can find in the library, retell one of these earlier adventures to the class.

RELATED READING

The full story of *The Iliad* and *The Odyssey* can be read in Padraic Colum's *The Adventures of Odysseus and the Tale of Troy*. The two poems have also been translated into blank verse by William Cullen Bryant, and *The Odyssey* into excellent and stirring prose by T. E. Shaw. Shaw is popularly known as "Lawrence of Arabia." E. V. Rieu has also made a good translation of *The Odyssey* in modern English.

◇◇◇◇◇

Here is a fleeting glimpse of the home life of the Prince of Peace. The poet paints a portrait of Mary, the spinner. He reveals to us Jesus' twofold love for his mother: a human love and a divine love.

The Spinner

CHARLES L. O'DONNELL, C.S.C.

Mary the Mother of Jesus,
  A lady of high degree,
Sat by her cottage spinning
  In Nazareth of Galilee.

A light fell over her shoulder
  As she sat in the plane-tree's shade
While a delicate lace of shadows
  The sun and the green leaves made.

"The Spinner" from *Collected Poems of Charles O'Donnell*, University Press, Notre Dame, Indiana, 1942. Reprinted by permission of Hugh J. O'Donnell.

6. PLANE-TREE—A sycamore or buttonwood tree.

Busy her foot on the treadle,
And her wheel busily whirled 10
As a Child looked out from the doorway,
A Child who had made the world.

Deftly she handled the distaff,
And happily whirred her wheel
As the Child came down from the doorway 15
And ran at her side to kneel.

"Mother," He said as He watched her
There while she sat and spun,
"Some things are more fair than I dreamed them
The day that I made the sun. 20

"And you are My heart of all beauty,
My star of all seas, of all lands—"
"Hush, Child," whispered Mary His Mother,
Her tears falling down on His hands.

13. DISTAFF—A vertical staff that holds the wool to be spun.

FOR DISCUSSION

1. By watching Mary and Jesus at home, you will surely find something good to imitate. What virtues do you recognize in the lines below?

a. "Sat by her cottage spinning."
b. "Some things are more fair than I dreamed."
c. "You are My heart of all beauty."
d. "Hush, Child."

2. Because Jesus was God, only His sense-knowledge could grow from day to day. Although as God, He knew everything from all eternity, He did not see things through human eyes until He became man. Can you pick out the lines of the poem which show He was pleased by this sense-knowledge?

3. What things mentioned in the poem are familiar to you? a plane-tree? the design made by sun and shade? the spinning machine? What are *not* familiar?

4. What ideas did you get from the poem about an ideal home life? Which lines helped you formulate your ideas?

5. If you can imagine some realistic details which might be added to the poem, it would be entertaining to write them down in good order and read them to the class. For instance, where was St. Joseph?

SENSE IMPRESSIONS

All that you learn of the world directly, that is, by your own experience, comes to you through your five senses. These experiences are stored in your mind as sense impressions. The poet tries to touch your mind in the same way, with sense words. See how often in this poem he appeals to your senses. The first appeal is made with the sound of the wheel, in the word "spinning." Now pick out as many other sense words as you can.

SOME PROJECTS

1. The poet gives a fairly realistic sketch here of a few minutes in the day of the Holy Family at Nazareth. What opportunities for similarly realistic description do you see in the life going on around *you?* Do not your classroom, the gymnasium, chapel, cafeteria, and your own home suggest picturesque descriptions to be written for someone not as accustomed to the scene as you are? Practice looking at familiar scenes with new vision, and write out realistically what you see.

2. Find out what you can about the geography of Nazareth and the customs of its residents. The librarian will readily supply you with material if you cannot find it yourself.

3. Suppose that you had been visiting Jesus and Mary that day. How would your presence have changed the story of the poem? Be as imaginative as you wish. What effects would such a visit have had upon *you?*

Clarence Day lived in the late nineteenth century on respectable Madison Avenue, New York City. In LIFE WITH FATHER *he has recorded many humorous recollections of his family life. The central figure in his book is Father, after whom Clarence was named. In the following selection from the book we learn much about both father and son. If you have laughed at any of the incidents taken from this book and portrayed on the stage or in television, you already know why Clarence Day's book has been so popular.*

FATHER OPENS MY MAIL

CLARENCE DAY

There was a time in my boyhood when I felt that Father had handicapped me severely in life by naming me after him, "Clarence." All literature, so far as I could see, was thronged with objectionable persons named Clarence. Percy was bad enough, but there had been some good fighters named Percy. The only Clarence in history was a duke who did something dirty at Tewkesbury,[1] and who died a ridiculous death afterwards in a barrel of malmsey.[2]

As for the Clarences in the fiction I read, they were horrible. In one story, for instance, there were two brothers, Clarence and Frank. Clarence was a "vain, disagreeable little fellow," who was proud of his curly hair and fine clothes, while Frank was a "rollicking boy who was ready to play games with anybody." Clarence didn't like to play games, of course. He just minced around looking on.

One day when the mother of these boys had gone out, this story went on, Clarence "tempted" Frank to disobey her and fly their kite on the roof. Frank didn't want to, but Clarence kept taunting him and daring him until Frank was stung into doing it. After the two boys went up to the roof, Frank got good and dirty, running up and down and stumbling over scuttles, while Clarence sat there, giving him orders, and kept his natty clothes tidy. To my horror, he even spread out his handkerchief on the trap door to sit on. And to crown all, this sneak told on Frank as soon as their mother came in.

This wasn't an exceptionally mean Clarence, either. He was just run-of-the-mill. Some were worse.

So far as I could ever learn, however, Father had never heard of these stories, and had never dreamed of there being anything objectionable in his name. Quite the contrary. And yet as a boy he

[1] TEWKESBURY—A district in Southwest England; the Yorkist party defeated the Lancastrians there in 1471.

[2] MALMSEY—A kind of wine.

had lived a good rough-and-tumble boy's life. He had played and fought on the city streets, and kept a dog in Grandpa's stable, and stolen rides to Greenpoint Ferry on the high, lurching bus. In the summer he had gone to West Springfield and had run down Shad Lane through the trees to the house where Grandpa was born, and had gone barefoot and driven the cows home just as though he had been named Tom or Bill.

He had the same character as a boy, I suppose, that he had as a man, and he was too independent to care if people thought his name fancy. He paid no attention to the prejudices of others, except to disapprove of them. He had plenty of prejudices himself, of course, but they were his own. He was humorous and confident and level-headed, and I imagine that if any boy had tried to make fun of him for being named Clarence, Father would simply have laughed and told him he didn't know what he was talking about.

I asked Mother how this name had ever happened to spring up in our family. She explained that my great-great-grandfather was Benjamin Day, and my great-grandfather was Henry, and consequently my grandfather had been named Benjamin Henry. He in turn had named his eldest son Henry and his second son Benjamin. The result was that when Father was born there was no family name left. The privilege of choosing a name for Father had thereupon been given to Grandma, and unluckily for the Day family she had been reading a novel, the hero of which was named Clarence.

I knew that Grandma, though very like Grandpa in some respects, had a dreamy side which he hadn't, a side that she usually kept to herself, in her serene, quiet way. Her romantic choice of this name probably made Grandpa smile, but he was a detached sort of man who didn't take small matters seriously, and who drew a good deal of private amusement from the happenings of everyday life. Besides, he was partly to blame in this case, because that novel was one he had published himself in his magazine.

I asked Mother, when she had finished, why I had been named Clarence too.

It hadn't been her choice, Mother said. She had suggested all sorts of names to Father, but there seemed to be something wrong with each one. When she had at last spoken of naming me after him, however, he had said at once that that was the best suggestion yet—he said it sounded just right.

Father and I would have had plenty of friction in any case. This identity of names made things worse. Every time that I had been more of a fool than he liked, Father would try to impress on me my responsibilities as his eldest son, and above all as the son to whom he had given his name, as he put it. A great deal was expected, it seemed to me, of a boy who was named after his father. I used to envy my brothers, who didn't have anything expected of them on this score at all.

I envied them still more after I was old enough to begin getting letters. I then discovered that when Father "gave" me his name he had also, not unnaturally, I had to admit, retained it himself, and when anything came for Clarence S. Day he opened it, though it was sometimes for me.

He also opened everything that came addressed to Clarence S. Day, Jr. He didn't do this intentionally, but unless the "Jr." was clearly written, it looked like "Esq." and anyhow Father was too accustomed to open all Clarence Day letters to remember about looking carefully every time for a "Jr." So far as mail and express went, I had no name at all of my own.

For the most part nobody wrote to me when I was a small boy except firms whose advertisements I had read in the *Youth's Companion* and to whom I had written requesting them to send me their circulars. These circulars described remarkable bargains in magicians' card outfits, stamps and coins, pocketknives, trick spiders, and imitation fried eggs, and they seemed interesting and valuable to me when I got them. The trouble was that Father usually got them and at once tore them up. I then had to write for such circulars again, and if Father got the second one too, he would explode with annoyance. He became particularly indignant one year, I remember, when he was repeatedly urged to take advantage of a special bargain sale of false whiskers. He said that he couldn't understand why these offerings kept pouring in. I knew why, in this case, but at other times I was often surprised myself at the number he got, not realizing that as a result of my postcard request my or our name had been automatically put on several large general mailing lists.

During this period I got more of my mail out of Father's wastebasket than I did from the postman.

At the age of twelve or thirteen, I stopped writing for these childish things and turned to a new field. Father and I, whichever of us got at the mail first, then began to receive not merely circulars but personal letters beginning:

> DEAR FRIEND DAY:
> In reply to your valued request for one of our Mammoth Agents' Outfits, kindly forward post-office order for $1.49 to cover cost of postage and packing, and we will put you in a position to earn a large income in your spare time with absolutely no labor on your part, by taking subscriptions for *The Secret Handbook of Mesmerism*, and our *Tales of Blood* series.

And one spring, I remember, as the result of what I had intended to be a secret application on my part, Father was assigned "the exclusive rights for Staten Island and Hoboken of selling the Gem Home Popper for Pop Corn. Housewives buy it at sight."

After Father had stormily endured these afflictions for a while, he and I began to get letters from girls. Fortunately for our feelings, these were rare, but they were ordeals for both of us. Father had forgotten, if he ever knew, how silly young girls can sound, and I got my first lesson in how unsystematic they were. No matter how private and playful they meant their letters to be, they forgot to put "Jr." on the envelope every once in so often. When Father opened these letters, he read them all the way through, sometimes twice, muttering to himself over and over: "This is very peculiar. I don't understand this at all. Here's a letter to me from some person I never heard of. I can't see what it's about." By the time it had occurred to him that possibly the letter might be for me, I was red and embarrassed and even angrier at the girl

than at Father. And on days when he had read some of the phrases aloud to the family, it nearly killed me to claim it.

Lots of fellows whom I knew had been named after their fathers without having such troubles. But although Father couldn't have been kinder-hearted or had any better intentions, when he saw his name on a package or envelope it never dawned on him that it might not be for him. He was too active in his habit to wait until I had a chance to get at it. And as he was also single-minded and prompt to attend to unfinished business, he opened everything automatically and then did his best to dispose of it.

This went on even after I grew up, until I had a home of my own. Father was always perfectly decent about it, but he never changed. When he saw I felt sulky, he was genuinely sorry and said so, but he couldn't see why all this should annoy me, and he was surprised and amused that it did. I used to get angry once in a while when something came for me which I particularly hadn't wished him to see and which I would find lying, opened, on the hall table marked "For Jr.?" when I came in; but nobody could stay angry with Father—he was too utterly guiltless of having meant to offend.

He often got angry himself, but it was mostly at things, not at persons, and he didn't mind a bit (as a rule) when persons got angry at him. He even declared, when I got back from college, feeling dignified, and told him that I wished he'd be more careful, that he suffered from these mistakes more than I did. It wasn't *his* fault, he pointed out, if my stupid correspondents couldn't remember my name, and it wasn't any pleasure to him to be upset at his breakfast by finding that a lunatic company in Battle Creek had sent

him a box of dry bread crumbs, with a letter asserting that this rubbish would be good for his stomach. "I admit I threw it into the fireplace, Clarence, but what else could I do? If you valued this preposterous concoction, my dear boy, I'm sorry. I'll buy another box for you today, if you'll tell me where I can get it. Don't feel badly! I'll buy you a barrel. Only I hope you won't eat it."

In the days when Mrs. Pankhurst and her friends were chaining themselves to lampposts in London, in their campaign for the vote, a letter came from Frances Hand trustfully asking "Dear Clarence" to do something to help Woman Suffrage—speak at a meeting, I think. Father got red in the face. "Speak at one of their meetings!" he roared at Mother. "I'd like nothing better! You can tell Mrs. Hand that it would give me great pleasure to inform all those crackpots in petticoats exactly what I think of their antics."

"Now, Clare," Mother said, "you mustn't talk that way. I like that nice Mrs. Hand, and anyhow this letter must be for Clarence."

One time I asked Father for his opinion of a low-priced stock I'd been watching. His opinion was that it was not worth a damn. I thought this over, but I still wished to buy it, so I placed a scale order with another firm instead of with Father's office, and said nothing about it. At the end of the month this other firm sent me a statement, setting forth each of my little transactions in full, and of course they forgot to put the "Jr." at the end of my name. When Father opened the envelope, he thought at first in his excitement that this firm had actually opened an account for him without being asked. I found him telling Mother that he'd like to wring their necks.

"That must be for me, Father," I said, when I took in what had happened.

We looked at each other.

"You bought this stuff?" he said incredulously. "After all I said about it?"

"Yes, Father."

He handed over the statement and walked out of the room.

Both he and I felt offended and angry. We stayed so for several days, too, but we then made it up.

Once in a while when I got a letter that I had no time to answer I used to address an envelope to the sender and then put anything in it that happened to be lying around on my desk—a circular about books, a piece of newspaper, an old laundry bill—anything at all, just to be amiable, and yet at the same time to save myself the trouble of writing. I happened to tell several people about this private habit of mine at a dinner one night—a dinner at which Alice Duer Miller and one or two other writers were present. A little later she wrote me a criticism of Henry James [3] and ended by saying that I needn't send her any of my old laundry bills because she wouldn't stand it. And she forgot to put on the "Jr."

"In the name of—," Father said bleakly, "this is the worst yet. Here's a woman who says I'd better not read *The Golden Bowl,* which I have no intention whatever of doing, and she also warns me for some unknown reason not to send her my laundry bills."

The good part of all these experiences, as I realize now, was that in the end they drew Father and me closer together. My brothers had only chance battles with him. I had a war. Neither he nor I relished its clashes, but they made us surprisingly intimate.

[3] HENRY JAMES—An American novelist.

◇◇◇◇◇◇◇◇◇◇◇◇◇◇◇◇◇◇◇◇◇◇◇◇◇◇◇◇◇◇◇◇

FOR DISCUSSION

1. How did the name Clarence get into the Day family? What was Junior's original objection to the name? Do you sympathize with him?

2. Why did Clarence, Jr. envy his brothers?

3. Which incident dealing with the mail difficulty strikes you as the funniest?

4. How would you characterize Father from what you have read about him in this story? Do you think Junior was like his father in any respect? Explain your answers by using details from the story.

DETERMINING EXACT WORD MEANINGS

1. Clarence on the roof "sat there . . . and kept his natty clothes *tidy.*" How does *tidy* differ from *neat, trim,* or *prim?*

2. Grandma had a side which she kept to herself in "her *serene,* quiet way." Could one properly substitute *calm, tranquil, placid,* or *peaceful* without changing Grandma? Explain.

3. "Letters from girls," says Clarence, Jr., "were *ordeals* for both of us." What is the original meaning of the word *ordeal?*

4. Father could not see why all the troubles growing out of identity of names "should *annoy*" Clarence, Jr. How does *annoy* differ from these words: *harass, vex, fret, worry, plague, torment, molest, tease, tantalize?*

RELATED READING

Life with Father either as a play or as a series of sketches is amusing and discloses another member of the Day family—Mother.

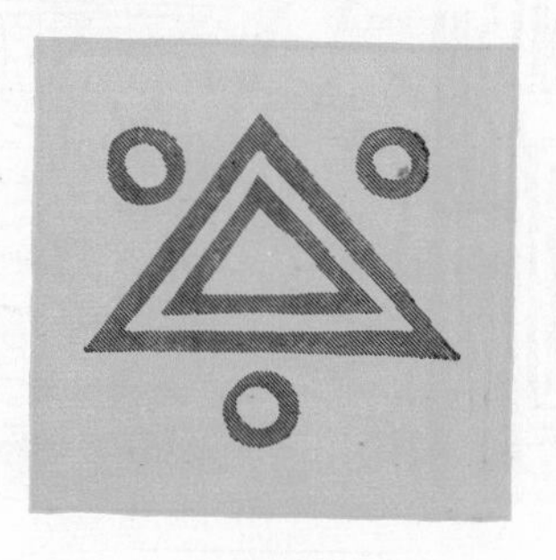

Christmas for the Catholic means not only one of the great religious feasts of the year but a day remarkable for its beautiful simplicity, its merry and blessed spirit of giving. In the following poem Joyce Kilmer captures much of the real Christmas message.

Gates and Doors

JOYCE KILMER

There was a gentle hostler
(And blessèd be his name!)
He opened up the stable
The night Our Lady came.
Our Lady and Saint Joseph, 5
He gave them food and bed,
And Jesus Christ has given him
A glory round his head.

So let the gate swing open
However poor the yard, 10
Lest weary people visit you
And find their passage barred;
Unlatch the door at midnight
And let your lantern's glow
Shine out to guide the traveler's feet 15
To you across the snow.

There was a courteous hostler
(He is in Heaven to-night)
He held Our Lady's bridle
And helped her to alight; 20
He spread clean straw before her
Whereon she might lie down,
And Jesus Christ has given him
An everlasting crown.

Unlock the door this evening 25
And let your gate swing wide,
Let all who ask for shelter
Come speedily inside.
What if your yard be narrow?
What if your house be small? 30
There is a Guest is coming
Will glorify it all.

There was a joyous hostler
Who knelt on Christmas morn
Beside the radiant manger 35
Wherein his Lord was born.
His heart was full of laughter,
His soul was full of bliss
When Jesus, on His Mother's lap,
Gave him His hand to kiss. 40

Unbar your heart this evening
And keep no stranger out,
Take from your soul's great portal
The barrier of doubt.
To humble folk and weary 45
Give hearty welcoming,
Your breast shall be to-morrow
The cradle of a King.

FOR DISCUSSION

1. Why is a hostler an appropriate figure to introduce into the Christmas scene?
2. In the second, fourth, and sixth stanzas the poet puts his message in imaginative language. State in your own words the thought of each of these stanzas.
3. What does this line mean: "Your breast shall be tomorrow the cradle of a King"?
4. Read the poem aloud. Do you think its rhythm is in keeping with the poet's mood and the spirit of the season?

DISCUSSING THE MEANING OF CHRISTMAS

The reading of *A Christmas Carol* by Charles Dickens has become part of the Christmas tradition. If you have not already read this English classic, you should get a copy of it at the library and read it. Why do you think this story has come to represent the meaning and spirit of Christmas? Is there any deeply religious meaning of Christmas which you think has been left out of the story? Prepare to explain what you think it is.

If three or four pupils have read the story thoroughly enough to discuss it well, you might plan to have a round-table discussion of it. Decide beforehand what questions you think are most important to talk about. Be sure that you know the story well enough to defend your answers with details from the book. You might even mark passages which you will want to read.

For Further Reading

Little Women by Louisa May Alcott is the delightful story of the March family. Jo, Amy, Beth, and Meg will become like sisters to anyone who reads this charming book.

Make Way for the Brave by Merritt Allen tells of the adventures of Red Dakin along the Oregon Trail in 1832. The story is full of action and offers sidelights on the ways of Indians, trappers, traders, animals, missionaries, and mountain-men.

This Way, Please by Eleanor Boykin. Here is an unusually intriguing book on modern manners.

Secret Garden by Frances Burnett. A hidden garden spells health and happiness for a little girl and contentment for her lonely uncle.

A Girl Grows Up by Ruth Fedder gives valuable aid to a teen-age girl in adjusting herself to her family and in meeting other social relationships.

Understood Betsy by Dorothy Canfield Fisher. Life in the country changes Betsy, a nervous child from the city, into a self-reliant and happy girl.

They Came from Sweden by Clara Judson. By dint of hard work, the Larssons made America the "land of opportunity" for every member of the family.

Lassie Come-Home by Eric Knight. A dog's unending courage and faithfulness bring her four hundred miles back to her friends.

Let the Hurricane Roar by Rose Lane is the forceful story of a recently married couple determined to keep their homestead despite the hardships of a pioneer life in the Dakotas.

The Three Brothers by Michael McLaverty is the story of a middle-class Irish family headed by the three brothers, Bob, D. J., and John. Mr. McLaverty recounts their fortunes and gives, at the same time, charming descriptions of the Irish landscape.

My Friend Flicka by Mary O'Hara. Life became real to Ken when his father gave him a colt of his own. Flicka's attempt to escape, her illness, and Ken's patient nursing highlight the real purpose of the book—to show the clash and weaving of personalities of a family of people who love each other.

The Yearling by Marjorie K. Rawlings tells about the life of a boy in the scrub regions of Florida just after the Civil War.

The Human Comedy by William Saroyan is the story of the Macauley family, and especially of Homer, the fifteen-year-old son—how they live and the impressions that living leaves with them. Birth, love, death, and joy all take on new meaning through the patient eyes of Ma Macauley. The loving-kindness of the author will help the reader to look with new eyes on the world around him.

Penrod by Booth Tarkington. Every boy and girl enjoys this humorous story of the life and loves, joys and sorrows of Penrod Schofield and his friends and family.

Lad: A Dog by Albert P. Terhune is the story of Sunnybank Lad, a collie that lived on Mr. Terhune's estate.

The Story of the Trapp Family Singers by Maria Augusta Trapp. Written with a deep religious feeling and a charming simplicity, this is the story of one of the most distinguished musical families in recent years.

Daddy-Long-Legs by Jean Webster. Judy Abbot writes about college life to an unseen benefactor who removed her from an orphanage.

Rebecca of Sunnybrook Farm by Kate D. Wiggins. High-spirited Rebecca wins the affection of two old maid aunts in this universally loved story.

LAND OF PROMISE

A purple cloak clung to his shoulders, and a flag embroidered with a cross waved above his head, as Columbus fell on his knees and kissed the ground. Then raising his forehead from the sand, he prayed:

> "Almighty and eternal God, Who by the energy of Your creative word have made the firmament and earth and sea, blessed and glorified be Your name in all places! May Your majesty and dominion be exalted forever, because You have permitted Your holy name to be made known and spread by the most humble of Your servants in this hitherto unknown portion of Your empire."

Then he baptized this land in the name of Christ—San Salvador.

With such godly dedication as this, our great land was inscribed on the list of Christian homelands. In the same breath, supernatural love of God was allied to natural love of country. Our national honor was then so consecrated that to be a perfect American, one must be a perfect Christian, too.

You will glimpse that kind of patriotism in the following stories. You will see young Abe Lincoln working at humble tasks and striving for an education. You will watch a pint-sized man find his own place in a strange land. You will find adventure in the journey of the rough frontiersman, George Rogers Clark, and his Virginian "Big Knives" as they wade one hundred and twenty miles through river-sloughs and tangled thickets to take the key colony in Illinois and make the townspeople free Americans. You will enjoy an expression of appreciation of America from the pen of a famous woman journalist. Look well at these people; they are true patriots.

COURTESY OF PHILADELPHIA MUSEUM OF ART

The other boys in the backwoods community where Lincoln grew up thought that there was "suthin' peculiarsome" about Abe. They admired his physical strength and athletic ability—qualities highly prized on the frontier and developed by all pioneer boys. What they did not understand in him were the moods and habits that made him different from themselves. They had no way of knowing that in cultivating his "peculiarsome" traits, Abraham Lincoln was preparing to become one of the great men of the world.

THE BOYHOOD OF LINCOLN

CARL SANDBURG

When he was eleven years old, Abe Lincoln's young body began to change. The juices and glands began to make a long, tall boy out of him. As the months and years went by, he noticed his lean wrists getting longer, his legs too, and he was now looking over the heads of other boys. Men said, "Land o' Goshen, that boy air a-growin'!"

As he took on more length, they said he was shooting up into the air like green corn in the summer of a good corn year. So he grew. When he reached seventeen years of age and they measured him, he was six feet, nearly four inches, high, from the bottoms of moccasins to the top of his skull.

These were years he was handling the ax. Except in spring plowing time and the fall fodder pulling, he was handling the ax nearly all the time. The insides of his hands took on callus thick as leather. He cleared openings in the timber, cut logs and puncheons,[1] split firewood, built pigpens.

He learned how to measure with his eye the half-circle swing of the ax so as to nick out the deepest possible chip from off a tree trunk. The trick of swaying his body easily on the hips so as to throw the heaviest possible weight into the blow of the ax—he learned that.

On winter mornings he wiped the frost from the ax handle, sniffed sparkles of air into his lungs, and beat a steady cleaving of blows into a big tree—till it fell—and he sat on the main log and ate his noon dinner of corn bread and fried salt pork—and joked with the gray squirrels that frisked and peeped at him from high forks of near-by walnut trees.

He learned how to make his ax flash and bite into a sugar-maple or a sycamore. The outside and the inside look of black walnut and black oak, hickory and jack oak, elm and white oak, sassafras, dogwood, grapevines, sumac—he came on their secrets. He could guess close to the

[1] PUNCHEONS—Upright supporting timbers.

time of the year, to the week of the month, by the way the leaves and branches of trees looked. He sniffed the seasons.

Often he worked alone in the timbers, all day long with only the sound of his own ax, or his own voice speaking to himself, or the crackling and swaying of branches in the wind, and the cries and whirs of animals, of brown and silver-gray squirrels, of partridges, hawks, crows, turkeys, sparrows, and the occasional wildcats.

The tricks and whimsies of the sky, how to read clear skies and cloudy weather, the creeping vines of ivy and wild grape, the recurrence of dogwood blossoms in spring, the ways of snow, rain, drizzle, sleet, the visitors of sky and weather coming and going hour by hour—he tried to read their secrets, he tried to be friendly with their mystery.

So he grew, to become hard, tough, wiry. The muscle on his bones and the cords, tendons, cross-weaves of fiber, and nerve centers,—these became instruments to obey his wishes. He found with other men he could lift his own end of a log—and more too. One of the neighbors said he was strong as three men. Another said, "He can sink an ax deeper into wood than any man I ever saw." And another, "If you heard him fellin' trees in a clearin', you would say there was three men at work by the way the trees fell."

He was more than a tough, long, rawboned boy. He amazed men with his man's lifting power. He put his shoulders under a new-built corncrib one day and walked away with it to where the farmer wanted it. Four men, ready with poles to put under it and carry it, didn't need their poles. He played the same trick with a chicken house; at the new, growing town of Gentryville near by, they said the chicken house weighed six hundred pounds, and only a big boy with a hard backbone could get under it and walk away with it.

A blacksmith shop, a grocery, and a store had started up on the crossroads of the Gentry farm. And one night after Abe had been helping thresh wheat on Dave Turnham's place, he went with Dennis Hanks, John Johnston, and some other boys to Gentryville, where the farm hands sat around with John Baldwin, the blacksmith, and Jones, the storekeeper, passed the whiskey jug, told stories, and talked politics and religion and gossip. Going home late that night, they saw something in a mud puddle alongside the road. They stepped over to see whether it was a man or a hog. It was a man—drunk—snoring—sleeping off his drunk—on a frosty night outdoors in a cold wind.

They shook him by the shoulders, doubled his knees to his stomach, but he went on sleeping, snoring. The cold wind was getting colder. The other boys said they were going home, and they went away leaving Abe alone with the snoring sleeper in the mud puddle. Abe stepped into the mud, reached arms around the man, slung him over his shoulders, carried him to Dennis Hanks's cabin, built a fire, rubbed him warm, and left him sleeping off the whiskey.

And the man afterward said Abe saved his life. He told John Hanks, "It was mighty clever of Abe to tote me to a warm fire that night."

So he grew, living in that Pigeon Creek cabin for a home, sleeping in the loft, climbing up at night to a bed just under the roof, where sometimes the snow and the rain drove through the cracks, eating sometimes at a table where the family had only one thing to eat—potatoes. Once at the table, when there were only potatoes, his father spoke a blessing to the Lord for potatoes; the boy murmured, "Those are mighty poor blessings." And Abe made jokes once when company came and Sally Bush Lincoln brought out raw potatoes, gave the visitors a knife apiece, and they all peeled raw potatoes, and talked about the crops, politics, religion, gossip.

Days when they had only potatoes to eat didn't come often. Other days in the year they had "yaller-legged chicken" with gravy, and corndodgers with shortening, and berries and honey. They tasted of bear meat, deer, coon, quail, grouse, prairie turkey, catfish, bass, perch.

Abe knew the sleep that comes after long hours of work outdoors, the feeling of simple food changing into blood and muscle as he worked in those young years, clearing timberland for pasture and corn crops, cutting loose the brush, piling it and burning it, splitting rails, pulling the crosscut saw and the whipsaw, driving the shovel-plow, harrowing, planting, hoeing, pulling fodder, milking cows, churning butter, helping neighbors at house-raisings, log-rollings, corn-huskings.

He found he was fast, strong, and keen when he went against other boys in sports. On farms where he worked, he held his own at scuffing, knocking off hats, wrestling. The time came when around Gentryville and Spencer County he was known as the best "rassler" of all, the champion. In jumping, foot-racing, throwing the maul,[2] pitching the crowbar, he carried away the decisions against the lads of his own age always, and usually won against those older than himself.

He earned his board, clothes, and lodgings, sometimes working for a neighbor farmer. He watched his father while helping make cabinets, coffins, cupboards, window frames, doors. Hammers, saws, pegs, cleats, he understood first-hand, also the scythe and the cradle[3] for cutting hay and grain, the corn cutter's knife, and the leather piece to protect the hand while shucking corn, and the horse, the dog, the cow, the ox, the hog. He could skin and cure the hides of coon and deer. He lifted the slippery two-hundred-pound hog carcass, head down, holding the hind hocks up for others of the gang to hook, and swung the animal clear of the ground. He learned where to stick a hog in the underside of the neck so as to bleed it to death; how to split it in two, and carve out the chops, the parts for sausage grinding, for hams, for "cracklings."[4]

Farmers called him to butcher for them at thirty-one cents a day—this when he was sixteen and seventeen years old. He could "knock a beef in the head," swing a maul and hit a cow between the eyes, skin the hide, halve and quarter it, carve out the tallow, the steaks, kidneys, liver.

And the hiding places of fresh spring water under the earth crust had to be in his thoughts; he helped at well-digging; the wells Tom Lincoln dug went dry one year after another; neighbors said Tom was always digging a well and had his land "honey-combed"; and the boy, Abe, ran the errands and held the tools for the well-digging.

When he was eighteen years old, he could take an ax at the end of the handle and hold it out in a straight horizontal line, easy and steady—he had strong shoulder muscles and steady wrists early in life. He walked thirty-four miles in one day, just on an errand to please himself, to hear a lawyer make a speech. He could tell his body to do almost impossible things, and the body obeyed.

Growing from boy to man, he was alone a good deal of the time. Days came often when he was by himself all the time except at breakfast and supper hours in the cabin home. In some years more of his time was spent in loneliness than in company of other people. It happened, too, that this loneliness he knew was not like that of people in cities who can look from a window on streets where faces pass and repass. It was the wilderness loneliness he became acquainted with, solved, filtered through body, eye, and brain, held communion with in his ears, in the temples of his forehead, in the works of his beating heart.

He lived with trees, with the bush wet with shining raindrops, with the burning bush of autumn, with the lone wild duck riding a north wind and crying down on a line north to south; the faces of open sky and weather, the ax, which is an individual one-man instrument—these he had for companions, books, friends, talkers, chums of his endless changing soliloquies.

His moccasin feet in the wintertime knew the white spaces of snowdrifts piled in whimsical shapes against timber slopes

[2] MAUL—A sledge hammer.
[3] CRADLE—A grain scythe.
[4] CRACKLINGS—The crisp rind of roasted pork.

or blown in levels across the fields of last year's cut corn stalks; in the summertime his bare feet toughened in the gravel of green streams while he laughed back to the chatter of bluejays in the redhaw trees or while he kept his eyes ready in the slough [5] quack grass for the cow snake, the rattler, the copperhead.

He rested between spells of work in the springtime, when the upward push of the coming out of the new grass can be heard; and in autumn weeks, when the rustle of a single falling leaf lets go a whisper that a listening ear can catch.

He found his life thrown in ways where there was a certain chance for a certain growth. And so he grew. Silence found him; he met silence. In the making of him as he was, the element of silence was immense.

The farm boys in their evenings at Jones's store in Gentryville talked about how Abe Lincoln was always reading, digging into books, stretching out flat on his stomach in front of the fireplace, studying till midnight and past midnight, picking a piece of charcoal to write on the fire shovel, shaving off what he wrote, and then writing more—till midnight and past midnight. The next thing Abe would be reading books between the plow handles, it seemed to them. And once trying to speak a last word, Dennis Hanks said, "There's suthin' peculiarsome about Abe."

He wanted to learn, to know, to live, to reach out; he wanted to satisfy hungers and thirsts he couldn't tell about, this big boy of the backwoods. And some of what he wanted so much, so deep down, seemed to be in the books. Maybe in books he would find the answers to dark questions pushing around in the pools of his thoughts and the drifts of his mind. He told Dennis and other people, "The things I want to know are in books; my best friend is the man who'll git me a book I ain't read." And sometimes friends answered, "Well, books ain't as plenty as wildcats in these parts o' Indianny."

This was one thing meant by Dennis when he said there was "suthin' peculiarsome" about Abe. It seemed that Abe made the books tell him more than they told other people. All the other farm boys had gone to school and read "The Kentucky Preceptor," but Abe picked out questions from it such as, "Who has the most right to complain, the Indian or the Negro?" and Abe would talk about it, up one way and down the other, while they were in the cornfield pulling fodder for the winter. When Abe got hold of a storybook and read about a boat that came near a magnetic rock, and how the magnets in the rock pulled all the nails out of the boat so it went to pieces and the people in the boat found themselves floundering in water, Abe thought it was funny and told it to other people. After Abe read poetry, especially Bobby Burns's poems, Abe began writing rhymes himself. When Abe sat with a girl, with their bare feet in the creek water, and she spoke of the moon rising, he explained to her it was the earth moving and not the moon—the moon only seemed to rise.

John Hanks, who worked in the fields barefooted with Abe, grubbing stumps,[6]

[5] SLOUGH (sloo)—Stagnant swamp or reedy inlet into which water backs up.

[6] GRUBBING STUMPS—Digging the stumps out of the ground.

plowing, mowing, said: "When Abe and I came back to the house from work, he used to go to the cupboard, snatch a piece of corn bread, sit down, take a book, cock his legs up high as his head, and read. Whenever Abe had a chance in the field while at work, or at the house, he would stop and read." He liked to explain to other people what he was getting from books; explaining an idea to someone else made it clearer to him. The habit was growing on him of reading out loud; words came more real if picked from the silent page of the book and pronounced on the tongue; new balances and values of words stood out if spoken aloud. When writing letters for his father or the neighbors, he read the words out loud as they got written. Before writing a letter he asked questions such as: "What do you want to say in the letter? How do you want to say it? Are you sure that's the best way to say it? Or do you think we can fix up a better way to say it?"

As he studied his books his lower lip stuck out; Josiah Crawford noticed it was a habit and joked Abe about the "stuck-out lip." This habit too stayed with him.

He wrote in his Sum Book or arithmetic that Compound Division was "When several numbers of Divers Denominations are given to be divided by 1 common divisor," and worked on the exercise in multiplication: "If 1 foot contains 12 inches I demand how many there are in 126 feet." Thus the schoolboy.

What he got in the schools didn't satisfy him. He went to three different schools in Indiana, besides two in Kentucky—altogether about four months of school. He learned his ABC's, how to spell, read, write. And he had been with the other barefoot boys in butternut jeans learning "manners" under the schoolteacher, Andrew Crawford, who had them open a door, walk in, and say, "Howdy do?" Yet what he tasted of books in school was only a beginning, only made him hungry and thirsty, shook him with a wanting and a wanting of more and more of what was hidden between the covers of books.

He kept on saying, "The things I want to know are in books; my best friend is the man who'll git me a book I ain't read." He said that to Pitcher, the lawyer over at Rockport, nearly twenty miles away, one fall afternoon, when he walked from Pigeon Creek to Rockport and borrowed a book from Pitcher. Then when fodder pulling time came a few days later, he shucked corn from early daylight till sundown along with his father and Dennis Hanks and John Hanks; but after supper he read the book till midnight, and at noon he hardly knew the taste of his corn bread because he had the book in front of him. It was a hundred little things like these which made Dennis Hanks say there was "suthin' peculiarsome" about Abe.

Besides reading the family Bible and figuring his way all through the old arithmetic they had at home, he got hold of *Aesop's Fables*, *Pilgrim's Progress*, *Robinson Crusoe*, and Weems's *The Life of Francis Marion*. The book of fables, written or collected thousands of years ago by the Greek slave known as *Aesop*, sank deep in his mind. As he read through the book a second and third time, he had a feeling there were fables all around him, that everything he touched and handled, everything he saw and learned had a fable wrapped in it somewhere. One fable was about a bundle of sticks and a farmer whose sons were quarreling and fighting.

There was a fable in two sentences which read, "A coachman, hearing one of the wheels of his coach make a great noise and perceiving that it was the worst one of the four, asked how it came to take such a liberty. The wheel answered that from the beginning of time creaking had always been the privilege of the weak." And there were shrewd, brief incidents of foolery such as this: "A waggish, idle fellow in a country town, being desirous of playing a trick on the simplicity of his neighbors and at the same time putting a little money in his pocket at their cost, advertised that he would on a certain day show a wheel carriage that should be so contrived as to go without horses. By silly curiosity the rustics were taken in, and each succeeding group who came out from the show were ashamed to confess to their neighbors that they had seen nothing but a wheelbarrow."

The style of the Bible, of Aesop's fables, the hearts and minds back of those books, were much in his thoughts. His favorite pages in them he read over and over. Behind such proverbs as, "Muzzle not the ox that treadeth out the corn," and "He that ruleth his own spirit is greater than he that taketh a city," there was a music of simple wisdom and a mystery of common everyday life that touched deep spots in him; while out of the fables of the ancient Greek slave he came to see the cats, rats, dogs, horses, plows, hammers, fingers, toes, people—all had fables connected with their lives, characters, places. There was, perhaps, an outside for each thing as it stood alone, while inside of it was its fable.

One book came, titled, *The Life of George Washington, with Curious Anecdotes, Equally Honorable to Himself and Exemplary to His Young Countrymen. Embellished with Six Steel Engravings, by M. L. Weems, formerly Rector of Mt. Vernon Parish.* It pictured men of passion and proud ignorance in the government of England driving their country into war on the American colonies. It quoted the far-visioned warning of Chatham to the British Parliament, "For God's sake, then, my lords, let the way be instantly opened for reconciliation. I say instantly; or it will be too late forever."

The book told of war, as at Saratoga. "Hoarse as a mastiff of true British breed, Lord Balcarras was heard from rank to rank, loud-animating his troops; while on the other hand, fierce as a hungry Bengal tiger, the impetuous Arnold precipitated heroes on the stubborn foe. Shrill and terrible, from rank to rank resounds the clash of bayonets—frequent and sad the groans of the dying. Pairs on pairs, Britons and Americans, with each his bayonet at his brother's breast, fall forward together faint—shrieking in death, and mingle their smoking blood." Washington, the man, stood out, as when he wrote, "These things so harassed my heart with grief that I solemnly declared to God, if I know myself, I would gladly offer myself a sacrifice to the butchering enemy, if I could thereby insure the safety of these my poor distressed countrymen."

The Weems book reached some deep

spots in the boy. He asked himself what it meant that men should march, fight, bleed, go cold and hungry for the sake of what they called "freedom."

"Few great men are great in everything," said the book. And there was a cool sap in the passage: "His delight was in that of the manliest sort, which, by stringing the limbs and swelling the muscles, promotes the kindliest flow of blood and spirits. At jumping with a long pole, or heaving heavy weights, for his years he hardly had an equal."

Such book talk was a comfort against the same thing over again, day after day, so many mornings the same kind of water from the same spring, the same fried pork and corn meal to eat, the same drizzles of rain, spring plowing, summer weeds, fall fodder pulling, each coming every year, with the same tired feeling at the end of the day, so many days alone in the woods or the fields or else the same people to talk with, people from whom he had learned all they could teach him. Yet there ran through his head the stories and sayings of other people, the stories and sayings of books, the learning his eyes had caught from books; they were a comfort; they were good to have because they were good by themselves; and they were still better to have because they broke the chill of the lonesome feeling.

He was thankful to the writer of Aesop's fables because that writer stood by him and walked with him, an invisible companion, when he pulled fodder or chopped wood. Books lighted lamps in the dark rooms of his gloomy hours. . . . Well—he would live on; maybe the time would come when he would be free from work for a few weeks, or a few months, with books, and then he would read. . . Then he would read. . . . Then he would go and get at the proud secrets of his books.

His father—would he be like his father when he grew up? He hoped not. Why should his father knock him off a fence rail when he was asking a neighbor, passing by, a question? Even if it was a smart question, too pert and too quick, it was no way to handle a boy in front of a neighbor. No, he was going to be a man different from his father. The books—his father hated the books. His father talked about "too much eddication"; after readin', writin', 'rithmetic, that was enough, his father said. He, Abe Lincoln, the boy, wanted to know more than the father, Tom Lincoln, wanted to know. Already Abe knew more than his father; he was writing letters for the neighbors; they hunted out the Lincoln farm to get young Abe to find his bottle of ink with blackberry brier root and copperas [7] in it and his pen made from a turkey buzzard feather, and write letters. Abe had a suspicion sometimes his father was a little proud to have a boy that could write letters, and tell about things in books, and outrun and outwrestle and rough-and-tumble any boy or man in Spencer County. Yes, he would be different from his father; he was already so; it couldn't be helped.

In growing up from boyhood to young manhood, he had survived against lonesome, gnawing monotony, and against floods, forest and prairie fires, snake bites, horse kicks, ague, chills, fever, malaria, "milksick." [8]

[7] COPPERAS—A green crystalline chemical.

[8] MILKSICK—A disease caused by eating dairy products or meat of poisoned cattle.

A comic outline against the sky he was, hiking along the roads of Spencer and other counties in southern Indiana in those years when he read all the books within a fifty-mile circuit of his home. Stretching up on the long legs that ran from his moccasins to the body frame with its long, gangling arms, covered with linsey woolsey,[9] then the lean neck that carried the head with its surmounting coonskin cap or straw hat—it was, again, a comic outline;—yet with a portent in its shadow. His laughing "Howdy," his yarns and drollery, opened the doors of men's hearts.

Starting along in his eleventh year came spells of abstraction. When he was spoken to, no answer came from him. "He might be a thousand miles away." The roaming, fathoming, searching, questioning operations of the minds and hearts of poets, inventors, beginners who take facts stark—these were at work in him. This was one sort of abstraction he knew; there was another: the blues took him; coils of multiplied melancholies wrapped their blue frustrations inside him, all that Hamlet,[10] Koheleth,[11] Schopenhauer [12] have uttered, in a mesh of foiled hopes. "There was absolutely nothing to excite ambition for education," he wrote later of that Indiana region. Against these "blues," he found the best warfare was to find people and trade with them his yarns and drolleries. John Baldwin, the blacksmith, with many stories and odd talk and eye slants, was a help and a light.

[9] LINSEY WOOLSEY—A cloth made of linen and wool mixed.

[10] HAMLET—The hero of Shakespeare's play of the same name.

[11] KOHELETH—A name applied to Solomon.

[12] SCHOPENHAUER—A German philosopher.

Days came when he sank deep in the stream of human life and felt himself kin of all that swam in it, whether the waters were crystal or mud.

He learned how suddenly life can spring a surprise. One day in the woods, as he was sharpening a wedge on a log, the ax glanced, nearly took his thumb off, and left a white scar after healing.

"You never cuss a good ax," was a saying in those timbers.

FOR DISCUSSION

1. Lincoln frequently worked alone. What effect did these hours of solitude have on his character? On page 407 Carl Sandburg says, "Silence found him; he met silence." Explain what this means.

2. Lincoln became strong physically. Did you every try to hold an ax at arm's length by the end of the handle? Is it difficult? Name three other signs of Lincoln's strength.

3. Lincoln is frequently described as awkward. Can you show from the reading of this passage that he was, on the contrary, rather agile?

4. Do you suppose that Lincoln's contact with "just plain folks" influenced his character and helped him in later life? Give examples.

5. Give one sign from Lincoln's life by which you can tell the difference between reading because of mere curiosity and reading for education.

6. Write in one clear sentence the main idea of the selection.

7. Cite all the instances you can in the selection which foretell Lincoln's attitude toward the slavery question.

DESCRIBING CHARACTER

Read through the selection again. Wherever a new quality of young Abe is mentioned, express it by a single specific adjective. Read over your list of adjectives. Do they show the features and character of Abe as portrayed in the selection?

WRITING AN APPRECIATION OF LINCOLN

Abraham Lincoln was a truly great American. He embodied the American ideal, the chance for the common man to aspire to the greatest heights. Abraham Lincoln was a common man. By his efforts he bettered not only himself but his people as well. Write an appreciation of Lincoln.

RELATED READING

To find out more about Lincoln read Carl Sandburg's book, *Abraham Lincoln, The Prairie Years.*

◇◇◇◇◇

Elias Lieberman, author of this poem, came to America when he was seven years old. In his poems he expresses his appreciation of the opportunities which life in America offers the immigrant. You probably know a recent immigrant to this country. Decide whether you think Mr. Lieberman is speaking for him, too.

The Chant of Loyalty

ELIAS LIEBERMAN

Firm as the furnace heat
Rivets the bars of steel,
Thus to thy destiny,
Flag, are we plighted;
One are the hearts that beat, 5
One is the throb we feel,
One in our loyalty,
Stand we united.

Many a folk has brought
Sinew and brawn to thee; 10
Many an ancient wrong
Well hast thou righted;
Here in the land we sought,
Stanchly, from sea to sea;
Here, where our hearts belong, 15
Stand we united.

Ask us to pay the price,
All that we have to give,
Nothing shall be denied,
All be requited; 20
Ready for sacrifice,
Ready for thee to live,
Over the country wide,
Stand we united.

One under palm and pine, 25
One in the prairie sun,
One on the rock-bound shore,
Liberty-sighted;
All that we have is thine,
Thine, who hast made us one, 30
True to thee evermore,
Stand we united.

FOR DISCUSSION

1. What is emphasized most of all in this poem? Read the lines to confirm your answer.

2. When a person becomes a naturalized citizen of this country he must take the oath of citizenship and repeat the Pledge of Allegiance to the Flag of the United States. Do you know the Pledge of Allegiance? How do the words in this pledge compare with the lines of Elias Lieberman's poem?

3. In 1954 the phrase "under God" was officially inserted in the Pledge of Allegiance to the Flag. Find out why this insertion was proposed. Do you agree that it is a necessary addition to the pledge of allegiance to the flag of this country? Explain.

A SCENIC VOCABULARY

To what part of our country does *palm* refer? *prairie? rock-bound?* Do you think these words are descriptive? Can you think of other words descriptive of particular sections of the country?

HOW AN ALIEN BECOMES A CITIZEN OF THE UNITED STATES

Do you know the requirements for becoming a citizen of the United States? What are the rights of a naturalized citizen? Your librarian can help you find the answers.

◇◇◇◇◇

The flag has ever been the inspiration of poets who have woven meaningful threads into its colors of red and white and blue.

The American Flag

JOSEPH RODMAN DRAKE

When Freedom, from her mountain height,
  Unfurled her standard to the air,
She tore the azure robe of night,
  And set the stars of glory there.
She mingled with its gorgeous dyes 5
The milky baldric of the skies,
And striped its pure celestial white
With streakings of the morning light;
Then, from his mansion in the sun,
She called her eagle bearer down, 10
And gave into his mighty hand
The symbol of her chosen land.

3. AZURE—The clear blue of the sky.
6. BALDRIC—A belt worn over the shoulder and across the body to support a sword or bugle.

Flag of the free heart's hope and home!
By angel hands to valor given;
Thy stars have lit the welkin dome, 15
And all thy hues were born in heaven.
Forever float that standard sheet!
Where breathes the foe but falls before us
With Freedom's soil beneath our feet,
And freedom's banner streaming o'er us? 20

15. WELKIN—The sky, the vault of heaven.

FOR DISCUSSION

1. According to the poet, who made our first flag? Where were the colors procured? Can you understand why the poet keeps his conception of the birth of the flag in a heavenly sphere? What is the "milky baldric of the skies" (l. 6)? To whom was the flag intrusted?

2. The poet, Joseph Rodman Drake, was born in 1795, not so long after the date on which the flag was born. The first Flag Day was celebrated on June 14, 1777, but it was not until April 14, 1818, that the flag was finally fixed by act of Congress. It was about the latter date that Drake wrote the poem. Do you think the flag might have meant more to him than it does to us?

Crosby Corners had no use for Velvet Pants, the "small, scared man" from nowhere. Who could have respect for a man who was afraid of lightning bugs?

THE UNFAMILIAR

RICHARD CONNELL

Who he was and what he was and where he came from no one knew. How he came to be in Crosby Corners was a mystery, and at harvest time Connecticut farmers are too busy to peer into mysteries. He could not speak much English beyond "Yes," "No," and "Hungry," but he could gesture—with his hands, his elbows, his eyes, his feet. He appeared to be trying by pantomime to convey the idea that he had been forcibly seized in his native land, which was remote; had been pressed into service aboard a ship; had been very ill at sea, had escaped at a port; had fled on a train; and had dropped, or been dropped, at Crosby Corners. The farmers, however, had no time to interpret pantomime. Farm hands were scarce, and, if a man had two hands and at least one good eye, they did not delve into his past or his pedigree: they put him to work.

It was thus that the small, scared man in the velvet trousers entered the employ of Ben Crosby, richest farmer in that region.

"I found the little rascal," Ben Crosby told his wife, "squealing like a pig in a hornet's nest, and frightened almost out of his wits, with Constable Pettit marching him along by the ear. 'Constable,' I says, 'what is that and where did you get it?' He says to me, 'I dunno what it is, Ben, but it looks foreign. I found it down by the railroad tracks trying to eat a raw potato. When I asked it what its name was, it said, "See."' I says to the Constable, 'He may be a Gypsy, or he may be a Hindu, and he looks as if he suspected you of being a cannibal. But,' I says, 'he seems wiry and he didn't get that lovely tobacco-brown finish of his at a pink tea or from working in an office. Now I need hands worse than ducks need ponds. So turn him over to me 'stead of sticking him in the calaboose, and I'll give him a job.' Pettit didn't want to be bothered with him, so he turned him over to me; and there he is out at the pump, washing the dirtiest pair of hands I ever saw and now and then rubbing his stomach to show how hungry he is. I'll send him to the back door, Hannah; you give him a lining of ham and eggs and pie, and then send him down to me. I'll be in the twenty-acre lot."

Presently there came a knock on the back door of the Crosby house. It was not at all a robust knock; it was a tap as faint and timid as a butterfly's kick.

Mrs. Crosby opened the door and saw a small man standing there; his face was a rich brown; his eyes were black and apprehensive; he appeared to be ready to flee if the occasion demanded it. When he saw Mrs. Crosby, however, he bowed deeply. Such a bow had never before been executed at Crosby Corners except in the moving pictures. It was a sweeping, courtly thing, that bow, in which the small man swept off his wide felt hat and dusted the steps with it.

Then he smiled; it was a humble, ingratiating smile. He looked toward the stove, where the sizzling ham was sending its aroma heavenward, and sighed. Mrs. Crosby pointed to a chair at the kitchen table, and he, with another bow, took it and presently was eating hungrily and freely. Mrs. Crosby now and then lifted an eye from her canning to regard the exotic stranger; she had a doubt or two at first whether it was safe for her to stay there. She glanced into the dining room where, above the mantel, hung Grandpa Crosby's Civil War sword, a long, heavy weapon; its presence reassured her. As she studied the man, she decided that any fear of him was groundless; if anything, he was afraid of her. His hair, she observed, was blue-black and long, but arranged in a way that suggested that he was a bit of a dandy. The stranger's trousers surprised her greatly; they were of black velvet, really painfully tight, except at the bottom of each leg, where they flared out like bells. He had no belt but, instead, a scarlet sash. His shirt, when new and clean, must have been a remarkable garment; it had been plaid silk, but it was now neither new nor clean. His boots were of patent leather and excessively pointed.

When he had eaten a very great deal, he arose, bowed, smiled beatifically, and made gestures of gratitude. Mrs. Crosby pointed in the direction of the twenty-acre lot, and he understood. She saw him picking his way down the path; he was the first man she had ever seen whose gait at one and the same time included a mince and a swagger.

When Ben Crosby came in to his late supper that evening he announced, "I was wrong about that new little fellow. He doesn't seem to have done farm work. He's willing enough, but he handles a hayfork as dainty as if it was a toothpick. And say, he certainly is the most scary human being I ever set eyes on. You should have seen him when the tractor came into the field with the mowing machine. He gave a yelp and jumped on the stone wall, and, if there'd been a tree handy, I guess he'd have climbed it. He looked as if he was afraid the machine would eat him. Pete High, who was driving it, said, 'I guess it ain't only his skin that's yellow.' I hope Pete is wrong. I hate a coward."

"Don't you let Pete High pick on him," admonished Mrs. Crosby. "Perhaps the man never saw a mowing machine before. I remember how scared I was when I saw the first automobile come roaring and snorting along the road. And so were you, Ben Crosby."

"Well, I didn't let on I was," replied her husband, harpooning a potato.

"No, you old hypocrite, maybe you didn't; but I saw you looking around for a tree."

He laughed, and was on the point of sending the potato to its final resting place when they both heard a cry—a high, terrified cry that came through the dusk. He started up.

"That's not Janey?" he asked.

"No; she's still in town taking her music lesson."

"Who is it, then?" he asked quickly.

They heard the patter of running feet on the path outside; they heard the sound of feet landing after a leap to the porch; they heard someone banging frantically on the front door. Ben Crosby called out:

"What's the matter?"

A flood of words in a strange tongue answered him.

"It's Velvet Pants," he exclaimed, and flung open the door. The small man, breathless, tumbled in.

"What in the name of thunderation!" demanded Ben Crosby. The small man pointed through the open door with quivering fingers.

"I don't see anything out there but the evening," said Ben Crosby.

"Ice!" cried the man, very agitated. "Ice!"

"What do you want ice for?" asked Ben Crosby.

The man made eloquent gestures; first he pointed at his own face, then he pointed outside; his index finger stabbed at the gloom once, twice, a dozen times.

"Ice! Ice! Ice! Ice! Ice! Ice!" he said.

"Why, Ben, he means 'eyes'!" exclaimed Mrs. Crosby.

"Eyes? What eyes, Hannah? I don't

see any eyes. There's nothing out there but lightning bugs."

One of the circling fireflies flew quite near the open door. The small man saw it coming, and made an earnest, but only partly successful, attempt to climb into the grandfather's clock that stood in the corner of the hall.

Ben Crosby threw back his head and laughed.

"Why, dog my cats! If the little cuss ain't afraid of lightning bugs!" he said. "Hey, Velvet Pants, look here."

He plucked the man out of the clock with one big hand, and with the other captured the firefly and held it near the stranger's wide eyes.

"Look!" said Ben Crosby in the loud tone that is supposed to make the American language intelligible to those who do not understand it when it is spoken in an ordinary tone of voice. "Bug! Bug! No hurt! Lightning bug! *Lightning bug!*"

The small man pulled away from the insect.

"Not know lightnong boogs," he said.

Ben released his hold on the small man and pointed upstairs; then he gave a highly realistic imitation of a snore. The man comprehended, and his velvet-clad legs twinkled upstairs toward his bedroom. Ben Crosby returned to his supper, shaking his head.

"It beats me," he remarked to his wife. "He's afraid of mowing machines and he's afraid of lightning bugs. I wonder if he's afraid of the dark. I need farm hands, but may I be fried like a smelt if I'll tell 'em bedtime stories or sing 'em to sleep. What's the world coming to, anyhow? Can you imagine a real, honest-to-goodness farm hand like Pete High being afraid of lightning bugs?"

"Boneheads are seldom afraid of anything," remarked Mrs. Crosby, pouring buttermilk.

They heard the front door open.

"There's Janey," said Mrs. Crosby. "Hello, dear. Come right to the table. I've made ice cream—coffee, the kind you like."

Janey, daughter of the household, came in, bearing her guitar. She kissed both her parents. Janey was nearly eighteen, a pretty, elf-like girl. All the masculine hearts in Crosby Corners beat a little faster when she went down the village street; her blue eyes had been the cause of many black eyes. Her father told her of the new man, of his extraordinary velvet trousers, and of his still more extraordinary fears.

"Poor little fellow!" she said.

As the harvest days hurried along, Velvet Pants atoned somewhat for his lack of expertness as a farmer by his unfailing good nature. He even learned to speak a little English of a certain hesitant species, but he had little opportunity to talk with his fellow workers. Mostly they ignored him, or, if they addressed him at all, did so loftily and with contempt; a man who paled at the sight of mowing machines and lightning bugs was not of their stout-hearted kind.

The incident at the swimming hole added little to Velvet Pants' reputation for bravery. The swimming hole was Sandy Bottom, where all the workers, hot from their day in the fields, went for a cool plunge after work. They noticed that Velvet Pants never went with them.

"How does he keep so neat and clean?"

they asked. It was Pete High who solved this mystery.

"Yesterday morning," said Pete, "I woke up earlier than usual, and what do you suppose I see? Well, I hear a tap, tap, tap, like somebody was stealing downstairs on his tiptoes. I peek out o' the door, and it's Velvet Pants. Just for fun, I follow him. He goes down the creek—not to Sandy Bottom, but a couple of rods downstream where the water ain't more than ankle-deep. He takes a stick and goes like this, 'Ah, ah, ah, ah, ah, ah,' and pokes at the bushes each time he says 'ah.' Then he gives one big loud 'Ahhhhhhh,' and lunges with his stick at the bushes; then he bows low, like he was an actor in a show. He takes a bath then, dabbling a little water on himself like a cat does; but he doesn't go in above his ankles. I guess he's afraid of the water."

"Mebbe he ain't much on swimming," said one of the other hands, "but he sure can twang a mean guitar. He's giving Janey Crosby lessons."

Pete High scowled.

"He is, is he? First I heard about it. Well, the first thing he knows he won't know nothing."

"She likes him," teased the other man. "Says he's got such lovely manners; just like what you ain't, Pete."

"She don't know how yella he is," Pete High growled, "but she will."

On Saturday afternoons most of Crosby Corners—men, women, and children—come to Sandy Bottom, bringing bathing suits. It is not a very big pool; at its deepest part it is not much over six feet deep.

How it happened that the small man with the velvet trousers should be passing Sandy Bottom that Saturday noon at the precise moment when the freckled Johnny Nelson was floundering in the water and calling loudly for help does not matter. Why Johnny Nelson should be drowning at all is something of a puzzle, for he was the best swimmer in the county. It also happened that just as Johnny was going down for the ninth or tenth time, and was calling piteously for Velvet Pants to dive in and save him, Janey Crosby and a party of girl friends came down to the pool.

They saw Velvet Pants, his dark face ivory-colored, trying to reach Johnny with a young tree wrenched from the bank. The small man was a picture of frantic helplessness.

"Save me, Velvet Pants! Save me!" bawled Johnny, submerging and coming up for the fourteenth time.

"Not know how," screamed Velvet Pants in agony. "Not know how."

Janey Crosby and her companions grew mildly hysterical; Johnny Nelson went down for the seventeenth time. Velvet Pants, finding that he could not reach Johnny with the tree, had fallen on his knees and with clasped hands was praying aloud in his own tongue. Then it also happened that Pete High came racing through the bushes.

"I'll save you, Johnny!" he cried dramatically. Overalls and all, he plunged in and brought the dripping Johnny to the bank. The prayers of Velvet Pants became prayers of thanksgiving. Pete High stood regarding him with disgust.

"Oh, Velvet Pants," said Janey Crosby, "why didn't you jump in and save him?"

Slowly, sadly, the small man shrugged his shoulders.

"Not know water," he said; "not know sweem."

He did not seem nearly so abashed as he said this as he might very well have been under the circumstances; he said it very much as if he were stating a fact—a lamentable fact the truth of which he regretted, but a fact nevertheless. He looked dismayed and surprised when Janey Crosby and the others turned away from him.

After that Velvet Pants was an outcast. The men spoke to him only when it was necessary to do so, and then briefly and even harshly. He did not seem to understand; he would try to tell them things, making many gestures; but he had not the words to make himself clear, nor had they the inclination to listen to him.

In the evening, when the men were sitting about the porch competing for Janey Crosby's smiles, there was no place for him there. He had tried to join in their talk and play, to be friendly, to be one of them; they froze him out, and still he did not seem to understand that they did it because he was so flagrant a coward. At last he seemed to accept his status as a pariah without really understanding it, for he would take his guitar, which he had constructed from the ruin of an old one, and go alone into the woods. It was said that he sang there to himself sad songs in his native tongue.

Janey Crosby's birthday came toward the end of the harvest season, and it was the most important social event of the year in Crosby Corners. All the village was invited, and all the village came—the girls in their fresh dimities; the men soaped and collared and uncomfortable, but happy. They brought presents as if they were bringing tribute to a queen, and Janey, as graciously as a reigning sovereign, took them all and smiled.

The party was held in the Masonic hall; it was an affair of considerable tone, with dancing, two helpings of ice cream all round, and a three-piece orchestra.

The dancing was half over. Janey and Pete High, her current partner, had gone out on the porch; a harvest moon silvered the village streets.

"Look!" exclaimed Pete. "What's that sitting down there on the horse block?"

"It's a man," said Janey, her eyes following his pointing finger.

"But who can it be?"

The girl looked again, and made out a small, bent figure sitting there, chin on hands, eyes turned toward the lighted hall, ears toward the music and the buzz and laughter of the guests.

"Why, it's Velvet Pants!" she exclaimed.

"Shall I chase him away?" asked Pete, swelling out his chest and looking belligerent. Janey laid a restraining hand on his arm.

"No; don't chase him, Pete. Let him stay. The poor fellow's probably lonesome. Everybody is here but him."

"He deserves to be lonesome," said Pete; "he's yella."

"Would you jump in to save a person from drowning if you didn't know how to swim?" asked Janey.

"Of course I would," replied Pete promptly. "Now, see here, Janey Crosby, don't you go sticking up for that chap. He's not fit to associate with white men."

She sat gazing at the small, miserable

figure; then she made a sudden resolution.

"I'm going to ask him to come up to the party," she said.

"No, you ain't."

"Whose birthday is this, Pete High? I guess it won't do any harm to give him a dish of ice cream. You don't have to associate with him. Run down and tell him I'd like to see him, Pete."

Pete mumbled protests, but he went. Very diffidently, as if he momentarily expected to be kicked, Velvet Pants approached the porch. Janey Crosby saw that he was wearing a new, clean shirt, that his black locks had been parted and buttered, and that his shoes had been rigorously shined. Over his shoulder was slung his wreck of a guitar.

"This is my birthday, Velvet Pants," said the girl. "I want you to help me celebrate it. Pete, will you get another plate of ice cream?"

The small man seemed overcome; he bowed twice very low. Then he spoke. He spoke mechanically, as if the words had been often rehearsed.

"I had no gif' for you on your birthday, Mees Crosby, but I haf learn a song American to seeng for you. I hear heem on funnygraf. I hope you like."

He said it humbly, but not without a certain pride that attends the accomplishment of a difficult feat.

Janey laughed delightedly.

"So you learned an American song just for my birthday? Well, now, wasn't that a sweet idea! Wait! I'll call the others; no, better still, you come into the hall and sing, so they can all hear."

Velvet Pants looked horrified at this suggestion.

"But, no," he protested. "I do not seeng good."

"That's all right. They won't know the difference," said Janey laughingly. "Come along."

She pushed him through the open doorway. The guests looked up. What would Janey Crosby do next?

"Folks," announced Janey Crosby, "Mr. Velvet Pants is going to sing for us. He learned a little American song just for my birthday. Wasn't that nice of him?"

It was evident from the face of Pete High, who stood in the doorway, that he did not think it was particularly nice.

The small brown man glanced uncertainly about the hall; then he began to play chords upon his guitar. Some of the girls tittered. In a round, clear tenor Velvet Pants began to sing:

> "Kees me hagain, kees me hagain,
> Kees me hagain, and hagain."

His memory seemed to go back on him at this point; he groped for a moment for the words. There was a slight, dubious ripple of applause that was checked suddenly. Pete High had stridden up to Velvet Pants and was facing him.

"Just a minute there," said Pete. "You and me has got a little bone to pick. What do you mean by singing a song like that to Miss Crosby?"

The small man looked puzzled.

"It ees only song American I know," he said.

"Yeah? Well, I'm going to teach you to sing it out of the other side of your mouth. Come outside with me."

"Pete High," broke in Janey, "don't you go fighting with him. He didn't mean any harm; he probably doesn't know what the words mean."

"I told him never to say anything to you whether he understood it or not," stormed Pete. "Come on, you."

Velvet Pants made an attempt to steal away, but Pete blocked his path.

"You're going out on the lawn with me," said Pete.

"And seeng?" asked the little man, who seemed somewhat dazed by what was happening.

"No; fight."

"Fight?"

"Yes; fight."

"But I do no hate you, Meester Pete."

"Well, I hate you. Come on."

"But how we fight?" inquired the small man; he was pale beneath his tan, and trembling. For answer Pete thrust a clenched fist under the man's nose. The man drew his head back and shivered.

"No!" he said, shaking his head. "No! No! No! No!"

"You won't fight?"

"No."

"You're a coward," declared Pete.

Velvet Pants shrugged his shoulders.

"Not know hand fights," he said.

Pete slapped him across the face with his open hand.

"Now will you fight?"

"Not know hand fights," said the man, drawing away. Pete, contempt on his face, gave him a push into the night. They heard the sound of feet on the path; Velvet Pants was running.

"Not know hand fights," Pete mimicked. "Did you ever in your life see such a rat?"

Next day excitement swept Crosby Corners. Defender Monarch had gone crazy; and when that news spread, they forgot all about the conduct of Velvet Pants on the night before. As for him, he went about his work with a puzzled and hurt look on his brown face; he seemed still uncertain why the others did not respond to his smiles and attempts at friendliness.

Defender Monarch was the pride, and the terror, of the county. His owner, Ben Crosby, had raised him from a gawky calf, wobbly on his legs, into a massive ton-and-a-half bull, with a chest like a haystack, a voice like thunder, and the temper of a gouty demon. Ben Crosby had not dehorned him, because in cattle shows a good pair of horns is considered a point of merit in judging bulls, and the giant bull had won many blue ribbons. On this day Ben Crosby wished most earnestly that he had forgone the blue ribbons and taken off those horns. A savage bull without horns is bad enough, but a savage bull with a pair of sharp, wicked horns is just about the most dangerous animal that walks.

Perhaps on that morning Defender Monarch had realized that he had reached the end of his usefulness and that before very long he was doomed to end a proud career ingloriously, as steak, roast, and stew. He stood in his pasture, roaring a challenge to the world that he would die fighting. By blind luck Ben Crosby was able to trick him into entering the big pen, but in the process Defender Monarch had given a sample of his viciousness by ripping Johnny Nelson's arm from elbow to shoulder and had failed by a hair's breadth in a sincere attempt to crush the life out of Ben Crosby himself. Once confined in a pen,

Defender Monarch's rage knew no bounds. He hurled himself against the thick board sides so furiously that they creaked and trembled, and the crowd that had gathered to see him darted back to places of greater safety.

Luckily the pen was a stoutly built affair; it was not really a pen at all, but a small corral perhaps fifty feet square. About it moved Defender Monarch, his small eyes blazing, alert. And, perched on boxes and ladders, Crosby Corners, fascinated as all men are by dangerous things, watched the mad king of the herd.

"Isn't he just too terrible?" said Janey Crosby to Pete High.

"Oh, I don't know," answered Pete airily. "I've worked round him often."

"But not since he went crazy, Pete."

"No," admitted Pete, "mebbe not. I'm used to cattle of all kinds, but I never saw one that acted this way. Just plain bulls I'm none too fond of fooling with, but a crazy one! Excuse me!"

"See how he's looking right at us with those mean little eyes of his," said Janey. "It's just as if he were saying, 'If I only had you down here for a minute!' I'm scared, Pete."

"I'm here," said Pete High reassuringly. "Look, Janey, he's getting another fit; he's going to try to buck that other opposite wall."

Janey Crosby, to get a better view, climbed to the very top of the stepladder that leaned against the wall of the corral. There was a sharp crack as the top rail gave way, then horrified cries. She had fallen into the pen and lay unconscious almost at the feet of the mad bull.

The women screamed; the men ran about aimlessly, wildly, shouting orders at one another.

"Help! Janey's fallen into the pen!"

"Oh, he'll kill her! He'll kill her! He'll kill her!"

"Get pitchforks!"

"Get a gun!"

"No use; we've only got bird shot. It would just make him madder to hit him with that."

"Someone will have to jump in."

"Where are you running to, Pete High?"

"To get a rope or something."

"You'll be too late."

Defender Monarch looked down at the girl, and his eyes were evil. Then he looked at the ring of white faces that lined the top of the corral. He seemed to understand the situation; he seemed to know that he had plenty of time, and he gloated. He turned away from Janey, trotted to the farther end of the corral, wheeled about, and surveyed the distance between himself and the girl's body; then he lowered his head, with its gleaming prongs, and gathered his body for a charge.

The aghast onlookers became aware that something was in the corral besides the girl and the bull. A figure had come through the gate of the inclosure silently and swiftly. It was a small man in velvet trousers, and he was strolling toward Defender Monarch as casually and placidly as if the bull were a rosebush. On the brown face of Velvet Pants there was not the slightest trace of fear; indeed, he was smiling a slight, amused smile. Otherwise he was as matter-of-fact as if he were about to sit down to his breakfast. A brown-paper cigarette hung limp from one corner of his lips; with the mincing strut they had noticed and made fun of, he walked slowly toward Defender Monarch. The animal, distracted, stood blinking at the little man. Within a few feet of the bull Velvet Pants halted; there was a flash of something red. It was Ben Crosby's red-flannel shirt that a few moments before had been drying on the line. The small man had flicked it across the bull's face. Defender Monarch forgot for the moment his plan for smashing Janey Crosby; he saw the red, and he plunged toward it. The women turned their heads away; the men clenched their teeth. They saw Velvet Pants slip aside with the quickness of a jungle cat and the bull, unable to check himself, jolt his head against one of the sides of the corral. Velvet Pants turned round, smiled pleasantly, and bowed very low to the spectators. They saw that he had in his right hand something long and bright that caught the rays of the sun; they realized that it was Grandpa Crosby's old Civil War sword that had hung in the dining room. He was holding it as lightly and as easily as if it were a butter knife.

Defender Monarch, recovering from his fruitless charge against the wall, spun about; once more the red shirt was deftly flapped before his bright, mad eyes. Once more, with a roar of wrath, he launched his bulk straight at Velvet Pants. Then something happened to Defender Monarch. It happened with such speed that all the onlookers saw was a flash; then the huge frame of the bull tottered, crumpled, and sank down. Sticking from his left shoulder was the hilt of Grandpa Crosby's sword; the spectators saw the hilt only, for Velvet Pants had driven the point into Defender Monarch's heart.

The people of Crosby Corners allege that Ben Crosby kissed the little tanned man on both cheeks, but this he denies; he admits, however, that he hugged him

and patted him, and said many husky words of gratitude and admiration to Velvet Pants, who seemed abashed and quite unable to understand why everyone was making so much of a fuss about him.

"And I called you a coward," Ben Crosby kept saying. "I called you a coward, and you went in and faced a mad bull without batting an eyelash."

"It was nuzzing," murmured the small brown man.

"Nothing to face a mad bull?"

Velvet Pants shrugged his shoulders.

"But I am toreador," [1] he said. "In my country, Andalusia,[2] I keel one, two, t'ree bull every Sunday for fun. Why should I fear bulls? I know bulls."

[1] TOREADOR—A bull fighter.
[2] ANDALUSIA—A province of Southern Spain.

◇◇◇◇◇◇◇◇◇◇◇◇◇◇◇◇◇◇◇◇◇◇◇◇◇◇◇◇◇◇

FOR DISCUSSION

1. What circumstances led Ben Crosby to employ Velvet Pants? What impression did this foreigner's unfamiliarity with American ways make upon the folks of Crosby Corners?

2. Did Velvet Pants' fear of tractors and lightning bugs indicate cowardice? What is the meaning of his statement, "Not *know* lightnong boogs"?

3. What incident at Sandy Bottom resulted in Velvet Pants' utter disgrace? Explain the circumstances in the light of Pete High's remark, "She don't know how yella he is, but she will."

4. If you had been Velvet Pants on the night of Janey's birthday party, would you have fought Pete High? Was it a matter of honor to remain and take Pete's beating, considering the odds and Pete's unreasonable provocation?

5. What mischance placed Janey in great danger? What did Velvet Pants accomplish in a situation familiar to him? To what extent do you suppose Ben and Pete changed their opinions of Velvet Pants?

WORD MEANINGS

1. Find the following words in the story. See whether you can determine their meanings from the context of the sentence. After you have decided what you think each word means, look up the dictionary definition. How close were you to the meaning in the dictionary?

ingratiating (p. 415)	abashed (p. 419)
exotic (p. 415)	flagrant (p. 419)
aghast (p. 422)	dubious (p. 419)

2. The word *pariah* (page 419) means a social outcast. It is derived from the name of an aboriginal, non-Hindu people of southern India whom the Hindus exclude from their religion. Why was Velvet Pants called a *pariah?*

FACING PREJUDICE

1. An important goal in education is the fight against unreasonable prejudices—judging people, for example, before one has any right to judge them. Prejudice against another's religion, race, or color still plays an ugly role in American life. In "The Unfamiliar," jealousy and ignorance made Pete High hate the small, awkward man from Andalusia. Relate a case in your own experience which illustrates the vicious effects of prejudice.

2. What is a coward? Is a man a coward because he is afraid, or a hero because he is not afraid? Mrs. Crosby said: "Boneheads are seldom afraid of anything." Can you give examples of situations in which lack of fear would indicate lack of intelligence?

3. How would you define *courage?* Do you think there were other occasions when Velvet Pants showed even greater courage than when he was facing the angry bull? Explain your answer. Do you think any of the characters were blinded by prejudice in not recognizing his courage? Explain your answer.

Into the following essay are packed numerous details which characterize America and the American ideal. For many years Miss Thompson has been writing a syndicated column concerned with foreign and domestic political affairs. Here is an essay from her book, LET THE RECORD SPEAK.

AMERICA

DOROTHY THOMPSON

When I think of America, I see it in a series of pictures—of moving pictures. I see the tight white and green farms of Vermont; the quick lush summers knee deep in fern and field flowers; the narrow faces and the ironic grins of the Vermonters; the love of thrift and the strange inhibited hospitality of the people; the deep quiet lakes, the hills that are never too high for cattle to graze on them, the long, long bitter winters; small friendly communities where free, independent farmers still help build each other's barns and cut each other's wood; where the hired man calls the farmer by his first name; where the women from the farms and villages will come to cook for you, 'to help out,' but where you never can find anyone with the spirit or attitude of a servant.

I think of the incredible city of Manhattan—sometimes I think it too incredible to last—where the languages of a dozen nations are heard on the streets; where there are more Italians than in any Italian city except Rome; more Jews than there are in Jerusalem or any other town on earth; where there are more Irish than there are in Dublin.

I think of the temperate and civilized —and uncivilized Carolinas; of Annapolis, the most beautiful eighteenth-century town in the whole English-speaking world; of the long quays [1] of Savannah and the opulent [2] laziness of the South, and the queer intellectual vigor that has always come up in the South whenever people thought that it was dead—from the South that has repeatedly given us our greatest statesmen.

I think of the great Southwest with a climate in which it is almost impossible to die. Texas, where you could settle a whole nation—yes, even now, when they say our frontiers are exhausted. And California, the earth's Eldorado,[3] bigger than all of Italy, with a population only one-seventh that of Italy; great glittery beaches out of which rise the towers of oil wells. The finest fruits on earth. The most enchanting American city: San Francisco.

This country would be monstrous with-

[1] QUAYS (kēz)—Wharfs, docks.
[2] OPULENT—Rich, luxuriant.
[3] ELDORADO—An imaginary place abounding in gold.

out a corresponding largeness and generosity of the spirit of its citizens.

This country is only five generations old. In the days of our great-great-great-grandfathers it was still a howling wilderness, still unexplored. Today it is the most powerful single nation on the face of the earth.

This country has seven million farms valued at thirty-three billion dollars. It produces three and a half times as much corn as any other nation in the world. It produces more wheat than any other nation on earth except Soviet Russia. In the great industrial towns of the East and the Middle West—in twenty-six counties of this vast nation—it produces almost as much steel and four times as many automobiles as all the rest of the world combined.

It is so enormous and so powerful that gigantic public works are lost in it; they are done casually without any ballyhoo.[4] We have the greatest roads ever built since the Romans, and they were built without Fascism and without forced labor. In our lifetimes we have undertaken one of the greatest reclamation jobs ever done in the history of mankind. We have taken the Columbia and the Colorado Rivers and bent them, diverted them, stopped them, and pushed them around to create a whole new province in which men can settle and live, to create a lake so vast that it is an internal sea—and most people in the United States don't even know about it.

Here is the imagination which could conceive Wilson's dream of a world-state.

[4] BALLYHOO—Noisy advertising of the fact.

Is it so fantastic? Is it more fantastic than what this country is? Here is the imagination which could conceive a frontier on another nation, three thousand miles long and at all places vulnerable, and without a single fort. You think that is not something to have accomplished in history? Maybe it is the greatest thing that we have accomplished in history: the idea that two continental nations could live in permanent friendship.

And because of our geography, our position between two oceans, the largeness of the nation, the necessary wideness of sympathy and imagination, this country is of all countries in the world the most susceptible to what happens outside its own boundaries. Throughout our history, we have counseled isolation. Never in our history have we been isolationists. Upon this country beat all the ideas and all the conflicts of the whole world—for in this country are the peoples of the whole world, and in this country is a certain type of mind, which is impatient of boundaries; which is able to contemplate things near and very far—nothing too far.

This country is itself the synthesis of many cultures. Its founders were Anglo-Saxons—one of the most remarkable groups of men that history ever produced at the right moment. But the inspiration for the constitution of the new world did not come only from English traditions.

These Anglo-Saxons who framed the Constitution did not make America. They broke loose from their old ties; they broke loose, I might even say, from their own race, in order to make a new world and a new race. But they did not build this nation. This nation was built by Germans, Swedes, Russians, Negroes, and Bohemians—men from the Danubian Basin—by Italians, by Anglo-Saxons, and by Jews. It was built by people who came here with a dream. For five generations people have been coming here with a dream. Sometimes the dream was grandiose. The men who built New England came here with a dream of religious freedom. They came here as refugees, persecuted because they wouldn't bend their consciences. Acadians trekked to Louisiana also to find a world in which they could be themselves. And some came here hoping to find gold in the streets. And some came because they were herded up in Hungarian and Slavic villages and brought over here like cattle under false pretensions, full of false hopes. But in all of their minds there was something common. For all of them there was a magnet. And the magnet was that they thought that here, in their own way, they could stand up, and look their neighbors in the face, and call themselves men, and not slaves.

And in five generations we have produced on this continent a race. You think there's not an American race? It's funny. Here we are made up of every stock in the world, and yet you can tell an American if you see him on the streets in Berlin, or Vienna, or Paris. What is an American? A typical American? An American is a fellow whose grandfather was a German forty-eighter who settled in Wisconsin and married a Swede, whose mother's father married an Englishwoman, whose son met a girl at college, whose mother was an Austrian and whose father was a Hungarian Jew and their son in the twentieth century right now is six feet tall—we are perhaps the tallest race on earth—goes to a state college, plays football, can't speak a word of any known language except American, and is doubtful whether he ever had a grandfather.

This American has several characteristics. He doesn't like to take orders. If you speak to him in a friendly way, he will do almost anything you ask him—inside reason. If you once get him into a war, he is a very good fighter, but he has a very low opinion of war, and, except when he is dressed up for a festival of the Elks or the American Legion, a pretty low opinion of uniforms. He doesn't like to commit himself to stay forever in one place. He is restless, and an inveterate traveler in his own country or elsewhere if he can afford it. He is incredibly ingenious. He can devise more ways to save himself work than any other known race of human beings; that's probably why he has invented so many gadgets. He will wear himself out playing golf, or tennis, or football, but he won't walk to get to the golf links. He is gregarious, but not at all herd-minded. He is not servile. He is enormously inventive. This is one of the greatest races of inventors ever produced. He was born free and he shows it by the way he moves. He is the best-nourished human being on the face of the earth.

Now, what I am saying is this: we have got as far as we have, not only because we have a continent rich in resources—there are other continents rich in resources—we have got as far as we have because we produced a certain kind of human being and a certain type of mind. That human being is, first of all, a fellow with his eye on the future and not on the past. He is skeptical, and yet he has eternal faith. He constantly tries to think why something doesn't work as well as it should and how you can make it better. He is the kind of human being who likes to go off on his own and start something. If anyone wants to come with him, that's all right, too. He's a born democrat—and democrats are born, not made. He hates a stuffed shirt and he doesn't like to be high-hatted. He is suspicious of anybody who pretends to be better than he is. Nobody except the Scots and the Jews has such a passion for education as has the American.

I say all this because I hope that we are going to keep this kind of race alive. This race has emerged out of the concept of equality. Now don't misunderstand this word 'equality.' Equality does not mean that everybody is as good as everybody else. You can't go into any classroom in a public school and keep that illusion for ten minutes. But the American concept of equality is that every person has a right to a break. Every human being shall be judged by what he is and does, and not by any purely arbitrary rule. As a matter of fact, the American concept is a profoundly religious one. It is based on the belief of the sanctity of the human personality, on the immense value of every individual, and the right of every individual to make out of himself the very best human being that he can. The questions that Americans naturally ask concerning other human beings are 'What does he do?' and, 'What sort of a guy is he?' and, 'Does he know his stuff?'

The attitude of Americans toward themselves and toward all other human beings, the fact that we are a race of races, and a nation of nations, the fact of our outlook upon two oceans—and the miracle of the creation of this country out of stock that for such a large part represents the frustrations of European dreams and the rejection of human material—all these combine to make us a messianic people,[5] with a feeling of mission not only for ourselves but for the world. This has been true from our very beginnings. Our whole political literature, which is one of the greatest possessed by any nation, reiterates the conception that the values that we cherish are of universal validity. The Declaration of Independence contains these words:

> 'We hold these truths to be self-evident, that all *men* are created equal—(not all Americans)—and that they are endowed by their Creator with certain unalienable rights, among them life, liberty, and the pursuit of happiness.'

And when we wrote the Constitution, we made one which is not confined to any geographic area, but is infinitely expandable.

In all the great speeches of Lincoln, there is the same sense of the American Mission. In his farewell speech at Springfield, he spoke of the United States as 'the last great hope of earth.' And he closed the Gettysburg Address, the great apostrophe[6] to popular government, with the words, 'shall not perish from the earth.' He did not say 'from this soil.' He, like all great Americans, and above all the poets, conceived that there was some cosmic significance[7] about this country and about this great experiment. And that feeling is still in the American heart. It is expressed in our reaction, our spontaneous reaction, to all assaults against human rights, to the degradation of personality, to all crimes against human freedom, to all persecutions and bigotries, and, above all, to all tyranny wherever it raises its head, in the most remote quarters of the globe. And since we are a free people, and are not inhibited in our expression, all such crimes have been protested by the American people as individuals long in advance of the protests of their government. Time and again in our history we have broken off diplomatic relations with countries because they have persecuted Jews or Armenians, or any other branch of the human race. We have been told that is none of our business; but in some undefined way, we know it is some of our business; that the sense and meaning of our life is that we should be sensitive to such things.

And I, for one, believe that if ever the time comes that the antennae[8] of this country are not sensitive to assaults on liberty, wherever these assaults may occur, then this country will have degenerated into an unvirtuous and defeatist senility. Like it or not, that is the way we are.

[5] MESSIANIC PEOPLE—A nation that believes it is divinely chosen and has a mission to perform.

[6] APOSTROPHE—An address to a person or thing in the second person.

[7] COSMIC SIGNIFICANCE—World-wide importance.

[8] ANTENNAE—Literally, aerial wires for receiving radio waves; used here in the adapted sense of conscience or moral awareness.

◇◇◇◇◇◇◇◇◇◇◇◇◇◇◇◇◇◇◇◇◇◇◇◇◇◇◇◇◇◇◇

FOR DISCUSSION

1. In what sense are the pictures that Miss Thompson draws of America "moving

pictures"? Why do you think she chose the cities and regions she mentions in preference to others?

2. What detail best brings home to you the idea of America's largeness? Americans are said to emphasize size too much. Why, then, does Miss Thompson stress the largeness of America and its works?

3. According to the author, why cannot Americans be isolationists? Do you agree?

4. What do Americans mean by saying that "all men are created equal"? What further does the Catholic understand the same words to mean? Can you explain how Americans, even Catholic Americans, can show prejudice against fellow Americans because of race or religion?

5. Find in the selection one sentence which sums up the idea the author wants to drive home, or express that idea in a sentence of your own.

STUDYING WORDS

1. ". . . the quick *lush* summers . . ." What is the difference between *lush, luxurious, rich, lavish,* and *abundant?*

2. *Isolation* is derived from the Italian word *isola,* island. What connection do you see between the present meaning of *isolation* and the original Italian word?

3. Use synonyms for the italicized words:

a. "Here is the imagination which could conceive a frontier . . . at all places *vulnerable* . . ."

b. "This country is itself the *synthesis* of many cultures."

c. "He is *gregarious,* but not at all herd-minded."

d. "And since we are a free people, and are not *inhibited* in our expression, all such crimes have been protested by the American people as individuals long in advance of the protests of their government."

A PICTURE OF YOUR COMMUNITY

Imitate the style of Dorothy Thompson and write a word-picture of your community. Consider the different elements that make your town or city a typical American community. What has it in common with other communities? What is different about it? What can you say about its religious spirit?

RELATED READING

What do immigrants think of our American ideal? To discover this for yourself read *The Making of an American* by Jacob Riis or *The Promised Land* by Mary Antin.

Love of country, or patriotism, is rooted in the very nature of man. It is one of his natural rights. The poet expresses this truth in stirring language.

My Native Land

WALTER SCOTT

Breathes there the man with soul so dead,
Who never to himself hath said,
"This is my own—my native land!"
Whose heart hath ne'er within him burned,

As home his footsteps he hath turned,
From wandering on a foreign strand?

If such there be, go, mark him well!
For him no minstrel's raptures swell.
High though his titles, proud his name,
Boundless his wealth as wish can claim,—
Despite those titles, power, and pelf,
The wretch, concentred all in self,
Living shall forfeit fair renown,
And, doubly dying, shall go down
To the vile dust from whence he sprung,
Unwept, unhonored, and unsung.

FOR DISCUSSION

Love of your country is, in reality, love of your home and family, though on a broader scale. It is easy to understand, therefore, why the poet speaks so harshly of the man who does not love his native land. Walter Scott can scarcely believe that such a man exists. List the hard things that he says about such a fellow. What penalties are paid by the unpatriotic person?

2. It is important that all of us understand the subject of the separation of Church and State. In two or three paragraphs explain why there can really be no conflict between love of one's country and love of God.

LATIN DERIVATIVES

The words, *native, foreign, title,* like the word *journey* have a picturesque Latin past. Originally *native* came from *natus*, the past participle of *nasci*, meaning *to be born; foreign* originally meant *out of doors*, coming from *foras; title* originally meant *an inscription*, coming from *titulus*.

While Washington was engaging the British across the Appalachians, George Rogers Clark was preparing an expedition in the West. Settlers had suffered too much from British-inspired Indian raids to stand for any more. The Indians had to be stopped; the British had to be smoked out of their Mississippi River lairs. Clark did it without firing a shot, the most unusual campaign in our military history.

THE MARCH OF THE BIG KNIVES

LOWELL THOMAS

The country toward which the expedition was headed, although occupied and controlled by British soldiers, was mostly inhabited by French. Clark well knew that the French hunters and trappers had no love for the British. But he also knew

"The March of the Big Knives" from *The Hero of Vincennes* by Lowell Thomas. Reprinted by permission of Houghton Mifflin Company.

that they looked to the British troops for protection against the Virginians, or "Big Knives" as they were called. The British had cunningly spread tales among them of the rapacity and barbarity of the Big Knives, who they said were far worse than the Indians. And George Rogers Clark was the chief of these Big Knives, and this very fear of the Americans Clark determined to turn to his advantage.

On the morning of June 24, 1778, before the heat of the day had set in, Corn Island [1] settlement was agog with excitement. The boats had been dragged to the upper end of the island and a steady stream of men marched between them and the supply rooms. Powder and shot were put aboard; a quantity of food to supply the men on their voyage down the river; and a few articles of clothing. But certain things were conspicuously absent. There were no tents to protect the men from the weather; nor were there any blankets; and even most of the iron pots and cooking utensils were being left behind. There were no cannon, no horses, no pack animals. The soldiers themselves could not have been distinguished from the civilian settlers mingling with them. There were no bright uniforms of swagger military cut, no uniforms at all in fact, merely the rough homely clothing of the frontiersman—leather shirt, leather leggins, and the bushy, coonskin cap. But what they lacked in appearance they more than made up in bravery and determination. Colonel Clark looked on, issuing an occasional order, lending a hand here, supervising some arrangements there, above all anxious to be off.

At last everything was stowed aboard, including the men. There were four companies under the command of Captain Bowman, Captain Harrod, Captain Montgomery, and Captain Helm, respectively—about one hundred and eighty men. Colonel Clark must have smiled to himself when he remembered how imperative he had thought it was to start the expedition with five hundred! He stepped aboard his boat and gave the order for the men to bend to their oars while the little garrison that remained on the bank cheered and shouted good luck to them on their adventure.

The boats pulled steadily upstream for about a mile, in order to reach the main channel. There they swung into the swift current that carried them toward the boiling falls. As they approached the churning water, the sky began to darken, though there was not a cloud in sight. The darkness increased. It was not like the dusk of twilight and evening. It seemed as though the light were being sucked from the sky. The roar of the rapids drowned the terrified shouts that broke from the throats of the superstitious men. They turned their eyes toward the sun and saw a great shadow advancing across it. The sun was in eclipse. By now the color of the trees, the grasses and the flowers on shore had faded, the rough boats, the men's equipment, even their hands and faces had turned to a muddy, ashlike gray. Their world was faded and ominous, and the

[1] CORN ISLAND—An island in the Ohio River between the present sites of Louisville, Kentucky, and Jeffersonville, Indiana. The expedition had left Redstone (now Brownsville), Pennsylvania, on May 12, 1778, proceeded by way of the Monongahela River to Pittsburgh, and then down the Ohio to Corn Island. There they encamped for several weeks. Corn Island no longer exists, having been worn away by erosion.

boats tossed and swirled and shot ahead in the mad, racing waters. They were hurled forward and shaken as though the spirits of the earth and sky would crush them and cover their end in darkness. Never did a handful of men start out "to conquer an empire" under more awesome circumstances!

The adventurers rowed on. Day and night they rowed, for success lay largely in speed. They must outrun the news of their coming. When they reached the mouth of the Tennessee River, about sixty miles above where the Ohio joins the Mississippi, Colonel Clark ordered the boats to put in to a little island where they could make final preparations for the overland march to Kaskaskia.[2]

Scouts were sent out to reconnoiter and bring word of any Indians in the vicinity. While the others were still busy setting up camp, two scouts returned with an unknown white man who gave his name as John Duff. He said he had been leading a party of hunters up the river. When this mysterious wanderer was taken before Colonel Clark, he told his story and said his party had put out from the British post at Kaskaskia eight days before on a mere hunting expedition and that no one at Kaskaskia dreamed of an attack by the Americans. However, the British were by no means asleep and of course kept spies along the Mississippi. Colonel Clark, suspecting this, had for this very reason landed above the Mississippi with the intention of marching overland against the fort. Duff, although not particularly talkative, did inform Colonel Clark that there were some eight hundred French inhabitants at Kaskaskia who would take up arms and join the British garrison. He said the French would do this because they had been led to believe that their women and children would be the victims of the most terrible atrocities if they ever fell into the hands of Clark and his blood-thirsty Big Knives. As to the British garrison, it would be able to give a good account of itself unless taken by surprise. This was substantially the same news Clark had received from the spies he had sent out the previous year.

Duff apparently gave honest answers to all of Colonel Clark's questions, and then even asked if he and his companions might be allowed to join the expedition. Clark then had Duff's entire party brought before him. They all seemed sincere in the interest of the Big Knives, and the Colonel naturally was glad to add all the able-bodied men possible to his little army. But before he permitted them to remain he told them how they should talk in the presence of his soldiers and just how much information they should pass on to his men. They apparently did their work well, for when the column got under way the next morning everyone was in high spirits and eager for the march.

First they dropped down the river for about ten miles to an abandoned French outpost called Fort Massac. Here they dragged their boats ashore and carefully hid them in the cane and brush, in the hope that they would be safe from the prying eyes of Indians or any passing hunters.

Clark's little army did not function quite as you might expect an army to. It was not formed in squads and platoons

[2] KASKASKIA—A British garrison, the key position in the Illinois territory.

with the officers marching ahead. Instead the men were scattered out so that each might pick his own path through the swamps and marshlands of southern Illinois. There was an excellent reason for this because it meant that little evidence would be left by the soldiers to show that they had passed. If they had formed a narrow column for the march, they would have beaten down a path that any chance woodsman would have recognized had he stumbled across it in the dark. Flung far out ahead and on the wings were scouts to give notice of any roving bands of Indians or hunting parties that might dash to Kaskaskia with the news and thus prevent a surprise attack by Clark's Big Knives.

The first fifty miles of their one-hundred-and-twenty-mile journey was an exhausting and heroic effort. When the men were not wading through the sloughs and sticky marshes, they were breaking their way through tangled thickets. Their food was scanty, for game was scarce; the water was bad, and some of the men came down with fever. Their fatigue after the day's march was nearly more than they could bear. But their indomitable leader, by word and example, inspired them to push on.

On the third day of the march the country grew better. From the edge of the dark and clinging forest they looked out on wide prairies and waving meadows dotted here and there with groves of maple, oak, and walnut. But now their caution had to be redoubled, for just as they could see a great distance, so could they be seen.

One of the hunters who, along with John Duff, had joined Clark at his camp on the Tennessee, was acting as chief guide. John Saunders was his name. They had not gone far across the open country before Colonel Clark noticed that this man John Saunders was acting queerly. On being questioned the man said he was lost. This news passed from man to man, like a grass fire running before the wind and immediately produced "the greatest confusion." Clark, of course, was angry and suspected that the man was trying to mislead them. It is easy to imagine what must have been the feeling of the troops and their officers. Here were less than two hundred men, without supplies and ammunition except for what they each carried, in the midst of a country filled with hostile Indians who far outnumbered them. If these Indians even so much as caught sight of them, word would soon get to Kaskaskia and the chance of its capture would be entirely gone and the Big Knives would be ambushed and fall victims to French and British rifles or the Indian torture stake.

Saunders begged that he be allowed to go a little way ahead and reconnoiter. This Colonel Clark agreed to let him do, but took the precaution of sending a couple of men along and warned him that if he did not find the way shortly, he would be put to death without hesitation. After a couple of hours' search, Saunders returned and reported that he had found the Hunters' Road. Apparently he had been honestly confused. At any rate, he was able to convince the Colonel and his men of his sincerity and eagerness to lead them right.

The following day their scant supply of food gave out. No game was seen near by and to send out a hunting party was considered inadvisable on the grounds that it might double the chances of the discovery of the whole party. There was nothing to do but push ahead on empty stomachs.

From the point where they had left the junction of the Tennessee and Ohio Rivers to Kaskaskia was, as we have noted, about one hundred and twenty miles. And the march was made in six days, an average of twenty miles a day. Of this the first fifty miles through the low lands consumed half the time. So on the last two days of the march they must have traveled between fifty and sixty miles. Truly these were sturdy men who could make thirty miles a day, every moment on the alert, with only water to sustain them.

On the evening of July 4, 1778, the frontiersmen reached the Kaskaskia River about three miles above the town. There they halted until dark so their movements might not be noticed by possible enemy guards or outposts on the opposite bank.

The Commandant of the British garrison happened to be Colonel Rocheblave,[3] a Frenchman. For a number of years he had served as a mercenary soldier in the British army. He hated the Americans, and he also hated the Spanish. Then, too, the British had promised him that if New Orleans were ever captured he would be made its first British governor. He knew the Spanish had been aiding the Americans by sending them supplies up the Mississippi. He also was astute enough to realize that some day he was pretty sure to be attacked by an American army. So he wrote various letters to headquarters in Canada begging that supplies and men be sent him, sufficient to hold the Mississippi Valley. In one of his letters he said: "We are upon the eve of seeing here a numerous horde of brigands who will establish a chain of communications which will not be easy to break, once formed." How prophetically he spoke, his superiors did not realize.

Probably even Rocheblave did not fully appreciate the determined spirit of the men marching against him. There they sat concealed in the high grass behind a fringe of trees close to the water's edge, worn out and hungry. But as Captain Bowman, one of Clark's Big Knives, expressed it later in a letter to an uncle in Virginia, "We were all determined to take the town, or die in the attempt."

A little while after dark Clark decided his moment to strike had come. Scouts had brought word that Kaskaskia was quiet. Here and there were lights, but one after another they were winking out. There was no activity at the fort. At one end of the town there was music and singing. The negroes and creoles were having a dance. This was the only sound that broke the stillness of the night. The word of command from Clark was passed from man to man. They rose as stealthily as Indians with their rifles ready.

Just across from the town stood a farmhouse. The first move was to surround it quietly and seize the terrified occupants, who were immediately taken before the rough-looking chief of the Big Knives, Colonel Clark. The farmer and family were so startled that it is no wonder that some of their information "seemed to vary." The Americans were informed that a couple of days before there had

[3] ROCHEBLAVE—Pronounced rōsh′bläv.

been an alarm and that most of the men had been under arms, but spies had been unable to find any trace of an approaching enemy force. So Kaskaskia had quieted down to normal again. There were a great many men in the town, said the farmer, but most of the Indians were camped at Cahokia, sixty miles away.

Clark's next move was quickly to divide his men into three units, and instruct two of them to proceed to the far end of town. His own unit he intended leading directly to the fort, and at a given signal the others were to rush upon the town and storm it.

Luckily enough boats were found on the south bank to transport all the men across at once. The rowlocks were wrapped with rags and skins to keep them from squeaking and the oarsmen dipped their oars so that not so much as a lone splash was heard. The men landed and silently marched to the positions determined upon. Colonel Clark, with John Saunders still as his guide, led his unit toward the main gate of the fort. The moccasined feet of the marching men made no sound to warn the sentinel. They found the gate open, and before the sentry had time to cry out he was disarmed and gagged. Then Clark and his men crept into the fort, still without a sound. Saunders led the way to Rocheblave's house. It was surrounded, and then the Colonel forced an entrance and found the redoubtable Commandant in nightshirt and nightcap coming out of his bedroom door to see what all the noise was about. Imagine his surprise and chagrin when Colonel Clark, travel-worn and haggard, announced that he was the prisoner of the Big Knives and that the town was already in the hands of an American force. Rocheblave was allowed to dress, and when he appeared a few minutes later, in the street between two soldiers, the troops burst into a shout of triumph.

This was the signal that the other two units had been waiting for. With a wild yell they rushed the town and seized every person who happened to be about. Those of Clark's men who could speak French then ran through the streets informing the inhabitants that the town had fallen into the hands of the Big Knives and that any person who so much as dared to stick his nose out of a window would be shot without a second's hesitation. But the work of the weary soldiers was not done. Colonel Clark ordered them to split up into small parties and patrol the streets, shouting and singing, and making as much noise as an Indian tribe in the midst of a massacre. Further, they were to go to each house and demand guns, powder, and shot. But they were not to harm so much as a hair of anyone's head. The young Colonel was determined that in appearance, at least, he would substantiate the Frenchmen's opinion of the Big Knives, and then by a show of leniency later he hoped he could win their gratitude and genuine friendship. A careful guard was maintained around the town to prevent anyone escaping to give the alarm to the neighboring villages and thus bring a rescuing force down upon them.

One of the first things Clark did was to send Simon Kenton with a couple of companions to spy out the country around Vincennes [4] and to determine the strength

[4] VINCENNES—Fort on the Wabash River.

and condition of the garrison there. The scouts started out that very night. Clark next turned his attention to interviewing some of the principal inhabitants. One after another they were called from their houses and taken in terror before the Big Knife. In general he found that the people were not overly fond of the British, and this encouraged him to believe that it might be possible to make them feel friendly to the Americans. There were even a few among them who declared that they really were not French or British, but were American hunters. Two of these, Richard Winston and Daniel Murry, immediately set out to procure food supplies for the victorious raiders, and by morning had the finest meal prepared that Kaskaskia could produce. This proved a joy to the famished soldiers. "After the troops had regaled themselves, they were withdrawn from within the town and posted in different positions on the borders of it."

George Rogers Clark had taken and subdued the key position in Illinois without a gun being fired, without a single blow of the tomahawk or scalping-knife, and with a band numbering less than a quarter of those he had attacked. It was a masterful stroke; it was consummate strategy. Now strategy must make these people his friends or his position so far from his base and reënforcements might become a fatal trap.

He issued orders to the people that they were at liberty to move about their town, but that no one should venture beyond its borders. This brought a general exodus from the houses and the people gathered in little knots, and in hurried whispers, with frightened glances, they expressed wonder and anxiety as to their probable fate. The young Colonel must have smiled as he looked out on them from his headquarters and issued an order that certain of the more important militia officers be arrested and put in irons. No reason was given to the people for the arrests; no explanation was given to the prisoners. "The worst was now expected by the whole."

The people of Kaskaskia were not his only concern. There were the towns to the north to be taken before they could prepare for a defense. Therefore, Colonel Clark ordered Captain Bowman to take thirty men and mount them on horses found in the town and proceed with the greatest haste toward St. Philippe, Prairie du Rocher, and Cahokia. The first two towns were merely trading-posts without military protection, but Cahokia had a small fort and a British Commandant.

When the people of Kaskaskia realized what Captain Bowman was about, some of the Frenchmen went to Colonel Clark and begged that they be allowed to accompany him, explaining that the people of these towns were their friends and relatives. Their idea obviously was to urge these "friends and relatives" to submit with good grace lest they be torn to pieces by the Big Knives; that Captain Bowman's troop was an insignificant detachment of a much larger force that would march upon them from Kaskaskia if they showed any resistance. The Colonel, seeing the advantage of having these men accompany his expedition, gave his permission, and about noon of the 5th of July, Captain Bowman set out for Cahokia.

In the meantime the priest, Father

Gibault,[5] with several of the oldest and most responsible members of the town, asked permission to speak to Colonel Clark. They were shown to the door of a dimly lighted room, fear deepening the lines of their creased, old faces. The sight that met their eyes was worse than they could have anticipated; it left no doubt in their minds of the hideous barbarity of the Big Knives. Gathered about a table, rough-hewn from a solid log, sat four or five men practically naked. Their bodies were scarred and bleeding; their eyes seemed to glare out of their sockets from drawn, cadaverous faces partly hid by a ten days' growth of beard. On the table lay tomahawks and scalping-knives and one man was inspecting the flint of the rifle he held across his knees. The faint sunlight that crept in through one dingy little window accentuated the somber shadows and made the general gloom more ominous. Is it any wonder that the delegation was, for some moments, speechless? They did not know that the new Commandant and his officers had been bathing in the river and that they had left their clothing spread out upon the bank to dry while they returned to the fort to dress the cuts and scratches they had received during their march from the Ohio.

Finally Father Gibault summoned enough courage to ask which was Colonel Clark. The Colonel made himself known and asked the men to sit down, but they preferred to stand near the door so that in case of necessity they could flee from the savages before them. Again they

[5] GIBAULT—Pronounced zhē·bō′.

seemed speechless. Finally Colonel Clark asked them, rather gruffly, what they wanted. Father Gibault told him that the people realized they must suffer the hardships of war; that they would soon be separated one from another, and through him they begged that they might be allowed to gather in the little church to say their farewells.

Colonel Clark shrugged his shoulders and said he had nothing to do with the church. If they wanted to gather there, they could do so and stay as long as they liked. He told Father Gibault, however, that he had better warn the people not to attempt to leave the town, and with a gesture indicated the dire consequences that would result from such rashness. The Colonel then dismissed them by saying he was not at leisure.

George Rogers Clark had a sense of humor and a sense of the dramatic and both qualities contributed to his success. He was a keen student of men, and he knew how to make his points impressive. His seemingly harsh treatment of the people of Kaskaskia came not from any viciousness in his character, nor from any actual intention of doing them any harm. It was merely necessary from the standpoint of the safety of his little army and the success of his undertaking. He himself wrote: "My principle would not suffer me to distress such a number of people, except, through policy, it was necessary."

Very soon, from every direction, the people were seen gathering at the church. Mothers carried their babies, young children were led by the hand, the old and infirm who could scarcely hobble were helped along, sweethearts walked tearfully side by side, the stalwart young *coureurs de bois* [6] were stooped and dejected. Solemnly they crowded into the church and the doors were closed. The town seemed deserted except for the dogs that lay in the dusty roads sunning themselves and the gaunt, weather-bitten soldiers who leaned like brown-stained statues on their long rifles, silent men keeping watch over a silent village.

After a time the door of the church swung open and Father Gibault came out, followed by a group of bearded patriarchs. They walked toward the fort speaking in furtive undertones among themselves, punctuating their remarks with gestures of hopelessness and despair. They begged to see Colonel Clark and were immediately admitted.

This time the scene at headquarters was entirely changed. Colonel Clark stood beside the long table fully dressed in the costume of the frontiersman, which suited his broad, erect shoulders and gave him as much added dignity as any tailored uniform. His sword hung at his side and across his shoulder was slung the ever-present powder-horn and shot-pouch. His face was clean-shaven and his unruly sandy hair was brushed back from his forehead. Never did a young man look more impressively a soldier and a leader.

Father Gibault began by thanking the Colonel in the name of the people for his indulgence in allowing them to gather at the church. Then he asked that he might be allowed to say a few words in behalf of his people. Colonel Clark told him to speak out whatever he had to say. So with great hesitation Father Gibault

[6] *Coureurs de bois* (kōō·rûr′ dĕ bwȧ′)—French or Canadian hunters. The literal meaning is "runners of the wood."

explained that since theirs was the fate of war they were reconciled to their lot. Their property and goods, they knew, belonged to their conquerors; their homes were in the hands of the enemy, and when they were driven forth they had little expectation of returning. They would be sold into slavery, it was the fortune of war; but would not the good commander try to prevent them from being separated from their families? They knew well what had happened to the Frenchmen of Acadia; how wives and husbands had been torn from each other, how children had been taken from parents, how lovers had been separated, never to meet again. And could the good commander be generous enough to let the women and the little children keep some of their clothing; they were not so hardy as the men and their suffering would be more severe? And could they be allowed a small quantity of food for the women and children, enough to tide them along until the men, through their industry, could again support them? It was true that their conduct had been influenced by the British Commandants and the emissaries who had been among them, and it was true that they had been made to take the oath of allegiance to King George and these they had been bound to obey. In their distant outpost they had had little opportunity to learn about the war in the East, but there had been some Americans among them, from time to time, and on more than one occasion Father Gibault had heard the Frenchmen express sympathy for the American cause. But, above all, could the good commander show a little leniency toward the women and children?

Colonel Clark had listened to the priest's simple appeal without giving a sign as to the effect it was having upon him. He now turned and, with head bent, paced back and forth before the table. He was convinced of their sincerity. This was the moment for which he had waited.

Suddenly he stopped and raised his head. He acted as though he were insulted and his deep voice fairly boomed at them. Did the people of Kaskaskia think that he and the Americans were savages? Obviously they did or they would never have spoken as they had. What sort of men were these Big Knives to make war on women and children, to strip them of their clothing, to turn them out of their homes into the wilderness, to take the bread out of their mouths? Did they think they were brothers of the painted savages that would revel in the horrors of the torture stake? It was only too clear that they had listened to the lies that had been told them by the British and they had believed them. Bah! It was because of these lies and because the British and the Frenchmen, too, were stirring up the Indians and supplying them with powder and guns and scalping-knives to use against the settlers from Virginia that the Big Knives had determined to come to Illinois and put a stop to it. The Big Knives did not want plunder. What they wanted was peace and they were going to have it, even if it meant the extermination of the Indians and their white supporters. Did they know that the French King had taken the side of the Americans and was sending men and ships and supplies to help the armies in the East? Apparently they did not. Did they know that this meant the war would soon be over and their land would come under the rule of the Americans and they would have all the privileges of free people? Why hadn't they been told these things? They were free men to go to their church and worship as they saw fit. One of the foundation principles of the Americans was that of religious freedom. The Big Knives would not molest their church; in fact, they would straightway punish anyone who dared to offer it an insult. Now the Big Knives offered them liberty and freedom. If they preferred the British masters, they were free to take their families and their property and go to live among the British. The Big Knives would not take their property away from them or destroy their families, whichever choice they made.

Then Colonel Clark told them that they should go back to their weeping families and tell them that they might go about their business as usual and choose whether or not they wanted to take the oath of allegiance to America and to its Congress. He would give immediate orders that their friends in prison should be released and that the soldiers patrolling the town should be withdrawn. Later he would issue a proclamation which they should read and obey, but this would not proscribe them in living their lives in freedom.

The little delegation was struck dumb with surprise. Could they believe what the Big Knife had told them? They weren't to have their property taken from them; they weren't to be separated from their families and sold into slavery! Father Gibault tried to stammer a few words of gratitude, but his emotions were too strong. They bowed awkwardly to the Colonel and withdrew.

Once outside the fort, these men who a few moments before had approached it with abject resignation now lost all semblance of dignity. They jumped in the air for joy and set off at a run for the church. A few minutes later bells were ringing madly and the people were rushing out of doors singing and weeping and shouting and embracing one another. They paraded the streets crying the praises of the good Commandant and his chivalrous Big Knives from Virginia. They were not conquered people; they were freemen and they too wanted to become Americans.

Thus did George Rogers Clark, a young man of twenty-six, in one dramatic and effective stroke win the friendship and support of the inhabitants of Kaskaskia, and lay a foundation that was to make possible the taking of the rest of the British forts in this vast wilderness country, without so much as firing a single rifle.

◇◇◇◇◇◇◇◇◇◇◇◇◇◇◇◇◇◇◇◇◇◇◇◇◇◇◇◇◇◇

FOR DISCUSSION

1. What incident marked the departure from Corn Island? What was its effect?

2. Why did Clark undertake to trek across Illinois instead of going down the Ohio to the Mississippi and up that river? How did he find his way through the forest?

3. Outline the plan of attack. What was the signal for the rush of the two waiting groups?

4. Who took the lead for the inhabitants in their dealing with Clark? Do you see anything significant in that?

5. What was the reason for Clark's campaign into Illinois? What war was being fought? What effect did his campaign have?

SYNONYMS

1. "The Commandant at Kaskaskia was *astute*. . . ." How does *astute* differ from *clever* or *sharp* or *shrewd?*

2. "The faint sunlight . . . *accentuated* the somber shadows." What more common word of much the same meaning could be used in place of *accentuate?*

3. "They seized the *terrified* occupants of the farmhouse." How many synonyms for *terrified* can you discover?

4. "Once outside the fort, these men who . . . had approached it with *abject* resignation. . . ." What is a synonym for *abject?* Would the sentence mean the same if you were to substitute the synonym?

GEORGE ROGERS CLARK

This incident is but one of many in the adventurous career of George Rogers Clark. From an encyclopedia, a history textbook, or from a book recommended by your librarian, read more about this early American. Prepare to tell the class about another of his accomplishments.

RELATED READING

Alice of Old Vincennes, by Maurice Thompson, is a story you will enjoy also.

◇◇◇◇◇

Father Damien looked over the years of his labor on Molokai. He had put order into the lives of the lepers and given them medical aid and spiritual care. But leprosy had claimed him, too, and he longed and prayed for a successor. In answer to his prayer, Ira Dutton, called Brother Joseph, came and labored until death forty-four years later.

THE FLEET AND BROTHER JOSEPH

ALEXANDER WOOLLCOTT

This is the story of naval action by certain American battleships in the waters of the Pacific just off the Hawaiian Islands —a fleet action involving the American flag and directed by the Commander in Chief of our armed forces. The month was July, the year 1908.

The story begins years before that—begins, let us say, on a certain Sunday more than half a century ago in a church at Molokai.[1] That is the gray, lofty, and most desolate Hawaiian island, long ago set aside as a place where lepers [2] might hastily and conveniently be hidden from the sight of healthy men. The church was one built for Father Damien, a laugh-

[1] MOLOKAI—Pronounced mō′lô·kä′ē.

[2] LEPER—A person affected with leprosy.

ing and violent peasant from Belgium—a crude little wooden church built for this priest of theirs by parishioners who had fashioned the homely tabernacle with their own rotting hands. On this Sunday came the first tidings of Damien's now historic martyrdom, for then it was that he changed the familiar beginning of his sermon. This time he did not start, as so often before, with the salutation "My brethren." Instead the first words that morning were "We lepers."

One day in 1887, when Damien's malady had so advanced that he could no longer walk and was able to move about his strange parish at all only by trundling himself in a home-made tricycle, he went down to watch the arrival of the periodic steamer from Honolulu, which usually lingered only long enough to toss the mailbags over the side before hurrying on her way. But this time she was landing a passenger, a lean fellow clad in blue denim and bearded like a prophet. This stranger toted enough luggage to give Damien the wild notion that he had come to stay. He had. He stayed forty-four years. It was he who nursed Damien in his last illness, buried him there on the island, administered his estate and, until his own death in 1931, carried on the work which the flaming little Belgian had so nobly begun. Back in Vermont, where he was born the son of the village schoolmarm by Ezra Dutton, the shoe-cobbler, he had been christened Ira but at Molokai they knew him as Brother Joseph.

About the uneasy years before this man Dutton sailed for Molokai we have much scattered information, but the crucial periods are blank. We know that after his service in the Union forces and after the wreck of his disastrous marriage he took his troubled heart to the Church of Rome. We know that even after months of meditation in the Trappist [3] monastery at Gethsemane in Kentucky he had found no peace. Then, when he was adrift in New Orleans, he came one day, through what we have the effrontery to call chance, upon a magazine article about Father Damien. A few months later he was in San Francisco, booking steerage-passage [4] for Honolulu.

Brother Joseph never saw his native land again, never would consider even a visit to it. But there was no day in those forty-four years when he was not homesick. The vast litter of letters and diaries left behind him bear witness to his love of his country, and the leper boys who learned about America from Brother Joseph were taught to think of it as an earthly paradise. He set up a flagpole on the Molokai shore at a point so high that the flag snapping in the breeze could be seen from far out at sea, and the old-timers there will tell you that no one else was ever allowed to run it up in the morning or take it in at sundown. They say that in that moment when the red and white folds fell tumbling to his shoulder, he would let them rest there just for the space that a breath is held. It was as if the flag caressed him.

Then in 1908 there came in letters from the States and in the newspackets from Honolulu word that our fleet was going around the world. Brother Joseph was beside himself with excitement. Each day, when he ran up the flag in the

[3] TRAPPIST—A member of a religious Order of very strict penance and fasting.

[4] STEERAGE—The cheapest passenger rate aboard ship.

morning and took it down at night, he used to point out to sea and tell the leper boys that maybe the ships would come near enough for them all to see them. Now someone happened to mention this unworded prayer in a letter to the White House in Washington. When Theodore Roosevelt read that letter his heart skipped a beat for he knew the fleet was not scheduled to pass by Molokai at all. There was no time to lose. In another moment he had the Navy Department on the telephone and in an hour the cable was catching the admiral in Honolulu with a change in sailing orders.

Thus it befell that there came a day on Molokai when Brother Joseph—he was getting on now and his beard was snow-white but his back was as straight as ever—a day when Brother Joseph stood on the promontory with the leper boys around him and his heart overflowing as they watched the long file of battleships go by. It is good to remember that to his gay bit of bunting, so bright in the afternoon sunlight—was ever a flag dearer or more honored?—each gray ship as she went by dipped her own colors in salute.

◇◇◇◇◇◇◇◇◇◇◇◇◇◇◇◇◇◇◇◇◇◇◇◇◇◇◇◇◇◇

FOR DISCUSSION

1. In explaining how Brother Joseph heard about Father Damien, the author says ". . . he came one day, through what we have the effrontery to call chance, upon a magazine article about Father Damien." Would you choose another word besides *chance?* Explain.

2. Brother Joseph was ardently patriotic. If patriotic, how could he justify his abandonment of his native land?

3. What motive do you believe led both Damien and Dutton to embrace life among the lepers? Can you name any other persons whose life work was determined by the same motive?

4. Why would *boldness* or *audacity* not quite substitute for *effrontery* in the sentence about Ira Dutton's reading of the magazine article? Use each word correctly in an original sentence.

WITH BROTHER JOSEPH

Stand at attention with Brother Joseph as the fleet steams by. See the proud glint in his eye, the snap of his salute. Hear him speak to the leper boys about his country, his America, his home. What does he say? What would *you* say? Express your thoughts in a paragraph.

RELATED READING

John Farrow in his *Damien the Leper* has given us a clear, intensely moving portrait of Father Damien and of his assistant and successor, Brother Joseph. *Man of Molokai* by Ann Roos is another dramatic account of Father Damien's life, work, and death.

"L'Envoi" is French for a postscript to a poem or book. Thus, it also means "a special message." The poet here looks forward to that day in heaven where there'll be no business worries and no "Society." It is a solemn poem, even though the measure is gay.

L'Envoi

RUDYARD KIPLING

When Earth's last picture is painted, and the tubes are twisted and dried,
When the oldest colors have faded, and the youngest critic has died,
We shall rest, and, faith, we shall need it—lie down for an æon or two,
Till the Master of All Good Workmen shall set us to work anew!

And those that were good shall be happy: they shall sit in a golden chair; 5
They shall splash at a ten-league canvas with brushes of comets' hair;
They shall find real saints to draw from—Magdalene, Peter, and Paul;
They shall work for an age at a sitting and never be tired at all!

And only the Master shall praise us, and only the Master shall blame;
And no one shall work for money, and no one shall work for fame; 10
But each for the joy of the working, and each, in his separate star,
Shall draw the Thing as he sees It for the God of Things as They Are!

FOR DISCUSSION

1. In this poem the following words have a special meaning to the oil painter: *tubes, dried, faded, critic, canvas, brushes, sitting.* Why does the poet use this special vocabulary? What is he comparing to the life of a painter? What does he mean by an "æon or two"? by "the Master of All Good Workmen"?
2. According to the poet, what will be the motive for working in heaven?
3. Why does the poet call God, "the God of Things as They Are"? In what way is he protesting against hypocrisy and sham convention, so common in worldly men?

ABOUT THE AUTHOR

Were you ever curious to know what an author was like when he was young and growing up? Rudyard Kipling, the author of "L'Envoi," went to school just as you are doing now. Prepare for the class an interesting report about Rudyard's boyhood and early manhood. There is a good account in *School Days with Kipling*, by G. C. Beresford.

For Further Reading

Young Trailers by Joseph Altsheler reenacts the exciting days of our country's past. These are stories of the men and boys who moved the frontiers westward.

Growing Up with America by May L. Becker, ed. Here is a collection of seven stories illustrating seven periods of American history, and "written by men and women with special reason to know what life in America was like in the period of which they were writing."

Drums by James Boyd tells of the exciting adventures of a North Carolina boy before and during the Revolutionary War.

Son of Thunder by Julia Carsons is an intimate biography of Patrick Henry. It presents a vivid picture of his dramatic career in a way which makes the reader share in the drama.

The Crossing by Winston Churchill is an account of the settlement of the Mississippi Valley. Exciting adventures await the reader of this book.

Twenty Modern Americans by Alice Cooper and C. Palmer. Here are studies of Walt Disney, J. Edgar Hoover, and other modern Americans, showing the qualities that have made them outstanding in their fields.

The Last of the Mohicans by James F. Cooper. The hero, Natty Bumppo, has many exciting adventures and narrow escapes from the Indians around Lake George in the French and Indian Wars.

Daniel Boone by James Daugherty exemplifies the life of the early frontiersman in a biography of the man who typifies pioneer America.

Our F.B.I. by John Joseph Floherty is the inside story of the scientific methods of investigation of the Federal Bureau of Investigation. Stories of outstanding cases add interest and excitement to an already fascinating subject.

Blockade Runner by H. J. Heagney is a novel based on the boyhood experiences of Father John Bannister Tabb aboard a blockade runner during the Civil War.

Boys Who Became President by William Heyliger relates the boyhoods of eighteen presidents of the United States.

Eagles Roar! by Byron Kennerly tells the thrilling experiences of Graham Berry, a member of the Eagle Squadron of the Royal Air Force.

Explorations of Père Marquette by James Arthur Kjelgaard is the breath-taking story of the Jesuit priest and his adventurer-companion, Joliet, based on the journals kept by Father Marquette.

The Captain Wears a Cross by William A. Maguire contains the reminiscences of twenty-seven years of service as a chaplain in the United States Navy.

A Plebe at West Point by Paul B. Malone is the story of the first year at West Point.

Falcons of France by Charles Nordhoff and James Hall is an account of the absorbing adventures of Charles Sheldon and Gordon Forbes, members of the Lafayette Flying Corps in World War I.

Davy Crockett by Constance Rourke not only relates the exciting adventures of this fabulous frontiersman but gives an excellent character study as well.

Abe Lincoln Grows Up by Carl Sandburg shows the early prairie life of this great President, with all its hardship and promise.

Our Land and Our Lady by Daniel Sargent tells of the growth of the Catholic faith in the United States from Columbus to the first martyr of Maryknoll, 1938.

Long May It Wave by Leslie Thomas contains incidents from American history that tell the story of our flag.

Kit Carson by Stanley Vestal is a breathless unfolding of events in the frontier life of a famous scout.

HIS PEOPLE AND MINE

One stormy day as Martin was going through the city gates, he spotted a shivering beggar. In three seconds he had flung off his raincoat and given it to the drenched man. That night in a vision St. Martin of Tours saw our Lord Himself wearing the raincoat. Such, in brief, is the history of the corporal and spiritual works of mercy. Time and again, a perfect act of charity has made saints out of sinners in the twinkling of an eye.

Such noblehearted men and women have discovered that happiness does not consist in dominating one's neighbor, nor in hankering after possessions. It consists in relieving the burdens of those less fortunate than ourselves. In doing so we actually *imitate* the provident God who dresses dandelions in gold, and furnishes excellent seed for the carefree starlings.

"I am the trunk of the vine," said our Lord, explaining to the first Christians how closely they were united to Himself and to each other, "and you are the branches." Then lest we fail to understand the full significance of that truth, He said explicitly, "This is an order: Love one another as I have loved you." That is the love which prompts us to be glad with those who are glad, and to cry with those who are crying. That is the love which should saturate public works with motives of justice and social charity.

You will find examples of that love in the stories of this section. There is a cobbler, Conrad, who sets his table with milk and honey for our Lord. There are the Lindberghs bringing doctors and medicine to thousands of Chinese trapped by a great river flood. There is a Venetian merchant about whom Shakespeare has written a tragi-comedy, compounded of a pound of flesh, three romantic jewel-cases, and a study of racial intolerance. Such men and women you must learn to understand and love. For, since all are *His* people, they must become *yours* too.

EWING GALLOWAY

Everybody likes to have company come. Here is a story in verse about a lonely, hard-working cobbler expecting a visit from a friend. As you read, try to feel his mood of expectancy.

How the Great Guest Came

EDWIN MARKHAM

Before the Cathedral in grandeur rose,
At Ingelburg where the Danube goes;
Before its forest of silver spires
Went airily up to the clouds and fires:
Before the oak had ready a beam, 5
While yet the arch was stone and dream—
There where the altar was later laid,
Conrad, the cobbler, plied his trade.

Doubled all day on his busy bench,
Hard at his cobbling for master and hench, 10
He pounded away at a brisk rat-tat,
Shearing and shaping with pull and pat,
Hide well-hammered and pegs sent home,
Till the shoe was fit for the Prince of Rome.
And he sang as the threads went to and fro: 15
"Whether 'tis hidden or whether it show,
Let the work be sound, for the Lord will know."

Tall was the cobbler, and gray and thin,
And a full moon shone where the hair had been.
His eyes peered out, intent and afar, 20
As looking beyond the things that are;
He walked as one who is done with fear,
Knowing at last that God is near.
Only the half of him cobbled the shoes:
The rest was away for the heavenly news. 25
Indeed, so thin was the mystic screen

2. INGELBURG—A town in Austria. 10. HENCH—Helper.

That parted the Unseen from the Seen,
You could not tell from the cobbler's theme,
If his dream were truth or his truth were dream.

It happened one day at the year's white end, 30
Two neighbors called on their old-time friend;
And they found the shop, so meager and mean,
Made gay with a hundred boughs of green.
Conrad was stitching with face ashine,
But suddenly stopped as he twitched a twine: 35
"Old friends, good news! At dawn today,
As the cocks were scaring the night away,
The Lord appeared in a dream to me,
And said, 'I am coming your guest to be!'
So I've been busy with feet astir, 40
Strewing the floor with branches of fir.
The wall is washed and the shelf is shined,
And over the rafter the holly twined.
He comes today, and the table is spread
With milk and honey and wheaten bread." 45

His friends went home; and his face grew still
As he watched for the shadow across the sill.
He lived all the moments o'er and o'er,
When the Lord should enter the lowly door—
The knock, the call, the latch pulled up, 50
The lighted face, the offered cup.
He would wash the feet where the spikes had been;
He would kiss the hands where the nails went in;
And then at last he would sit with Him,
And break the bread as the day grew dim. 55

While the cobbler mused there passed his pane
A beggar drenched by the driving rain.
He called him in from the stony street
And gave him shoes for his bruiséd feet.
The beggar went and there came a crone, 60
Her face with wrinkles of sorrow sown.
A bundle of fagots bowed her back,
And she was spent with the wrench and rack.
He gave her his loaf and steadied her load

60. CRONE—An old woman.

As she took her way on the weary road. 65
Then came to his door a little child,
Lost and afraid in the world so wild,
In the big, dark world. Catching it up,
He gave it the milk in the waiting cup,
And led it home to its mother's arms, 70
Out of the reach of the world's alarms.

The day went down in the crimson west
And with it the hope of the blesséd Guest,
And Conrad sighed as the world turned gray:
"Why is it, Lord, that your feet delay? 75
Did You forget that this was the day?"
Then soft in the silence a Voice he heard:
"Lift up your heart, for I kept my word,
Three times I came to your friendly door;
Three times my shadow was on your floor, 80
I was the beggar with bruiséd feet;
I was the woman you gave to eat;
I was the child on the homeless street!"

FOR DISCUSSION

1. Did you suspect how the story would end? If you did, you must be familiar with the *New Testament,* Matthew, Chapter 25: 34–40. At which line did you begin to foresee the ending?

2. What would you have done if you had been waiting for the divine Guest and these other people constantly rang your doorbell? Would you have treated them as the cobbler did? Do you think Conrad went beyond the limits of strict justice? Explain your answer.

3. What solid truth is in this story? State it in one clear sentence.

TWO PROJECTS

1. Can you think of anyone to whom you might play "Conrad" if you could recognize our Lord in the disguise of your fellowmen? Consider all the people you meet at home, at school, and elsewhere. Then write down five instances, without mentioning actual names. Explain how you could help.

2. Draw a picture of the cobbler waiting for our Lord.

When disaster strikes close to home, we sympathize with the victims and do everything we can to relieve their suffering. However, we are usually not much disturbed by accounts of similar tragedies when they happen in distant lands to people we know little about. In the cold statistics of dead, sick, and injured we are unable to see the misery of the individual human beings like ourselves that such figures represent.

In the following selection from her book, North to the Orient, *Anne Morrow Lindbergh, wife of the famous flier, Charles Lindbergh, makes these kinds of statistics more meaningful.*

THE FLOODS

ANNE MORROW LINDBERGH

Before we left Japan we knew that the lower Yangtze[1] valley was badly flooded. But we had no picture in our minds of the size or character of this valley. Only someone who has been there can imagine the amount of damage a flood can do.

Looking down on it from the air on our flight to Nanking, we saw that there was nothing to stop a flood. Flat fields for miles and miles—and the great massive river. The impression of magnificence is perhaps similar from any great river and its valley. And yet if one compares this yellow river to the Mississippi, one is

[1] YANGTZE—A very large river in China.

aware of a vast difference. The Yangtze valley, despite the immense expanse of land, still seems crowded. Every inch of ground is cultivated, not in big tracts, like our farms, but in narrow strips of rice fields, slivering off at right angles to the river. No wild land, no forests; just thin back-yard strips of field with occasionally a crowded village of mud huts, representing thousands of people.

One did not have to be told that this was a land in which there could be no waste; that people here lived literally from day to day; that there was no "extra" stored away; that even the shucks of the crop and the dry grass were saved for fuel, because the trees had gone long ago.

This was the type of country into which the floods came, destroying crops, homes, and people. And this was the type of country over which we did most of our survey flying. For on our arrival in Nanking we offered to help the National Flood Relief Commission by mapping the damaged areas.

On the first day's flight we left our anchorage at Lotus Lake in the morning and for a time followed the river east until it met the Grand Canal, then turned and flew north. At first we noticed only the obviously flooded fields along the banks of the river, the green of late crops showing through the water. Then gradually we became aware of a number of "lakes" which constantly increased until finally they gave the impression of one big lake, enormous, stretching as far as we could see. I realized with a shock that this was not "lake"; it was all flood. Yet it did not have the look of fields covered with water. Deep and wide, horribly still and permanent, it looked as though it had always been there and would always stay. (There was in fact no hope of its going down before spring, and this was early fall.)

Flying lower we could see suggestions of what the land was like under the flood: fields under water; hundreds of small villages standing in water, many of them up to their roofs; towns whose dykes and walls had given way, whose streets were canals; in some places, nothing but the tops of a few trees, with here and there a smear of brown on the surface, where a dyke or a road or a mud village had once been. In this last territory one dared not think how many lives had been lost. There was no trace left. In less badly flooded country the people had built up temporary mud dykes around their villages and pulled inside their first crop. But it was a hopeless fight. For these hastily slapped-up walls, guarding a group of huts and a rescued grain stack, were rapidly crumbling before the constant lapping of little waves, whipped up by the wind.

There was no dry land for miles around. Most of the people who were near enough to the border to escape had crowded into the outlying cities. Thousands of refugees had put up temporary grass shelters along the dykes lining the Grand Canal and on an uncompleted road just south of the flooded area. But there were thousands more who would never get out, who, their homes completely destroyed, were living in flat-bottomed sampans,[2] with a grass roof rigged up in one end for shelter. Moored in the old streets or floating about the flooded

[2] SAMPAN—A Chinese flat-bottomed river boat.

fields, these refugees were apparently living only on the few straws of grain they had saved and what fish they might catch.

The small sampan driven by oar or pole seemed to be the only possible means of transportation in this vast area. Looking down on them, myriads of gnats on the surface of the water, we began to realize the hopelessness of the situation. How could relief ever reach these people? The water was not deep enough for large boats. There were no roads and probably never had been. There were almost no large centers from which food could be distributed, just thousands of small isolated villages—or what remained of them —stretched out over an area larger than Massachusetts.

Some things could be and were being done by the Relief Commission. Food could be taken to the refugee camps in or near the few larger centers, and, what was even more needed, medical supplies and assistance to stop the epidemics which inevitably follow a flood. We could not help to carry food, as the weight would be prohibitive in a plane; but we could perhaps carry medical supplies and a doctor.

My husband was trying to do this the day he set out for Hinghwa. We had seen the walled city from the air on our first day's flight. It was marooned in the center of a large flooded area; the nearest dry ground was more than twenty-five miles to the south. Medical aid, the Commission felt, was probably as badly needed there as anywhere, and it would be a good center for distribution. So one morning my husband took off from Nanking, carrying with him in the plane a Chinese doctor, an American doctor, and several packages of medical supplies. I had given up my place to one doctor. The baggage compartment had been cleared of much emergency equipment to lighten the load and make room for the second.

In less than an hour they completed a trip which would have taken days by canal. The plane landed on flooded fields outside the city walls. A few stray sampans were the only signs of life on the calm waters. The Chinese doctor, who was to land with supplies, waved at them and finally persuaded one boat to pull up alongside. Others straggled behind curiously. Slowly the doctor climbed down out of the cockpit and stepped from the pontoon into the sampan. Carefully a package of medicines was handed down after him. An old woman took it in her arms, put it down on the floor of the sampan, and sat on it firmly.

There was a stir of curiosity in the surrounding boats. By now there were ten or twenty of them poling about. Men, women, and children, sullen and hungry, looked at the package and began to murmur among themselves. "Food," they were saying, "there must be food in the box." They pushed forward and soon surrounded the doctor's boat as it poled out. Others pressed nearer the plane.

My husband stood up in the cockpit and motioned them back. (One of the heavy prows could easily knock a hole in our pontoons.) But they paid no attention to him. And there were more sampans coming every minute, attracted by the strange craft. They sprang up from nowhere like flies on a summer day. The American doctor began to shout to them in Chinese, telling them to keep back. But the starving people were thinking only of one thing. They made cups out of their hands and pretended to be eating with chopsticks. "The foreigners must understand now; we want food." The word spread like fire leaping across a field in a high wind. It reached the outer circle of boats, and people began jumping from one boat to another toward the plane. For they could no longer pole any nearer. There were literally hundreds of sampans now, boat jammed against boat on all sides. The nearest were right under the wings and tail surfaces. A sampan under the left wing had a small fire dangerously near its grass hood. Shouting, either in English or Chinese, had no effect and—worse still—there were even more coming. In the distance one could see a solid stream of boats rounding the city wall.

"Have you a gun?" the American doctor shouted.

"Yes—" said my husband, "a thirty-eight revolver—but someone in that crowd"—looking out at thousands of sullen and desperate faces—"may have a rifle—probably several—fatal to show a gun in a crowd like that."

Nevertheless he hid it under his parachute, planning not to use it unless they started to board the plane. People were hanging on to wings, pontoons, and tail surfaces but no one had yet actually tried to climb on.

Suddenly a man stood up and put his foot on the left pontoon. As though at a signal the rest surged forward. Now a man was on the other pontoon. They had begun to board.

My husband grabbed his revolver and covered the nearest man. He stopped but did not move back. My husband turned to the right side. Those faced with the gun hesitated, but the men on the other side moved up. He whipped the gun from the right side to the left

quickly, shooting straight up in the air as he turned. Each side thought someone had been shot on the other. He moved it back and forth quickly, covering always the nearest person. Slowly they edged back.

The two men in the plane stopped to breathe and to look for the Chinese doctor. He had completely lost track of the package soon after leaving the plane. It had been seized from his sampan and fought over as a crust of bread is torn apart by gulls. His own boat, overloaded with men who had jumped in from other sampans, had sunk under the weight. With the water curling over the edges, he stepped quickly into another. The crowd followed him, thinking where he went the package would eventually go too. Three boats sank under him. In the middle of an island of sampans, people fighting and pushing around him, he knew there was no hope of rescuing the vaccines or of reaching the city. He hoped he could get back to the plane alive. Finally, arguing with a boatload that there was a larger package in the plane, he managed to reach the front ring of sampans only to be faced with a pistol! He stood up and shouted excitedly before he was recognized. In the cleared space in front of him, he was able to reach the plane and climbed hurriedly into the back cockpit.

The American doctor in the meantime was hauling up the anchor as fast as he could. There was no time to stow it in the pontoon anchor-hatch, where it usually fitted in the neat coils of rope. He stuffed it, rope and all, in the baggage compartment, and started to climb in on top. They were clear, ready to go.

No—there was a single sampan just in front of the plane, an old man and an old woman poling it. My husband raised himself up in the cockpit and covered them with his gun. The American doctor jumped out on the wing and shouted, "Get out of the way! We'll kill you!"

They made no move. The old woman looked up sullenly, "What does it matter?" she said slowly. "We have nothing."

The plane swung slightly in the wind, pointing clear of the sampan. My husband pressed the starter. The engine caught—an answering roar. They took off dead ahead, over flooded fields, between fences, collapsed roofs, and grave-mounds, regardless of wind direction—anything to get off, to shake that trailing wake of hundreds of sampans, those arms paddling as fast as they could in a vain attempt to follow.

The plane left the water, rising easily, roaring upwards in one wide circle. Men, boats, fields, and huts dropped off below the wing and were left behind. In a few seconds it was high above that flooded world. The milling mass of sampans was a swarm of gnats on the water's surface. Even the city of Hinghwa (from whose gates boats were still streaming) looked insignificant, a small island of roofs in the vast sea of flood that surrounded it.

Looking down on the spot they had just left, the men in the plane were acutely conscious of the miracle of their escape. A moment before they had been down in that crowd of starving people, some of whom might live until spring; many would die before the waters receded. Now, headed for Nanking, safety, food, and shelter were assured to the fliers as in their own homes. Separated from those desperate people below only by a few seconds in time, only by a few hundred feet in distance, they were yet irretrievably removed in some fourth dimension. The two worlds were separated by a gulf which, although not wide, was deep, perilous, and unbridgeable. At least it was unbridgeable to the owners of the sampans. The fliers had crossed over from one world to another as easily, as swiftly, as one crosses from the world of nightmare to the world of reality in the flash of waking.

They had a gun; they had a plane—powerful as any genii to be summoned from a magic lamp. And yet, magic rests on a knife-edge—a lamp, a tinderbox, an "open sesame." [3] It is a hair bridge between captivity and escape; safety and danger; life and death. The pull of a trigger, the press of a switch—without these, the three magicians flying back to Nanking would have been simply three people in a starving, dying, and devastated land.

[3] "OPEN SESAME"—A charm to secure admission, originally to the robbers' cave, in the story of "Ali Baba and the Forty Thieves."

◇◇◇◇◇◇◇◇◇◇◇◇◇◇◇◇◇◇◇◇◇◇◇◇◇◇◇◇◇◇◇◇

FOR DISCUSSION

1. You have, no doubt, seen a flood—perhaps even one of the big Ohio or Mississippi floods. But America has nothing to compare with the great Yangtze River floods. How long, for example, would the flood described in this selection last?

2. Imagine a flood so extensive that it gave the impression even from a plane of one vast lake. How did the people live in such a flood? What conditions made it difficult or impossible to aid these people?

3. What was the purpose of the flight by Colonel Lindbergh and the two doctors? What did the people think their visitors had come for?

4. The take-off path of the plane was blocked by an old man and woman. Did they hurry to get out of the way? What did they reply to the doctor's threat? How can you explain the behavior of the crowd?

5. In case of a devastating flood in the United States, how is relief brought to the sufferers?

DESCRIPTIVE WORD STUDY

The following words from the selection accentuate its somber tone: *crumble, angry, desperate, perilous.* Find in the dictionary synonyms for these words. Can you find other words in the story which help to impress upon the reader the tragedy of this flood?

FOR BETTER UNDERSTANDING

On a map of China locate the Yangtze River. Compare its length with that of our great American rivers. Tell in a paragraph why a Yangtze flood is more disastrous than one in America.

RELATED READING

Charles Lindbergh's autobiography *We* tells the thrilling story of the first non-stop airplane flight over the Atlantic Ocean.

What happens when a young girl's generosity arouses the rage of a proud father? The answer is given in this legend of St. Brigid.

St. Brigid

DENIS A. McCARTHY

Brigid, the daughter of Duffy, she wasn't like other young things,
Dreaming of lads for her lovers, and twirling her bracelets and rings;
Combing and coiling and curling her hair that was black as the sloes,
Painting her lips and her cheeks that were ruddy and fresh as the rose.
Ah, 'twasn't Brigid would waste all her days in such follies as these— 5
Christ was the Lover she worshipped for hour after hour on her knees;
Christ and His Church and His poor,—and 'twas many a mile that she trod
Serving the loathsome lepers that ever were stricken by God.

Brigid, the daughter of Duffy, she sold all her jewels and gems,
Sold all her finely-spun robes that were braided with gold to the hems; 10
Kept to her back but one garment, one dress that was faded and old,
Gave all her goods to the poor who were famished with hunger and cold.
Ah, 'twasn't Brigid would fling at the poor the hard work like a stone—
Christ the Redeemer she saw in each wretch that was ragged and lone;
Every wandering beggar who asked for a bite or a bed 15
Knocked at her heart like the Man who had nowhere to shelter His head.

Brigid, the daughter of Duffy, she angered her father at last.
"Where are your dresses, my daughter? Crom Cruach! You wear them out fast!
Where are the chains that I bought you all wrought in red gold from the mine?
Where the bright brooches of silver that once on your bosom would shine?" 20
Ah, 'twas he was the man that was proud of his name and his race,
Proud of their prowess in battle and proud of their deeds in the chase!
Knew not the Christ, the pale God Whom the priests from afar had brought in,
Held to the old Gaelic gods that were known to Cuchulain and Finn.
Brigid, the daughter of Duffy, made answer, "O father," said she, 25
"What is the richest of raiment, and what are bright jewels to me?

3. SLOES—Wild plums.
18. CROM CRUACH—The chief idol of pagan Ireland.
24. CUCHULAIN AND FINN—Irish heroes.

Lepers of Christ must I care for, the hungry of Christ must I feed;
How can I walk in rich robes when His people and mine are in need?"
Ah, but 'twas she didn't fear for herself when he blustered and swore,
Meekly she bowed when he ordered his chariot brought to the door; 30
Meekly obeyed when he bade her get in at the point of his sword,
Knowing whatever her fate she'd be safe with her Lover and Lord.

Brigid, the daughter of Duffy, was brought to the court of the King,
(Monarch of Leinster, MacEnda, whose praises the poets would sing).
"Hither, O monarch," said Duffy, "I've come with a maiden to sell; 35
Buy her and bind her to bondage—she's needing such discipline well!"
Ah, but 'twas wise was the King. From the maid to the chieftain he turned;
Mildness he saw in her face, in the other 'twas anger that burned;
"This is no bondmaid, I'll swear it, O chief, but a girl of your own.
Why sells the father the flesh of his flesh and the bone of his bone?" 40

Brigid, the daughter of Duffy, was mute while her father replied—
"Monarch, this maid has no place as the child of a chieftain of pride.
Beggars and wretches whose wounds would the soul of a soldier affright,
Sure, 'tis on these she is wasting my substance from morning till night!"
Ah, but 'twas bitter was Duffy; he spoke like a man that was vext. 45
Musing, the monarch was silent; he pondered the question perplexed.
"Maiden," said he, "if 'tis true, as I've just from your father heard tell,
Might it not be, as my bondmaid, you'd waste all my substance as well?"

Brigid, the daughter of Duffy, made answer. "O monarch," she said,
"Had I the wealth from your coffers, and had I the crown from your head— 50
Yea, if the plentiful yield of the broad breasts of Erin were mine,
All would I give to the people of Christ who in poverty pine."
Ah, but 'twas then that the King felt the heart in his bosom upleap,
"I am not worthy," he cried, "such a maiden in bondage to keep!
Here's a king's sword for her ransom, and here's a king's sword to decree 55
Never to other than Christ and His poor let her in servitude be!"

55. RANSOM—The king buys her from her father and sets her free to continue her Christian social service.

FOR DISCUSSION

1. Are there girls today like Brigid? Discuss. What made Brigid's father swear? Was he justified in trying to sell her to the king? Why or why not?

2. Should everybody be as concerned about the welfare of "His people and mine" as Brigid was? Explain your reasons. Does the wealthy man have an obligation to give alms in proportion to his wealth? What

does the story of the camel and the needle have to do with this poem?

THE LIFE STORY OF A SAINT

Some saints' names are surely familiar to you. Perhaps you live on San Juan or Santa Barbara Drive, or do business with a St. Lawrence haberdashery, or go to a St. John's High School. Tomorrow bring to class the life story of some such familiar saint so that you can read it to the class. Be sure to choose your saint for some *special* reason.

RELATED READING

For another appreciation in verse of St. Brigid, by all means read "The Giveaway," in *The Love Letters of Phyllis McGinley*. As a result of the reading you will see how differently two writers can treat the same saint.

Christians usually associate the serious and sacred side of life with their religion. But there are lighter moments, too, in the practice of religion, as this story told with delightful Irish humor proves.

THE CONFESSIONAL

SEAN O'FAOLAIN

In the wide nave the wintry evening light was faint as gloom and in the shadows of the aisle it was like early night. There was no sound in the chapel but the wind blowing up from the river-valley, or an occasional tiny noise when a brass socket creaked under the great heat of a dying flame. To the three small boys crouched together in a bench in the farther aisle, holding each other's hands, listening timidly to the crying wind, staring wide-eyed at the candles, it seemed odd that in such a storm the bright flames never moved.

Suddenly the eldest of the three, a red-headed little ruffian, whispered loudly; but the other two, staring at the distant face of the statue, silenced him with a great hiss like a breaking wave. In another moment the lad in the center, crouching down in fear and gripping the hand on each side of him, whispered so quietly that they barely heard: "She's moving."

For a second or two they did not even breathe. Then all three expelled a deep sigh of disappointment.

It was Monday afternoon, and every Monday, as they had each heard tell over and over again in their homes, Father Hanafin spoke with the Blessed Virgin in the grotto. Some said she came late at night; some said in the early morning before the chapel was opened; some said it was at the time when the sun goes down, but until now nobody had dared to watch. To be sure Father Hanafin was not in the chapel now, but for all that the three little spies had come filled with high hope. The eldest spoke their bitter disappointment aloud.

"It's all my eye," he said angrily. The other two felt that what he said was true, but they pretended to be deeply shocked.

"That's an awful thing you said, Foxer," whispered the boy in the middle.

"Go away, you, Philpot!" said Foxer.

". . . I think it's a cause for confession, Foxer!" whispered Philpot again.

"It's a mortal sin, Foxer!" said the third, leaning over to say it.

"Don't you try to cod[1] me, Cooney, or I'd burst yer jaw!" cried Foxer angrily.

Philpot hushed them sternly and swiftly, but the spell was broken. They all leaned back in the bench.

Beside them was Father Hanafin's confession-box, its worn purple curtain partly drawn back, his worn purple stole hanging on a crook on the wall inside, and as Foxer gazed into the box with curiosity the Adversary tempted him in his heart.

"Come on, Cooney!" he invited at last. "Come on, and I'll hear yer confession."

"Gor! Come on," said Cooney, rising.

"That's a sin," said Philpot, though secretly eager to sit in the priest's chair.

"You're an awful ould Aunt Mary!" jeered Foxer, whereupon all Philpot's scruples vanished and the three scrambled for the confessor's seat. But Foxer was there before either of them, and at once he swished the curtains together as he had seen Father Hanafin do, and put the long stole about his neck. It was so nice in there in the dark that he forgot his two penitents waiting beyond the closed grilles on either side, and he was putting imaginary snuff[2] into his nostrils and flicking imaginary specks of snuff from his chest when Cooney's angry face appeared between the curtains.

"Are you going to hear me confession, Foxer, or are ye not?" he cried in a rage, eager for his turn to be priest.

"Go back, my child," said Foxer crossly, and he swished the curtains together again. Then, as if in spite, he leaned over to the opposite grille and slowly and solemnly he drew the slide and peered into the frightened eyes of Philpot.

"Tell me how long since your last confession, my child," he said gravely.

"Twenty years," whispered Philpot in awe.

"What have you done since then?" intoned Foxer sadly.

"I stole sweets, Father. And I forgot my prayers. And I cursed, Father."

"Cursed!" thundered Foxer. "What curse did you say?"

"I said that our master was an ould sod, Father," murmured Philpot timidly.

"So he is, my child. Is there anything else?"

"No, Father."

"For your penance say two hundred and forty-nine Rosaries, and four hundred and seventy Our Fathers, and three hundred and thirty-two Hail Marys. And now be a good obedient boy. And pray for me, won't you? Gawd bless you, my child."

And with that Foxer drew the slide slowly before the small astonished face.

[1] COD—To trick, fool.

[2] SNUFF—Powdered tobacco taken into the nose.

As he turned to the other side his hand fell on a little box—it was Father Hanafin's consolation during the long hours spent in that stuffy confessional listening to the sins and sorrows of his parishioners. Foxer's awkward fingers lifted the cover and the sweet scent rose powerfully through the darkness as he coaxed the loose snuff down from the cover. Then drawing the slide on Cooney, he gravely inhaled a pinch and leaned his ear to the cool iron of the grille.

Outside a footstep sounded on the marble floor, and peering out Foxer saw the priest walk slowly up the farther aisle, turn and walk slowly down again, his breviary held high to the slanting radiance of the Virgin's altar.

"It's Father Hanafin," whispered Foxer to Cooney; and to Philpot: "Keep quiet or we're all ruined."

Up and down the solemn footsteps went, and high above their heads in the windows of the clerestory [3] and along the lath and plaster of the roof the wind moaned and fingered the loose slates, and now and again they heard the priest murmur aloud the deep, open vowels of his prayer, *Gaudeamus Domine,* or *Domine, Domine meo,* in a long breathing sigh.

"He's talking to the Virgin," breathed Cooney to Foxer.

"He's talking to the Virgin," breathed Foxer in turn to Philpot.

"Amen," sighed the priest, and went on his knees before the candles that shone steadily and were reflected brilliantly in the burnished brass.

The three spies had begun to peep from their hiding-place when the snuff fell on Foxer's lap and the grains began to titillate his nose. In agony he held his mouth for a full minute and then burst into a furious sneeze. In astonishment the priest gazed about him and once again Foxer held his breath and once again he sneezed. At the third sneeze the priest gazed straight at the box.

"Come out!" he said in a loud voice. "Come out of that box!"

And as the three guilty forms crept

[3] CLERESTORY—Upper part of a church wall, having windows above the roofs of the aisles.

from the three portals he commanded again: "Come here!"

Awkwardly they stumbled forward through the seats, trying to hide behind one another, pushing and upbraiding one another until they stood before him.

"What were you doing in there?" he asked Foxer.

"I was hearing their confession, Father," trembled Foxer, and half raised his arm as if to ward off a blow.

For a moment the priest glared at him and then he asked: "And what penance did you give?"

"I—I gave three hundred and thirty Hail Marys, Father, and I think it was four hundred Our Fathers, Father, and two hundred and forty-nine Rosaries, Father."

"Well!" pronounced the priest in a solemn voice, "go home and let each one of ye say that penance three times over before nine o'clock tomorrow morning."

Stumbling over one another's heels the three crept down the dark aisle and crushed out through the green baize door and into the falling night that was torn by the storm. The street-lamps were lit and under one of these they halted and looked at each other, angry and crestfallen.

"Nine hundred and ninety Hail Marys!" wailed Philpot, and Cooney squared up to Foxer with clenched fists.

"Yerrah!" said Foxer. "It's all a cod!"

And he raced suddenly away to his supper, followed by the shouts and feet of the other two.

◇◇◇◇◇◇◇◇◇◇◇◇◇◇◇◇◇◇◇◇◇◇◇◇◇◇◇◇◇◇◇◇

FOR DISCUSSION

1. How would you defend the three boys' spying on Father Hanafin, if you think their action was defensible?

2. From details given in the story how do you imagine that the report got around that "Father Hanafin spoke with the Blessed Virgin in the grotto"?

3. Who is the "Adversary" that tempted Foxer in his heart?

4. Where do you suppose Foxer learned the instruction that he gave Philpot after imposing on him the mountainous penance: "And now be a good obedient boy. And pray for me, won't you? Gawd bless you, my child"?

5. At fifteen minutes a Rosary, how long would it take the boys to say three times two hundred and forty-nine Rosaries?

6. Did Father Hanafin have a sense of humor? How do you know?

7. A writer carefully sets the scene of his story in such a way that the reader can feel in imagination that he is actually there. Select some of the details that help you feel as though you are actually in the little church.

8. The characters in the story express themselves in a distinctively Irish manner. Make a list of these expressions. How would an American boy say the same things?

WORD MEANINGS

Use each of the following words in a sentence to show its meaning: *ruffian, peer, burnish, crestfallen.*

YOUR OPINION

Think over this statement and say whether or not you agree, giving your reasons: "Any piece of literature in order to be truly Catholic must teach a lesson."

RELATED READING

With a Merry Heart, edited by Paul Phelan, is an entertaining collection of prose and poetry by modern Catholic humorists.

The Merchant of Venice

WILLIAM SHAKESPEARE

Told in the form of a play, "The Merchant of Venice" is one of the world's most famous stories. It has a double romance, with a third minor love affair on the side; it has a villain who plots murder —legalized murder—and a thrilling courtroom scene. It has tears and shudders and jokes and poetry—a bundle of characters and circumstances as varied as life.

The play was written by the greatest storyteller and poet of all time—William Shakespeare. Because Shakespeare lived almost 400 years ago, his English is quite different from ours. At first sight his words may seem very strange. But if you will read the lines aloud, conversationally, you will soon fall into the swing of it.

If you are to understand the story, you must have a picture in your mind of two kinds of life: one, of living conditions in Venice in the early 1500's; and the other of living conditions in Elizabethan England in the last years of the 1500's. The second picture is the more important. For though Shakespeare was a genius as a poet and playwright, he was not a careful student of history or historical backgrounds. He knew how men and women think and act in any age; but he was not concerned about the details of living in one particular place or generation. No matter in what country or century one of his plays is laid, his characters are likely to follow the outward customs of Elizabethan England, in which he lived.

In the first place, the England of Shakespeare's day was enjoying a period of prosperity. It was a time of high spirits and gaiety. People had awakened to a great interest in poetry and music. It was said that all the young men about the court and in the cities could write verses and compose songs. They could play different kinds of musical instruments, like mandolins, guitars, and flutes.

Then, because the ruler of England was a queen and a witty one, men were inclined to give greater credit to the intelligence of women. Shakespeare's women characters show an independent mind and resourcefulness that makes them the equal of the men—or even their superiors. In "The Merchant of Venice" it is a woman who is the star. It is her wit and good judgment that save the "hero." You will find the women joking and punning with each other and with their servants. You will find them playing tricks on their husbands. You will find them talking poetry and literature and music.

You will also discover that Elizabethan England was—like the rest of Europe—sharply aware of racial distinctions. There was distrust and bitterness between men of different nations and different creeds. You will find that justice was pretty much a local affair, with the magistrate of a community being also the court of last appeal. All through Europe, cruel and unusual punishments might prevail.

On the continent, cities like Florence and Venice had independent governments. They were really city-states.

The play, then, has its setting in the flourishing merchant city of Venice and the near-by country seat, Belmont. The characters, for the most part, are romantic, gay young men and women. They can talk like Elizabethan poets, strum mandolins, sing songs, joke; be cruel or kind or generous by turn. The main incident of the plot could not happen in this same fashion now, though our own day has seen mass hatred and cruelty on a staggering scale. Perhaps this particular story of Antonio and Shylock never did happen in any day; but there were centuries in Europe when it could have happened in a regular court of law. In the play, Shakespeare makes it the core of a plausible, gripping tale.

As you probably know, Shakespeare's plays were presented on a simple stage with little or no scenery and with very few "props." The imagination of the audience and the descriptions of the poet furnished the background. The exuberance of the actors and the fine presentation of their lines made the whole thing come alive. Once you get your own imagination working and get into the *feel* of the play, you will find that you too can give it a lively presentation with your own classroom serving for a stage.

The footnotes are to help you understand the lines. Unfamiliar words have been defined, and expressions that are puzzling have been explained. Many of the words that seem strange are made clear by the lines in which you find them. For them, there are no notes. The special introductions to each scene of the play will give you a picture of sixteenth century Venice and will set the stage for the scene, with time and place and people.

Now let us dissolve away four centuries of history and slip across the Atlantic to an odd island city in the calm waters of the Adriatic. Our city is the sea-queen, Venice—at that time the greatest commercial port in Europe.

It is bright morning, and the citizens stroll about or stand talking in the broad, sun-splashed square before St. Mark's golden-domed cathedral. Men and women are dressed in gay colors, in the long hose and doublets or in the flowing gowns and cloaks of the period.

And what are the men talking of? Perhaps of the morning's arrival of ships from abroad—from Spain and England, even from India—for world-wide trade is the life of this bustling city. The price of silks and spices, the latest doings of the ever-menacing Turk, developments on the Rialto—the business mart in Venice—all figure in the morning news. A man-of-war, to have no less than sixty-four cannon, is building at the city arsenal. This formidable galleon is to make the sons of Mohammed trim their sails a bit.

Out of the shadow shuffles a slight, bent figure, wearing a loose brown cloak and yellow cap. He is the aged money-lender Shylock, off to his shop near the Rialto. A shift of the salt-laden breeze floats a voice bearing news to our ears. We learn that Antonio, one of the city's richest merchants, yesterday saw the last of his ships on its way to England. Shylock has also caught the mention of Antonio and, stopping short, spits angrily. With a shake of the head, he is lost to sight around the corner.

It is time for week-day High Mass. The bells of St. Mark's boom out, their great iron voices disturbing the nesting pigeons and white sea gulls. With flapping wings these lumber into the sky, to find perches atop the Duke's great lemon-colored palace or in the slim, brown-brick tower that dominates the cobbled square.

With a laugh, the groups congregating near the regal-looking lions of St. Mark's break up for a day's trading. From the edge of the canal on the left, two men hail a gondola—the Venetian water-tax—for their trip to the ferry landing.

If we turn left off the square onto a narrow street paralleling the dark waters of the canal, we can see ahead the riggings of high-decked ships, with sails furled. The vessels look top-heavy as they sidle up to wharfs on either side, to be loaded with casks and chests. Three men step out from a side street. The merchant Antonio, in conversation with two close friends, sweeps us into the first act of the play.

DRAMATIS PERSONAE

THE DUKE OF VENICE
THE PRINCE OF MOROCCO } *suitors*
THE PRINCE OF ARRAGON } *to Portia*
ANTONIO, *a merchant of Venice*
BASSANIO, *his friend, suitor likewise to Portia*
SALANIO } *friends to*
SALARINO } *Antonio and*
GRATIANO } *Bassanio*
LORENZO, *in love with Jessica*
SHYLOCK, *a rich Jew*
TUBAL, *a Jew, Shylock's friend*
LAUNCELOT GOBBO, *the clown, servant to Shylock*
OLD GOBBO, *father to Launcelot*
SALERIO, *a messenger*
LEONARDO, *servant to Bassanio*
BALTHASAR } *servants to Portia*
STEPHANO }
PORTIA, *a rich heiress*
NERISSA, *her waiting-maid*
JESSICA, *daughter to Shylock*

Magnificoes of Venice, Officers of the Court of Justice, Jailer, Servants to Portia, and other Attendants.

SCENE: *Partly at Venice, and partly at Belmont, the seat of Portia on the Continent.*

ACT I

SCENE 1. *Venice. A street.*

Enter ANTONIO, SALARINO, *and* SALANIO

ANTONIO. In sooth, I know not why I am so sad:
It wearies me; you say it wearies you;
But how I caught it, found it, or came by it,
What stuff 'tis made of, whereof it is born,

1. IN SOOTH—In truth.

I am to learn, 5
And such a want-wit sadness makes of me
That I have much ado to know myself.

SALARINO. Your mind is tossing on the ocean;
There, where your argosies with portly sail,
Like signiors and rich burghers on the flood, 10
Or, as it were, the pageants of the sea,
Do overpeer the petty traffickers,
That curtsy to them, do them reverence,
As they fly by them with their woven wings.

SALANIO. Believe me, sir, had I such venture forth, 15
The better part of my affections would
Be with my hopes abroad. I should be still
Plucking the grass, to know where sits the wind,
Peering in maps for ports, and piers, and roads;
And every object that might make me fear 20
Misfortune to my ventures, out of doubt
Would make me sad.

SALARINO. My wind, cooling my broth,
Would blow me to an ague, when I thought
What harm a wind too great might do at sea.
I should not see the sandy hour-glass run, 25
But I should think of shallows and of flats,
And see my wealthy *Andrew* dock'd in sand,
Vailing her high top lower than her ribs
To kiss her burial. Should I go to church,
And see the holy edifice of stone, 30
And not bethink me straight of dangerous rocks,
Which, touching but my gentle vessel's side,
Would scatter all her spices on the stream,

6. WANT-WIT—Dunce. The word is a noun, the object of *makes*.
9. ARGOSIES—Great merchant ships.
10. SIGNIORS (sē'nyôrz) AND RICH BURGHERS—Like lords and wealthy townsmen.
11. PAGEANTS—The ships with their high decks, elaborate woodwork, and painted sails were like gay show-wagons in the famous Mardi Gras parades.
12. OVERPEER—Look down on.
12. PETTY TRAFFICKERS—Small merchant ships.
14. WOVEN WINGS—Cloth sails.
15. VENTURE FORTH—Risk or investment out on the sea.
17–18. STILL PLUCKING THE GRASS—Always throwing blades of grass in the air to see which way the wind is blowing.
19. ROADS—Places where ships may ride at anchor; not as sheltered as a harbor.
27. ANDREW—The name of Salarino's fancied ship.
28. VAILING—Lowering.
29. BURIAL—Grave. The ship is pictured as beached on a sand flat and lying over on one side, its masts down in the sand.

Enrobe the roaring waters with my silks;
And, in a word, but even now worth this, 35
And now worth nothing? Shall I have the thought
To think on this; and shall I lack the thought,
That such a thing bechanc'd would make me sad?
But tell not me; I know, Antonio
Is sad to think upon his merchandise. 40

ANTONIO. Believe me, no: I thank my fortune for it,
My ventures are not in one bottom trusted,
Nor to one place; nor is my whole estate
Upon the fortune of this present year:
Therefore my merchandise makes me not sad. 45

SALARINO. Why, then you are in love.

ANTONIO. Fie, fie!

SALARINO. Not in love neither? Then let us say you are sad,
Because you are not merry; and 'twere as easy
For you to laugh, and leap, and say you are merry,
Because you are not sad. Now, by two-headed Janus, 50
Nature hath fram'd strange fellows in her time:
Some that will evermore peep through their eyes,
And laugh like parrots at a bagpiper;
And other of such vinegar aspect,
That they'll not show their teeth in way of smile, 55
Though Nestor swear the jest be laughable.

[*Enter* BASSANIO, LORENZO, *and* GRATIANO.]

SALANIO. Here comes Bassanio, your most noble kinsman,
Gratiano, and Lorenzo. Fare ye well:
We leave you now with better company.

SALARINO. I would have stay'd till I had made you merry, 60
If worthier friends had not prevented me.

ANTONIO. Your worth is very dear in my regard.
I take it, your own business calls on you,
And you embrace the occasion to depart.

SALARINO. Good morrow, my good lords. 65

35. EVEN NOW WORTH THIS—The actor's gesture suggests a great amount.
42. BOTTOM—Ship.
43–44. MY WHOLE ESTATE—All my property is not risked in the investments of this year.
47. NEITHER—That is, "either." The double negative was common in Shakespeare's day.
50. JANUS—The Roman god of gates and doorways, represented as having two faces. Can you guess why?
52. PEEP—Look through eyes half-shut with laughter.
56. NESTOR—An aged Greek famed for wisdom and gravity. Anyone therefore would enjoy a joke which Nestor declared to be laughable.

BASSANIO. Good signiors both, when shall we laugh? say, when?
You grow exceeding strange: must it be so?
SALARINO. We'll make our leisures to attend on yours.
[*Exeunt* SALARINO *and* SALANIO.]
LORENZO. My lord Bassanio, since you have found Antonio,
We two will leave you; but, at dinner-time, 70
I pray you, have in mind where we must meet.
BASSANIO. I will not fail you.
GRATIANO. You look not well, Signior Antonio;
You have too much respect upon the world:
They lose it that do buy it with much care, 75
Believe me, you are marvellously chang'd.
ANTONIO. I hold the world but as the world, Gratiano;
A stage, where every man must play a part,
And mine a sad one.
GRATIANO. Let me play the fool:
With mirth and laughter let old wrinkles come; 80
And let my liver rather heat with wine
Than my heart cool with mortifying groans.
Why should a man, whose blood is warm within,
Sit like his grandsire cut in alabaster?
Sleep when he wakes, and creep into the jaundice 85
By being peevish? I tell thee what, Antonio,—
I love thee, and it is my love that speaks,—
There are a sort of men whose visages
Do cream and mantle like a standing pond;
And do a willful stillness entertain, 90
With purpose to be dress'd in an opinion
Of wisdom, gravity, profound conceit;
As who should say, "I am Sir Oracle,
And when I ope my lips, let no dog bark!"
O my Antonio, I do know of these, 95

66. WHEN SHALL WE LAUGH—When is our next merry meeting? The next lines say: You act like strangers nowadays. Must you go now?

74. RESPECT UPON THE WORLD—Regard for worldly affairs or prosperity.

79. FOOL—Play the part of court fool or jester. Gratiano does not intend to take life too seriously.

85. SLEEP WHEN HE WAKES—Show no more life when awake than he does asleep.

85. JAUNDICE—A disease resulting from a disordered liver. Peevishness was popularly regarded as a symptom of a disordered liver; hence, figuratively, jaundice might come from being peevish.

88–89. VISAGES . . . CREAM AND MANTLE—Their faces, always set and stern, are covered as with the scum of a stagnant pool.

91–92. BE DRESS'D IN AN OPINION OF . . . CONCEIT—Be considered as having deep thoughtfulness and wisdom.

93. AS WHO SHOULD SAY—As though one should say, "I am Sir Know-it-all."

That therefore only are reputed wise
For saying nothing; when, I am very sure,
If they should speak, would almost damn those ears,
Which, hearing them, would call their brothers fools.
I'll tell thee more of this another time: 100
But fish not, with this melancholy bait,
For this fool gudgeon, this opinion.
Come, good Lorenzo. Fare ye well awhile:
I'll end my exhortation after dinner.

LORENZO. Well, we will leave you, then, till dinner-time. 105
I must be one of these same dumb wise men,
For Gratiano never lets me speak.

GRATIANO. Well, keep me company but two years moe,
Thou shalt not know the sound of thine own tongue.

ANTONIO. Farewell: I'll grow a talker for this gear. 110

GRATIANO. Thanks, i' faith; for silence is only commendable
In a neat's tongue dried, and a maid not vendible.

[*Exeunt* GRATIANO *and* LORENZO.]

ANTONIO. Is that anything now?

BASSANIO. Gratiano speaks an infinite deal of nothing, more than any man in all Venice. His reasons are as two grains of wheat hid in two bushels 115 of chaff: you shall seek all day ere you find them; and when you have them, they are not worth the search.

ANTONIO. Well, tell me now, what lady is the same
To whom you swore a secret pilgrimage,
That you today promis'd to tell me of? 120

BASSANIO. 'Tis not unknown to you, Antonio,
How much I have disabled mine estate,
By something showing a more swelling port
Than my faint means would grant continuance:
Nor do I now make moan to be abridg'd 125

98. DAMN THOSE EARS—Others, thinking such men to be fools, would therefore fall under Our Lord's condemnation in Matt. 1:22—"Whoever says, 'Thou fool!' shall be in danger of hell-fire."
101–102. BAIT, FOR THIS FOOL GUDGEON—Do not try to win an empty reputation for wisdom by appearing sad. (The gudgeon was a proverbially stupid fish and easily caught.)
108. MOE—More.
110. GEAR—Stuff. Antonio jests that his friend's argument will almost induce him to grow talkative.
112. NEAT'S TONGUE—Cow's tongue.
112. VENDIBLE—Marriageable.
113. IS THAT ANYTHING NOW?—Is there any sense in that last remark?
115. REASONS—Sensible remarks.
122. DISABLED MINE ESTATE—Squandered my property.
123. A MORE SWELLING PORT—A more expensive style of living than I can afford.
125. MAKE MOAN—I do not complain now of having to economize.

From such a noble rate; but my chief care
Is to come fairly off from the great debts,
Wherein my time, something too prodigal,
Hath left me gag'd. To you, Antonio,
I owe the most, in money and in love; 130
And from your love I have a warranty
To unburthen all my plots and purposes
How to get clear of all the debts I owe.

ANTONIO. I pray you, good Bassanio, let me know it;
And if it stand, as you yourself still do, 135
Within the eye of honor, be assur'd,
My purse, my person, my extremest means,
Lie all unlock'd to your occasions.

BASSANIO. In my school days, when I had lost one shaft,
I shot his fellow of the selfsame flight 140
The selfsame way with more advised watch,
To find the other forth; and, by adventuring both,
I oft found both. I urge this childhood proof,
Because what follows is pure innocence.
I owe you much; and, like a willful youth, 145
That which I owe is lost: but, if you please
To shoot another arrow that self way
Which you did shoot the first, I do not doubt,
As I will watch the aim, or to find both,
Or bring your latter hazard back again, 150
And thankfully rest debtor for the first.

ANTONIO. You know me well; and herein spend but time
To wind about my love with circumstance;
And out of doubt you do me now more wrong
In making question of my uttermost, 155
Than if you had made waste of all I have:
Then do but say to me what I should do,
That in your knowledge may by me be done,
And I am prest unto it: Therefore, speak.

BASSANIO. In Belmont is a lady richly left; 160
And she is fair, and, fairer than that word,

127. FAIRLY—Honorably.
128–129. WHEREIN . . . GAG'D—In which my extravagant youth has left me pledged to pay.
131. WARRANTY—Permission.
140. FELLOW OF THE SELFSAME FLIGHT—An arrow of the same carrying power.
144. INNOCENCE—Foolishness.
150. LATTER HAZARD—Your second risk; that is, the loan that Bassanio is now asking.
153. TO WIND ABOUT . . . WITH CIRCUMSTANCE—To talk in a roundabout way.
159. PREST UNTO IT—Ready to do it.

Of wondrous virtues: sometimes from her eyes
I did receive fair speechless messages.
Her name is Portia; nothing undervalu'd
To Cato's daughter, Brutus' Portia: 165
Nor is the wide world ignorant of her worth;
For the four winds blow in from every coast
Renowned suitors; and her sunny locks
Hang on her temples like a golden fleece;
Which makes her seat of Belmont Colchos' strand, 170
And many Jasons come in quest of her.
O my Antonio, had I but the means
To hold a rival place with one of them,
I have a mind presages me such thrift,
That I should questionless be fortunate. 175

ANTONIO. Thou know'st that all my fortunes are at sea;
Neither have I money, nor commodity,
To raise a present sum: therefore go forth;
Try what my credit can in Venice do:
That shall be rack'd, even to the uttermost, 180
To furnish thee to Belmont, to fair Portia.
Go, presently inquire, and so will I,
Where money is; and I no question make,
To have it of my trust, or for my sake. [*Exeunt.*]

165. PORTIA—Wife of Brutus, the hero of *Julius Caesar,* and distinguished for her honor and wifely virtues.
169. GOLDEN FLEECE—The allusion is to the story of Jason who set out for Colchos to bring back the golden fleece.
170. SEAT OF BELMONT—Her estate at Belmont, on the mainland west of Venice.
174. PRESAGES ME SUCH THRIFT—Which foretells to me such success.
180. RACK'D—Stretched.
182. PRESENTLY—At once.
184. OF MY TRUST—On my credit or as a personal favor.

SCENE 2. *Belmont. A room in* PORTIA'S *house.*

Portia, the heroine, lives on the Italian mainland on a rich estate. We meet her at high noon in a small room off the great hall of her home. The scent of flowers and drowsy sounds of country life are carried in through the open window on a mellow sea breeze. Sunlight touches a wall portrait of Portia's father and splashes gold on Portia's hair as she enters with her friend and maid-in-waiting, Nerissa. Portia looks troubled.

[*Enter* PORTIA *and* NERISSA.]

PORTIA. By my troth, Nerissa, my little body is aweary of this great world.

NERISSA. You would be, sweet madam, if your miseries were in the same abundance as your good fortunes are: and yet, for aught I see, they are as sick that surfeit with too much, as they that starve with nothing. It is no mean happiness, therefore, to be seated in the mean: superfluity comes sooner 5 by white hairs, but competency lives longer.

PORTIA. Good sentences, and well pronounc'd.

NERISSA. They would be better, if well follow'd.

PORTIA. If to do were as easy as to know what were good to do, chapels had been churches, and poor men's cottages princes' palaces. It is a good 10 divine that follows his own instructions: I can easier teach twenty what were good to be done, than be one of the twenty to follow mine own teaching. The brain may devise laws for the blood; but a hot temper leaps o'er a cold decree: such a hare is madness the youth, to skip o'er the meshes of good counsel the cripple. But this reasoning is not in the fashion 15 to choose me a husband. O me, the word "choose"! I may neither choose whom I would, nor refuse whom I dislike; so is the will of the living daughter curb'd by the will of a dead father. Is it not hard, Nerissa, that I cannot choose one, nor refuse none?

NERISSA. Your father was ever virtuous; and holy men, at their death, have 20 good inspirations: therefore the lottery that he hath devis'd in these three chests of gold, silver, and lead,—whereof who chooses his meaning chooses you,—will, no doubt, never be chosen by any rightly, but one who you shall rightly love. But what warmth is there in your affection towards any of these princely suitors that are already come? 25

PORTIA. I pray thee, over-name them; and, as thou namest them, I will describe them; and, according to my description, level at my affection.

NERISSA. First, there is the Neapolitan prince.

PORTIA. Ay, that's a colt indeed, for he doth nothing but talk of his horse; and he makes it a great appropriation to his own good parts, that he can shoe 30 him himself.

NERISSA. Then is there the County Palatine.

PORTIA. He doth nothing but frown; as who should say, "If you will not have me,

4–5. MEAN . . . MEAN—Small . . . middle (in comfortable circumstances). A characteristic play on the double meaning of words.

5. SUPERFLUITY—Those who have too much are likely to indulge themselves to excess and grow old sooner than those who have only enough to satisfy their needs.

11. DIVINE—Preacher.

14. MESHES—Snares set for a rabbit.

22. WHO CHOOSES HIS MEANING—Whoever rightly understands the meaning of the inscriptions put on the caskets by Portia's father.

26. OVER-NAME—List, name them over.

27. LEVEL AT—Guess at.

30. APPROPRIATION—Credit.

32. COUNTY—Count.

choose." He hears merry tales, and smiles not: I fear he will prove the weeping philosopher when he grows old, being so full of unmannerly 35 sadness in his youth. I had rather be married to a death's-head with a bone in his mouth than to either of these. God defend me from these two!

NERISSA. How say you by the French lord, Monsieur Le Bon?

PORTIA. God made him, and therefore let him pass for a man. In truth, I know it is a sin to be a mocker: but, he! why, he hath a horse better than 40 the Neapolitan's; a better bad habit of frowning than the County Palatine: he is every man in no man: if a throstle sing, he falls straight a-capering; he will fence with his own shadow. If I should marry him, I should marry twenty husbands. If he would despise me, I would forgive him; for, if he love me to madness, I shall never requite him. 45

NERISSA. What say you then to Falconbridge, the young baron of England?

PORTIA. You know I say nothing to him; for he understands not me, nor I him: he hath neither Latin, French, nor Italian; and you will come into the court and swear that I have a poor pennyworth in the English. He is a proper man's picture; but, alas, who can converse with a dumb-show? How 50 oddly he is suited! I think he bought his doublet in Italy, his round hose in France, his bonnet in Germany, and his behavior everywhere.

NERISSA. What think you of the Scottish lord, his neighbor?

PORTIA. That he hath a neighborly charity in him; for he borrow'd a box of the ear of the Englishman, and swore he would pay him again when he was 55 able: I think the Frenchman became his surety, and seal'd under for another.

NERISSA. How like you the young German, the Duke of Saxony's nephew?

PORTIA. Very vilely in the morning, when he is sober; and most vilely in the afternoon, when he is drunk; when he is best, he is little worse than a man; and when he is worst, he is little better than a beast: an the worst fall 60 that ever fell, I hope I shall make shift to go without him.

NERISSA. If he should offer to choose, and choose the right casket, you should refuse to perform your father's will, if you should refuse to accept him.

34. CHOOSE—Do as you please.
38. MONSIEUR LE BON—Pronounced mẽ·syû′ lĕ bōN′.
45. REQUITE HIM—Return his love.
48. HATH—Speaks. At least one of these languages was held necessary in a cultured man of Shakespeare's time.
49. HAVE A POOR PENNYWORTH—Know little about.
50. DUMB-SHOW—Pantomime, because he cannot speak any language that Portia knows.
51. SUITED—Dressed.
51. DOUBLET—Jacket.
51. ROUND HOSE—Short, full breeches.
54–55. A BOX OF THE EAR OF THE ENGLISHMAN—Apparently Falconbridge had boxed the ears of the Scottish lord, and the latter swore vengeance. The next lines allude to the Scottish-French alliance in which the French undertook to aid Scotland in the war against England. The meaning is that the Scots generally got the worst of it. Shakespeare's English audience had a good laugh here at the expense of the Scots.
60. AN THE WORST FALL—If worst comes to worst.
61. MAKE SHIFT—Manage.

PORTIA. Therefore, for fear of the worst, I pray thee, set a deep glass of Rhenish wine on the contrary casket; for, if the devil be within and that temptation without, I know he will choose it. I will do anything, Nerissa, ere I'll be married to a sponge. 65

NERISSA. You need not fear, lady, the having any of these lords: they have acquainted me with their determinations; which is, indeed, to return to their home, and to trouble you with no more suit, unless you may be won by some other sort than your father's imposition depending on the caskets. 70

PORTIA. If I live to be as old as Sibylla, I will die as chaste as Diana, unless I be obtain'd by the manner of my father's will. I am glad this parcel of wooers are so reasonable; for there is not one among them but I dote on his very absence: and I pray God grant them a fair departure. 75

NERISSA. Do you not remember, lady, in your father's time, a Venetian, a scholar, and a soldier, that came hither in company of the Marquis of Montferrat?

PORTIA. Yes, yes, it was Bassanio; as I think he was so call'd.

NERISSA. True, madam: he, of all the men that ever my foolish eyes look'd upon, was the best deserving a fair lady. 80

PORTIA. I remember him well; and I remember him worthy of thy praise.

[*Enter a* SERVING-MAN.]

How now! what news?

SERVING-MAN. The four strangers seek for you, madam, to take their leave: and there is a forerunner come from a fifth, the Prince of Morocco; who brings word the prince his master will be here tonight. 85

PORTIA. If I could bid the fifth welcome with so good heart as I can bid the other four farewell, I should be glad of his approach: if he have the condition of a saint and the complexion of a devil, I had rather he should shrive me than wive me. Come Nerissa. Sirrah, go before.
Whiles we shut the gates upon one wooer, another knocks at the door. 90 [*Exeunt.*]

72. SIBYLLA—A prophetess of Cumae in southern Italy, to whom Apollo granted long life.
72. DIANA—A goddess who never married.
87. CONDITION—Disposition.
88. COMPLEXION—The dark, swarthy skin of Morocco.
88. SHRIVE—To hear confession and give absolution for sins. The expression is today retained in the phrase, "Shrove-tide," referring to the three days before Ash Wednesday.
89. SIRRAH—Fellow, sir—addressed to the serving-man.

SCENE 3. *Venice. A public place.*

Bassanio has found the money-lender, Shylock. The two men stand on a corner of the great square before St. Mark's. Bassanio's youthfulness and gay dress contrast sharply with Shylock's bent figure and worn clothes.

The old man wears the yellow cap required of all Jews. Shylock has an arresting face with gaunt, bearded features and a shrewd glance. Bassanio, having just raised the question of the loan, awaits Shylock's answer.

[*Enter* BASSANIO *and* SHYLOCK.]

SHYLOCK. Three thousand ducats,—well.

BASSANIO. Ay, sir, for three months.

SHYLOCK. For three months,—well.

BASSANIO. For the which, as I told you, Antonio shall be bound.

SHYLOCK. Antonio shall become bound,—well. 5

BASSANIO. May you stead me? will you pleasure me? shall I know your answer?

SHYLOCK. Three thousand ducats for three months, and Antonio bound.

BASSANIO. Your answer to that.

SHYLOCK. Antonio is a good man.

BASSANIO. Have you heard any imputation to the contrary? 10

SHYLOCK. Ho! no, no, no, no: my meaning in saying he is a good man is to have you understand me that he is sufficient. Yet his means are in supposition: he hath an argosy bound to Tripolis, another to the Indies; I understand, moreover, upon the Rialto, he hath a third at Mexico, a fourth for England; and other ventures he hath, squander'd abroad. But ships are but 15 boards, sailors but men: there be land-rats and water-rats, water-thieves and land-thieves, I mean pirates: and then there is the peril of water, winds, and rocks. The man is, notwithstanding, sufficient. Three thousand ducats;—I think I may take his bond.

BASSANIO. Be assur'd you may. 20

SHYLOCK. I will be assur'd I may; and, that I may be assur'd, I will bethink me, May I speak with Antonio?

BASSANIO. If it please you to dine with us.

SHYLOCK. Yes, to smell pork; to eat of the habitation which your prophet the Nazarite conjur'd the devil into. I will buy with you, sell with you, 25 talk with you, walk with you, and so following; but I will not eat with you, drink with you, nor pray with you. What news on the Rialto? Who is he comes here?

1. DUCAT (dŭk'ăt)—A coin worth about two dollars.
6. STEAD ME . . . PLEASURE ME—Help me . . . do me the favor.
10. IMPUTATION—Hint.
12. SUFFICIENT—His wealth is sufficient to guarantee payment of the loan.
12. IN SUPPOSITION—Tied up in business ventures.
14. RIALTO (rē·äl'tō)—The business Exchange of Venice, somewhat like Wall Street in New York City.
15. SQUANDER'D—Scattered.
21. WILL BE ASSUR'D—Emphatically spoken. Shylock will not take Antonio's word without full security.
24. HABITATION—The reference is to Matt. viii: 28–32, where Our Lord cast out the devils from two men, and the devils went into a herd of pigs.

[*Enter* ANTONIO.]

BASSANIO. This is Signior Antonio.

SHYLOCK. [*Aside.*] How like a fawning publican he looks! 30
I hate him for he is a Christian;
But more for that, in low simplicity,
He lends out money gratis and brings down
The rate of usance here with us in Venice.
If I can catch him once upon the hip, 35
I will feed fat the ancient grudge I bear him.
He hates our sacred nation; and he rails,
Even there where merchants most do congregate,
On me, my bargains, and my well-won thrift,
Which he calls interest. Cursed be my tribe, 40
If I forgive him!

BASSANIO. Shylock, do you hear?

30. FAWNING PUBLICAN—A flattering tax-gatherer. The words are spoken of Antonio in hatred and refer to the universal scorn felt by the Jews for tax collectors in New Testament times.
32. LOW SIMPLICITY—Base folly.
33. GRATIS—Free, without interest.
34. USANCE—Interest on a loan.
35. CATCH HIM . . . UPON THE HIP—Get him at a disadvantage (a wrestling term).
37–39. RAILS . . . ON ME—Taunts me.

SHYLOCK. I am debating of my present store;
And, by the near guess of my memory,
I cannot instantly raise up the gross
Of full three thousand ducats. What of that? 45
Tubal, a wealthy Hebrew of my tribe,
Will furnish me. But, soft! how many months
Do you desire?—[*To* ANTONIO.] Rest you fair, good signior;
Your worship was the last man in our mouths.

ANTONIO. Shylock, although I neither lend nor borrow, 50
By taking nor by giving of excess,
Yet, to supply the ripe wants of my friend,
I'll break a custom.—Is he yet possess'd
How much ye would?

SHYLOCK. Ay, ay, three thousand ducats.

ANTONIO. And for three months. 55

SHYLOCK. I had forgot,—three months; you told me so.
Well then, your bond; and, let me see; but hear you:
Methought you said you neither lend nor borrow
Upon advantage.

ANTONIO. I do never use it.

SHYLOCK. When Jacob graz'd his uncle Laban's sheep,— 60
This Jacob from our holy Abram was,
(As his wise mother wrought in his behalf)
The third possessor; ay, he was the third,—

ANTONIO. And what of him? did he take interest?

SHYLOCK. No, not take interest; not, as you would say, 65
Directly interest: mark what Jacob did.
When Laban and himself were compromis'd
That all the eanlings which were streak'd and pied
Should fall as Jacob's hire,
The skillful shepherd pill'd me certain wands; 70

42. PRESENT STORE—Cash on hand.
44. GROSS—The total.
47. SOFT!—Stop!
48. REST YOU FAIR—God rest you well—equivalent to our "Good day." Shylock pretends he has just seen Antonio.
49. LAST MAN IN OUR MOUTHS—We were just speaking of you.
51. EXCESS—Interest.
52. RIPE WANTS—Pressing needs.
53. POSSESS'D—Informed—spoken to Bassanio. "He" is Shylock.
61. JACOB . . . ABRAM—The story is in Genesis xxx. Jacob, the grandson of Abraham, was the third possessor of Abraham's lands and flocks. His mother, Rebecca, contrived that Jacob should receive his father Isaac's blessing instead of Esau.
67. WERE COMPROMIS'D—Had mutually agreed.
68. EANLINGS—Newborn lambs.
68. PIED—Spotted.
70. PILL'D—Peeled.
70. WANDS—Rods of green wood.

He stuck them up before the fulsome ewes,
Who, then conceiving did in eaning time
Fall parti-color'd lambs, and those were Jacob's.
This was a way to thrive, and he was blest:
And thrift is blessing, if men steal it not. 75

ANTONIO. This was a venture, sir, that Jacob serv'd for;
A thing not in his power to bring to pass,
But sway'd and fashion'd by the hand of heaven.
Was this inserted to make interest good?
Or is your gold and silver ewes and rams? 80

SHYLOCK. I cannot tell; I make it breed as fast.
But note me, signior.

ANTONIO. Mark you this, Bassanio,
The devil can cite Scripture for his purpose.
An evil soul, producing holy witness,
Is like a villain with a smiling cheek; 85
A goodly apple rotten at the heart:
O, what a goodly outside falsehood hath!

SHYLOCK. Three thousand ducats,—'tis a good round sum.
Three months from twelve,—then, let me see; the rate—

ANTONIO. Well, Shylock, shall we be beholding to you? 90

SHYLOCK. Signior Antonio, many a time and oft
In the Rialto you have rated me
About my moneys and my usances:
Still have I borne it with a patient shrug,
For sufferance is the badge of all our tribe. 95
You call me misbeliever, cut-throat dog,
And spit upon my Jewish gaberdine,
And all for use of that which is mine own.
Well then, it now appears you need my help:
Go to, then; you come to me, and you say, 100
"Shylock, we would have moneys": you say so;
You, that did void your rheum upon my beard,
And foot me as you spurn a stranger cur
Over your threshold: moneys is your suit.
What should I say to you? Should I not say, 105

73. FALL—Bear, give birth to.
76. VENTURE—Chance.
79. INSERTED—Put into the Bible to justify usury.
92. RATED—Berated, scolded.
97. GABERDINE—Gown.
100. GO TO, THEN—Very well, then.
102. VOID YOUR RHEUM (rōōm)—Spit.
104. SUIT—Request.

"Hath a dog money? is it possible
A cur can lend three thousand ducats?" or
Shall I bend low, and in a bondman's key,
With bated breath and whispering humbleness,
Say this,— 110
"Fair sir, you spit on me on Wednesday last;
You spurn'd me such a day; another time
You call'd me dog; and for these courtesies
I'll lend you thus much moneys?"

ANTONIO. I am as like to call thee so again, 115
To spit on thee again, to spurn thee too.
If thou wilt lend this money, lend it not
As to thy friends; for when did friendship take
A breed of barren metal of his friend?
But lend it rather to thine enemy; 120
Who if he break, thou mayest with better face
Exact the penalty.

SHYLOCK. Why, look you, how you storm!
I would be friends with you, and have your love,
Forget the shames that you have stain'd me with,
Supply your present wants, and take no doit 125
Of usance for my moneys, and you'll not hear me:
This is kind I offer.

BASSANIO. This were kindness.

SHYLOCK. This kindness will I show.
Go with me to a notary, seal me there
Your single bond; and, in a merry sport, 130
If you repay me not on such a day,
In such a place, such sum or sums as are
Express'd in the condition, let the forfeit
Be nominated for an equal pound
Of your fair flesh, to be cut off and taken 135
In what part of your body pleaseth me.

ANTONIO. Content, in faith; I'll seal to such a bond,
And say there is much kindness in the Jew.

BASSANIO. You shall not seal to such a bond for me:

108. BONDMAN'S KEY—A slave's tone of voice.
109. BATED—Lessened; lowered; diminished.
119. BREED . . . OF HIS FRIEND—Increase . . . from his friend.
121. BREAK—Defaults, fails to pay on time.
125. DOIT—Penny.
128. THIS WERE KINDNESS—"Were" is emphatic. Bassanio does not trust Shylock; he means that Shylock's offer would be a kindness in anyone else.
130. SINGLE BOND—Bond without security.

I'll rather dwell in my necessity. 140

ANTONIO. Why, fear not, man; I will not forfeit it:
Within these two months, that's a month before
This bond expires, I do expect return
Of thrice times the value of this bond.

SHYLOCK. O father Abram, what these Christians are, 145
Whose own hard dealings teaches them suspect
The thoughts of others!—Pray you, tell me this:
If he should break his day, what should I gain
By the exaction of the forfeiture?
A pound of man's flesh taken from a man 150
Is not so estimable, profitable neither,
As flesh of muttons, beefs, or goats. I say,
To buy his favor, I extend this friendship:
If he will take it, so; if not, adieu;
And, for my love, I pray you wrong me not. 155

ANTONIO. Yes, Shylock, I will seal unto this bond.

SHYLOCK. Then meet me forthwith at the notary's:
Give him direction for this merry bond;
And I will go and purse the ducats straight;
See to my house, left in the fearful guard 160
Of an unthrifty knave; and presently
I will be with you.

ANTONIO. Hie thee, gentle Jew. [*Exit* SHYLOCK.]
The Hebrew will turn Christian: he grows kind.

BASSANIO. I like not fair terms and a villain's mind.

ANTONIO. Come on: in this there can be no dismay; 165
My ships come home a month before the day. [*Exeunt.*]

151. ESTIMABLE—Valuable.
155. WRONG ME NOT—Do not misjudge my friendly intentions.
160. FEARFUL—Untrustworthy.
162. HIE—Haste.

FOR DISCUSSION

ACT I, SCENE 1 (*pages* 466–472)

1. In movies the musical score often sets the mood for the action. Does Shakespeare accomplish the same thing with the opening lines of the play? What does Antonio's mood hint at? What information do Salarino and Salanio give about Antonio?

2. Antonio's character grows throughout the first scene. How, for example, can you tell that he is much admired and loved? How does Shakespeare enlist your sympathy for Antonio?

3. Bassanio owns up frankly to past misdemeanors. Is this in his favor? What plan does Bassanio advance to mend his fortunes? Is it "within the eye of honor"? How can Antonio help him?

ACT I, SCENE 2 (*pages* 472–475)

Portia is one of Shakespeare's most carefully drawn and vital heroines. As you play this scene in your mind, what picture do you form of Portia? Has she intelligence? beauty? insight? sense of honor? moral character? What may account for her unhappiness?

ACT I, SCENE 3 (*pages* 475–481)

1. This scene introduces the pound-of-flesh story, and therefore is decisive in the further action of the play. Would Bassanio have approached Shylock, if there had been another way out? Why not? Has Shylock's hatred for Antonio a history? What is Shylock's particular grievance? Is Antonio without blame? List what you consider the rights and wrongs on both sides. In what precise passage does Shylock's hatred come into the open?

2. With the signing of the contract, any retreat for Antonio is barred and bolted shut. For Bassanio, Antonio has taken the decisive step. At this point, then, we reach what is called the "incentive moment"—the starting point—of the play. Had Antonio any misgivings? Had Bassanio? State the conditions of the bond.

3. In casting the most important characters, what well-known movie actors would you choose for the roles of Antonio, Bassanio, Shylock, Portia, and Nerissa? Justify your choice.

ACT II

SCENE 1. *Belmont. A room in* PORTIA'S *house.*

It is an afternoon several days later. The Prince of Morocco has enjoyed Portia's hospitality for the greater part of a week. A brusque soldier, Morocco is impatient of further delay. Tonight he will make his choice of the three caskets.

[*Flourish of cornets. Enter the* PRINCE OF MOROCCO *and his train;* PORTIA, NERISSA, *and others attending.*]

MOROCCO. Mislike me not for my complexion,
The shadow'd livery of the burnish'd sun,
To whom I am a neighbor and near bred.

1. MISLIKE—Dislike.
2. SHADOW'D LIVERY—Dark dress.

Bring me the fairest creature northward born
Where Phoebus' fire scarce thaws the icicles, 5
And let us make incision for your love,
To prove whose blood is reddest, his or mine.
I tell thee, lady, this aspect of mine
Hath fear'd the valiant: by my love, I swear
The best-regarded virgins of our clime 10
Have lov'd it too. I would not change this hue,
Except to steal your thoughts, my gentle queen.

PORTIA. In terms of choice I am not solely led
By nice direction of a maiden's eyes;
Besides, the lottery of my destiny 15
Bars me the right of voluntary choosing:
But, if my father had not scanted me,
And hedg'd me by his wit, to yield myself
His wife who wins me by that means I told you,
Yourself, renowned Prince, then stood as fair 20
As any comer I have look'd on yet
For my affection.

MOROCCO. Even for that I thank you:
Therefore, I pray you, lead me to the caskets,
To try my fortune. By this scimitar
That slew the Sophy, and a Persian prince 25
That won three fields of Sultan Solyman,
I would outstare the sternest eyes that look,
Outbrave the heart most daring on the earth,
Pluck the young sucking cubs from the she-bear,
Yea, mock the lion when he roars for prey, 30
To win thee, lady. But, alas the while!
If Hercules and Lichas play at dice
Which is the better man, the greater throw
May turn by fortune from the weaker hand:
So is Alcides beaten by his page; 35
And so may I, blind fortune leading me,
Miss that which one unworthier may attain,
And die with grieving.

PORTIA. You must take your chance;
And either not attempt to choose at all,

5. PHOEBUS—The sun. 9. FEAR'D—Frightened.
17. SCANTED—Limited, restricted. 18. WIT—Foresight, judgment.
20. STOOD AS FAIR—Would stand as fair a chance. 25. SOPHY—An emperor of Persia.
26. SOLYMAN—Suleiman, Sultan of the Ottoman Turks.
32. HERCULES—A Greek hero. Lichas was his servant. (Supply "to decide" after *dice*.)
35. ALCIDES (ăl·sī'dēz)—Another name for Hercules.

Or swear, before you choose, if you choose wrong 40
Never to speak to lady afterward
In way of marriage: therefore be advis'd.

MOROCCO. Nor will not. Come, bring me unto my chance.

PORTIA. First, forward to the temple: after dinner
Your hazard shall be made.

MOROCCO. Good fortune then! 45
To make me blest or cursed'st among men. [*Cornets, and exeunt.*]

43. NOR WILL NOT—Nor will I speak to lady afterward in way of marriage.
44. TEMPLE—The chapel, where Morocco will take the oath required of those who make choice of the caskets.

SCENE 2. *Venice. A street.*

This same afternoon introduces an impudent but engaging character, Launcelot Gobbo, Shylock's house-boy. He is a youth given to breaking dishes, wearing out clothes, and similarly adding to household expenses. At the moment he is pondering a serious question. Shall he desert his present employer to go to work for a more generous man? Launcelot considers the problem in the street outside Shylock's house.

[*Enter* LAUNCELOT.]

LAUNCELOT. Certainly my conscience will serve me to run from this Jew my master. The fiend is at mine elbow, and tempts me, saying to me, "Gobbo, Launcelot Gobbo, good Launcelot," or "good Gobbo," or "good Launcelot Gobbo, use your legs, take the start, run away." My conscience says, "No; take heed, honest Launcelot; take heed, honest Gobbo," or, as aforesaid, "honest 5 Launcelot Gobbo; do not run; scorn running with thy heels." Well, the most courageous fiend bids me pack: "Via!" says the fiend; "away!" says the fiend; "for the heavens, rouse up a brave mind," says the fiend, "and run." Well, my conscience, hanging about the neck of my heart, says very wisely to me, "My honest friend Launcelot, being an honest man's son,"— 10 or rather an honest woman's son; for, indeed, my father did something smack, something grow to, he had a kind of taste;—Well, my conscience says, "Launcelot, budge not." "Budge," says the fiend. "Budge not," says my conscience. "Conscience," say I, "you counsel well"; "Fiend," say I, "you counsel well": to be ruled by my conscience, I should stay with the 15 Jew my master, who, God bless the mark, is a kind of devil; and, to run away from the Jew, I should be ruled by the fiend, who, saving your reverence, is

1. SERVE—Permit. 2. FIEND—Satan, the tempter.
7. VIA—Italian for "Away" or "Be off."
11–12. SOMETHING SMACK . . . GROW TO—Taste somewhat of dishonesty.

the devil himself. Certainly the Jew is the very devil incarnal; and, in my conscience, my conscience is but a kind of hard conscience, to offer to counsel me to stay with the Jew. The fiend gives the more friendly counsel: I will run, fiend; my heels are at your commandment; I will run. 20

[*Enter* OLD GOBBO, *with a basket.*]

GOBBO. Master young man, you, I pray you, which is the way to master Jew's?

LAUNCELOT. [*Aside.*] O heavens, this is my true-begotten father! who, being more than sand-blind, high-gravel-blind, knows me not: I will try confusions with him. 25

GOBBO. Master young gentleman, I pray you, which is the way to master Jew's?

LAUNCELOT. Turn up on your right hand at the next turning, but, at the next turning of all, on your left; marry, at the very next turning, turn of no hand, but turn down indirectly to the Jew's house.

GOBBO. By God's sonties, 'twill be a hard way to hit. Can you tell me whether one Launcelot, that dwells with him, dwell with him or no? 30

LAUNCELOT. Talk you of young Master Launcelot?—[*Aside.*] Mark me now: now will I raise the waters.—Talk you of young Master Launcelot?

GOBBO. No master, sir, but a poor man's son: his father, though I say 't, is an honest exceeding poor man, and, God be thank'd, well to live. 35

LAUNCELOT. Well, let his father be what a will, we talk of young Master Launcelot.

GOBBO. Your worship's friend, and Launcelot, sir.

LAUNCELOT. But, I pray you, ergo, old man, ergo, I beseech you, talk you of young Master Launcelot?

GOBBO. Of Launcelot, an't please your mastership. 40

LAUNCELOT. Ergo, Master Launcelot. Talk not of Master Launcelot, father; for the young gentleman—according to Fates and Destinies, and such odd sayings, the Sisters Three, and such branches of learning—is, indeed, deceas'd; or, as you would say in plain terms, gone to heaven.

GOBBO. Marry, God forbid; the boy was the very staff of my age, my very prop.

18. INCARNAL—Incarnate, in the flesh. Launcelot likes to use big words and often misjudges their meaning. Note the humorous result in succeeding lines.

24. SAND-BLIND—Half-blind. Launcelot plays with the word, comparing it. His superlative would be the well-known term "stone-blind."

24. CONFUSIONS—Launcelot's slip for "conclusions." *To try conclusions* means "to argue."

28. MARRY—At first an oath "by the Virgin Mary"; then, as here, merely "indeed."

30. SONTIES—Saints.

32. MASTER—"Master" was a title applied only to gentlemen, not to servants.

33. RAISE THE WATERS—Cause excitement; that is, "start something."

35. WELL TO LIVE—In good health. 36. A—He.

37. WORSHIP—A term addressed to persons of rank. Old Gobbo thinks there must be an actual Master Launcelot, friend of the "worshipful" stranger. His son, Gobbo insists, is called plain *Launcelot*. 38. ERGO—Latin for "therefore." 40. AN'T—If it.

41. FATHER—A common form of address from young men to old, even where no relationship existed. Launcelot doesn't yet disclose his identity.

42. SUCH ODD SAYINGS—Launcelot is doing his best to talk in what he thinks is the learned manner. The Three Fates, the Destinies, and the Three Sisters are one and the same.

LAUNCELOT. [*Aside.*] Do I look like a cudgel or a hovel-post, a staff or a prop?—Do you know me, father? 46

GOBBO. Alack the day, I know you not, young gentleman: but, I pray you, tell me, is my boy—God rest his soul!—alive or dead?

LAUNCELOT. Do you not know me, father? 50

GOBBO. Alack, sir, I am sand-blind; I know you not.

LAUNCELOT. Nay, indeed, if you had your eyes, you might fail of the knowing me: it is a wise father that knows his own child. Well, old man, I will tell you news of your son: give me your blessing. Truth will come to light; murder cannot be hid long,—a man's son may; but, in the end, truth will out. 55

GOBBO. Pray you, sir, stand up: I am sure you are not Launcelot, my boy.

LAUNCELOT. Pray you, let's have no more fooling about it, but give me your blessing: I am Launcelot, your boy that was, your son that is, your child that shall be.

GOBBO. I cannot think you are my son. 60

LAUNCELOT. I know not what I shall think of that: but I am Launcelot, the Jew's man; and I am sure Margery your wife is my mother.

GOBBO. Her name is Margery, indeed: I'll be sworn, if thou be Launcelot, thou art mine own flesh and blood. Lord worshipp'd might he be! what a beard hast thou got! thou hast more hair on thy chin than Dobbin my fill-horse has on his tail. 65

LAUNCELOT. It should seem, then, that Dobbin's tail grows backward: I am sure he had more hair of his tail than I have of my face, when I last saw him.

GOBBO. Lord, how art thou chang'd! How dost thou and thy master agree? I have brought him a present. How 'gree you now? 70

LAUNCELOT. Well, well; but, for mine own part, as I have set up my rest to run away, so I will not rest till I have run some ground. My master's a very Jew: give him a present! give him a halter: I am famish'd in his service; you may tell every finger I have with my ribs. Father, I am glad you are come: give me your present to one Master Bassanio, who, indeed, gives rare new liveries: if I serve not him, I will run as far as God has any ground.—O rare fortune! here comes the man:—to him, father; for I am a Jew, if I serve the Jew any longer. 75

[*Enter* BASSANIO, *with* LEONARDO *and other followers.*]

BASSANIO. You may do so; but let it be so hasted, that supper be ready at the farthest by five of the clock. See these letters deliver'd; put the liveries to making; and desire Gratiano to come anon to my lodging. 80

[*Exit a* SERVANT.]

64. BEARD—Launcelot knelt with his back to his father who, therefore, felt the back of Launcelot's head, not his face.

65. FILL-HORSE—Work horse. 71. SET UP MY REST—Made up my mind.

81. TO MAKING—Look after having the costumes made.

LAUNCELOT. To him, father.

GOBBO. God bless your worship!

BASSANIO. Gramercy! wouldst thou aught with me?

GOBBO. Here's my son, sir, a poor boy,— 85

LAUNCELOT. Not a poor boy, sir, but the rich Jew's man; that would, sir,—as my father shall specify,—

GOBBO. He hath a great infection, sir, as one would say, to serve,—

LAUNCELOT. Indeed, the short and the long is, I serve the Jew, and have a desire,—as my father shall specify,— 90

GOBBO. His master and he—saving your worship's reverence—are scarce cater-cousins,—

LAUNCELOT. To be brief, the very truth is, that the Jew having done me wrong doth cause me,—as my father, being, I hope, an old man, shall frutify unto you,— 95

GOBBO. I have here a dish of doves that I would bestow upon your worship; and my suit is,—

LAUNCELOT. In very brief, the suit is impertinent to myself, as your worship shall know by this honest old man; and, though I say it, though old man, yet, poor man, my father. 100

BASSANIO. One speak for both.—What would you?

LAUNCELOT. Serve you, sir.

GOBBO. That is the very defect of the matter, sir.

BASSANIO. I know thee well; thou hast obtain'd thy suit:
Shylock thy master spoke with me this day, 105
And hath preferr'd thee, if it be preferment
To leave a rich Jew's service, to become
The follower of so poor a gentleman.

LAUNCELOT. The old proverb is very well parted between my master Shylock and you, sir: you have the grace of God, sir, and he hath enough. 110

BASSANIO. Thou speak'st it well.—Go, father, with thy son.—
Take leave of thy old master, and inquire
My lodging out. Give him a livery
More guarded than his fellows'; see it done.

84. GRAMERCY—French for "many thanks"—usually, as here, an expression of surprise or protest.
88. INFECTION—Old Gobbo mistakes the word for "affection"; that is, "desire."
91. SCARCE CATER-COUSINS—Not good friends.
94. FRUTIFY—Certify. Like his father, Launcelot in excitement is blundering into using the wrong words.
98. IMPERTINENT—Launcelot means "pertinent."
103. DEFECT—Effect or substance.
106. PREFERR'D—Recommended. 106. PREFERMENT—Promotion.
109. PROVERB—It ran, "The grace of God is gear enough."
113–114. LIVERY . . . MORE GUARDED—A servant's suit . . . more decorated, as befitting Launcelot's humorous character.

LAUNCELOT. Father, in.—I cannot get a service, no; I have ne'er a tongue 115
in my head.—Well, if any man in Italy have a fairer table which doth offer
to swear upon a book, I shall have good fortune! Go to; here's a simple line
of life! here's a small trifle of wives: alas! fifteen wives is nothing! a'leven
widows and nine maids is a simple coming-in for one man; and then to 'scape
drowning thrice, and to be in peril of my life with the edge of a 120
feather-bed,—here are simple 'scapes! Well, if Fortune be a woman, she's
a good wench for this gear.—Father, come; I'll take my leave of the Jew in
the twinkling of an eye. [*Exeunt* LAUNCELOT *and* OLD GOBBO.]

BASSANIO. I pray thee, good Leonardo, think on this:
These things being bought and orderly bestow'd, 125
Return in haste, for I do feast tonight
My best-esteem'd acquaintance: hie thee, go.

LEONARDO. My best endeavors shall be done herein.

[*Enter* GRATIANO.]

GRATIANO. Where is your master?

LEONARDO. Yonder, sir, he walks. [*Exit.*]

GRATIANO. Signior Bassanio,—

BASSANIO. Gratiano! 130

GRATIANO. I have a suit to you.

BASSANIO. You have obtain'd it.

GRATIANO. You must not deny me: I must go with you to Belmont.

BASSANIO. Why, then you must. But hear thee, Gratiano:
Thou art too wild, too rude, and bold of voice,—
Parts that become thee happily enough, 135
And in such eyes as ours appear not faults;
But where thou art not known, why, there they show
Something too liberal. Pray thee, take pain
To allay with some cold drops of modesty
Thy skipping spirit; lest, through thy wild behavior, 140
I be misconstru'd in the place I go to,
And lose my hopes.

GRATIANO. Signior Bassanio, hear me:
If I do not put on a sober habit,

115. IN—That is, enter Shylock's house. The talking has been going on outside in the street.
115–123. NO—Launcelot congratulates himself on his new position and begins to tell his own fortune by reading his palm or "table." The "table," "line of life," and indications of marrying are technical details as he reads his future.
117. SIMPLE—Ordinary—implying in tone just the opposite.
119. COMING IN—Income. 122. GEAR—Business.
125. BESTOW'D—Put on shipboard.
131. SUIT TO YOU—A favor to ask you.
138. LIBERAL—Reckless.

Talk with respect, and swear but now and then,
Wear prayer-books in my pocket, look demurely; 145
Nay more, while grace is saying, hood mine eyes
Thus with my hat, and sigh, and say "amen";
Use all the observance of civility,
Like one well studied in a sad ostent
To please his grandam, never trust me more. 150

BASSANIO. Well, we shall see your bearing.

GRATIANO. Nay, but I bar tonight: you shall not gage me
By what we do tonight.

BASSANIO. No, that were a pity:
I would entreat you rather to put on
Your boldest suit of mirth, for we have friends 155
That purpose merriment. But fare you well:
I have some business.

GRATIANO. And I must to Lorenzo and the rest;
But we will visit you at supper-time. [*Exeunt.*]

146. HOOD MINE EYES—In those days men were accustomed to wear hats while eating; during grace, they held them over their eyes.
149. SAD OSTENT—Grave appearance.
152. GAGE—Judge.

SCENE 3. *The same. A room in* SHYLOCK'S *house.*

It is only a few minutes later. In high spirits, Launcelot has just confided news of his new employment to Shylock's only daughter, Jessica.

[*Enter* JESSICA *and* LAUNCELOT.]

JESSICA. I am sorry thou wilt leave my father so:
Our house is hell; and thou, a merry devil,
Didst rob it of some taste of tediousness.
But fare thee well; there is a ducat for thee:
And, Launcelot, soon at supper shalt thou see 5
Lorenzo, who is thy new master's guest:
Give him this letter; do it secretly:
And so farewell: I would not have my father
See me in talk with thee.

LAUNCELOT. Adieu! tears exhibit my tongue. Most beautiful pagan, most 10
sweet Jew! if a Christian do not play the knave and get thee, I am much deceiv'd. But, adieu: these foolish drops do something drown my manly spirit: adieu.

10. TEARS EXHIBIT MY TONGUE—My tears talk for me. Or it may be Launcelot's mistake for tears *inhibit*—that is, "restrain."

JESSICA. Farewell, good Launcelot.— [*Exit* LAUNCELOT.]
Alack, what heinous sin is it in me 15
To be asham'd to be my father's child!
But though I am a daughter to his blood,
I am not to his manners. O Lorenzo,
If thou keep promise, I shall end this strife,
Become a Christian, and thy loving wife! [*Exit.*] 20

15. HEINOUS (hā'nŭs)—Hateful.
19. THIS STRIFE—Jessica's inner conflict between loyalty to her father and her love for Lorenzo.

SCENE 4. *The same. A street.*

Gratiano has met Lorenzo and his other confederates in the evening's venture. They are putting the finishing touches to a plan in which Jessica has a leading role.

[*Enter* GRATIANO, LORENZO, SALARINO, *and* SALANIO.]

LORENZO. Nay, we will slink away in supper-time,
Disguise us at my lodging, and return
All in an hour.

GRATIANO. We have not made good preparation.
SALARINO. We have not spoke us yet of torch-bearers. 5
SALANIO. 'T is vile, unless it may be quaintly order'd,
And better in my mind not undertook.
LORENZO. 'T is now but four o'clock: we have two hours
To furnish us.—

[*Enter* LAUNCELOT, *with a letter.*]

Friend Launcelot, what's the news?
LAUNCELOT. And it shall please you to break up this, it shall seem to signify. 10
LORENZO. I know the hand: in faith, 't is a fair hand;
And whiter than the paper it writ on
Is the fair hand that writ.
GRATIANO. Love-news, in faith.
LAUNCELOT. By your leave, sir.
LORENZO. Whither goest thou? 15
LAUNCELOT. Marry, sir, to bid my old master the Jew to sup tonight with my new master the Christian.
LORENZO. Hold here, take this: tell gentle Jessica
I will not fail her; speak it privately;
Go.—Gentlemen, [*Exit* LAUNCELOT.] 20
Will you prepare you for this masque tonight?
I am provided of a torch-bearer.
SALARINO. Ay, marry, I'll be gone about it straight.
SALANIO. And so will I.
LORENZO. Meet me and Gratiano
At Gratiano's lodging some hour hence. 25
SALARINO. 'T is good we do so. [*Exeunt* SALARINO *and* SALANIO.]
GRATIANO. Was not that letter from fair Jessica?
LORENZO. I must needs tell thee all: She hath directed
How I shall take her from her father's house;
What gold and jewels she is furnish'd with; 30
What page's suit she hath in readiness.
If e'er the Jew her father come to heaven,
It will be for his gentle daughter's sake;
And never dare misfortune cross her foot,
Unless she do it under this excuse, 35
That she is issue to a faithless Jew.

5. SPOKE US YET—Yet engaged.
6. VILE, UNLESS . . . QUAINTLY ORDERED—No good unless cleverly arranged.
10. BREAK UP THIS—Break the seal and open Jessica's letter.
14. BY YOUR LEAVE—May I have your permission to go now?
21. MASQUE—Masquerade. 25. SOME HOUR—About an hour.
36. ISSUE TO A FAITHLESS JEW—Child of an unbelieving Jew.

Come, go with me: peruse this as thou goest.
Fair Jessica shall be my torch-bearer. [*Exeunt.*]

SCENE 5. *The same. Before* SHYLOCK'S *house.*

Shylock has just received Launcelot's notice. Now that Launcelot is giving up a "generous" master, Shylock prophesies lean times for him.

[*Enter* SHYLOCK *and* LAUNCELOT.]

SHYLOCK. Well, thou shalt see, thy eyes shall be the judge,
The difference of old Shylock and Bassanio:—
What, Jessica!—thou shalt not gormandize,
As thou hast done with me,—what, Jessica!—
And sleep and snore, and rend apparel out.— 5
Why, Jessica, I say!

LAUNCELOT. Why, Jessica!

SHYLOCK. Who bids thee call? I do not bid thee call.

LAUNCELOT. Your worship was wont to tell me I could do nothing without bidding.

[*Enter* JESSICA.]

JESSICA. Call you? what is your will?

SHYLOCK. I am bid forth to supper, Jessica: 10
There are my keys.—But wherefore should I go?
I am not bid for love; they flatter me:
But yet I'll go in hate, to feed upon
The prodigal Christian.—Jessica, my girl,
Look to my house.—I am right loth to go: 15
There is some ill a-brewing towards my rest,
For I did dream of money-bags tonight.

LAUNCELOT. I beseech you, sir, go: my young master doth expect your reproach.

SHYLOCK. So do I his. 19

LAUNCELOT. And they have conspir'd together,—I will not say you shall see a masque; but if you do, then it was not for nothing that my nose fell a-bleed-

3. WHAT, JESSICA—Oh, Jessica! Shylock is impatiently calling Jessica and at the same time talking to Launcelot.
3. GORMANDIZE—Overeat.
5. REND APPAREL OUT—Tear your clothes.
8. WAS WONT—Was accustomed. Launcelot is enjoying his new freedom by calling Jessica without Shylock's bidding.
13–14. TO FEED UPON THE PRODIGAL CHRISTIAN—To help the spendthrift Bassanio spend his three thousand ducats.
15. RIGHT LOTH—Very unwilling.
18. REPROACH—Launcelot means "approach." Shylock grimly takes advantage of the mistake to say he expects Bassanio's reproach for what he himself is planning to do about the loan.

ing on Black-Monday last at six o'clock i' the morning, falling out that year on Ash-Wednesday was four year in the afternoon.

SHYLOCK. What, are there masques?—Hear you me, Jessica:
Lock up my doors; and, when you hear the drum, 25
And the vile squealing of the wry-neck'd fife,
Clamber not you up to the casements then,
Nor thrust your head into the public street,
To gaze on Christian fools with varnish'd faces;
But stop my house's ears,—I mean my casements: 30
Let not the sound of shallow foppery enter
My sober house.—By Jacob's staff, I swear
I have no mind of feasting forth tonight:
But I will go.—Go you before me, sirrah;
Say I will come. 35

LAUNCELOT. I will go before, sir.—Mistress, look out at window for all this;
There will come a Christian by,
Will be worth a Jewess' eye. [*Exit.*]

SHYLOCK. What says that fool of Hagar's offspring, ha?

JESSICA. His words were, "Farewell, mistress"; nothing else. 40

SHYLOCK. The patch is kind enough; but a huge feeder,
Snail-slow in profit, and he sleeps by day
More than the wild-cat: drones hive not with me;
Therefore I part with him; and part with him
To one that I would have him help to waste 45
His borrow'd purse.—Well, Jessica, go in:
Perhaps I will return immediately:
Do as I bid you; shut doors after you:
Fast bind, fast find,—
A proverb never stale in thrifty mind. [*Exit.*] 50

JESSICA. Farewell; and if my fortune be not crost,
I have a father, you a daughter, lost. [*Exit.*]

22. BLACK-MONDAY LAST—Last Easter-Monday.
23. ASH WEDNESDAY WAS FOUR YEAR—Four years ago last Ash Wednesday.
26. WRY-NECK'D FIFE—The instrument had a crooked mouthpiece.
29. VARNISH'D FACES—Masks with painted faces.
39. HAGAR—Hagar and her descendants, the Ishmaelites, were considered outcasts by the Old Testament Hebrews.
41. PATCH—Fool.

SCENE 6. *The same.*

Two conspirators in holiday masques skulk in the evening shadows outside Shylock's house, waiting to carry out Lorenzo's plan. As we come on the scene, Lorenzo is late, and Gratiano and Salarino are trying to account for this lover's tardiness.

[*Enter* GRATIANO *and* SALARINO, *masqued.*]

GRATIANO. This is the penthouse under which Lorenzo
Desir'd us to make stand.

SALARINO. His hour is almost past.

GRATIANO. And it is marvel he out-dwells his hour,
For lovers ever run before the clock.

SALARINO. O, ten times faster Venus' pigeons fly 5
To seal love's bonds new-made than they are wont,
To keep obliged faith unforfeited!

GRATIANO. That ever holds. Who riseth from a feast
With that keen appetite that he sits down?
Where is the horse that doth untread again 10
His tedious measures with the unbated fire
That he did pace them first? All things that are,
Are with more spirit chased than enjoy'd.
How like a younker or a prodigal
The scarfed bark puts from her native bay, 15
Hugg'd and embraced by the strumpet wind!
How like the prodigal doth she return,
With over-weather'd ribs, and ragged sails,
Lean, rent, and beggar'd by the strumpet wind!

SALARINO. Here comes Lorenzo: more of this hereafter. 20

[*Enter* LORENZO.]

LORENZO. Sweet friends, your patience for my long abode;
Not I, but my affairs, have made you wait:
When you shall please to play the thieves for wives,
I'll watch as long for you then. Approach;
Here dwells my father Jew. Ho! who's within? 25

[*Enter* JESSICA, *above, in boy's clothes.*]

JESSICA. Who are you? Tell me, for more certainty,
Albeit I'll swear that I do know your tongue.

LORENZO. Lorenzo, and thy love.

1. PENTHOUSE—Here a shed-roof, projecting over a doorway.
5. VENUS—The Roman goddess of love, whose chariot in classic mythology was drawn by doves.
7. OBLIGED—Bound by a contract of marriage.
14. YOUNKER—Youngster. 15. SCARFED—Decked with flags and streamers.
21. ABODE—Delay. 27. ALBEIT—Although.

JESSICA. Lorenzo, certain; and my love, indeed;
For who love I so much? And now who knows 30
But you, Lorenzo, whether I am yours?
LORENZO. Heaven and thy thoughts are witness that thou art.
JESSICA. Here, catch this casket; it is worth the pains.
I am glad 't is night, you do not look on me,
For I am much asham'd of my exchange: 35
But love is blind, and lovers cannot see
The pretty follies that themselves commit;
For, if they could, Cupid himself would blush
To see me thus transformed to a boy.
LORENZO. Descend, for you must be my torch-bearer. 40
JESSICA. What, must I hold a candle to my shames?
They in themselves, good sooth, are too, too light.
Why, 't is an office of discovery, love;
And I should be obscur'd.
LORENZO. So are you, sweet,
Even in the lovely garnish of a boy. 45
But come at once;
For the close night doth play the runaway,
And we are stay'd for at Bassanio's feast.
JESSICA. I will make fast the doors, and gild myself
With some more ducats, and be with you straight. [*Exit above.*] 50
GRATIANO. Now, by my hood, a Gentile, and no Jew.
LORENZO. Beshrew me, but I love her heartily;
For she is wise, if I can judge of her;
And fair she is, if that mine eyes be true;
And true she is, as she hath prov'd herself; 55
And therefore, like herself, wise, fair, and true,
Shall she be placed in my constant soul.

[*Enter* JESSICA, *below.*]

What, art thou come?—On, gentlemen; away!
Our masquing mates by this time for us stay.
[*Exit, with* JESSICA *and* SALARINO.]

[*Enter* ANTONIO.]

ANTONIO. Who's there? 60

41. SHAMES—Referring to her boy's attire.
42. LIGHT—Here, in its double meaning of "visible" and "frivolous."
43. DISCOVERY—To act as torch-bearer is a service which invites discovery.
51. GENTILE—Pronounced "gentle," a play upon the words *gentle* and *gentile* being intended.
52. BESHREW—A mild, playful oath, literally "Curse me."

GRATIANO. Signior Antonio!
ANTONIO. Fie, fie, Gratiano! where are all the rest?
'T is nine o'clock; our friends all stay for you.
No masque tonight: the wind is come about;
Bassanio presently will go abroad: 65
I have sent twenty out to seek for you.
GRATIANO. I am glad on't: I desire no more delight
Than to be under sail and gone tonight. [*Exeunt.*]

64. IS COME ABOUT—Has changed (to a favorable direction).

SCENE 7. *Belmont. A room in* PORTIA'S *house.*

This same evening Morocco at Belmont has made his solemn vow and comes to make choice of the fateful caskets. The scene is taut with suspense for both Morocco and Portia.

[*Flourish of cornets. Enter* PORTIA, *with the* PRINCE OF MOROCCO, *and their trains.*]

PORTIA. Go draw aside the curtains, and discover
The several caskets to this noble prince.—
Now make your choice.
MOROCCO. The first, of gold, who this inscription bears,
"Who chooseth me shall gain what many men desire;" 5
The second, silver, which this promise carries,
"Who chooseth me shall get as much as he deserves;"
This third, dull lead, with warning all as blunt,
"Who chooseth me must give and hazard all he hath."
How shall I now if I do choose the right? 10
PORTIA. The one of them contains my picture, prince:
If you choose that, then I am yours withal.
MOROCCO. Some god direct my judgment! Let me see;
I will survey the inscriptions back again.
What says this leaden casket? 15
"Who chooseth me must give and hazard all he hath."
Must give,—for what? for lead? hazard for lead?
This casket threatens. Men that hazard all
Do it in hope of fair advantages:
A golden mind stoops not to shows of dross; 20
I'll then nor give nor hazard aught for lead.
What says the silver with her virgin hue?

1. DISCOVER—Reveal.
20. SHOWS OF DROSS—Worthless appearances.
22. VIRGIN—Fresh, bright.

"Who chooseth me shall get as much as he deserves."
As much as he deserves! Pause there, Morocco,
And weigh thy value with an even hand: 25
If thou be'st rated by thy estimation,
Thou dost deserve enough; and yet enough
May not extend so far as to the lady:
And yet to be afeard of my deserving
Were but a weak disabling of myself. 30
As much as I deserve! Why, that's the lady:
I do in birth deserve her, and in fortunes,
In graces, and in qualities of breeding;
But more than these, in love I do deserve.
What if I stay'd no further, but chose here? 35
Let's see once more this saying grav'd in gold:
"Who chooseth me shall gain what many men desire."
Why, that's the lady; all the world desires her:
From the four corners of the earth they come,
To kiss this shrine, this mortal breathing saint: 40
The Hyrcanian deserts and the vasty wilds
Of wide Arabia are as throughfares now
For princes to come view fair Portia:
The watery kingdom, whose ambitious head
Spits in the face of heaven, is no bar 45
To stop the foreign spirits; but they come,
As o'er a brook, to see fair Portia.
One of these three contains her heavenly picture.
Is't like that lead contains her? 'T were damnation
To think so base a thought: it were too gross 50
To rib her cerecloth in the obscure grave.
Or shall I think in silver she's immur'd,
Being ten times undervalu'd to tried gold?
O sinful thought! Never so rich a gem
Was set in worse than gold. They have in England 55
A coin that bears the figure of an angel
Stamped in gold, but that's insculp'd upon;
But here an angel in a golden bed

30. DISABLING—Undervaluing.
40. KISS THIS SHRINE—To pay respect to Portia, as if in pilgrimage to the shrine of a saint.
41. HYRCANIAN DESERTS—Deserts south of the Caspian Sea.
44. WATERY KINGDOM—The ocean.
51. RIB HER CERECLOTH—Enclose her burial garment.
52. IMMUR'D—Entombed, enclosed.
57. INSCULP'D UPON—Carved upon.

Lies all within.—Deliver me the key:
Here do I choose, and thrive I as I may! 60

PORTIA, There, take it, prince; and if my form lies there,
Then I am yours. [*He unlocks the casket.*]

MOROCCO. O hell! what have we here?
A carrion Death, within whose empty eye
There is a written scroll! I'll read the writing.

[*Reads.*] All that glisters is not gold 65
Often have you heard that told:
Many a man his life hath sold
But my outside to behold:
Gilded timber do worms infold.
Had you been as wise as bold, 70
Young in limbs, in judgment old,
Your answer had not been inscroll'd:
Fare you well; your suit is cold.

Cold indeed, and labor lost;
Then, farewell, heat, and welcome, frost! 75
Portia, adieu. I have too griev'd a heart
To take a tedious leave: thus losers part.
[*Exit, with his train. Flourish of cornets.*]

PORTIA. A gentle riddance.—Draw the curtains; go:
Let all of his complexion choose me so. [*Exeunt.*]

63. CARRION DEATH—A bare skull.
69. GILDED TIMBER—Tombs ornamented with gold.

SCENE 8. *Venice. A street.*

During the night Bassanio and Gratiano have put off for the mainland; Jessica has eloped with Lorenzo. This morning a great hue and cry is being raised by Shylock for his daughter and his stolen ducats. Salarino and Salanio have other news also.

[*Enter* SALARINO *and* SALANIO.]

SALARINO. Why, man, I saw Bassanio under sail:
With him is Gratiano gone along;
And in their ship I'm sure Lorenzo is not.

SALANIO. The villain Jew with outcries rais'd the Duke,
Who went with him to search Bassanio's ship. 5

SALARINO. He came too late, the ship was under sail;
But there the Duke was given to understand

That in a gondola were seen together
Lorenzo and his amorous Jessica:
Besides, Antonio certified the Duke 10
They were not with Bassanio in his ship.

SALANIO. I never heard a passion so confus'd,
So strange, outrageous, and so variable,
As the dog Jew did utter in the streets:
"My daughter! O my ducats! O my daughter! 15
Fled with a Christian! O my Christian ducats!
Justice! the law! my ducats, and my daughter!
A sealed bag, two sealed bags of ducats,
Of double ducats, stolen from me by my daughter!
And jewels, two stones, two rich and precious stones, 20
Stolen by my daughter! Justice! find the girl!
She hath the stones upon her, and the ducats!"

SALARINO. Why, all the boys in Venice follow him,
Crying, his stones, his daughter, and his ducats.

SALANIO. Let good Antonio look he keep his day, 25
Or he shall pay for this.

SALARINO. Marry, well remember'd.
I reason'd with a Frenchman yesterday,
Who told me, in the narrow seas that part
The French and English, there miscarried
A vessel of our country richly fraught: 30
I thought upon Antonio when he told me;
And wish'd in silence that it were not his.

SALANIO. You were best to tell Antonio what you hear;
Yet do not suddenly, for it may grieve him.

SALARINO. A kinder gentleman treads not the earth. 35
I saw Bassanio and Antonio part:
Bassanio told him he would make some speed
Of his return: he answer'd, "Do not so;
Slubber not business for my sake, Bassanio,
But stay the very riping of time;
And for the Jew's bond which he hath of me,
Let it not enter in your mind of love:
Be merry; and employ your chiefest thoughts

25. LOOK HE KEEP HIS DAY—Take care to pay Shylock when the bond falls due. Shylock's rage prepares us for his extreme bitterness against Antonio later.
27. REASON'D—Talked.
28. NARROW SEAS—The English Channel.
29. MISCARRIED—Was wrecked.
30. FRAUGHT—Freighted.
39. SLUBBER NOT—Do not neglect your mission.

To courtship, and such fair ostents of love
As shall conveniently become you there:" 45
And even there, his eyes being big with tears,
Turning his face, he put his hand behind him,
And with affection wondrous sensible
He wrung Bassanio's hand; and so they parted.

SALANIO. I think he only loves the world for him. 50
I pray thee, let us go and find him out,
And quicken his embraced heaviness
With some delight or other.

SALARINO. Do we so. [*Exeunt.*]

48. SENSIBLE—Evident.
52. QUICKEN HIS EMBRACED HEAVINESS—Cheer him up.

SCENE 9. *Belmont. A room in* PORTIA'S *house.*

It is somewhat later, the same evening. The lure of the caskets has brought yet another suitor, the noble Spanish Prince of Arragon, to Portia's house. Arragon waits upon little ceremony. Having taken his oath, he is on the way to the room of the caskets. Again Portia's fate hangs on a moment's choice.

[*Enter* NERISSA, *with a* SERVITOR.]

NERISSA. Quick, quick, I pray thee; draw the curtain straight:
The Prince of Arragon hath ta'en his oath,
And comes to his election presently.

[*Flourish of cornets. Enter the* PRINCE OF ARRAGON, PORTIA, *and their trains.*]

PORTIA. Behold, there stand the caskets, noble prince:
If you choose that wherein I am contain'd, 5
Straight shall our nuptial rites be solemnized:
But if you fail, without more speech, my lord,
You must be gone from hence immediately.

ARRAGON. I am enjoin'd by oath to observe three things:
First, never to unfold to anyone 10
Which casket 't was I chose; next, if I fail
Of the right casket, never in my life
To woo a maid in way of marriage;
Lastly, if I do fail in fortune of my choice,
Immediately to leave you and be gone. 15

1. DRAW—Open.
3. ELECTION—To make his choice.

PORTIA. To these injunctions everyone doth swear
That comes to hazard for my worthless self.

ARRAGON. And so have I address'd me. Fortune now
To my heart's hope!—Gold, silver, and base lead.
"Who chooseth me must give and hazard all he hath." 20
You shall look fairer, ere I give or hazard.
What says the golden chest? ha! let me see:
"Who chooseth me shall gain what many men desire."
What many men desire! That "many" may be meant
By the fool multitude, that choose by show, 25
Not learning more than the fond eye doth teach,
Which pries not to the interior, but, like the martlet,
Builds in the weather on the outward wall,
Even in the force and road of casualty.
I will not choose what many men desire, 30
Because I will not jump with common spirits,
And rank me with the barbarous multitudes.
Why, then to thee, thou silver treasure-house;
Tell me once more what title thou dost bear:
"Who chooseth me shall get as much as he deserves." 35
And well said too; for who shall go about
To cozen fortune, and be honorable
Without the stamp of merit? Let none presume
To wear an undeserved dignity.
O, that estates, degrees, and offices 40
Were not deriv'd corruptly! and that clear honor
Were purchas'd by the merit of the wearer!
How many then should cover that stand bare!
How many be commanded that command!
How much low peasantry would then be glean'd 45
From the true seed of honor! and how much honor
Pick'd from the chaff and ruin of the times,
To be new-varnish'd! Well, but to my choice:
"Who chooseth me shall get as much as he deserves."
I will assume desert.—Give me a key for this, 50
And instantly unlock my fortunes here. *[He opens the silver casket.]*

18. ADDRESS'D ME—Prepared myself. 25. BY—For. 27. MARTLET—House swallow.
29. IN THE FORCE AND ROAD OF CASUALTY—Exposed to the force of every accident.
31. JUMP—Agree. 37. COZEN—Cheat. 41. DERIV'D—Obtained.
43. SHOULD COVER THAT STAND BARE—Would put on hats as masters who now are servants.
45–46. GLEAN'D FROM THE TRUE SEED—Picked from the genuine children of honor.
48. NEW-VARNISH'D—Freshly polished, recognized.
50. ASSUME DESERT—Take merit for granted.

PORTIA. Too long a pause for that which you find there.

ARRAGON. What's here? the portrait of a blinking idiot,
Presenting me a schedule! I will read it.
How much unlike art thou to Portia! 55
How much unlike my hopes and my deservings!
"Who chooseth me shall have as much as he deserves."
Did I deserve no more than a fool's head?
Is that my prize? are my deserts no better?

PORTIA. To offend, and judge, are distinct offices, 60
And of opposed natures.

ARRAGON. What is here?

[*Reads.*] The fire seven times tried this:
Seven times tried that judgment is,
That did never choose amiss.
Some there be that shadows kiss; 65
Such have but a shadow's bliss:
There be fools alive, I wis,
Silver'd o'er; and so was this.
Take what wife you will to bed,
I will ever be your head: 70
So be gone: you are sped.

Still more fool I shall appear
By the time I linger here:
With one fool's head I came to woo,
But I go away with two. 75
Sweet, adieu. I'll keep my oath,
Patiently to bear my wroth.

[*Exeunt* ARRAGON *and train.*]

PORTIA. Thus hath the candle sing'd the moth.
O, these deliberate fools when they do choose,
They have the wisdom by their wit to lose. 80

NERISSA. The ancient saying is no heresy,—
Hanging and wiving goes by destiny.

54. SCHEDULE—Document.

61. NATURES—Portia means that one cannot be at the same time both prisoner and judge. Having had his chance and having made the wrong choice, Arragon ought not to complain of the justice of the agreement.

67. I WIS—I know.

70. HEAD—You will always have a fool's head.

79. DELIBERATE—Slow and careful.

80. THEY HAVE THE WISDOM—Their attempts to be wise defeat their own purposes. This defeat is the only truly wise thing they accomplish.

PORTIA. Come, draw the curtain, Nerissa.

[*Enter a* SERVANT.]

SERVANT. Where is my lady?
PORTIA. Here: what would my lord?
SERVANT. Madam, there is alighted at your gate 85
A young Venetian, one that comes before
To signify the approaching of his lord,
From whom he bringeth sensible regreets;
To wit, besides commends and courteous breath,
Gifts of rich value. Yet I have not seen 90
So likely an ambassador of love:
A day in April never came so sweet,
To show how costly summer was at hand,
As this fore-spurrer comes before his lord.
PORTIA. No more, I pray thee: I am half afeard 95
Thou wilt say anon he is some kin to thee,
Thou spend'st such high-day wit in praising him.—
Come, come, Nerissa; for I long to see
Quick Cupid's post that comes so mannerly.
NERISSA. Bassanio, lord Love, if thy will it be! [*Exeunt.*] 100

84. MY LORD—Playfully spoken to the servant who has just inquired for "my lady."
88. SENSIBLE REGREETS—Substantial greetings—the rich gifts mentioned below.
89. COMMENDS—Compliments.
93. COSTLY—Rich, lavish.
94. FORE-SPURRER—Advance rider.
97. HIGH-DAY—Holiday, uncommon.
99. POST—Messenger.

FOR DISCUSSION

ACT II, SCENE 1 (*pages* 482–484)

What did each suitor have to agree to before choosing one of the caskets? What is Morocco's opinion of himself? What is Portia's opinion of him?

ACT II, SCENE 2 (*pages* 484–489)

1. What boy of your acquaintance would you cast as Launcelot? Why might Launcelot's conscience warn him not to run away? What circumstance permitted Launcelot to deceive old Gobbo?

2. With what was Bassanio preoccupied just before meeting Launcelot? Give two considerations prompting him to hire the boy. Why does Bassanio suggest that Gratiano alter his personality?

ACT II, SCENE 3 (*pages* 489–490)

Some have characterized Jessica as a light-minded, unfeeling daughter. Would you agree with this in view of the genuine tears Launcelot sheds at his leave-taking? What can be said in Jessica's favor? What sub-plot is forming in this short scene? Are you in sympathy with it?

ACT II, SCENE 4 (*pages* 490–492)
How does Jessica plan to take advantage of Shylock's absence that night? Is any other course possible to Jessica, in the light of Shylock's certain objections to her marriage with Lorenzo?

ACT II, SCENE 5 (*pages* 492–493)
A passion to possess and hold fast to his own—to daughter, ducats, race, religion, and revenge—is the keynote to Shylock's character. Read the lines in which Shakespeare highlights this passion in the present scene.

ACT II, SCENE 6 (*pages* 493–496)
Under what circumstances did Jessica elope with Lorenzo? Is the taking of the ducats and jewels completely unjustified? What two lines spoken by Jessica are rather famous? Do they apply to Jessica and Lorenzo? Explain your answers.

ACT II, SCENE 7 (*pages* 496–498)
Portia's father foresaw that only a noble and truly deserving man could make the winning choice of the caskets. What defect of character, then, would you consider responsible for Morocco's failure? Why would one "in judgment old" have avoided the golden casket?

ACT II, SCENE 8 (*pages* 498–500)
What part of Shylock's loss has priority in his affections—daughter or ducats? Had Antonio any direct connection with Shylock's loss? Why must Antonio, in the wake of Shylock's injury, "look he keep his day"? What report promises disaster for Antonio?

ACT II, SCENE 9 (*pages* 500–503)
Portia respected Morocco as a brave, stalwart soldier. Did she react as favorably to Arragon? What argument decided Arragon in favor of the silver casket? How does the choice reveal his character? Which epitaph is more damning—Morocco's or Arragon's?

ACT III

SCENE 1. *Venice. A street.*

More than two months have passed, and within two weeks Antonio's bond will be due. Report has it that he has lost a ship with rich cargo. As time runs out and none of his investments bring returns, storm clouds gather on Antonio's horizon.

[*Enter* SALANIO *and* SALARINO.]

SALANIO. Now, what news on the Rialto?

SALARINO. Why, yet it lives there uncheck'd, that Antonio hath a ship of rich lading wreck'd on the narrow seas; the Goodwins, I think they call the place; a very dangerous flat, and fatal, where the carcasses of many a tall ship lie buried, as they say, if my gossip Report be an honest woman of her word.

SALANIO. I would she were as lying a gossip in that as ever knapp'd ginger, 6 or made her neighbors believe she wept for the death of a third husband. But it is true, without any slips of prolixity, or crossing the plain highway of talk, that the good Antonio, the honest Antonio,—O, that I had a title good enough to keep his name company!— 10

SALARINO. Come, the full stop.

SALANIO. Ha! what sayest thou? Why, the end is, he hath lost a ship.

SALARINO. I would it might prove the end of his losses.

SALANIO. Let me say "amen" betimes, lest the devil cross my prayer, for here he comes in the likeness of a Jew. 15

[*Enter* SHYLOCK.]

How now, Shylock! what news among the merchants?

SHYLOCK. You knew, none so well, none so well as you, of my daughter's flight.

SALARINO. That's certain: I, for my part, knew the tailor that made the wings she flew withal.

SALANIO. And Shylock, for his own part, knew the bird was fledg'd; and 20 then it is the complexion of them all to leave the dam.

SHYLOCK. She is damn'd for it.

SALARINO. That's certain, if the devil may be her judge.

SHYLOCK. My own flesh and blood to rebel!

SALANIO. Out upon it, old carrion! rebels it at these years? 25

SHYLOCK. I say my daughter is my flesh and blood.

SALARINO. There is more difference between thy flesh and hers than between jet and ivory; more between your bloods than there is between red wine and Rhenish. But tell us, do you hear whether Antonio have had any loss at sea or no? 30

2. UNCHECK'D—The report goes uncontradicted.
3. GOODWINS—The Goodwin Sands, dangerous shoal waters off the English coast.
6. KNAPP'D—Nibbled, bit off. The habit of nibbling on ginger root was common in Shakespeare's day.
8. SLIPS OF PROLIXITY—Wasting words.
11. THE FULL STOP—Come to the point.
18. WINGS—The boy's suit Jessica wore.
21. COMPLEXION—Inclination, disposition.
21. DAM—Mother.
23. DEVIL—No good man can blame Jessica for running away.
29. RHENISH—A white wine.

SHYLOCK. There I have another bad match: a bankrupt, a prodigal, who dare scarce show his head on the Rialto; a beggar, that was us'd to come so smug upon the mart. Let him look to his bond: he was wont to call me usurer; let him look to his bond! he was wont to lend money for a Christian courtesy; let him look to his bond! 35

SALARINO. Why, I am sure, if he forfeit, thou wilt not take his flesh: what's that good for?

SHYLOCK. To bait fish withal: if it will feed nothing else, it will feed my revenge. He hath disgrac'd me, and hinder'd me half a million; laugh'd at my losses, mock'd at my gains, scorn'd my nation, thwarted my bargains, cool'd 40 my friends, heated mine enemies; and what's his reason? I am a Jew. Hath not a Jew eyes? hath not a Jew hands, organs, dimensions, senses, affections, passions? fed with the same food, hurt with the same weapons, subject to the same diseases, heal'd by the same means, warm'd and cool'd by the same winter and summer, as a Christian is? If you prick us, do we not 45 bleed? if you tickle us, do we not laugh? if you poison us, do we not die? and if you wrong us, shall we not revenge? if we are like you in the rest, we will resemble you in that. If a Jew wrong a Christian, what is his humility? Revenge. If a Christian wrong a Jew, what should his sufferance be by Christian example? Why, revenge. The villainy you teach me, I 50 will execute; and it shall go hard but I will better the instruction.

[*Enter a* SERVANT.]

SERVANT. Gentlemen, my master Antonio is at his house, and desires to speak with you both.

SALARINO. We have been up and down to seek him.

SALANIO. Here comes another of the tribe: a third cannot be match'd, unless 55 the devil himself turn Jew.

[*Exeunt* SALANIO, SALARINO, *and* SERVANT.]

[*Enter* TUBAL.]

SHYLOCK. How now, Tubal! what news from Genoa? hast thou found my daughter?

TUBAL. I often came where I did hear of her, but cannot find her.

SHYLOCK. Why, there, there, there, there! a diamond gone, cost me two thousand ducats in Frankfort! The curse never fell upon our nation till now; I 60

32. SMUG—Finely dressed.
34. FOR A CHRISTIAN COURTESY—Without interest.
39. DISGRAC'D . . . HINDER'D—Put me in disgrace . . . prevented my making a half-million ducats. Shylock's charge should not be taken quite at face value. At the moment he makes Antonio the scapegoat for all the insults and injuries he has ever endured from the Christians.
48. HIS HUMILITY—What kind of Christian humility or humanity does he show?

never felt it till now: two thousand ducats in that; and other precious, precious jewels. I would my daughter were dead at my foot, and the jewels in her ear! would she were hears'd at my foot, and the ducats in her coffin! No news of them?—Why so:—and I know not what's spent in the search: why, thou loss upon loss! the thief gone with so much, and so much 65 to find the thief; and no satisfaction, no revenge, nor no ill luck stirring but what lights on my shoulders; no sighs but of my breathing; no tears but of my shedding.

TUBAL. Yes, other men have ill luck too: Antonio, as I heard in Genoa,—

SHYLOCK. What, what, what? ill luck, ill luck? 70

TUBAL. Hath an argosy cast away, coming from Tripolis.

SHYLOCK. I thank God, I thank God!—Is it true, is it true?

TUBAL. I spoke with some of the sailors that escap'd the wreck.

SHYLOCK. I thank thee, good Tubal: good news, good news! ha, ha!—Where? in Genoa? 75

TUBAL. Your daughter spent in Genoa, as I heard, in one night fourscore ducats.

SHYLOCK. Thou stick'st a dagger in me: I shall never see my gold again: fourscore ducats at a sitting! fourscore ducats!

TUBAL. There came divers of Antonio's creditors in my company to Venice, that swear he cannot choose but break. 80

SHYLOCK. I am very glad of it: I'll plague him; I'll torture him: I am glad of it.

TUBAL. One of them show'd me a ring that he had of your daughter for a monkey.

SHYLOCK. Out upon her! Thou torturest me, Tubal: it was my turquoise; I had it of Leah when I was a bachelor: I would not have given it for a wilderness of monkeys. 85

TUBAL. But Antonio is certainly undone.

SHYLOCK. Nay, that's true, that's very true. Go, Tubal, fee me an officer; bespeak him a fortnight before. I will have the heart of him, if he forfeit; for were he out of Venice, I can make what merchandise I will. Go, Tubal, and meet me at our synagogue; go, good Tubal; at our synagogue, Tubal. 90

[*Exeunt.*]

63. HEARS'D—Lying in her coffin.
80. BREAK—Go bankrupt.
84. LEAH—Shylock's wife.
87. OFFICER—A sheriff's officer paid in advance to make the arrest.
87. BESPEAK—Engage.
89. MERCHANDISE—Business, bargains.

SCENE 2. *Belmont. A room in* PORTIA'S house.

It is two weeks later and the bond is past due. At Belmont, Bassanio has had no news of Antonio's plight. Two months have seen him and

Portia grow deeply in love. Today Bassanio makes his choice of the caskets, and Portia struggles with her fears for the outcome.

[*Enter* BASSANIO, PORTIA, GRATIANO, NERISSA, *and* ATTENDANTS.]

PORTIA. I pray you, tarry; pause a day or two
Before you hazard; for, in choosing wrong,
I lose your company: therefore forbear awhile.
There's something tells me—but it is not love—
I would not lose you; and you know yourself, 5
Hate counsels not in such a quality.
But, lest you should not understand me well,—
And yet a maiden hath no tongue but thought,—
I would detain you here some month or two
Before you venture for me. I could teach you 10
How to choose right, but then I am forsworn;
So will I never be: so may you miss me;
But, if you do, you'll make me wish a sin,
That I had been forsworn. Beshrew your eyes,
They have o'erlook'd me, and divided me; 15
One half of me is yours, the other half yours.—
Mine own, I would say; but if mine, then yours,
And so all yours! O, these naughty times
Puts bars between the owners and their rights!
And so, though yours, not yours. Prove it so, 20
Let fortune go to hell for it, not I.
I speak too long; but 't is to peize the time,
To eke it, and to draw it out in length,
To stay you from election.

BASSANIO. Let me choose;
For, as I am, I live upon the rack. 25

PORTIA. Upon the rack, Bassanio! then confess
What treason there is mingled with your love.

BASSANIO. None but that ugly treason of mistrust,
Which makes me fear the enjoying of my love:
There may as well be amity and life 30
'Tween snow and fire, as treason and my love.

6. HATE COUNSELS NOT—*Hate* does not give this kind of advice.
11. AM FORSWORN—Should break my oath.
15. O'ERLOOKED—Bewitched.
18. NAUGHTY—Evil, wicked.
20. PROVE IT SO—*If* it prove so.
22. PEIZE—Retard.
23. EKE—Lengthen, draw out. 25. UPON THE RACK—In torture.
26. CONFESS—The torture of the rack was used to make persons confess to crimes.

PORTIA. Ay, but I fear you speak upon the rack,
Where men enforced do speak anything.
BASSANIO. Promise me life, and I'll confess the truth.
PORTIA. Well then, confess and live.
BASSANIO. Confess and love 35
Had been the very sum of my confession:
O happy torment, when my torturer
Doth teach me answers for deliverance!
But let me to my fortune and the caskets.
PORTIA. Away, then! I am lock'd in one of them: 40
If you do love me, you will find me out.
Nerissa, and the rest, stand all aloof.
Let music sound while he doth make his choice;
Then, if he lose, he makes a swan-like end,
Fading in music: that the comparison 45
May stand more proper, my eye shall be the stream
And watery death-bed for him. He may win;
And what is music then? Then music is
Even as the flourish when true subjects bow
To a new-crowned monarch: such it is 50
As are those dulcet sounds in break of day
That creep into the dreaming bridegroom's ear,
And summon him to marriage. Now he goes,
With no less presence, but with much more love,
Than young Alcides, when he did redeem 55
The virgin tribute paid by howling Troy
To the sea-monster: I stand for sacrifice;
The rest aloof are the Dardanian wives,
With bleared visages come forth to view
The issue of the exploit. Go, Hercules! 60
Live thou, I live: with much, much more dismay
I view the fight than thou that mak'st the fray.

[*Music, whilst* BASSANIO comments on the caskets to himself.]

44. SWAN-LIKE END—The old belief was that a dying swan uttered a beautiful musical sound.
54. PRESENCE—Dignity.
55–57. ALCIDES . . . SEA-MONSTER—*Alcides* refers to Hercules. The reference is to a Greek myth. Hesione, daughter of a Trojan king, was demanded by the sea monster as a sacrifice. Hercules slew the monster, not out of love for Hesione, but to win the horses offered as a reward by the king.
57. I STAND FOR SACRIFICE—Like Hesione.
58. DARDANIAN—Trojan. If their men lost the siege the women became slaves of the victors.
59. BLEARED VISAGES—Tear-stained faces.
60. ISSUE—Outcome.
61. LIVE THOU—If you succeed.

SONG

Tell me where is fancy bred,
Or in the heart or in the head?
How begot, how nourishèd? 65
Reply, reply.
It is engender'd in the eyes,
With gazing fed; and fancy dies
In the cradle where it lies.
Let us all ring fancy's knell; 70
I'll begin it,—Ding, dong, bell.

ALL. Ding, dong, bell.
BASSANIO. So may the outward shows be least themselves:
The world is still deceiv'd with ornament.
In law, what plea so tainted and corrupt, 75
But, being season'd with a gracious voice,
Obscures the show of evil? In religion,
What damned error, but some sober brow
Will bless it, and approve it with a text,
Hiding the grossness with fair ornament? 80
There is no vice so simple, but assumes
Some mark of virtue on his outward parts:
How many cowards, whose hearts are all as false
As stairs of sand, wear yet upon their chins
The beards of Hercules and frowning Mars; 85
Who, inward search'd, have livers white as milk!
And these assume but valor's excrement
To render them redoubted! Look on beauty,
And you shall see 'tis purchas'd by the weight;
Which therein works a miracle in nature, 90
Making them lightest that wear most of it:
So are those crisped snaky golden locks,
Which make such wanton gambols with the wind,

73. OUTWARD SHOWS—Appearances. Bassanio means that the appearances of the caskets are no indication of their contents.
79. APPROVE—Prove.
81. SIMPLE—Unmixed, so clearly a vice.
85. MARS—The god of war.
87. EXCREMENT—Outgrowth, the beard.
88. REDOUBTED—Dreaded, feared.
89. PURCHAS'D BY THE WEIGHT—Cosmetics (beauty) are bought by weight.
91. LIGHTEST—Loosest, most frivolous; also fairest—another word-play on the double meaning of *light*.
93. WANTON GAMBOLS—Carefree tossing.

Upon supposed fairness, often known
To be the dowry of a second head, 95
The skull that bred them in the sepulcher.
Thus ornament is but the guiled shore
To a most dangerous sea; the beauteous scarf
Veiling an Indian beauty; in a word,
The seeming truth which cunning times put on 100
To entrap the wisest. Therefore, thou gaudy gold,
Hard food for Midas, I will none of thee;
Nor none of thee, thou pale and common drudge
'Tween man and man: but thou, thou meager lead,
Which rather threatenest than dost promise aught, 105

94. UPON SUPPOSED FAIRNESS—Worn by make-believe beauty.

95. DOWRY—Property; the blonde curls are sometimes wigs made from the hair of other beauties who have died.

97. GUILED—Deceptive, treacherous.

99. INDIAN BEAUTY—A black, swarthy beauty which fair-skinned Europeans would regard as ugly.

102. HARD FOOD FOR MIDAS—King Midas, whose touch turned everything to gold, found his food (turned to gold) impossible to eat.

103. DRUDGE—Servant—that is, silver, the ordinary currency of the day.

104. MEAGER—Worthless, poor.

Thy paleness moves me more than eloquence;
And here choose I: joy be the consequence!

PORTIA. [*Aside.*] How all the other passions fleet to air,
As doubtful thoughts, and rash-embrac'd despair,
And shuddering fear, and green-eyed jealousy! 110
O love, be moderate; allay thy ecstasy;
In measure rain thy joy; scant this excess!
I feel too much thy blessing: make it less,
For fear I surfeit!

BASSANIO. What find I here? [*Opening the leaden casket.*]
Fair Portia's counterfeit! What demi-god 115
Hath come so near creation? Move these eyes?
Or whether, riding on the balls of mine,
Seem they in motion? Here are sever'd lips,
Parted with sugar breath: so sweet a bar
Should sunder such sweet friends. Here in her hairs 120
The painter plays the spider, and hath woven
A golden mesh to entrap the hearts of men
Faster than gnats in cobwebs. But her eyes!—
How could he see to do them? having made one,
Methinks it should have power to steal both his 125
And leave itself unfurnish'd. Yet look, how far
The substance of my praise doth wrong this shadow
In underprizing it, so far this shadow
Doth limp behind the substance. Here's the scroll,
The continent and summary of my fortune: 130

[*Reads.*] You that choose not by the view,
Chance as fair, and choose as true!
Since this fortune falls to you,
Be content, and seek no new.
If you be well pleas'd with this, 135
And hold your fortune for your bliss,
Turn you where your lady is,
And claim her with a loving kiss.

A gentle scroll.—Fair lady, by your leave; [*Kissing her.*]

112. SCANT—Limit this excessive joy which I feel.
114. SURFEIT—Suffer from having too much. 115. COUNTERFEIT—Likeness.
115. WHAT DEMI-GOD—What man with godlike powers has come so near creating a living person (as the painter of Portia's picture)?
118. SEVER'D—Open. 126. UNFURNISH'D—Without a mate.
129. THE SUBSTANCE—The reality—that is, Portia herself.
130. CONTINENT AND SUMMARY—That which contains and sums up.

I come by note, to give and to receive. 140
Like one of two contending in a prize,
That thinks he hath done well in people's eyes,
Hearing applause and universal shout,
Giddy in spirit, still gazing, in a doubt
Whether those peals of praise be his or no; 145
So, thrice-fair lady, stand I, even so;
As doubtful whether what I see be true,
Until confirm'd, sign'd, ratified by you.

PORTIA. You see me, Lord Bassanio, where I stand,
Such as I am: though for myself alone 150
I would not be ambitious in my wish
To wish myself much better; yet for you
I would be trebled twenty times myself;
A thousand times for fair, ten thousand times more rich;
That, only to stand high in your account, 155
I might in virtues, beauties, livings, friends,
Exceed account: but the full sum of me
Is sum of—something: which, to term in gross,
Is an unlesson'd girl, unschool'd, unpractic'd:
Happy in this, she is not yet so old 160
But she may learn; happier than this,
She is not bred so dull but she can learn;
Happiest of all is that her gentle spirit
Commits itself to yours to be directed,
As from her lord, her governor, her king. 165
Myself and what is mine to you and yours
Is now converted: but now I was the lord
Of this fair mansion, master of my servants,
Queen o'er myself; and even now, but now,
This house, these servants, and this same myself, 170
Are yours, my lord: I give them with this ring;
Which when you part from, lose, or give away,
Let it presage the ruin of your love,
And be my vantage to exclaim on you.

BASSANIO. Madam, you have bereft me of all words; 175
Only my blood speaks to you in my veins;

140. BY NOTE TO GIVE AND TO RECEIVE—According to the direction to give (a kiss) and to receive (the lady).
158. SUM OF . . . —Portia hesitates, uncertain how to conclude so as to avoid either boasting or false modesty. With a smile she ends on "something."
158. TO TERM IN GROSS—To speak in general terms.
174. VANTAGE TO EXCLAIM ON YOU—Chance to cry out against you.

And there is such confusion in my powers,
As, after some oration fairly spoke
By a beloved prince, there doth appear
Among the buzzing pleased multitude; 180
Where every something, being blent together,
Turns to a wild of nothing save of joy,
Express'd and not express'd. But when this ring
Parts from this finger, then parts life from hence:
O, then be bold to say Bassanio's dead! 185

NERISSA. My lord and lady, it is now our time,
That have stood by and seen our wishes prosper,
To cry, good joy. Good joy, my lord and lady!

GRATIANO. My Lord Bassanio and my gentle lady,
I wish you all the joy that you can wish; 190
For I am sure you can wish none from me.
And, when your honors mean to solemnize
The bargain of your faith, I do beseech you,
Even at that time I may be married too.

BASSANIO. With all my heart, so thou canst get a wife. 195

GRATIANO. I thank your lordship, you have got me one.
My eyes, my lord, can look as swift as yours:
You saw the mistress, I beheld the maid;
You lov'd, I lov'd; for intermission
No more pertains to me, my lord, than you. 200
Your fortune stood upon the caskets there,
And so did mine too, as the matter falls;
For, wooing here, until I sweat again,
And swearing, till my very roof was dry
With oaths of love, at last, if promise last, 205
I got a promise of this fair one here
To have her love, provided that your fortune
Achiev'd her mistress.

PORTIA. Is this true, Nerissa?

NERISSA. Madam, it is, so you stand pleas'd withal.

BASSANIO. And do you, Gratiano, mean good faith? 210

GRATIANO. Yes, faith, my lord.

BASSANIO. Our feast shall be much honor'd in your marriage.

191. NONE FROM ME—You cannot wish any joy away from me. The meaning is: I wish you all the joy that you yourself can wish to have, for I am sure that even at that you cannot lessen my joy.
198. MAID—Nerissa is Portia's companion, not her servant.
199. INTERMISSION—Delay.
205. IF PROMISE LAST—If Nerissa's promise endures.

GRATIANO. But who comes here? Lorenzo and his infidel?
What, and my old Venetian friend, Salerio?

[*Enter* LORENZO, JESSICA, *and* SALERIO.]

BASSANIO. Lorenzo and Salerio, welcome hither; 215
If that the youth of my new interest here
Have power to bid you welcome. By your leave,
I bid my very friends and countrymen,
Sweet Portia, welcome.

PORTIA. So do I, my lord;
They are entirely welcome. 220

LORENZO. I thank your honor.—For my part, my lord,
My purpose was not to have seen you here;
But, meeting with Salerio by the way,
He did entreat me, past all saying nay,
To come with him along.

SALERIO. I did, my lord; 225
And I have reason for it. Signior Antonio
Commends him to you. [*Gives* BASSANIO *a letter.*]

BASSANIO. Ere I ope his letter
I pray you, tell me how my good friend doth.

SALERIO. Not sick, my lord, unless it be in mind;
Nor well, unless in mind: his letter there 230
Will show you his estate.

GRATIANO. Nerissa, cheer yon stranger; bid her welcome.—
Your hand, Salerio: what's the news from Venice?
How doth that royal merchant, good Antonio?
I know he will be glad of our success; 235
We are the Jasons, we have won the fleece.

SALERIO. I would you had won the fleece that he hath lost!

PORTIA. There are some shrewd contents in yon same paper,
That steals the color from Bassanio's cheek:
Some dear friend dead; else nothing in the world 240
Could turn so much the constitution
Of any constant man. What, worse and worse?
With leave, Bassanio; I am half yourself,

213. INFIDEL—Jessica, so called because she is a Jewess.
216. IF THAT THE YOUTH—If my new interest here, young as it is, justifies me in welcoming you.
218. VERY—True.
227. COMMENDS HIM—Sends you his regards.
238. SHREWD—Evil.
242. CONSTANT—Steadfast; one not disturbed by trifles.
243. WITH LEAVE—With your permission. Portia asks to read the letter or know its contents.

And I must freely have the half of anything
That this same paper brings you.

BASSANIO. O sweet Portia, 245
Here are a few of the unpleasant'st words
That ever blotted paper! Gentle lady,
When I did first impart my love to you,
I freely told you, all the wealth I had
Ran in my veins,—I was a gentleman; 250
And then I told you true: and yet, dear lady,
Rating myself at nothing, you shall see
How much I was a braggart. When I told you
My state was nothing, I should then have told you
That I was worse than nothing; for, indeed, 255
I have engag'd myself to a dear friend,
Engag'd my friend to his mere enemy,
To feed my means. Here is a letter, lady;
The paper as the body of my friend,
And every word in it a gaping wound, 260
Issuing life-blood. But is it true, Salerio?
Hath all his ventures fail'd? What, not one hit?
From Tripolis, from Mexico, and England,
From Lisbon, Barbary, and India?
And not one vessel 'scape the dreadful touch 265
Of merchant-marring rocks?

SALERIO. Not one, my lord.
Besides, it should appear that, if he had
The present money to discharge the Jew,
He would not take it. Never did I know
A creature, that did bear the shape of man 270
So keen and greedy to confound a man:
He plies the Duke at morning and at night;
And doth impeach the freedom of the state,
If they deny him justice: twenty merchants,
The Duke himself, and the magnificoes 275
Of greatest port, have all persuaded with him;
But none can drive him from the envious plea

250. GENTLEMAN—That is, well-born, and that was all.
256. ENGAG'D—Pledged. 257. MERE—Out-and-out, worst.
262. HIT—Succeeded.
268. DISCHARGE—Repay.
271. CONFOUND—Ruin. 272. PLIES—Urges.
273. IMPEACH—Accuse—that is, he makes the charge that Venice does not grant equal rights to everyone, as it claims to do by law.
275–276. MAGNIFICOES . . . HAVE PERSUADED—The chief magistrates have argued.

Of forfeiture, of justice, and his bond.
JESSICA. When I was with him, I have heard him swear,
To Tubal and to Chus, his countrymen, 280
That he would rather have Antonio's flesh
Than twenty times the value of the sum
That he did owe him: and I know, my lord,
If law, authority, and power deny not,
It will go hard with poor Antonio. 285
PORTIA. Is it your dear friend that is thus in trouble?
BASSANIO. The dearest friend to me, the kindest man,
The best-condition'd and unwearied spirit
In doing courtesies; and one in whom
The ancient Roman honor more appears 290
Than any that draws breath in Italy.
PORTIA. What sum owes he the Jew?
BASSANIO. For me three thousand ducats.
PORTIA. What, no more?
Pay him six thousand, and deface the bond;
Double six thousand, and then treble that, 295
Before a friend of this description
Shall lose a hair through Bassanio's fault.
First go with me to church and call me wife,
And then away to Venice to your friend;
For never shall you lie by Portia's side 300
With an unquiet soul. You shall have gold
To pay the petty debt twenty times over:
When it is paid, bring your true friend along.
My maid Nerissa and myself meantime
Will live as maids and widows. Come, away! 305
For you shall hence upon your wedding-day:
Bid your friends welcome, show a merry cheer:
Since you are dear bought, I will love you dear.
But let me hear the letter of your friend.
BASSANIO. [*Reads.*]

Sweet Bassanio, my ships have all miscarried, my creditors grow 310
cruel, my estate is very low, my bond to the Jew is forfeit; and since in paying it, it is impossible I should live, all debts are cleared between you and me, if I might but see you at my death. Notwithstanding, use your pleasure; if your love do not persuade you to come, let not my letter.

277. ENVIOUS PLEA—Spiteful claim.
288. BEST-CONDITION'D AND UNWEARIED—With the best disposition and most unwearied
294. DEFACE—Cancel.

PORTIA. O love, dispatch all business, and be gone! 315

BASSANIO. Since I have your good leave to go away,
I will make haste; but, till I come again,
No bed shall e'er be guilty of my stay,
Nor rest be interposer 'twixt us twain. [*Exeunt.*]

315. DISPATCH—Finish quickly.

SCENE 3. *Venice. A street.*

Back at Venice this same day, we find Antonio under arrest. It now appears that Shylock is in deadly earnest about collecting the forfeiture. The two men meet when a jailer takes Antonio out for a walk.

[*Enter* SHYLOCK, SALARINO, ANTONIO, *and* JAILER.]

SHYLOCK. Jailer, look to him: tell not me of mercy.—
This is the fool that lends out money gratis.—
Jailer, look at him.

ANTONIO. Hear me yet, good Shylock.

SHYLOCK. I'll have my bond; speak not against my bond:
I have sworn an oath that I will have my bond. 5
Thou call'dst me dog before thou hadst a cause;
But, since I am a dog, beware my fangs:
The Duke shall grant me justice.—I do wonder,
Thou naughty jailer, that thou art so fond
To come abroad with him at his request. 10

ANTONIO. I pray thee, hear me speak.

SHYLOCK. I'll have my bond; I will not hear thee speak;
I'll have my bond; and therefore speak no more.
I'll not be made a soft and dull-eyed fool,
To shake the head, relent, and sigh, and yield 15
To Christian intercessors. Follow not;
I'll have no speaking: I will have my bond. [*Exit.*]

SALARINO. It is the most impenetrable cur
That ever kept with men.

ANTONIO. Let him alone:
I'll follow him no more with bootless prayers. 20
He seeks my life; his reason well I know:
I oft deliver'd from his forfeitures
Many that have at times made moan to me;
Therefore he hates me.

9. SO FOND—So foolish as.
18. IMPENETRABLE CUR—Merciless dog that ever dwelt among men.
20. BOOTLESS—Useless. 22. FORFEITURES—Legal seizures.

SALARINO. I am sure the Duke
Will never grant this forfeiture to hold. 25

ANTONIO. The Duke cannot deny the course of law:
For the commodity that strangers have
With us in Venice, if it be denied,
Will much impeach the justice of the state;
Since that the trade and profit of the city 30
Consisteth of all nations. Therefore, go:
These griefs and losses have so bated me,
That I shall hardly spare a pound of flesh
Tomorrow to my bloody creditor.
Well, jailer, on. Pray God, Bassanio come 35
To see me pay his debt, and then I care not! [*Exeunt.*]

27. COMMODITY—The right of alien merchants to equal protection of the laws.
31. ALL NATIONS—Venice at this time was the chief commercial city of Europe.
32. BATED—Reduced, weakened.

SCENE 4. *Belmont. A room in* PORTIA'*s house.*

While her husband hurries to Antonio, Portia has a plan afoot that will require her own and Nerissa's absence from Belmont for a few days. She is making hurried arrangements with Lorenzo.

[*Enter* PORTIA, NERISSA, LORENZO, JESSICA, *and* BALTHASAR.]

LORENZO. Madam, although I speak it in your presence,
You have a noble and a true conceit
Of god-like amity, which appears most strongly
In bearing thus the absence of your lord.
But, if you knew to whom you show this honor, 5
How true a gentleman you send relief,
How dear a lover of my lord your husband,
I know you would be prouder of the work
Than customary bounty can enforce you.

PORTIA. I never did repent for doing good, 10
Nor shall I now: for in companions
That do converse and waste the time together,
Whose souls do bear an equal yoke of love,
There must be needs a like proportion

2. CONCEIT—Conception, idea.
3. AMITY—Friendship. Lorenzo means that Portia understands well what true friendship is; the best proof of her understanding, he thinks, is her willingness to let Bassanio go to his friend.
9. CUSTOMARY BOUNTY—Than your usual goodness can make you.
12. WASTE—Spend, pass.

Of lineaments, of manners, and of spirit; 15
Which makes me think that this Antonio,
Being the bosom lover of my lord,
Must needs be like my lord. If it be so,
How little is the cost I have bestow'd
In purchasing the semblance of my soul 20
From out the state of hellish cruelty!
This comes too near the praising of myself;
Therefore no more of it: hear other things.
Lorenzo, I commit into your hands
The husbandry and manage of my house 25
Until my lord's return: for mine own part,
I have toward heaven breath'd a secret vow
To live in prayer and contemplation,
Only attended by Nerissa here,
Until her husband and my lord's return: 30
There is a monastery two miles off,
And there we will abide. I do desire you
Not to deny this imposition,
The which my love and some necessity
Now lays upon you.

15. LINEAMENTS—Features.
20. SEMBLANCE—Likeness. Antonio is the image of Bassanio whom I love as my soul.
25. HUSBANDRY AND MANAGE—Care and management.
33. DENY THIS IMPOSITION—Refuse this charge.

LORENZO. Madam, with all my heart, 35
I shall obey you in all fair commands.
PORTIA. My people do already know my mind,
And will acknowledge you and Jessica
In place of Lord Bassanio and myself.
So fare you well, till we shall meet again. 40
LORENZO. Fair thoughts and happy hours attend on you!
JESSICA. I wish your ladyship all heart's content.
PORTIA. I thank you for your wish, and am well pleas'd
To wish it back on you: fare you well, Jessica.
[*Exeunt* JESSICA *and* LORENZO.]
Now, Balthasar, 45
As I have ever found thee honest-true,
So let me find thee still. Take this same letter,
And use thou all the endeavor of a man
In speed to Padua: see thou render this
Into my cousin's hand, Doctor Bellario; 50
And, look, what notes and garments he doth give thee,
Bring them, I pray thee, with imagin'd speed
Unto the tranect, to the common ferry
Which trades to Venice. Waste no time in words,
But get thee gone: I shall be there before thee. 55
BALTHASAR. Madam, I go with all convenient speed. [*Exit.*]
PORTIA. Come on, Nerissa; I have work in hand
That you yet know not of: we'll see our husbands
Before they think of us.
NERISSA. Shall they see us?
PORTIA. They shall, Nerissa; but in such a habit, 60
That they shall think we are accomplished
With that we lack. I'll hold thee any wager,
When we are both accoutred like young men,
I'll prove the prettier fellow of the two,
And wear my dagger with the braver grace; 65
And speak between the change of man and boy
With a reed voice; and turn two mincing steps
Into a manly stride; and speak of frays,
Like a fine-bragging youth; and tell quaint lies,

52. WITH IMAGIN'D SPEED—With all possible speed.
53. TRANECT—The ferry between Venice and the mainland.
60. HABIT—Costume, disguise.
61. ACCOMPLISHED WITH THAT—Furnished with what we lack (that is, manhood).
67. REED VOICE—As a boy speaks when his voice is changing.
68. FRAYS—Fights.

How honorable ladies sought my love, 70
Which I denying, they fell sick and died;
I could not do withal: then I'll repent,
And wish, for all that, that I had not kill'd them.
And twenty of these puny lies I'll tell;
That men shall swear I have discontinued school 75
Above a twelvemonth. I have within my mind
A thousand raw tricks of these bragging Jacks,
Which I will practice.
But come; I'll tell thee all my whole device
When I am in my coach, which stays for us 80
At the park gate; and therefore haste away,
For we must measure twenty miles today. [*Exeunt.*]

72. COULD NOT DO WITHAL—I could not help it (if they did). 74. PUNY—Youthful.
75. DISCONTINUED SCHOOL—That I have not been out of school a year.
77. JACKS—Conceited fellows.

SCENE 5. *The same. A garden.*

It is late morning, the following day. Portia is gone on her mysterious errand, and Lorenzo and Jessica keep the house. Outside, Jessica and Launcelot are talking. With a change of masters, Launcelot has not lost his bouncing wit. As the scene opens, he is playing father confessor to sprightly Jessica.

[*Enter* LAUNCELOT *and* JESSICA.]

LAUNCELOT. Yes, truly; for, look you, the sins of the father are to be laid upon the children: therefore, I promise ye, I fear you. I was always plain with you, and so now I speak my agitation of the matter: therefore be of good cheer; for, truly, I think you are damn'd. There is but one hope in it that can do you any good; and that is but a kind of bastard hope neither. 5

JESSICA. And what hope is that, I pray thee?

LAUNCELOT. Marry, you may partly hope that you are not the Jew's daughter.

JESSICA. That were a kind of bastard hope, indeed: so the sins of my mother should be visited upon me.

LAUNCELOT. Truly then I fear you are damn'd both by father and mother: 10 thus when I shun Scylla, your father, I fall into Charybdis, your mother: well, you are gone both ways.

2. I FEAR YOU—I fear for you.
3. AGITATION—He means to say "cogitation" or "thought." 5. BASTARD—False.
11. SCYLLA AND CHARYBDIS—The rock and the whirlpool in the narrow strait between Sicily and the foot of Italy. They were dangers equally great; shipmen trying to avoid one were often wrecked by the other. In classic mythology the rock and the whirlpool were described as evil monsters.

JESSICA. I shall be sav'd by my husband; he hath made me a Christian.

LAUNCELOT. Truly, the more to blame he: we were Christians enow before; e'en as many as could well live, one by another. This making of Christians 15 will raise the price of hogs: if we grow all to be pork-eaters, we shall not shortly have a rasher on the coals for money.

JESSICA. I'll tell my husband, Launcelot, what you say: here he comes.

[*Enter* LORENZO.]

LORENZO. I shall grow jealous of you shortly, Launcelot, if you thus get my wife into corners. 20

JESSICA. Nay, you need not fear us, Lorenzo: Launcelot and I are out. He tells me flatly there is no mercy for me in heaven, because I am a Jew's daughter: and he says you are no good member of the commonwealth; for, in converting Jews to Christians, you raise the price of pork.

LORENZO. I think the best grace of wit will shortly turn into silence, and 25 discourse grow commendable in none only but parrots. Go in, sirrah; bid them prepare for dinner.

LAUNCELOT. That is done, sir; they have all stomachs.

LORENZO. Goodly Lord, what a wit-snapper are you! then bid them prepare dinner.

LAUNCELOT. That is done too, sir; only, "cover" is the word. 30

LORENZO. Will you cover, then, sir?

LAUNCELOT. Not so, sir, neither; I know my duty.

LORENZO. Yet more quarreling with occasion! Wilt thou show the whole wealth of thy wit in an instant? I pray thee, understand a plain man in his plain meaning: go to thy fellows, bid them cover the table, serve in the 35 meat, and we will come in to dinner.

LAUNCELOT. For the table, sir, it shall be serv'd in; for the meat, sir, it shall be cover'd; for your coming in to dinner, sir, why, let it be as humors and conceits shall govern. [*Exit.*]

LORENZO. O dear discretion, how his words are suited! 40
The fool hath planted in his memory
An army of good words; and I do know
A many fools, that stand in better place,
Garnish'd like him, that for a tricksy word

16. RAISE THE PRICE OF HOGS—The Jews did not eat pork—that is, the flesh of swine.
17. RASHER—A slice of bacon, for our money.
25. BEST GRACE OF WIT—The most becoming form of wisdom.
26. DISCOURSE GROW COMMENDABLE—Talk grow praiseworthy.
30. "COVER"—The word has a double sense, to "lay the table cloth" and to "put on one's hat." Launcelot puns here, using the first meaning at the outset and the second in the line below. Gentlemen wore hats to table.
33. QUARRELING WITH OCCASION—Quibbling at every opportunity.
38–39. HUMORS AND CONCEITS—Whims and fancies.
40. O DEAR DISCRETION—An ironic comment on Launcelot's serious attempt to speak precisely.
44. GARNISH'D—Equipped. 44. TRICKSY—Fantastic, extraordinary.

Defy the matter.—How cheer'st thou, Jessica? 45
And now, good sweet, say thy opinion:
How dost thou like the Lord Bassanio's wife?

JESSICA. Past all expressing. It is very meet
The Lord Bassanio live an upright life;
For, having such a blessing in his lady, 50
He finds the joys of heaven here on earth;
And if on earth he do not mean it, then
In reason he should never come to heaven.
Why, if two gods should play some heavenly match,
And on the wager lay two earthly women, 55
And Portia one, there must be something else
Pawn'd with the other; for the poor rude world
Hath not her fellow.

LORENZO. Even such a husband
Hast thou of me as she is for a wife.

JESSICA. Nay, but ask my opinion too of that. 60

LORENZO. I will anon: first, let us go to dinner.

JESSICA. Nay, let me praise you while I have a stomach.

LORENZO. No, pray thee, let it serve for table-talk;
Then, howsoe'er thou speak'st, 'mong other things
I shall digest it.

JESSICA. Well, I'll set you forth. [*Exeunt.*] 65

45. DEFY THE MATTER—Sacrifice accuracy to effect.
45. HOW CHEER'ST THOU—How are you?
52. MEAN IT—Possibly "intend to live an upright life" now that he has won Portia.
57. PAWN'D—Pledged, wagered.
58. FELLOW—Equal.
62. A STOMACH—A word-play upon stomach in the sense of "appetite for dinner" and "inclination to praise Lorenzo."
65. SET YOU FORTH—Serve you up at table—that is, tell my opinion of you at table.

FOR DISCUSSION

ACT III, SCENE 1 (*pages* 504–507)

Shakespeare's plays are built on the pyramid or arch scheme of development. That is, the tension of events, already begun earlier, grows stronger up into the third act and there snaps at the highest point of strain. This high point serves as the pivot or "turning point" of the play for good or evil.

1. In this scene we are in the upward swing of events. What events here narrated bring closer the fatal conflict between Antonio and Shylock? Would you say Shylock is striking only at Antonio, or rather through Antonio at the whole Christian environment thwarting his happiness? What key does Shylock provide to the latter explanation?

2. Note that Shakespeare, through Tubal, interweaves good and bad news for Shylock, alternately closing and re-opening his wounds. How do the details about

Jessica fan Shylock's hatred for Antonio? Can you understand the reason for his feelings?

ACT III, SCENE 2 (*pages* 507–518)

1. The casket story is on the brink of decision. The outcome of conflict between Antonio and Shylock, as you will see, also depends on that decision. At such a dramatic point, a good movie director slows down the action to achieve suspense. Does Shakespeare use the same trick? How? Why does Bassanio reject the gold and silver caskets in favor of the lead casket? What pledge does Portia demand from Bassanio in return for the ring she gives him? What other engagement is announced?

2. Up to the present, Bassanio and Portia have been young, light-hearted lovers. Now Shakespeare brings them hard to earth with extremely bad news. What form does the news take? Can you trace its maturing effect in the speech and actions of the two lovers? For example, do you discover a new and tender humility in Bassanio? a spirit of sacrifice and a quick, practical tendency in Portia? Quote lines from the play to support your answers.

ACT III, SCENE 3 (*pages* 518–519)

The revenge Shylock means to exact seems at first sight too inhuman to be true to life. How has Shakespeare made it credible? List the successive blows of fortune which drive Shylock to his revenge. Why cannot the Duke interfere?

ACT III, SCENE 4 (*pages* 519–522)

Why did Portia not confide her intentions to Lorenzo? How does Portia intend to act when she is disguised as a boy? About how old will she pretend to be? What lines tell you? Do modern youths have any of the characteristics that Portia refers to in this passage? Discuss.

ACT III, SCENE 5 (*pages* 522–524)

Does this scene contribute anything to the story? Why do you think Shakespeare included it?

ACT IV

SCENE 1. *Venice. A court of justice.*

It is early afternoon of the same day. Antonio is about to go on trial in the courtroom of the Duke's palace. The plight of this well-loved man has brought together the senators and grandees of Venice. We hear the usual hubbub of a crowded room until the Duke enters and the major-domo pounds his mace for silence. The scene is set for Antonio's hearing.

[*Enter the* DUKE, *the* MAGNIFICOES, ANTONIO, BASSANIO, GRATIANO, SALERIO, *and others.*]

DUKE. What, is Antonio here?
ANTONIO. Ready, so please your Grace.
DUKE. I am sorry for thee: thou art come to answer
A stony adversary, an inhuman wretch
Uncapable of pity, void and empty 5
From any dram of mercy.
ANTONIO. I have heard
Your Grace hath ta'en great pains to qualify
His rigorous course; but, since he stands obdurate,
And that no lawful means can carry me
Out of his envy's reach, I do oppose 10
My patience to his fury; and am arm'd
To suffer, with a quietness of spirit,
The very tyranny and rage of his.
DUKE. Go one, and call the Jew into the court.
SALERIO. He is ready at the door: he comes, my lord. 15

[*Enter* SHYLOCK.]

DUKE. Make room, and let him stand before our face—
Shylock, the world thinks, and I think so too,
That thou but lead'st this fashion of thy malice
To the last hour of act; and then 'tis thought
Thou'lt show thy mercy and remorse, more strange 20
Than is thy strange apparent cruelty;
And where thou now exact'st the penalty,
Which is a pound of this poor merchant's flesh,
Thou wilt not only loose the forfeiture,
But, touch'd with human gentleness and love, 25
Forgive a moiety of the principal;
Glancing an eye of pity on his losses,
That have of late so huddled on his back,
Enow to press a royal merchant down,

9. THAT—Since. 10. ENVY'S—Hatred's.
18. LEAD'ST THIS FASHION—That you only keep up this show of malice until the last minute when you will relent.
24. LOOSE—Release, forego. 26. MOIETY—Part.

And pluck commiseration of his state 30
From brassy bosoms and rough hearts of flint,
From stubborn Turks and Tartars, never train'd
To offices of tender courtesy.
We all expect a gentle answer, Jew.

SHYLOCK. I have possess'd your Grace of what I purpose; 35
And by our holy Sabbath have I sworn
To have the due and forfeit of my bond:
If you deny it, let the danger light
Upon your charter and your city's freedom.
You'll ask me why I rather choose to have 40
A weight of carrion-flesh than to receive
Three thousand ducats: I'll not answer that:
But, say, it is my humor; is it answer'd?
What if my house be troubl'd with a rat,
And I be pleas'd to give ten thousand ducats 45
To have it ban'd! What, are you answer'd yet?
Some men there are love not a gaping pig;
Some that are mad if they behold a cat;
And others, when the bag-pipe sings i' the nose.
Masters of passion sway it to the mood 50
Of what it likes or loathes. Now, for your answer.
As there is no firm reason to be render'd,
Why he cannot abide a gaping pig;
Why he, a harmless necessary cat;
Why he, a woolen bag-pipe, but of force 55
Must yield to such inevitable shame
As to offend, himself being offended;
So can I give no reason, nor I will not,
More than a lodg'd hate and a certain loathing
I bear Antonio, that I follow thus 60
A losing suit against him. Are you answer'd?

30. COMMISERATION OF—Sympathy for.
33. OFFICES—Services.
35. POSSESS'D—Fully informed.
38. DANGER—Consequences.
43. HUMOR—Whim.
46. BAN'D (bān'd)—Poisoned. The point of Shylock's questions is that his reason for wanting the pound of flesh is his own business, and no one else's.
47. GAPING PIG—A whole roast pig served at table, its mouth held open by an apple or a lemon.
49. SINGS I' THE NOSE—An allusion to the drone of the pipes.
50. MASTERS OF PASSION SWAY—The things that control feeling bend it—that is, bend feeling.
53. HE—One man. "He" in the following lines refers to a second and a third man.
61. LOSING SUIT—Shylock will lose three thousand ducats if he insists on the forfeiture—that is, on the penalty of a pound of flesh.

BASSANIO. This is no answer, thou unfeeling man,
To excuse the current of thy cruelty.
SHYLOCK. I am not bound to please thee with my answer.
BASSANIO. Do all men kill the things they do not love? 65
SHYLOCK. Hates any man the thing he would not kill?
BASSANIO. Every offense is not a hate at first.
SHYLOCK. What, wouldst thou have a serpent sting thee twice?
ANTONIO. I pray you, think you question with the Jew.
You may as well go stand upon the beach, 70
And bid the main flood bate his usual height;
You may as well use question with the wolf,
Why he hath made the ewe bleat for the lamb;
You may as well forbid the mountain pines
To wag their high tops, and to make no noise, 75
When they are fretted with the gusts of heaven;
You may as well do anything most hard,
As seek to soften that—than which what's harder?—
His Jewish heart: therefore, I do beseech you,
Make no more offers, use no further means; 80
But with all brief and plain conveniency
Let me have judgment, and the Jew his will.
BASSANIO. For thy three thousand ducats here is six.
SHYLOCK. If every ducat in six thousand ducats
Were in six parts, and every part a ducat, 85
I would not draw them; I would have my bond.
DUKE. How shalt thou hope for mercy, rendering none?
SHYLOCK. What judgment shall I dread, doing no wrong?
You have among you many a purchas'd slave,
Which, like your asses and your dogs and mules, 90
You use in abject and in slavish parts,
Because you bought them: shall I say to you,
Let them be free, marry them to your heirs?
Why sweat they under burthens? let their beds
Be made as soft as yours, and let their palates 95
Be season'd with such viands? You will answer,
"The slaves are ours."—So do I answer you:
The pound of flesh, which I demand of him,

63. EXCUSE THE CURRENT—Justify the course.
69. THINK YOU QUESTION—Remember you are arguing with the Jew.
71. MAIN FLOOD BATE—The ocean tide lower . . .
81. BRIEF AND PLAIN COVENIENCY—With all the speed and straightforward procedure which the law permits.
91. IN ABJECT AND SLAVISH PARTS—In manual and degrading duties.

Is dearly bought; 'tis mine, and I will have it.
If you deny me, fie upon your law! 100
There is no force in the decrees of Venice.
I stand for judgment: answer; shall I have it?

DUKE. Upon my power I may dismiss this court
Unless Bellario, a learned doctor,
Whom I have sent for to determine this, 105
Come here today.

SALERIO. My lord, here stays without
A messenger with letters from the doctor,
New come from Padua.

DUKE. Bring us the letters; call the messenger.

BASSANIO. Good cheer, Antonio! What, man, courage yet! 110
The Jew shall have my flesh, blood, bones, and all,
Ere thou shalt lose for me one drop of blood.

ANTONIO. I am a tainted wether of the flock,
Meetest for death: the weakest kind of fruit
Drops earliest to the ground; and so let me: 115
You cannot better be employ'd, Bassanio,
Than to live still, and write mine epitaph.

[*Enter* NERISSA, *dressed like a lawyer's clerk.*]

DUKE. Came you from Padua, from Bellario?

NERISSA. From both, my lord. Bellario greets your Grace. [*Presents a letter.*]

BASSANIO. Why dost thou whet thy knife so earnestly? 120

SHYLOCK. To cut the forfeiture from that bankrupt there.

GRATIANO. Not on thy sole, but on thy soul, harsh Jew,
Thou mak'st thy knife keen; but no metal can,
No, not the hangman's ax, bear half the keenness
Of thy sharp envy. Can no prayers pierce thee? 125

SHYLOCK. No, none that thou has wit enough to make.

GRATIANO. O, be thou damn'd, inexecrable dog!
And for thy life let justice be accus'd.
Thou almost mak'st me waver in my faith,
To hold opinion with Pythagoras, 130
That souls of animals infuse themselves
Into the trunks of men: thy currish spirit

104. DOCTOR—Doctor of laws, lawyer.
113–114. TAINTED WETHER . . . MEETEST FOR DEATH—An infected sheep . . . most fit for death.
127. INEXECRABLE—That cannot be cursed enough. 128. FOR THY LIFE—For letting you live.
130. PYTHAGORAS—A Greek philosopher who taught that souls at death pass into other bodies.
132. TRUNKS—Bodies.

Govern'd a wolf, who, hang'd for human slaughter,
Even from the gallows did his fell soul fleet,
And, whilst thou lay'st in thy unhallow'd dam, 135
Infus'd itself in thee; for thy desires
Are wolfish, bloody, starv'd, and ravenous.

SHYLOCK. Till thou canst rail the seal from off my bond,
Thou but offend'st thy lungs to speak so loud:
Repair thy wit, good youth, or it will fall 140
To cureless ruin. I stand here for law.

DUKE. This letter from Bellario doth commend
A young and learned doctor to our court.—
Where is he?

NERISSA. He attendeth here hard by,
To know your answer, whether you'll admit him. 145

DUKE. With all my heart. —Some three or four of you
Go give him courteous conduct to this place.—
Meantime the court shall hear Bellario's letter.

CLERK. [*Reads.*] Your Grace shall understand, that at the receipt of your letter I am very sick: but in the instant that your messenger came, in 150 loving visitation was with me a young doctor of Rome; his name is Balthasar. I acquainted him with the cause in controversy between the Jew and Antonio the merchant: we turn'd o'er many books together: he is furnish'd with my opinion; which, better'd with his own learning,—the greatness whereof I cannot enough commend,—comes with him, 155 at my importunity, to fill up your Grace's request in my stead. I beseech you, let his lack of years be no impediment to let him lack a reverend estimation; for I never knew so young a body with so old a head. I leave him to your gracious acceptance, whose trial shall better publish his commendation. 160

DUKE. You hear the learn'd Bellario, what he writes:
And here, I take it, is the doctor come.—

[*Enter* PORTIA, *dressed like a doctor of laws.*]

Give me your hand. Came you from old Bellario?

PORTIA. I did, my lord.

DUKE. You are welcome: take your place.

134. FELL SOUL FLEET—Cruel soul flit.
135. UNHALLOW'D DAM—Unholy mother.
138. RAIL—Insult.
157. LET HIS LACK OF YEARS—Let his youth not stand in the way of enjoying your highest respect.
159. WHOSE TRIAL—If you put him to the test, the result will justify his praise better than any words of mine.

Are you acquainted with the difference 165
That holds this present question in the court?

PORTIA. I am informed throughly of the cause.
Which is the merchant here, and which the Jew?

DUKE. Antonio and old Shylock, both stand forth.

PORTIA. Is your name Shylock?

SHYLOCK. Shylock is my name. 170

PORTIA. Of a strange nature is the suit you follow;
Yet in such rule, that the Venetian law
Cannot impugn you as you do proceed.—
You stand within his danger, do you not?

ANTONIO. Ay, so he says.

PORTIA. Do you confess the bond? 175

ANTONIO. I do.

PORTIA. Then must the Jew be merciful.

SHYLOCK. On what compulsion must I? tell me that.

PORTIA. The quality of mercy is not strain'd:
It droppeth as the gentle rain from heaven
Upon the place beneath: it is twice blest; 180
It blesseth him that gives, and him that takes:
'Tis mightiest in the mightiest: it becomes
The throned monarch better than his crown;
His scepter shows the force of temporal power,
The attribute to awe and majesty, 185
Wherein doth sit the dread and fear of kings;
But mercy is above the sceptered sway;
It is enthroned in the hearts of kings,
It is an attribute to God himself;
And earthly power doth then show likest God's 190
When mercy seasons justice. Therefore, Jew,

167. THROUGHLY—Thoroughly.
172. IN SUCH RULE—Your suit comes so under the rules of law that . . .
173. IMPUGN—Call in question, attack.
176. MUST—Not used in the sense that the law compels him to be merciful. Portia means that nothing can save Antonio unless Shylock exercises mercy. In the next line you will see that Shylock has misunderstood what Portia means by "must."
178. THE QUALITY OF MERCY IS NOT STRAIN'D—Mercy cannot be forced. There is no power which can make a man merciful if he is not naturally so, just as there is no power which can make a man brave if he is naturally a coward.
180. TWICE BLEST—Doubly full of blessings.
182. MIGHTIEST IN THE MIGHTIEST—Mercy is greatest when displayed by the strong and powerful.
187. ABOVE THE SCEPTERED SWAY—Mercy is a personal quality, not a power that comes with authority.
191. SEASONS—Tempers, moderates.

Though justice be thy plea, consider this,—
That, in the course of justice, none of us
Should see salvation: we do pray for mercy;
And that same prayer doth teach us all to render 195
The deeds of mercy. I have spoke thus much
To mitigate the justice of thy plea;
Which if thou follow, this strict court of Venice
Must needs give sentence 'gainst the merchant there.

SHYLOCK. My deeds upon my head! I crave the law, 200
The penalty and forfeit of my bond.

PORTIA. Is he not able to discharge the money?

BASSANIO. Yes, here I tender it for him in the court;
Yea, twice the sum: if that will not suffice,
I will be bound to pay it ten times o'er, 205
On forfeit of my hands, my head, my heart:
If this will not suffice, it must appear
That malice bears down truth. And I beseech you,
Wrest once the law to your authority:
To do a great right, do a little wrong; 210
And curb this cruel devil of his will.

PORTIA. It must not be; there is no power in Venice
Can alter a decree established:
'Twill be recorded for a precedent;
And many an error, by the same example, 215
Will rush into the state. It cannot be.

SHYLOCK. A Daniel come to judgment! yea, a Daniel!
O wise young judge, how I do honor thee!

PORTIA. I pray you, let me look upon the bond.

SHYLOCK. Here 'tis, most reverend doctor; here it is. 220

PORTIA. Shylock, there's thrice thy money offer'd thee.

SHYLOCK. An oath, an oath, I have an oath in heaven:
Shall I lay perjury upon my soul?
No, not for Venice.

193. IN THE COURSE OF JUSTICE—If God judged us only in view of what we deserve, without recourse to His divine mercy.

195. THAT SAME PRAYER—The Lord's Prayer in which we ask: And forgive us our debts, as we forgive our debtors.

197. TO MITIGATE—To soften.

200. MY DEEDS UPON MY HEAD—I will answer for the consequences.

203. TENDER—Offer.

208. MALICE BEARS DOWN TRUTH—Wickedness is, after all, greater than honesty.

209. WREST ONCE—Use your authority this once to nullify or circumvent the law. Bassanio urges that a good end justifies evil means.

217. DANIEL—The reference is to the great wisdom shown by the youthful prophet Daniel in the Old Testament, in deciding the case between Susanna and the Elders.

217. COME TO JUDGMENT—Come to give judgment.

PORTIA. Why, this bond is forfeit;
And lawfully by this the Jew may claim 225
A pound of flesh, to be by him cut off
Nearest the merchant's heart. —Be merciful;
Take thrice thy money; bid me tear the bond.
SHYLOCK. When it is paid according to the tenor.
It doth appear you are a worthy judge; 230
You know the law, your exposition
Hath been most sound: I charge you by the law,
Whereof you are a well-deserving pillar,
Proceed to judgment. By my soul I swear
There is no power in the tongue of man 235
To alter me: I stay here on my bond.
ANTONIO. Most heartily I do beseech the court
To give the judgment.
PORTIA. Why then, thus it is:
You must prepare your bosom for his knife.
SHYLOCK. O noble judge! O excellent young man! 240
PORTIA. For the intent and purpose of the law
Hath full relation to the penalty,
Which here appeareth due upon the bond.
SHYLOCK. 'Tis very true. O wise and upright judge!
How much more elder art thou than thy looks! 245
PORTIA. Therefore lay bare your bosom.
SHYLOCK. Ay, his breast:
So says the bond:—doth it not, noble judge?
Nearest his heart: those are the very words.
PORTIA. It is so. Are there balance here to weigh
The flesh? 250
SHYLOCK. I have them ready.
PORTIA. Have by some surgeon, Shylock, on your charge,
To stop his wounds, lest he do bleed to death.
SHYLOCK. Is it so nominated in the bond?
PORTIA. It is not so express'd; but what of that? 255
'T were good you do so much for charity.
SHYLOCK. I cannot find it; 'tis not in the bond.
PORTIA. Come, merchant, have you anything to say?

229. TENOR—Meaning, the express terms of the bond.
242. HATH FULL RELATION—Fully applies to any penalty, even to that mentioned in the present bond.
249. BALANCE—Scales.
252. BY . . . ON YOUR CHARGE—Near by . . . at your expense.
254. NOMINATED—Named, specified.

ANTONIO. But little: I am arm'd and well prepar'd.
Give me your hand, Bassanio: fare you well! 260
Grieve not that I am fall'n to this for you;
For herein Fortune shows herself more kind
Than is her custom: it is still her use
To let the wretched man outlive his wealth,
To view with hollow eye and wrinkled brow 265
An age of poverty; from which lingering penance
Of such a misery doth she cut me off.
Commend me to your honorable wife:
Tell her the process of Antonio's end;
Say how I lov'd you, speak me fair in death; 270
And, when the tale is told, bid her be judge
Whether Bassanio had not once a love.
Repent not you that you shall lose your friend,
And he repents not that he pays your debt;
For, if the Jew do cut but deep enough, 275
I'll pay it instantly with all my heart.

BASSANIO. Antonio, I am married to a wife
Which is as dear to me as life itself;
But life itself, my wife, and all the world,
Are not with me esteem'd above thy life: 280
I would lose all, ay, sacrifice them all
Here to this devil, to deliver you.

PORTIA. Your wife would give you little thanks for that,
If she were by to hear you make the offer.

GRATIANO. I have a wife, whom, I protest, I love: 285
I would she were in heaven, so she could
Entreat some power to change this currish Jew.

NERISSA. 'Tis well you offer it behind her back;
The wish would make else an unquiet house.

SHYLOCK. [*Aside.*] These be the Christian husbands! I have a daughter; 290
Would any of the stock of Barrabas
Had been her husband rather than a Christian!
[*Aloud.*] We trifle time: I pray thee, pursue sentence.

PORTIA. A pound of that same merchant's flesh is thine:
The court awards it, and the law doth give it. 295

SHYLOCK. Most rightful judge!

263. STILL HER USE—Ever her custom.
269. PROCESS—Story.
270. SPEAK ME FAIR—Speak well of me when I am dead.
272. A LOVE—A friend.
291. BARRABAS—The murderer whom Pilate released instead of Our Lord.

PORTIA. And you must cut this flesh from off his breast:
The law allows it, and the court awards it.
SHYLOCK. Most learned judge! A sentence! Come, prepare!
PORTIA. Tarry a little; there is something else. 300
This bond doth give thee here no jot of blood;
The words expressly are, a pound of flesh:
Take then thy bond, take thou thy pound of flesh;
But, in the cutting it, if thou dost shed
One drop of Christian blood, thy lands and goods 305
Are, by the laws of Venice, confiscate
Unto the state of Venice.
GRATIANO. O upright judge! Mark, Jew: O learned judge!
SHYLOCK. Is that the law?
PORTIA. Thyself shalt see the act:
For, as thou urgest justice, be assur'd 310
Thou shalt have justice, more than thou desirest.
GRATIANO. O learned judge!—Mark, Jew: a learned judge!
SHYLOCK. I take this offer, then;—pay the bond thrice,
And let the Christian go.
BASSANIO. Here is the money.
PORTIA. Soft! 315
The Jew shall have all justice; soft! no haste:
He shall have nothing but the penalty.
GRATIANO. O Jew! an upright judge, a learned judge!
PORTIA. Therefore prepare thee to cut off the flesh.
Shed thou no blood; nor cut thou less nor more 320
But just a pound of flesh: if thou cut'st more
Or less than a just pound,—be it but so much
As makes it light or heavy in the substance,
Or the division of the twentieth part
Of one poor scruple, nay, if the scale do turn 325
But in the estimation of a hair,—
Thou diest, and all thy goods are confiscate.
GRATIANO. A second Daniel, a Daniel, Jew!
Now, infidel, I have thee on the hip.
PORTIA. Why doth the Jew pause? take thy forfeiture. 330
SHYLOCK. Give me my principal, and let me go.
BASSANIO. I have it ready for thee; here it is.

315. SOFT!—Wait, don't be in a hurry.
325. SCRUPLE—One twenty-fourth part of an ounce.
331. LET ME GO—Shylock says this after a brief, violent struggle between his hatred and his prudence. Had hatred won out and had Shylock insisted on the pound of flesh at peril of his life, the play would have turned out a tragedy, not a comedy.

PORTIA. He hath refus'd it in the open court:
He shall have merely justice and his bond.
GRATIANO. A Daniel, still say I, a second Daniel!— 335
I thank thee, Jew, for teaching me that word.
SHYLOCK. Shall I not have barely my principal?
PORTIA. Thou shalt have nothing but the forfeiture,
To be so taken at thy peril, Jew.
SHYLOCK. Why, then the devil give him good of it! 340
I'll stay no longer question.
PORTIA. Tarry, Jew:
The law hath yet another hold on you.
It is enacted in the laws of Venice,
If it be proved against an alien
That by direct or indirect attempts 345
He seek the life of any citizen,
The party 'gainst the which he doth contrive
Shall seize one half his goods; the other half
Comes to the privy coffer of the state;

341. STAY NO LONGER QUESTION—Wait for no further argument.
348. SEIZE—Take by law.
349. PRIVY COFFER—Treasury.

And the offender's life lies in the mercy 350
Of the Duke only, 'gainst all other voice.
In which predicament, I say, thou stand'st;
For it appears, by manifest proceeding,
That indirectly, and directly too,
Thou hast contriv'd against the very life 355
Of the defendant; and thou hast incurr'd
The danger formerly by me rehears'd.
Down, therefore, and beg mercy of the Duke.

GRATIANO. Beg that thou mayst have leave to hang thyself:
And yet, thy wealth being forfeit to the state, 360
Thou has not left the value of a cord;
Therefore thou must be hang'd at the state's charge.

DUKE. That thou shalt see the difference of our spirits,
I pardon thee thy life before thou ask it:
For half thy wealth, it is Antonio's; 365
The other half comes to the general state,
Which humbleness may drive unto a fine.

PORTIA. Ay, for the state; not for Antonio.

SHYLOCK. Nay, take my life and all; pardon not that;
You take my house, when you do take the prop 370
That doth sustain my house; you take my life,
When you do take the means whereby I live.

PORTIA. What mercy can you render him, Antonio?

GRATIANO. A halter gratis; nothing else, for God's sake.

ANTONIO. So please my lord the Duke and all the court 375
To quit the fine for one half of his goods,
I am content; so he will let me have
The other half in use, to render it,
Upon his death, unto the gentleman
That lately stole his daughter: 380
Two things provided more—that, for this favor,
He presently become a Christian;
The other, that he do record a gift,
Here in the court, of all he dies possess'd,
Unto his son Lorenzo and his daughter. 385

351. 'GAINST ALL OTHER VOICE—Against any appeal from the Duke's final decision.
357. FORMERLY . . . REHEARS'D—Just now . . . described.
367. WHICH HUMBLENESS—Which submission on your part may lead me to change to a fine.
368. FOR THE STATE—That is, the Duke may waive the state's share of Shylock's wealth, but not Antonio's.
376. QUIT—Release, remit.
378. IN USE—In trust. Shylock must sign over to Antonio one-half of his wealth, but will retain its use until his death, when the money will go outright to Lorenzo and Jessica.

DUKE. He shall do this; or else I do recant
The pardon that I late pronounced here.

PORTIA. Art thou contented, Jew? what dost thou say?

SHYLOCK. I am content.

PORTIA. Clerk, draw a deed of gift.

SHYLOCK. I pray you, give me leave to go from hence; 390
I am not well: send the deed after me,
And I will sign it.

DUKE. Get thee gone, but do it.

GRATIANO. In christening shalt thou have two godfathers:
Had I been judge, thou shouldst have had ten more,
To bring thee to the gallows, not the font. [*Exit* SHYLOCK.]

DUKE. Sir, I entreat you home with me to dinner. 396

PORTIA. I humbly do desire your Grace of pardon:
I must away this night toward Padua,
And it is meet I presently set forth.

DUKE. I am sorry that your leisure serves you not. 400
Antonio, gratify this gentleman:
For, in my mind, you are much bound to him.

[*Exeunt the* DUKE *and his train.*]

BASSANIO. Most worthy gentleman, I and my friend
Have by your wisdom been this day acquitted
Of grievous penalties; in lieu whereof, 405
Three thousand ducats, due unto the Jew,
We freely cope your courteous pains withal.

ANTONIO. And stand indebted, over and above,
In love and service to you evermore.

PORTIA. He is well paid that is well satisfied; 410
And I, delivering you, am satisfied,
And therein do account myself well paid:
My mind was never yet more mercenary.
I pray you, know me when we meet again:
I wish you well, and so I take my leave. 415

BASSANIO. Dear sir, of force I must attempt you further:
Take some remembrance of us, as a tribute,
Not as a fee: grant me two things, I pray you,

386. RECANT—Withdraw.
393. IN CHRISTENING—At baptism.
394. TEN MORE—Making in all twelve jurymen for Shylock's trial and condemnation.
401. GRATIFY—Reward.
405. IN LIEU WHEREOF—In return for which.
407. COPE—Repay.
413. MY MIND—I had no intention of asking other pay than setting you free.
416. ATTEMPT—Tempt.

Not to deny me, and to pardon me.
PORTIA. You press me far, and therefore I will yield.— 420
[*To* ANTONIO.] Give me your gloves, I'll wear them for your sake;—
[*To* BASSANIO.] And, for your love, I'll take this ring from you.
Do not draw back your hand; I'll take no more;
And you in love shall not deny me this.
BASSANIO. This ring, good sir,—alas, it is a trifle! 425
I will not shame myself to give you this.
PORTIA. I will have nothing else but only this;
And now methinks I have a mind to it.
BASSANIO. There's more depends on this than on the value.
The dearest ring in Venice will I give you, 430
And find it out by proclamation:
Only for this, I pray you, pardon me.
PORTIA. I see, sir, you are liberal in offers:
You taught me first to beg; and now methinks
You teach me how a beggar should be answer'd. 435
BASSANIO. Good sir, this ring was given me by my wife;
And when she put it on, she made me vow
That I should neither sell nor give nor lose it.
PORTIA. That 'scuse serves many men to save their gifts.
And if your wife be not a mad-woman, 440
And know how well I have deserv'd this ring,
She would not hold out enemy for ever
For giving it to me. Well, peace be with you!
[*Exeunt* PORTIA *and* NERISSA.]
ANTONIO. My Lord Bassanio, let him have the ring:
Let his deservings, and my love withal, 445
Be valued 'gainst your wife's commandment.
BASSANIO. Go, Gratiano, run and overtake him;
Give him the ring, and bring him, if thou canst,
Unto Antonio's house. Away! make haste.— [*Exit* GRATIANO.]
Come, you and I will thither presently; 450
And in the morning early will we both
Fly toward Belmont: come, Antonio. [*Exeunt.*]

419. PARDON ME—Pardon my insistence.
428. MIND TO IT—A real desire for the ring itself.

SCENE 2. *The same. A street.*

It is just after the trial. Still flushed with the courtroom victory and still in clerk's costume, Portia stands outside the courthouse door confer-

ring with Nerissa. In her hand is Shylock's deed of gift drawn up by the court clerk as Portia had directed.

[*Enter* PORTIA *and* NERISSA.]

PORTIA. Inquire the Jew's house out, give him this deed,
And let him sign it: we'll away tonight,
And be a day before our husbands home.
This deed will be well welcome to Lorenzo.

[*Enter* GRATIANO.]

GRATIANO. Fair sir, you are well o'erta'en: 5
My Lord Bassanio, upon more advice,
Hath sent you here this ring, and doth entreat
Your company at dinner.
PORTIA. That cannot be:
His ring I do accept most thankfully;
And so, I pray you, tell him: furthermore, 10
I pray you, show my youth old Shylock's house.
GRATIANO. That will I do.
NERISSA. Sir, I would speak with you.—
[*Aside to* PORTIA.] I'll see if I can get my husband's ring,
Which I did make him swear to keep for ever.
PORTIA. [*Aside to* NERISSA.] Thou mayst, I warrant. We shall have old swearing
That they did give the rings away to men; 16
But we'll outface them, and outswear them too.
Away! make haste: thou know'st where I will tarry.
NERISSA. Come, good sir; will you show me to this house? [*Exeunt.*]

5. WELL O'ERTA'EN—I am lucky to have caught up with you.
11. YOUTH—Young attendant (Nerissa).
15. OLD SWEARING—Elizabethan slang for *great, hard*—as in our "a high old time."
17. OUTFACE—Outwit, get the better of them.

FOR DISCUSSION

ACT IV, SCENE 1 (*pages* 525–539)

1. The opposing characters now face in final conflict, and it seems Antonio is doomed to utter defeat. What factors are against him? As Shylock comes on stage, notice how his personality now dominates the play and gives its action a terrible strength. What way out, with honor, does the Duke first offer Shylock? What are Shylock's reasons for demanding the exact nature of the bond? Throughout the trial scene, we note that Antonio is despondent. Is this out of character, or has Shakespeare already prepared us for such a pass? Discuss.

2. At Portia's entrance, the pound-of-flesh story rises swiftly to its climax. Thus far, Shylock's will has been locked against all argument, insult, and threats. Now what plea does Portia advance? What

very familiar prayer is invoked at the close of her speech? Does Shylock's answer recall a similar tragic instance in the history of his people? What is Portia's response when Bassanio urges that a good end—Antonio's release—justifies an evil means? On the other hand, can Shylock rightly urge that heaven supports his evil oath?

3. By what brilliant legal technicality does Portia win Antonio's freedom? Does it violate actual justice? On what score is Shylock no longer the accuser but the accused? Observing the letter of the law, do Portia and the Duke also observe the dictates of Christian charity? In what respect does Antonio grievously violate a basic human right of Shylock? In what lies the tragedy of Shylock's life?

4. At the scene's end, how does Bassanio unwittingly invite future grief?

ACT IV, SCENE 2 (*pages* 539–540)

What are the details of the deed of gift which Shylock must sign? Why must Portia and Nerissa precede their husbands to Belmont?

ACT V

SCENE 1. *Belmont. Avenue to* PORTIA'S *house.*

It is the evening of the following day, nearing midnight. Stars are out, looking big as oranges. The moon, like a silver sail, rides high through wispy clouds. The young lovers, Lorenzo and Jessica, are enjoying the evening in Portia's garden, while they await the return of their friends.

[*Enter* LORENZO *and* JESSICA.]

LORENZO. The moon shines bright. In such a night as this
When the sweet wind did gently kiss the trees,
And they did make no noise—in such a night
Troilus methinks mounted the Trojan walls,
And sigh'd his soul toward the Grecian tents, 5
Where Cressid lay that night.

JESSICA. In such a night

4. TROILUS—The faithful lover of Chaucer's poem of that name—the youngest son of Priam, king of Troy. Cressida, his sweetheart, was given to the Greeks in exchange for a Trojan captive.

Did Thisbe fearfully o'ertrip the dew,
And saw the lion's shadow ere himself,
And ran dismay'd away.

LORENZO. In such a night
Stood Dido with a willow in her hand 10
Upon the wild sea banks, and waft her love
To come again to Carthage.

JESSICA. In such a night
Medea gather'd the enchanted herbs
That did renew old Æson.

LORENZO. In such a night
Did Jessica steal from the wealthy Jew, 15

7. THISBE—A Babylonian maiden, beloved by Pyramus, whom she went to meet one night. Arriving beforehand, Thisbe was frightened away by a lioness that bloodied her scarf, which she dropped in flight. When Pyramus came on the scene, he saw the scarf and supposed her dead. Thereupon he killed himself for grief, and Thisbe, discovering her dead lover, took her own life.

10. DIDO—Queen of ancient Carthage and lover of Trojan Æneas. He deserted her at the command of the gods, fleeing away by ship at night in order to found the city of Rome.

10. WILLOW—The sign of grief and forsaken love.

11. WAFT—Waved.

13. MEDEA (mē·dē'ȧ)—Daughter of the King of Colchis and an enchantress, by whose aid Jason secured the Golden Fleece. Medea fled to Greece with Jason and, according to legend, restored Jason's father to youthfulness by the use of magic herbs gathered by moonlight.

15. STEAL—Steal away.

And with an unthrift love did run from Venice
As far as Belmont.

JESSICA. In such a night
Did young Lorenzo swear he lov'd her well,
Stealing her soul with many vows of faith,
And ne'er a true one.

LORENZO. In such a night 20
Did pretty Jessica, like a little shrew,
Slander her love, and he forgave it her.

JESSICA. I would out-night you, did nobody come:
But, hark, I hear the footing of a man.

[*Enter* STEPHANO.]

LORENZO. Who comes so fast in silence of the night? 25

STEPHANO. A friend.

LORENZO. A friend! what friend? your name, I pray you, friend?

STEPHANO. Stephano is my name; and I bring word
My mistress will before the break of day
Be here at Belmont: she doth stray about 30
By holy crosses, where she kneels and prays
For happy wedlock hours.

LORENZO. Who comes with her?

STEPHANO. None but a holy hermit and her maid.
I pray you, is my master yet return'd?

LORENZO. He is not, nor we have not heard from him.— 35
But go we in, I pray thee, Jessica,
And ceremoniously let us prepare
Some welcome for the mistress of the house.

[*Enter* LAUNCELOT.]

LAUNCELOT. Sola, sola! wo, ha, ho! sola, sola!

LORENZO. Who calls? 40

LAUNCELOT. Sola! did you see Master Lorenzo? Master Lorenzo, sola, sola!

LORENZO. Leave hollaing, man: here.

LAUNCELOT. Sola! where? where?

LORENZO. Here.

16. UNTHRIFT LOVE—Poor lover (Lorenzo).
21. SHREW—A scolding woman.
24. FOOTING—Footsteps.
31. BY HOLY CROSSES—By wayside shrines.
33. HOLY HERMIT—A friar.
39. SOLA SOLA!—Accented on the last syllable. Launcelot pretends to be the mail courier and comes in as though blowing the post horn carried by the courier around his neck.

LAUNCELOT. Tell him there's a post come from my master, with his horn full of good news: my master will be here ere morning. 45 [*Exit.*]

LORENZO. Sweet soul, let's in, and there expect their coming.
And yet no matter: why should we go in?—
My friend Stephano, signify, I pray you,
Within the house, your mistress is at hand. 50
And bring your music forth into the air. [*Exit* STEPHANO.]
How sweet the moonlight sleeps upon this bank!
Here will we sit, and let the sounds of music
Creep in our ears: soft stillness and the night
Become the touches of sweet harmony. 55
Sit, Jessica. Look how the floor of heaven
Is thick inlaid with patens of bright gold:
There's not the smallest orb which thou behold'st
But in his motion like an angel sings,
Still quiring to the young-eyed cherubims: 60
Such harmony is in immortal souls;
But, whilst this muddy vesture of decay
Doth grossly close it in, we cannot hear it.—

[*Enter* MUSICIANS.]

Come, ho, and wake Diana with a hymn!
With sweetest touches pierce your mistress' ear, 65
And draw her home with music. [*Music.*]

JESSICA. I am never merry when I hear sweet music.

LORENZO. The reason is, your spirits are attentive:
For do but note a wild and wanton herd,
Or race of youthful and unhandled colts, 70
Fetching mad bounds, bellowing and neighing loud,
Which is the hot condition of their blood;
If they but hear perchance a trumpet sound,
Or any air of music touch their ears,

45. POST—Messenger. Compare our "postman."
49. SIGNIFY—Make known.
55. BECOME THE TOUCHES—Befit the strains.
57. PATENS—Little plates—the stars. Compare with the *paten* used by the priest in celebrating Mass.
58. ORB—Star.
59. LIKE AN ANGEL SINGS—In ancient astronomy, the stars were thought to revolve about the earth, their majestic march across the skies making a kind of harmony of motion comparable to the cadences of music.
60. STILL QUIRING—Always singing. Compare our *choir*.
62. THIS MUDDY VESTURE—The body, which comes of dust.
64. DIANA—The moon, so named for Diana the moon goddess. Apparently, a wandering cloud has for the moment obscured the moon.
70. UNHANDLED—Unbroken.

You shall perceive them make a mutual stand, 75
Their savage eyes turn'd to a modest gaze,
By the sweet power of music: therefore the poet
Did feign that Orpheus drew trees, stones, and floods;
Since nought so stockish, hard, and full of rage,
But music for the time doth change his nature. 80
The man that hath no music in himself,
Nor is not mov'd with concord of sweet sounds,
Is fit for treasons, stratagems, and spoils;
The motions of his spirit are dull as night,
And his affections dark as Erebus: 85
Let no such man be trusted. Mark the music.

[*Enter* PORTIA *and* NERISSA.]

PORTIA. That light we see is burning in my hall.
How far that little candle throws his beams!
So shines a good deed in a naughty world.
NERISSA. When the moon shone, we did not see the candle. 90
PORTIA. So doth the greater glory dim the less:
A substitute shines brightly as a king,
Until a king be by; and then his state
Empties itself, as doth an inland brook
Into the main of waters. Music! hark! 95
NERISSA. It is your music, madam, of the house.
PORTIA. Nothing is good, I see, without respect:
Methinks it sounds much sweeter than by day.
NERISSA. Silence bestows that virtue on it, madam.
PORTIA. The crow doth sing as sweetly as the lark, 100
When neither is attended; and I think
The nightingale, if she should sing by day,
When every goose is cackling, would be thought
No better a musician than the wren.
How many things by season season'd are 105

78. FEIGN—Relate in fable.
78. ORPHEUS—According to the story told by the poet Ovid, Orpheus invented the lyre and was so great a musician that he moved stones and trees with his melodies.
79. STOCKISH—Blocklike, unfeeling.
83. STRATAGEMS AND SPOILS—Cunning plots and robbery.
85. EREBUS—The lower world, Hades.
93. STATE—Dignity, majesty.
95. MAIN—Sea.
97. WITHOUT RESPECT—Without regard to other things. Portia means that everything gains by being given its proper surroundings. Thus the music that she hears sounds much sweeter in the quiet beauty of the moonlit night than it would by day.
105. BY SEASON SEASON'D ARE—By being rightly timed are made effective.

To their right praise and true perfection!—
Peace, ho! the moon sleeps with Endymion,
And would not be awak'd. [*Music ceases.*]

LORENZO. That is the voice,
Or I am much deceiv'd of Portia.

PORTIA. He knows me, as the blind man knows the cuckoo, 110
By the bad voice.

LORENZO. Dear lady, welcome home.

PORTIA. We have been praying for our husbands' welfare,
Which speed, we hope, the better for our words.
Are they return'd?

LORENZO. Madam, they are not yet;
But there is come a messenger before, 115
To signify their coming.

PORTIA. Go in, Nerissa;
Give orders to my servants that they take
No note at all of our being absent hence;—
Nor you, Lorenzo;—Jessica, nor you. [*A tucket sounds.*]

LORENZO. Your husband is at hand; I hear his trumpet: 120
We are no tell-tales, madam; fear you not.

PORTIA. This night methinks is but the daylight sick;
It looks a little paler; 'tis a day,
Such as the day when the sun is hid.

[*Enter* BASSANIO, ANTONIO, GRATIANO, *and their followers.*]

BASSANIO. We should hold day with the Antipodes, 125
If you would walk in absence of the sun.

PORTIA. Let me give light, but let me not be light;
For a light wife doth make a heavy husband,
And never be Bassanio so for me:
But God sort all! You are welcome home, my lord. 130

BASSANIO. I thank you, madam. Give welcome to my friend:
This is the man, this is Antonio,
To whom I am so infinitely bound.

PORTIA. You should in all sense be much bound to him,

107. ENDYMION—In Greek legend, a very beautiful youth whom Selene, one of the moon goddesses, loved and came to kiss as he lay sleeping. The expression "the moon sleeps with Endymion" is a poetic way of saying that the moon has set, or gone behind a cloud.

113. SPEED—Prosper.

125. HOLD DAY WITH THE ANTIPODES (ăn·tĭp′ô·dēz)—Have day at the same time as the other side of the world—that is, if Portia would walk out at night, she would turn night into day.

127. LIGHT—Another pun on the word *light* in the sense of "illumination" and of "frivolous."

130. GOD SORT ALL—God dispose all things!

134. IN ALL SENSE—On every account.

For, as I hear, he was much bound for you. 135
ANTONIO. No more than I am well acquitted of.
PORTIA. Sir, you are very welcome to our house:
It must appear in other ways than words,
Therefore I scant this breathing courtesy.
GRATIANO. [*To* NERISSA.] By yonder moon I swear you do me wrong; 140
In faith, I gave it to the judge's clerk.
PORTIA. A quarrel, ho, already! what's the matter?
GRATIANO. About a hoop of gold, a paltry ring
That she did give me; whose poesy was
For all the world like cutler's poetry 145
Upon a knife, "Love me, and leave me not."
NERISSA. What talk you of the poesy or the value?
You swore to me, when I did give it to you,
That you would wear it till your hour of death;
And that it should lie with you in your grave: 150
Though not for me, yet for your vehement oaths,
You should have been respective, and have kept it.
Gave it a judge's clerk! no, God's my judge,
The clerk will ne'er wear hair on 's face that had it.
GRATIANO. He will, and if he live to be a man. 155
NERISSA. Ay, if a woman live to be a man.
GRATIANO. Now, by this hand, I gave it to a youth,
A kind of boy; a little scrubbed boy,
No higher than thyself, the judge's clerk;
A prating boy, that begg'd it as a fee: 160
I could not for my heart deny it him.
PORTIA. You were to blame, I must be plain with you,
To part so slightly with your wife's first gift;
A thing stuck on with oaths upon your finger,
And so riveted with faith unto your flesh. 165
I gave my love a ring, and made him swear

136. ACQUITTED OF—Freed from.
139. SCANT . . . COURTESY—Cut short these courtesies which are made up of breath alone.
141. IT—The ring Nerissa got from Gratiano. Tongue in cheek, she has just now asked why the ring is absent from Gratiano's finger.
144. POESY—Inscription.
145. CUTLER'S POETRY—It was customary for cutlers to etch mottoes on the blades of knives. "Cutler's poetry" came to signify any sentimental love poetry, as in the present instance: "Love me and leave me not," where "leave" is equivalent to "lose" or "part with."
152. RESPECTIVE—Careful.
158. SCRUBBED—Stunted, undersized. Gratiano has no idea that the original little scrubbed boy is listening.
163. SLIGHTLY—Carelessly. This speech of Portia's is meant, of course, to "raise the waters" with Bassanio. Your imagination should have little trouble in picturing his mounting embarrassment.

Never to part with it; and here he stands:
I dare be sworn for him, he would not leave it,
Nor pluck it from his finger, for the wealth
That the world masters. Now, in faith, Gratiano, 170
You give your wife too unkind a cause of grief:
And 'twere to me, I should be mad at it.

BASSANIO. [*Aside.*] Why, I were best to cut my left hand off,
And swear I lost the ring defending it.

GRATIANO. My Lord Bassanio gave his ring away 175
Unto the judge that begg'd it, and indeed
Deserv'd it too; and then the boy, his clerk,
That took some pains in writing, he begg'd mine:
And neither man nor master would take aught
But the two rings.

PORTIA. What ring gave you, my lord? 180
Not that, I hope, which you receiv'd of me.

BASSANIO. If I could add a lie unto a fault,
I would deny it; but you see my finger
Hath not the ring upon it,—it is gone.

PORTIA. Even so void is your false heart of truth.

BASSANIO. Sweet Portia, 185
If you did know to whom I gave the ring,
If you did know for whom I gave the ring,
And would conceive for what I gave the ring,
And how unwillingly I left the ring,
When nought would be accepted but the ring, 190
You would abate the strength of your displeasure.

PORTIA. If you had known the virtue of the ring,
Or half her worthiness that gave the ring,
Or your own honor to contain the ring,
You would not then have parted with the ring. 195
What man is there so much unreasonable,
If you had pleas'd to have defended it
With any terms of zeal, wanted the modesty
To urge the thing held as a ceremony?
Nerissa teaches me what to believe: 200
I'll die for 't but some woman had the ring.

172. MAD AT IT—Insane with rage at it.
192. VIRTUE—Power (of the ring to hold Portia's love).
194. CONTAIN—Retain, keep.
198. WANTED THE MODESTY TO URGE—Would be so inconsiderate as to insist on having what you plainly regarded as a sacred token.

BASSANIO. No, by mine honor, madam, by my soul,
No woman had it, but a civil doctor,
Which did refuse three thousand ducats of me,
And begg'd the ring; the which I did deny him, 205
And suffer'd him to go displeas'd away;
Even he that did uphold the very life
Of my dear friend. What should I say, sweet lady?
I was enforc'd to send it after him:
I was beset with shame and courtesy; 210
My honor would not let ingratitude
So much besmear it. Pardon me, good lady;
For, by these blessed candles of the night,
Had you been there, I think you would have begg'd
The ring of me to give the worthy doctor. 215

ANTONIO. I am the unhappy subject of these quarrels.

PORTIA. Sir, grieve not you; you are welcome notwithstanding.

BASSANIO. Portia, forgive me this enforced wrong;
And, in the hearing of these many friends,
I swear to thee, even by thine own fair eyes, 220
Wherein I see myself,—

PORTIA. Mark you but that!
In both my eyes he doubly sees himself;
In each eye, one:—swear by your double self,
And there's an oath of credit.

BASSANIO. Nay, but hear me:
Pardon this fault, and by my soul I swear 225
I never more will break an oath with thee.

ANTONIO. I once did lend my body for his wealth;
Which, but for him that had your husband's ring,
Had quite miscarried: I dare be bound again,
My soul upon the forfeit, that your lord 230
Will never more break faith advisedly.

PORTIA. Then you shall be his surety. Give him this;
And bid him keep it better than the other.

ANTONIO. Here, Lord Bassanio; swear to keep this ring.

203. CIVIL DOCTOR—Doctor of civil law.
210. SHAME AND COURTESY—The shame of being discourteous.
213. CANDLES—The stars.
223. DOUBLE—False. Compare the phrases "two-faced" and "to double-cross."
224. OF CREDIT—To be believed. Said ironically.
227. WEALTH—Benefit.
228. WHICH—That is, Antonio's body.
229. QUITE MISCARRIED—Entirely perished, been lost.
231. ADVISEDLY—Deliberately.
232. SURETY—Guarantor.

BASSANIO. By heaven, it is the same I gave the doctor! 235
PORTIA. I had it of him. You are all amaz'd:
Here is a letter; read it at your leisure;
It comes from Padua, from Bellario:
There you shall find that Portia was the doctor;
Nerissa there her clerk: Lorenzo here 240
Shall witness I set forth as soon as you,
And even but now return'd; I have not yet
Enter'd my house.—Antonio, you are welcome;
And I have better news in store for you
Than you expect: unseal this letter soon; 245
There you shall find three of your argosies
Are richly come to harbor suddenly:
You shall not know by what strange accident
I chanced on this letter.
ANTONIO. I am dumb.
BASSANIO. Were you the doctor, and I knew you not? 250
ANTONIO. Sweet lady, you have given me life and living;
For here I read for certain that my ships
Are safely come to road.
PORTIA. How, now, Lorenzo!
My clerk hath some good comforts too for you.
NERISSA. Ay, and I'll give them him without a fee.— 255
There do I give to you and Jessica,
From the rich Jew, a special deed of gift,
After his death, of all he dies possess'd of.
LORENZO. Fair ladies, you drop manna in the way
Of starved people.
PORTIA. It is almost morning, 260
And yet I'm sure you are not satisfied
Of these events at full. Let us go in;
And charge us there upon inter'gatories,
And we will answer all things faithfully.
GRATIANO. Well, while I live I'll fear no other thing 265
So sore as keeping safe Nerissa's ring. [*Exeunt.*]

247. SUDDENLY—Unexpectedly.
253. ROAD—Harbor.
259. MANNA—A reference to the "manna" from heaven with which God fed the Israelites in the desert.
262. OF THESE EVENTS AT FULL—Concerning the full story of these events.
263. CHARGE US . . . UPON INTER'GATORIES—Ask us questions. Interrogatories were formal questions put to a defendant according to the legal procedure of the day.
265. FEAR—Worry about.

FOR DISCUSSION

ACT V, SCENE 1 (*pages* 541–550)

1. The drama of the trial over, the shadows of Venice and the somber, tragic figure of Shylock vanish from memory with the enchanting night scene at Belmont—a jewel in literature. Shakespeare "concludes" his play. Near the opening of the scene occurs one of the loveliest poetic passages in our language. What do the references to mythology add to the moonlight scene? What shows that Lorenzo is something of a philosopher? Quote the lines. How do you interpret Jessica's sad remark, "I am never merry when I hear sweet music"?

2. With the arrival of the two parties from Venice, one last commotion remains before the play glides to an end. How has Portia prepared for her return home? How do Bassanio and Gratiano try to defend themselves in regard to the rings? Are Portia and Nerissa enjoying their discomfiture? How does all this quarreling end? What good news ends the play? Is the ending satisfactory?

SHAKESPEARE'S VOCABULARY, RICH IN MEANING

You have discovered for yourself the variety, visual imagery, and emotional richness of Shakespeare's language. Many of the words we take for granted were fixed in our literature by Shakespeare. His phrases have greatly influenced our modern-day vocabulary. Scores of quotations —some, as you notice, from "The Merchant of Venice"—have become the common heritage of English-speaking peoples. On the other hand, you have recognized (doubtless it was your greatest stumbling-block in reading) that the English language has changed since Shakespeare's time: some of his words have passed out of use, while others no longer carry the meaning intended by Shakespeare.

Shakespeare's words and expressions divide into several groups.

A. *Elizabethan expressions.* You have met many phrases like "in sooth," "Hie thee," and "by my troth." An amusing trick is to introduce such expressions into your conversation. List all such expressions in any particular act, together with their meaning. Then try using them in your own sentences.

B. *Words with changed meanings.* All the following words will appear familiar to you. But notice what different meanings they had as used by Shakespeare in these lines from Act I, Scene 1:

line 17 *still* (always)
line 61 *prevented* (expected)
line 92 *conceit* (thought)
line 126 *rate* (manner)

What do the above words mean in modern usage? Go through another act of the play for words which had different meanings in Shakespeare's day. Put down both the old and modern meanings.

C. *Mythological allusions.* To sixteenth-century England, as earlier to Italy and the Continent, the Renaissance ("Rebirth of Learning") brought a tremendous enthusiasm for the literature of ancient Greece and Rome. The educated Englishman, therefore, caught on the fly the legendary background of expressions like "two-headed Janus," "Colchos' strand," and "Nestor," which quite escape the modern reader unless he thumbs the footnotes. Perhaps you already know who Hercules was and can recall the story of Jason and the Golden Fleece. If you are to appreciate a passage like the conversation between Lorenzo and Jessica at the beginning of the last act, you must understand these references to classic mythology.

Make a list of the names of classic gods and heroes. Let each pupil look up the story connected with at least four of these names and prepare to give short oral reports on them to the class.

D. *Imaginative comparisons.* Colorful pictures and glowing figures of speech flow from Shakespeare's pen as if by habit. Here is a vivid picture of a shipwreck.

Should I go to Church,
And see the holy edifice of stone,
And not bethink me straight of dangerous rocks,
Which, touching but my gentle vessel's side,
Would scatter all her spices on the stream,
Enrobe the roaring waters with my silks;
And, in a word, but even now worth this,
And now worth nothing? (*Act I, Scene 1, lines* 29–36)

Catch the image: a clumsy galleon of olden days breaking up on a reef . . . pounded by green ocean waves . . . sea casks splintering and floating away . . . the rich cargo broken open and drifting in sloshing waters. Such a picture is only one tiny scene on Shakespeare's colorful canvas. What poetic comparisons do you remember particularly? Find lines to read to the class, if you can.

DRAMATIZING

1. At least some portion of "The Merchant of Venice" can be presented before the class. Act IV, Scene 1 is especially good for the purpose. It is not necessary that the scene be acted out as on the stage. Neither need the lines actually be memorized. Reading stands in front of the class may be used, the actors being grouped about them. If you are chosen for a part, read your lines carefully beforehand to determine how you will interpret them. If necessary, consult with your teacher about it. Above all, speak out confidently and with feeling, as though you *are* the character whose part you have.

2. For memorization or solo reading, these passages are especially recommended:

a. Shylock's speech, beginning "Signior Antonio, many a time and oft . . ." (*Act I, Scene* 3, *lines* 91–114).

b. Portia's "mercy" speech, beginning: "The quality of mercy is not strained . . ." (*Act IV, Scene* 1, *lines* 178–199).

c. Lorenzo's speech, beginning: "Sweet soul, let's in . . ." (*Act* V, *Scene* 1, *lines* 47–63).

3. The Casket Scene in Act III and Portia's Mercy Speech in Act IV by E. H. Sothern and Julia Marlowe, are available on Victor record No. 6297.

RELATED READING

Shakespeare Without Tears by Margaret Webster provides a good introduction to Shakespeare and his plays. *Forty-Minute Plays from Shakespeare,* by Fred G. Barker, offers excellent condensed versions of Shakespeare's better-known dramas.

For Further Reading

Commodore Barry by Francis Benz is a biography of the first commodore of the American Navy, John Barry, a young Irishman who fought in our Revolutionary War.

Lorna Doone by Richard Blackmore takes place in seventeenth-century England. It tells how Lorna Doone, sister of the famous outlaws, and her lover, John Ridd, overcome a family feud.

13 Against the Odds by Edwin Embree contains inspiring biographies of thirteen of the greatest living Negroes.

The Sacred Scimitar by Mabel Farnum is a biography of Blessed John de Brito. It is an inspiring story of his success in winning converts in seventeenth-century India.

Jack London: Magnet for Adventure by Shannon Garst is a biography of the famous writer of adventure stories. It is a sympathetic but frank account of a man who was forced to struggle with his own nature.

St. Martin of Tours by Henri Ghéon is the story of the life of a soldier and monk of France who was loved by his countrymen.

Goodby, Mr. Chips by James Hilton is the story of a schoolmaster, loved and honored by three generations of schoolboys.

Tales from the Rectory by Francis C. Kelley is a collection of short stories drawn from the experiences of a priest and bishop.

Tales from Shakespeare by Charles Lamb. Shakespeare's famous plays, adapted in prose form, are easy to read and help to make Shakespeare a favorite with young readers.

North to the Orient by Anne Morrow Lindbergh relates the air travels of Colonel and Mrs. Lindbergh throughout Asia.

Father Tim by Harold J. McAuliffe, S.J., is the biography of Father Timothy Dempsey. This beloved priest was the apostle and good samaritan of the slums of St. Louis.

If I Were King by Justin McCarthy is a brilliant romance of François Villon, the beggar-poet, who was made Constable of France for one week.

Men of Mexico by James A. Magner contains biographies of seventeen outstanding men in Mexican history.

Human Harvest by Theophane Maguire, C.P., is a simple but inspiring narrative of Father Maguire's mission work in China twenty years ago.

Black Fire by Covelle Newcomb. This is the story of Henri Christophe, a slave, who shares his people's struggle for freedom and becomes Henry I of Haiti.

Through the Desert by Henryk Sienkiewicz is the thrilling story of a Polish boy and an English girl who are carried off captive through the desert by agents of the Mahdi.

The Foundling by Francis Cardinal Spellman is the story of an abandoned baby raised in a Catholic Foundling home and of Paul Taggart to whom the foundling meant so much.

Heidi by Johanna Spyri is the story of a girl who goes to live with her grandfather in the Swiss Alps.

All-American by John Tunis. A very popular sports story writer presents the problem of racial discrimination and anti-Semitism in the activity of a football team.

Jane Addams of Hull House by Winifred Wise is the story of Miss Addams' long struggle, against constant misunderstanding, to do something for the poor about her.

An Adventure Novel

When Conrad Richter was a boy, he once tried to run away from home to find the country of the Indians. There, it seemed to him, would be the glorious freedom and adventure that all boys long for.

Years later, when Mr. Richter was studying old records of life in colonial America, he came across notes about white people who had been captured by the Indians and who had fought against being returned to their own families when the Indians were forced to give up their prisoners. Those references led him to wonder about the captives who had come to prefer the Indian way of life to the civilization of the white man. The result was THE LIGHT IN THE FOREST, a novel about a fifteen-year-old white boy who had been stolen by Indians when he was four years old and had lived with them as the adopted son of a member of the tribe for eleven years.

Read this novel as you would read any other adventure story, for pure enjoyment. It will take you deep into the forests of early America. You will learn to know True Son, the white boy who wanted to be an Indian; Half Arrow, his loyal friend; and many others.

Shades of the prison-house begin to close
Upon the growing Boy,
But he beholds the light, and whence it flows,
He sees it in his joy. WORDSWORTH

THE LIGHT IN THE FOREST

CONRAD RICHTER

The boy was about fifteen years old. He tried to stand very straight and still when he heard the news, but inside of him everything had gone black. It wasn't that he couldn't endure pain. In summer he would put a stone hot from the fire on his flesh to see how long he could stand it.

In winter he would sit in the icy river until his Indian father smoking on the bank said he could come out. It made him strong against any hardship that would come to him, his father said. But if it had any effect on this thing that had come to him now, the boy couldn't tell what it was.

For days word had been reaching the Indian village that the Lenni-Lenape and Shawanose[1] must give up their white prisoners. Never for a moment did the boy dream that it meant him. Why, he had been one of them ever since he could remember! Cuyloga[2] was his father. Eleven years past he had been adopted to take the place of a son dead from the yellow vomit.[3] More than once he had been told how, when he was only four years old, his father had said words that took out his white blood and put Indian blood in its place. His white thoughts and meanness had been wiped away and the brave thoughts of the Indian put in their stead. Ever since, he had been True Son, the blood of Cuyloga and flesh of his flesh. For eleven years he had lived here, a native of this village on the Tuscarawas,[4] a full member of the family. Then how could he be torn from his home like a sapling from the ground and given to the alien whites who were his enemy!

The day his father told him, the boy made up his mind. Never would he give up his Indian life. Never! When no one saw him, he crept away from the village. From an old campfire, he blackened his face. Up above Pockhapockink,[5] which means the stream between two hills, he had once found a hollow tree. Now he hid himself in it. He thought only he knew the existence of that tree and was dismayed when his father tracked him to it. It was humiliating to be taken back with his blackened face and tied up in his father's cabin like some prisoner to be burned at the stake. When his father led him out next morning, he knew everybody watched: his mother and sisters, the townspeople, his uncle and aunt, his cousins and his favorite cousin, Half Arrow, with whom he had ever fished, hunted, and played. Seldom had they been separated even for a single day.

All morning on the path with his father, crazy thoughts ran like squirrels in the boy's head. Never before had he known his father to be in the wrong. Could it be that he was in the right now? Had he unknowingly left a little white blood in the boy's veins and was it for this that he must be returned? Then they came in sight of the ugly log redoubts[6] and pale tents of the white army, and the boy felt sure there was in his body not a drop of blood that knew these things. At the sight and smells of the white man, strong aversion and loathing came over him. He tried with all his young strength to get away. His father had to hold him hard. In the end he dragged him twisting and yelling over the ground to the council house of the whites and threw him on the leaves that had been spread around.

[1] LENNI-LENAPE AND SHAWANOSE—Lenni-Lenape (lĕn′ĭ-lĕn′ȧ·pē) is the Indian name for the Delaware Indians. Shawanose (shä·wä′nōz) is a variant of Shawnee.

[2] CUYLOGA—Pronounced kī·lō′gȧ.

[3] YELLOW VOMIT—Probably whooping cough.

[4] TUSCARAWAS (tŭs′kȧ·rô′wȧs)—A river in Ohio.

[5] POCKHAPOCKINK—Pronounced pōk′ä·pō′-kĭnk.

[6] LOG REDOUBTS—Fortified structures, such as forts, buildings, or barricades.

"I gave talking paper [7] that I bring him," he told the white guards. "Now he belong to you."

It was all over then, the boy knew. He was as good as dead and lay among the other captives with his face down. He was sure that his father had stayed. He could feel his presence and smell the sweet inner bark of the red willow mixed with the dried sumach leaves of his pipe. When dusk fell, a white guard came up. The other soldiers called him Del, perhaps because he could talk Delaware, the strange name the whites gave the Lenni-Lenape and their language. True Son heard Del tell his father that all Indians must be out of the camp by nightfall. From the sounds the boy guessed his father was knocking out his pipe and putting it away. Then he knew he had risen and was standing over him.

"Now go like an Indian, True Son," he said in a low, stern voice. "Give me no more shame."

He left almost at once and the boy heard his footsteps in the leaves. The rustling sound grew farther and farther away. When he sat up, his father was gone. But never before or since was the place his father was going back to so clear and beautiful in the boy's mind. He could see the great oaks and shiver-bark hickories standing over the village in the autumn dusk, the smoke rising from the double row of cabins with the street between, and the shining, white reflection of the sky in the Tuscarawas beyond. Fallen red, brown, and golden leaves lay over roofs and bushes, street and forest floor. Tramping through them could be made out the friendly forms of those he knew, warriors and hunters, squaws, and the boys, dogs, and girls he had played with. Through the open door of his father's cabin shone the warm red fire with his mother and sisters over it, for this was the beginning of the Month of the First Snow, November. Near the fire heavy bark had been strewn on the ground, and on it lay his familiar bed and the old worn half-grown bearskin he pulled over himself at night. Homesickness overwhelmed him, and he sat there and wept.

After a while he was conscious of eyes upon him. When he looked up, he saw the white guard they called Del, standing there in the dusk that to the Indian is part of the day and part of the night. The white soldier was about twenty years old, with red hair and a hunting shirt of some coarse brownish cloth. The bosom stuck out like a pouch from his belongings carried in it. His belt was tied in the back and his cape fringed with threads that in the daylight were raveled scarlet and green. But what affronted the boy was that the white guard laughed at him.

Instantly True Son turned and lay on his face again. Inside of him hate rose like a poison.

"Once my hands are loose, I'll get his knife," he promised himself. "Then quickly I'll kill him."

II

When Del Hardy had left Fort Pitt [1] in October, he reckoned he was looking on the Allegheny River for the last time. It

[7] TALKING PAPER—Probably Cuyloga means that he signed a paper promising to return True Son to his white parents.

[1] FORT PITT—A British fort on the site of modern Pittsburgh.

was his first stint with the army and his only one with Colonel Bouquet.[2] Afterwards he was to serve under Generals Sullivan, Broadhead, and Wayne,[3] but Bouquet was the one he claimed he'd go through anything for the willingest. The Colonel was the peacefullest man, Del used to say, but mad as a wolverine. He marched his men out of Fort Pitt that fall day like they were going to a celebration.

And what was the celebration? Why, they were setting out on a suicide march! They were heading more than a hundred miles into hostile Indian territory! Mind you, this was plumb wilderness, with no roads, and no forts or white settlements to fall back on. Every day the savages would be lying thick as copper snakes[4] in the woods around them. The whites would be outnumbered two to one, maybe worse. And yet the peace-palavering[5] Colonel swore he wouldn't halt till he'd reach the Forks of the Muskingum,[6] which only a few of his men had ever seen.

Del never expected to reach those Forks alive. Nor did a lot of older and more

[2] COLONEL BOUQUET (bōō·kā′)—Henry Bouquet was a British officer who fought in the French and Indian War and later helped to suppress Indian uprisings.

[3] GENERALS SULLIVAN, BROADHEAD, AND WAYNE—American officers in the Revolutionary War.

[4] COPPER SNAKES—Probably another name for the copperhead, a poisonous snake.

[5] PEACE-PALAVERING—The word *palaver* means *idle talk.* Here it is used as a reference to the Colonel's constant talk of peace.

[6] FORKS OF THE MUSKINGUM—A place in eastern Ohio where the Muskingum (mŭs·kĭng′-[g]ŭm) River is formed by the joining of the Tuscarawas and Walhonding (wôl·hŏn′dĭng) Rivers.

seasoned men. But the Colonel looked after them like they were his own sons. He marched them in matching lines to protect each other, with the pack horses and stock in the middle. He let no man on the march bandy[7] words with his neighbor. All day he kept ordering Del and the others to be on guard against ambush. But his hardest order was that, unless attacked, they hadn't dare lay hands on a savage.

"Mind you," Del liked to tell later, "half of us were volunteers. We had risked our hair with him for one reason. We'd lost kin captured or scalped, and our one idea was to get them back or get back at the Injuns. When we came to Injun sign or towns, our fingers itched like fire on our hatchets and triggers. We cursed the Colonel's orders right and left. But that's as far as we went. We never touched hair nor hide of those Injun hostages[8] we had marchin' beside us, though we knew the devils had scalped plenty of our people in their time."

Del couldn't believe it when they got there. But according to them that knew, this miserable spot in the wilderness was the wonderful, Indian-sacred Forks of the Muskingum. There from the northeast came the Tuscarawas. Yonder from the northwest the Waldhoning, or White Woman's River, flowed into it. And now they were so deep in Indian country it looked as if they'd never get out, the Colonel got doughtier and spunkier than ever.

[7] BANDY—Exchange.

[8] INJUN HOSTAGES—Captives whom Bouquet planned to hold until the Indians fulfilled their promise to return their white prisoners.

He sassed back the Indian messengers who came into camp. He said they could have no peace till they'd bring in their white prisoners.

"I told the Colonel they'd never give in on that," Del said. "I'd lived with the Delawares my own self when I was little, and I told him if white prisoners weren't killed right off, they were adopted, mostly for some dead relative. They were made brother or sister or son or daughter or wife. It wasn't any mock or make-believe business either. Those Injuns actually looked on their new white relations like full-blooded Injuns. And they'd never give them up any more than their own people."

Del used to rub his chin.

"But I was plumb wrong. They hated to give them up all right. But they hated worse to see a white man's town a settin' there on the banks of their own river. They hated like poison the sight of our tents and redoubts. They couldn't wait to clear out our axes from cuttin' down their Injun woods and our cattle from eatin' the grass on their river bottoms. They were scared we were takin' over the country. So they started fetchin' in their white relations."

That was a sight Del Hardy never would forget. The Colonel himself rubbed his eyes to find savages, whose names were a terror on the frontier, crying like women as they gave up some white child or wife. They held to them, gave them presents to take along, and begged the white captain to be good to them. But what many of the men couldn't get over was the ungratefulness of the captives. They didn't want to have anything to do with the whites who had risked their lives to rescue them. They called out in Delaware to their Indian masters to take them back again to their Indian homes.

Of all the prisoners Del saw brought in, the fifteen-year-old boy from Pennsylvania was the wildest and most rebellious. He had to be tied up with strips of buffalo hide, and then he struggled like a panther kit trussed up on a pole. His name in Delaware, his father said, was True Son, but never had Del seen anybody so unwilling to go back to his true father and mother.

Del had gone up to the North Tuscarawas redoubt when he first saw the pair on the path. The boy wore a brand-new calico hunting shirt, probably made by his mother and sisters for the occasion to show they could dress him as well as the whites. It covered the boy's upper parts and half way down his leggings. His hair was black and his face and arms brown as an Indian's, but you couldn't mistake the English cast of his features. He was plainly white, and yet when he came in sight of the white camp, he stopped dead, a wild expression flew in his face, and he fought like a bobcat to get away. Squaws and Indian children who had come with other prisoners watched and stared. Their faces never moved a muscle, but you could tell they understood and felt for the prisoner.

When Del got back to duty at the council house, the boy lay flat on his face. After dark when the fires burned low, the guard caught him tearing with his teeth at the knots that bound him.

"If you know what's good for you, you won't try to get away!" he warned sharply in Delaware.

The boy turned on him.

"I spit on white people!" he told him.

"Don't forget you're white your own self," Del retorted.

"I'm Indian!" the boy said and looked up at him straight in the eye. The guard didn't laugh. There were times when Indian feelings still came up in him strong.

"Well, your father and mother were white anyway," Del tried to reason with him.

"My father is Cuyloga. My mother, Quaquenga," [9] he said.

"Yes, lately. But you had another father and mother before them. The ones you were born to."

"Nobody can help how he is born," he informed with dignity.

"You can argue like an Injun all right," Del agreed. "But your skin is still white."

"You call this white?" He held out his arm.

"Let's see the skin under that shirt." But the boy hit savagely at the extended hand. He wouldn't let the guard touch him.

"You've been away from us a long time," Del soothed him. "When you're back in our country a while, you'll get used to us."

"I'll never go back to your country."

"It's your country, too."

"This is my country!" he called out with such passion that Del shrugged his shoulders and walked away.

By daylight, True Son still lay on his face.

"You better get up and eat." Del nudged him with the toe of his moccasin.

[9] QUAQUENGA—Pronounced kwŏ·kwēn′gȧ.

The boy shrank with loathing.

"*Palli aal!* [10] Go away."

"You got to eat. You can't tramp back to Pennsylvania on air."

"I'll never go back to Pennsylvania."

"Then where do you reckon you're goin'?"

"A place where you can't tramp me with your big foot."

Now what did the young varmint mean by that, Del wondered. But the boy closed his mouth and would not say more.

[10] *Palli aal!*—Pronounced päl′ĭ äl.

III

The third day a change came among the tents and log redoubts along the Tuscarawas. The camp quickened. You could close your eyes and feel the nervous bustle and excitation of the white man. Soldiers moved quickstep at their tasks. They called lively to each other and hummed strange-sounding ditties.

"Does it mean something?" True Son asked a captive who knew all the talk of the Yengwes.[1]

"Tomorrow we leave for Pennsylvania," she told him.

That day the boy lay with despair in his breast. His life had been short but now it must come to its end. Never would he go to this enemy land. How could he exist among a race of aliens with such slouching ways and undignified speech! How could he live and breathe and not be an Indian!

He would have to act now. He remembered his father's friend, Make Daylight,

[1] YENGWES (yĕn′gēz)—English settlers. The word is a corruption of *English* by North American Indians.

who lived in the next village. Make Daylight had been forsaken, too. His squaw had gone to another Indian's cabin to live. She had taken Make Daylight's children with her. Make Daylight had stood his abandonment and disgrace a few days. Then he went in the forest and ate the root of the May apple.[2] He had been brave in war. No one thought him a coward now. So no one would think True Son a coward when they found him lying silent and superior to the white man. They would say True Son had triumphed over his enemies. Never could they carry him off to Pennsylvania now. No, his body would stay in his beloved land along the Tuscarawas. Word would be sent to Cuyloga, his father. Through the village the mourning cry would pass, "He is no more!" His father and mother, his sisters, his uncle and aunt and cousins would come to him. They would put logs and posts on the fresh earth against the wolves. Under the ground near his head they would set good Lenni-Lenape food to feed him on his journey.

Three times that day the boy tried to get the root of the May apple. His white guard, Del, gave him no chance. When he went from the council house, the guard kept hold of him like a haltered beast. He would have to wait till he was on the march. Some time tomorrow they would pass through a wooded meadow. At the place of the May apple he would fall on the ground. When they lifted

[2] MAY APPLE—The root of this plant is poisonous.

him up, he would have the death medicine in his hands.

It was a gray morning when they left the Forks of the Muskingum. For a while their way lay on the path by which the boy and his father had come. True Son's heart rose. It was almost as if he were going home. When they came to the parting of the trails, something in him wanted to cry out. An ancient sycamore stood at the forks, one dead limb pointing to the gloomy trace[3] to Pennsylvania. On the far side, a live branch indicated the path running bright and free toward home. The boy's moccasins wanted to race on that path. He could feel himself light as a deer leaping over roots and logs, through the deep woods, over the hills and by the narrows to the village on the bank of the Tuscarawas. Violently he struggled to escape, but the guard pushed him on.

Through the blackness in his heart, he heard a voice calling in Delaware.

"True Son! Look! Not yonder. I am here."

The boy's eyes found a young Indian in leggings, breech clout, and strouding.[4] He was moving in the woods abreast of him. Never had he believed that such a feeling of joy and hope would sweep over him again. He would know that form anywhere.

"Is it you, Half Arrow? Do you still live?" he called.

"No, it's Between-the-Logs," Half Arrow called back in delight, for Between-the-Logs was very old and lame and that was a joke between them. "I wait a long time. I think you never come. Then you come but I see you bound up. How is such a thing? I thought you were among friends and your people!"

"I am not among my people, but my enemies," the boy said bitterly.

"Well, anyway, I am your people and am with you," his cousin cheered him. "If Little Crane marches with his white squaw, I can march with you and keep you company."

"I cannot believe it. What will my father say?"

"He says plenty, but let's talk of pleasant and cheerful things. How we can kill these white devils so you can come back to the village with me."

"*Jukella!*[5] If only I could! But there are too many for us."

"The more they are, the more scalps and loot we get!" Half Arrow declared eagerly.

"*Sehe!*[6] Watch out. Some can understand our language," True Son warned him, but Half Arrow laughed, and True Son knew he was talking as he always did, just for Indian cheerfulness and companionship, half in joke and half in earnest, but mostly in joke, for there were nearly two thousand armed white men, and not all the Delaware and Shawanose warriors in the woods had dared attack them.

Most of the day Half Arrow kept up his talking and calling to him. The pair had been apart for three days, and now his chatter ran on to make up for it. All the time he talked he kept tirelessly leaping

[3] TRACE—A beaten path or marked trail through the woods.

[4] BREECH CLOUT, AND STROUDING—The first is a cloth wrapped around the hips; the second is a coarse material obtained from white traders and used for blankets.

[5] *Jukella!*—Pronounced jo͞o·kĕl′ȧ.

[6] *Sehe!* (sē·ē′)—A sound like our English *sh*, meaning *hush*.

over rocks and logs and brushing limbs aside. To see and hear him did True Son good like medicine. It seemed an age since he had heard an Indian joke and seen a dark face break into a wonderful Indian smile. Even Little Crane went sad as a bear near his white bride. But Half Arrow was bright and full of village and family news.

True Son did not notice now when they passed the bare and withered stalks of the May apple. At midday he could even joke a little.

"Half Arrow. Come out of the woods. You're burned too red for the white man to want to take back to Pennsylvania."

"But not too red to shoot me and take my scalp back," Half Arrow said quickly.

"They could have shot you any time all day," True Son pointed out.

"Yes, but not so easy. They might have missed me with all the trees and bushes between. They are poor shots anyway, especially at Indians who jump and dance. But if I came in close to you like a cousin, they could reach me with their tomahawks and long knives."

"They haven't tomahawked Little Crane."

"Well, then, in that case I'll take a chance on the white devils," Half Arrow said and started to edge a little nearer. When at last he came cautiously out of the timber onto the trace, True Son looked with interest at the pack on his back, although it wasn't polite to acknowledge its existence. Half Arrow ate greedily the bread True Son shared with him. At the same time he made a wry grimace over the meat.

"What kind of flesh is this they give you?"

"White man's beef."

"So that's why they're so pale and bandy-legged," he nodded, "having to eat such old and stringy leather while Indian people have rich venison and bear meat."

All afternoon the two cousins marched together, and at times True Son could almost forget the bitterness of his destination. At supper they ate together, but the red-haired guard would not let them sleep side by side. You couldn't trust an Indian. Half Arrow would have to go off in the woods by himself to sleep, like Little Crane.

"I will sleep in the wood," Half Arrow said with dignity. "But first I bear presents to my cousin." He lifted from his pack a small buckskin sack of parched corn. It was so True Son would go well fed with the whites and remember his uncle who sent it. After that, he fetched out moccasins embroidered in red by True Son's mother and sisters so he would go back to his white people newly shod and remember his mother and sisters. Finally all that was left of the pack was its covering, the old worn bearskin that had been True Son's bed in the cabin.

"Your father sent it so you could go warm at night to your white people and remember your father," Half Arrow told him.

In a concealed rush of emotion, True Son held it up in his hands. With the feel of it against his body and the familiar smell of it in his nostrils, he could almost believe that he was back home again in the beloved cabin.

"But what will you have on such a cold night for yourself?" he asked.

"Me! I'll have plenty and more!" Half Arrow boasted. "I have my strouding. Then I'll scrape myself a hill of leaves, yes a whole mountain to crawl inside of. I'll have a soft bed of leaves below me and a thick blanket of sweet-smelling leaves above me. I'll bounce and flex my muscles till I sweat. Then I'll be snug and warm as Zelozelos,[7] the cricket, in a wigwam."

[7] ZELOZELOS—Pronounced tsē′lō·tsē′lōs.

IV

All the way to the ominous-sounding Fort Pitt, True Son tried to keep his mind from the gloomy hour when Half Arrow must turn back and leave him. Only rarely did his cousin mention it.

"I think now I have tramped enough toward the sun's rising," he would soberly begin the subject.

True Son would put on a strained and formal face.

"Yes, tomorrow you must go back. *Elkesa!* [1] What does your father say?"

"He doesn't say because he doesn't know how far I am," Half Arrow would remind him.

"He knows you're not home yet."

"Yes, but he knows Little Crane must come back too, and we can travel together."

"Little Crane might not come back. He's lovesick for his white squaw. He would like to stay with her."

"Then I'll go back by myself. Never could I get lost on such a wide road. All I need do is follow horse droppings."

"Some white devil might ambush you."

"Never could he hit me," Half Arrow boasted. "When he shoots, I jump. Let me hear his rifle, and Achto,[2] the deer, has no legs like mine. Ten jumps from campsite to campsite. My feet won't even get wet in the rivers. I'll fly over, like Ploeu,[3] the turkey."

Now that the subject of Half Arrow's return had been duly mentioned, it could be put away till another time. To keep it covered up and out of sight, they talked of many things. One was the respective qualities of the white man's horses and which ones they would steal and ride home on if they got the chance. Another pleasant subject was the white guards they disliked and with what strokes, if they met them alone in the woods, they would kill and scalp them.

Sometimes Little Crane left his white squaw to walk with the cousins, and then they talked of the foolish ways of the white people.

"The reason they act so queer," Little Crane pointed out, "is because they're not an original people. Now we Indians are an original people. The Great Being made us from the beginning. Look! Our hair is always black, our eyes and skin dark, even True Son's here. But the whites are of colors like horses. Some are light, some are dark, some are in-between. Some have black hair, some have light hair. Some have hair the color of a rotting log. Some have hair like the Colonel's horse, and some have even red like his blanket. Their eyes are fickle as their hair. It's because they are a mixed people, and that's what makes them so foolish and troublesome. The Great Being knows their disposition. He had to give them a Good Book and teach them to

[1] *Elkesa!*—Pronounced ĕl·kē′sȧ.

[2] ACHTO—Pronounced äk′tō.

[3] PLOEU—Pronounced plō′oi.

read so they could learn what is good and bad. Now we Indians know good and bad for ourselves without a book or the cumbersome labor of reading."

"I think," Half Arrow said, "they are all nearsighted. Do you notice how when we come upon them they crowd close to stare at us? They almost tread on our toes. Now an Indian's eyes are keen and farsighted. He can stand at a distance and see all that he wants to."

"They must be hard of hearing too," True Son mentioned. "They talk loud though they stand close enough to each other to touch with a stick."

"And they all talk at once like waterfowl," Half Arrow declared. "How can they understand what is being said? Why don't their elders teach them to keep silent and listen till the speaker's done?"

"It's because they're such a new people," Little Crane explained. "They are young and heedless like children. You can see it the way they heap up treasures like a child, although they know they must die and can't take such things with them. It would be no use anyhow because the next world has plenty of everything a man wants. Their house isn't big enough for all they gather, so they have to build another house they call the barn. That's why you find so many thieves among the whites. All white people must put what they call a lock on their door. It's made of iron and you must carry another piece of iron with you to open it."

"If they shared with their brothers like the Indian, they wouldn't have the work of building a second house," Half Arrow said. "Don't they see the sense of this?"

"Oh, they're a peculiar race and no sensible man can understand them," Little Crane answered. "Have you never noticed them on the march? What do we Indians look for? We look for game or tracks or how the Great Being made our country beautiful with trees for the forest, water for the river, and grass for the prairies. But the white man sees little of this. He looks mostly at the ground. He digs it up with his iron tool to see how black and deep it goes. Sometimes he makes a fuss of the trees. He says, look, here are walnut and hickory and cherry and white ash and locust and sugar trees. But it's not for the trees, only because the ground is black and deep that such trees stand in. Yet if there is much white oak and beech that feed the squirrels and bear and turkey, he makes a face. He says such country is good for nothing."

"I've noticed the white man's foolishness in the woods," Half Arrow nodded. "When the time grows near to camp for the night, they keep their eyes half closed. They don't look for a high and dry place but set themselves down in any wet and dirty place, just so it's under some big trees. They don't even look which way the wind blows before they make their campfire. When the smoke blows on them, they try to hit it with their hands and caps like mosquitoes."

"*Bischik!*"[4] True Son agreed. "And they hang their kettles right away before the blackest of the smoke has passed. They burn any kind of wood that's handy. Green oak or cherry or walnut or chestnut that throws many sparks. You can see their blankets and clothing always have holes burned in them."

"All you say is true," Little Crane declared. "But one thing they do I would

[4] *Bischik!*—Pronounced bĭs′kĭk.

not like to change. That's the way they lie down at night. They never look up first to see if heavy dead branches hang over their heads. Sometime I hope the Great Being sends a big wind to knock down the dead wood and kill them in their beds."

The three laughed. True Son didn't know what he would do when Half Arrow and Little Crane weren't there to keep him company. And now there were signs that they wouldn't be with him long. A Mohawk [5] from the north fell in with them that day. He said soon they would meet a large river and that Fort Pitt was on this river. The very next day it happened as he said, but the waters were swollen with rains. They would have to wait for the flood to go down before crossing.

Next morning when Half Arrow and Little Crane came back from the forest, they found the body of the Mohawk near camp. He had been tomahawked and scalped. Now a Delaware sheds no tears for a Mingo,[6] and especially a Mohawk, but though dogs may fight among themselves they are one against the wolf.

"I think white soldiers did this," Little Crane said. "One of them made friendly talk to him in front. Another came up and tomahawked him from behind."

Inside of him, True Son felt bitterness for all the white soldiers. The Mohawk might be ugly, but he was an Indian. It was hard to hold in his feelings next morning when the red-haired guard said that this was the day True Son and Half Arrow must part. In a little while they would be crossing the river, and his cousin must stay on this side.

"Why do you spit on my cousin?" True Son asked.

"Little Crane can't come either. We're getting close to white people now. Some of them have suffered from the Indians and might kill him."

"They could kill him just as easy on this side, like they did the Mohawk."

"It's the Colonel's orders."

"He's not Half Arrow's colonel. Why does he have to obey him?"

The guard flushed. He said nothing more. But when the column started to move toward the ford, he took his rifle and, holding it at Half Arrow's breast, forced him out of line. True Son felt fresh hate for the white man. His arms had been freed to let him carry his pack above the water. Now he dropped his belongings and made a lunge at the guard. He knocked him down, tried to pull out first the guard's knife and then his hatchet. Over the ground they rolled, while a second soldier drew a bead on Half Arrow and others came running to pull True Son off.

"You Injun-crazy young fool!" the red-haired guard panted as he got up. "I wasn't trying to shoot him—just to save his hair."

As they tied his arms again True Son still struggled. Half Arrow stood by, grave and impassive.

"Once long ago my cousin had white blood," he apologized to the guard. "Now you can rest your mind. I will stay on this side like you say. But first I

[5] MOHAWK—An Indian of the Mohawk tribe, which once lived in the Mohawk Valley, New York.

[6] MINGO—Mingo or Mingue is the Lenni-Lenape name for Iroquois. The Iroquois Confederacy, of which the Mohawk tribe was perhaps the most aggressive, attacked the Delaware Indians in 1720 and dominated them until 1763.

would like to give True Son a message from his father before we are separated by the waters."

"You can give him a message," the guard said sharply. "But don't try to give him a knife. If you do, you'll get a bullet between your ribs."

At the order to march Half Arrow moved beside True Son. Through the trees ahead they could see the river.

"I talk now for your father, True Son," he began. "He said I should tell you this. On no account must I forget. These are his words: 'True Son. Remember what happens to the white prisoner the Indian takes. If the white prisoner bears his hardship with patience and cheerfulness, his Indian master likes him. He knows he will make a good Indian. So he treats him well and adopts him. True Son. If the white prisoner fights him or hangs back or tries to escape or if he complains all the time, the Indian knows he will never make one like himself. Then there is nothing to do but scalp him. True Son. If you fight and hang back, maybe the white man will scalp you. True Son. It is better to wait for your cause to be ripe like a persimmon on the snow before you fight back. True Son. It is wiser to be willing and be alive than be defiant and be dead so your father and mother and sisters have to mourn you.' "

True Son bowed his head. The words were so like his father's, he could hear the sound of his father's voice in his mind. Half Arrow went on.

"Your father said more. He said, True Son. Remember the time we hunted on the White Woman's River. We came on a bear and the shot broke its backbone. The bear fell down and started to cry like Long Tail, the panther. Your father went up and struck it with his ramrod across the nose. He said, 'Listen, bear. You are a coward and not the warrior you pretend to be. You know our tribes are at war. Had you conquered me, I would have borne it with courage and died like a warrior. But you, bear, sit and whimper like an old woman. You disgrace your tribe with your behavior.' True Son. Do you remember?"

"I remember," the boy groaned. "Tell my father so. Tell him I will bear my disgrace like an Indian and will wait to strike till the time is in my favor."

The two marched on in silence. When they came to the river's edge, Half Arrow stepped aside and True Son waded in alone. The water grew steadily higher till it reached above his waist. He shivered, but he did not turn around. Not till he was out and dripping on the other side and following the trail on the bank with the column did he look back. Far across the water he could make out two figures. They were Half Arrow and Little Crane, standing at the water's edge. Their eyes, he knew, strained after him. He wished he could hold up his hand in farewell, but his arms were tied. Then he passed with his companions into the forest.

V

From now forward he was on his own, the boy told himself. He would have to think his own Indian thoughts and follow his own Indian counsel. He gave no sign of the constriction in his throat or the loathing in his breast when they entered the white man's stronghold of Fort Pitt; the gloomy stone, the dark passageways, the drunken soldiers, all the swaggering of the white-skinned legion and among them a few turncoat Indians [1] looking pitiful and slavish among their enemies.

But it was when they had left Fort Pitt and crossed the eastern mountains that the full weight of his exile fell on him. Never along the Tuscarawas had he seen such tremendous mounds of earth and rock heaped to the sky and running farther than the eye could see. Once behind him, they were like unscalable stockades separating him from his people. And now he saw he had reached a point he had often heard about, the sad, incredible region where the Indian forest had been cut down by the white destroyers and no place left for the Indian game to live. Here the desolate face of the earth had been exposed to dead brown weeds and stubble, lorded over by the lodges of the white people and the fat storehouses of their riches. Fort Pitt had been ugly, but it had still been Indian country. This now, he knew, was the barbarous homeland of his white enemies.

He could feel them all around him. His moccasins tramped no longer soft mossy forest trails but a hard-rutted roadway. Curious wooden barriers ran alongside in a regular crooked fashion with spreading wooden horns at each angle. He was told they were meant to keep the white man's cattle from running free. The cattle stood tame and stolid as the soldiers passed, but the white people came running from their lodges to line the road. From the noise they made you might have thought the white army came from a great battle with loot and scalps instead of only children captives and without a shot having been fired.

Every hour the forest receded and the lodges of the whites grew more numerous. Late that afternoon they encamped near a white man's village. How could human beings, he wondered, live in such confinement! Here the whites had shut themselves up in prisons of gray stone and of red stone called brick, while the larger log houses had been covered over with smooth painted boards to give them the glittering ostentation and falseness so dear to the whites. Evidently their coming had been expected, for many people awaited them. Herds of saddled horses stood around. Men and women must have come a long way. Small crowds tried to storm the captives as soon as they arrived, but the soldiers held them off.

That evening the red-headed guard spoke to True Son in Delaware.

"Well, thank the Almighty I won't have to wet-nurse you much more. Your father's taking you over in the morning."

The boy gave no answer but the realization of who these people were swept over him. They were the captives' future masters, who would claim them and drag them off to a life of subjection in their own lodges. Among this company staring at him now was likely the one who pretended to be his own father.

The sun rose red and cold next morning. Through a frosty mist they were herded to the middle of the town where for a blocklike space no houses had been built, for what reason the boy did not know. It was early, but already the white people had gathered around fires trying to keep warm. Hardly had the captives arrived before they were stormed, taken

[1] TURNCOAT INDIANS—Those who had deserted their tribes and worked for white men.

by the hand, their faces sharply looked into, their scanty dress lifted apart for birthmarks, all the while their ears bombarded with questions that True Son could only in part understand. Then the Colonel and his staff put an end to it. They showed they had learned at least one thing from the Indians. They announced there would be no more confusion. All would be conducted according to rule and order.

Nothing of the scene that followed was missed by True Son—the swarming whites in cloaks and greatcoats,[2] their heads scarved and hatted, and in their midst the sacrificial cluster of captives, mostly young, bareheaded, in simple Indian dress, with parts of their bodies exposed to the early winter wind. One unwilling young captive after another was brought forward, what was known about him or her announced, then a hearing given those who claimed relationship. Several times the crowd gave way to emotion, wiping eyes and blowing noses with a great fluttering of red, blue, white, and other colored cloths. Even many of the white soldiers showed their feelings. Only the captives took it dry-eyed and restrained. True Son thought their Indian fathers and mothers would be proud of them.

At the end a very few were left unclaimed, including himself and two girls of twelve or fourteen years. The boy felt relief and hope creep over him. His white father didn't want him after all. He couldn't believe his good fortune. Now perhaps they would let him go back to his far-off home along the Tuscarawas.

But presently above the murmurs of the departing crowd he heard the hoofbeat of horses in the strange town. Soon afterward a rider approached and the boy saw a small man on a sweated bay horse leading a saddled but riderless gray. In front of the Colonel and his staff, the rider dismounted. The Colonel shook hands with him and, smiling, led him over to where True Son and the unclaimed girls stood awaiting their fate. A chill ran up the boy's backbone. Surely he had nothing in common with this insignificant man with black boots, a face colorless as clay, and a silly hat on his head. He came up anxiously, and his very light blue eyes misted into the boy's face while the ashen hand he held out visibly trembled.

True Son stood rigid and unmoving.

"Put out your hand and shake his," Del Hardy ordered in Delaware.

Reluctantly the boy gave his hand. The man spoke a stammer of strange-sounding words.

"Your father welcomes you back," Del translated. "He thanks God you're safe and sound." When the boy's lips compressed, "Can't you say you're glad after all these years to see your own father?"

True Son's heart felt like a stone. How could this fantastic and inferior figure in a long fawn-colored garment like a woman be possibly anything to him—this pallid creature who revealed his feelings in front of all! In the boy's mind came the picture of his Indian father. How differently he would have looked and acted. With what dignity and restraint he could conduct himself in any situation, in peace or war, in council or the hunt, with pipe or tomahawk, rifle or scalping knife. This weak and pale-skinned man was nothing beside him.

[2] GREATCOATS—Overcoats.

"He's not my father," he said.

Del Hardy made a face. When he repeated it to the white man, the latter seemed to recoil. The Colonel had been standing by following intently with his foreign eyes. Now he began to talk. The boy couldn't understand much of his mixed-up Yengwe tongue, but it looked and sounded like the Colonel was giving an order.

When they finished, the red-haired guard turned to the boy with a scowl.

"I thought I was rid of you," he spoke in Delaware. "Now I've got to go along and translate you to your own family."

The boy said nothing. His eyes gave a hard unwelcome. He knew instinctively that translating wasn't the chief reason for Del's going. No, the armed soldier was being sent along mostly to guard him, perhaps also to protect this slight presumptuous white man who claimed to be his father. Bitter disappointment came over the boy. Now he wouldn't be able to carry out his plan as soon as he had expected.

VI

When Del Hardy saw Fort Pitt through the trees, he threw his cap in the air. For weeks he had lived among savages in the wilderness. Now, thank God, he was laying eyes on a white man's settlement again. Sight of chimneys, of the certain slant of roofs with the British flag flying over them, stirred him deeply inside. These walls of mortared stone bespoke his own people. English or French, they had built to stay. This might be their farthest outpost now, but it wouldn't be long. He had heard a dozen soldiers say they were coming back to clear and settle the rich black land they had found along Yellow Creek beyond the Ohio.

His feet felt light as deer hooves climbing the mountains and jogging down the eastern slopes. He reckoned one of the pleasantest feelings a white man could have was, after tramping days in the everlasting forest, to come out on cleared land and look across open fields. Same way with a road. He had marched nigh onto three hundred miles on savage trails and traces, stumbling over roots and logs, slopping through runs [1] and bogs. Now the hard firm ground of a cartway under foot lifted him up. His eye ran warmly over the good ruts, and the familiar zigzag of rail fences. Tame cattle in the fields stood quiet and decent as they passed. Here neither man nor beast had to be afraid of his shadow. The log barns and sheds on the land had an air of white man's industry and their houses of peace. From all of them young folk and old came to the road to rejoice as the army and its delivered captives passed.

That had been a day or two ago. Yesterday at Carlisle [2] the freed white captives had been given back to the bosom of their families. You'd reckon by this time they'd learned to appreciate it. Yet, look at this Butler boy [3] on ahead riding with his father, sullen as a young spider, making as though he didn't understand a word his father said. To watch him and listen to his Indian talk, you'd reckon English a questionable tongue and Delaware the only language fit to put in your mouth. You could see he still reckoned himself a savage and all those were blackguards and slavers who had anything to do with fetching him back to his own people. But then Indians were a strange lot. Del himself had lived neighbors to them as a boy. He knew their ways but never could he make them out.

Thank the Lord, he told himself, when they came to the home river. It would take his mind off the boy for a spell. The great stream flowed south from the mountains, a noble tide a mile wide. Just to let his eye roam over it gave him peace and wonder. The ferry pushing off from the far shore was a mark of civilization and the white race. To the north a squadron of islands swam like ships pointing downstream, and still farther northward were the majestic gaps of the Blue Mountains,[4] one after the other, where the great river poured through.

It was to Del the greatest sight in his world. The narrower if deeper Ohio couldn't compare to it. And yet when he looked at the boy, he found him sitting his saddle unnoticing and unmoved. Not till they were on the ferry did he wake up to it. That was when his father called the river Susquehanna.[5] Quickly, as if he had heard that name before, the boy lifted his head. His eyes took in the great stretch of water with the fields and houses on its far shore. Then he poured out bitter words in Delaware.

"What's he saying?" his father asked.

[1] RUNS—Brooks.

[2] CARLISLE (kär·līl′)—A town in southern Pennsylvania near Harrisburg.

[3] BUTLER BOY—True Son's real name was John Butler.

[4] BLUE MOUNTAINS—A mountain range in northeastern Pennsylvania.

[5] SUSQUEHANNA—Pronounced sŭs′kwē·hăn′ȧ.

Del made a face.

"He says the Susquehanna and all the water flowing into it belongs to his Indian people. He says his Indian father lived on its banks to the north. The graves of his ancestors are beside it. He says he often heard his father tell how the river and graves were stolen from them by the white people."

Mr. Butler looked weary.

"Tell him we'll talk about that some other time. Tell him he's getting close to home now. If he'll look up at those hills across the river, he'll see Paxton township where he was born."

Even before he translated it, Del was sure the boy had understood. He gazed at the far bank with a sudden look of terror.

"Place of Peshtank white men?" he asked in thick, Indian English.

His father looked pleased. He put an affectionate hand on the boy's shoulder.

"That's right, Son. Peshtank or Paxton. It's the same thing. We call them the Paxton boys. Many of them, I'm proud to say, are your own kin."

The boy looked as if a whiplash had hit him. He stared wildly up at the facing hills. The ferryman pushed by with his pole. The water curled around the flat bow of the scow.[6] On the eastern bank, the sycamores and maples grew steadily nearer. Suddenly, before the boat touched shore, the boy kicked his moccasin heels into the sides of his horse and plunged with him into the shallow water. At once he was urging the gray with sharp Indian yells up the high steep bank. By the time Del and Mr. Butler reached the shore level, all they got was a glimpse of horse and boy vanishing into the northern forest.

"They'll stop him at Fort Hunter," the boy's father said.

But before reaching the fort, they came on the boy's horse standing riderless in the trail. Del jumped from the saddle and bent over the ground. In the thawed earth he could make out where the gray had shied at a white rag tied to a bush at a fork in the trail. In the ground were marks where the boy had landed. His tracks on foot were harder to follow, but Del ran down a path that led to the river. In a tangle of alders and sweetbrier he stopped and soon pulled out the kicking and biting boy. Mr. Butler had to help drag him back to his horse and lift him on the saddle. Then, with the gray firmly tethered between the two men, they rode back down the river trail.

They passed a mill, open fields, log and stone buildings. Their road climbed the rising hills. Now they could see rich, cleared farms with solid-looking houses and barns. The boy's father turned into a lane lined with young walnuts. Ahead of them a barn with stone ends had the greatest space between them that Del Hardy thought he had ever seen in a building. Nearby was a limestone tenant house and, beyond the spring, a stone mansion house with a wide front door. As the riders approached, a boy and servant girl came out on the porch with a determined-looking woman beside them.

Del glanced at Mr. Butler. His face was uneasy. Likely he had looked forward to a time when his son would come back to him. But hardly had he counted on a homecoming like this. It would be

[6] scow—A large flatbottomed boat with square ends.

an ordeal they would all have to go through.

The two men swung to the ground in front of the house, but the boy had to be ordered from the saddle. Del took him by the arm and led him to the porch steps.

"Your brother is home," the father said uncomfortably to the small boy standing there, then to True Son, "You never saw Gordie. He was born while you were away. But you ought to recollect your Aunt Kate."

The older boy stood silent in his Indian dress, ignoring all. The servant girl had started toward him. Now she stopped painfully, while Aunt Kate stared in frank disapproval and disbelief. Only the small boy seemed to see nothing unusual in the scene, gazing at his brother with open delight and admiration.

"Well, let's go in," the father said, clearing his throat, and they moved into the wide hall.

"Harry!" a lady's voice called eagerly from upstairs.

Mr. Butler and Aunt Kate exchanged glances.

"Harry!" the voice called again. "Aren't you bringing him up?"

The father gave a look as if there was no help for it.

"You better come along," he told the soldier significantly, then with the small boy running ahead and the aunt coming after, they urged True Son toward the stairs.

It wasn't easy to get him up. Plenty of times, Del knew, this boy must have shinned up cliffs and trees higher than this. But he eyed the stairs and bannister rail as an invention of the devil. For a while the guard figured this short distance from floor to floor might be the hardest part of their journey. Then Gordie, running ahead, turned the tide. He bounced up those steps so easy, looking around as he ran, that his brother shook off the hands that tried to help him. For a moment his eyes measured this white man's ladder, wide enough for two or three men abreast, the oaken treads shaven smooth as an ax handle and polished with a kind of beeswax. Then half crouching and taking two steps at a time, he climbed to the second-floor hall. It ran from one end of the house to the other, with doors branching off on both sides.

"This way, Son," Mr. Butler said, and took him toward an open doorway where his small brother stood waiting.

The room they entered was large and sunny, with green-figured white walls. The broad flooring held much furniture, a red cherry bureau and washstand, a high polished chest of drawers, two or three small tables and twice as many chairs, a large bed with impressive posts, and by the window a couch on which a lady in a blue dressing gown half sat and half lay. You could tell by the black hair and eyes and by the eager loving look she gave the boy that she was his mother. Just the same his father had to push him to the couch, and for all the notice he took of her, she might not have been there. Only when she pulled down his head and kissed him did he acknowledge her presence, stiffening painfully.

"Why, you look like an Indian, John!" she exclaimed. "You even walk like one. You've had a hard fate, but thank God your life was spared and you're home with us again. Are you happy?"

True Son had wrapped himself again in aloofness like a blanket. His mother turned with quick compassion.

"Doesn't he remember any English?"

"He understands a good deal, we think," his father said. "But not everything. We don't know how much he can talk it. So far he's only said a few words in English. Del has to talk to him in Indian."

"I'm sure he understands me," his mother declared. "I can tell by his eyes when I speak. You do understand me, don't you, John?"

The boy gave no response. She went on quickly, sympathetically.

"You've been away a long time, John. Your education has been arrested. You've had to live in heathen darkness and ignorance. Now you must make up for lost time. You're almost a young man. The first and most important thing to know is your native English tongue. We'll start right now. I am your mother, Myra Butler. This is your father, Harry Butler. Your brother is Gordon Butler. And you are John Cameron Butler. Now repeat it after me, John Cameron Butler."

The boy said nothing, only stood there impassively. Aunt Kate turned from the room as if she could stand no more.

"He don't know his own name. He don't even know when it's Sunday," Del heard her tell the servant girl on the stairs.

But back in her bedroom Mrs. Butler had far from given up. She might be an invalid, but you could tell she was the mistress of this house.

"I want you to repeat your name after me. Say John, John!" She seized his arm and shook it, then turned helplessly.

"Maybe he's deaf and dumb, Mamma!" little Gordie said.

That broke the strain for a moment and all smiled, all except the boy in Indian dress. Gradually his insistent, somber silence overtook the others. You could see Mrs. Butler come to a decision.

"Very well, John," she said, tightening her lips. "I see you are willful and stubborn as your Uncle Wilse. We will have to act accordingly. Your family and friends are coming to see you tomorrow, and I won't have you standing up crude and ignorant as a savage in front of them. You'll have to stay in this room till you speak your own name."

You could see that the boy understood. Resentment crept into his dark face. He spoke rapidly in Delaware. Del had to translate it.

"He says his name is Lenni Quis. In English you'd call it Original Son or True Son."

Mrs. Butler heard him.

"But he's not with the Delawares any more. He's at home under our roof, and here he'll have to recognize his real name."

The boy regarded her with burning dark eyes so like her own.

"True Son my real name," he said in thick English, having trouble with the letter *r*. "My father and mother give me this name."

"He means his Indian father and mother," Del explained.

Mrs. Butler had flushed.

"Well, I think that will be enough today," she said. "He has spoken a few words in English at any rate."

She took from beside her on the couch

some clothing she had been mending. A feeling of constriction crept over the boy when he saw they were a pair of light gray Yengwe pantaloons and a youth's yellow jacket. She went on. "When I heard you were coming home, I borrowed these from your cousin Alec. Now I'd like you to put them on and see how they fit you."

The boy made no effort to take them.

"Do you understand, John?" she repeated earnestly. "You're to put these on so we can see what you look like in civilized dress."

The boy stared with loathing at the pants and jacket. They were symbols of all the lies, thefts, and murders by the white man. Now he was asked to wear them. You might as well ask a deer to dress itself in the hide of its enemy, the wolf.

"Do you hear your mother?" Del said sharply and repeated the request in Delaware.

The boy still held back. How could he touch these things? Had there been small wood by the fireplace, he might have picked up the clothes with the end of a stick and carried them out, holding them as far from his body as possible. But there was no stick. Then Gordie took them for him.

"When you put these on, will you give me your Indian clothes, True Son?" he asked eagerly as they went from the room. "Then I can be an Indian."

The older boy did not say anything, nor did he take off his Indian dress when they reached the room where Gordie took him, but for a moment a look of mutual respect and understanding passed between the two brothers.

VII

That night the boy lay in the alien place provided him and Del. Walls and ceiling had been closed up with some kind of thick white mud. To make it airtight, his white people had covered the dried mud with paper. The only holes in the walls had been blocked off by wooden doors and glass squares.

He felt sealed up as in the grave. He knew now why the English looked so pale. They shut themselves oft from the living air. They were like green grass bleached white under a stone or the pallid ghost pipes [1] that grow in the dark woods where no sun reaches. The heart of the whites must be different from the Indian as sheep from the deer. The Indian and deer would wither and die in such confinement, but the white man flourished in the stale sickly air of his house like fleas in his wall and borers in the cabin logs. He could rise refreshed from a suffocating bed of feathers high as a turkey roost off his mother, the Earth. He could even survive that instrument of torture called a bolster,[2] which bent white people from the straightness of the Indian, curving their necks forward like a crane's.

But what kept the boy most wakeful this first night was the feel of his enemies around him. He could still hear in his mind the "Peshtank story" that had swept through his village and the other Indian towns like a pestilence. He could see the dark Indian faces of the teller and his listeners.

[1] PALLID GHOST PIPES—Indian pipes. The single nodding flower on these waxy white plants resembles a white clay pipe.

[2] BOLSTER—A long cushion placed under the pillows to support the head.

"It was the month that the white men claim their good, kind Lord and master was born in," his father had told them. "Our Conestogo [3] cousins had taken the white man's religion. They were only a handful, living at peace among the white men. Then the white savages from Peshtank came. They came on horseback with guns and hatchets. The Conestogo were true to their religion.[4] They made no resistance. Only those away from the village escaped."

"How many escaped?" True Son's sister, A'astonah,[5] had asked piteously.

"None escaped in the end," her father had said harshly. "When the Conestogo who were away came home, there was no village. Their cabins had been burned. Their brothers were killed. So they went to the white man's town of Lancaster.[6] They asked to stay in the white man's gaol.[7] Here they would be safe, they thought. They had lost their Indian caution. They had lived too long among the white people. A day or two before the birthday of their Christian chief and God [8] the white barbarians came again. They broke down the doors of the gaol, and no white man in the town lifted a hand to stop them. The young Conestogo called out not to kill them, that they liked the Yengwes. Now you know it is the custom of us Indians to adopt prisoners who like us. We make them one of us and everything we have, they have. But the white men do not want the Indians even to share the common air."

True Son could still hear in his mind his father's great wrath and scorn for the white cowards as he spoke the names of their victims.

"Shalehaha,[9] a little boy, and Exundas, another boy. Tonquas was just a whip of a boy and Hyyenaes not much bigger. Koquaeunquas was the name of a little girl, Karendouah another girl, and Canukiesung the littlest girl of all. Not satisfied, the white barbarians scalped them. They chopped off the hands of the men and squaws. They put guns in the mouth of one of our Conestogo cousins while he was yet speaking and blew his head to pieces."

Tonight True Son lay cold with hate just to remember. And now tomorrow some of these very men and their women were coming to welcome him. Their bloody hands would press his, calling him nephew and cousin. It gave him a feeling of abhorrence. Hardly could he bear even this white soldier, now in deep sleep beside him. At each snore, the boy began moving away from him, little by little, first one foot, then the other. It took a long time to work his way to the bed's edge and still longer to lower himself clear. Like a panther kit he crawled to the fireplace where embers still glowed. Here he stretched out. It was good to feel the hardness and coolness of the hearthstone beneath him. A little air drifted under

[3] CONESTOGO (kŏn′ĕs·tō′gȧ)—Indians who once lived along the Susquehanna River.

[4] TRUE TO THEIR RELIGION—Here the Christian religion.

[5] A'ASTONAH—Pronounced ä'ä·stō′nä.

[6] LANCASTER (lăng′kăs·tẽr)—A town in southeastern Pennsylvania.

[7] GAOL—Jail.

[8] CHRISTIAN CHIEF AND GOD—Christ.

[9] SHALEHAHA—This and the other Indian names in the paragraph are pronounced as follows: Shalehaha (shä·lē·hä′hä), Exundas (ĕx-o͞on′dȧs), Tonquas (tŏn′kwäs), Hyyenaes (hī·ē′-nēz), Koquaeunquas (kō·kwē·o͞on′kwäs), Karendouah (kăr·ĕn·dou′ȧ), Canukiesung (kä·no͞o·kē′-so͞ong).

the door and across his face to be drawn up the chimney. He pulled his worn bearskin over him. Its familiar smell calmed him. It took him back to his father's cabin, blotting out the offensive scent of these white people. With the fur moving from his breath, he fell asleep.

At daylight he awoke with a jerk. He left the unpleasant jacket and pantaloons hanging from the peg in the wall of his room. At breakfast his white father and Aunt Kate looked disapprovingly at his Indian dress. He did not see his mother. Gordie told him that you didn't go into her room of a morning. When True Son came to midday dinner still in hunting frock and leggings, his Aunt Kate was very stern. As he got up from his chair, she got up with him.

"Now I've had enough of this, Johnny," she said. "Your own kin are coming this afternoon to see you, and we won't have you rigged out in your father's house like a naked and dirty savage. If you won't wash and dress, I'm coming up to wash and dress you my own self."

True Son didn't know every word she said, but he understood enough so that cold horror shook him. This strong, ugly-looking white squaw looked as if she meant it.

"I go look at clothes," he said with dignity in English.

"You're not just going to look at them!" she informed him sharply. "You're going to put them on. And you're going to wash yourself first or I'll do it for you."

He flinched. Gordie saw it with his quick eyes.

"I'll show him how, Aunt Kate!" he promised.

"Well, see that he does a good job or I will!" she warned. "Now come out in the kitchen, Johnny, and I'll give you some hot water to wash with."

He felt debased. He was an Indian male obeying a white squaw, made to carry with his own hands a bucket of steaming water up the stairs. That was woman's work back along the Tuscarawas. His only consolation was that his Indian father wasn't here to see. He thought he felt amusement on Del's face as he and Gordie instructed him to stand in a wooden tub. Then they showed him how to sop soap and water on his body from the white crockery basin.

When that was done, he could no longer postpone the crisis of the clothes. Gordie pointed out which was front and back. Revulsion grew as he drew the despised garments over his skin. Just to feel them about his flesh stung and bound him. Now he was thrice imprisoned—first in this alien land, then in this Yengwe house and room, and last in this white boy's clothing. He turned away from the window as he saw the first visitors riding up the lane, none on foot, all proud with horses.

Gordie had to come for him twice before he would go down. He must remember what his real father had said—to conceal his true feelings from his enemies. First he had to present himself to his mother in her room and to the strange woman he found with her. Then slowly he went down the stairs. His father led him around the big parlor. A dozen people shook his hand, white uncles, aunts, and cousins. He couldn't tell one from the other. It was true what Cut Fingers back along the Tuscarawas had once said, that all white people looked alike. Only one stood out, a fattish boy who stared at his clothes, and True Son knew by his peculiar expression that this was Alec, whose jacket and pantaloons he wore.

At the end his father left him by his two uncles. Both sat back smoking. The lean and rangy one with loose skin on his jaw was his Uncle George Owens.

"Well, you can thank your lucky stars you're out of the clutches of those devils, Johnny," he said.

His Uncle Wilse, a powerful, heavy-set man, swept the boy with slaty, less friendly eyes.

"He still looks like an Indian to me," he grunted, and True Son remembered what Gordie had told him, that his Uncle Wilse was a leader of the "Paxton boys." He tried to take no notice of either comment. His Uncle Wilse went on. "How long was he with those savages? Twelve years. Well, once an Indian, always an Indian. You can make an Indian out of a white man, but you can never make a white man out of an Indian."

"Johnny is no Indian," the boy's father said uneasily. "He has the same white blood as you and I."

"It might have been white once," Uncle Wilse admitted. "But those savages brought it up red. It's the heathen notions they drill into him. Bad is good and good is bad. Stealing's a virtue. Lying's an art. Butchering and scalping white women and young ones is the master accomplishment."

The boy stood impassive, although he could feel the blood creeping up his neck and face. Uncle Wilse watched him darkly.

"Look at him now. Standing there cold-blooded as any redskin. I'll warrant he's hatching out deviltry in his heart." He looked at True Son, and his slate eyes flamed with a dangerous smoky violet light that had only smoldered in them before. "Tell the truth, boy! Isn't that what you're doing right now?"

True Son gave no indication that he had heard.

"What's the matter with him?" Uncle Wilse growled. "Is he deaf or why doesn't he give his betters a civil answer?"

Del Hardy, who had been listening, moved up and repeated the questions to the boy in Delaware. Uncle Wilse interrupted.

"What kind of language is that?" And when he was told, "Can't he talk English, only that scrub Indian stuff? Well, if that's all he can talk, why doesn't he talk it?"

Del translated. The boy felt he could be honorably silent no longer. Holding himself erect as he could, he made an answer in Delaware.

"What did he say?" Uncle Wilse asked.

"He said Delaware isn't the scrub language you say. He says when Indians of different tribes meet, they talk to each other in Delaware. It's the master language of the Indians, and that's true. Most all tribes learn some of it so they can get along with other tribes."

Uncle Wilse had an expression of derision.

"What does it matter what gibberish Indians talk?"

True Son, listening closely, poured out a flood of words. Del translated it again.

"He says white people talk the Delaware language, too. He says we say tomahawk and wigwam and Susquehanna and other Delaware words. He says it's not a poor but a rich language. There's so many different ways of saying the same thing. You can always say just what you mean. He says, in English we say, God. But his Indian father, Cuyloga, told him there were more than twenty ways to say God in Delaware and each one means something different. There's Eliwuleck.[10] That means, He that's above everything. There's Eluwitschanessik. That means, the strongest and most powerful One. Then there's Eluwilissit. That means, the One greatest in goodness—"

Uncle Wilse interrupted. His face was a picture.

"I can't stand that! You mean this heathen Indian, Cuyloga, who stole Johnny and claims to be his father, talks about God before he goes out and murders Christian men and women!"

At the reference to his Indian father, True Son felt his hackles[11] rise. Suddenly a translator was too slow for him. He spoke to his Uncle Wilse direct, in English as best he could.

"Uncle. You talk about being Christian, but you murder the Conestogo!"

The heavy face flared.

"So you were lying to us when you said you couldn't talk English?"

"I no lie. I say nothing."

"No, but you tried to deceive us just the same, keeping quiet and making believe you didn't understand. That's an Indian trick, and that's why the Conestogo got their just deserts at last. They pretended they were Christians so they could murder white people without being suspected or caught. If you tried to arrest them and put them to trial like anybody else, the Quakers took them to Philadelphia. They were only poor pagan Christians there. Rubbish! They were no more Christians than wolves!"

"I don't know," True Son said. "But they were people. Some good people, some bad maybe. But you were Christians! You had forty, fifty men. You had horses, knives, tomahawks, and rifles. You blow heads off of Indian men. You kill Indian women and young ones. Not one is left. You scalp. You chop. You cut off hands and try to cut off feet—"

Uncle Wilse's face was distorted. He got halfway to his feet.

"Yes, and that's the best thing that could have happened to them. They got what they deserved. We fixed them so they wouldn't butcher any more of our people."

His shouting brought Alec to his side. The latter stood glaring at True Son.

"We give him my clothes," he said. "Then he stands there and insults us."

True Son flushed.

"I don't ask for clothes. I take clothes off and don't put them on again."

"Now that's enough!" Mr. Butler came to life. "Johnny, you can't talk this way to your elders. Tell your Uncle Wilse you're sorry."

The boy closed his lips tightly. His Uncle Wilse threw an angry, meaning glance at his brother-in-law.

"All I have to say, Harry, you better watch him. If he goes around siding against his own kin and neighbors, he's liable to get hurt."

[10] ELIWULECK—This and the following names are pronounced: Eliwuleck (ē·lĭ·wōō′-lĕk), Eluwitschanessik (ē·lōō·wĭt′skän·ĕs′·ĭk), Eluwilissit (ē·lōō·wĭl′ĭ·sĭt).

[11] HACKLES—Here the author means hair. Usually hackle refers to the neck plumage on domestic fowls.

For the first time since his initial greeting, the other uncle spoke.

"My boy, I want to tell you something. I'd hate to see you get the wrong impression of your family and especially of your father, Uncle Wilson, and other Paxton men. In private life we're decent and respected citizens. We're members of Colonel Elder's church and subscribe to public benefits. But nobody can tell us anything about Indians. We've had too much experience. If a white man kills an Indian, he's called a murderer. He daren't be tried here where he'd surely be acquitted. No, he has to be taken to Philadelphia where he's convicted and hanged. But if an Indian kills a white man, he's just a poor pagan who doesn't know any better. He daren't be tried here either or he'd surely be convicted and hanged. So he's taken to Bucks County [12] or Philadelphia where he's petted and sheltered and made a fuss of and never even goes to trial. That's the way it is between us and Indians, and why we've had to take the law in our own hands."

Uncle Wilse nodded grimly to the boy. "I'll tell you something else. No Indian friends of yours better come to see you around here. If you expect that heathen abductor of yours, you better send him word to stay away."

A sudden fear struck the boy as he thought of the possible coming of his father. Bitter words poured out at his white uncle.

"Once a white man lived with Indians. He married Indian woman along the Muskingum. They had three young ones. All girls. One day white man makes mind he goes back to his people. He kills his squaw and three girls. He takes their scalps back to Philadelphia for scalp money. His name David Owens. Maybe you are his brother."

With the quickness of a giant cat, his Uncle Wilse moved to his feet and slapped the boy. The force of the blow almost knocked him down.

"No, I'm not his brother!" he shouted. "But I wish I was. He did his duty to his country and his people. He believed in getting rid of vermin and so do I."

With great difficulty, True Son regained his posture. Now he stood straight and rigid. No more words, he told himself, would come from his mouth today. Around that mouth the white mark of his uncle's heavy hand still lay. At the owner of the hand his eyes burned with black, consuming hatred.

VIII

True Son kept his word. That evening he pulled off the tainted clothes of his cousin Alec, and no one could induce him to let them touch his body again. Mornings he put on his Indian dress. When his father forbade him coming downstairs in it, he made a prison of his room. In a few days Peter Wormley, the Derry township tailor, came. He drew a painful face at the rude hunting-frock and leggings. What was he coming to, he complained, having to leave Captain Rebuck's fine broadcloth coat to dress a half-naked Indian boy!

Peter Wormley turned out two suits for the boy while he was there, one out of new cloth for Sunday, and one for weekdays from an old suit of his white father.

[12] BUCKS COUNTY—A county in southeastern Pennsylvania.

"Now take care of these!" he charged when he left. "Remember you're no young Injun running wild in the brush any more!"

Later Andy Goff, the shoemaker, arrived. The tailor's fitting and fussing had been trial enough, the clothes he made were ugly as Alec's. But the shoemaker was worse. The boots he pounded out were like half-hollowed logs. They gripped the boy's feet, wedged his toes, cramped his ankles. He felt that he stood in millstones. How could white men endure such things when they might run light and free in moccasins? Next day True Son went back to his Indian footgear. Then one night when he lay half asleep, Aunt Kate came in and took both pairs of moccasins. She carried off his Indian dress, too, and now if the boy didn't want to languish in bed, there was nothing for him to do but put on his prisoner garb and clatter about in his hard leather boots.

It was done, he suspected, so he wouldn't run away, for no man or boy could hope to get far through the woods in such encumbrances. Already Del Hardy had gone back to his regiment. At first True Son welcomed his going, but once away, he missed him keenly. Of all these white people he had known the guard the longest. He was the only link to Half Arrow and his people along the Tuscarawas. He had no one to speak Lenni-Lenape to any more.

And now all the odious and joyless life of the white race, its incomprehensible customs and heavy ways, fell on him like a plague. Every afternoon but the sixth and seventh he must be a prisoner in his mother's bedroom learning to read, making the tiresome Yengwe marks on a slate. On the seventh morning he must sit, a captive between his father and Aunt Kate in what they called the Great Spirit's lodge, with the strong scent of the white people and their clothing about him. The whites were very childish to believe that the God of the Whole Universe would stay in such a closed-up and stuffy place. The Indians knew better—that the Great Spirit loved the freedom of woods and streams where the air blew pure, where the birds sang sweet, and nature made an endless bower of praying-spots and worship-places.

Sometimes he felt the Great Spirit had utterly forgotten him in the white man's land. Then he would remember what Kringas[1] back along the Tuscarawas had told them. Kringas was old and rheumatic, a great-uncle to Half Arrow. True Son could recall most every word.

"Nephews. Never think the Great Spirit forgets you. Some Indians think he favors the white people. They say the white people have their flocks of cattle to kill from when they are hungry. They have their barns filled with grain for their pots when they need it. The Indian has none of these. Nephews. Some think this is bad, but of truth it is good. It shows the Indian he is not supported by storehouses but by the Ruler of Heaven. Nephews. I have been young and now am very old. I have often been in want. It taught me that the Great Spirit suffers us Indians to be so for a purpose. It's to show us our dependence on Him who is the Father of us all and to let us know that if we do our part he will always supply us at just the right time. If we wait

[1] KRINGAS—Pronounced krĭn'gàs.

and are worthy, he will deliver the enemy into our hands."

Today True Son wondered if the Great Spirit had anything to do with his being sent out for a new bushel basket. Aunt Kate had sent Gordie along to show him where the basketmaker lived, but he suspected that Gordie was really the string to lead him back again. She need have no fear that he would run away on a day like today, for this was still the Month When Cold Makes the Trees Crack. The sun on the treeless white countryside blinded him, and his boots slipped in the snow as moccasins never would.

By and by they came to a little dark patch of woods near a run. In the woods was a log cabin. Blue smoke rose from the chimney. The door opened to their knock, and a very old man with a brown wrinkled face stood there welcoming them. For a moment it was almost like being in the village at home. The ancient Negro basketmaker might have been an Indian. The cabin had a dirt floor like cabins along the Tuscarawas. The chinked logs and white-oak baskets had such a smell of the Ohio woods that the boy was overwhelmed with homesickness.

He sat on the earth floor on a mat plaited from shavings, watching the wrinkled brown hands split the splints and weave them into a bushel basket.

"You're the Butler boy took by the Injuns?" the basketmaker said. "I heerd about you. I was took myself when I was a little tyke. The Wyandottes [2] got me down in Virginny. Before I was twenty a Pennsylvany captain got me out, and I been working for him ever since."

[2] WYANDOTTES (wī′ăn·dŏtz)—Another name for the Huron (hū′rŏn) tribe.

"You're a slave, 'Bejance," little Gordie said.

"I reckon I am, child," he agreed equably. "And so are you and your brother, though you don't know it yet. Now I know it too well. For nigh onto sixty years I been wantin' to go fishin' in the spring and summer, and huntin' fall and winter. But every spring and summer I had to work in the fields and every fall and winter in the woods. Now when I kain't work in the woods and fields no more, I kain't go out huntin' or fishin' neither. All I'm good for is sit on my bench and braid up hampers for the white folks."

"You're not free like us," Gordie declared.

"No. I'm never free from white folks," the Negro assented. "And neither are you and your brother. Every day they drop another fine strap around you. Little by little they buckle you up so you don't feel it too much at one time. Sooner or later they have you all hitched up, but you've got so used to it by that time you hardly know it. You eat with a fork and spoon. You sleep in a bed. You own a house and a piece of land and pay taxes. You hoe all day in the cornfield and toil and sweat a diggin' up stumps. Piece by piece you get broke in to livin' in a stall by night, and by day pullin' burdens that mean nothin' to the soul inside of you."

True Son felt a constriction in his chest.

"I'll never be a slave to the white people," he declared.

"Oh, you don't aim to, boy. Neither did I. I reckoned I was gettin' out of the woods. I was a goin' back home to fine folks and good livin'. I was gettin' back to good houses and barns and tools and wheat and barley fields, to clocks that told the time, and preachers that preached out of books and prayed your soul to heaven. Now I'm eighty-four years old near as I can make out, and the best I remember of my time is when I was a boy in the woods. I kin look back and see my whole life stretchin' like a cordstring behind me. And the brightest piece was when I ran free in the woods. It had a glory I ain't seen since."

True Son looked at him hungrily.

"Can you talk Lenape?"

"When I was young I could. Not Lenape but Wyandotte. I could rattle it off like I was born to it. But the Wyandottes and Lenni-Lenape can't understand each other. Now the Shawanose and the Lenape kin."

"Not too good but they can make each other out," True Son said.

"That's what I say. The Shawanose and the Lenape kin make each other out. Once I could talk a little Lenape. All I recollect now is: *nitschu*, friend, and *auween kachev*, who are you, and *kella*, yes, and *matty*,[3] no. I kain't even recollect much Wyandotte any more. Once when I was workin' up the river for Mr. McKee, a Wyandotte came through. I could understand everything he said, but it shamed me that I couldn't talk it back to him."

"I was hoping you could talk Lenape with me." True Son was disappointed.

"No, they's only one left around here who can talk Lenape, or Delaware as they call it around here. That's old Corn Blade up on the Third Mountain, and I reckon he's a hundred years old."

"Where's the Third Mountain?"

"You know the Kittaniny Mountain?[4] You kin see it from all over Paxton township. Well, that's what some call the First Mountain. The Second Mountain lays just beyond. Still farther north is a short mountain they sometimes call the Stony Mountain. It don't run out to the river. That's the Third Mountain. On top the Almighty left a pile of rocks like a church and on top of that a pulpit. Up in those rocks is where Corn Blade lives. How he keeps alive, nobody knows because he never comes down. He's afeard the Paxton Boys'll scalp him."

All the boy could think of when he got back to the house was the old Indian on the Third Mountain who could talk Lenape. Most of January, the Month When the Ground Squirrels Begin to Run, he stood at the window looking north through the small panes. He couldn't see the Third but he could see the First Mountain. It rose from the fields dark brown and furry like the back of an immense beast. After a fresh snowfall the paths of the mountainside stood out clear. The deer paths were short. The wolves' paths were longer, crossing the mountain at dips in the ridges. Near the foot of the mountain a broad path ran level to the westward. It must be an Indian path, the boy told himself. In his mind he could see it running on and on, fording the Saosquahanaunk,[5] crossing the mountains and rivers beyond till it reached the Tus-

[3] NITSCHU . . . MATTY—*Nitschu* (nĭt′skōō); *auween kachev* (ou·wēn′ kȧ·kĕf′); *kella* (kĕl′ȧ); *matty* (mät′ĕ).

[4] KITTANINY MOUNTAIN—Probably a reference to the Kittatinny (kĭt′ȧ·tĭn′ĭ) Mountains, an extension of the Blue Mountains.

[5] SAOSQUAHANAUNK (sous′kwä·hä′nounk)—The English version is Susquehanna.

carawas where blue smoke rose from the dark weathered cabins, and quiet and peace lay over all.

Then it was February, the Month When the First Frog Croaks. One day the cold went and the rains came. Almost overnight the paths vanished, and the mountain turned from white to something dark, shaggy, and comfortingly wild. Just to look at it did something to the boy. He thought he could smell the forest as it smelled along the Tuscarawas after a rain, with the trees soaked black as ebony, and mosses on the bark and ground, green as splashes of paint. The ragged bark-flags of the river birches would be flying redder than ever. The buck's tail would lift white and unconstrained as he sprang. The boy's heart filled with wild longing. He could almost hear the sharp, fierce shout of his Indian father's gun along the river and taste the aroma of Kaak,[6] the northern goose, roasting on the coals along with his favorite cakes baked from Indian corn and bean meal.

What he hungered for most was the sight of an Indian face again—his father's, deep red, shaped like a hawk's, used to riding the wind, always above the earth, letting nothing small or of the village disturb him—his mother's, fresh and brown yet indented with great arching cheek wrinkles born of laughing and smiling, framing the mouth, and across the forehead, horizontal lines like the Indian sign of lightning, not from laughing but from war and talk of war, from family cares and the strain of labor—and his sisters' smooth young moon faces, not pale and sickly like the faces of white girls, but the rich blooming brown of the earth, their lively black eyes looking out from under the blackest and heaviest of hair, always with touches of some bright red cloth that set them off and made them handsome. Even the ancient face of Corn Blade, which must be no more than a wrinkled brown mask, would do him good, the boy felt, just to see it.

The Pawpawing Days passed. The Month of the Shad came.[7] The roots of grasses scented the thawing earth and air. He could hardly wait. One day he took a loaf of bread and piece of cold beef from the wooden safe[8] hanging in the cellar. Like a half-grown panther playing at stalking its own den, he made his stealthy way to the barn. Dock, the gray horse he had ridden from Carlisle, stood long-haired in his stall. Bridle and saddle hung from oaken pins. It did not take the boy long to ready him, stowing meat and bread in the saddlebags. Then keeping the barn between him and the house, he led the horse toward freedom.

"True Son! Where are you going? Take me along!" Gordie called, running after.

He lifted the boy to the front of the saddle and climbed up behind. Once out of sight of the house, he turned Dock through the half-down bars[9] to the open road. In time they passed a two-and-a-half-story house with a cooperage[10] near by.

[6] KAAK—Pronounced käk.

[7] PAWPAWING DAYS . . . MONTH OF THE SHAD—The month in which the pawpaw tree blossoms . . . the time of year when the shad leaves the ocean to spawn in fresh water.

[8] SAFE—A ventilated closet in which food is stored to keep it safe from insects.

[9] BARS—Wooden bars serving as a barrier across a road or path.

[10] COOPERAGE—A shop where barrels and casks are made and repaired.

"That's Uncle Wilse's!" Gordie said. "And there's Cousin Alec. He's running in the shop to tell Uncle Wilse that we went by."

True Son didn't care. The earth was wide. The sky was the spread wings of a giant bluebird overhead. The sun shone warm. Dock splashed through runs that flowed full and wild. Down a long hill the road entered a dark green woods of pine and hemlock. Mysterious paths led through. A savage creek foamed in the hollow and delicious untamed scents rose from the ground and thicket.

He stopped the horse for a long time.

"True Son, what do you see? Do you hear something?" Gordie kept asking, but how could the older boy tell even his brother what he saw and heard! He let Dock stand in the woods cropping at twigs and buds. Why did the white race imprison itself in houses and barns when the life-giving forest stood all around? Kringas had spoken true. Perhaps the Ruler of Heaven and Earth had imprisoned him to make him value freedom when he got out. Never even along the Tuscarawas had he tasted such savor in the open trail, the sweet air, the green forest. Ahead lay the wide riches of the Saosquahanaunk, the shadowy watergaps, the unseen valleys and streams, and then the Short Mountain with Corn Blade calling in good Lenape from the rocks on its summit.

They were coming in sight of the Narrows when the sound of hooves rose from behind them. Here in this deep, holy place where the river broke through the Kittaniny Mountain, True Son wished he could have been alone. He steeled himself against the strange men on horseback overtaking him. Then looking up with surprise he saw his father, Uncle Wilse, and Neal, the farmer.

"So you were running away!" his father accused him.

"We were going to see Corn Blade," the boy said.

"Don't lie to your father!" Uncle Wilse threatened and True Son braced himself to be struck.

"Corn Blade is dead long ago," his father told him.

True Son said nothing. His Uncle Wilse reached into the bulging saddlebags.

"What's this?" he asked when he brought out the bread and cold meat.

"They were for Corn Blade," True Son said, but he saw that no one believed him.

"Did you know you were taking this stuff to Corn Blade?" Uncle Wilse put to Gordie who looked unhappy and kept still.

"So you lie and steal!" True Son's father reproached him.

"I told you what to expect, Harry," Uncle Wilse said.

"Well, we'll keep him under closer watch from now on," his father promised.

The boy tried to show no feeling. He kept the muscles of his face smooth as he had so often seen his Indian father do. The hardest thing, now that he had come so far, was to turn around and go back. He had lost all the precious beckoning things ahead. They had almost been his, the unseen valleys, the unforded streams, the untrodden forest and the great shaggy, unclimbed mountains that tried to push the white man, when he passed, into the river.

IX

It was one of those unusually mild days that sometimes come to the lower Susquehanna in late March. Outside, the sun shone. A song sparrow sang. The low grass in the orchard already looked green. Two maples in blossom stood red against the distant dark mountain. You could smell the good, upturned earth where Neal and a hired man were ploughing, with chickens and a robin following the furrows.

But inside the big upstairs bedroom, Myra Butler had her windows closed and the curtains drawn. She lay on her couch in the welcome dimness with her eyes half closed. She was thinking, as she had so much, of that day in July eleven years ago. It was harvest time and Harry was helping the cradlers.[1] He had taken little Johnny along. They were cutting wheat in the farthest field that curved like a wide snaith [2] into the timber surrounding it on three sides. This timber and most of the other woods that used to stand between here and the Susquehanna was gone now, cut down and destroyed in the Indian wars. But then it stood thick and heavy as it had when the first settler came.

A hundred times she had heard the story and a hundred times had she told it, how the savages had hid in the woods and watched the cradlers. How long they had been there no one knew, but with devilish cunning they waited till the harvesters were in the middle of the field far from their rifles stacked along the fence. Then they opened fire. Tom Galaugher was killed, and Mary Awl, who helped in the binding, was wounded. The other harvesters made their escape, all but little Johnny who had been left in the shade of a big hickory, building a playhouse with shagbark.[3] When the men came back with help and fresh arms, the boy was gone. They had kept the news from his mother as long as they could, but in the end they had to tell her that the savages had her child. That was when Myra Butler had first taken to her bed.

Lying here this March morning with her eyes half closed, she thought she heard someone ride up to the house. Afterward there was the sound of feet on the stairs, a knock, and Kate's vigorous red face peered around the edge of the door.

"Parson Elder's come!" she said and came in. Swiftly she redded the room,[4] drew back the curtains, combed her sister-in-law's hair and helped her into another gown.

Afterward a lean gray-haired man in black smallclothes,[5] stockings, and slippers with fine silver buckles entered. He was much beloved in the two townships. His keen face seldom lost its gravity, and it didn't lose a shred of it now as he quietly crossed the room and pressed the invalid woman's hand.

"I saw Harry at the mill yesterday. He said you were poorly."

"It's nothing unusual, Parson," Myra Butler said. "But I'm always glad when you come."

"It's unusual enough, Parson!" Kate corrected bluntly.

[1] CRADLERS—Harvesters. Years ago grain was cut by hand with a cradle scythe.

[2] SNAITH (snāth)—Scythe handle.

[3] SHAGBARK—The shaggy bark of the hickory tree that can be peeled off in large slabs.

[4] REDDED THE ROOM—Cleaned up or tidied the room.

[5] SMALLCLOTHES—Close-fitting, fine-woven knee breeches.

Parson Elder glanced at one face, then the other. He was a leading citizen of the county, long pastor of the Derry church, a colonel in the militia, a shrewd and successful farmer, and not easily affected by complaints and circumstances. Now he pulled a chair to the side of the couch and seated himself much as Dr. Childsley might have done.

"Tell me about it."

"There is nothing to tell," Myra Butler said. "As you know, I haven't been a well woman for more than eleven years."

"But she's worse lately," Kate put in. "And I'll tell you why, Parson. It's Johnny. You remember how often you prayed with her in this room that the Lord would restore him to her. Your prayers were righteous and the Lord answered them. Now you must do something about it, because you're the one responsible for getting him back."

The parson didn't look at Kate, only at Mrs. Butler.

"What's he done now?" he asked quietly.

The mother's lips closed tight, but Kate was quick to go on.

"You know how he tried to run off and take little Gordie along? It's lucky Harry and Wilse found him before he got away. Well, that's only a small part of it. He's a trial to all of us but Gordie. He's ungrateful. He won't own to his white skin. He still thinks he's Indian. He says Indians don't have regular meal hours so he doesn't want to come to meals except when he's hungry. He shames us in front of the relations and neighbors. He won't join in our talk. He says we only know uninteresting things. He means we don't talk of savage things like beaver and panthers and bears and skins and scalps like the Indians. He believes Indians are sinless and perfect. He even believes it's right to lie and steal."

"I'm sure that's untrue!" Myra Butler declared quickly.

"Well, if it's untrue, then things here walk off by themselves," her sister-in-law answered tartly. "First it was one of your butcher knives. Then Harry's rifle went. Fortunately it wasn't his best. The brass part to the patch box [6] is broken, and Harry said he never liked it too much anyway because curly maple rusts the barrel. But it shoots to kill, and Harry says some powder and lead are gone, too. I've missed Indian meal. In fact, twice the bin was lower than I remembered."

"But you don't know definitely if anything was taken!" Myra Butler insisted.

"Not a hundred per cent. I only know somebody around here who doesn't like us. It don't matter about me but it galls me to see him treat his own mother and father like strangers. The Bible says, 'Honor thy father and mother that thy days may be long upon the land which the Lord thy God giveth thee.' [7] But he only honors his false Indian father and mother and that's what's the matter with Myra."

"Kate—"

"It's true, Myra, and you know it. You've heard him talk almost every chance he gets of this Cuyloga and Queen Haga [8] or whatever her name is. He may live in this house, but he's still a savage

[6] PATCH BOX—A block under the front sight of a gun.

[7] 'HONOR THY FATHER . . . GIVETH THEE'—Referring to the Fourth Commandment.

[8] QUEEN HAGA—Kate is referring to John's Indian mother, Quaquenga.

through and through. If he wasn't the image of his Grandfather Espy, I'd swear Colonel Bouquet made a mistake and sent us the offshoot of some squaw and no-account trader."

Myra Butler winced. The Reverend Elder saw it and sat back in his chair. He could afford to take his time and deliberate. It was a difficult subject.

"Perhaps I can talk to the boy for you," he said.

"I was hoping you would. I'll get Johnny for you," Kate told him and left the room.

Neither the parson nor Mrs. Butler heard the boy come in. One minute the two were talking together, and the next he stood inside the doorway, a lithe, dark-faced figure. In his jacket, pants, and boots he might have been one of several well-to-do boys in the township. But on second glance there was something different in the way he held himself, an erectness, an intensity, an alien unmanageable quality you could not lay your finger on. Most boys brought in front of the formidable Parson Elder were reluctant, some terrified, all uneasy. This boy stood before him without fear or inferiority. Only his eyes showed traces of unhappiness and concealed hostility.

Before any of them could speak, Aunt Kate came brushing through with pitcher and glasses on a brass tray.

"You don't need to stand, Johnny," she told him.

He dropped down to sit on the floor, and the clergyman noted the instant passage of pain across his mother's face.

"There's a chair here by me, Johnny," he invited.

"I am used to sit on the floor," he answered. "Always I sit on the ground outside. It is the lap of my mother, the Earth."

Aunt Kate flashed a look at the parson. "You see!" it said. The sweetish perfume of whisky penetrated the room as she poured the glasses. It was the custom of the times, a full one to the clergyman, slightly lesser ones to her sister-in-law and self, and one mixed with water to Gordie who had followed her upstairs. Now she held up the fifth glass already partly prepared with water.

"Johnny?" she asked but you could see she didn't expect him to take any.

The parson observed his refusal quietly.

"It would be more dutiful if you would join us, Johnny," he said. "Your aunt invited you, and it's well to be obedient and of the same mind."

The boy's dark eyes met the minister's.

"I don't like," he said briefly.

"I'm not sure that all of us particularly like everything we do on earth," the Reverend Elder commented slowly. "However, there's such a thing among civilized people as putting off things of the flesh and showing charity and things of the spirit, especially in the home. If you practiced politeness and took a dram with us, you might feel more friendly towards God and man."

"My father told me why white people give rum to the Indian," the boy answered. "Get Indian drunk. Buy his furs cheap. Afterward Indian gets sober. Has no money, no furs, no nothing. Hates white people. Kills them some day. Now Aunt Kate gives rum to Gordie. You want give rum to me. You want make us hate you? You want make us kill you some day?"

Aunt Kate turned on him angrily.

"Now that's enough, Johnny," she threatened.

"I'll talk to him, Mrs. Stewart," the parson said. He turned to the boy. "John, what you say about some white traders is probably true. I've never seen it but I've heard of it and don't condone it. There are evil whites like everything else. But this fellowship between us isn't evil. It's just sociable. We are friends here together. We don't want to get anything out of you."

The boy's eyes showed disbelief.

"You want me your friend, you say. Maybe you want me to do like you. Want me baptize or pray to your God or believe things I be sorry for afterward."

There was an awkward silence. The parson flushed.

"I do want you to believe certain things that are good for your soul," he admitted. "Things that nearly all your white race believe in and practice. And I do want you to do some of the things I say. For instance, to treat your mother with kindness. Also not to lie, steal, or swear."

"Indian only swear like he learns from the white man," the boy said. "My father says when he is a boy he hears white man say God damn. God damn when it rain and God damn if powder don't go off. So my father says God damn too. Then somebody tells him what God damn mean—that the Great Spirit must burn it in hell fire forever. He is surprise. How could the Great Spirit bother to burn in hell fire forever powder that don't go off? Why would he burn rain when he made rain and sent it on earth? After that my father don't swear. He tells me never swear. It's the white man's lie."

"Well, I'm glad to hear such precepts from a pagan," the Reverend Elder said with dignity and just a little sarcasm. "Did he also instruct you to treat your mother and father with love and obedience?"

"Always I treat my father and mother with love and obedience."

"He means his Indian father and mother," Aunt Kate explained. "He won't believe that his Indian father ever did anything bad and horrible like scalping white children and dashing their poor brains out against a tree."

"Is not true!" the boy cried, getting to his feet swiftly. "But is true that white Peshtank men killed Conestogo children, and Colonel Elder is captain of Peshtank men."

The shape of sarcasm rounding and modeling Parson Elder's mouth slowly disintegrated. His face showed pain.

"No one knows better than a preacher of the gospel the dark unfathomable heart of man," he said sadly. "Sometimes even the most exemplary Christians get out of hand."

"Does good man like preacher get out of hand, too?" the boy asked.

The parson gazed at him steadily.

"No, not often," he said. "I did what I could. As their military leader, I ordered them to disperse and go home. But they refused. Had I persisted, they would have killed my favorite horse."

"Better your favorite horse dead than the favorite young ones of the poor Indian," the boy asserted.

The Reverend Elder sat more powerful and self-restrained than Myra Butler had ever seen him.

"It's not only the white man who

breaks the fifth commandment,[9] Johnny," he said humbly. "Evil and ugly things have been committed against the will of God on both sides. Eight and nine years ago I never dared preach without a pair of loaded rifles in the pulpit. The men in my congregation kept their rifles standing by their pews. It was to discourage any of your red friends peeping in the window from trying to scalp us and our children. You say your foster Indian father never harmed a white child. It may be true. But I'm sorry to tell you that I know personally the authentic cases of many white children who were killed and mutilated by Indians. In one case the head was used as a football."

"Is not true!" the boy cried. "I see many scalp but no children scalp in our village. My father says men are cowards who fight children."

Aunt Kate had stepped up quickly to stop the boy, but the parson deterred her. His face was white. Despite that, he lifted his glass to his lips with great self-control. Sipping the whisky coolly from time to time, he talked with strong earnestness to the boy of the brotherhood of man and the duties of Christians, red and white, to each other. He asked no questions that required answer, made no provocative statements and brooked no interruption. He closed with a long fervent prayer and then dismissed the boy.

When the latter was gone, the veteran parson wearily asked if he could have another glass.

"Living here near the frontier, we have our own particular trials and tribulations,"[10] he said. "This case of Johnny is not an easy one. But I don't think we should be too discouraged. It seems fairly natural under the circumstances for the boy to act this way. He's been in the hands of heathen for more than ten years. He's been virtually raised by them. Their character and philosophy was above the average savage, I'm glad to say, and you can be thankful for that. Just the same they were not white people, certainly not Christians, and you'll have to bear with their influence for a while. Ten years' teaching takes a long time to break down. You know what Proverbs says, 'Train up a child in the way he should go and when he is old he will not depart from it.'[11] John has been brought up in the way he was not intended by his Maker to go, and it will take some effort to make him depart from it. But time is on our side."

"What can we do, Parson?" Myra Butler asked piteously.

"Just what you have been doing. Be grateful that God has given Johnny back while he's still a youth with a pliable mind. Teach him daily. Don't get discouraged. You see him every day and don't notice his improvement. But I see him only on the Sabbath or once in a while when I come here, and I can see a great change in him already. Despite himself, his English is better. Already he walks and gestures less like an Indian. You can't expect him to turn into a seraph[12] or saint overnight. Don't push him too hard. Guide him little by little.

[9] FIFTH COMMANDMENT—"Thou shalt not kill," Exodus 20:13.

[10] TRIALS AND TRIBULATIONS—Sufferings and sorrows.

[11] 'TRAIN UP A CHILD . . . DEPART FROM IT'—Referring to command in Proverbs 22:6.

[12] SERAPH—One having the characteristics of a seraph, a celestial being.

Spring is here and soon he'll be working in the fields, getting up an appetite for the table. One of these days he'll notice some pretty and desirable girl. Pray God he takes a fancy to her. Then it won't be long till he's settled in our white way of life."

X

Harry Butler stood just inside the door. This was his son's room. It seemed curious that he hadn't been here since Johnny was back and probably wouldn't be now save for the boy's sickness. What that sickness was none of them exactly knew. Dr. Childsley had been here twice, the last time this very day when he had bled the boy's feet [1] into a wicked-looking gallipot [2] from his saddlebags.

But he wouldn't diagnose the trouble. The brusque Lancaster County doctor only looked grim, and muttered as he did the other time that the boy had lived too many years among the Indians, subject to their uncivilized fare, hardship, and mode of life. Indians were liable to mysterious forest miasmas,[3] he said, and at times they died like pigeons. Despite all curative knowledge, white physicians didn't know very much about these savage ailments. Cut them up, and the heathen had the same organs and muscles as civilized peoples, even to the exact shape and size of their bones. The blood they hemorrhaged was as rich and red as any white man's, but there were obscure primitive tendencies and susceptibilities in the aboriginal race, and they weren't helped by the superstition lurking in the dark and hidden recesses of the untutored mind. All he knew definitely was that the boy had some unknown fever, probably a result of his long unhappy captivity. This fever had remained unchanged now for nearly a week. It had refused to yield to powerful teas and powders. Sooner or later it would reach a crisis, and send the boy either into slow recovery or the grave.

The latter statement had shaken Harry Butler. He wished he could do something. The boy had been the victim of unhappy chance. If he hadn't taken him that day eleven years ago to play at the side of the wheat field, the Indians would never have got their heathen hands on him. Today he would be a different being, brought up on Christian precepts and the nourishing food and drink suitable to his race.

He wished he could talk to the boy, expressing these thoughts. It might release the burden long on his breast. Of course, he himself had really not been guilty, only the unwitting means that evil had used. Just the same if he bared his heart, it would relieve him, and Johnny might bare his in return, expressing filial regret for his persistent and unhealthy passion for Indian ways and for his stubborn antagonism toward the decent thrifty ways of his white people. He might even confess his part in the disappearance of the curly maple rifle and ask forgiveness. In that event Harry Butler would completely pardon him and tell him that he meant to make him a present of it anyhow.

[1] BLED THE BOY'S FEET—Blood-letting was once a common way of treating disease.

[2] GALLIPOT (găl′ĭ·pŏt)—A small vessel once used by doctors.

[3] LIABLE TO MYSTERIOUS FOREST MIASMAS—Exposed to or unprotected from miasmas (mī-ăz′măz), an infectious material once believed to be a part of the night air.

But for all the eager anxiety in the father's mind, the boy remained deaf to him, lying flat in bed without benefit of a bolster, the dark eyes in his flushed face gazing straight up at the ceiling. When his father spoke to him, he gave no sign except eventually to answer. But there was little warmth or affection in it, only a kind of brief and mechanical response. The older man might as well have been a stranger with no right to invade the boy's solitude and privacy.

It was curious how at such a time in the shadow of death all the belongings of the helpless victim affected a father to a degree he dared not speak of even to his wife. There from a row of wooden pins on the wall hung the still and mute clothing Johnny had worn in the sunlight of health—the weekday coat and pants made over from a suit the Reading[4] tailor had cut for the father when he was still a young man—the boy's Sabbath clothes in which he attended divine service and listened to the word of God—also the miserable and pitiful Indian dress in which he had come home from captivity. Since the boy's illness, Aunt Kate had hurried to take it out of hiding and put it back, hoping it might console him and her own conscience as well.

In the end, the father left the bedside saddened and unrelieved. Going to a small room downstairs which had once been used as a cloak room but was now his office-room, he stood at the high desk and opened his heavy leather-bound account book. Hardly had he begun to set down the day's entries when he heard someone ride up to the house. There was a knock and Kate called him. When he got to the hall he found Parson Elder's son standing there in restrained excitement. He waited till Aunt Kate had gone.

"My father sent me over. There's Indians around and he wanted to warn you."

At once Mr. Butler took the younger man to his office-room and closed the door. Here he turned around, shocked.

"Indians! Why, we're at peace!"

"Maybe we are but they aren't," the other said. "One was shot tonight at Mehargue's[5] pasture. He's lying down there now. Since Papa's head of the militia, Mr. Mehargue came right over."

"Any of our people attacked?"

"We don't know yet. They've seen only two of the savages so far. They stopped first down at the mill asking for the white boy that was taken from the Indians. The men at the mill sent them to Mr. Owens' cooper shop. At least, that's where the Indians went. My father thinks the men at the mill told them Mr. Owens was Johnny's uncle and that the Indians couldn't understand English very well and thought that Johnny lived there. But some think the men at the mill did it on purpose, for devilment. They know how much your brother-in-law hates Indians. But evidently Mr. Owens was very kind and hospitable. When one of the Indians asked for 'lum,'[6] Mr. Owens gave him some. I believe the Indian had two or three mugs. Then he started boasting about himself and abusing the whites. There were some cronies

[4] READING (rĕd′ĭng)—A town in southeastern Pennsylvania.

[5] MEHARGUE'S—Pronounced mĕ·är′gūz.

[6] 'LUM'—Rum. There was no sound for *r* in the Delaware language. When they tried to make the sound, the result was more like an *l*.

with Mr. Owens, and they said the Indian told degrading stories on the white people. Anyhow about sundown the two Indians left. It was just getting dark when the Mehargues heard two shots. Some others heard them, too. When the Mehargues investigated, they found the Indian lying dead and scalped in their pasture. Mr. Mehargue said it looked like somebody had ambushed him from behind the trees because the Indian had been shot from the side and back. My father said he'd have him buried in the morning."

Harry Butler heard all this with a mixture of emotion. Troubles seldom came singly. Never had he known it to fail.

"Did your father say who he believed shot him?"

"He didn't say, sir." The younger man moved uneasily and declined to meet Mr. Butler's eyes.

"Did he say what happened to the other Indian?"

"Nobody's seen him since. If there were only two, my father thinks he's back across the river by this time and still going. But you never know how many might be hiding in the mountain. My father thought you ought to hear right away. He said you'd likely want to keep it from Johnny. It might aggravate his sickness."

For a while after the rider had gone, Harry Butler stood thinking. If he told Kate, she would invariably tell Myra and that would upset her. Let her hover around for news. He would confide in no one for the present but keep his guns handy and loaded. When he heard Gordie trotting downstairs from his mother's room, he went back to his office. It was a relief at such a time to stand at his desk and straighten out his business affairs, to reckon up his accounts and property. When he opened the heavy brown-leathered book, the double pages with their solid lines of physical and financial items looked back at him, stable and reassuring. Presently the rough nib of his quill scratched roughly over the smooth blue and red lined surface of the thick page.

May 31, 1765

Sold this day holdover grain to one, Achmuty

248 bus.[7]	*Wheat*	*at 4*	*Shillings*	*a bus.*	
191	*do*	*Rey*	*do 3*	*do*	*do*
82	*do*	*Oats*	*do 1*	*do*	*do*

Opened last Kag of Cydar. Very Potent Sow Campbell sold me has Litter of 11

He wished there might be more things to set down. Dealing with valid material things seldom failed to calm him. For a while he occupied himself counting the paper pound notes and silver shillings.[8] The considerable sum steadied him. A pity his eldest son hadn't been raised to evaluate and enjoy the satisfaction and benefits of honest work, the solace and support of ready cash, and the remuneration and accumulation of active property.

[7] *Bus.*—An abbreviation for bushels. *Do* in the same paragraph is an abbreviation for *ditto* meaning *the same.* *Rey* is an old spelling of rye.

[8] PAPER POUND NOTES AND SILVER SHILLINGS—In the colonial period Americans used the British monetary system.

XI

For a long time True Son had felt the sickness coming on. The pain in his forehead refused to be wiped away. It was just his eyes, at first he told himself, and came from looking too hard for word from his Indian people. All winter his eyes had stared down the road and to the far hills across the river, straining for sight of a word-bringer from his people.

Now and then letters duly came for his white father and mother. His Indian father, he remembered, would get messages, too, mostly by messenger. His white parents' letters were quickly broken apart, read, and thrown aside. His Indian father had more respect for words that somebody went to such trouble to send him. First the messenger was received and welcomed. He was made comfortable after his long journey and his wants supplied. Then when all was meet [1] and ready, perhaps in the presence of others who had been called to hear, the message was given in words and dignity sometimes noble as an oration.

The boy knew it was a long way from the Tuscarawas to the banks of the Susquehanna, but word of mouth had been passed farther than that. There was always a way. Traders and hunters traveled back and forth. A message could even be sent by hand. The whites were not the only people able to make marks on wood or paper. He had seen his Indian father carve signs on the bark of a tree far in the woods, telling how he had shot a bear at this spot and that if the traveler left the path toward the west, he could find a spring of water where the elk or woods horse came to drink.

But winter passed and no word for him ever came that he knew about. The first green leaves of the Schka'ak lettuce [2] scented the marshes. Birch buds stung the tongue, and the blossoms of the Tree of the Schwanammek [3] lay in drifts on the mountainside like remnants of last year's snow. Hardly dare he look at them for homesickness. But it was the call of Memedhakemo,[4] the turtle dove, that spoke to the very center of his being. Whenever he heard its note of lonely solitude, it carried him back on swift wings to the village on the Tuscarawas. It could almost be the same bird that used to sit on the hill of the High Spring and call in the early morning when the sun was breaking through the river mists. Then he could feel the bark town [5] coming to life around him. Soon he and Half Arrow would be leaving for their day's freedom in the forest, chewing hunks of dried venison as they went. Where the river widened into a cattail swamp,[6] their blood would race with the noisy talk of ducks and their fingers itch for the guns denied them. They complained of lost arrows shot across the water, but their fathers said if they had guns, they wouldn't get the bullets back either.

Other times they fished for Namespema,[7] the rock fish, and waded in riffles [8] for Machewachtey,[9] the red-bellied

[1] MEET—Proper.
[2] SCHKA'AK (skä'äk)—Skunk cabbage.

[3] SCHWANAMMEK—Pronounced skwän′ā-mĕk.
[4] MEMEDHAKEMO—Pronounced mĕ·mĕ·däk′-ē·mō.
[5] BARK TOWN—Indian village. All the Eastern woodland Indians constructed their homes from bark.
[6] CATTAIL SWAMP—A swamp or marsh where there grew many tall plants with furry spikes called cattails.
[7] NAMESPEMA—Pronounced nä·mĕs·pē′mȧ.
[8] RIFFLES (rĭf″lz)—Shallow places in the stream.
[9] MACHEWACHTEY—Pronounced mäk·ē·wäk-tē.

terrapin. Often they didn't come back till Memedhakemo called again from the hill, and the village hung wreathed in woodsmoke flavored with the scent of roasting meat and of burning red-willow tobacco.

Oh, that was the life of young gods in the forest, and how could one think to live without it! All through the winter and early spring he told himself that when Hattawaniminschi,[10] the dogwood, bloomed, he would have some word of greeting and encouragement from his Indian father, some message to keep up his courage and to say that the time of deliverance was near. But the fragile petals fell from the shad tree.[11] Dogwood came into broad bloom. Now the leaves of Wipunquok,[12] the gnarled and powerful white oak, hung tiny, pink, and furry on massive branches. And still he heard nothing on the breeze that blew most every day from the Tuscarawas. It came over him that he was dead to his Indian people, his body buried, his grave neglected, his name forgotten as last autumn's leaves that had floated down the river never to be seen again.

The worst of it was that something had happened to his unquenchable Indian soul. When first they had taken him from the Lenni-Lenape, he would have fought an army for the chance of returning. But now he had stayed in the insidious company of white people too long. Their milk-warm water had got into his blood. He had become tamed, submissive as a plough horse in the field. At first he had rebelled against the hoe. He had told his white father how once as a small boy the squaws had got him to help them hoe their corn. His Indian father had sternly reproved him. He was a man-child and should never dishonor himself with the labor of squaws.

But his white father could see no point in the story.

"We look at things differently here," he said.

A day or two later, old black Bejance came hobbling up the road on his two sticks. He gazed gravely over the fence at True Son and his hoe.

"They got the harness on you, Injun boy," he said. "The straps is buckled and the singletree lugged." [13]

The boy kept on down the row. That evening his white father spoke to him in the house.

"It wasn't so bad, was it, Johnny?" he smiled. "You did tolerable well for the first time."

His praise meant little to the boy, coming as it did from this man whose fondest place was his desk, his bald head bulging like a storehouse with useless figures of land, crops, and money. He was still incomprehensible to his son, in dress and sex like a man and yet unable to rule his own squaw, but being ruled by her, obeying her slightest wish, paying others to do her work while she spent her life in her room like a sleek white rat in its cage, concerned mostly with newspapers, books, and letters such as white rats liked to

[10] HATTAWANIMINSCHI—Pronounced hät′ä-wän·ĭ·mĭn′skē.

[11] SHAD TREE—A small tree or shrub that produces white blossoms in early spring and edible berries in summer.

[12] WIPUNQUOK—Pronounced wĭ·po͞on′kōk.

[13] SINGLETREE LUGGED—A swinging bar to which the traces, a part of the horse's harness, are fastened. The singletree is attached to the wagon or plow that the horse must draw.

chew upon. Beside her, the memory of his Indian mother was like a spreading sugar maple providing them all with food and warmth, while beside this feeble white man at his desk, his Indian father had been an oak sheltering them from both the heat of the sun and the fury of the thunderbolt.

When they had put him to bed, his white mother, supported by his father and Aunt Kate, came to his room to read to him from the black book she said God had given the white people. Later the white medicine man appeared, smelling of horses, practicing the white man's superstition of bleeding the feet and purging with powders. The boy let them do with him as they would. In his heart he felt there was no use. Let the whites tie the Indian, imprison him, surround him with guards night and day, still they couldn't hold him. There was provided for him a way of escape. He need not walk or run in it, only yield to the inward voice telling him what to do, let himself sink, permit the light of day to close over him, and the prison cell would be left empty above him.

He was dimly aware this evening that something out of the ordinary had happened. He heard the gallop of a horse. Later the sounds of commotion rose from the back porch.

"Go 'way! Vamoose!"[14] he heard Aunt Kate call. She sounded very cross.

Soon Gordie came to bed in excitement. He said Aunt Kate had seen an Indian looking through the kitchen window. The Indian had run like a coward when she went to the door with her broom.

True Son lay very still, letting the words sink into his mind. So one of his people was near! Perhaps the long-awaited message had come. At the thought, a lump long hard and dried up inside of him melted. A door he had never seen opened in his breast, and the first trickle of life-giving substance came through. Motionless he waited till Gordie slept in bed beside him. Then he sat up.

He felt very weak but stronger than he expected. The room stretched about him, faintly light with the night. After a while he put his feet to the floor. His Indian dress, he saw, hung beside his white clothes from a peg. He had not been forgotten by the Great Spirit. Everything had been provided. From time to time he rested on the chair from his small exertions. At last he climbed out of the open window, lowering himself till his moccasins touched the roof tiles of the low kitchen wing. Then he let himself fall and slide like a crumpled ball of spider down to the lap of his mother, the Earth.

His aunt, the Night, with her cool hands, received him. His brother-in-law, the West Wind, with his clear breath revived him. His very old uncle, the Moon, shone down upon him. When from the shadow of the barn he looked back, the big white stone house stood like some monster created by the white people, staring after him with one hostile yellow lamplit eye. It was good to look the other way in the soft, endless Indian moonlight, which was never shut up in houses, never having to be bought in white man's posts or lighted in a pot, but free to all the earth and its creatures.

[14] VAMOOSE (vă·mōōs')—A slang expression meaning go away.

Across the big field of tiny corn, he stopped where the fence row of sassafras trees made a shadow in which he could hide. There was no sound save of distant hounds. Into the stillness he threw out the regular spaced notes of Chingokhos,[15] the big-eared owl. Utter quiet followed as if even the dogs listened. After an interval he called again, telling a listener what white men would never notice that, although owls called from near and far in flight, his own calls came from the same place. Still there was silence. He called the third time, and now he added the unmistakable rasping whoo-haw of Schachachgokhos,[16] the barred owl, on the end.

This time an answer rang so close from across the fence row in front of him that he almost jumped. He guessed that all the time the answerer had been moving noiselessly toward him.

"*Auween khackev?* Who are you?" he called very low in Delaware.

"*Lenape n'hackey.*[17] I am Indian," a guarded voice he was sure he had heard before, answered. "*Auween khackev?*"

"I am Lenape, too. Come out and let me look on you."

But the unseen speaker in the fence row did not stir. True Son moved closer and still he could see nothing.

"*Lenni-Lenape ta koom?*[18] Delaware, where do you come from?" he asked.

"*Otenink Tuscarawas noom.*[19] From

[15] CHINGOKHOS—Pronounced shĭn·gōk′ōs.

[16] SCHACHACHGOKHOS—Pronounced shäk·äk-gōk′ōs.

[17] *Lenape n'hackey*—Pronounced lĕn′ȧ·pē n'häk′ē.

[18] *Lenni-Lenape ta koom*—Pronounced lĕn′-ĭ-lĕn′ȧ·pē tä ko͞om.

[19] *Otenink Tuscarawas noom*—Pronounced ō·tĕn·ĭnk′ tŭs′kȧ·rô′wăs no͞om.

the town on the Tuscarawas," the answer came, and now True Son was sure of the voice. A surge of joy lightened him.

"Half Arrow! *Ili kleheleche!*[20] Do you still breathe!" he cried. A bush detached itself from another bush and in the dim light the two boys rushed to each other. They embraced and cried out, gripping each other's arms. Half Arrow's fingers were iron.

"Cousin! I didn't know you. Your voice was like a Yengwe's trying to be Indian."

"*Ekih!*[21] Am I that bad?" True Son muttered.

"But now with me you will soon talk better!" Half Arrow promised.

"I hope. Let us go to the house."

But Half Arrow drew back.

"Cousin. It's better not to. I don't dare trust the white people. Already I am chased off by your white mother. She called bad names. She would not like to see me again."

"It wasn't my white mother, only Piwitak,[22] the aunt. You mustn't let the rudeness of white people affect you. They are young and haven't learned yet the hospitality of our Indian houses. If I ask them to, they will feed you."

"No, I am not hungry. I ate yesterday with Little Crane."

"Little Crane!" True Son said the name with delight. "Does he still breathe! Is he already a papa and how is his feeling for his young white squaw?"

"All the way from the Tuscarawas he talked of her. But she is still two days' journey off."

[20] *Ili kleheleche!*—Pronounced ĭ·lĭ′ klĕ·hĕl-ē′kē.

[21] *Ekih!*—Pronounced ĕk′ĭ.

[22] PIWITAK—Pronounced pĭ·wĭ·täk′.

"I hope he's not gone to her so I can still see him," True Son said.

"No, he's not gone, and you can see him," Half Arrow promised, but his voice sounded strange.

On the way, one ahead of the other, True Son plied questions, and Half Arrow answered. It was like medicine to hear the familiar boyhood tongue with the good whistling sound of the Indian consonant which white people did not have, and to speak without having to set his lips or tongue for the foolish Yengwe *v* and *r* which the Lenape did not need. All the way his spirits lifted so that he didn't notice where they were going. Then suddenly he saw they approached Mehargue's pasture and that Half Arrow had stopped speaking and was moving with slowness and caution.

"Why do you drag?" True Son asked. "If you whistle like the crane, then he will answer unless now since he is a papa he has become deaf."

"He is deaf enough," Half Arrow answered, moving from tree to tree where he paused and listened as if not for a friend but an enemy. At last he halted.

"I said I would bring you to him. Here he is," he said in a dull voice.

"Where? I see no one, unless he's a tree."

"He is something like a tree. Do you see him now?"

True Son strained his eyes through the shadows. All the trees he saw bore limbs and leaves. Then slowly he became conscious of a dark mark on the ground. He had taken it for one of the short logs of the white people.

"That which lies like a cut tree isn't he?" he asked.

For answer Half Arrow ran and knelt at the dark mound.

"Ai, for the Lenni-Lenape!" he cried and gave a long Indian moan.

True Son came slowly closer. Even in the dimness he could make out the design of the familiar matchcoat [23] Little Crane had worn last fall. It had been spread like a blanket, but the body beneath it neither moved nor spoke. True Son stared in rigid disbelief.

"Cousin. It was not sickness that brought him down?"

"No, it was not the sickness."

"It was not the Frightener that white people call the rattlesnake?"

"No, it was not the Frightener."

As True Son bent over the body, he felt a terrible hate for the ones who had done this. Could this hard and dried blood on the matchcoat be the life fluid that only a few hours ago had flowed through Little Crane's veins and had brought him all this distance but now could carry him no farther?

"Cousin. Who did this evil thing?"

"The shots came from behind. When I looked the butchers were over there behind the trees."

"Cousin. Where were you and what did you do that men would shoot after you in peace?"

"We did nothing and stopped at only two places. The first place we asked for you. They sent us to the second place. It was your white uncle who has men making kegs and barrels. But you were not there."

"Did you or Little Crane say anything to make him cross?"

[23] MATCHCOAT—A sort of mantle or wrap of coarse woolen cloth worn by American Indians.

"Cousin. Before we went in, Little Crane said we must remember we are guests of the white man. We must be polite. If you look at the skin of a white man, he said, you can see how thin and weak it is. Even such a small thing as words will bruise and cut it open. So we must not remind the white man what he knows very well, that his land rightfully belongs to the Indian from whom he stole it. No, we must be happy and tell happy stories. So when we went in, Little Crane was happy and told happy stories."

"Do you remember any of these happy stories?"

"Two I remember. They were very funny. Once some Mingue [24] stopped with a white missionary overnight and put their horses in his grass field. The missionary chased their horses out of the field. He said he intended mowing the grass for hay. The Mingue said, Friend, the field is on Indian land. Then how is it your grass? Oh, yes it is my grass, the missionary said. I fenced it in. But who grew the grass, you or the Great Spirit? the Mingue asked. The Great Spirit grew it, the missionary had to say. Then our horses have a right in it, the Mingue said, because we are the Great Spirit's children. Little Crane said you had to laugh at the missionary's face when the Mingue put their horses back in and ate up the grass. He was not a real Quekel [25] but wore a big hat like the Quekel. Little Crane himself had to laugh when he told it. Is there anything so funny, he asked the white men, as a

[24] MINGUE—A variant of Mingo, the Lenni-Lenape's name for Iroquois.

[25] QUEKEL—Quaker.

man thinking he owns Indian land if he fences it in?"

True Son stirred uneasily.

"Cousin. You said there was another story."

"That was very happy, too. It was about a Shawano who owed the white man he gave his trade to. The trader said he must pay up. He daren't even wait for winter when his pelts of the beaver and fisher fox would be prime. The Shawano asked if cattle hides taken in the summer time would be good in trade, and the trader said, yes he would salt them down. So the Shawano settled his debt with cattle hides, and not till the Shawano was gone did the trader find out the hides were from his own cattle. Cousin, it was a very happy story. I heard it once at home in the village, and the squaws had to hold their sides with laughing."

True Son stirred again. This was the bold, full-flavored Indian humor he had longed for. But he couldn't laugh tonight.

"Did the men at my white uncle's laugh?" he asked.

"Cousin. They didn't laugh. When we left your white uncle, Little Crane said to me, the white men are beyond Indian understanding. No matter how happy we talk, they won't laugh with us."

Half Arrow lifted the blanket from the body, and True Son saw with horror that his friend had been scalped. His cold savage rage rose and consumed him.

"First let us give Little Crane rest," he said. "Then we go to my white uncle and ask him who is the murderer."

With Half Arrow's knife and tomahawk, they cut out a shallow grave. On the mound they laid branches from the bushes in Indian fashion. Weak with exertion and covered with sweat, True Son led the way to the two-story house with the cooperage beside it. A shed was piled with hoop poles and stacked with new barrels and kegs shining white as skeletons in the moonlight.

The cooper shop was dark but light still showed in the house. True Son knocked and the short thick form of Uncle Wilse came to the door. At the sight of him, the boy's hate for this man who had slapped him rose and his voice with it.

"Where's Little Crane?" he accused shrilly.

His uncle stood stocky and untouched, peering out at him.

"If that's one of those Indians that was here," he said, "he's where he won't do any more mischief." He suddenly recognized the caller. "So it's you, boy! I thought you were sick and going to die. Does your father know where you're at? I reckon I better keep you till I tell him."

His quick stubby fingers shot out and caught hold of the boy. True Son struggled to free himself but the powerful hairy hands easily held him fast.

"*Itschemil!* [26] Help me!" he gasped and, with a rush, Half Arrow came out of the shadows.

He struck with such force that the unprepared man went down. Even so, he was more than a match for the two boys. Half rising, he threw Half Arrow back with one hand while he choked the kicking and writhing True Son into submission with the other. Things were going black before the boy's eyes when he saw

[26] *Itschemil!*—Pronounced ĭts′kē·mĭl.

Half Arrow return with a rush. The good Indian hate was on his face and a hoop pole swinging in his hands. It struck the heavy head of the white man who grunted and fell forward. True Son felt his own breath and sight come back as the death grip on his throat relaxed.

Quickly Half Arrow threw down the pole and pulled out his knife.

"*Pennau!* [27] Now watch me cut out his black heart!"

"*Matta.*[28] No," True Son said with regret. "He calls himself my uncle."

"Then let us skin him like a beast."

"*Tah.*[29] It takes too long."

"Well, anyhow, we will take his hair like he took Little Crane's. *Lachi!* [30] Quick!" Half Arrow gave him his tomahawk, and the two set to work together, one cutting, one hacking. At the pain, the heavy white man stirred, groaning loudly, and before they had got very far, steps sounded on the floor above them. One of the cooper hands who boarded with his master appeared suddenly on the stairs. With an exclamation of dismay, he hurried back.

"When we are done with this one, we will scalp him too," Half Arrow declared confidently.

"No, he goes for his gun," True Son said. "*Kshamehellatan!* [31] Let us run together."

Giving up their trophy with regret, the two youths faded into the night. True Son led the shortest way across fields to his father's farm. The big stone house, the small house, and barn all stood dark.

In the pitch blackness of the barn floor, he felt his whispering way to a mow [32] where he burrowed deep under the hay. From here he brought mysterious articles that out in the moonlight became a bag of meal, a tow wallet [33] of lead balls, a knife, a horn heavy with powder, his old bearskin, and a long rifle with the brass patch [34] broken off.

"*Ju!*" [35] Half Arrow exclaimed with delight at the sight of the rifle. He took it admiringly in his hands. "What a pity we did not have this at your white uncle's. Then we could have got his scalp and the other white devil's too. Now we could dance around the scalps. We could spit on them and sing revenge for the murder of our brother."

"Listen!" True Son said. "Somebody goes for help against us."

They could hear plainly the gallop of a horse across the valley. Most of their way to the wall of the First Mountain the sounds followed them, of other horses pounding the roads, raising the alarm in Paxton township.

XII

When True Son woke, he didn't know at first where he was. All he could remember was his sickbed in the house of his white father. He had expected he would die. Could this be the bright land of death, where all was made right? He remembered he had been weak. Now he

[27] *Pennau!*—Pronounced pĕn·ou′.
[28] *Matta*—Pronounced mät′ȧ.
[29] *Tah*—Pronounced tä.
[30] *Lachi!*—Pronounced läk′ī.
[31] *Kshamehellatan*—Pronounced kshä·mĕ-hĕl′ȧ·tȧn.

[32] MOW (mou)—The place in the barn where hay or sheaves of grain are stored.
[33] TOW WALLET—A bag made of tow cloth, a kind of material made from flax.
[34] BRASS PATCH—A block under the front sight of a gun.
[35] *Ju!*—Pronounced jo͞o.

felt strong. He had been bound. Now he was free. He had lain for days sealed in by the white man's plaster. Now he lay in the infinite open with green leaves moving over him and fresh air blowing on his face. His father, the Sun, had already risen. Around him his sisters, the Birds, sang. His brother, the Black Squirrel, coughed at him. His mother, the Earth, bore him up on her breast, while all his small cousins that stood or ran upon the earth spoke their scents to him—the Fox and the Pine, the Hemlock that men used for tanning, the Medicine Plants, the aromatic Spice Bush that bloomed in the spring and the Hazel that bloomed in the fall.

Then he thought he couldn't be dead, for somebody snored beside him. He turned his head and found Half Arrow's coal-black hair close to his face. Seeing that coarse hair sent the love for his cousin through him. He had come all the long way across mountains and rivers through a dangerous land just to reach his side. Through the night they had lain like brothers, close as chestnuts in a burr for warmth. His old worn bearskin below served them both, Half Arrow's blanket above.

And now he remembered what had happened last night and that where they camped was the top of the Kittaniny Mountain he had watched so long from his white father's farm. Joy rose in him at the thought that he couldn't go back, for, if he did, they would surely put him and Half Arrow in irons. And if his white uncle died, they would hang them by the neck in the barbarous custom of white people. Even if freed, the friends of his white uncle would never let him live. He and Half Arrow would be ambushed and scalped, their hands cut off like the young boys, Shalekaha, Exundas, and Tonquas of the Conestogo.

"Cousin!" he breathed, and he knew by the quickly halted breath that Half Arrow was awake. "We waste daylight. Let's go before the white men catch us."

Half Arrow sat up instantly.

"Where are the white devils?" he demanded.

"They're not here yet but they soon will be."

"*Elke!*[1] That's good. Then I can sleep again."

"No, we have many hundred miles to go."

Half Arrow gave him a look. He jumped to his feet like a deer.

"Cousin. You mean I don't go back all that long way alone?"

At True Son's answer, he broke off two branches of hemlock. Holding one in each hand above his head, he began to dance around his cousin chanting foolish Lenape words of triumph.

"*Sehe!* Not so loud," True Son cautioned. "They will hear you down in the valley."

"They are too deaf," Half Arrow boasted. "They can hear only the war whoop and money rattle. Maybe we better go just the same," he said and started to scoop up his carrying share of the belongings.

Down the north side of the mountain, they avoided white hunters' paths. Their moccasins sought to disturb no leaves or sticks, stepping from stone to stone. Now and then both boys stopped to listen. At the first run they clapped palms of

[1] *Elke!*—Pronounced ĕl·kē′.

meal from the sack to their mouths, washing it down with water in Indian fashion.

Half Arrow smacked his lips.

"Now I can go till evening," he promised.

Under cover of trees and brush they crept among the next valley's clearings. They climbed the second mountain, fording the second creek when they came down on the other side. Always they avoided the river trail. The third mountain they did not have to climb. As the old basketmaker said, it stood drawn back from its companions like a noble chief aloof from his fellows. True Son pointed out to Half Arrow the pile of rocks at the top where Bejance said the old Lenni-Lenape lived. But they had no time to look for him now.

Cutting northwest, they crossed the trail, forded the third stream at a cliff red with rock flowers, and pressed on toward the point of the fourth mountain where the great river broke through. Here True Son's strength gave out, and the rest of the day they lay in the woods. Twice they heard parties of white men crossing the valley, some on horseback, calling to each other and talking noisily. Once the sound of a rifle echoed from mountain to mountain.

For a while Half Arrow was gone to spy. He said on his return he had seen half the world from a tree on the mountain. A large creek flowed into the other side of the river, and a ford of rocks led to it. Before daylight both boys were at the river's edge, wet by the heavy mist, trying to peer across. At the first streaks of daylight they set their feet in the water. They found the rocks wet and slippery, tilting up sharply from the foundations of the mountain that once must have stood here. It was a hard crossing. Where the rocks failed, the boys had to wade. When the friendly screen of mist dissolved, most of the wide river lay behind.

True Son shivered with wet and cold. Since day before yesterday he had tasted no food save raw meal and water. And yet now as he climbed out on the western Saosquahanaunk shore, he felt around him a golden and purple brightness as if the sun had risen over the mountains behind him. He had escaped from his Peshtank prison at last. The very trees of the forest looked different over here. The unknown creek from the west flowed brown and primitive as a naked Lenni-Lenape.

His only shaft of regret was leaving Gordie. He could see him in his mind now, lying alone on their wide bed, a chattering squirrel by day, a bedwarming stone by night, only a little minny of a fellow waiting for his Indian brother who would never return. For a long count while Half Arrow watched silently, True Son stood on the point of land between the two streams, gazing down the broad watery road through the mountain gaps that opened like majestic gates toward his white father's house.

"You sorry! You don't want to go?" Half Arrow asked.

"Cousin. Nothing holds me now," True Son told him. "Cousin. I leave a small white brother. Out along the Tuscarawas I have only sisters. Cousin. From today on, you must be my brother."

For a long time they traveled blind, for there were high cliffs, thick woods, and no paths. Then suddenly they broke out on a narrow well-worn trail coming over the hills to meet the small river. Their feet took to it like wings. The very breath of the path was Indian. It dipped through the dim pungency of pine groves where hardly would you know the season, and it broke out into the bright new greenness of the hardwoods where even the blind could tell that this was the Month When the Deer Turns Red.

Always the endless Indian forest stood above them. When it thinned, there were the crimson Indian Hearts that white people call strawberry and the purple swords of Indian raspberries. Fish leaped from the creek and pheasants made thunder through the trees. Not often was Half Arrow silent. He pointed out the meaning of signs and droppings as if his companion so long among the whites had forgotten. Oh, never, True Son told himself, would he forget this path, this westward, ever westward path, deep in their Indian forest, with his cousin tramping before him, pointing and talking, giving thanks to every spring that ran across their path, for hadn't this water they cupped to drink lain deep in the dark caverns of their mother, the Earth, to be brought out just for their refreshment as they passed!

Only once, when the forest gave way to the cleared fields of a colony of whites, did Half Arrow's good humor leave him.

"*Lennau!*[2] Look at them. Cutters down of the Indian forest! Stealers of the Indian land. Let's give them a present of Indian lead. In return we'll take presents for our Indian brothers."

But all the time he talked, Half Arrow kept to the path, berating the thieving whites, regretting there were only two against so many and that he and True Son would have so far to carry booty.

"Ah well, lead is scarce," he said. "We will let them breathe this time. But didn't we fix that old *schwannack*[3] of your white uncle who scalped Little Crane! He won't forget us in a hurry. If he lives, he is rubbing his head right now. *Yuh allacque!*[4] What a pity we didn't finish him when we had the chance."

It made them a little uneasy when their path joined a deeper and wider path. It came pouring down through a mountain gap. You could see that white men and their horses had trod this path. But its makers must have been Indian, for it looked as if long before white men came it had been here. His own people, the Lenni-Lenape, must have traveled it, the Shawonose, the Nanticokes,[5] the Ganawese and Saosquahanaunks. Even distant nations had helped to pack it, the Sankhicani or Gunlock people that the whites call Mohawks; the W'Tassone or stone-pipe makers, called the Oneidas; the Onandagos or hilltop people; the Cuyugas or lake dwellers; the Meachachtinny or mountaineers that the whites call the Senecas; and the Tuscarawas, called by all Tuscarawas, for the word rolls easy from the tongue so that wherever they go

[2] *Lennau!*—Pronounced lĕn·ou′.

[3] *Schwannack*—Pronounced skwän′äk.

[4] *Yuh allacque!*—Pronounced yo͞o äl·ä′kē.

[5] NANTICOKES . . . ABENAKIS—The various tribes mentioned here are pronounced as follows: Nanticokes (năn·tĭ·kōkz); Ganawese (găn·ä-wēz′ē); Sankhicani (sän·khĭ·kän′ĭ); W'Tassone (w'täs′ō·nĕ); Oneidas (ō·nī′dȧz); Onandagos (ŏn·ŏn·dô′gäz); Cuyugas (kī·yo͞o′gȧz); Meachachtinny (mĕ·ä·käk′tĭ·nē); Cherokees (chĕr·ȯ-kēz′); Catawbas (kȧ·tô′bȧz); Kanahawas (kăn-ȧ·hô′wȧz); Canai (kän·ī′); Mohican (mȯ·hē′-kȧn); Abenakis (ä·bĕ·näk′ēz).

mountains, streams, and valleys are called after them. All these latter were the Mengue which the whites called the Mingoes or Six Nations, and the French, the Iroquois. But many others must have tramped this path, too, the Cherokees and Catawbas, the Kanahawas who should be called the Canai; the Mohican or River Indians, the Wyandottes that the French call Huron; and perhaps even the far eastern Abenakis who are brothers of the Lenni-Lenape and speak a dialect of the Lenni-Lenape tongue.

And yet for all those red peoples and nations who had trod it, not an Indian did they see that day. So far had the whites driven them from this country. Only twice did the two boys have to lie in the woods while parties passed, once when three white men came suddenly on foot, and another time when a train of nineteen pack horses slid down the mountain. Armed traders guarded them. Every bale of pelts on the horses' backs was a message from home. Surely, Half Arrow chattered, they were on the right track, for those pelts could only have come from Indian country, perhaps even from the Forks of the Muskingum and their own village on the Tuscarawas.

That night they lay on the western side of a mountain. Now not a river alone but a great wall was between them and the Peshtank country. Next morning their legs put a still bigger mountain behind them, and now they went on the path with less caution. Freely they baked cakes of Indian meal over their fire and roasted game shot by the striped rifle. Oh, they hid quickly enough from any armed men they saw who might take a fancy to their hair. But the deeper they went in the forest, the nearer they felt to home. They tramped a deep, long valley; saw sleeping cabins for white traders; drank from a spring around which you could see great numbers of red and white men had once camped; passed the Shades of Death where two mountains stood close and dark with ancient pines and hemlocks between.

At a fork in the trail, they took the north branch. Always they kept apart from the Bedford road to the south where the Peshtank men might seek them. Three times in one day the trail forded the same river. They passed an old Indian town and traversed the longest Narrows either of them had ever seen, stopping to see a curious stone as high as three men and only a few inches square, pointing to the heaven.

"I have heard of this stone," Half Arrow said. "Now if those that spoke knew the truth, only one mountain stands between us and the Tuscarawas."

They came on that mountain next day. Their breath grew short on the way up, for this was the tallest hill of all. But when they reached the top they found this was no mountain like the others, a steep way up, a steep way down and a sharp summit. The top of this mountain was very wide, stretching on and on, a high country with immense timber. They passed a few cleared fields, old Indian cabins, some beaver dams, and a deer lick [6] many miles long. So they kept on for two days until they met a river flowing strong and deep through the forest.

An Indian track went up and down,

[6] DEER LICK—A place where wild animals come to lick the salt that dries on the surface of the earth, or drink from a salt spring or brook.

and on the bank stood the log buildings of a trader. A few Indians loafed in front. Through the open door the eyes of the two boys caught the glitter of much goods. Once the trader himself came out to take oars from one of the smaller of two dugouts bobbing at the landing. The two boys did not venture close but sat on the roots of a buttonwood [7] at the edge of the water.

"I have heard of this river," Half Arrow told. "They call it the Alleghi Sipu.[8] From here, it is said, a fish can swim to the Forks of the Muskingum."

[7] BUTTONWOOD—A kind of tree.

[8] ALLEGHI SIPU (ä·lĕg'ĭ sĭ'po͞o)—The Allegheny River.

"Maybe it is so," True Son agreed, "but we are not fish."

"No, but if a fish can swim, a boat can float, and the Father of Heaven has already provided two boats at the landing."

True Son considered.

"I see the two boats. But they belong to the trader."

"Cousin. You have been too long among the whites. They have corrupted you in your thinking. You have believed their false claims that justify their plunder and pillage. Now, all we Indians know it is not stealing to take back from the whites what they took from us. Cousin. What have they taken from us? Land, woods, game, streams, fish, and our happiness. Cousin. Look at the white trader's fine house and all his possessions. Think how much he must have stolen from the poor Indians who trade with him."

"He is only half white and half Indian, I think."

"Then we will take only half of his boats," Half Arrow answered brightly. "I think we will choose the larger, for there are two of us and only one of him. He will thank us tomorrow morning for leaving him any boat at all."

"The trader has dogs," True Son reminded him. "The dogs won't thank us for coming to the landing at night."

"Only a white man would go up on a trader's landing at night," Half Arrow said. "First my father would cut a dry wind-fallen pole. Then he would float down the river like two sticks of wood in the night. His knife would cut the boat's thong. The dugout would float willingly downstream with him till out of scent and hearing. Then my father would climb in. I wonder that the trader never lost these fine dugouts before."

Later True Son went down the river trail alone. He carried the packs, the almost empty sack of meal, the powder horn [9] and the rifle. Far out of sight of the post, he cut a pole and waited in the woods. At sundown he piled his things on a point of land at the bend of the river. When it grew dark, he waded in like Half Arrow told him. The water was cold and he did not go far. After a while he called the call of the Schachachgokhos as they had agreed. But there was no reply, only the faint gurgling sounds of the river.

He had given up calling and almost hope when the impatient whoo-haw of the barred owl sounded in the river. Quickly he answered and waded farther out. Presently in the darkness he made out a shadow approaching over the water. When it reached him, he found a wet and dripping Half Arrow in a dugout but it was not the larger.

"The big one has an iron rope," Half Arrow told him.

"Let's be glad the trader hadn't two iron ropes," True Son said. He pulled the boat to shore and made haste to load it with their things. Then quickly he climbed in and they shoved off.

All night they lay floating on the current of the Alleghi Sipu, listening for falls ahead, peering through the darkness to avoid rocks and logs, poling quickly to the side at shallows and Indian fish weirs.[10] Before daylight they pulled the dugout into hiding on the thickly wooded shore, smoothing the telltale marks in the mud. All day they lay hidden, resting, watching the boats that went up and down. When no one was in sight, they split strips from a fallen pine and whittled them into paddles. After nightfall they were on the river again.

It was just before daylight when Half Arrow woke him with a sharp word of caution.

"*Nechi!*" [11] he said.

Looking ahead, True Son glimpsed a dull red campfire winking from the western shore. Then suddenly to the east there came into view the dark outlines of

[9] POWDER HORN—A container, often the horn of a cow, in which gunpowder was stored.

[10] FISH WEIRS—Barriers of brushwood or stakes placed in a stream to catch fish.

[11] *Nechi!*—Pronounced nĕ·kĭ'.

a settlement dotted already at this early hour with two or three burning candles and wood fires. Almost at once it flew into True Son's head where they were. Every moment he felt surer from the gleam of more water beyond.

"It's the great fort of the Plantscheman [12] that is now of the Yengwes!" he whispered to Half Arrow.

It was risky to pass, they told each other, but still more risky to stop and camp. Here the half-white, half-Indian trader and even the men from Peshtank might be waiting. Lying tense and low in the boat, they rode the gantlet [13] through. Never, True Son told his cousin, would he forget this morning in the Month That the Deer Turns Red, with the sight of Fort Pitt standing bristling on the point of land between the two rivers, its lights small and few, its strong stockade, redoubts, and houses dark and sinister against the faint murky streaks of red and orange in the eastern sky.

"The last time I saw it, I was heavy and a prisoner," he said. "Now I go light and free."

Then their dugout sped silently to the great meeting of the waters and passed into the sweep of the Ohio beyond.

[12] PLANTSCHEMAN (plănt′chē·mȧn)—Probably the Indian word for *Frenchmen*. In 1754 the French built Fort Duquesne (dü′kān′) at the junction of the Monongahela (mȯ·nŏn′gȧ·hē′lȧ) and Allegheny Rivers. Four years later they abandoned the position and burned the fort. The English then built Fort Pitt on this site.

[13] GANTLET (gônt′lĕt)—In frontier days the gantlet was a form of punishment in which the transgressor ran between two lines of men who struck him with clubs, switches, etc. Here the word is used figuratively with the white settlement and Fort Pitt representing the two lines of men.

XIII

Once the ominous point of Fort Pitt was past, they hid their boat and selves by day no longer.

"Indian world now," Half Arrow said. "Nobody comes after us here."

All that day they drifted with the current, paddling a little from either shore where white land-spies, traveling where they had no right, might covet their dugout. Most of the time they lay back dozing in the sun, for last night they had little sleep. Opening their eyes, they feasted on the passing richness of the Indian forest. Mile after mile it stood, untouched as the Great One had made it. Here were no roads bringing a plague of Yengwe carts, no prison fields, no unjust fences, no clocks enslaving the sun. Once a flock of noisy paroquets [1] with the bright feathers that warriors coveted flew overhead. Where small rivers flowed into the larger, they saw the good bark shelter of Indian camps and villages. Twice canoes shot out to hail them in their own tongue for news from the English fort. All the while, there was before them the constant, wheeling unfoldment of the river.

At sunset the deserted mouth of a creek drew them in. Cautiously they paddled up to find a place for the night. The great butts of the forest stood on either hand guarding the watery glade. It was utterly still. Only the drip from the lifted paddles ringed the glassy water. The last slanting rays of their father, the Sun, laid a red benediction upon them.

[1] PAROQUETS (păr′ȯ·kĕts)—Probably the Carolina Parakeet. This colorful bird, now extinct, was once found as far north as Albany, New York.

Then suddenly the thick darkness of the forest fell.

What kind of place it was they could not be sure of till morning. When it came, they found themselves lying on a ferny bank looking up through a lofty network of branches. Their father, the Sun, was back, smiling on them. The whole beautiful day lay ahead. There was no mist. All their little world stood in the crystal clarity of early forest morning. Their sister-in-law, the Creek, crept slowly past them. Their brother-in-law, the South Wind, rippled her with his breath.

"It's a place prepared for us," True Son said. "We mustn't offend the Preparer by going away without tasting it."

"I think the Preparer knows our corn meal is gone from the sack," Half Arrow agreed.

They set to work on a brush net at once. Often had they seen their fathers at the task. First they laid down the pliant new whips of the soft maple. Then they gathered vines from the forest grape, the Five Fingers,[2] and other creepers. Weaving them in and out of the branches, they tied each with a knot as it passed through. It took most of the hungry day. Then their brush seine[3] was ready. It was not so large as they had hoped. It looked still smaller dragged behind the dugout. The little fish swam through it. But the second time they drew it out, two longish white moons[4] came rising from the watery depths, and soon a pair of big and shiny fish threw themselves about on the ferny bank.

[2] FIVE FINGERS—Probably woodbine or Virginia creeper.

[3] SEINE—A net for catching fish.

[4] WHITE MOONS—Crescent-shaped shadows of the fish.

Half Arrow's fierce shout of joy whooped through the woods.

"Now already I am strong!" he cried.

They didn't leave next day or the next. As boys in the village, this was the fortune they had dreamed about, the greatest boon the Lord of Heaven could give them, a life of fishing and hunting, forgetting all else and by all else forgot, abandoning themselves to the forest and the bounty of its wild beasts. Always up to now they had gone as wards and lackeys[5] of their fathers. Now at last they were their own masters. No one stood between them and life. They took their joy and meat direct from its hand.

They passed their days in a kind of primitive deliciousness. The past was buried. There was only the present and tomorrow. By day they lived as happy animals. Moonlight nights in the forest they saw what the deer saw. Swimming under water with open eyes, they knew now what the otter knew.

The change in the weather was always foretold them by their uncle, the Moon. They could hear the rain before it reached them, a fine unmistakable roar in the forest. They lay snug under the upturned dugout, watching the trees drink in the wetness. Sometimes it thundered on their wooden roof. Then they knew it was a shower and soon over. But some days it fell with a long, soft, beautiful sound through the woods, so light at times they only knew it continued by the leaves on trees and bushes delicately nodding. The great butts turned darker with the wet. The mold under foot grew browner. Roots above ground were al-

[5] LACKEYS—Servile followers.

ways black enough. Now they looked blacker. Nothing but their brother-in-law, the East Wind, moved among the trees. After a long day of rain it seemed that this small dry spot where they lay was the only place left on earth. All the rest of the world did not exist, had never been.

But next morning after the rain, the mist drifted through the woods, vanishing like smoke, and they knew that all the drowned and blotted-out world was freshly created again. The mosses and trailing pine, the wintergreen, the mats of arbutus and partridge berry had never been so new and green. Lichens [6] stood up risen from the dead. You walked the thick leaves from last fall and underfoot there was no sound. Neither was there mud like in the white man's fields and roads. The forest floor lay clean and springy from ancient logs long since rotted level with the ground and now returned to a kind of youth by the rain from heaven.

When the two boys tired of fishing, they gathered shag bark and pine knots. Then they waited for a night when their uncle, the Moon, lay abed. First they set a clump of freshly picked branches in the dugout's bow. Behind it sat Half Arrow holding high a blazing torch of bark and pine tied by creepers. In the rear behind a second clump of green leaves, True Son paddled silently. His rifle lay ready across the thwarts.[7] The fire lighted up the road of the creek through the forest like day. They saw coons illumined and transfixed at the water's edge where they hunted frogs and crayfish. The boat glided through an unreal world. Submerged logs like Water Bulls of the southern rivers passed below them. Above them from either side trees mingled the white bellies of their leaves while before them on the forest bank a buck, with jaws adrip from his drink, waited for the fatal bullet.

Part of each day they squatted by the fire, cutting each other's ears to make them seemly, pulling the other's unnecessary hair, their wet fingers dipped in ashes. Only the long center growth on the head was left hanging. They were in no hurry, drifting with the day, mingling with slow time. Always the fertile forest spread around them. Abundance supported them. Completeness was for the taking. Days unfolded, rich and inexhaustible. After the Month When the Deer Turns Red came the Honey Bee Month. Soon would follow the Month When Corn Is in the Milk.[8] Even though they wished it, they couldn't stay forever. Their families would be wondering. They hated to go but they hated worse to stay. The sun had passed its northern meridian and was beginning its slow return. The foliage of the great forest wall had turned from light green to dark. It was time to leave.

The first thing they did when at last they reached the mouth of the Muskingum was to bathe in the home waters. And now as they paddled north there opened up before them the sacred heart of their Indian country, the beloved Forks of the Muskingum. Hurrying from the

[6] LICHENS (lī'kĕnz)—Small primitive plants that grow on tree trunks and rocks.

[7] THWARTS—Rowers' seats in a boat.

[8] MONTH WHEN CORN IS IN THE MILK—The season when the corn kernels are plump with a milklike substance.

northwest came the White Woman's River and from the northeast sprang the brave Tuscarawas. From here on the two boys never halted. Every bank and sandbar was familiar until they rounded the final bend and there among the great trees stood the bark village with blue smoke rising from the high-pitched roofs, with the forms of home villagers moving among the cabins and the sun throwing long shadows across the river over bank and street. It was as True Son had seen it so often in his mind, but never had he trembled like this at the sight.

They heard dogs barking at the strange dugout and saw brown faces turn toward them while quick hands shielded eyes from the sun. They had a glimpse of Shangas,[9] the Exhorter, already dressed in his bufflalo head and bearskins to preach against evil to whosoever would listen. And there lounging easily with his pipe was Nischa, strong as two men, with Wapahamink, his crippled son who drew himself backward on the ground; and Nungasa, the girl whom True Son used always to find looking so steadily at him; and Moschaigeu, the old scalped one who wore a rag of beaver to cover his ancient wound; and Tsuchechin, the fat squaw, who had once defended True Son, hiding him from a beating when his father and uncle were away; and Suskit, the big black dog that always wanted to go with him; and Wikiwon, who had a difficulty of speech and was mocked by boys singing war songs through their noses.

[9] SHANGAS—The Indian names in this paragraph are pronounced as follows: Shangas (shän′gȧs); Nischa (nĭs′kȧ); Wapahamink (wäp·ä·hä′mĭnk); Moschaigeu (mōsk·ī′gū); Tsuchechin (tso͞o·kĕk′ĭn); Suskit (so͞os′kĭt); Wikiwon (wĭk·ĭ·wŏn′).

"Now they know us and run to tell our cabins!" Half Arrow exulted. By the time they beached the dugout, a little group of squaws and young people stood smiling and chattering to them from the high bank. The two youths answered with fitting restraint. Weren't they men now, and hunters, home from an alien land? With dignity they picked up their belongings and stalked up the bank, trying to see no farther to the right or left than they had to.

"True Son, is it really you!" a soft voice hailed him, and there was his younger sister, A'astonah, her long hair streaming behind her, running with the children who had come to the cabin.

True Son looked at her with love and aloofness, carrying his rifle, passing her by, striding on with Half Arrow, past his older sister, Mechelit,[10] who stood halfway with bright vermilion cloth in her black hair, on to the door of his cabin where his mother waited. He saw her look of joy and that she had quickly fastened buckles to her strouding at news of his coming, but now she drew back to let him pass first to his father who stood straight in the shadows.

Cuyloga's face was strong and impassive. Not a line could you read from its muscles, but from his eyes True Son thought he discerned a deep welcome. Here in the shelter of the cabin, while others who had the right crowded in and many eyes watched from the doorway, they embraced.

"*Elke!* Do you live yet, True Son! And are you come home to stay?" his father said, breathing heavily.

[10] MECHELIT—Pronounced mĕk′ĕ·lĭt.

XIV

True Son slept that night in the bosom of his family. He lay at his accustomed place. He felt close around him the presence and affections of those dear to him. The good awareness of their rich brown skin, of their gray deer hide and bright calico garments, the rise and fall of their breath pervaded him. Familiar Indian odors of family and cabin that had been part of him since childhood lulled him to sleep. Even in unconsciousness he knew them. They spoke to his heart. They said now it could beat softly and at ease, for he was home again.

For several days the village celebrated the boys' return. The cabins of True Son's father and uncle stood open to friends to come and share their rejoicing. The delicacies of bear's oil and tree sugar were poured on hominy and venison and offered to the men. Warriors and hunters went from one house to the other, visiting, smoking, eating up all the two houses had. They shook bowls of plum stones for dice, the stones painted black on one side and white on the other. The sounds of their calling for black or white and then of their loud and triumphant counting could be heard through the village. There were the twanging of jew's harps [1] and the high whistling of hollowed cane flutes. True Son had thought nothing could approach the joy of hunting in the forest. But now he felt contentment in the deep summer days of the village. Afterwards they seemed to him like a dream.

It was a dream even then with shadows in it. Each day he was aware that not all the men of the village joined in the festivities. The cousins of Little Crane, who lived only a stone's throw away, did not come. They sat on a log in a group with their cronies and refrained from greeting True Son when he passed.

"If we had fetched back your white uncle's scalp, this would not have happened," Half Arrow spoke in True Son's ear. "But take no notice. My father says it will pass. Time will dry it up like carrion."

Just the same both boys felt uneasiness when the brother of Little Crane came from the Killbuck. His name was Thitpan,[2] which means Bitter, and his mouth was puckered up as from a mockernut.[3] With him were High Bank, his father-in-law, with only one eye; and Niskitoon,[4] which means Put-on-Paint, whose skin was tattooed from head to foot with signs of valor; also others, including Cheek Bone, a Shawano. They carried rifles, mallets, tomahawks, packs for the trail, and an old keg. One end of the latter had been knocked out and deer hide stretched over. With Thitpan's cousins they took up in the council house, which stood very near the cabin of Cuyloga. Here they started beating the drum.

True Son knew instantly from his father's face that this was serious. Not often had he seen his father so unbent and even jovial as since he had returned to him. But now his father's joking and easy bearing were gone. Grimly he listened to the drum and the songs for vengeance and war.

"When will the white man learn!" he

[1] JEW'S HARPS—Small musical instruments.

[2] THITPAN—Pronounced tĭt′pän.

[3] MOCKERNUT—North American hickory nut.

[4] NISKITOON—Pronounced nĭs′kĭ·tōōn.

muttered. "He says to the Indian, brother, have peace. The Indian buries the tomahawk. He hides it deep under a stump. He believes his brother, the white man. He visits his brother, the white man. Then his brother, the white man, murders him, a guest under his roof. He thinks no more of it than killing a snake in his cabin. The white man talks to other Indians. He says, brother, what's the matter? Why do you go to war? Why dig up the tomahawk? *Ekih!* The white man is a strange creature of the Almighty. He is hard to fathom. How can you reason with him? He is like a spoiled child without instruction. He has no understanding of good and evil."

Sumakek,[5] Black Fish, the father of Half Arrow, nodded. But True Son, standing with his cousin behind the men, could feel his mother and sisters stir uneasily at the talk and at the cries of recruiting.

"Look this way!" Little Crane's brother kept calling from the council house. "The cause of my brother is loud! It cries for blood! It's high in the sight of Heaven!"

"It's not necessary for everybody to join," True Son's mother ventured in the cabin.

"No, but I am not everybody," her brother, Black Fish, answered. "My son was Little Crane's companion. He walked with him on the journey when he was scalped. How can I turn my back?"

"Your back and mine are too broad to turn," Cuyloga agreed gravely. "It was going to visit my son that Little Crane was deprived of his life. *Ekih!* In my son's own white village."

[5] SUMAKEK—Pronounced so͞om′ä·kĕk.

"If you go, you wouldn't take True Son and Half Arrow along! They are only boys!" his mother begged them.

There was no answer from the two fathers. Behind their backs, Half Arrow and True Son exchanged glances. Anyone could see they were bursting to go. When the war party in the council house sang its war songs, both were filled with excitement. The chanting moved them so that scarcely could they contain themselves at the fearful scalp yells that followed. The long Ow-w-w-w-w-w turning into a sudden uw-w-w-w-w-w-w-w-w and held on a fierce tingling note set their blood on fire. Eagerly to each other they made the swift motions of tomahawking and scalping.

True Son's mother watched bitterly.

"Cuyloga. Think what the whites will do to our son if they catch him. They will burn him as a traitor to their side."

"Woman. Stay home and boil your pots," Cuyloga reproved her. "It is something I have no choice in. True Son is nearly a man. It would not look good for him to stay behind. Our friends would say he is surely white, see he is unwilling to fight against his white people."

"*Bischik,*" his brother-in-law grunted in agreement.

"But he needn't go unless he wants to," Cuyloga added.

"I go!" True Son said quickly. He felt the flush of a great exultation. He stood very straight, looking away not to see the quick pain in his mother's and sisters' faces. They were women and couldn't be expected to understand.

Much was healed between the friends of Little Crane and themselves when Cuyloga and Black Fish with their sons joined. Now they were all brothers in arms against the white murderers. Under-the-Hill, with an old purple wound in his cheek, also joined, as did Pepallistank,[6] Disbeliever, who with his bobbing lameness was about the fastest on his feet in the village; and Kschippihelleu,[7] whose name in English was Strong Water; and several others.

Now it is the custom that he who first proposes going to war is the leader. As Thitpan did, the others followed. When he tied up his pack, they tied up theirs. When he took his musket, tomahawk, and death mallet, the others took up theirs. When he sang his war song of farewell and promise not to return save with scalps and captives, the others made the chorus of brave ferocity and deserving death noises that can't be spoken in words but only in memory sounds that have come down in the ancient deeds of the race. True Son felt a savage sweetness he had never known before. He saw before his eyes a redness that colored all things like blood. He tasted a violence wilder than any root or game. Then Thitpan led the way out of the council house, followed in a single line by the rest.

Half Arrow and True Son brought up the rear. The latter remembered how it had been when last he had left the village. Then with everybody watching as today, his mother and sisters, his aunt and cousins, his friends and neighbors, his father had dragged him off like a dog. Now he went as a warrior, painted, his eyebrows and hair plucked, on his back his small pack and in his hands his hatchet and striped rifle with brass fittings that was the envy of everybody who watched. Once out of sight of the village, Thitpan shot off his gun and the others followed in a blast of farewell and promise to those at home who listened.

As guide for the party, Thitpan chose Disbeliever. This was a slight on his father, the boy knew. Why, there was no greater He-Who-Knows-the-Marks in the forest than his father. He could follow the trail of the most careful and secretive stranger, sometimes naming both his tribe and age. More than once he had taught True Son his art, how to read the smallest sign on the ground or bushes, a leaf turned back or a blade of grass down, a bit of mud on a stone, gravel turned up, how in snow men would tread in each other's tracks to look like one instead of two or many.

But today his father betrayed no flicker of disappointment, and his son stayed impassive like him. In silence he followed where Thitpan and Disbeliever led, on a path neither he nor Half Arrow had ever trod before. By the tree moss [8] and slant of the sun, True Son knew they traveled with the east wind on one side and the south wind on the other. By a deep riffle they crossed the Ohio and climbed hills strange to him.

In a forest valley they divided. One party under Black Fish stayed on the path, and another with Thitpan, Cuyloga, and others turned to the south where Disbeliever said were white men's cabins. They made out to meet at a spring across the mountain. The two boys went with the party under Black Fish.

[6] PEPALLISTANK—Pronounced pĕ·päl'ĭs·tänk.

[7] KSCHIPPIHELLEU—Pronounced kskĭ·pĭ·hĕl'-oi.

[8] TREE MOSS—The moss grows thickest on the north side of a tree.

Late that afternoon when all were met again, True Son noticed at once that Thitpan's party carried booty and something else. A leaping ran through his blood like quicksilver as he saw their first scalps, one an ugly dark roan like rusted iron, one brown streaked with gray, and a smaller one with long fine hair the color of willow shoots in the spring.

"*Jukella!* Oh, that I had been a lucky one!" Half Arrow wished.

By the fire that evening the two boys listened to a recital of the battle. Not a detail was left out from the time the Indians drew near the unlawful fields the white people had cut from the Indian forest and the cabins they had wrongfully built. The whole course of stratagem was recounted, every sign and movement, the successful deception and ambush, all the fearful and cowardly efforts of the whites to escape and appease them, together with the foolish and fruitless words they cried in their religion which was no help to them now.

Eagerly the two boys watched the takers of the scalps skillfully dry them, stretching them on red hoops and trimming off the uneven pieces with their knives. Each time a piece was dropped, Half Arrow picked it up. With deerhide thread he sewed a small, pied,[9] makeshift scalp for himself. The two boys put it on a pole and danced around it, singing fierce words of scorn and victory. But all the time the tender pieces of discarded scalp with long soft hairs the color of willow shoots in the spring kept entering True Son's blood like long worms clotting the free wild flow. He tried to forget what he had said to his white mother, that never had he seen a child's scalp taken by his Indian people.

Before he lay down for the night, he spoke to his father.

"Then the very young of the whites are our enemies, too?" he asked.

His father did not answer, only sat there strong with a look of aloofness, as if to say this was none of his doing. But Thitpan, who claimed the young scalp, answered angrily.

"They are our enemies, yes. Was my brother young or old? *Bischik*, he was not much more than a youth and yet he was murdered by your white uncle."

"It is clear to me now, cousin," True Son said humbly. "I ask you to forget my ignorance. I did not know we fought children."

To his surprise, his words produced a murmur of disapproval.

"Young cousin. I don't fight children. On our way home I should have taken her prisoner. But a child holds us back on our way forward. Young cousin. It was lighter for us to carry her scalp than her body."

True Son said nothing more, but he was conscious of dark eyes resentful at criticism from a boy.

Next day they came on a wide river. When Under-the-Hill joined them from downstream, he said that a boat of whites had just passed. Had they been an hour earlier they might have enticed it to shore and enriched themselves with rifles and powder. His report enlivened the eyes of the warriors. They held quick council. They would wait for another boat. This was a favorite river to the whites. Many from the Quekel provinces used it as a watery road to the west.

[9] PIED—Variegated in color.

Sometimes traders and even settlers, seeking to steal Indian lands, could be found floating on it.

"Now your son will be good for something," Thitpan said to Cuyloga. "Tomorrow he can call in his white cousins. When the boat comes close, we will fall on them with lead and hatchet."

It was strange, True Son thought to himself, that here among his Indian brothers this night he should dream of his white father and mother. He saw them in his dream as clear and real as in life. It was wintertime in the dream and their sled hunted him in the forest. "Johnny! Johnny!" they called as the sled went over the snowy ground. Then suddenly the sled was a boat, the snow was water and other white people stood with his parents in the boat. For the first time he saw that a white child was with his mother. He tried to see the face of the child, but it kept looking the other way. It was afraid of something. At last True Son heard what it heard, the roar of Sokpehellak,[10] the waterfall, just ahead of them on the river.

True Son woke in a sweat. He could still clearly see his white father's bulging head, the high cloak around the shoulders of his mother, and the frightened crouch of the child.

In the morning, Thitpan and Disbeliever instructed the boy in the meritorious art of decoy. First they had him wade in the river and wash off his war paint with sand. Then they bade him pull on a pair of pantaloons they had taken from one of the white cabins. The legs were too long and the warriors gravely consulted what to do. In the end they cut them short with their knives. Also, the blouse they gave him to wear was wrong. Perhaps it had belonged to the slain girl. It was too small and constrained him. He showed them he could scarcely move his arms or shoulders in it, but they told him what mattered only was that he look like a white boy. The smaller he looked, the better to melt the whites' cruel and stony hearts. Then Disbeliever took Cheek Bone along up the river to watch.

All day True Son waited for word that a boat was in sight. But the day passed and the next, and the only creatures that passed on the river were Those-Which-Go-Self-Suspended, the birds, and Those-Which-Go-Crooked, the butterflies. By the third day Thitpan said they had waited long enough. They took a vote to cross the river, but then Disbeliever, who had never deserted his post, came running and hopping down the path. He said a large flatboat of whites had just hove around the upper bend. Hurriedly True Son was given back his pantaloons to cover his breechclout. He was helped on with his white blouse and sent into the river.

"Remember," Thitpan instructed him, "you are not Lenape now. You are white. You must talk and act white. You must make their foolish white hearts bleed so they come close to help you."

The water felt mild enough as he waded in, and yet the boy found himself shivering. He had to stand in the river a long time. Once or twice he thought Disbeliever might have mistaken a floating log for a distant boat of white people. When he looked back to shore he could see nothing. Thitpan had picked a place

[10] SOKPEHELLAK—Pronounced sōk·pē·hēl′äk.

where the bank was thick with wipochk.[11] Not a wisp of smoke arose, nor was there a sign of life among the bushes. Even the footprints on the bank had been smoothed out. The river shore looked peaceful and unpeopled as the deepest forest. Then he turned back to the water and saw an actual boat pushing around the bend above him.

It was larger than he expected, filled with white people and their possessions. For a moment the thought of all the scalps and plunder gave his blood a fierce upward surge. Surely some should be allotted to him, for without him the others could do nothing. In his mind he recounted Yengwe words to call.

He felt sure that the boat had seen him. At first when it cleared the bend, it had kept to the middle of the river as if to be reasonably safe from either shore. But now he could see it pushing farther away from him. Although still a distance off, he lifted his empty hands and sent Yengwe words across the water.

"Brothers. Help! Brothers. I am English. I have white skin like you!"

The boat slowed visibly. There were both oars and poles among the men, but their use was suspended now. With its passengers staring, the craft drifted on the current. Presently it had lessened its distance enough for True Son to recognize the dress of several women.

"Mothers! Take me with you! Mothers! See, I am white boy! Mothers! Take me or I starve."

He called so piteously that now he

[11] WIPOCHK (wī·pōk′)—Indian word for *bushes* or *thicket*.

could hear the voice of one of the women remonstrating with the unwilling men. He couldn't make out the words, but her tone had the same imperial quality of his white mother when she forced her wishes on his white father.

"Brothers. Listen to her!" he cried. "Mothers. Don't pass by!"

Slowly he saw the boat make its first movement toward him. A man's harsh voice shouted to him.

"If you're white, wade out to the middle and we'll pick you up."

True Son waded only a little farther. He crouched low in the water making it seem to cover his shoulders.

"Is deep! I can't swim!" he whimpered.

He could hear the burden of argument rising from the boat and understand most of the words. Some believed in him and wanted to pick him up. Others shouted to the boatmen to go on. They mistrusted this strange youth in the river. Why did he say Brothers and Mothers, like the savages, and why was his hair cut around the edges in the Indian fashion? Why hadn't he chosen a shallow place where he could wade out? The man with the harsh voice declared he would come no closer even though the boy had a Bible in his hands. But one of the women was True Son's friend. She called them cowards. She said with spirit that if they were afraid to pick him up, she would take an oar and do it herself.

Some of the men gave in to her. Little by little the heavily loaded flatboat slanted across the river. At his back True Son could feel the rising exultation of his hidden friends. Then someone in the boat moved and disclosed a child. It was a boy about Gordie's age, dressed in a dark gray dress with a broad light band around it such as his small white brother used to wear. True Son stared and his begging abruptly ceased. Like a flash he remembered his dream. Could it be that his white father and mother were on this boat, coming west to find him, and that they had taken Gordie along? For the moment he forgot who and where he was. He was conscious only of this child so like Gordie coming closer and closer to the unseen rifles and tomahawks of his companions.

Once the child spoke to its mother and at the sound of the slender voice, True Son felt himself shaken.

"Take him back! It's an ambush!" he suddenly screamed.

For a moment the men on the boat stood startled. True Son saw terror and incredulity on the face of the white woman. Then in a panic the men bent their oars and poles to return the boat out of range. When it was seen that the prize was escaping, a volley of Indian shots rang out. True Son ducked as bullets went over him. He saw a stout man in the boat fall back as if too gross a mark to be missed. But distance kept most of the shots from taking effect. While the Indians came out on the bank yelling, reloading and firing again, the boat made off downstream, hugging the farther bank.

XV

Not until the boy turned back to shore did he realize the gravity of what he had done. He had betrayed his own brothers. None had welcome for him as he climbed the bank. Even Half Arrow turned away. Thitpan especially looked down on him angry and grim.

"Why don't you go with your friends? Why come back to us?" he asked scornfully.

True Son didn't answer. What could he say that they would understand? He didn't understand himself. He stood wet and miserable while the warriors withdrew to discuss him, his father and uncle among them. From time to time he caught the words: *tipatit*, chicken; *achgook*, snake; *putschiskey*, poison vine; *schwannack*, bad white people; and *schupijaw*, spy.[1] When he started to take off his dripping blouse, Thitpan called to him angrily.

"It is fitting to a white person. Let it stay."

"It is wet and cold," True Son told him.

"Maybe soon it will be dry and hot enough," Thitpan promised.

He spoke to Disbeliever and Under-the-Hill, who seized the boy. They bound his hands and feet with creepers. Then they let him stand. Disbeliever took charcoal from the fire and blacked half of True Son's face. Under-the-Hill fetched white clay from the river bank. With this he chalked the remaining side.

The boy knew well what it meant. They were divided in council about him, were going to try him in the Lenape fashion. Here in their court under the roof of the Indian forest they would decide his fate, whether to do to him as the char-

[1] TIPATIT . . . SCHUPIJAW—*Tipatit* (tĭp·ä-tĭt′); *achgook* (äk·gōōk′); *putschiskey* (pōōt-skĭsk′ē); *schwannack* (skwän′äk); *schupijaw* (skōōp′ĭ·jô).

coal signified or let him remain alive. Thitpan and his cousins were for burning. True Son, they said, had been sent by the white people. His tongue was like the crooked stripes of the whites' talking papers. His heart would always be with the whites. There was no Indian blood in him.

True Son stood hearing, waiting. It was strange that, with all their talk of his white badness, never had he felt more Indian than at this moment. All the stories he knew of his Indian people who with calmness of mind accepted their death sentence came to his mind. He remembered Be-Smoke, whom the Lenni-Lenape gave a reprieve of two years to live among his own clan, the Unamis.[2] Easily he might have stayed away the rest of his life but came back on the prescribed day for his execution. Also there was Heavy Belt freed at night by his brothers-in-law but who stayed to die because it had been decreed against him by the village. True Son understood them perfectly. How could life mean anything to you if already your people had killed you in their minds?

Thitpan voted first, throwing a heavy stick on the fire to show his strong choice for burning. One after the other followed, tossing sticks. When he saw how it was going, Half Arrow turned and stumbled off in the forest. True Son in pity watched him disappear among the leaves. His own father, he noticed, waited as if till last. When it came to the turn of his uncle, Black Fish, the latter motioned his brother-in-law to go ahead, signifying he would vote with him.

[2] UNAMIS (ōō·nä′mēz)—The Unami or Turtle Tribe was one of the three Delaware tribes.

The boy's father stood there a moment. Then deliberately he went to the fire. True Son's heart sank. He felt sure that his father joined in the vote against him. Then he saw that his father carried no stick. Instead he picked up a charred one from the fire. Silently he began blacking his own face, not one side, but both and the backs of the hands also. When he was done, he faced them.

All had watched him puzzled and a little disquieted. Now they waited, fastening their eyes on him. Cuyloga looked powerful and forbidding, his eyes in the black face flashing with whiteness.

"Brothers," he spoke. "I have listened to the council. I hear that my son is a spy from the whites, that his tongue is the fork of a tree and his heart black. Brothers. You know me. I am Cuyloga. Cuyloga knows his son. It was Cuyloga who raised and instructed him. He is like Cuyloga. If he is double-tongued and a spy, then Cuyloga is also. Why don't you bind and burn Cuyloga, for he is the father and responsible for the bad instruction?"

There was only a kind of displeasure and uneasiness from his hearers. Cuyloga went on. Never had he appeared more formidable and magnificent to his son than at this moment.

"Brothers. What do you expect of me—to stand idly by while you burn my son? My son has brought death to none of us. The scratches he gave us are not on our bodies but our pride. Brothers. How if my son is burnt do I go back and face her who lives with me in my house? How do I look in the eyes of his sisters who think the rainbow arches over him? Brothers. It is easier for me to fight you all than go back and say that Cuyloga stood by and did nothing while his brothers in anger put his son to the fire."

With the quickness of Long Tail, the panther, he took his knife and cut the boy's thongs. Then he stood there waiting for the attack but none came. The warriors were too astonished. They watched, sullen and yet fascinated by the drama. This was the great Cuyloga at his bravest that they looked upon, and none knew what he would do next.

When he saw that they hesitated to fight him, he turned to the boy. His manner was not softened. He spoke, if anything, with sterner dignity.

"True Son. I have things also to say to you. It is not easy to say them. When you were very small, I took you in. I adopted you in my family. You were to me like my own son. I taught you to speak with a straight tongue. I showed you right and wrong. I bound you to my heart with strong new vines. The old rotten vines that held you to the white people I tore apart. True Son. Now I find these old rotten vines have new life. They have sprouted again to pull you back to the white people.

"True Son. From your early days you were not neglected. You were taught the kinds and signs of game. You were taught their habits and where to find them. You were taught to hunt and shoot. You gave me no shame as a hunter. I told myself that when I am old, you, my son, will support me. When my bones creak, you will keep me in bear's oil and venison. When the ashes of life cool, you will be the fire to warm my old age. Never did I think that you would turn against me and that I would have to send you back to your white people. All this time I looked on you as Indian. I leaned on you as a staff. Now it is broken."

True Son heard with emotion.

"My father. Never will I go back to whites. They are strange to me. They are my enemies. My father. If you send me away, I must go, but never to the white people."

His father looked at him with sternness and pity for a long time.

"True Son. Maybe not now, you think. But after you are away from us for a while, you will go back. True Son. I look into your heart. I look into your head. I look into your blood. Your heart is Indian. Your head is Indian. But your blood is still thin like the whites. It can be joined only with the thin blood of the white people. It does not mix with the brave redness of Indian blood. True Son. I and you must leave here together. When we come to a white man's road, that will be the place of our parting. You must go one way. I must go the other. Afterwards the path will be closed between us. True Son. On the way to that road, no harm will come to you. Cuyloga will watch over his son. After that road, we are son and father no longer. We are not even cousins but enemies. You must have no pity for me or I for you. When sometime you meet me in battle, you must kill me, for that is what I must do to you."

The boy's mouth was stopped. He could say nothing, only look at his parent whom he had never loved or yearned for so much as at this moment. From behind a bush where he had returned, he saw Half Arrow's look of bitter emotion.

Even Little Crane's brother and cousins had been powerfully moved by the scene and oration. What they might do to his father in ambush later, he could not guess, but there would be no attempt to molest either of them now.

At a sign from his father, True Son kept on the white blouse and pantaloons. Both gathered up their packs. There was no leavetaking. The two boys looked at each other a long farewell. Cuyloga had already left and True Son moved up the riverbank path after him.

In the afternoon, Cuyloga shot a turkey. They roasted and ate it before evening. The boy could hardly touch it, and he thought that the meat stuck in his father's mouth also. Near noon next day they came to a ford. A wide trail led down from the north and crossed the river. With a sickening feeling, the boy saw the track was rutted by white men's carts.

His father spoke bleakly.

"This is the parting place. This is where the path must be closed between us. My place is on this side. Your place is on that. You must never cross it. If you come back, I cannot receive you and they will kill you."

The boy stood there a long time. He knew his father was waiting for him to go. At last he made the first movement, but at the edge of the water he turned. He hoped he would see in his father the faintest sign of relenting, but he found only fixed purpose in those dark eyes.

"My father. Do we say good-by to each other now?"

"Enemies do not do so," Cuyloga told him harshly. "I am no longer your father, nor you my son."

"Then who is my father?" the boy cried in despair and turned quickly to hide the blinding wetness in his eyes.

There was no reply from behind him. After a moment he forced himself into the water. It came to him then that this was the second time he was made to go through this living death. Not a year ago he had been forced to part from Half Arrow and Little Crane. Then, like his father today, they had stayed on the afternoon side [3] of the river. Then he had felt the same bitter grief as now. Then as today he was made against his will to take up his life among the white people.

But gladly would he exchange today for yesterday, if he only could. Then, no matter the ordeal, he could always go back. Then Half Arrow and Little Crane had waited faithfully on the bank while he crossed. So long as his trail ran by the water, he had seen them still standing on the afternoon side, raising their hands to him in loyalty and affection. But today when he came to the morning side and turned, no one stood watching him from the distant shore. His father was gone. He stood alone in the forest by the river.

Ahead of him ran the rutted road of the whites. It led, he knew, to where men of their own volition constrained themselves with heavy clothing like harness, where men chose to be slaves to their own or another's property and followed empty and desolate lives far from the wild beloved freedom of the Indian.

[3] AFTERNOON SIDE—West side.

EVALUATING A NOVEL

As you have probably discovered, the principal difference between a novel and the short stories you read in this book is that a novel is longer. Both are fiction; that is, they tell about imaginary happenings of imaginary people. In both short stories and novels the happenings form a chain of events called the *plot* which holds the interest of the reader by keeping him in suspense.

CHAPTER I

In *The Light in the Forest* the plot is the conflict between the Indians and the white settlers. Each race thought the other race inferior; each race thought its own way of life superior to the other's way of life.

1. What does Conrad Richter tell you about True Son's birth and parents? How do these facts show you that this conflict between the Indians and the white settlers is going to be particularly bitter for True Son?
2. Describe True Son's memory of his life in the Indian village on the Tuscarawas River. Can you show how this memory indicates True Son will hate his white rescuers?
3. Why was True Son surprised when Cuyloga, his Indian father, surrendered him to the white soldiers?
4. Do you think that True Son was justified in not wanting to return to his true parents?
5. Why does True Son want to kill Del Hardy? How does True Son's hatred for Del Hardy help develop the plot?

CHAPTER II

There are two sides to a conflict. In the first chapter, by presenting True Son's view of the white people, Conrad Richter showed you how the Indians felt toward the whites. In this chapter, Conrad Richter, by presenting Del Hardy's attitude toward the Indians, shows you how the white men felt about the Indians.

1. Can you recall some of Del Hardy's remarks that show he and the white men felt the Indians to be inferior to them?
2. How does Conrad Richter bring both sides into active conflict at the end of this chapter?
3. When people in a novel act, their actions do not seem real to us unless the author gives us a motive or a reason for their actions. What reason does Conrad Richter give that explains why the Indian Cuyloga was so willing to surrender True Son to the white soldiers? Do you think the reason a good enough one? Why?

CHAPTER III

1. True Son thought he could escape his enemies by committing suicide. Why did his suicide seem good and justified in his eyes? How would you judge such an action?
2. Who was Half Arrow? Why was Half Arrow surprised to find True Son bound?
3. What are some of the remarks Half Arrow makes that show you he thought the white men inferior to the Indians?

In the last part of this chapter, Half Arrow gives True Son the presents from his Indian father, mother, and sisters. Notice how each present is a tie between True Son and a member of Indian family, and how each one expresses deep love for True Son. Remember this incident. When True Son is returned to his white parents, you will want to compare their treatment of True Son with the way his Indian family treated him.

CHAPTER IV

1. What did Little Crane mean by saying that the white men were not an original people?
2. Little Crane refers to God as the Great Being. He says that the Great Being had to teach the white men to read and had to give them a Good Book (the Bible) in order to teach them the difference between good and bad, whereas the Indian could decide for himself what was good and what was bad. Do you agree with Little Crane? Do you think any man can decide

for himself what is right and what is wrong? Explain.

3. What was Little Crane's reason for saying there were so many thieves among the whites? Do you think it is better for men to own goods in common, as Little Crane says the Indians did, or for men to own their goods privately? Was it really wrong for the white men to be looking for good soil and timber? Do you think God created the forests to shelter animals or to serve men?

4. What are some of the things the white men did in the woods that made them appear stupid in the Indians' eyes?

5. What two incidents at the end of the chapter make the conflict between the Indians and the white men more bitter?

6. Comment on the advice Cuyloga gave True Son.

CHAPTER V

Besides a plot, the novel must have a *setting,* a specific time and place in which the events occur.

1. Can you describe the time in which the conflict of *The Light in the Forest* took place? Can you describe the parts of the country where the action happened?

2. The setting in this novel is divided by the great river (the Ohio) flowing past Fort Pitt. The land to the west belongs to the Indians; the land to the east belongs to the white men. Describe the way the people lived in each section.

3. Describe the way the white man's country appeared to True Son? How did his love of the Indian's way of life distort his view of the white man's civilization?

4. Compare Cuyloga with True Son's white father.

5. Do you feel True Son's white father gave his son the proper kind of welcome? Do you think Conrad Richter deliberately made True Son's white father appear inferior to Cuyloga so that he could make Cuyloga and the Indian way of life look better to you than the white man's way of life? Or do you think the things Conrad Richter describes in this meeting are only the things True Son, with his strong Indian preferences, saw?

CHAPTER VI

In Chapter V Conrad Richter showed you how the white settlement appeared to True Son. In this chapter, by describing the joy Del Hardy felt at returning to his own people, he shows you how the settlement looked to Del Hardy.

1. Describe Del Hardy's outlook on the white settlement. How does it differ from True Son's? What causes this difference?

2. Show how in the description of Harry Butler's farm Conrad Richter gives you the impression that Harry Butler is a wealthy man.

3. Do you think that True Son's mother and father gave him the kind of welcome an ordinary mother and father would give a fifteen-year-old son who had been away from them for eleven years? Do you think they made any effort to understand what had happened to True Son's outlook on life?

4. If you were a member of the Butler family, how would you have reacted to True Son's stubbornness?

5. Do you think Conrad Richter is giving a true picture of the way an average white mother and father would act in such a situation, or is he trying to convince the reader that the Indians treated even their adopted children better?

6. How do you explain the fact that little Gordie seems to understand True Son?

CHAPTER VII

The conflict that is the plot of the novel is always portrayed through the actions of the *characters,* or people in the novel. An effective character, by his words and actions, strongly manifests and develops the conflict of the novel. In *The Light in the Forest,* therefore, a character must strongly show his hatred of the Indians or the white men.

1. Tell some of the words and actions of Uncle Wilse that show he hates all Indians.

2. Review the words and actions of True Son that show he hates most white men because they are the Indian's enemy.

3. In Chapter VI, Conrad Richter, you remember, showed that Paxton had a meaning for True Son. How does he develop the Paxton incident so that in this chapter it becomes the real cause for the hatred between True Son and his Uncle Wilse?

4. In describing the Paxton incident, Conrad Richter says that the Indians accepted the religion of the white man and thought, because of it, they could be friends and live together. Do you think that by having the Christian white men murder the Indians, especially the Indian children, Conrad Richter is saying that Christianity has had little effect on the white men? What do you think of Christians, even Catholics, who today are unjust in their treatment of other races? What do you think of people who do not live according to their religion—like the white men who murdered the Indians at Paxton?

5. Harry Butler (True Son's father) and Uncle George were more tolerant in their attitudes toward the Indians. Why does this make them weaker characters than True Son or Uncle Wilse, as far as the development of the plot goes?

CHAPTER VIII

1. Describe True Son's idea of God. What did he believe the white men thought about God? According to Kringas, why did it sometimes seem that God treated the white men better than the Indians?

2. Bejance, the old Negro slave who makes baskets, tells True Son that the white men will make him a slave, too. By this he means that True Son's white parents will deprive him of the freedom he had as an Indian by forcing him to follow a way of life in which he must work, obey laws, and acquire property. Do you think this is true? Do you think the commands of your parents, the laws of the Church, the laws of the city in which you live, and the regulations of your school make you a slave? What would life be like without laws and regulations?

In the following chapters, watch how Conrad Richter comes back to this idea that the civilization of the white man has made men slaves. Watch closely to see if he makes this the real reason for the conflict between the whites and the Indians: the desire of the white man to deprive the Indian of his freedom, and the Indian's desire to remain free.

CHAPTER IX

The novelist develops his characters by making them take part in the conflict of the novel, or by having them shy away from it. In this chapter notice how Conrad Richter further develops Myra Butler's character by having her recall the story of True Son's abduction and by having her, in the conversation with Parson Elders, attempt to defend True Son.

1. What does Aunt Kate do in this chapter that shows you the kind of woman she is?

2. True Son is stubborn and resents his white kin. What does True Son say to Parson Elders that shows you he is stubborn and resentful?

3. Parson Elders wants to be kind and understanding. What does he say to True Son that shows you this? What does he say to Myra Butler after True Son leaves that further shows his kindness and understanding? Is there any reason to suspect that Parson Elders is also severe?

4. Conrad Richter did not want the parson to be perfect. How do you know this? What particular fault in the parson would make True Son despise him?

CHAPTER X

Until this chapter Conrad Richter has presented Harry Butler as a colorless man who seemed to take little or no interest in his son. What does he tell us in this chapter to change, just a bit, his original picture of Harry Butler?

1. How does the news that there are Indians in the neighborhood affect Harry Butler? Does this tell you anything more about his character? Does it explain why Harry Butler is able to return to his accounts?

2. How does the delight with which he goes over his accounts complete the picture of Harry Butler?

3. Back in Chapter IV, Little Crane said that white men heap up treasures like children, although they know they must die and can't take such things with them. Do you think by showing you how Harry Butler delights in amassing treasures, that Conrad Richter is telling you all white men are wasting their lives? What place does property have in the life of a man? Do you think it is necessary for each man to own property of his own? What happens when a man becomes too interested in property?

CHAPTER XI

1. In this chapter, how does Conrad Richter return to the conflict in True Son between the freedom of the Indian and the slavery of the white man?

2. True Son's sickness seems to have been caused by the fact that he had received no word from his Indian friends. Does this fact prepare you for the appearance of Half Arrow? Explain.

3. When True Son slips from his white father's house, he speaks of his mother the Earth, his aunt the Night, his brother-in-law the West Wind, his uncle the Moon. Do you think he is identifying the earth, night, west wind, and moon with the Great Being he worships as God? Does he think of them as spirits? Or what does he mean?

4. Why did the men at Uncle Wilse's barrel factory fail to see any humor in Little Crane's stories?

5. At the end of this chapter, Conrad Richter has brought the conflict between the Indians and the white men to a crisis. Why did True Son and Half Arrow attack Uncle Wilse? Do you think they were justified?

CHAPTER XII

This chapter describes the passage of True Son and Half Arrow through the forest wilderness occupied by the white settlers to the frontier of Indian Country on the Ohio River. Did you notice that the author shifted his attention from the conflict between the Indians and the white men to a kind of quiet and contented description of the forest and the rivers? No white men are encountered at all.

1. Why does True Son tell himself that he can never return to his white family? Remember this reason. It will make you want to ask a question about the way Conrad Richter ends the novel.

2. Both True Son and Half Arrow hate their white enemies; yet the character of each boy is different. Recalling previous incidents, and using incidents that occur in this chapter, can you describe this difference in their characters?

3. What do you think of the reasons Half Arrow gives for saying that they may justly steal the white trader's dugout?

CHAPTER XIII

This chapter describes the crossing of the barrier separating the white settler's world from the Indian's world, and tells how the two Indian boys passed into a land of complete freedom.

1. Conrad Richter does not mention the word *freedom*, but you are always aware that it is present. Can you describe the actions of True Son and Half Arrow that make them feel that they are completely free?

2. If they were completely free, why did True Son and Half Arrow feel they should return to their families in the village on the Tuscarawas River?

3. Do you think True Son is deceiving himself when he thinks of the Indian's life as one in which there are no duties and obligations? True Son refuses to speak to anyone on his return to the village until he first speaks with his father Cuyloga. Does

this fact show that True Son feels he has an obligation? What obligation? To whom?

CHAPTER XIV

Many early eye-witness accounts of Indian life described the Indian as being poor, often hungry, poorly dressed, filthy, lazy, and immoral.

1. Do you think the description of Indian life in this village is true? Have you read any other accounts of Indian life with which you can compare it?
2. What is the cause of the new war against the white settlers?
3. What effect did the scalping of the little white girl have on True Son's faith in the Indian way of life?
4. Why did True Son warn the white settlers in the flatboat that they were coming into an Indian ambush? Do you think this reason is strong enough to make True Son warn the settlers? Do you think that if the Indians had not scalped the little white girl True Son would have warned the settlers of the ambush?

CHAPTER XV

Recall the setting for *The Light in the Forest,* the part of America and the time in which the novel took place. Recall that the plot of the novel was the conflict between the Indians and the white men. Recall that Conrad Richter developed the characters in his novel by having them take part in the conflict, or by having them shy away from it.

In *The Light in the Forest,* the land to the west of the Ohio River is the land of the Indians; it represents freedom. The land to the east of the Ohio River is the land of the white settlers; it represents slavery to material possessions, work, a way of life. The Ohio River is the barrier separating these two lands.

1. At the end of the novel, Conrad Richter leaves True Son standing on the white man's side of the Ohio River. Why do you feel that, by ending the novel this way, Conrad Richter has not settled the main conflict, the enmity between the Indians and the white men?
2. The author has True Son return to his own people, constrain himself in heavy clothing, and thus become a slave to his own or to another's property. How can a boy take up the burdens of a man without becoming a slave?
3. Because he warned the flatboat of the Indian ambush, True Son can never return to the land of the Indians, the land of freedom. In Chapter XII, True Son said he could never return to his own people because he had attacked his Uncle Wilse.

Do you think True Son has a place to go? Do you think Conrad Richter may be saying that the life of the Indian was the better life, but man left it to lead a more civilized life and can never return to it? Do you think he is saying that our way of life, because it makes men slaves to property, offers us no meaning for our lives? Is he saying our way of life has destroyed us because it has taken away our freedom? If he is saying these things, how would you answer him?

For Further Reading

Heroines of the Sky by Jean Adams and Margaret Kimball contains sketches of seventeen women aviators.

The Stolen Spruce: A Mystery Adventure in the Maine Woods by Kenneth Andler. The search for an ancient boundary line and a long-lost corner tree form the core of this fast-moving novel.

Master Skylark: A Story of Shakespeare's Time by John Bennett. The young hero of this book runs away and joins a troupe of actors.

A Son of the Land by Ivy May Boltón. Roger, an English serf who lived during the Middle Ages, tries to win his freedom.

Lost Kingdom by Chester Bryant. The mystery of the cobra sign is solved in this story of modern India.

Haunted Airways by Thomson Burtis. Some strange happenings which have plagued the airlines are brought to a climax in the Mohave Desert.

Girl of Urbino by Mary K. Corbett is an adventure story of Italy during the time of Da Vinci and the Borgias.

The Black Stallion by Walter Farley. Alex Ramsey is shipwrecked on a desert island, finds and tames a wild Arabian horse, is rescued and returns to New York where he enters his horse in an exciting race.

Ghosts, Ghosts, Ghosts edited by Phyllis Fenner. These stories are well described in the subtitle: "Stories of spooks and spirits, haunts and hobgoblins, werewolves and will-o'-the-wisps."

The Avion My Uncle Flew by Cyrus Fisher takes an American boy to France for exciting adventures with his uncle who is building a new type of avion, or airplane.

Moon Ahead by Leslie Greener. Here is a novel of the first rocket trip to the moon.

Thirty Seconds over Tokyo by Ted Lawson. During World War II Mr. Lawson flew on a bombing mission with General Doolittle. This is the thrilling account of the raid, a plane crash, and great personal suffering.

The Spirit of St. Louis by Charles Lindbergh. The author piloted the first transocean flight over the Atlantic. His story is an absorbing account.

Jonathan Goes West by Stephen Meader is a tale of Jonathan's adventures with river boats and highwaymen in the 1880's.

Who Rides in the Dark by Stephen Meader tells of a fifteen-year-old boy's adventures with night riders in early New Hampshire.

The Ship Without a Crew and *Wind in the Rigging* by Howard Pease are two novels of murder and intrigue aboard ship.

Girl Without a Country by Martha Lee Poston. The daughter of an American medical missionary in China, who is captured by the Japanese, disguises herself as a Chinese widow in order to escape.

Ivanhoe by Walter Scott. Ivanhoe returns to England and fights to drive the Normans from his land. You will meet Robin Hood again in this exciting novel.

The White Stag by Kate Seredy is the story of Attila the Hun and his followers who are led in search of a promised land by the White Stag.

A Bridle for Pegasus by Katherine B. Shippen. This book follows the story of aviation from its beginning to the present day.

Thunder Mountains Mine by Kenneth L. Sinclair. In joining an expedition to find an old Spanish mine Frank Wayne finds exciting adventure.

Treasure Island by Robert Louis Stevenson. This is probably the most famous pirate story ever written.

Adam of the Road by Elizabeth Janet Gray Vining. Two minstrel boys travel through England in the thirteenth century.

Meet the Authors

THOMAS BAILEY ALDRICH (1836–1907). As a child, Thomas Bailey Aldrich visited every state in the Union, spending long periods in New York City and New Orleans. His first verses were published before he was fifteen years old in a New England journal, but most of his inspiration came from the South. He used to write a verse or two every morning before going to work at his uncle's office. Soon he took the job of junior literary critic for the *Evening Mirror*, and so began a career lasting thirty-five years. The best-known samples of his jaunty, confident prose are the short story, "Marjorie Daw," and the novel, *The Story of a Bad Boy*, with a setting around Portsmouth, New Hampshire, where he was born.

ROBERT ARTHUR (1909–), the son of a U. S. Army officer, was born on Corregidor Island, Philippines. Educated at the University of Michigan, Mr. Arthur is a writer of short stories and radio scripts of mystery, fantasy, and science fiction. Creator of the program, "The Mysterious Traveler," Robert Arthur twice won the "Edgar" award of the Mystery Writers of America, Inc., for the Best Radio Mystery Program of the Year. A free-lance writer, Mr. Arthur says that he appropriately lives in an old house with an attic full of bats.

ALFRED BARRETT, S.J. (1906–). Born in Flushing, Long Island, Father Barrett attended Xavier High School and then entered the Society of Jesus at St. Andrew-on-Hudson. He was professor of poetry at Canisius College and from 1940–45 was chaplain of the Catholic Poetry Society of America. As a First Lieutenant in World War II, he was the 101st Jesuit to enter the Armed Forces. After the war he became an instructor of literature at Fordham. His volume of poetry, *Mint by Night*, has been highly praised for its precise and illuminating poetic style. Father Barrett's favorite sources are "the Fathers of the Church and the metaphysical poets of the seventeenth century."

WILLIAM BEEBE (1877–). Scientist and nature writer, William Beebe is director of the department of scientific research for the New York Zoological Society. His work in the depths of the sea and his subsequent delicate description—see *Beneath Tropic Seas* and *Half-Mile Down*—have made him justly famous and honored.

HILAIRE BELLOC (1870–1953). A Parisian by birth, but British citizen by choice, Hilaire Belloc began to write immediately after his graduation from Oxford. Interested in a variety of subjects, Mr. Belloc wrote books on history, politics, and travel, as well as children's stories and light verse. His delightful sense of humor as expressed in his nonsense verse has endeared him to readers young and old.

STEPHEN VINCENT BENÉT (1898–1943). The son of an army man, Stephen Vincent Benét traveled from army post to army post with his family. He became well acquainted with the country itself and loved to read of America's history and traditions. It is not surprising that his best work was devoted to American themes. *John Brown's Body*, a long poem of the Civil War period, won the Pulitzer Prize in 1928. *Western Star*, an epic celebrating the American pioneer, although unfinished at the time of Benét's death, won for him again the Pulitzer Prize.

RICHARD BREEN was outstanding in dramatics at Fordham University, a school noted for its dramatic productions. He won the annual play-writing contest in 1938 with *The Rain Has Eyes* and again in 1939 with *The Dreamslayers.* From 1936 to 1940, the year of his graduation, this Catholic student acted in all the major productions of the university. He was vice-president of the "Mimes and Mummers," student theatrical organization, in 1940. He has since done work in radio, including the writing and directing of the radio drama, *Are These Our Children?* Now a screen writer for 20th Century-Fox Corporation, Richard Breen is president of the Screen Writer's Guild.

HEYWOOD BROUN (1888–1939). The striking similarities between Broun and G. K. Chesterton in talent, appearance, and temperament caused many to hope that his conversion, like the latter's, would be of considerable significance to the Church. Correspondent, critic, columnist, Broun graduated from Harvard to champion the cause of the underprivileged. The accusation of Communism leveled against him was unfounded, but so radical had he and these accusations been that his conversion to Catholicism a few months before his death came as a shock to everyone. "The Broun Nobody Knew," the funeral sermon preached at St. Patrick's Cathedral, New York City, by Monsignor Fulton Sheen, gives an insight into his character.

ROBERT BROWNING (1812–1889). Born near London, Robert Browning inherited his love of literature, music, and art from his parents. He began to write poetry early, but success did not come until after his marriage to Elizabeth Barrett, who was also a poet. Browning was especially interested in the drama of everyday life, and he could turn an incident in the life of an ordinary man such as Hervé Riel into a heroic event. Some of Browning's most familiar works are *The Ring and the Book,* "Pippa Passes," and "Home Thoughts from Abroad."

AMELIA JOSEPHINE BURR was born in 1878. During World War I, Miss Burr published several volumes of poetry, including *The Silver Trumpet* and *Hearts Awake!* Her chief theme was the war in progress, and one of her best war poems is "Evening Prayer." She tried to express the spiritual meaning of the war and to show how God can work good even from the horror and destruction of war. Miss Burr married the Reverend Carl Hopkins Elmore in 1921.

RICHARD E. BYRD (1888–) is a Virginian. As a grammar school boy he traveled around the world alone. An injury to his foot at Annapolis forced him to retire from what promised to be a brilliant career in the Navy. In 1916 he persuaded naval authorities to accept his services as an aviator, and he was the first to fly across the North and South Poles. His books, *Skyward, Little America, Discovery, Exploring with Byrd,* and *Alone,* manifest his qualities of courage, sympathy, and devotion to duty and friends.

WILLA CATHER (1875–1947). Born in Virginia, Willa Cather received her first education from her grandmother. After her family moved to Nebraska, she attended high school there, and by doing newspaper correspondence, worked her way through the University of Nebraska. After a brief trial of newspaper work, she turned to teaching, then to editing *McClure's Magazine.* Finally the success of her books made it possible for her to write without the encumbrance of editorial work. She was a lover of music and was intensely loyal to the friends of her childhood and youth. Among her most prominent works are *O Pioneers!, My Ántonia,* and *Death Comes for the Archbishop.*

ROBERT P. TRISTRAM COFFIN (1892–1955) belonged to a famous old New England family of whalers. He grew up in Brunswick, Maine, and attended a little red schoolhouse which he later purchased to show people what the old one-room schools were like. His college education was obtained at Bowdoin, and he was a Rhodes Scholar at Oxford University. After serving in the army during World War I, Coffin became an English instructor at Wells College and later at Bowdoin. His volume of poetry, *Strange Holiness*, received the 1936 Pulitzer Prize. Mr. Coffin's poems express his love of New England and his affection for simple farm people.

PADRAIC COLUM (1881–). In his boyhood this noted Catholic poet and storyteller absorbed the richness of Irish folklore from his grandmother. In his twenties, Colum wrote *The Land*, which proved to be the first successful play of the Irish Theater. In 1912 he married Mary Gunning Maguire, now a well-known literary critic. Two years later they came to America. His poetry and folk stories reflect his knowledge and love of the land of his birth.

RICHARD EDWARD CONNELL (1893–1949) entered professional writing in Poughkeepsie, New York, at the age of ten, writing up baseball games for his father's paper at ten cents a game. At sixteen he became city editor of the paper. For a year he attended Georgetown College. After his father's death, he went to Harvard, graduating in 1915. At Harvard he edited the *Daily Crimson* and the *Lampoon*. The years following his graduation were filled with various writing activities, with one year's intermission when he served with the American Expeditionary Forces in France during World War I. A writer of short stories, novels, and screen plays, Connell won the O. Henry Memorial Award in 1924 for his short story, "The Most Dangerous Game."

JAMES B. CONNOLLY was born in 1868. Engineer, athlete, soldier, sailor, politician, war correspondent—he is most at home when writing of the sea and the New England fishing fleets. He has fished all over the world, knows the task of the deep-sea fisherman and the workings of his boat, the deep-water fishing schooner. An ardent Catholic, he was received in audience by the Holy Father shortly before World War I. His stories and essays mirror the action of his life. *Sea-Borne* is an excellent example.

ALOYSIUS CROFT (1906–) received his M.A. degree from St. Francis Seminary in 1932. He has been an editor for the Bruce Publishing Company. His *Twenty-One Saints* was written for the boys he knew and loved in the C.Y.O. Among his works are *With Heart and Lips*, *The Greatest Prayer: the Mass*, and *Symbols of the Church*.

A. J. CRONIN (1896–). Honest love of simple humanity, as illustrated in "The Doctor of Lennox," explains much of A. J. Cronin's success as a writer. Though secretly cherishing literary ambitions, "England's new Dickens" studied medicine, became a successful physician in London, and only in 1931 when convalescing from overwork did he take up writing. *Hatter's Castle*, his first novel, was an instantaneous success. Other very popular books were *The Green Years*, *The Citadel*, and *Keys of the Kingdom*. Dr. Cronin is a Catholic, is married, and has two sons.

THOMAS AUGUSTINE DALY (1871–1948) was born in Philadelphia, Pennsylvania. He attended college at Villanova and at Fordham University, where his chief claim to fame was as a baseball star. One of the first newspaper columnists, Daly used many of his everyday experiences with human nature to make the characters in his poems warm men's hearts. He is best known for his verses in the Italian dialect, describing with a gentle understanding the life of immigrants. *Canzoni* and *McAroni Ballads* are representative of his work.

CLARENCE DAY (1874–1935). While in active service in the Navy during the Spanish-American War, Clarence Day contracted arthritis, which confined him to his bed for the rest of his life. In spite of it he continued to write and sketch. His first book, *This Simian World*, self-illustrated, was only moderately successful, but his *Life with Father*, written during his last year of life, became a Broadway hit and best-seller. There is hardly a literate American today who is not familiar with "Father's" booming voice and "Mother's" frantic attempts at budget-balancing. This group of delightful essays is the crown of a life of humor and inspiration.

GUY DE MAUPASSANT (1850–1893). At one time Guy de Maupassant announced that he wished to write only what he had seen, felt, and understood. This fits in with the fact that in "The Necklace" he gave Henry Loisel the position he once held himself in the Department of Instruction. He surprised his friends by the quality of his first short story. Fame followed with each publication, but he demanded too much of his physical strength. Overwork caused a brain lesion, and after a brief period of insanity he died.

EMILY DICKINSON (1830–1886). Because she seemed to be only an ordinary Massachusetts girl who went to school, helped her mother, and wrote letters and poems for her own pleasure, Emily Dickinson won fame only after her death, when her thousand-and-more poems were published by her friends. Comic valentines sent to her brother's college friends, music, gardening, Shakespeare, and dancing during her school days are in strong contrast to the solitude she preferred in later years. In that solitude she composed her finest poems.

ARTHUR CONAN DOYLE (1859–1930). Since his family was strongly Catholic, Arthur Conan Doyle was trained at Hodder, an elementary school, and Stonyhurst—both Jesuit institutions. After graduating from Edinburgh University with a medical degree, he began the practice of medicine. He met so little success in this field that he wrote stories to fill his spare time and gave the world its number one detective—Sherlock Holmes. The stories proved so profitable that he abandoned medicine in favor of writing. He was knighted in 1902 for his defense of the British cause in *The Great Boer War*. At Edinburgh he had ceased to practice his faith. After his son's death, he became a strong exponent of spiritualism.

JOSEPH RODMAN DRAKE (1795–1820). The American poet and satirist, Joseph Rodman Drake, was born in New York City and became a practicing physician there. Writing under the name of "The Croakers," Drake and Fitz-Greene Halleck did a series of light satirical verses for the New York *Evening Post*. At Drake's death Halleck wrote his elegy, "Green be the turf above thee." Drake's longest serious poem is "The Culprit Fay."

SISTER M. ELEANORE, C.S.C. (1890–1940) studied at St. Mary's College, Notre Dame, Indiana, at the University of Notre Dame, and at Cambridge. A member of the Congregation of the Holy Cross, she lectured in English and administered high schools after she received her doctorate. She wrote widely, publishing a dozen volumes of poetry and prose as well as contributing to numerous periodicals.

ROBERT FARREN (1909–). By ancestry and birth Robert Farren is a native Dubliner; by occupation he was for some years a school teacher, graduating from St. Patrick's College and taking a master's degree in Scholastic Philosophy from the National University. In recent years his energies and talents have gained for him two new posts of more far-reaching influence: the directorship of Gaelic broadcasts for Radio Eireann and a membership on the board for Ireland's famed Abbey Theatre. Farren's style has a certain rugged strength that lends tang and expressiveness to his poetry. He has played an important part in Ireland in the revival of reciting poetry.

ST. FRANCIS OF ASSISI (1182–1226). St. Francis was born Giovanni Francesco Bernadone in Assisi, a hill town of central Italy, of a well-to-do merchant family. A merry-hearted and generous youth, Francis prepared by day for a commercial career, but at night freely spent large sums entertaining his gay companions. After a severe illness, Francis began to lose interest in this frivolous way of life and in 1207 turned completely to God. Before the Bishop and his angry father, he renounced his inheritance, stripped off his fine clothes, and barefoot and in rags set forth to serve Christ in self-denial, poverty, and preaching. Many men followed the example of the *Poverello* —the little poor man, as Francis was known. Francis founded the great Order of Friars Minor, which quickly spread throughout Europe. With St. Clare, daughter of an Assisi nobleman, Francis helped found the Poor Clares, sister Order of the Poor Friars of Assisi. A sign of Francis' remarkable union with Our Lord is found in the "stigmata," or five wounds of the Crucifixion, which appeared on Francis' body toward the close of his life. As he lay ill, he composed the famous "Song of the Creatures," in whose theme of gratitude to God is found the soul of St. Francis' humble and joyous spirit.

HELEN FRAZEE-BOWER was born in Moosa, California, in 1896. She received her education at San Diego State College and at the University of California at Los Angeles. She began writing poetry and short stories in 1920. Besides having poems appear in leading periodicals, Mrs. Frazee-Bower published two volumes—*Beauty for Ashes* and *Inner Pilgrim*. She has received the "Browning Award" for the best of 3500 poems submitted by California residents. A teacher in the Los Angeles City School System, Mrs. Frazee-Bower is the mother of five children and has nine grandchildren.

HAMLIN HANNIBAL GARLAND (1860–1940) grew up in Iowa, the center of the "middle border" of which he wrote so vividly. After a year teaching school, Hamlin went to Boston to embark on a career of letters. His *Main Travelled Roads*, published in 1891, became the first of a series of books about the Middle West. Garland found the road to recognition a long and difficult one, but when *A Daughter of the Middle Border*, a biography of his mother, was published he was awarded the Pulitzer Prize for literature.

JOHN GIBBONS (1882–). An English journalist, John Gibbons was converted to the Catholic Church in 1899. As his books—*Tramping to Lourdes, Tramping Through Ireland, Afoot in Italy*—and his tales testify, much of his time has been spent in travel throughout Europe. His easily aroused wonder makes his books fresh and alive.

GIOVANNI GUARESCHI (1908–) is a modern journalist with a talent for drawing as well as writing. Someone has aptly described him as an Italian O. Henry with a dash of James Thurber in him. His stories are snapshots that skillfully catch in moments of pathos and humor the simple, sunny peasants of the Po Valley where

Guareschi was born. Failing to co-operate with the Germans during World War II, he spent many long and terrible months in various concentration camps. Never a bitter man, Guareschi tells us that he survived the ordeal only by sticking fast to his slogan —"I will not die even if they kill me." Guareschi now lives in Milan with his wife and two children.

ARTHUR GUITERMAN (1871–1943). Born in Vienna, Austria, of American parentage, Arthur Guiterman is principally known for his humorous verses and historical ballads. After graduation from the College of the City of New York, Guiterman went into newspaper work. As a free lance writer, Mr. Guiterman contributed regularly to both the New York *Times* and *Life* magazine. To clear up the puzzling pronunciation of Guiterman's name, an editorial associate of his once wrote:

"There ain't no better, fitter man
Than Mister Arthur Guiterman."

HERMANN HAGEDORN (1882–). The American writer, Hermann Hagedorn, is chiefly noted for his interest in Theodore Roosevelt. His *Boys' Life of Roosevelt* is an interesting and sympathetic portrayal of that historical figure. He is also a poet and novelist. Among his novels are *Faces in the Dawn, The Great Maze,* and *The Heart of Youth. This Darkness and This Light* and *Harvard Poems* are volumes of his poetry.

CECILY HALLACK (1898–1938), the daughter of an Anglican minister, was converted to Catholicism by a chance visit to a Catholic church. Convinced that she had discovered the true Church, she had to wait two years to gain parental consent to be received into it. Her essays, novels, and short stories are characterized by a spirit of joyful Catholicism. Among her best works are *A Mirror for Toby, Sword-Blade of Michael,* and *The Adventures of the Amethyst.*

KATHARINE TYNAN HINKSON (1861–1931). Writing from the age of seventeen until seventy, Katharine Tynan Hinkson produced over a hundred novels, four volumes of memoirs, and numerous volumes of poems (which she prized most of all). As an outstanding leader in the Celtic revival of literature, she was hostess to all the Irish celebrities of her day.

FRANK HORNE was born in New York City in 1899. He wrote his first poetry at the College of the City of New York, where he was also on the track team. Frank Horne has a graduate degree in ophthalmology from Northern Illinois College, and he has taught at Fort Valley High and Industrial School in Fort Valley, Georgia. His poetic style is distinctly modern, being sinewy and muscular and unadorned. His ideas are clear and direct both in their conception and expression, lending to his message authentic impact.

LANGSTON HUGHES (1902–) was born in Joplin, Missouri. His first poems were written and published in the school magazine during his high school days in Cleveland. But despite good education and poetic ability, his color prevented him from securing any really good job. He worked as doorman and waiter in famous hotels at home and abroad. It was in the Wardman Park Hotel that Vachel Lindsay discovered the bus-boy who was a poet. His poems, generally in Negro dialect, emphasize the suffering of his race: *Weary Blues* and *Not Without Laughter.* Many of his poems have been set to music.

JAMES WELDON JOHNSON (1871–1938). Mr. Johnson's career includes that of teaching school and serving as consul for the United States to Venezuela and Nicaragua. When he died, he was a successful song-writer on Broadway. His *Autobiography of an Ex-Colored Man* and four books of poems did much to win appreciation for Negro writing in America. Two of his works are *God's Trombones* and *Black Manhattan.*

OSA JOHNSON (1894–1953). Her life was as full of excitement as the breath-taking stories she wrote. For many years she worked with her husband, Martin, in the jungles of Australia and Africa. She had no fear of the most fierce animals, and was often able to win their friendship. Her husband's death in 1937 left Osa to carry on the work he had been doing, and she continued the study of wild life in those far-away lands.

JOYCE KILMER (1886–1918) was a convert to Catholicism. Editor of his school paper, prize-winning public speaker, Latin teacher, collaborator on a revision of the *Standard Dictionary*, book-reviewer for the New York *Times*, university lecturer on English literature, husband of a writer, Kilmer promised greater poetry than his thirty-two years allowed him. "Rouge Bouquet" is a good example of his vibrant yet mellow style. His best-known poem, though not his finest, is "Trees."

RUDYARD KIPLING (1865–1936). Born in Bombay, India, Kipling learned Hindustani at the same time he learned English. In India, too, he got his start as a journalist, and much of his subject matter is about that country. No one has produced a more perfect expression of the British soldier's language and viewpoint during the reign of Victoria than Kipling has in *Barrack-Room Ballads.* Other famous works are *Departmental Ditties, Plain Tales from the Hills, The Jungle Books, Captains Courageous, Just So Stories,* and *Kim.* Among the many honors conferred upon him were the Nobel Prize for literature in 1907 and the medal of the Royal Society of Literature in 1926.

CLIFFORD J. LAUBE was born in Telluride, Colorado, in 1891. He lived in Mount St. Vincent Orphanage in Denver for six years. Ink got into his blood at the age of twelve, when he became a printer's apprentice on the Rico, Colorado, *News.* Elected to the Colorado state legislature when he was twenty-five, Mr. Laube joined the staff of the New York *Times* in 1929. After twenty-four years of service, he retired as national news editor in 1953. He was one of the founders and editors of *Spirit,* a national Catholic poetry magazine. Clifford Laube started The Monastine Press in the cellar of his home where he wrote, illustrated, handset, printed, and bound his first book, *Crags,* in 1938. Although Clifford Laube had no college education, the honorary degree of Doctor of Letters was conferred upon him by St. Bonaventure University and Boston College. Manhattan College also awarded him the degree of Doctor of Humane Letters. Mr. Laube was elected president of the Catholic Poetry Society of America in 1954, and is now working on an autobiographical novel.

WINIFRED M. LETTS was born in Manchester, England, and attended Alexandra College in Dublin. She was a physio-therapist in World War I and worked in a hospital until her marriage in 1926. Winifred Letts started writing when she was a child but did not start publishing until the 1920's. She claims that her luck changed with a visit of a red-haired woman selling blackberries. "Honey, they'll bring you luck from the red-haired woman," she was told. Her poem about the blackberry seller was accepted by the editor of the English *Spectator,* who thus became her "literary godfather . . . and . . . fast friend . . ." Winifred Letts has written novels, children's books, and plays, two of which were performed at the Abbey Theatre in Dublin. But her poems, which reflect her deep love for Ireland and the Irish people, are her "best sellers." *Songs from Leinster* is probably her best known collection, and thirteen of her songs have been set to music. Winifred Letts now lives in a cottage outside Dublin, where she enjoys gardening and country life. Having no car, she uses a bicycle for her means of transportation.

ELIAS LIEBERMAN (1883–) was born in St. Petersburg, Russia, and came to America when he was seven years old. He graduated *cum laude* from the College of the City of New York, where he had been elected a member of Phi Beta Kappa. After receiving his M.A. and Ph.D. degrees from New York University, Mr. Lieberman was a teacher of English and later held many supervisory and administrative positions in New York City schools. Writing professionally since his graduation from college, Mr. Lieberman has won many honors with his distinguished poetry. Former lecturer in poetry technique and appreciation, he is now devoting himself exclusively to his literary career. His latest collection of verse is *To My Brothers Everywhere.*

ANNE MORROW LINDBERGH (1906–). Two years after graduating from Smith College, Anne Morrow married a national hero, Charles A. Lindbergh. As her husband's companion in his world flying and as author of *North to the Orient* and *Listen, the Wind* she is deservedly famous. She holds the United States Flag Association's Cross of Honor and the Hubbard Gold Medal of the National Geographic Society.

JACK LONDON (1876–1916). In his youth the world of books was Jack London's one consolation. To aid his poverty-stricken parents, Jack worked long hours for excessively small pay at odd jobs. At fifteen he became a tramp, serving a term in prison as a vagrant. He was lured to Alaska by the promises of the "gold rush." He found no gold, but his experiences form the background of some of his best writing. Outstanding among his novels are *The Call of the Wild* and its sequel, *White Fang.*

EDWIN MARKHAM (1852–1940) was born in a log cabin in Oregon, of parents who had come West from Michigan. A bag of buried gold-pieces which he found gave him money for college. After his studies were finished, he became a school principal. At this time he published his famous poem in honor of the workingman, "The Man with the Hoe," which has been translated into thirty-seven languages. His works are saturated with Americanism and include "Lincoln," "The Shoes of Happiness," "Gates of Paradise," and "California, the Wonderful."

CYRIL CHARLES MARTINDALE was born in England in 1879. He attended Harrow and was converted to Catholicism in 1897. He entered the Society of Jesus and had a brilliant career at Stonyhurst and Oxford. C. C. Martindale acted as English Army chaplain during World War I and in 1940 went to Copenhagen, Denmark, where he was interned in the German Jesuit House during World War II. Although dangerously ill in 1941, he managed to finish writing the lives of Frassati and St. Camillus de Lellis. His health broken, he returned to England in 1945.

JOHN MASEFIELD (1874–). As a boy in Herefordshire, England, John Masefield loved any kind of adventure more than study. His mother and father died when he was still a youngster, so at fourteen he began his nine-year career as a sailor. The titles of his books show that these years impressed him—*Salt Water Ballads, Captain Margaret, The Wanderer of Liverpool.* Now he bears the highest honor England can give a poet—the title of "Poet Laureate."

DENIS A. McCARTHY was born in Ireland in 1870. After coming to America, he began a journalistic career. McCarthy is known best for his Irish ballads and patriotic American poems, many of which have been set to music.

TIMOTHY J. MULVEY (1913–). A pioneer in the field of radio drama, Father Mulvey was born in New York City and attended Canisius College in Buffalo, New York. After his ordination into the priesthood, Father Mulvey was sent to Shikoku, Japan, where he helped open a Japanese missionary center. At college he had studied speech and radio, and his skill in the use of sound and music for emotional effect in radio plays has been instrumental in the success of his scripts. In 1944 the Institute for Education by Radio singled out his radio plays as some of the most effective religious programs.

ROBERT NATHAN (1894–). A New Yorker by birth, Robert Nathan was educated in private schools both at home and abroad. He attended Harvard but left before receiving a degree. Later he worked in an advertising agency and taught at the Columbia University School of Journalism. In 1925 Mr. Nathan began to devote his entire time to writing. Today, besides being a successful writer, he is also a talented painter and musician and a member of the National Institute of Arts and Letters.

ALFRED NOYES (1880–). Noted at Oxford chiefly for his oarsman's ability, this convert to the Catholic Church continues, as he did from the time he wrote his very first poem, to earn his living by writing poetry. His first book was published when he was twenty-two. His best-known works are *Drake*, *Tales of the Mermaid Tavern*, and *The Torch Bearers*.

HOWARD VINCENT O'BRIEN (1888–1947) received his A.B. degree from Yale University. He founded and edited the magazine, *Art*. In the field of journalism he was both literary editor and columnist for the Chicago *Daily News*.

CHARLES L. O'DONNELL, C.S.C. (1884–1934). After his ordination and the completion of higher studies, Charles O'Donnell served for a time as professor at Notre Dame University and as associate editor of the *Ave Maria*. He went overseas as chaplain with the American Expeditionary Forces during World War I. From 1920 to 1926 he was Provincial of his religious congregation; from that office he became Assistant-General of the congregation. In 1928 he was appointed President of Notre Dame University, retaining this post until his death. His poetry is contained in three volumes—*The Dead Musician*, *Cloister*, and *A Rime of the Rood and Other Poems*.

SEAN O'FAOLAIN (1900–). Among the foremost writers of modern Ireland, O'Faolain is by trade a critic, a storyteller, and a journalist. He has taken degrees at the National University and at Harvard. *A Purse of Coppers* is one of his most highly acclaimed literary efforts.

JOSEPH MARY PLUNKETT (1887–1916). This Irishman has the triple distinction of having been a student of languages, a poet, and a patriot. A native of Dublin, Plunkett attended Belvedere College and the English Jesuit College at Stonyhurst. Interest in the Arabic language and literature took him to Algiers for a time. Returning to Ireland, he joined forces with another poet-patriot, Thomas MacDonogh. They studied Gaelic at the National University and edited the "Irish Review." In the ill-fated Easter Week Rebellion of 1916 Plunkett was captured by the English authorities, tried for treason, and executed. Published after his death, *The Poems of Joseph Mary Plunkett* contains his most representative work.

WILLIAM SYDNEY PORTER (1862–1910). The story of William Sydney Porter, who in prison took the pen name,

O. Henry, reads like one of his own famous stories. Born in North Carolina, he left school at fifteen and began work in a drugstore. Later, because of illness, he went to Austin, Texas, where he made a reputation by his cartoons and caricatures. Successful in both his public and private life, O. Henry became first a bank teller and finally a newspaper editor. He moved to Houston and had just embarked on a journalistic career when he was summoned back to Austin for trial on the charge of embezzling funds. According to all evidence he was innocent, but for some reason he left the country. When he received word that his wife was dying, he returned to Austin, stood trial, and was sentenced to five years in prison. It was there that he began writing short stories. Upon his release he went to New York and agreed to a contract with the New York *World* for a story a week at a hundred dollars a story. During his entire career, O. Henry wrote more than six hundred pieces.

ARTHUR T. QUILLER-COUCH (1863–1944). Using the pseudonym of "Q," Arthur T. Quiller-Couch wrote several novels of his native Cornwall. He finished Stevenson's novel, *St. Ives,* and later became professor of English literature at Cambridge. He is said to have had the supreme gift of being able to charm while he lectured. An editor of many anthologies, including the *Oxford Book of English Verse,* Arthur T. Quiller-Couch was knighted in 1910.

JAMES RYDER RANDALL (1839–1908) was descended from the Acadian exiles who found a home in Philadelphia after the English had driven them from their farms in Acadia (Nova Scotia). He was, in fact, a great-great-grandson of René Leblanc, the notary portrayed by Longfellow in *Evangeline.* As a boy, Randall studied in Baltimore under Joseph H. Clarke, who had previously been Edgar Allan Poe's tutor. As a result of excellent training, Randall was able to enter Georgetown College at the age of ten. He achieved renown in later years as the author of "Maryland, My Maryland." The poem, printed in the New Orleans *Delta,* was quickly adapted to the music of an old German song and became the battle cry of the whole South.

FRANKLIN M. RECK (1896–). Upon completion of his first year at Iowa State College, Franklin Reck joined the United States Army to fight in World War I. After the war he returned to college, where he became editor of the college agricultural magazine. For a year after graduation he remained as assistant to the president of the college. Afterwards he joined the staff of *American Boy* magazine. There he became managing editor and a popular writer of sports stories.

JAMES B. REUTER, S.J. (1916–). Upon the completion of his novitiate and juniorate in the Society of Jesus in 1938, James Reuter was assigned to the Philippines to study philosophy. Three years later he taught at the Ateneo de Manila. There he acted as basketball coach, director of dramatics, and radio script writer. He was interned in Los Baños prison camp by the Japanese in 1942. Released from Los Baños in 1945, he returned to the United States to study theology at Woodstock College, Maryland. Father Reuter has since returned to the Philippines where he is again teaching at the Ateneo de Manila.

QUENTIN REYNOLDS was born in New York City in 1902. Although a graduate of law school, Mr. Reynolds preferred to be a writer. At first, sports writer for the New York *World Telegram,* Mr. Reynolds later was a war correspondent during World War II. Associate editor of *Collier's* magazine from 1933 to 1945, Quentin Reynolds still contributes articles and short stories to this and other magazines.

CONRAD RICHTER (1890–). The author of *The Light in the Forest* was born in Pine Grove, Pennsylvania. For a few years following graduation from high school he drove teams, pitched hay, served as a bank teller, cut timber, and finally became a reporter for the Johnstown, Pennsylvania, *Journal.* Later, while working as a private secretary in Cleveland, Ohio, he sold his first story. Turning to children's stories, Mr. Richter began to write for *John Martin's Book.* One of his books was the first serial printed by that magazine. With this success behind him he launched his own children's publication, *The Junior Magazine Book.* After World War I, Mr. Richter spent five years collecting data on the history of the Southwest. This information was used in three colorful novels and a volume of short stories all centering in this locale. *The Trees* is one of his most popular books.

S. ROBERT RUSSELL is known for his popular magazine feature articles on porpoises, sharks, and fish. His most thrilling sea experience, the attempt to capture a giant ray with a rod and reel, might have proved disastrous. The ray dragged his canoe twenty miles in the open Pacific before it broke away and escaped.

CARL SANDBURG (1878–), a son of Swedish immigrant parents, was born in the Mid-West. He worked as a milk wagon driver, porter in a barber shop, scene-shifter in a theater, and truck driver at a brick kiln. After his service in the Spanish-American War he was persuaded to attend college. Upon graduating, he tried business, then moved into journalism. He is now established as a poet of considerable merit. He is a poet of the worker, a man of intense vigor but capable also of great tenderness, as demonstrated in his prose tales for children and in the lyrical passages of his biography of Abraham Lincoln, ranked by many critics as his most brilliant literary contribution.

HARRY SCHNIBBE was president of the "Mimes and Mummers," Fordham University dramatic association, in 1940, the year of his graduation. His play, *Men of the Valley,* had received special honors in the annual play-writing contest at the university in 1937. In two years he had built twenty-two sets for Fordham dramatic productions. In 1940 he edited the *Fordham Ram,* student publication, in addition to his dramatic activities. He served in the Navy during World War II.

WALTER SCOTT (1771–1832). "One of the manliest men of the English race," Scott was a victim of infantile paralysis which left him lame. He spent his boyhood with shepherds on the hills trying to strengthen his health. He collected stories from everyone and never tired of learning more of his country's history and legend. His own tales became so popular with the people of his day, that novel-reading then began to be the widespread amusement we know today. For entertainment value, *Ivanhoe, Kenilworth,* and his series of Waverly novels rank with any of the best-sellers today.

ROBERT W. SERVICE (1876–) was born and educated in England. His traveling steerage to Canada with just five dollars in his pocket was his first taste of the hardships he was to suffer for the next seven years. Jack-of-all-trades up and down the Pacific coast, he then spent eight years in the Yukon, where he was attracted by Kipling's books and began to imitate them. So successful was he that he is now called the Canadian Kipling. He now lives in France, where he continues his writing.

WILLIAM SHAKESPEARE (1564–1616), the greatest of English dramatists, was born in Stratford-on-Avon, a small town in central England. His father was chief alderman or mayor of the town at the time.

William probably attended the King Edward VI Grammar School, but his plays show that he learned most from his personal observation of men and of nature. Reverses in his father's business forced him to withdraw from school to help his family. In 1582 at the age of eighteen he married Anne Hathaway. After the birth of three children, William went to London to improve the family fortune. Several years of his life are lost to the historian. In our next contact with him we find him doing odd jobs connected with the theater, taking small parts, revising plays, and helping in stage productions. Finally, he began to write his own plays and to act in them. They were immediately successful. In 1594 he became a shareholder in the Lord Chamberlain's Company, a noted group of actors. From then on, his fortune improved. He was an intelligent business man. He bought New Place, a fine home in Stratford, for his family. He made many other good investments in property. Having done well and having taken such good care of his money, he was able to retire from the stage and establish himself as a country gentleman in Stratford in 1613. He died there in 1616. Among his greatest plays are the tragedies, *Hamlet*, *King Lear*, *Macbeth*, and *Julius Caesar*; and the comedies, *Midsummer Night's Dream*, *As You Like It*, *The Merchant of Venice*, and *The Tempest*. His works include many famous poems also.

DALLAS LORE SHARP (1870–1929). After attending Brown University and Boston University, Dallas Lore Sharp entered the ministry of the Methodist Episcopal Church in 1895. He is known as a nature writer. Among his works are *Watchers in the Woods*, *Where Rolls the Oregon*, and *The Better Country*.

HENRYK SIENKIEWICZ (1846–1916). A Polish Catholic writer and editor, Henryk Sienkiewicz has made the inherent rich Catholicity of his nation the background of his novels. He lived a great part of his life in Warsaw and Krakow, editing the Warsaw newspaper *Slowo*. In 1905 he received the Nobel Prize for literature. He traveled extensively, visiting England, France, Italy, Spain, Greece, Africa, and the East. The early years of World War I found him organizing relief for Polish victims of the war. While engaged in this work of mercy, he died in Switzerland in 1916. Outstanding among his works are *With Fire and Sword*, *The Deluge*, *Without Dogma*, *Quo Vadis?* and *Knights of the Cross*.

ROBERT LOUIS STEVENSON (1850–1894). The Scottish poet, essayist, and novelist, Robert Louis Stevenson, was born in Edinburgh. Despite frequent withdrawals from school because of ill health, he received a good education at various private schools. He became a lawyer but never practiced his profession. He began writing essays for magazines about 1876. All his life Robert Louis Stevenson wandered about Europe and America in search of a healthier climate. At last he settled in Samoa in the South Seas. There he continued to write, and the natives called him *Tusitala*, meaning "Teller of Tales."

JOHN BANNISTER TABB (1845–1909). Rejected from the Confederate Army because of weak eyesight, John Bannister Tabb became a blockade runner for a year before he was captured and imprisoned. In the cell next to him he discovered the Southern poet, Sidney Lanier. They became close friends, and soon after Tabb began writing verse in earnest. Upon his release he turned to the Catholic faith and was ordained a priest. His poetic talent was a ready tool with which to express his rare love of nature and his faith in God.

SARA TEASDALE (1884–1933). Although born in St. Louis, Missouri, the Gateway to the West, Sara Teasdale's poems have none of the ruggedness associated with the Great West. On the contrary, they are delicately musical: *Rivers to the Sea, Flame and Shadow, Dark of the Moon.* She was a systematic reader all her life and even as a young girl kept a list of all the books she read. She edited *Rainbow Gold,* an anthology for young people.

LOWELL THOMAS (1892–). As author, lecturer, and news commentator, Lowell Thomas is well known to American readers. His experiences as a newspaper correspondent, as chief of the commission to prepare a historical record of World War I, included work with nearly all the Allied armies. His travels to all parts of the world are reflected in his lectures and books, among which are *With Lawrence in Arabia, The First World Flight,* and *Back to Mandalay.*

DOROTHY THOMPSON (1894–). Having taken her undergraduate studies at Lewis Institute, Chicago, and Syracuse University, Dorothy Thompson did graduate work at the University of Vienna. She has received honorary L.H.D. degrees from six universities, including Columbia and Dartmouth. In 1920 she became foreign correspondent for the Philadelphia *Public Ledger* and the New York *Evening Post.* In 1936 she became political commentator of the New York *Herald Tribune.* Her contributions include a syndicated newspaper column, magazine articles, and radio broadcasts.

WILLIAM THOMAS WALSH (1891–1949) was born in Waterbury, Connecticut of Irish parents. He was educated at Yale, where he conducted the Yale University Symphony Orchestra, and he received his Litt.D. from Fordham. He was a reporter for several Connecticut papers and from 1911–1917 he worked for the Philadelphia *Public Ledger.* He later was head of the English department at Roxbury School, and then became Professor of English at Manhattanville College of the Sacred Heart in New York, a position he held until 1947. The author of several biographies, including *Isabella of Spain, St. Theresa of Avila,* and *Our Lady of Fatima,* William Thomas Walsh was awarded the Laetare medal by Note Dame University and also received honors from Spain.

ELLA WHEELER WILCOX (1850–1919) began to contribute verse to magazines at the age of seven. She was born in Johnstown Center, Wisconsin, but following her marriage in 1884 she made her home in New York City. For many years she wrote a daily poem for a newspaper syndicate, and she published over twenty volumes of verse.

ALEXANDER WOOLLCOTT (1877–1943). When little Alexander Woollcott heard that newspaper critics got free tickets to plays, he made up his mind to become a newspaperman. He was then six. A graduate of Hamilton College, he served as drama critic on the New York *Times,* as editor of *Stars and Stripes* during the first World War, and as "Town Crier" over the radio. From 1934 until his death he was a freelance writer of great popularity. Among his books are *Shouts and Murmurs* and *While Rome Burns.*

GLOSSARY

A

abash (ȧ·băsh′). To shame; to embarrass.
abductor (ăb·dŭk′tẽr). One who kidnaps.
abet (ȧ·bĕt′). To aid.
abhorrence (ă̆b·hôr′ĕns). Hatred; disgust.
abject (ăb·jĕkt′). Low spirited; downhearted.
abjure (ăb·jo͝or′). To renounce or reject; to abandon.
abominable (ȧ·bŏm′ĭ·nȧ·b'l). Very hateful; detestable; loathsome.
aboriginal (ăb′ô·rĭj′ĭ·năl). Primitive; native.
abridge (ȧ·brĭj′). To cut down; to lessen.
abstraction (ăb·străk′shŭn). Absent-mindedness; attention to other matters.
abyss (ȧ·bĭs′). A bottomless pit.
accede (ăk·sēd′). To agree; to yield.
acclaim (ă·klām′). To applaud.
accouterment (ă·ko͞o′tẽr·mĕnt). Equipment.
acme (ăk′mē). The highest point.
acquiescence (ăk′wĭ·ĕs′ĕns). Acceptance, but not necessarily agreement.
acquit (ȧ·kwĭt′). To release; to clear from blame.
adamantine (ăd′ȧ·măn′tĭn). Very hard.
adherence (ăd·hēr′ĕns). Loyalty; attachment.
admonish (ăd·mŏn′ĭsh). To warn.
adulation (ăd′ū·lā′shŭn). Extravagant praise and applause.
adversary (ăd′vẽr·sẽr′ĭ). An opponent.
advocate (ăd′vô·kāt). A defender.
affluent (ăf′lů·ĕnt). Wealthy.
affront (ă·frŭnt′). To insult; to offend.
aghast (ȧ·găst′). Terrified; horrified.
agitation (ăj′ĭ·tā′shŭn). A movement or swaying.
ague (ā′gū). A recurrent malarial fever; or, a chill accompanying such a fever.
alabaster (ăl′ȧ·băs′tẽr). A white, marble-like stone.
alacrity (ȧ·lăk′rĭ·tĭ). Readiness; eagerness; willingness.
allay (ă·lā′). To control.
allege (ă·lĕj′). To declare; to maintain.
alleviate (ă·lē′vĭ·āt). To relieve.
allusion (ă·lū′zhŭn). A reference to.
aloofness (ȧ·lo͞of′nĕs). Indifference.
altercation (ôl·tẽr·kā′shŭn). An angry dispute; a quarrel.
amber (ăm′bẽr). A yellowish hard resin.
ambush (ăm′bo͝osh). A surprise attack.
amethyst (ăm′ê·thĭst). Violet-colored.
amiable (ā′mĭ·ȧ·b'l). Friendly; pleasant.
amity (ăm′ĭ·tĭ). Friendliness; affection.
anatomy (ȧ·năt′ô·mĭ). The science of physical appearance; the body.
anteroom (ăn′tê·ro͞om). A hall; a lobby.
apathetic (ăp′ȧ·thĕt′ĭk). Listless; without feeling or hope.
apparition (ăp′ȧ·rĭsh′ŭn). A miraculous appearance of a supernatural figure.
appease (ă·pēz′). To calm; to pacify.
appendage (ă·pĕn′dĭj). Something attached to the main body.
apprehension (ăp′rê·hĕn′shŭn). Anxiety; fear of something that might happen.
apprentice (ă·prĕn′tĭs). Beginning; as done by a learner.
arbitrary (är′bĭ·trẽr′ĭ). Decided upon without consideration of the circumstances.
armada (är·mā′dȧ). A fleet of armed ships.
arras (ăr′ăs). A tapestry; a curtain.
arrogance (ăr′ô·găns). Pride; sense of superiority.
articulate (är·tĭk′ū·lāt). To speak or utter distinctly.

āte, chåotic, dâre, ădd, ăccuse, bär, cȧsk, ȧfar; ēat, dẹar, ėlude, ĕgg, quiĕt, centẽr; īdle, ĭf, activĭty; ōpen, ôbey, ôr, ŏrange, ŏffer, ŏccur, co͞ol, co͝ok; our, boil; cūte, ūnite, bûrn, cŭt, ŭnless, menü; check; goat, sing, this, thick, scriptūre, verdūre.

astute (ăs·tūt′). Shrewdly wise; crafty.
atrocity (*ȧ*·trŏs′*ĭ*·tĭ). A savagely cruel deed.
attribute (ăt′r*ĭ*·būt). A characteristic.
authentic (ô·thĕn′tĭk). Real or genuine.
avaricious (ăv′ȧ·rĭsh′*ŭ*s). Greedy.
averse (*ȧ*·vûrs′). Unwilling; reluctant.
aversion (*ȧ*·vûr′zh*ŭ*n). Dislike or disgust.

B

baize (bāz). A coarse wool fabric, dyed in plain colors.
barbarity (bär·băr′*ĭ*·tĭ). Cruelty; inhumanity.
barrier (băr′ĭ·ĕr). Anything that hinders approach; an obstacle; an obstruction.
bastion (băs′ch*ŭ*n). A defense work projecting from a fortress wall.
beachcomber (bēch′kōm′ĕr). A loafer living on the seacoast.
beatific (bē′*ȧ*·tĭf′ĭk). Happy; contented.
belated (bē·lāt′ĕd). Delayed; late.
belligerent (bĕ·lĭj′ĕr·ĕnt). Warlike.
bemuse (bē·mūz′). To daze.
benediction (bĕn′ē·dĭk′sh*ŭ*n). A blessing; an expression of kind wishes.
benefactor (bĕn′ē·făk′tĕr). One who gives a gift to someone else.
benign (bē·nīn′). Kind and gentle.
bereft (bē·rĕft′). Deprived; dispossessed.
bigotry (bĭg′*ŭ*t·rĭ). Intolerant conduct; disrespect for the views of others.
bolster (bōl′stĕr). To support; to hold up.
boudoir (bōō′dwär). A small, elegantly furnished room for a lady.
bow (bou). The front part of a ship.
bowline (bō′lĭn). The rope used to tie a vessel up to the dock.
brace (brās). A pair; a couple.
brawn (brôn). Strong muscles.
breach (brēch). 1. An opening made by breaking or battering. 2. A violation.
brigantine (brĭg′*ă*n·tēn). A two-masted warship.
buckaroo (bŭk′*ȧ*·rōō). A cowboy.
buoyant (bōō′y*ă*nt). Floating lightly.
burnish (bûr′nĭsh). To polish.

C

cadaverous (k*ȧ*·dăv′ĕr·*ŭ*s). Pale; ghastly.
cajolery (k*ȧ*·jōl′ĕr·ĭ). The use of deceptive promises; flattery.
calliope (kă·lī′ô·pē). A circus organ, operated by steam.
cantankerous (kăn·tăng′kĕr·*ŭ*s). Showing ill nature; irritable.
canticle (kăn′tĭ·k′l). A Bible hymn or song of praise.
caparison (k*ȧ*·păr′*ĭ*·s*ŭ*n). To decorate with rich clothing.
carrion (kăr′ĭ·*ŭ*n). 1. The decaying body of a person or animal. 2. Something corrupt; vile; rotten.
cataclysmic (kăt·*ȧ*·klĭz′mĭk). Violent; sudden; disastrous.
cataract (kăt′*ȧ*·răkt). 1. A growth over the eyeball. 2. A waterfall.
cauterize (kô′tĕr·īz). To burn; to sterilize by applying a red-hot iron.
cavalier (kăv′*ȧ*·lēr′). A horseman.
celestial (sē·lĕs′ch*ă*l). Heavenly.
chafe (chāf). To rub together.
chaff (chȧf). To make fun of.
chagrin (sh*ȧ*·grĭn′). A feeling of failure or humiliation.
chastise (chăs′tīz). To punish.
chide (chīd). To scold.
chronic (krŏn′ĭk). Continuous; constant.
chronometer (krō·nŏm′ē·tĕr). A very accurate timepiece.
cimeter (sĭm′ĭ·tĕr). A sword.
clannish (klăn′ĭsh). Apt to cling or group together, as in clans.
cleat (klēt). A piece of wood or iron used to secure ropes or lines.
clutch (klŭch). A nest of eggs.
collaborate (kŏ·lăb′ô·rāt). To work together.
colleague (kŏl′ēg). An associate, usually a professional one.
comely (kŭm′lĭ). Attractive to look at.
commodity (kŏ·mŏd′*ĭ*·tĭ). Merchandise.
commute (kŏ·mūt′). To change a penalty to an easier one.

āte, chāotic, dâre, ădd, *ă*ccuse, bär, cȧsk, *ȧ*far; ēat, dēar, ēlude, ĕgg, qui*ĕ*t, centĕr; īdle, ĭf, activ*ĭ*ty; ōpen, ōbey, ôr, ŏrange, ŏffer, *ŏ*ccur.

compassion (kŏm·păsh′ŭn). The quality of mercy or sympathy.
complacent (kŏm·plā′sĕnt). Self-satisfied.
compromise (kŏm′prô·mīz). To endanger the reputation.
concentre (kŏn·sĕn′tēr). To focus; to draw into a common point.
conception (kŏn·sĕp′shŭn). Idea; thought.
concoction (kŏn·kŏk′shŭn). A mixture of different ingredients.
condone (kŏn·dōn′). To forgive; to excuse.
confiscate (kŏn′fĭs·kāt). Appropriated by the government.
conflagration (kŏn′flȧ·grā′shŭn). A blaze or flaring up; a sudden fire.
congenial (kŏn·jēn′yăl). Pleasant.
conjectural (kŏn·jĕk′tūr·ăl). Imaginative; pertaining to a guess.
conjurer (kŏn′jēr·ēr). A magician.
connive (kŏ·nīv′). To plan secretly.
consensus (kŏn·sĕn′sŭs). A collective or general agreement.
conspicuous (kŏn·spĭk′ū·ŭs). Outstanding; attracting attention; obvious.
consummate (kŏn·sŭm′ĭt). Perfect; complete.
contemn (kŏn·tĕm′). To treat with contempt; to despise.
contemplate (kŏn′tĕm·plāt). To consider; to think upon.
contempt (kŏn·tĕmpt′). Low regard for someone or something; scorn.
contend (kŏn·tĕnd′). To fight; to struggle.
contiguous (kŏn·tĭg′ū·ŭs). Nearby.
contrive (kŏn·trīv′). To make; to build.
corroborate (kŏ·rŏb′ô·rāt). To confirm; to strengthen.
covenant (kŭv′ĕ·nănt). A pact; an agreement.
covet (kŭv′ĕt). To wish to possess.
cowl (koul). A monk's hood.
crave (krāv). To desire very strongly.
craven (krā′vĕn). Frightened.
credence (krē′dĕns). Belief.
creole (krē′ōl). One of mixed Negro and French or Spanish descent.
crestfallen (krĕst′fôl·ĕn). Dejected.
crevasse (krĕ·văs′). A deep crack in the glacier ice.
cringe (krĭnj). To cower in fear.
critical (krĭ′tĭ·kăl). Decisive; at the turning point.
crony (krō′nĭ). A friend or chum.
crucial (krōō′shăl). Most important.
crypt (krĭpt). A chapel or vault beneath a church; any hidden recess.
cudgel (kŭj′ĕl). A short, heavy stick.
cumbersome (kŭm′bēr·sŭm). Heavy and awkward; clumsy.
curtail (kûr·tāl′). To shorten; to reduce; to cut off.
custodian (kŭs·tō′dĭ·ăn). One who takes care of a public building.

D

däis (dā′ĭs). A throne platform.
dandy (dăn′dĭ). One who pays great attention to dress.
dastard (dăs′tērd). A coward.
debase (dê·bās′). To reduce in value.
debonair (dĕb′ô·nâr′). Gracious.
debouch (dê·bōōsh′). To come out; to emerge.
deceptive (dê·sĕp′tĭv). Misleading.
decipher (dê·sī′fēr). To find out the meaning of.
decree (dê·krē′). A command; a rule.
decrepit (dê·krĕp′ĭt). Worn; broken down.
deference (dĕf′ēr·ĕns). Respect.
define (dê·fīn′). To give meaning.
degenerate (dê·jĕn′ēr·ĭt). Degraded, physically, mentally, or morally.
degradation (dĕg′rȧ·dā′shŭn). A cheapening or lowering in value.
demur (dê·mûr′). Hesitation.
demure (dê·mūr′). Composed; modest.
depose (dê·pōz′). To remove from office.
deprecation (dĕp·rê·kā′shŭn). A protest.
desolation (dĕs·ô·lā′shŭn). Emptiness; forsaken region.
despicable (dĕs′pĭ·kȧ·b'l). Deserving to be despised.
despondency (dê·spŏn′dĕn·sĭ). Loss of courage or hope.

cōōl, cŏŏk; **our**, **boil**; cūte, ūnite, bûrn, cŭt, ŭnless, menü; **ch**eck; **g**oat, si**ng**, **th**is, **th**ick, scriptūre, verdūre.

deter (dē·tûr′). To restrain; to hold back.
detrimental (dĕt′rĭ·mĕn′tăl). Harmful.
dexterity (dĕks·tĕr′ĭ·tĭ). Skill.
diabolical (dī′ȧ·bŏl′ĭ·kăl). Devilish; wicked and cruel.
diadem (dī′ȧ·dĕm). A crown.
diagnose (dī′ăg·nōs′). To recognize a condition, as sickness.
diesel (dē′zĕl). An oil-burning combustion engine.
diffident (dĭf′ĭ·dĕnt). Lacking confidence; timid.
diffusion (dĭ·fū′zhŭn). A spreading.
dimity (dĭm′ĭ·tĭ). A dress made of a thin corded cotton cloth.
dire (dīr). Evil; horrible; deadly.
disconsolate (dĭs·kŏn′sō·lĭt). Sad and downhearted; not able to be comforted.
discreet (dĭs·krēt′). Careful; showing good judgment.
disheveled (dĭ·shĕv′ĕld). Untidy.
disintegrate (dĭs·ĭn′tē·grāt). To fall apart; to crumble.
disperse (dĭs·pûrs′). To scatter; to separate.
disport (dĭs·pōrt′). To carry on in a playful manner.
dissect (dĭ·sĕkt′). To cut up bodies for examination and study.
distort (dĭs·tôrt′). To twist out of shape.
distract (dĭs·trăkt′). To charm or amuse.
distraught (dĭs·trôt′). Confused; upset.
divers (dī′vẽrz). Many different; several.
divert (dī·vûrt′). To change the course of.
divertissements (dē′vĕr′tēs′mäɴ′). Amusements.
docile (dŏs′ĭl). Easy going; gentle.
dolor (dō′lẽr). Grief; distress.
domain (dō·mān′). Land; territory.
dote (dōt). To be excessively fond of.
doughtier (dou′tĭ·ẽr). Stronger and more courageous.
dowry (dou′rĭ). The money or goods which a bride brings to her husband.
dram (drăm). A small drink or portion.
draught (dråft). A current of air.
drollery (drōl′ẽr·ĭ). Comical manners; joking.
dubious (dū′bĭ·ŭs). Wavering; doubtful.
dulcet (dŭl′sĕt). Gentle; sweet.
dynamo (dī′nȧ·mō). A machine for creating electrical energy.

E

eclipse (ē·klĭps′). The passing of any heavenly body between the sun or moon and the earth, which shades the earth.
ecstasy (ĕk′stȧ·sĭ). Extravagant delight.
edifice (ĕd′ĭ·fĭs). A large imposing building.
effete (ĕ·fēt′). Exhausted; barren.
ejaculate (ē·jăk′ū·lāt′). To exclaim; to cry out.
elaborate (ē·lăb′ō·rāt). To explain further, in detail.
elated (ē·lāt′ĕd). Overjoyed; excited.
eloquence (ĕl′ō·kwĕns). Forceful and vivid speech.
emblazoned (ĕm·blā′z′nd). Inscribed; adorned with bright colors.
embrasure (ĕm·brā′zhẽr). An opening in the wall.
eminent (ĕm′ĭ·nĕnt). Prominent; important.
emissary (ĕm′ĭ·sĕr·ĭ). An agent; one who is sent on a mission.
enamor (ĕn·ăm′ẽr). To charm; to fascinate.
encumber (ĕn·kŭm′bẽr). To burden.
enhance (ĕn·håns′). To increase in value.
enigmatical (ē′nĭg·măt′ĭ·kăl). Puzzling.
enlighten (ĕn·līt′n). To inform; to free from ignorance.
ensconce (ĕn·skŏns′). To settle comfortably.
entice (ĕn·tīs′). To lure; to persuade.
entrails (ĕn′trālz). The insides of animal bodies.
epaulet (ĕp′ō·lĕt). The fringed shoulder ornament of a commissioned officer.
epigram (ĕp′ĭ·grăm). A witty saying.
epithet (ĕp′ĭ·thĕt). An expression describing a special trait or quality.

āte, chāotic, dâre, ădd, ăccuse, bär, cåsk, ȧfar; ēat, dēar, ēlude, ĕgg, quiĕt, centẽr; īdle, ĭf, activĭty; ōpen, ōbey, ôr, ŏrange, ŏffer, ŏccur.

epitomize (ē·pĭt′ō·mīz). To summarize in a brief expression.
epoch (ĕp′ŏk). A period of time.
equanimity (ē′kwȧ·nĭm′ĭ·tĭ). Even-temper; calmness.
equivocation (ē·kwĭv′ō·kā′shŭn). An expression of doubtful meaning.
erosion (ē·rō′zhŭn). Disintegration; a wearing away.
essay (ĕ·sā′). To try; to make an effort.
essence (ĕs′ĕns). The inner, basic meaning.
ethics (ĕth′ĭks). The science of moral conduct.
etiquette (ĕ′tĭ·kĕt). Rules of behavior.
evasive (ē·vā′sĭv). Avoiding the issue.
execration (ĕk′sē·krā′shŭn). Cursing.
exemplary (ĕg·zĕm′plȧ·rĭ). Worthy of praise and respect.
exhort (ĕg·zôrt′). To encourage; to urge.
exile (ĕk′sīl). A long absence from one's native land.
exodus (ĕk′sō·dŭs). A departure.
exotic (ĕks·ŏt′ĭk). Foreign; strange.
extort (ĕks·tôrt′). To obtain by force or torture.
extraneous (ĕks·trā′nē·ŭs). Not essential; added on.
exultation (ĕk′sŭl·tā′shŭn). Great happiness; joyful triumph.

F

fain (fān). Glad; satisfied.
fallibility (făl·ĭ·bĭl′ĭ·tĭ). Possibility of error; unsureness.
fanatic (fȧ·năt′ĭk). Frenzied; wildly intolerant.
farce (färs). A ridiculous proceeding; a comedy.
Fascism (făsh′ĭz′m). A political and social system which uses force and violence on all opposition.
fathom (făth′ŭm). To penetrate and comprehend; to get to the bottom of a matter.
ferocity (fē·rŏs′ĭ·tĭ). Fierceness; rage.
fervent (fûr′vĕnt). Eager and full of earnestness.
fervid (fûr′vĭd). Showing intense feeling.
fissure (fĭsh′ẽr). A narrow opening.
flaccid (flăk′sĭd). Flabby; limp.
flagrant (flā′grănt). Openly scandalous; obviously wicked.
flayed (flād). With the skin stripped off.
fluent (flū′ĕnt). Flowing; graceful.
foil (foil). To frustrate; to defeat.
ford (fōrd). A place where a river can be crossed by wading.
foreboding (fōr·bōd′ĭng). A feeling that something bad is going to happen.
formidable (fôr′mĭ·dȧ·b'l). Causing fear or dread.
fracas (frā′kȧs). An uproar; a disturbance.
frigate (frĭg′ĭt). A light, swift vessel propelled both by sails and oars.
frugal (frōō′găl). Economical; very plain.
frustration (frŭs·trā′shŭn). Disappointment.
furl (fûrl). To curl tightly.
furtive (fûr′tĭv). Stealthy; secret.
futile (fū′tĭl). Useless.

G

gait (gāt). A walk; a manner of walking.
gallantry (găl′ăn·trĭ). Politeness, especially polite attention to ladies.
galley (găl′ĭ). A large sailing vessel used in the Middle Ages.
gargoyle (gär′goil). A stone water spout, usually in a grotesque form.
gaunt (gônt). Thin; haggard.
genealogist (jĕn′ē·ăl′ō·jĭst). One who studies the descent of families.
genial (jēn′yăl). Pleasant; cheerful.
genii (jē′nĭ·ī). The plural of *genie:* a powerful spirit which serves a human master.
gesticulate (jĕs·tĭk′ū·lāt). To use expressive motions of the body or limbs.
glib (glĭb). Speaking smoothly, sometimes with insincerity.
gluttonous (glŭt′'n·ŭs). Greedy.
gonfalon (gŏn′fȧ·lŏn). A flag with several streamers.

cōōl, cŏŏk; our, boil; cūte, ûnite, bûrn, cŭt, ŭnless, menü; check; goat, sing, this, thick, scriptūre, verdūre

gouty (gout′ĭ). Affected with an inflammation of the foot joints; hence, ill-tempered, peevish.
grandiose (grăn′dĭ·ōs). Lavish; overly magnificent.
gratis (gră·tĭs). Free of charge; without receiving interest.
gregarious (grē·gâr′ĭ·ŭs). Fond of being with others.
grisly (grĭz′lĭ). Horrible; ghastly.
gross (grōs). Outrageous.
grotesque (grō·tĕsk′). Queer; strange; fantastic.
grotto (grŏt′ō). A cave-like opening.
guise (gīz). Disguise; appearance.
gunnel (gŭn′ĕl). The outside edge of the deck.
gyration (jī·rā′shŭn). A rapid whirling.

H

haggard (hăg′ērd). Careworn; gaunt.
haggle (hăg′'l). To dispute; to make difficulties in bargaining.
harass (hăr′ăs). To trouble; to distress.
harpoon (här′po͞on′). To spear; to stick.
havoc (hăv′ŭk). Confusion; great disorder.
heresy (hĕr′ĕ·sĭ). An opinion opposed to the generally popular belief.
hew (hū). To cut; to carve.
hibiscus (hī·bĭs′kŭs). A flowering shrub.
homage (hŏm′ĭj). Respect; reverent regard.
hostile (hŏs′tĭl). Unfriendly.
humiliate (hū·mĭl′ĭ·āt). To embarrass; to shame.
husky (hŭs′kĭ). An Alaskan dog.

I

ignominious (ĭg′nō·mĭn′ĭ·ŭs). Dishonorable; humiliating.
impale (ĭm·pāl′). To pierce with anything pointed; to fasten upon.
impassive (ĭm·păs′ĭv). Not showing signs of emotion; calm.
impediment (ĭm·pĕd′ĭ·mĕnt). An obstacle; a hindrance.
impending (ĭm·pĕnd′ĭng). On the point of happening.
imperative (ĭm·pĕr′ȧ·tĭv). Absolutely necessary; essential.
impetuous (ĭm·pĕt′ū·ŭs). Hasty; rash.
impetus (ĭm′pē·tŭs). The force which pushes an object forward.
impious (ĭm′pĭ·ŭs). Irreverent; profane.
importunity (ĭm′pôr·tū′nĭ·tĭ). Urgent request; persistent demand.
imposition (ĭm′pō·zĭsh′ŭn). A requirement; a burden.
impotence (ĭm′pō·tĕns). Lack of power or strength; weakness.
impregnable (ĭm·prĕg′nȧ·b'l). Not able to be conquered; resistant to attack.
impromptu (ĭm·prŏmp′tū). Done without previous thought or planning.
impunity (ĭm·pū′nĭ·tĭ). Freedom from punishment or injury.
inarticulate (ĭn′är·tĭk′ū·lȧt). Not like regular speech; indistinct.
incalculable (ĭn·kăl′kū·lȧ·b'l). Not able to be foreseen.
incantation (ĭn′kăn·tā′shŭn). A set of words spoken as a magic charm.
incarnadine (ĭn·kär′nȧ·dĭn). To dye red.
inclination (ĭn·klĭ·nā′shŭn). Willingness.
inconceivable (ĭn′kŏn·sēv′ȧ·b'l). Unthinkable; unbelievable.
inconsequential (ĭn·kŏn·sē·kwĕn′shăl). Trivial; of no importance.
incontinent (ĭn·kŏn′tĭ·nĕnt). Without restraint.
incredible (ĭn·krĕd′ĭ·b'l). Unbelievable.
incredulity (ĭn′krē·dū′lĭ·tĭ). Unbelief.
indefatigable (ĭn′dē·făt′ĭ·gȧ·b'l). Untiring; not yielding to fatigue.
indictment (ĭn·dīt′mĕnt). A formal charge; accusation.
indomitable (ĭn·dŏm′ĭ·tȧ·b'l). Unconquerable; not to be defeated.
indulgence (ĭn·dŭl′jĕns). Favor.
ineffable (ĭn·ĕf′ȧ·b'l). Indescribable; inexpressible.
inference (ĭn′fēr·ĕns). A conclusion; a meaning drawn from facts.
infidel (ĭn′fĭ·dĕl). A non-believer.
infidelity (ĭn′fĭ·dĕl′ĭ·tĭ). Unfaithfulness.

āte, chāotic, dâre, ădd, ăccuse, bär, cȧsk, ȧfar; ēat, dḙar, ēlude, ĕgg, quiĕt, centẽr; īdle, ĭf, activĭty; ōpen, ōbey, ôr, ŏrange, ŏffer, ŏccur.

infinity (ĭn·fĭn′ĭ·tĭ). That which is numberless; unlimited.
ingratiating (ĭn·grā′shĭ·āt′ĭng). Pleasing; winning favors.
inherent (ĭn·hĕr′ĕnt). Belonging by nature; essential.
inhibited (ĭn·hĭ′bĭt·ĕd). Quiet; restrained.
inimitable (ĭn·ĭm′ĭ·tȧ·b'l). Not capable of being imitated; matchless.
injunction (ĭn·jŭngk′shŭn). An order; a rule.
inordinate (ĭn·ôr′dĭ·nĭt). Excessive.
insignia (ĭn·sĭg′nĭ·ȧ). Typical mark or sign by which anything is known.
intangible (ĭn·tăn′jĭ·b'l). Not able to be touched or seen.
intelligible (ĭn·tĕl′ĭ·jĭ·b'l). Capable of being understood.
intercede (ĭn′tẽr·sēd′). To beg or plead in behalf of another.
intercessor (ĭn′tẽr·sĕs′ẽr). One who comes between two quarrelers.
interminable (ĭn·tûr′mĭ·nȧ·b'l). Unending; very tedious.
intermittent (ĭn′tẽr·mĭt′ĕnt). Now and then; at intervals.
intervene (ĭn′tẽr·vēn′). To enter (a fight) in order to throw weight on one side, or to settle it.
intoxicate (ĭn·tŏk′sĭ·kāt). To excite with enthusiasm; to elate.
intrepid (ĭn·trĕ′pĭd). Fearless; undaunted.
intuition (ĭn′tū·ĭsh′ŭn). Knowing, without the aid of reason.
invariable (ĭn·vâr′ĭ·ȧ·b'l). Always.
inveterate (ĭn·vĕt′ẽr·ĭt). Firmly established as a habit; deep-rooted.
inviolability (ĭn·vī′ô·lȧ·bĭl′ĭ·tĭ). Safety from harm or corruption.
irrelevancy (ĭr·rĕl′ê·văn·sĭ). The quality of being unrelated to the matter at hand.
irrevocable (ĭ·rĕv′ô·kȧ·b'l). Incapable of being recalled or revoked.

J

jade (jād). A worthless young woman.
jest (jĕst). A joke.
joust (joust). A combat; a tournament.
jurisprudence (jo͝or′ĭs·pro͞o′dĕns). A system of laws.

K

kaleidoscopical (kȧ·lī′dô·skŏp′ĭ·kăl). With varying, shifting colors.
Kanaka (kăn′ȧ·kȧ). Hawaiian.
keel (kēl). The principal timber of a ship, running the length of the hull.
kilometer (kĭl′ô·mē′tẽr). 1000 meters, a little over .6 mile.

L

lacerate (lăs′ẽr·āt). To cut or to tear the flesh.
lackadaisical (lăk′ȧ·dā′zĭ·kăl). Lazy; slow-moving; listless.
laggard (lăg′ẽrd). A slow fellow; one who hesitates.
lath (làth). A strip of wood nailed to the rafters making a groundwork for the ceiling.
latitude (lăt′ĭ·tūd). Broadness; freedom.
lee (lē). The side or part sheltered from the wind.
leech (lēch). Either edge of a square sail.
legitimate (lê·jĭt′ĭ·mĭt). Lawful.
leniency (lē′nĭ·ĕn·sĭ). Mercy; mild treatment.
liability (lī′ȧ·bĭl′ĭ·tĭ). A disadvantage; an obligation.
libation (lī′bā′shŭn). A liquid poured out in token of honor or sacrifice.
literal (lĭt′ẽr·ăl). According to the usual meaning.
livery (lĭv′ẽr·ĭ). Distinctive dress; esp. a servant's uniform.
loath (lōth). To have disgust for; to despise.
logy (lō′gĭ). Heavy in motion; sluggish.
lowering (lou′ẽr·ĭng). Threatening; frowning.

M

maelstrom (māl′strŏm). Turmoil.
malady (măl′ȧ·dĭ). A sickness.

co͞ol, co͝ok; **our**, **boil**; cūte, ûnite, bûrn, cŭt, ŭnless, menü; **ch**eck; **g**oat, si**ng**, **th**is, **th**ick, script**ū**re, verd**ū**re.

malicious (mȧ·lĭsh′ŭs). Intending evil or harm.
manifest (măn′ĭ·fĕst). Obvious; clear.
mastiff (măs′tĭf). An old English breed of large watchdog.
maul (môl). To beat; to handle roughly.
mediocre (mē′dĭ·ō′kẽr). Medium; average.
meet (mēt). Fitting.
mercenary (mûr′sê·nĕr′ĭ). Acting solely for money or gain.
meritorious (mĕr′ĭ·tō′rĭ·ŭs). Deserving high praise or honor.
mettle (mĕt′'l). Courage or spirit.
militia (mĭ·lĭsh′ȧ). A body of civilians enrolled as a military force, but not usually called on for active service.
mince (mĭns). A delicate walk; a walk using short, quick steps.
minstrel (mĭn′strĕl). A musical entertainer.
misconstrue (mĭs′kŏn·stro͞o′). To misunderstand; to misjudge.
mite (mīt). A small sum of money.
mock (mŏk). False; pretending.
modify (mŏd′ĭ·fī). To change; to alter.
monitor (mŏn′ĭ·tẽr). A person in charge in an advisory capacity.
monstrous (mŏn′strŭs). Deformed; unnatural.
morass (mô·răs′). A swamp or bog.
morbid (môr′bĭd). Interested in gruesome happenings.
mortification (môr′tĭ·fĭ·kā′shŭn). A cause of shame or embarrassment.
mundane (mŭn′dān). Earthly or worldly.
mutilate (mū′tĭ·lāt). To disfigure; to injure seriously.
myriad (mĭr′ĭ·ăd). A very large indefinite number.
mystic (mĭs′tĭk). Strange; unknown; highly spiritual.

N

naïve (nä·ēv′). Simple and child-like; innocent.
natty (năt′ĭ). Neatly fine; tidy.
nocturnal (nŏk·tûr′năl). Occurring in the night.
notorious (nô·tō′rĭ·ŭs). Widely known.
noxious (nŏk′shŭs). Harmful; unwholesome.
nucleus (nū′klē·ŭs). The center.
nuptial (nŭp′shăl). A marriage.

O

obdurate (ŏb′dû·rȧt). Unyielding.
obeisance (ô·bā′săns). A gesture of respect; a bow.
odious (ō′dĭ·ŭs). Bad or hateful.
omen (ō′mĕn). A prophetic sign.
ominous (ŏm′ĭ·nŭs). Predicting evil; threatening.
omnipotent (ŏm·nĭp′ô·tĕnt). All-powerful.
opaque (ô·pāk′). Unable to be seen through.
opportune (ŏp′ŏr·tūn′). Lucky; coming at the right moment.
oratory (ŏr′ȧ·tō′rĭ). A chapel set apart for private devotions.
ordeal (ôr·dēl′). A test of strength or endurance.
ostentation (ŏs′tĕn·tā′shŭn). Gaudiness; showiness.
overwhelm (ō′vẽr·hwĕlm′). To overpower; to crush.

P

pagan (pā′găn). An irreligious person; a heathen.
palate (păl′ĭt). Mouth.
pall (pôl). 1. A dark, gloomy covering. 2. To become dull and tasteless.
pallet (păl′ĕt). A small, mean bed or mattress of straw.
pallid (păl′ĭd). Pale and colorless.
palpitate (păl′pĭ·tāt). To throb with excitement.
palsied (pôl′zĭd). Trembling; shaking.
paltry (pôl′trĭ). Insignificant; of little worth.
paradox (păr′ȧ·dŏks′). A statement that seems to be contradictory.
parka (pär′kȧ). An outer garment of undressed skins.

āte, chȧotic, dâre, ădd, ăccuse, bär, cȧsk, ȧfar; ēat, dẹar, ėlude, ĕgg, quiĕt, centẽr; īdle, ĭf, activĭty; ōpen, ôbey, ôr, ŏrange, ŏffer, ŏccur.

paroxysm (păr′ŏk·sĭz′m). A convulsive movement.

pate (pāt). Head.

patriarch (pā′trĭ·ärk). A ruler of the tribe; hence, an old and wise man.

patronize (pā′trŭn·īz). To treat as an inferior.

pedigree (pĕd′ĭ·grē). A list of ancestors.

peerless (pēr′lĕs). Without equal.

pelf (pĕlf). Money; riches; gain.

perceptible (pẽr·sĕp′tĭ·b′l). Noticeable.

peremptory (pẽr·ĕmp′tô·rĭ). Positive; showing authority.

perfunctory (pẽr·fŭngt′tô·rĭ). Done merely as a duty or routine matter.

perjury (pûr′jẽr·ĭ). Lying; false swearing.

permeate (pûr′mê·āt). To penetrate; to seep through and fill thoroughly.

peroration (pĕr′ô·rā′shŭn). The concluding part of a speech.

perpetrate (pûr′pê·trāt). To perform; to commit.

perverse (pẽr·vûrs′). Contrary; willful.

pestilence (pĕs′tĭ·lĕns). A contagious and deadly disease.

phosphorescence (fŏs′fô·rĕs′ĕns). The faint light given off by phosphorus.

pippin (pĭp′ĭn). A highly admired person. (*slang*).

pittance (pĭt′ăns). A very small amount.

plaintive (plān′tĭv). Sad; melancholy.

pliable (plī′ȧ·b′l). Able to be bent or twisted easily.

plight (plīt). To promise; to pledge.

ply (plī). To work at continuously.

poltroon (pŏl·tro͞on′). A coward.

ponderous (pŏn′dẽr·ŭs). Weighty; hard to understand.

pontoon (pŏn·to͞on′). A float which enables a seaplane to land on water.

porpoise (pôr′pŭs). A playful fish, commonly called the dolphin.

port (pōrt). The left side of a ship.

portal (pōr′tăl). A door or entrance.

portent (pôr′tĕnt). A warning of coming evil; an omen.

potentate (pō′tĕn·tāt). A ruler; a prince; one who has great power.

prate (prāt). To talk foolishly; to chatter.

precedent (prĕs′ê·dĕnt). A decision that serves as an example for future decisions of the same kind.

precept (prē′sĕpt). A law or rule.

precipitate (prê·sĭp′ĭ·tât). To throw out; to cast headlong.

predatory (prĕd′ȧ·tō·rĭ). Like a beast of prey; for example, like a panther.

predestined (prê·dĕs′tĭnd). Decided upon beforehand.

prelude (prĕl′ūd). An introduction.

premature (prē′mȧ·tūr′). Untimely; too early.

premonitory (prê·mŏn′ĭ·tō′rĭ). Giving warning of what is to come.

preponderance (prê·pŏn′dẽr·ăns). A superiority in power and weight.

preposterous (prê·pŏs′tẽr·ŭs). Utterly absurd; ridiculous.

presage (prê·sāj′). To predict; to warn.

prescribe (prê·skrīb′). To rule; to direct.

prodigious (prô·dĭj′ŭs). Huge; tremendous.

prodigy (prŏd′ĭ·jĭ). Something extraordinary; a marvel.

profess (prô·fĕs′). To take vows of formal acceptance of a religious order.

prohibitive (prô·hĭb′ĭ·tĭv). Preventing the use of.

promontory (prŏm′ŭn·tō·rĭ). A high point of land extending into the sea.

proscribe (prô·skrīb′). To outlaw; to limit one's freedom.

prostrate (prŏs′trāt). To lie down full length, as in adoration.

protract (prô·trăkt′). To draw out; to lengthen.

protuberance (prô·tū′bẽr·ăns). A bulge or swelling.

providential (prŏv′ĭ·dĕn′shăl). Lucky; miraculous.

provincial (prô·vĭn′shăl). Rural; in the country.

provocation (prŏv′ô·kā′shŭn). A challenge; a stirring up.

prow (prou). The front of a ship.
prowess (prou′ĕs). Strength and skill.
punctilious (pŭngk·tĭl′ĭ·ŭs). Very careful.

Q

quay (kē). A wharf; a dock.
quiescence (kwī·ĕs′ĕns). Calm; silence.
quip (kwĭp). A joke or pun.
quizzical (kwĭz′ĭ·kăl). Slightly puzzled.

R

rack (răk). 1. An instrument of torture; suffering. 2. To torture.
rally (răl′ĭ). To revive; to recover.
rampart (răm′pärt). A defense.
rapacity (rȧ·păs′ĭ·tĭ). Fierce greediness.
rapturous (răp′tųr·ŭs). Blissful; delighted.
raspy (răs′pĭ). Harsh; sore.
ravenous (răv′ĕn·ŭs). Greedily devouring.
rebuttal (rê·bŭt′ăl). An argument answering another's argument.
recede (rê·sēd′). To withdraw from view; to fade into the distance.
reck (rĕk). To care.
reclamation (rĕk·lă·mā′shŭn). Restoration; cultivation of wild land.
reconcile (rĕk′ŏn·sīl). To bring to contentment; to restore to harmony.
reconnoiter (rĕk′ŏ·noi′tẽr). To survey what might lie ahead; to look around.
recruit (rê·kro͞ot′). To supply men for an army.
redoubtable (rê·dout′ȧ·b'l). Inspiring fear; valiant.
reek (rēk). Unpleasant fumes or smells.
regale (rê·gāl′). To feast merrily.
reiterate (rê·ĭt′ẽr·āt). To repeat.
remonstrance (rê·mŏn′străns). A protest; a complaint.
renegade (rĕn′ê·gād). A rebel; one who turns from a cause.
renown (rê·noun′). Fame.
replica (rĕp′lĭ·kȧ). A picture of; an image; a likeness.
reproach (rê·prōch′). To scold or condemn; to blame.
repulse (rê·pŭls′). To reject; to throw out.
repute (rê·pūt′). To consider.
requite (rê·kwīt′). To return; to repay.
resonance (rĕz′ô·năns). Depth of tone or sound; quality; richness.
respiration (rĕs′pĭ·rā′shŭn). Breathing.
resplendent (rê·splĕn′dĕnt). Shining brilliantly.
restive (rĕs′tĭv). Uneasy; restless; fidgeting.
retract (rê·trăkt′). To withdraw, to take back something one said.
revile (rê·vīl′). To abuse or insult in speech or act.
rhetoric (rĕt′ô·rĭk). The art of forceful speech and writing.
ricochet (rĭk′ô·shā′). To glance off.
rigorous (rĭg′ẽr·ŭs). With strict exactness.
rollicking (rŏl′ĭk·ĭng). Frolicsome; playful and full of fun.
rudiment (ro͞o′dĭ·mĕnt). A fundamental; a basic part.
ruffian (rŭf′ĭ·ăn). A boisterous, rough fellow.
ruth (ro͞oth). Sorrow; mercy.

S

sadistic (sȧ·dĭs′tĭk). Getting pleasure from inflicting pain on others.
sagacity (sȧ·găs′ĭ·tĭ). Wisdom; good judgment.
sage (sāj). Low underbrush found on the western plains.
sardonic (sär·dŏn′ĭk). Scornful; mocking; bitter.
sate (sāt). To supply with too much; to satisfy fully.
savant (să·väɴ′). A learned or wise man.
scimitar (sĭm′ĭ·tẽr). A sword with a curved, flat blade.
scourge (skûrj). A lash or whip.
scruple (skro͞o′p'l). A doubt; a hesitation.
scrupulous (skro͞o′pû·lŭs). Exact; correct.
scuttle (skŭt′'l). An opening in a roof, with a lid or cover.
sedative (sĕd′ȧ·tĭv). A drug which calms and soothes the nerves.
seer (sēr). One who foretells the future.

āte, chȧotic, dâre, ădd, ăccuse, bär, càsk, ȧfar; ēat, dẹ̄ar, ėlude, ĕgg, quiĕt, centẽr; īdle, ĭf, activĭty; ōpen, ôbey, ôr, ŏrange, ŏffer, ŏccur.

semblance (sĕm′blăns). Appearance; resemblance.
senility (sĕn·ĭl′ĭ·tĭ). The weakness of old age.
sepulcher (sĕp′ŭl·kẽr). A tomb.
serrated (sĕr′rāt·ĕd). Edged as with saw teeth.
servile (sûr′vĭl). Slavish; behaving with lack of spirit.
sextant (sĕks′tănt). A navigation instrument.
shaft (shăft). Figuratively, a joke at someone else's expense.
shingly (shĭng′lĭ). Strewn with rounded, water-worn fragments of rock.
shoal (shōl). A crowd or school of fish.
shroud (shroud). The burial garment; a veil.
sidle (sī′d′l). To move sidewise, in a furtive manner.
singular (sĭng′gû·lẽr). Odd; peculiar; particular.
sinister (sĭn′ĭs·tẽr). Evil or harmful.
sinuous (sĭn′û·ŭs). Twisting and turning.
sluggard (slŭg′ẽrd). A lazy, idle, inactive person.
sluice (sloōs). A passageway through which water is conducted.
slough (sloō). A stagnant swampland.
smelt (smĕlt). A small, salmon-like fish.
solace (sŏl′ĭs). To comfort; to console.
solicitor (sô·lĭs′ĭ·tẽr). A lawyer.
solicitude (sô·lĭs′ĭ·tūd). Anxiety for a person's welfare; concern or care.
soliloquy (sô·lĭl′ô·kwĭ). A talking to oneself.
sovereign (sŏv′ẽr·ĭn). Supreme.
spasmodic (spăz·mŏd′ĭk). Sudden; violent.
spawn (spôn). To produce or deposit eggs; to bring forth.
species (spē′shĭz). A distinct kind or sort.
specter (spĕk′tẽr). A haunting vision; a ghost.
speculative (spĕk′û·lā′tĭv). Thoughtful.
spume (spūm). Foam.
squeamish (skwēm′ĭsh). Unduly sensitive; easily shocked.
starboard (stär′bōrd). The right side of a ship.
stark (stärk). Bare; unadorned; stripped down to the essentials.
stead (stĕd). The place which belongs to another.
stern (stẽrn). The rear part of a ship.
stigmatize (stĭg′mȧ·tīz). To mark with disgrace.
stint (stĭnt). A task.
stipulation (stĭp′û·lā′shŭn). A term or condition in an agreement.
strand (strănd). Land, usually, far away.
stringent (strĭn′jĕnt). Rigid; severe.
stupefy (stū′pê·fī). To stun.
stymie (stī′mĭ). To stop; to prevent. (*slang*).
subsist (sŭb·sĭst′). To live; to feed.
substantiate (sŭb·stăn′shĭ·āt). To prove; to confirm.
succor (sŭk′ẽr). Comfort; help; aid.
sumac (shoō′măk). A kind of bush.
sumptuous (sŭmp′tū·ŭs). Lavish; luxurious.
sundry (sŭn′drĭ). Several different.
supercilious (sū′pẽr·sĭl′ĭ·ŭs). Haughty.
superimpose (sū′pẽr·ĭm·pōz′). To layer; to put one upon the other.
supplement (sŭp′lê·mĕnt). To add to.
suppleness (sŭp′'l·nĕs). Softness; flexibility.
suppliant (sŭp′lĭ·ănt). One who begs.
supposition (sŭp′ô·zĭsh′ŭn). A guess.
surfeit (sûr′fĭt). To over-indulge; to overeat.
surreptitious (sûr′ĕp·tĭsh′ŭs). In a quiet or secret manner; sly.
susceptibility (sŭ·sĕp′tĭ·bĭl′ĭ·tĭ). Sensitivity; state of being impressionable.
swagger (swăg′ẽr). A conceited or lordly strut or swing in one's walk.
sylvan (sĭl′văn). Peaceful; quiet, as in the forest.
synthesis (sĭn′thê·sĭs). The sum; the blending of many parts into a whole.

cōōl, cŏŏk; **our**, **boil**; cūte, ûnite, bûrn, cŭt, ŭnless, menü; **ch**eck; **g**oat, si**ng**, **th**is, **th**ick, scriptūre, verdūre.

T

tarry (tăr′ĭ). To linger; to stay.
taut (tôt). Tight; full of tension.
tawny (tô′nĭ). Yellow-brown colored.
tediousness (tē′dĭ·ŭs·nĕs). Boredom; weariness.
temperate (tĕm′pēr·ĭt). Free from extremes; mild.
tempest (tĕm′pĕst). A storm with especially high winds.
temporal (tĕm′pō·răl). Civil; political; worldly, as opposed to spiritual.
terminus (tûr′mĭ·nŭs). An end; a final goal.
terrain (tĕ·rān′). The area or ground under observation.
theory (thē′ō·rĭ). An explanation based on observation and reasoning.
throstle (thrŏs′'l). A song thrush.
throttle (thrŏt′'l). To choke.
timorous (tĭm′ēr·ŭs). Timid.
titillate (tĭt′ĭ·lāt). To tickle.
tonsured (tŏn′shērd). With a shaven head.
topaz (tō′păz). A yellow gem.
torrential (tŏ·rĕn′shăl). Violent and rapid flow; vigorous and rushing.
tract (trăkt). A large area of land or water.
travail (trăv′āl). Toil; labor.
treadle (trĕd′'l). A pedal which operates a machine.
tremulous (trĕm′ū·lŭs). Quivering; shaking; vibrating.
tribulation (trĭb′ū·lā′shŭn). Trouble; grief or sorrow.
trophy (trō′fĭ). A prize.
troth (trŏth). Faith.
truss (trŭs). To tie or bind.
tumultuous (tū·mŭl′tū·ŭs). Violent; noisy.
tycoon (tī·ko͞on′). A prominent businessman.

U

ultimate (ŭl′tĭ·mĭt). Final.
unalienable (ŭn·āl′yĕn·ȧ·b'l). Cannot be taken away.
undulate (ŭn′dū·lāt). To wave; to move with a regular rise and fall.
unfeigned (ŭn·fānd′). Real; sincere.
ungirded (ŭn·gûrd′ĕd). Unbelted; unbound.
unrelenting (ŭn′rê·lĕn′tĭng). With unceasing force.
unscalable (ŭn·skāl′ȧ·b'l). Not capable of being climbed.
unstinted (ŭn·stĭnt′ĕd). Unrestrained; abundant.
unwonted (ŭn·wŭn′tĕd). Unexpected; unusual.
upbraid (ŭp·brād′). To accuse; to find fault with.
usurer (ū′zho͞o·rēr). One who lends money at a high rate of interest.

V

vagrant (vā′grănt). Wandering.
valorous (văl′ēr·ŭs). Courageous; brave.
vanguard (văn′gärd). Military forces at the front of the main body.
veer (vēr). To change course; to turn.
vehemence (vē′ĕ·mĕns). Forcefulness; violence.
venerable (vĕn′ēr·ȧ·b'l). Worthy of respect because of age.
veneration (vĕn′ēr·ā′shŭn). Praise; admiration; reverence.
vermin (vēr′mĭn). Small, troublesome animals like fleas, lice, rats.
versatile (vûr′sȧ·tĭl). Apt; many-sided.
vestibule (vĕs′tĭ·būl). Outer room; hall.
vesture (vĕs′tūr). Clothing.
viand (vī′ănd). Food; a meal.
viceroy (vīs′roi). A man who governs as the king's representative.
victuals (vĭt′'lz). Food.
vigil (vĭj′ĭl). Evening or night devotions and prayers.
vindication (vĭn′dĭ·kā′shŭn). Defense; justification.
vindictive (vĭn·dĭk′tĭv). Revengeful; bearing a grudge.
visage (vĭz′ĭj). Face; appearance.
void (void). Empty.

āte, chắotic, dâre, ădd, ăccuse, bär, cȧsk, ȧfar; ēat, dẹar, ėlude, ĕgg, quiĕt, centẽr; īdle, ĭf, activĭty; ōpen, ōbey, ôr, ŏrange, ŏffer, ŏccur.

volition (vô·lĭsh′ŭn). Will; desire.
vulnerable (vŭl′nēr·ȧ·b'l). Open to attack.

W

wanderlust (vän′dēr·lo͝ost′; wŏn′dēr·lŭst). Strong longing for travel.
wanton (wŏn′tŭn). Without restriction; careless.
wax (wăks). To grow.
weir (wēr). A dam.
whet (hwĕt). To sharpen.
whey (hwā). The watery part of milk.
whimsical (hwĭm′zĭ·kăl). Humorous; quaint.
windlass (wĭnd′lȧs). A machine on a ship used to raise the anchor.
wistful (wĭst′fo͝ol). Wishful; longing.
wizened (wĭz′'nd). Withered; shrunken.
wraith (rāth). A wisp; a filmy remainder.
wrath (răth). Anger.
wrench (rĕnch). Distress; anguish.
writhe (rīth). To twist; to squirm.
wrought (rôt). Worked.

X, Y

yeomanry (yō′măn·rĭ). A group of small landowners; commonmen.

co͞ol, co͝ok; **ou**r, b**oi**l; cūte, ûnite, bûrn, cŭt, ŭnless, menü; **ch**eck; **g**oat, si**ng**, **th**is, **th**ick, scrip**t**ûre, ver**d**ûre.

INDEX